W9-BQJ-395

VESTAL PUBLIC LIBRARY
0 00 10 0273458 8

The Rock of Anzio

Also by Flint Whitlock

Soldiers on Skis:
A Pictorial Memoir of the 10th Mountain Division
(with Bob Bishop)

The Rock of Anzio

From Sicily to Dachau:
A History of the
45th Infantry Division

Flint Whitlock

Westview Press
A Member of the Perseus Books Group

Grateful acknowledgment is made for permission to quote from the following:

Brave Men, by Ernie Pyle. Copyright © 1944. Reprinted by permission of Henry Holt & Co.

Calculated Risk, by Mark W. Clark. Copyright © 1950 by Mark W. Clark. Copyright renewed © 1978 by Mark W. Clark. Reprinted by permission of HarperCollins.

Vertrauensmann: Man of Confidence, by Henry Kaufman. Copyright © 1994 by Henry Kaufman. Reprinted by permission of the author.

Scouts Out! by William Whitman. Copyright © 1990 by William Whitman. Reprinted by permission of the author.

The Liberation of KZ Dachau, a video documentary by James Kent Strong. Copyright © 1990. Used by permission of J. K. Strong, Strong Communications, P.O. Box 181652, Coronado, CA 92178.

Epigraphs are reprinted from *The Divine Comedy of Dante Alighieri: Inferno,* by Allen Mandelbaum; translation copyright © 1980 by Allen Mandelbaum. Used by permission of Bantam Books, a division of Bantam Doubleday Dell Publishing Group, Inc.

Published in 1998 in the United States of America by Westview Press, 5500 Central Avenue, Boulder, Colorado 80301-2877, and in the United Kingdom by Westview Press, 12 Hid's Copse Road, Cumnor Hill, Oxford OX2 9JJ

ISBN 0-8133-3399-7

In memory of
my parents

Contents

Illustrations

Photos

Maps

Acknowledgments

I am deeply indebted to the many veterans of the 45th Infantry Division who helped me with this project by taking the time to answer my seemingly endless stream of questions and share with me their memories of their wartime service. Many have painful memories of lost buddies, lost limbs, and lost innocence. It is telling of the ferocity of war that the first three veterans I interviewed had each lost a leg in combat.

Although the book has "Anzio" in the title, it covers considerably more ground than that one momentous battle in Italy. In fact, it is a rather complete history of one infantry division, from its inception through its training and more than 500 days of combat to its eventual deactivation at war's end. It is also more than merely a parochial division history; it is a stark and realistic view of war as seen and lived and remembered by those who were there. Men in many other units went through similar experiences, and so it becomes a universal account of men at war, of interest to anyone studying what war does to the human psyche.

Although most of the narrative involves and celebrates the lowly, noble infantryman, each infantryman (and I) acknowledges the vital role played by those in other branches—the artillerymen, the medics, the cooks and clerks and quartermasters, and everyone else who had a hand in victory. Each one I interviewed is fiercely proud to have served his division, and his nation, so well. When the proverbial chips were down, when it would have been easier to run away from the German onslaught that claimed so many lives on so many occasions, it is an inspiration that these brave men held their ground and denied the enemy the victory it paid so dearly to achieve. These Thunderbirds are men to whom this nation should forever be deeply grateful.

Those whom I interviewed or who shared with me their letters, diaries, photographs, manuscripts, and other memorabilia or who performed a great service by introducing me to other 45th Division veterans who they thought would have stories to share are listed below. (An asterisk indicates those who received the Congressional Medal of Honor.)

Edward J. "Don" Amzibel, L Company, 157th Infantry Regiment
Van T. Barfoot, L Company, 157th Infantry Regiment *
Clay A. Barnes, Anti-Tank Company, 157th Infantry Regiment
J. Allen "Al" Bedard, HQ Company, 157th Infantry Regiment
Hubert L. Berry, I Company, 157th Infantry Regiment

James R. Bird, A Battery, 160th Field Artillery Battalion
Joseph Bosa, HQ, 171st Field Artillery Battalion
Theodore F. Bottinelli, HQ, 179th Infantry Regiment
Robert E. Brasher, Regimental Band, 179th Infantry Regiment
Robert L. Bryan, HQ Company, 179th Infantry Regiment
Dr. Philip B. Burke, E, H, and HQ Companies, 157th Infantry Regiment
Mortimer "Morty" Carr, HQ Company, 157th Infantry Regiment
Ernest Childers, C Company, 180th Infantry Regiment *
John D. Coffey, HQ Company, 3rd Battalion, 157th Infantry Regiment
Pete Conde, Anti-Tank Company, 157th Infantry Regiment
Carmen A. Cook, M Company, 179th Infantry Regiment
Ben Cooper, Medical Detachment, 3rd Battalion, 179th Infantry Regiment
Ross P. Copeland, I Company, 157th Infantry Regiment
Mel Craven, A Battery, 158th Field Artillery Battalion
Nicholas J. Defonte, Attached to British 1st Infantry Division
Fr. Alex Dryden, 45th Reconnaissance Squadron
Charles D. Dunham, E Company, 157th Infantry Regiment
Everett W. Easley, E Company, 179th Infantry Regiment
George Ecker, Medical Detachment, 179th Infantry Regiment
Trevor Evans, I and M Companies, 157th Infantry Regiment
Bernard F. Fleming, Anti-Tank Company, 157th Infantry Regiment
Daniel Ficco, C Company, 157th Infantry Regiment
Ralph W. Fink, D Company, 157th Infantry Regiment
Robert Joseph ("Doc Joe") Franklin, Medical Detachment, I Company, 157th Infantry Regiment
Peter Galary, Medical Detachment, I Company, 157th Infantry Regiment
William H. Gordon, Anti-Tank Company, 179th Infantry Regiment
John P. Griffin, HQ Company, 3rd Battalion, 157th Infantry Regiment
Glen K. Hanson, L Company, 157th Infantry Regiment
Harold C. Hanson, I Company, 157th Infantry Regiment
Henry J. Havlat, B and I Companies, 157th Infantry Regiment
R. Herbert Hill, Anti-Tank Company, 179th Infantry Regiment
Sidney C. Horn, I Company, 157th Infantry Regiment
Dr. Treadwell L. Ireland, Medical Detachment, 1st Battalion, 157th Infantry Regiment
Henry Kaufman, H Company, 157th Infantry Regiment
Charles A. Keffler, Medical Detachment, 3rd Battalion, 179th Infantry Regiment
Kenneth Kindig, I Company, 157th Infantry Regiment
Ralph Krieger, HQ, 1st Battalion, 157th Infantry Regiment
Dr. Robert W. LaDu, F Company, 179th Infantry Regiment
John Lee, I Company, 157th Infantry Regiment
Donald M. Lesch, I and HQ Companies, 157th Infantry Regiment

Leland L. Loy, HQ Company, 3rd Battalion, 157th Infantry Regiment
Walter E. Mack, I Company, 157th Infantry Regiment
Karl O. Mann, HQ Company, 3rd Battalion, 157th Infantry Regiment
Alvin "Bud" McMillan, K Company, 157th Infantry Regiment
Jack McMillion, L Company, 157th Infantry Regiment
Henry "Hank" Mills, I Company, 157th Infantry Regiment
Jeremiah W. Moher, E Company, 157th Infantry Regiment
Jack C. Montgomery, I Company, 180th Infantry Regiment *
George Nalley, K Company, 157th Infantry Regiment
Oren L. Peters, HQ Company, 2nd Battalion, 179th Infantry Regiment
Sid Pollock, C Company, 157th Infantry Regiment
Chester A. Powell, M Company, 180th Infantry Regiment
William C. Pullum, K Company, 157th Infantry Regiment
Robert Reckling, I Company, 157th Infantry Regiment
Charles R. Reiman, G Company, 179th Infantry Regiment
Robert L. Rogers, Service Company, 180th Infantry Regiment
John William "Bill" Rolen, I Company, 180th Infantry Regiment
Minor S. Shirk, Service Company, 157th Infantry Regiment
Felix L. Sparks, E Company, 157th Infantry Regiment
Anse H. "Eddie" Speairs, C Company, 157th Infantry Regiment
Kenneth P. Stemmons, B Company, 157th Infantry Regiment
Kenneth L. Vogt, E Company, 157th Infantry Regiment
Howard W. Walton, I Company, 157th Infantry Regiment
W. Scott Wells, B Company, 180th Infantry Regiment
William H. Whitman, B Company, 180th Infantry Regiment
Kenneth Wickham, Division HQ, Chief of Staff
Robert F. Wiley, C Company, 157th Infantry Regiment
Ray N. Williams, HQ Company, 1st Battalion, 179th Infantry Regiment
Vere L. "Tarzan" Williams, K Company, 157th Infantry Regiment
Daniel H. Witts, Anti-Tank Company, 179th Infantry Regiment

Much controversy about the liberation of the Dachau concentration camp has arisen among members of the 45th and 42nd Infantry Divisions, both of which were involved, as is detailed in Chapter 13. Helping me sort out the myriad details and often conflicting accounts were Curtis Whiteway and David Israel, both of whom have done considerable research into the Dachau liberation and who generously provided me with maps, time lines, and other material concerning the camp and its liberation.

I am deeply indebted to Lieutenant Colonel (Ret.) Hugh Foster III, who uncovered material concerning the liberation of Dachau at the National Archives that was thought for decades to be lost. An expert as well on the battle of Reipertswiller in the Vosges Mountains of France, he carefully critiqued Chapters 12 and 13, making them more accurate than they otherwise would have been.

I also wish to thank Dr. George Daoust of the DuPuy Institute and Colonel John Linden, son of Brigadier General Henning Linden, assistant division commander of the 42nd ("Rainbow") Division, along with several 42nd men—John R. Veitch, William P. Donahue, Guido N. Oddi, and Carl E. Tinkham—all members of General Linden's party at Dachau. Chapter 13 is, I believe, the first overall account of what actually happened at Dachau on 29 April 1945, although, because of the fallibility of human memory and the lack of hard evidence, some contradictory issues still remain that, in all likelihood, will never be resolved.

Words are inadequate to express my gratitude to Dr. Richard Sommers, chief archivist of the U.S. Army Military History Institute at Carlisle Barracks, Pennsylvania, whose help was invaluable and whose friendship is immeasurable. Others who assisted me in my research and deserve mention for their assistance include Mack C. O'Quinn, Jr.; Thera Dickson; Antonio J. Muñuz, editor of *Axis Europa* magazine; Dwight Strandberg, archivist with the Eisenhower Library in Abilene, Kansas; and Tony Dudman and Giancarlo Bendini, longtime friends and fellow historians in England and Italy, respectively.

This list would not be complete without also expressing my deep appreciation to Major General (Ret.) Fred Daugherty, archivist of the 45th Infantry Division Museum in Oklahoma City, and Major (Ret.) Mike Gonzales, 45th Infantry Division Museum Curator, for all their guidance and assistance through the museum's extensive holdings, and to General Daugherty and Brigadier General (Ret.) W. Rex Wilson, National Secretary of the 45th Infantry Division Association, for reviewing the manuscript and offering their suggestions and corrections. Any errors are mine, not theirs.

I must also thank my editors at Westview, Peter Kracht and Rob Williams, for their insight and wisdom, and, for their untiring efforts, my agent Jody Rein and her assistant Sandra Bond, who did much to make this project a reality. My wife, Dr. Mary Ann Watson, was also unflagging in her support during the innumerable days and nights I spent at the word processor.

Most of all, I am indebted to the veterans of the 45th for sharing their personal experiences with me, either in interviews or in written form. Many of them, too, lent me their precious personal photographs for inclusion in this book. Generally speaking, the men of the 45th were not men of letters. Most had a high school education and little else at that time. Yet, in the unadorned simplicity of their language, they speak eloquently about the horrors of war and the resiliency of the human spirit. The pride in what they endured and the inevitable victory that they helped achieve is evident in their words.

Flint Whitlock

Introduction

During the Second World War, the United States Army fielded ninety-one combat divisions. Of these, fifty-two were deployed to the European and Mediterranean theaters of operation. And, of the Army's ninety-one divisions, eighteen were National Guard divisions—originally and primarily composed of nonprofessional "citizen soldiers" who voluntarily joined their local units before Pearl Harbor for a variety of reasons: the camaraderie, the extra pay that came in handy during the final years of the Great Depression, the manly pursuits of military training, and, not inconsequentially, because it was the patriotic thing to do.

This book is the story of one of those eighteen National Guard divisions—the 45th Infantry Division, nicknamed the "Thunderbirds." The 45th initially was made up of men from Arizona, Colorado, New Mexico, and Oklahoma—men who grew up in lean times and under hard conditions. The men who joined its ranks were tough, and the Army's grueling training regimen and spartan living conditions made them tougher. For the most part, they were men who never shirked an assignment, no matter how difficult. They were men who never whined when the burden of battle fell on their shoulders, as it did so often. They were men who never asked, "Why us?" or complained that life had dealt them a bad hand. They just did their job, and they did it well.

Generally regarded as the Army's "poor stepchildren," the National Guard outfits, prior to the outbreak of the Second World War, were a very secondary second line of defense, shackled with obsolete equipment and hamstrung with substandard training. Army Chief of Staff George Catlett Marshall would change all that. Streamlining the Army for the war he saw coming, Marshall made sure that the National Guard divisions would be as strong, as well trained, and as well equipped as the Regular Army divisions. In the case of the 45th, it was fortuitous that the men were the equal of those in any other division in the Army, for their valor and determination would be tested on numerous occasions, not the least of which was the struggle for the beachhead at Anzio.

While doing research for an article on Anzio for the January 1994 issue of *World War II* magazine, I was struck by a simple fact—had the men of the 45th not held their ground in February 1944 when the Germans launched their furious counterattack against them, the Anzio beachhead, in all likelihood, would have been wiped out and Hitler would have won a major victory. And so, more than fifty years after the smoke had cleared from Anzio and the din of battle had faded away, I decided to contact as many survivors of the 45th as practical and plumb the depths of their memories, which remain amazingly clear to this day. The more I dug into their story, the more fascinated by it I became and the more resolved I was to write a book about them. I also came to discover that what the 45th accomplished in World War II in general, and at Anzio in particular, has been largely forgotten by history.

Here was a National Guard division the roots of which go back to the settling of the Wild West; the early antecedents of which saw service in the Civil War, the Spanish-American War, and the Punitive Expedition against Pancho Villa, as well as World War I; and that was brought into active federal service before Pearl Harbor. The 45th was a 14,000-man division that included thousands of Native Americans integrated into its ranks, a division that landed in North Africa in 1943; played a major role in the invasion of Sicily; saved the landings at Salerno; and took part in the agony at Anzio, the capture of Rome, the invasion of southern France, the drive into Germany, the liberation of the Dachau concentration camp, and the occupation of a defeated Germany—and for its efforts suffered over 20,000 men killed, wounded, or missing in action during its 511 days of combat.

These young but battle-hardened men were not part of what the Army considered an "elite" outfit. They did not apparently possess any of the "glamour" of the airborne troops or the rangers or Marines or the mountain troops or the flyboys in the Army Air Corps. But, just like the men in these elite units, they possessed an incredible esprit de corps—the feeling, no, the *belief*, that they were the best damned outfit in the whole U.S. military establishment—and probably in the world. As one of the division's veterans told me, "No Marine has more love for the Corps than we have for the 45th."

In the 45th's long and distinguished service, no period of combat more exemplifies the determination of its members to overcome overwhelming odds than the weeks they spent absorbing every punishment the mighty German war machine could throw at them at Anzio.

Anzio.

The name of this beautiful, peaceful Italian resort town lying on the western coast of Italy, a mere thirty-five miles from Rome, has become synonymous with the horrors of modern warfare. Anzio has taken its place beside such infamous bleeding grounds as Antietam, Gettysburg, Passchendaele, the Somme, Verdun, and Stalingrad.

At Anzio, the amphibious landings (in which the Allies had little faith and for which they had allocated inadequate resources) took the Germans totally by surprise. The stunning early success was not exploited and the delay allowed the Germans to react swiftly to throw a solid defensive perimeter around the beachhead. Four months of agony lay ahead for both sides.

At Anzio, young men from Germany, Britain, and the United States engaged in a titanic struggle where the stakes were high. If the Allies won, it would be one more nail in the coffin of the world's most evil regime. Were the Germans to win, it would be Hitler's first major victory since his defeats at Stalingrad, at Kursk, and in North Africa. A German victory would also have had serious repercussions for the Allies, not only in the Italian campaign but also in the conduct of war in the rest of the European theater. Both sides, therefore, threw everything they could spare into the battle.

At Anzio, hundreds of thousands of men were pitted against each other in life-and-death struggles that frequently resembled the grim tableaux of the previous world war: a muddy, underground existence for the combatants, immense artillery duels, and human-wave assaults across no-man's land where death and destruction were meted out without mercy.

At Anzio, young men lost their limbs, their lives, their innocence. Those who survived would never view the world in quite the same way again.

Although a number of historians of Anzio have touched upon the deeds of the 45th in the larger context of the battle, none has focused specifically on this division or explored the significance of what the 45th accomplished. In my view, the 45th's stand at Anzio must be regarded as on a par with the greatest defensive actions in military history: Wellington's stand against Napoleon's legions at Waterloo, Chamberlain's defense of the left flank of the Union line at Gettysburg, and the 101st Airborne's stand at Bastogne, to name but a few. By concentrating this book on the deeds of the 45th I do not mean to imply that the courageous contributions of the other units at Anzio were insignificant or that the 45th accomplished something that the other units could not have accomplished given the same set of circumstances. But fate had placed the 45th directly in the path that the Germans had chosen for their all-out counteroffensive, and homage must be paid to the dedication to duty that enabled the 45th to stop the enemy's assaults, for the final analysis clearly shows that the 45th was the rock that anchored the Allied line at Anzio at its most critical moments.

Comparisons of the conditions at Anzio with Dante's terrible, yet imaginary, visions of the netherworld are inevitable. Almost to a man, the surviving veterans of Anzio described it as "hell." Therefore, each chapter of this book begins with a quotation from the Italian poet Dante's *Inferno*. It seems exceedingly appropriate. Yet the ghastliness of the battle of Anzio is no fictional vision. The reality consists of scenes of soldiers battling each other with knives, bayonets, entrenching tools, and bare hands; thirst-crazed soldiers drinking from streams flowing red with blood; men roasting to death in burning tanks; pigs devouring corpses; soldiers being torn to pieces or decapitated by the bursting of shells, leaving no earthly trace that they had ever existed. In the hell of Anzio, grizzled veterans and frightened teenagers—each one someone's son, father, husband, lover, brother, nephew, or uncle—died together, their torn bodies intermingled in death and mixed with the mud churned up by unceasing artillery duels, or crushed flat and beyond recognition by armored vehicles. Many soldiers from both sides who came to do battle in this terrible place were never seen again. Individual soldiers and whole units simply vanished into the nightmarish landscape.

Yet, almost unbelievably, there were men—tens of thousands of them—who survived the ordeal at Anzio, and many more who survived the entire war—wounded, nicked up, and emotionally scarred, but otherwise alive. Although the story of vast armies marching across whole continents has often been told, the small, personal stories of the dogface living and fighting for survival in unbearable conditions has rarely been incorporated in the larger picture. My goal was to change that. To give this work the personal focus it required and to keep it from being just another reworking of old histories, I interviewed over sixty 45th Division veterans to gain—and share—the reality of what they endured and to include the type of personal remembrances not found in most history books. As one veteran whom I interviewed said, "I hope you'll be able to get down in the mud with us and tell people what it was like."

Sadly, with the passing of a half century since the guns fell silent, many of the veterans, now in their seventies and eighties, have not much time left to tell succeeding generations of their deeds and recount their experiences. This work may, in fact, be one of the last major World War II histories to include extensive oral histories of the participants. Before what the 45th endured and accomplished fades entirely from the overall tapestry of mankind's most destructive war—indeed, at a time when America needs heroes—the story of the Thunderbirds' struggle, of their endurance, and of their heroism, deserves to be told again.

1

Ancient Spirits

1846–1943

Therefore, I think and judge it best for you to follow me, and I shall guide you, taking you from this place through an eternal place, where you shall hear the howls of desperation and see the ancient spirits in their pain, as each of them laments his second death. . . .

—Dante Alighieri, *The Inferno,* Canto I

PRIVATE FIRST CLASS VERE "TARZAN" WILLIAMS was, quite literally, not a happy camper.

Here he was at Fort Sill, standing in grass up to his knees, his brawny farmer's hands on his hips, unhappily surveying the Oklahoma landscape while another dawn hit him squarely in the face. It was bad enough that his division—the 45th Infantry Division, a National Guard outfit—had to live in tents while the other units, Regular Army units, stationed at the post were housed in permanent barracks. But, for the fifth straight day, the promised wooden floors for the 45th's tents had not been delivered. That meant that he and the other members of K Company were required, for the fifth straight day, to disassemble the heavy canvas tents, fold them up, and hope that the floors would arrive while the unit was out performing close order drill or firing on the rifle range or doing the thousands of other make-work projects a peacetime army dreams up to keep its troops busy.

Like so many of the other fellows, Tarzan Williams—so called because of his broad chest and shoulders and dark, movie-star looks—had a few additional gripes. The 45th Division, a month previously, in August 1940, had just finished taking part in the Louisiana Maneuvers—the largest peacetime maneuvers in the history of the United States Army. No sooner had the boys returned home, turned in their rifles at the armory, and gone back to their civilian occupations than the Army decided to mobilize the 45th and place it on active-duty status. Everybody knew why. War with either Japan

Vere "Tarzan" Williams, K Company 157th Infantry Regiment. (Courtesy of V. L. Williams)

or Germany, or both, was coming. But nobody cared much for the idea of interrupting their normal civilian lives and their tolerable part-time military commitment and becoming full-time soldiers. Sure, they knew, when they joined the Guard, that that risk was part of the deal. Still, it didn't sit well with any of them.

Williams felt especially put out by the activation of the 45th. He was an essential part of the family farm at Snyder, Colorado, a tiny community near Brush and Fort Morgan in the semiarid northeast corner of the state. His father and mother, Claude and Eva, and his two younger brothers and younger sister would have to get by without his help on their 160-acre farm that grew corn, beets, and alfalfa. Farming was never easy during the best of times and now, with the dust bowl days of the Depression still lingering, it would be especially hard on the family. One of the reasons Williams had joined the Guard in 1938 was for the extra twelve dollars the government paid him every quarter—a sum that nicely supplemented the family's meager income.

Then, on September 16, 1940—or, as the Army prefers to write it, 16 September—President Franklin D. Roosevelt signed the papers that made the 45th the first of four National Guard infantry divisions (the other three were the 30th Division from Tennessee, North Carolina, and South Carolina; the 41st Division from Washington, Oregon, Idaho, Montana, and Wyoming; and the 44th Division from New York and New Jersey)[1] to became a part of the active army for a period of one year. Maybe by that time the war will be over and we can get back home, Williams hoped. At least the money will still be coming in, he thought, even if I'm not on the farm to share the work.

His thoughts flew back to a time, three weeks earlier, when the train from Denver pulled into the sprawling fort and chugged close to blocks of three-story brick barracks. Boy, these barracks will be all right, Williams and the other soldiers agreed. But the train didn't stop. It kept going to an area of the post filled with two-story, white-painted wooden barracks. These will be swell, too, they assured themselves. Still the train continued on. When it finally stopped, the men shouldered their duffle bags, got off, and marched out into a big open field with grass two feet high. There they found stakes pounded in the ground to indicate where each company's tents were to go. With six men assigned to each tent, the field conditions were tolerable, but barely. Two weeks of tent living went by before an officer told the men to take down the tents so carpenters could install wooden floors. The 45th Division took the tents down and folded up them up, then went off to their training regime. Williams recalled, "When we came in that evening, no floors. So we put the tents back up. Then, next morning, we took them down again. This went on for five days."

The drill, by this time, was getting old, and no one in the outfit believed that they would actually get floors under their tents. On the fifth day, Williams looked around the grassy field at the other soldiers, already sweating in the morning sun in their sleeveless, olive-drab undershirts, bitching and moaning as they struggled with the bulky tents. As far as the eye could see, the field was filled with the boys of the 45th Infantry Division—thousands of them, garbed in obsolete, World War I–vintage uniforms. Besides the 157th Infantry Regiment from Colorado, there was the 158th from Arizona, and the 179th and 180th from Oklahoma. There also were men from the division's four organic field artillery battalions, the lads from the Engineer battalion, the medics, the signalmen, the cavalry recon troopers, the Military Police, and the Quartermasters. The field was alive with the division.

Although his feelings toward being on active duty were mixed, Williams felt a special kinship with the other boys, even though he didn't know all their names. A lot of them came from farms, as he did. They knew how to handle a rifle and live off the land. They knew how to fix a balky tractor engine or a broken windmill. And, when pushed to a fight, they knew how to use their fists. The officers and sergeants were good fellows, too, even though some of them were city fellows, accustomed to soft living. And he liked the thousands of Hispanic and Indian boys in the division. He didn't know too many of them personally, but he knew they were a tough bunch—and he was glad they were on *his* side. Everybody pulled together. This is going to be some fighting outfit, Williams thought, and he felt a little surge of pride rush through him. Heck, he thought, they already *were* a fighting outfit. They proved that during the Louisiana Maneuvers.[2]

Of course, not everybody agreed with that assessment. *Nobody* did well in the Louisiana Maneuvers, especially not the 45th Division. In the early 1940s, the American Army was a pitiful force—only eighteenth in the world in terms of size. Undermanned and armed with obsolete weapons and obsolete tactics, the American military would not have lasted long on a modern battlefield against the millions of fanatical, superbly trained German or Japanese soldiers. Although the United States was officially neutral, everyone knew that the time of peace for America was rapidly running out.

First Sergeant Ernest Childers, a Creek Indian and a member of C Company, 180th Infantry Regiment, striking a fearsome pose during training at Fort Sill, Oklahoma. Childers would later win the Medal of Honor. (Courtesy of E. Childers)

One only had to read the newspapers to see that. Japan had been running roughshod over China, Inner Mongolia, and Manchuria since the early 1930s and now, in September 1940, was making incursions into southern French Indochina. And Burma, the Netherlands East Indies, and the Federated Malay States were all on Japan's takeover list.

The previous September, Germany had invaded Poland, and it was beginning to look like another world war was unavoidable. The Germans, with the *Anschluss,* had already incorporated Austria into the Third Reich, and Nazi storm troopers had overrun Poland, Denmark, Norway, Holland, Belgium, Luxembourg, and France. Germany's Axis partner Italy had declared war on Britain, and the battle for North Africa, with the British standing alone against the Germans and Italians, was heating up. The British had been routed at Dunkirk in June 1940, barely escaping from France with most of their army intact, and a German invasion of the British Isles loomed large. Only the determined but badly outnumbered British pilots had kept Hermann Göring's *Luftwaffe* from dominating the skies over England. But no one knew how long Britain would be able to hold out; ships transporting military hardware to Britain and the Soviet Union under Roosevelt's "lend-lease" program were being sent to the bottom of the Atlantic by German U-boats at an alarming rate.

With the war clouds darkening the horizon, training in the U.S. Army began to take on a new seriousness, and a large-scale field exercise, known as the Louisiana Maneuvers, was held to gauge the depth—or lack—of America's military preparedness. The results were appalling. In summer 1940, the 45th was sent to swampy western Louisiana for three weeks of maneuvers with several other divisions. Along with the active-duty 2nd Infantry Division and the 36th Division of the Texas National Guard, the 45th was made a part of the VIII Army Corps for the exercises. Lodged in a tent city near Pitkin, Louisiana, the 45th was soon to discover the special joys of living, working, and surviving in mud. During the maneuvers, the men spent as much, if not more, time battling the hurricane-force winds, torrential rains, and bloodthirsty mosquitoes as they did the opposing army. The high winds and steady downpours turned the ground into a bog of no mean proportions. The rain and mud were so bad, in fact, that the ground was covered with crayfish digging their nests in the open, and because so many vehicles were mired in the muck, the Army canceled much of the first week of maneuvers. During the war games, the men of the division were used as guinea pigs for the Army's tests of atabrine (an antimalarial agent) and a new delicacy: C rations.[3]

The second week saw units working in the field on a variety of regiment and brigade tactical problems, but the training, by all accounts, was farcical at best. Although nearly a full year had passed since Germany touched off the war in Europe, proper military equipment in America's army was sorely lacking. In the maneuvers, tree limbs and lengths of pipe doubled for anti-tank guns (with soldiers presumably saying "bang" when they "fired" them), Coke bottles filled with molasses became "Molotov cocktails," and bags of flour simulated grenades. Bridges had signs nailed to them declaring them to be knocked out, and obsolete trucks, with the word "tank" painted on their sides, were poor stand-ins for the real thing.

The 45th performed so ineptly during the 1940 exercises that an officer assigned to the division wrote, "The inefficiency of the Forty-fifth is so obvious, it is a pity the dumb public could not get down to see the feebleness of the nation's second line of defense," suggesting that if the public were aware of how ill prepared the nation's military was for the upcoming global conflict, America's isolationists would finally realize the vital importance of upgrading the fighting capabilities of the armed forces. The men who previously had trained only one night a week now found themselves on full-time, active duty in the regular Army. They dropped out of school, closed up or turned over their businesses to others, said good-bye to their families and loved ones, and prepared for an uncertain future. And now, in September, the 45th was here at Fort Sill, Oklahoma, undergoing the thirteen-week basic training course. Here, their skills in the art of war were being honed. They would climb over obstacles and crawl under barbed wire with

Part of A Company, 157th Infantry Regiment, in formation at Fort Sill, Oklahoma, autumn 1940. (Courtesy of K. Kindig)

machine gun bullets cracking overhead and run for hours until their muscles screamed for relief. They would become deadly shots with rifles, pistols, and machine guns, learning how to disassemble and reassemble the weapons until they could do it with their eyes closed. They would learn how to fight with knives and bayonets and bare hands. To learn the value of their gas masks, they would be exposed to choking, eye-stinging tear gas. They would practice throwing hand grenades until they gained the accuracy of a major league pitcher. They would become experts at map reading and orientation, proficient in the use of a wide variety of field radios and telephones, and masters of the art of cover and concealment. The "citizen soldiers" would, in short order, learn everything they needed to become real soldiers, ready to plunge into the cauldron of war.[4]

• • •

In actuality, soldiering was in the blood of many of the 45th's soldiers. For the men of America's Southwest, the profession of arms had come, if not naturally, at least out of necessity. Many of the units that made up the division could trace their military lineage back to the middle of the nineteenth century, when the federal government was expanding its borders westward. Settlers were pushing toward the new opportunities to be found west of the

Mississippi. Rumors of gold deposits were the lure for many, and soon small bands of hunters, trappers, and prospectors arrived in this parched land. These were followed by wagon trains full of homesteaders, then by the fire-belching "iron horses" snaking their way across the vast prairies, over rivers, and into the Rocky Mountains.

None of this would have mattered much had the land into which these newcomers came been barren and uninhabited. The problem was that this westward expansion (a direct result of President James K. Polk's earnest pursuit of the policy of "manifest destiny") was on a collision course with the hundreds of thousands of Native Americans who already lived there. The coming of the whites brought a drastic, irreversible change to the lives of the Indian tribes for which the plains and mountains were not merely home, but also their sacred lands. The buffalo herds on which they depended for food and clothing were decimated, the open range was fenced off, permanent settlements were built, and previously unknown forms of disease and pestilence were introduced that wiped out whole populations of Indians. It was predestined that war between the whites and Indians would be the bitter harvest reaped in the name of manifest destiny.

Although some tribes grudgingly accepted this incursion and befriended the whites, knowing that it was in their best self-interest to coexist with, rather than try to oppose, this strange race with its powerful weapons, other tribes resisted fiercely. Wagon trains and railroads were ambushed, settlements burned, livestock stolen, and homesteaders killed. It was guerrilla warfare in one of its earliest and most vicious forms. Naturally, the federal government did not take kindly to this kind of activity directed against its citizens by a people it deemed "savage" and "uncivilized" and thus took steps to prevent further violence and bloodshed and to punish the perpetrators. One of the first responses was to build forts in Indian country where detachments of soldiers could be barracked and nearby settlers could take refuge in the event of hostilities. But, as more and more whites moved westward, this burden on Washington became increasingly heavy to bear.

Because the United States often had too few resources of both men and money to spend on overseeing its newly won land, the task fell to the territorial governors and their legislatures. These governmental bodies, to varying degrees, passed laws that formed militia groups charged with protecting settlers and settlements, the railroads, the mail routes, the mines, and other features and groups considered to be valuable—not only from the hostile natives but also from agitators and criminal elements who were beyond the ability of local law enforcement officials to control. These militia groups were the forerunners of today's National Guard units.

The roots of the 45th Infantry Division can be traced back to the southwest territory known today as New Mexico. In 1846, during the war with Mexico, Brigadier General Stephen Watts Kearny led a military force into

New Mexico Territory and established a Territorial Militia to keep the peace. Sporting such names as the "New Mexico Dragoons," "First New Mexico Volunteer Cavalry," and "New Mexico Volunteers," Kearny's militiamen stood guard against raids by hostile Indians and incursions by the army of Antonio Lopez de Santa Anna, who had defeated the Texans at the Alamo a decade earlier. Soon the fortunes of the New Mexico and Colorado Territories would become linked.[5] On 26 February 1861, the U.S. Congress created the Colorado Territory, the mountains of which were home to newly discovered deposits of gold. This fact did not go unnoticed in the cash-strapped Confederate States of America, which needed vast sums to help finance its side of the Civil War.

At the outbreak of the Civil War, little attention was paid to the West by Washington, since the region was some 2,000 miles from where the major battles were taking place. But Washington's neglect was the South's opportunity, and Jefferson Davis's government began laying plans for a major western campaign. When Lincoln's administration learned of this, the mineral-rich Colorado Territory grew in importance in Washington's eyes, for deposits of Colorado gold and silver were also essential to financing the Union cause. Although Colorado was a "Northern" territory, many of its settlers had come from below the Mason-Dixon line and had definite Southern sympathies. After agitators displayed the Confederate flag in Denver, the federal government acted to forestall a Southern takeover. In 1861, all of the white male residents of the Colorado Territory were required to serve in the Territorial Militia, and two small companies of pro-North militia—the "Denver Guards" and "Jefferson Rangers"—were organized. They proved to be inadequate to maintain security throughout the territory. Therefore, in July of that year, the territorial governor took steps to form the 1st Regiment of Colorado Volunteers.

In autumn 1861, the 2nd Regiment of Colorado Volunteers was organized, and in December the 2nd marched off to Fort Garland, in the southern part of the state, to assist Colonel Edward R.S. Canby's men in stopping a rumored Confederate incursion into the West. So serious was the threat that Acting Governor Lewis Weld of the Colorado Territory requested a federal force from Fort Leavenworth, Kansas, be dispatched to reinforce Canby.[6]

These steps were taken none too soon, for in early 1862 a force of Texas Confederates led by Brigadier General Henry H. Sibley moved into New Mexico Territory with the purpose of driving northward, seizing the fabulous Colorado gold mines, and forging a route to the California ports. Federal troops and local militia in New Mexico and Colorado soon learned of the Rebel plans and dispatched a joint force from Fort Garland to literally head them off at the pass—Glorieta Pass, in the Sangre de Cristo Mountains, east of Santa Fe. For three days—from 26 to 28 March 1862—the

New Mexico Territorial Militia and the 1st Colorado Regiment hammered at Sibley's Confederates at the Battle of Glorieta Pass—a small-scale battle that has been called the "Gettysburg of the West"—and soundly defeated them. The Confederates would never again threaten the Colorado or New Mexico Territories.[7]

Following the Union victory at Glorieta Pass, the 1st Colorado was broken up and assigned to duty in Colorado, Kansas, and Nebraska, where the Indians had become a major threat to the western settlements. Considerable federal resources were diverted from the war against the South to keep the native population in check. The 2nd Regiment was joined by a 3rd, and in October 1863 the two units were designated the "2nd Regiment of Colorado Volunteer Cavalry."

By 1864, eight companies of Colorado militia had been formed, with such names as "The Central City Light Guards," "Boulder County Mounted Rifles," and "The Buckskin Guards." Meanwhile, another Indian uprising in Colorado was claiming lives, destroying property, and alarming Washington. Major John M. Chivington, a Methodist preacher and maverick officer who had distinguished himself at Glorieta Pass, was now in command of the 3rd Colorado Volunteer Cavalry and committed one of the worst atrocities in American military history. On 29 November 1864, over the protests of several officers, his force of 700 soldiers massacred a camp of defenseless Arapahoes and Cheyennes at Sand Creek in eastern Colorado, and the bodies were scalped and mutilated. This senseless, tragic act only served to further inflame Indian hostility and ensure that many years of bloodshed would follow.

During 1864, the Colorado Volunteer Cavalry was engaged in Missouri, fighting Rebel guerrilla units and Major General Sterling Price's Confederates. Following this campaign, the regiment was stationed at Fort Riley, Kansas, where it remained until 1865.[8]

While the war between the North and South raged on, so did the war between the whites and the Indians. In 1864, Colonel Christopher "Kit" Carson, in command of the New Mexico Volunteer Cavalry Regiment, engaged in ongoing battles with the Kiowas, Comanches, and Kiowa-Apaches, finally routing Chief Santana and his Kiowa warriors in the Texas panhandle in an encounter known as the Battle of Adobe Walls.[9] During this period, an additional eight companies, some of which were known as the "Denver Guards," "Colorado Rangers," and "Arvada Light Cavalry," were organized in the Colorado Territory. In 1865, a regiment of six mounted companies, known as the 1st Colorado Mounted Militia, also was formed.[10]

In 1865, at the conclusion of the Civil War, the unit that would one day become the 158th Regiment was born in Arizona. This contingent of civilian soldiers, known as the 1st Regiment of Infantry, Arizona Volunteers, was authorized to have a strength of eighty to one hundred men and was involved in scouting, escorting shipments of ore and other valuable cargo, and, of course, fighting hostile Indian tribes. Indians friendly to the white government made up a large proportion of Arizona's initial regiment. Although A and E Companies were primarily white, B Company was composed mostly of Maricopa Indians and C Company was filled with members of the Pima tribe. After only sixteen months, the regiment disbanded. Poor equipment, sickness, terrible weather, and a lack of pay afflicted the white soldiers; only the Native Americans held up well in Arizona's unforgiving climate. For the next four years, the Arizona Territory had no organized militia.

In 1870, another small military force in the Arizona Territory was formed, with a further boost from the legislature in 1877 to help combat the growing Apache problem. Among the newly formed troops were the "Galeyville Militia" and "Phoenix Rangers," who concerned themselves with protecting the citizens from outlaws, rustlers, and marauding bands of Apaches.[11]

As the decade of the 1860s waned, so did Indian unrest in the Colorado Territory and the need for a sizeable militia. By 1873, only two companies—"The Denver Scouts" and "Pikes Peak Rangers"—existed as cavalry units, and just prior to statehood in 1876 there were only five companies in the entire territory. With the coming of statehood, however, additional infantry and cavalry companies were added and, in 1879, the state legislature called for the reorganization of the militia groups into the "Colorado National Guard." During this year, another major clash between whites and Indians in Colorado took place near the present town of Meeker. A detachment of cavalry was ambushed and the White River Agency was attacked. The uprising was put down with force and the tribes involved were relocated to the Uintah reservation in Utah.[12]

Conflicts with the Indians in the Arizona Territory had grown so worrisome by 1881 that the legislature reorganized the militia groups and formed the National Guard of Arizona, which consisted of ten companies of infantry, artillery, or cavalry, for the main purpose of fighting the natives, especially the Chiricahua Apache leader, Geronimo. (Geronimo eventually was captured and sent to prison at Fort Sill, Oklahoma, where he remained on display as a tourist attraction until his death in 1909.)[13]

By 1888, the Colorado National Guard had grown to nearly a thousand officers and men. New settlers moved in and built homes and ranches in what once had been Indian territory. The remaining Indians, upset by the whites' often-illegal appropriation of their land, began harassing the settlers, burning homes and crops, and stealing livestock. Settlers appealed to Governor Alva Adams for protection, and soon troops were dispatched to quell the disturbances. The war between the whites and Indians in Colorado flared anew, then finally cooled.[14]

In Oklahoma, which had been open to settlement only since April 1889, the militia came later than in Arizona, Colorado, and New Mexico, but got off to a fast start. Seeing the value of a well-trained militia in neighboring states, the territorial government authorized the formation of a militia in 1895, naming it the "Oklahoma National Guard."[15]

During the next several years, Colorado's state legislature continued to alter the organization of the Guard, adding or deleting units and personnel, moving units to different locales, and revising its mission. A number of state emergencies required the Guard's assistance. A political dispute between the city of Denver and the state of Colorado erupted into violence in March 1894. Governor Davis H. Waite ordered elements of the Guard to surround City Hall with their rifles and cannon trained on the building. Cooler heads prevailed and the siege was called off. Also that same month, labor disputes erupted in the booming (and often lawless) gold-mining district of Cripple Creek, a town west of Pikes Peak, and the Guard was dispatched to add the force of arms to the force of law. In June of that year, riots in Colorado Springs required the presence of the Guard, and another civil war threatened to explode again in Cripple Creek. In 1896, a major fire that leveled Cripple Creek and a mining strike in Leadville were two more incidents that brought out the Guard, and for two more decades the hostilities between the whites and Indians continued to alternately simmer and erupt.[16]

In February 1898, however, the United States faced a new enemy—Spain. The American battleship USS *Maine* exploded under mysterious circumstances in Havana's harbor, touching off the Spanish-American War, and the Colorado and New Mexico Guardsmen found themselves in the thick of it. A unit from New Mexico, known as the 2nd Squadron, 1st U.S. Volunteer Cavalry, gained nationwide fame in 1898 as part of Teddy Roosevelt's "Rough Riders" in Cuba.[17] Arizona and Colorado also were represented in Cuba. In the battle for Santiago, the 250 men from the Arizona National Guard fought with considerable bravery. Although Oklahoma's Guard was not federalized for service in the Spanish-American War, it did contribute several individual units that saw action.[18]

A Colorado contingent—a regiment of infantry and two troops of cavalry—headed for the Pacific. Under Brigadier General Irving Hale (after whom Camp Hale, the Colorado training ground of the famed 10th Mountain Division, would be named fifty-six years later), the 1st Colorado Volunteers sailed from San Francisco to do battle with the Spanish, first landing unopposed on, and raising the flag over, Wake Island, later to become famous in the early days of World War II. The 1st Colorado also made another seaborne landing in the Philippines and took part in assaulting Manila on 13 August. The Coloradans were the first unit to enter the city, and an officer from the 1st Colorado raised the first American flag over the walled capital. While the battle was in progress, the regimental band kept spirits up with a peppy rendition of "There'll Be a Hot Time in the Old Town Tonight," a popular tune of the day which became the 157th Regiment's official march.[19]

After the war, appropriations for the Arizona National Guard were cut by the state legislature, but the officers kept the units functioning by paying for their units' expenses out of their own pockets. Funding was restored in 1901 and regular encampments were established. At Camp O'Neill, named after their beloved Captain Bucky O'Neill, killed at San Juan Hill, according to the Arizona National Guard's history, "Strict military discipline was maintained . . . and ladies visiting the camp were never embarrassed by any language, regardless of how unexpectedly they arrived."[20]

The short-lived war with Spain officially ended on 10 December 1898, with the United States gaining control of Panama, Puerto Rico, Guam, and the Philippine Islands and finding itself regarded as an emerging world power. The boys came sailing home, but the home to which they returned was anything but peaceful. The early years of the twentieth century continued to be a time of great civil unrest in Arizona, Colorado, and New Mexico. Colorado's Governor, Alva Adams, serving a second term, required the 1st's services to put down a number of labor strikes, riots, shootings, and incidents of arson in various parts of the state.[21]

As in Colorado, labor disturbances, sparked by intolerable working conditions and paltry wages, greatly affected Arizona. In 1903, the Guard was called out to quell a violent strike by 3,500 copper miners at Morenci. So impressed with the conduct of the militia were the citizens of Morenci that they petitioned the Territorial governor for their own company of Guardsmen. They received it. Over the next few years, public support and funding for the Arizona Guard increased, as did its overall military effectiveness.[22]

In 1910, Colorado's coal miners went on strike, armed themselves to the teeth, and declared war on heavy-handed mine owners, security guards, and deputies. Again, the Guard was the government's response. A state of anarchy and civil war soon followed, and full-scale battles erupted in the southern Colorado communities of Berwind, Walsenburg, La Veta, and other mining camps. The most tragic and controversial episode took place in April 1914, when the Guard was involved in destroying a camp of some 1,000 striking miners and their families in what has been called the Ludlow Massacre. So uncontrollable was the uprising in southern Colorado that the Guard was withdrawn and federal troops brought in. Law and order were shortly reestablished, but civil unrest was soon supplanted by more international troubles south of the border.[23]

Relations with Mexico had been deteriorating since 1910, and Mexico was beset by internal strife that threatened to boil over into the United States. Furthermore, in 1914, war in Europe had erupted, a war that would eventually involve the United States. Complicating the situation was the fact that the United States learned Germany was trying to turn Mexico into an ally. For the Guardsmen, however, defense of the country's border took priority over the war in Europe. National Guard units from Arizona, Colorado, New Mexico, and Oklahoma were called to duty along the U.S.-Mexican border after raids by followers of Francisco "Pancho" Villa created considerable panic. Under the command of Brigadier General John J. Pershing, 12,000 regulars, in an action that became known as the Punitive Expedition, were dispatched to the Southwest to keep order and, if necessary, pursue Villa and his men into Mexico. At Pershing's side was a young lieutenant who would "earn his spurs" during the expedition and launch his own considerable military career: George Smith Patton, Jr.[24]

On 9 March 1916, Villa struck at the border town of Columbus, New Mexico, burning and looting as he and his men searched for weapons, horses, and money. Although wounded in the early morning rampage, Susie Parks, the town's telephone operator, managed to call Camp Furlong where a National Guard unit was posted. About thirty mounted soldiers, led by Major Frank Tompkins, and another fifty troops under Lieutenant James Castleman, arrived on the double and took the estimated 600–700 *banditos* under fire with machine guns. Eighteen Americans and some 234 Mexicans were killed in the engagement; the surviving Mexicans were chased back across the border.[25] The situation remained volatile as Pershing launched a campaign 400 miles deep into the Mexican state of Chihuahua. On 23 October 1916, two battalions of Colorado infantry were sent to the Arizona-Mexico border to reinforce Pershing's troops.[26] Like the Guard units in Arizona, Colorado, and New Mexico, the Oklahoma force also was mobilized in 1916 and sent to patrol the Mexican-American border to guard against Villa's raiders. But Villa remained at large, and, in January 1917, Pershing's force was withdrawn.[27]

A new crisis now arose. On 6 April 1917, America declared war on Germany and the Central Powers. Combat-experienced American troops were in short supply, and the National Guard units of the Southwest were highly prized. In August 1917, the National Guard units were released from duty along the Mexico border and drafted into federal service, followed by a year of intensive combat training. It was during this period that Colorado's infantry component was redesignated the 157th Infantry Regiment, the Arizona Guard's designation was changed to the 158th Infantry Regiment, and the Oklahoma Guard was formed into two regiments: the 179th and 180th Infantry. The New Mexico Guard was broken up and reconstituted as the 120th Engineer Combat Battalion, with its infantry components made part of the 179th Regiment. These National Guard regiments, along with state units from Nevada and Utah, were sent to France in 1918 as part of the 40th ("Sunshine") Division. On reaching France, the 40th was used as a "depot division" and its troops were parceled out as replacements for other frontline units.[28]

Following the Armistice in November 1918, the 158th was detailed to guard President Woodrow Wilson briefly while he was in residence in

France; the rest of the troops were sent home, where peace was still a long way off.[29] The Colorado regiment found itself again battling disgruntled miners, this time in northern Colorado and at the steel mill in Pueblo in the southern part of the state. After calm had been restored once more, the 157th's infantry, artillery, and support units were reorganized, with companies assigned to armories in nineteen towns and cities throughout the state. The 157th as well as the 158th, 179th, and 180th Regiments found themselves part of a new organization—the 45th Infantry Division.

The 45th Infantry Division began life in 1923, with its headquarters in Oklahoma City. Major General Baird H. Markham of Oklahoma was the division's first commanding officer, followed in 1931 by another Oklahoman, Major General Roy Hoffman. He, in turn, was followed by Major General Alexander M. Tuthill, who had commanded the Arizona National Guard. In 1935, Tuthill retired from the service and was replaced by Major General Charles E. McPherren. The next year, Major General William S. Key took command. It was Key who would lead the division into the modern era.

William Shaffer Key was born in 1889 in Alabama and had been a soldier ever since he enlisted in the Georgia National Guard as a private at age eighteen, becoming a first lieutenant three years later. In 1911, he gave up his commission to move to Oklahoma, went into the hardware business, enlisted in the Oklahoma National Guard as a private, became a second lieutenant, rose to captain, and commanded an infantry company during the Punitive Expedition on the U.S.-Mexican border in 1916. In 1917, he served with the 42nd Division in France, participating in the battles of the Marne Defensive, Chateau-Thierry, St. Mihiel, and Meuse-Argonne. After World War I, Key was a captain of Field Artillery in the Oklahoma National Guard. He became executive officer of the 160th Field Artillery and that unit's commander and a full colonel in 1923. In 1928, he received his first star and was in command of an artillery brigade when he was appointed commander of the 45th Infantry Division.[30]

The economic boom following the Great War proved to be short lived and, on 24 October 1929, the Wall Street bubble burst, plunging the world into social and economic chaos. America's military also suffered from the Great Depression, and the funding for, and development of, weapons and training severely lagged behind that of Germany and Japan. Despite the cutbacks, planning for a modern army went forward and the nation's military organization was entirely revamped. The United States was divided into nine Army Corps areas, with each Corps area authorized to have one "Regular" division and two National Guard divisions. Arizona, Colorado, New Mexico, Oklahoma, and Texas became part of the VIII Corps area. At this time, the Army's infantry divisions were built on the "square" organizational concept—four regiments divided into two brigades. In the mid-1930s, in the 45th Division, the 157th from Colorado and the 158th from

Arizona composed the 89th Brigade, and the 179th and 180th Regiments, both from Oklahoma, made up the 90th Brigade. The 70th Field Artillery Brigade, made up of the 158th, 160th, 171st, and 189th Field Artillery Battalions, was also incorporated into the 45th, along with the division's necessary supporting formations—120th Medical, Engineer, and Quartermaster Battalions and various Headquarters units.[31]

The period between the world wars was a difficult time for National Guard units. Besides having little money to spend on military preparedness, the public and Congress were antimilitary at worst, indifferent at best. In 1939, while Germany, Japan, and Italy were building up their forces at a staggering pace, there were less than a half-million men in America's Army, Navy, and Air Corps.[32] National Guard units especially felt this neglect keenly, receiving the military's version of hand-me-downs: the obsolete uniforms, weapons, vehicles, and equipment no longer authorized for use by the few active-duty divisions. For example, whereas "Regular" Army soldiers received the new, lace-up canvas leggings, the National Guard troops were forced to continue wearing out-of-date puttees—cloth strips wrapped from ankle to knee. Ammunition for target practice was often in short supply or nonexistent, and some officers kept trucks and tanks running only by paying for gasoline out of their own pockets. Training was often sporadic, unrealistic, and taken lightly by the troops. Some people even joked that the "N.G." stenciled on unit property stood for "no good."[33]

In 1927, more coal mining troubles broke out, this time near Boulder, Colorado, and the 157th was again required to keep the peace. In 1937, the Guard was even called upon to help fight a plague of locusts in Colorado's eastern wheat fields.[34] No one could foresee, however, that these matters would soon be seen merely as minor annoyances; the world was about to face a challenge that would shake civilization to its very foundations.

Despite the often unpleasant task of marching against their fellow citizens with bayonets drawn or spraying DDT in farm fields alive with locusts or trying to operate on shoestring budgets, men continued to be attracted to the Guard, joining their local units for various reasons—for the few extra dollars they could earn while attending weekly drill and the two-week summer camp, for a relief from boredom, for the friendship and camaraderie of others from their communities, for the sense of patriotism it fostered, and even for the way the girls smiled at a man in a uniform. Anse "Eddie" Speairs, who would later command C Company, 157th, joined the Oklahoma National Guard in 1938 and recalled the social nature of the unit: "We were paid twelve dollars per quarter and privates got a dollar-a-day for the two-week summer camp. Other ranks earned a little more. It was like a club. Everybody who got in really loved it. People were from all walks of life. There were no promotions and no money, but everybody had a good time."[35]

• • •

From the Civil War through World War II, the American Army was a racially segregated one. Black soldiers were kept strictly to their own divisions and separate battalions, usually under the aegis of white officers. Even Japanese Americans were generally segregated from the white soldiers. The 45th is considered to be the first largely racially mixed division since the Civil War, when many blacks and individual Indians served in Union regiments. The experiment worked surprisingly well; no other division had more Native Americans. Because of the large population of Native Americans in the four states, a significant percentage of the 45th's men from the 1920s through the division's mobilization shortly before the start of World War II were Indians—Cherokee, Choctaw, Seminole, Apache, Sioux, Kiowa, Pawnee, Comanche, Osage, Creek, Navajo, and Hopi, to name but a few of over fifty tribes represented in the ranks. Some 200 Native Americans from Oklahoma's Chilocco Indian School formed a company in the 180th Regiment, and a large number of Hispanics also served with the 157th Regiment.[36]

Although most of the 45th's officers were Anglo, the whites and Indians, from all accounts, got along well, and the Native Americans were held in high regard by their white counterparts, especially when it came to matters of courage and physical endurance. One author who has studied the contributions of Native Americans during World War II concluded, "It is likely that Indians tried to live up to their own, as well as the whites', perceptions of them as warriors," falling back on their traditions of being tough, wily, and resourceful.[37] Whatever the reasons, the Native American soldier aroused the admiration of those who saw him in training and in combat. At Fort Devens, Massachusetts, an Army major commented, "Indians have better muscular coordination than any other race . . . they have the physical qualifications for a perfect soldier."[38]

Shortly after the 45th Infantry Division was established in 1923, its insignia was a gold swastika on a red square, the four sides of which represented the four states that furnished troops for the division. This emblem soon would be surrounded by controversy. Long before anyone had ever heard of Adolf Hitler, the leader of Germany's National Socialist Democratic Workers' Party—in fact, long before he was born—the swastika was considered a magical, mystical symbol to be revered. Ancient peoples used the symbol in untold ways. They wove it in their blankets and painted it on their pottery. The Byzantines carved it on their buildings and the Greeks stamped it on coins. The Buddhists used it in their temples and their writings, and the Celts employed its supposed magical powers on their monuments.

The simple hooked cross is often found in the designs of, and identified with, the Indian peoples of North and South America. Because of its southwestern U.S. regional identity, it became the obvious emblem of the 45th.

On 11 August 1924, the approved patch design was officially adopted and remained the division's insignia until 1938, when its more sinister German counterpart began to overshadow the symbol's peaceful origins. With some grumbling from tradition-minded members who did not yet understand the political ramifications behind Hitler's *Hakenkreuz,* the Thunderbird, another southwestern Indian symbol of good luck, replaced the swastika on the left sleeve of 45th Division uniforms in April 1939. But, besides bringing luck, the Thunderbird is also believed, in Indian mythology, to be a magic bird that brings rain, thunder, and lightning to the parched regions of the Southwest. In this regard, the Thunderbird's meteorological powers also seemed to plague the men of the division, as snow, wind, and rain would follow the 45th wherever it went.[39] As further indication of the 45th Division's proud southwestern heritage, the heraldic crests of the infantry regiments all sported designs that reflected Native American themes and symbols. The 157th's crest included two Indian teepees, the 179th's had a crossed tomahawk and peace pipe beneath an Indian head in full warbonnet, and the 180th's crest displayed three arrows in a shield beneath another warbonneted Indian head. The 180th Regiment's motto is a Choctaw phrase, meaning "Ready in Peace or War."[40]

One of the Native Americans in the division was Jack C. Montgomery, a Cherokee from Woodward, Oklahoma. As a boy in the 1930s, he had attended the Chilocco Indian School—a boarding school run by the federal government. He said, "There were maybe 300 or 400 students in the school. I started in the seventh grade and stayed through my sophomore year." The nineteen-year-old Montgomery joined the 180th Infantry Regiment in 1936 while attending Bacone College, an all-Indian college in Oklahoma. He remained with the unit for two years, attaining the rank of sergeant. In 1938, he transferred to Redlands University in California where, despite his wiry stature, he starred at football. Following graduation in 1940, he returned to Muskogee, Oklahoma, hoping to look up his old friends and find a job as a teacher and a coach. But his unit had been mobilized, his friends were gone, and he discovered that he couldn't teach in Oklahoma because he didn't have the right educational credits. He went to work for one of his older brothers. Then the Japanese struck at Pearl Harbor and Montgomery reenlisted in the 180th, then stationed at Camp Barkeley, Texas, as a private.

Relations between the whites and Native Americans in the division were comfortable, and racial tensions were few or nonexistent. Montgomery said, "In the Forty-fifth, there wasn't any problem between the Indians and the whites that I know of. I Company of the 180th Regiment was an entirely Indian company that consisted of students from Bacone College, but there were very few full-bloods; most were mixed blood. The captain was white and the first lieutenant was Indian. In 1941, there were five Indian sergeants in I Company, 180th, that got direct commissions."[41]

• • •

After the 45th began its period of federal service at Fort Sill in autumn 1940, unusually cold, wet weather hit Oklahoma in November and December of that year, and some 2,500 men of the canvas-housed 45th came down with the flu. Basic training went on, however, and the division completed its training in mid-January 1941, the first of the four federalized National Guard divisions to do so.[42] The 180th Regiment's official historian details life at Fort Sill that winter:

> While the soldiers at the Regular post, living in their heated barracks and individual quarters, had the latest type of clothing, our first issue of winter clothing contained many decrepit blouses of the World War I variety, and many of the . . . overcoats common to the first conflict. The fact, of course, that our men were out in the cold training while the men of the post were pursuing "inclement weather schedules" on blackboards and the like were not taken into consideration. General Key raised all sorts of protests about this situation. Then one morning it was announced that, in addition to commanding the Forty-fifth, he was also commander of Fort Sill! Things really broke loose then and in a short time overcoats and other clothing of the latest type was procured.[43]

The 45th's tenure at Fort Sill was brief. In late February and early March 1941, the division moved 226 miles to Camp Barkeley, Texas, near Abilene, for more advanced training. Immediately, the troops took a liking to the new, unfinished camp, despite the fact they were still housed in tents. At least these tents were equipped with new, gas stoves with pilot lights instead of the old Sibley stoves that constantly needed to be fed with wood to maintain heat.[44]

The city of Abilene, population 30,000, had a love affair with the 45th and the feeling was mutual. The Chamber of Commerce raised $125,000 in four days to purchase the ranch land on which Camp Barkeley was built. The town's citizens also raised $4,500 so the United Services Organization (USO) could equip two new recreation halls built for the soldiers. The locals even organized a series of "convalescent convoys" in which citizens would pick up sick and injured soldiers from the camp hospital and drive them around in the country for fresh air. The mayor of Coleman, an Abilene suburb, went out of his way to laud the conduct of the division's soldiers. Mayor E. P. Scarborough sent a letter to General Key, proclaiming "without hesitation that they are a group of the best behaved boys that it has ever been my pleasure to see. They conducted themselves as a whole in a fine, gentlemanly manner and we sincerely hope that it will be our pleasure to have them visit us again."[45] As a further show of their support, the townspeople hung a banner that said "Welcome Forty-fifth" from the railroad overpass in the downtown area.[46]

Thunderbirds getting acquainted with the new 37mm anti-tank gun at Camp Barkeley, Texas, April 1941. In combat, the gun proved virtually worthless against German armor. (Courtesy of U.S. Army Military History Institute)

While at the Texas post, in an April 1941 field exercise, the 45th was pitted against a well-trained Regular Army unit, the 2nd Infantry Division. The objective was to see which division could first reach a certain pass on a plateau near Abilene. Although the 45th had farther to go, over more difficult terrain than the 2nd faced, the National Guard outfit won the race. By a swift night movement, the Thunderbirds arrived to take possession of the pass hours before the surprised Regular Army division made it. The humiliated 2nd was ordered back to its home base for more training.[47]

In August 1941, the 45th prepared for a new, improved version of the Louisiana Maneuvers. The 1941 war games were held two full years after Germany had invaded Poland and a scant four months before the Japanese would attack the American naval and military installations in Hawaii. The new Army Chief of Staff, General George C. Marshall, and the planners at the War Department sensed the danger and tried to prepare the nation's forces for another shooting war, adding more realism than was found in the 1940 maneuvers. The 45th was again one of a number of divisions ordered to take part in the largest peacetime field maneuvers ever held in the United States. From early August until late September, the war games ranged over 3,400 square miles of public and private lands, through towns and villages, and involved some 470,000 troops. Several officers who were to gain prominence in the upcoming global war—including Major General George S. Patton, Jr., Colonel Dwight D. Eisenhower, and Lieutenant Colonel Mark W. Clark—played important roles in these maneuvers that tested men, equipment, logistics, and tactics.[48]

The climatic conditions in Louisiana were brutal. On the first day, the division drove nearly ninety miles in August heat that climbed to 107 degrees in the shade, with the humidity index at nearly the same figure. At least one of the 45th's regiments also conducted a twenty-three-mile march in the sultry weather on the first day. But the 45th prevailed. In fact, when the 1st Cavalry Division was surrounded by the 45th, the Third Army's commander called a halt to the field problem because the 1st Cavalry's horses were in danger of dying from lack of food and water. The 45th was declared the victor in more than one field problem.[49]

While on maneuvers, the members of the 45th learned that their one year of active federal service had been extended to two-and-a-half years by an act of Congress—by one vote. Some men groaned, but others realized that the division was finally beginning to coalesce as a potentially superb fighting force. With the war in Europe and the Pacific heating up, there was no telling when the 45th might see real action.[50] Unlike their inept performance in 1940, this time the men of the 45th performed so well that the General Staff, as the 179th Regiment's history states, singled it out "for special commendation and to mark it as an efficient combat force to remember in the future." For better or for worse, Eisenhower, Patton, and Clark would all remember the 45th when the time came.[51]

• • •

The war clouds building over the United States continued to darken throughout fall 1941. Each soldier was convinced that war was coming and praying that it wouldn't. Chaplain Leland Loy of the 157th recalled, "It was a time of great anxiety, like we kept waiting for the other shoe to drop."[52] When the shoe fell, it was a very large Japanese combat boot, and it landed squarely on an unexpected target: Pearl Harbor. The shock waves of the attack were felt everywhere. By the time the United States declared war on Japan on 8 December 1941, the 45th had already been on active duty for over a year, and its officers, noncommissioned officers (NCOs), and enlisted men could be said to be the equal of practically any other infantry division in the American Army.

During winter 1939–1940, General Marshall had proposed reorganizing the structure of the standard infantry division. He "triangularized" the Army's divisions, reducing the number of regiments in a standard infantry division from four to three, thus eliminating the brigade structure, and cutting the number of men in a division from about 18,000 to slightly more than 15,000. Each division was now composed of three infantry regiments (each with an assigned strength of about 3,000 officers and men); each regiment had three infantry battalions; and each battalion had three rifle or infantry companies of approximately 200 men each, plus a heavy-weapons company in which the bulk of the machine guns and mortars were concentrated. Each company was further subdivided into four platoons of about fifty men each. In addition, approximately 160 officers and enlisted men were assigned to Division Headquarters and Headquarters Company. Each division also had a Military Police Platoon; an Ordnance Light Maintenance Company to keep vehicles and weapons in top condition; a Quartermaster Company for maintaining and distributing authorized levels of supply items; a Signal Company charged with operating and maintaining radio equipment as well as photographic needs; a Cavalry Reconnaissance Troop; an Engineer Battalion trained in bridge building, field fortifications, road building, and the laying and clearing of minefields; a Medical Battalion; and a Division Artillery component with four battalions. In addition each regiment had an Anti-Tank Company outfitted with 37mm (later 57mm) guns, a Regimental Headquarters Company, and a Service Company. In April 1942, a Cannon Company with 75mm and 105mm guns mounted on tracked vehicles was added to each regiment. Later, once the infantry divisions had been committed to combat, independent tank and tank destroyer battalions would be attached. Also, once deployed to a combat area, the regiments often operated as Regimental Combat Teams, or RCTs, meaning that everything a regiment needed to accomplish a mission was assigned to it—an artillery battalion, an engineer company, a medical company, a signal detachment, an anti-aircraft battalion, or whatever other subunits might be deemed necessary.[53]

This more flexible, streamlined structure enabled the Army to carry out Marshall's doctrine of the "holding attack," in which one regiment could pin down the enemy with fire and the second could maneuver to attack the enemy from the flanks or rear, while the third could be held in reserve. Unfortunately, Marshall's triangularization meant one of the 45th's regiments would have to be separated from the division. In February 1942, the 158th (Arizona) Regiment was detached from the division and sent to the Panama Canal Zone before eventually seeing combat in the Pacific theater as a separate regiment not permanently attached to any specific division. The 158th's first taste of combat would be at Arawe, New Britain, on 27 December 1943. The unit would also see action on New Guinea, on Noemfoor Island, and in several engagements in the Philippines. Many men in the division were sad to see their friends in the 158th depart, for they had forged a strong bond with the Arizona boys over the years.[54]

• • •

In April 1942, after eighteen months at Camp Barkeley, the 45th received orders to relocate again, this time to Fort Devens, Massachusetts. In a farewell parade on a rainy day, the division marched down Abilene's main street to the cheers, and a few tears, of the citizens, who were truly sorry to see them go. For many of the men, the journey would be the first time in their lives they had ever left the Great Southwest. The train trip to Fort Devens took five days, at the end of which the 45th was delighted to discover that it would be housed in real barracks rather than under canvas. Shortly after its arrival, the division began to receive an infusion of draftees, mostly from New York and Massachusetts, that gradually altered its southwestern makeup. According to the 180th Regiment's history, "The Selective Service men speedily took their places as efficient working cogs in the machinery of the organization."[55]

Although the division thought it had been well conditioned over the past year, it was in for a rude surprise. The commander of the U.S. V Corps, whose headquarters were at Fort Dix, New Jersey, but who spent considerable time at Fort Devens, turned out to be a martinet. One of the general's favorite pastimes was requiring that when he came within one hundred yards of an officer instructing a group of subordinates the officer sprint as fast as he could to the general, come to attention, and salute. If he didn't run fast enough to suit the general (which was most of the time), the officer would have to dash back to his troops and then return to the general at a full gallop. If this second lap also proved to be unsatisfactory, the officer was directed to sprint to some distant tree, building, or other geographical feature. Needless to say, the officers of the 45th did not much care for this method of whipping them into shape.[56] As a way of preparing themselves for the general's sprints, a rigorous training regime was instituted at Devens. Every man in the 45th—from the cooks and clerks to the highest-ranking officers—was required to be able to run five miles in an hour or less.[57]

While in the Northeast, the division participated in a number of patriotic parades, including the 1942 Fourth of July parade in New York City, as well as others in Boston, New Haven, Bridgeport, and other cities where patriotic fervor and support for the war effort were running high. Always attracting attention and comment was the 45th's contingent of Native Americans, their broad, brown faces and black hair contrasting sharply with those of the "Anglo" soldiers. Sometimes the mere sight of the Indians elicited negative responses from a population unaccustomed to seeing them. On occasion, the New Englanders—descendants of those starving pilgrims who were cared for and fed by the Native Americans during the first Thanksgiving—would intentionally cross the street to avoid having any contact with them, thanks to rumors that portrayed the Indians as bloodthirsty savages. But the 45th's Native Americans scoffed at such rumors and set about to change the public's perception of them. Making replicas of their tribes' drums and flutes and traditional dress, including feathered headdresses, a large contingent of the Indians began presenting dances, ceremonies, and lessons in Native American culture to schools, Boy Scout troops, and church gatherings throughout New England, culminating in a war dance on the Boston Common in support of a war bond rally.[58]

Second Lieutenant Ernest Childers, C Company, 180th, and a member of the Creek tribe, wearing a ceremonial headdress. (Courtesy of E. Childers)

The Army had determined that any invasion of enemy-held territory was sure to involve amphibious landings and so embarked on a program of preparing its divisions for just such an eventuality. That summer, the 45th received training in amphibious assaults near Camp Edwards and Buzzard Bay on Cape Cod.[59] Tarzan Williams recalled that at Fort Devens,

> We done a lot of amphibious training there. Although there was no water, they had a large tower that simulated a ship that had a rope net that hung over the side to the ground. We had a full field pack and rifles and we had to climb to the top of the platform on the tower, then crawl over the side of the net to the ground to simulate a landing boat. We also went to Cape Cod for more amphibious training. The amphibious training battalion that trained us had the old-type boats. We had to climb over the sides to get in and jump over the sides when we made a landing. We even made a landing at Martha's Vineyard.[60]

Also that summer, Major General George S. Patton, Jr., spoke to a gathering of the division's officers, telling them that the 45th had been selected to take part in a task force that would land in North Africa as part of Operation Torch and strike the first blow by an American army against the German war machine. The 45th's role, however, was later canceled, to the great disappointment of the officers, who were eager to prove the division's mettle in combat.[61]

In October 1942, a significant change occurred in the division. Major General William S. Key, who had commanded the 45th for two years, was reassigned to become the Provost Marshal General of the European Theater of

Major General Troy Middleton took command of the division in 1942. (Courtesy of the 45th Infantry Division Archives)

Operations, and reluctantly relinquished the reins of his beloved division to the assistant division commander, Major General Troy Houston Middleton. The Mississippi-born Middleton's life and career closely matched that of General Key's. Both were born in the South in the same year. Like Key, Middleton had enlisted in the Army as a private, was commissioned a second lieutenant, and served in the Punitive Expedition into Mexico in 1916. Key, however, never saw combat in France during the First World War. When his unit, the 4th Infantry Division, was sent overseas, Middleton took part in several major engagements, including the battles of Aisne-Marne, St. Mihiel, and Meuse-Argonne. After the 47th Regiment's commander was disabled in a gas attack, Middleton, the executive officer for the 39th Regiment, assumed command and, at twenty-nine, became the youngest full colonel in the Allied Expeditionary Force. After the war, he reverted to the rank of captain, as was the custom, and remained in the Army for nineteen more years, retiring in 1937 after having served his country for thirty-seven years and reattaining his colonelcy. In civilian life, he became dean of administration, as well as comptroller and acting vice president of Louisiana State University but, with war breaking out in Europe, Middleton volunteered to return to active duty. His initial request was turned down, but after Pearl Harbor he was recalled to the Army with the rank of lieutenant colonel and saw duty with the 4th (the same division in which he had served during World War I) and the 36th Infantry Divisions. Now, in autumn 1942, at age fifty-three, he was a major general in command of the 45th.[62]

• • •

In November, the Thunderbirds moved again, this time to the winter wonderland of Pine Camp (today known as Fort Drum), near Watertown, New York. For two months, the division, more accustomed to the scorching summers of the desert Southwest, became acclimated to the harsh realities of winter near the eastern end of Lake Ontario. Ten-foot snow drifts and temperatures that plunged, depending on which report one believes, to 35,

46, or even 54 degrees below zero were commonplace that winter. According to the outspoken Felix Sparks, then a captain in the 157th, the transfer of the division to upstate New York was "a monumental blunder." He recalled that "heavy snowfall and constant subzero temperatures made training almost impossible. The first night maneuver was called off before it was completed because of the intense cold. Adequate cold weather clothing was not available, and frostbitten hands and ears were common."[63]

Tarzan Williams also remembered, "It wasn't too cold when we got there, but winter really socked in on us and the cold took its toll on the boys. The Army issued us fur-lined coats but not fur-lined pants. We were on overnight maneuvers when we stopped and were told to dig in. We dug holes to get out of the wind, but it was still cold. I was on guard duty one night. It was 42 degrees below zero and the moon was shining. I had on all the clothes the Army issued to us but my legs still froze."[64]

Despite the arctic conditions, the 45th continued to train, practicing the fine arts of marching, marksmanship, and mayhem—the latter not always on the maneuver field. The division gained quite a reputation for itself both on post and off. When the men trained, they trained hard; when they played, they apparently had forgotten the manners that had impressed the locals in Abilene. At Pine Camp, the Thunderbirds frequently went beyond the bounds of what polite society considered appropriate behavior. Even Watertown, a town that supposedly was familiar with the boisterous behavior of young soldiers, was unprepared for the antics of some of the young soldiers, who were not shy about settling an argument with fists, chairs, or beer bottles.[65]

A Thunderbird frolicking in the snow of Pine Camp, New York, December 1942. (Courtesy 45th Infantry Division Archives)

More serious problems also erupted. Two members of the 157th Regiment were arrested for robbing a Watertown bank and spent the duration of the war in the federal penitentiary at Fort Leavenworth, Kansas. Felix Sparks attributed the breakdown in discipline and morale to the substandard housing, clothing, and training conditions at Pine Camp.[66] In January 1943, the 45th slipped out of Pine Camp with no parade, no fanfare—just a sigh of "good riddance" by the locals. This time the Thunderbirds were on the move to the warmer climes of Camp Pickett, Virginia, near the town of Blackstone, which had recently been home to the 3rd Infantry Division. The 45th's infamy, however, continued to linger in Watertown long after its departure.

After the division made itself known to the Italians and Germans defending Sicily, two news items appeared in the Watertown newspaper. The first, an editorial, read:

> The Forty-fifth Division, as all will recall, was at Pine Camp for two months. They came just as the leaves were departing from the trees in early November last fall and remained until the middle of January. They were a rugged, rollicking group. They made the Fourth Armored, which preceded them, appear as docile as Dagwood Bumstead. It took us a few weeks to get used to them and frankly speaking, the town was considerably quieter after they were shifted elsewhere. Raw November and December weather never cooled their spirits. They cut high, wide, and handsome capers on our streets. They broke up a tavern or two. They gave local police and MPs a real workout. Yet we look back with affection upon the Forty-fifth. They were fighting men. Woe to anyone who fell in their path. Now, if it is true they are in Sicily, they will find conditions exactly to their liking. If General Eisenhower wants Catania taken, let him shove the Forty-fifth in battle. They will deliver any town, mussed up perhaps, but thoroughly conquered.[67]

The second notice came in a letter to the editor:

> Each day, as I read the accounts in the newspaper of the swell job the Forty-fifth Division has been doing in Sicily, I think back to last winter. . . . The Forty-fifth had just pulled into Pine Camp from Fort Devens, Massachusetts, and what a load of unfavorable publicity had accompanied it; how the boys had wrecked the town of Ayer, Massachusetts, and what a relief to the townsfolk of Ayer when the Forty-fifth pulled out. Consequently the people around Pine Camp were a little wary of these Oklahoma boys, when they first arrived and it was tough going at first to make friends in Watertown. There were the usual fights. People just didn't like them very much because they were too wild. . . . What the smug citizens who censured these soldiers did not realize was that here, in their midst, had been one of the roughest, toughest infantry divisions in the whole United States Army. Those fellows were just itching for combat duty. They had to blow off steam some way or other, so there were a few rows in beer joints or other public places. However, when those same holier-than-thou critics read the newspaper accounts of what the Forty-fifth has been doing, I'm sure they feel a bit of guilt. Because, in order to win, this army of ours has got to be the roughest, toughest of any army in the world.[68]

One of the "roughest, toughest infantry divisions in the whole United States Army" was now testing that reputation against the peaks in the Blue Ridge Mountains, as well as on the amphibious warfare practice beaches at Little Creek, Virginia, and Solomons Island, Maryland—two aspects of training that would serve the division well throughout the remainder of the war.[69] Tarzan Williams remembered one of the mountain maneuvers:

The Army had a small airplane for the officers to observe the maneuvers. We were moving through the trees and there was an open clearing where there was a house. Every time the plane would fly over, the old woman who lived there would come out and throw up her arms and yell at the plane. When we asked her what the problem was, she said she was afraid the flying machine would knock the chimney off her house. We told her the plane had to fly high enough to clear the tops of the trees. I don't know if we convinced her or not, because she would watch the plane every time it flew over.[70]

While the division went through its paces, Middleton and his staff were ordered to meet with General Patton in Morocco in April to discuss invasion plans that would involve the 45th in the near future. Flying to North Africa by way of Brazil, the 45th's "brain trust" was informed that the division would get its first taste of combat during the planned invasion of Sicily that July. Middleton and staff remained with Patton for a month, poring over the thousands of details that an amphibious landing entails. The original plan called for the 45th to land at Palermo, on the northern coast of Sicily. After Middleton had returned to Pickett, the plans were altered. Instead of the north coast, the division would land on the south.[71] Felix Sparks recalled that the division received a stepped-up emphasis on amphibious training: "We learned that climbing down a swaying landing net with full combat gear into the small landing craft below was a trying experience. Injuries from the final fall into the landing craft were not infrequent."[72]

At Pickett, training took on a new seriousness as the officers readied their men—and themselves—for their baptism of fire. The 45th would be fighting alongside two infantry divisions that had already seen combat—the 1st and 3rd—and no one wanted the sole National Guard outfit assigned to this operation to perform with any less professionalism.

Bit by bit, rumors of the impending deployment leaked out until the Army's Chief of Staff let almost the entire cat out of the bag. Louis Scott, a veteran of the division, recalled that General George C. Marshall addressed the 45th's officers at Camp Pickett, telling them, "You are going to make an amphibious landing in Europe. Your job and that of the few divisions who will land with you is to keep the enemy busy and occupied while we prepare a huge American Army." Scott added,

Most of those in the audience had no idea what General Marshall meant that day. He spoke in football terms that told us little that we could understand about the mission of the division. . . . The gist of what he said was, "In football, often the quarterback takes the ball and fakes to a back who runs into the center of the line and gets clobbered. Then the quarterback carries the ball around end and gets all the glory." At that time, the division didn't know if it was going to be the quarterback that got all the glory—or the back who ran up the middle and got clobbered.[73]

• • •

Except for a few of the officers' wives, the women who had followed their soldier-husbands, like soldiers' wives everywhere across the country, had no on-post housing. Life was difficult. While their husbands lived in the barracks, the women lived in whatever cheap hotels, boarding houses, and rented rooms might be available in the towns surrounding the military bases, often seeing their men only on weekends, or sometimes seeing them not at all. Tarzan Williams said, "We got the word we were going overseas. Every camp and fort we had been in always had a lot of girls and women in the towns and cities around the camps. A lot of the girls married the soldiers and they lived in town close to the camp while their husbands lived in the camp. So when the orders came down that we were going overseas, the men had to send their wives back home. Some were pregnant and some had babies."[74]

On 25 May, with its training complete, the rough-and-ready 45th Division moved from Camp Pickett to Camp Patrick Henry, near the huge, bustling naval base at Norfolk, Virginia, and at Newport News was combat-loaded into ships (meaning that men, equipment, and vehicles are arranged on board a vessel in the most effective order they will disembark on a hostile shore).[75] On 4 June, the division began a two-week voyage in convoy across the U-boat–infested Atlantic Ocean, screened from submarine attack by Navy destroyers.[76] Williams recalled, "We didn't know where we were going until we were out to sea, then we were told we were going to North Africa. There were twenty-five large ships in the convoy and twelve or fourteen escort ships."[77] The convoy's journey proved uneventful and, at 1500 hours on 22 June, the division dropped anchor off the North African coast at Mers-el-Kébir, near Oran, Algeria.[78]

The battle for North Africa had been over since May, when the surviving elements of Panzer Army Africa, under *Feldmarschall* Irwin Rommel's successor *General der Panzertruppen* Jürgen von Arnim, were utterly destroyed. The triumphant Allies were on the doorstep of Hitler's and Mussolini's home, and the 45th Division was one of the uninvited guests who would soon be kicking in the door. The reason for the combat loading became clear on the morning of 23 June. The 45th's entry into North Africa would take the form of another practice amphibious landing, this time in the darkness. The Thunderbirds climbed down cargo nets into landing craft, then made their run in to shore at Arzew in full combat gear. Unfortunately, only one of the regiments was landed on the correct beach; the other two were delivered some ten to twelve miles away by the inexperienced Navy coxswains. General Omar N. Bradley, who would command the II Corps during the Sicily operation, turned to Bill Kean, his chief of staff, and commented, "Good Lord! Suppose they miss it by that much in Sicily?"[79]

After the landing, the 45th moved into bivouac at Oran for a few days of physical conditioning for the men to work out the kinks from the long voyage; clean the sand out of their uniforms, equipment, and weapons; write

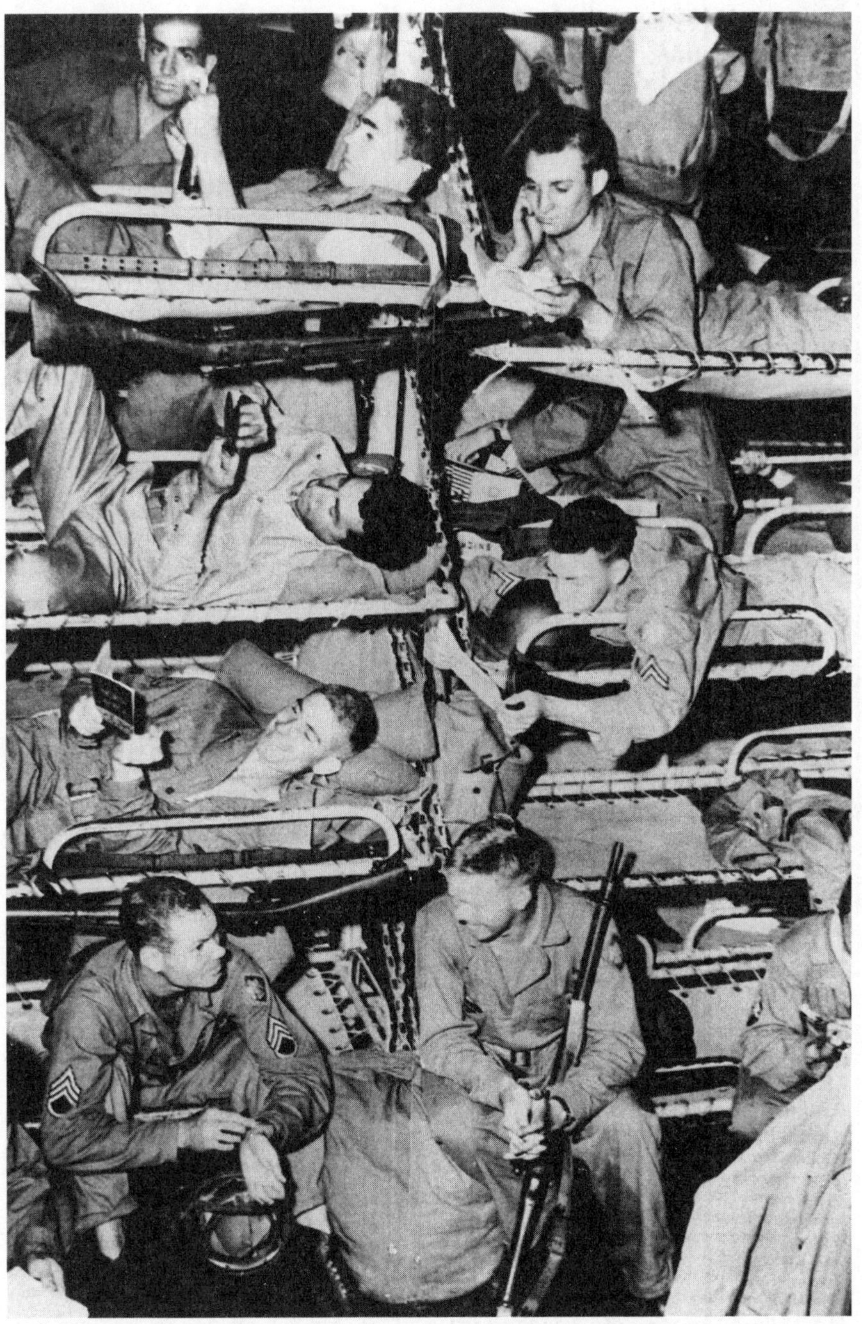

45th Division troops below decks on a crowded troop transport heading for North Africa, June 1943. (Courtesy of 45th Infantry Division Archives)

letters home; and prepare for their first combat experience.[80] On 27 June, George S. Patton, Jr., now sporting a third star as commander of the Seventh Army for the invasion of Sicily, an operation known as "Husky," assembled the eager but inexperienced men of the 45th around him and gave them a lecture few of the Thunderbirds would ever forget. Patton cautioned the men to watch out for dirty tricks when it seemed a group of enemy soldiers wanted to surrender. A favorite tactic, the general said, was for a small group to suddenly drop their weapons and raise their hands or wave a white flag. When unsuspecting Americans moved into the open to take the enemy prisoner, the "surrendering" troops would hit the dirt and their comrades, lying in wait, would spring up and mow down the exposed Americans. Patton warned the Thunderbirds to be always on their guard for this sort of treachery and to show no mercy if the Germans or Italians attempted this trick. His words would have fateful repercussions.[81]

Although General Middleton and his staff knew what lay ahead, the green troops were kept in the dark until the last minute. On 5 July, in the port of Oran, the 45th and its attached units loaded onto the same ships that had carried them across the Atlantic and steamed eastward on a calm sea under sunny skies. Once aboard the vessels, the division's mission and destination were finally revealed to the rest of the officers and men, who were given maps and detailed plaster topographical models of their objectives to study. Nearly five years of training for the 45th was about to be put to the test. Everything was as ready as it could be. Along the thousand-mile route to Sicily, the 45th's convoy linked up with LSTs (Landing Ship, Tank*) and LCIs (Landing Craft, Infantry†) carrying the 1st Infantry Division from Algiers and the 3rd Infantry Division from Bizerte.[82]

The invasion of Sicily was on, and the first major Allied dagger thrust against what Churchill had termed the "soft underbelly of Europe" was about to begin.

---

*An LST was 327 feet long, displaced nearly 4,500 tons, and could carry dozens of tanks and 150 soldiers. By comparison, the smaller LCT was over 200 feet in length, weighed from 123 to 143 tons, had a hinged ramp door, and could carry five tanks, ten or twelve trucks or jeeps, or a large number of soldiers.

†An LCI was 160 feet long, weighed 200 tons, and could carry an infantry company (200 men). If landing on a nonhostile beach, the soldiers would walk down long ramps on either side of the bow. If the beach were hostile ("hot"), the soldiers would climb down cargo nets hung over the side and transfer into smaller LCAs (Landing Craft, Assault) or LCVPs (Landing Craft, Vehicle and Personnel) that would carry them to shore before dropping the front ramp. These LCVPs were often referred to as "Higgins" boats, after their designer, Andrew Jackson Higgins. So vital to the overall war effort were the LCVPs that, after the war, Eisenhower remarked that Higgins was "the man who won the war for us" (G. A. Shepperd, *The Italian Campaign: 1943–45* [New York: Praeger, 1968], p. 413; and Stephen E. Ambrose, *D-Day; June 6, 1944: The Climactic Battle of World War II* [New York: Simon & Schuster, 1994], pp. 43–45).

2

Those Malign Gray Slopes

10 July–8 September 1943

When it has reached the foot of those malign gray slopes, that melancholy stream descends, forming a swamp that bears the name of Styx. And I who was intent on watching it, could make out muddied people in that slime, all naked and their faces furious. These struck each other not with hands alone, but with their heads and chests and with their feet, and tore each other piecemeal with their teeth.

—Dante Alighieri, *The Inferno*, Canto VII

THE ISLAND OF SICILY, lying like a deflated football just off the toe of the "boot" of Italy, is no stranger to warfare. Since the days of the ancient Greeks, Phoenicians, Carthaginians, Romans, Normans, and Spaniards who battled across the hot, hostile, volcanic island, Sicily has seen more than its share of bloodshed. The modern armies, with their guns and tanks and airplanes and more sophisticated methods of killing, were merely the latest to add to the litany of misery in the island's unhappy history.

Operation Husky, the invasion of Sicily, was, in many ways, a blueprint for Operation Overlord, and many of the lessons learned here would be incorporated in the Normandy invasion eleven months later. Both operations were massive in scale, requiring close coordination between air, ground, and sea forces. Both operations would involve both British and American troops. Both operations would begin before dawn, come out of a stormy sea, and catch the defenders off guard. Both operations would employ highly trained and motivated Rangers and Commandos, plus paratroops and glider-borne troops to achieve surprise and create confusion behind enemy lines. Even the overall commander of both Husky and Overlord would be the same—Dwight David Eisenhower. Under Ike, both Lieutenant General Omar Nelson Bradley and General Sir Bernard Law Montgomery would have significant commands. And both operations would have their share of mistakes, foul-ups, snafus, and tragedies. Both, too, would involve the flamboyant Lieutenant General George S. Patton, Jr., although in the case of Overlord, it would be as a decoy to deceive the Germans that the Normandy operation was merely a diversion and that the real blow would fall at the Pas de Calais.

Nine Allied divisions were slated to take part in Husky's initial phase. With 115,000 British and 66,000 American soldiers scheduled to assault Sicily, along with the participation of 3,200 ships and over 4,000 aircraft, Operation Husky was the largest amphibious operation up to that point of the war. Overlord, by comparison, would involve 7,000 ships and landing craft, 160,000 men to be landed on D day, 20,000 vehicles, and 11,000 aircraft.

Facing the invaders initially were over 50,000 German troops (primarily from the Hermann Göring Panzer Division, commanded by *Generalleutnant* Paul Conrath, and the 15th Panzer Grenadier Division, under *Generalmajor* Eberhardt Rodt) and 315,000 Italian soldiers, plus considerable numbers of aircraft and warships. An additional 40,000 German troops would be rushed to the island during the course of the monthlong battle. Commanding the Axis forces was *General der Infanterie* Hans Valentin Hube of XIV Panzer Corps, who had lost an arm at Verdun in the First World War. No one knew exactly what kind of resistance the Axis partners would offer.[1]

The opening notes of the battle would be sounded by over 3,000 paratroopers of the 82nd Airborne Division, flying in from North Africa in 266 C-47 transport planes, who would parachute down near the Ponte Olivo airfield on the night of 9–10 July to prevent any enemy force from attacking the landing beaches near Gela. It was the first of two scheduled drops.[2] Before dawn on the morning of 10 July, Montgomery's Eighth Army of some 115,000 British and Empire troops would land on the southeastern tip of the island, then drive north up the coast to take Syracuse, Catania, and Messina. The Eighth Army force consisted of the 5th and 50th Divisions, 1st Canadian Division, 51st Highland Division, 231st Independent Infantry Brigade, 4th and 23rd Armoured Brigades, 40th and 41st Royal Marine Commandos, an anti-aircraft brigade, and an air landing brigade from the 1st Airborne Division that would land in gliders south of Syracuse. The 46th and 78th Divisions would stand by as reserves in North Africa for follow-up operations. Patton's smaller Seventh Army, consisting of approximately 66,000 soldiers (minus the paratroops), would have only a supporting role to play, that of protecting Monty's left flank by driving northward through Sicily's mountainous center.[3]

The American invasion contingent was divided into three forces designated "Joss," "Dime," and "Cent." Operating under the aegis of Bradley's II Corps were Major General Terry Allen's 1st Infantry Division and a Ranger force

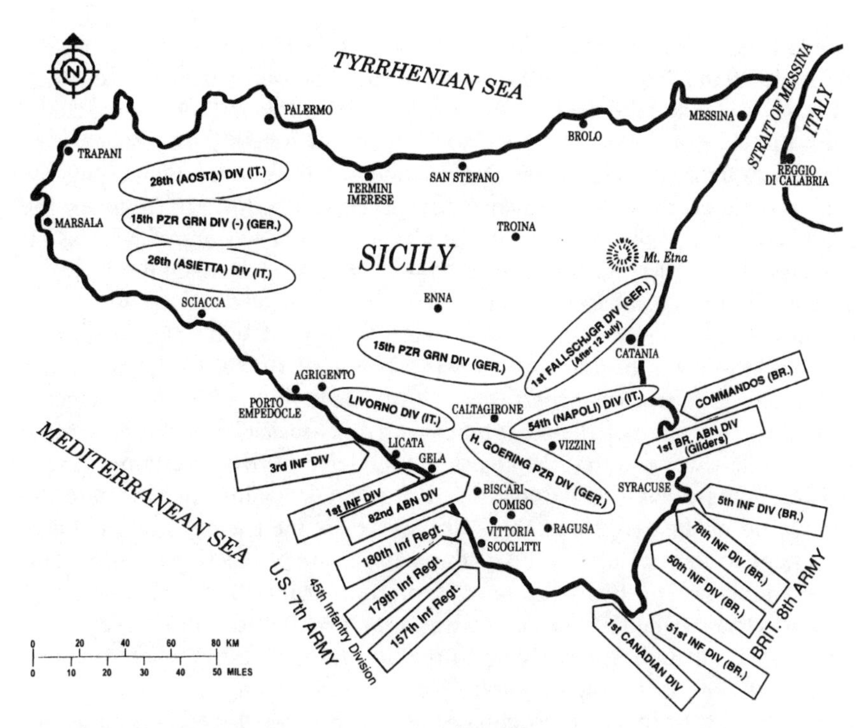

MAP 2.1 Operation Husky: The Invasion of Sicily
The Thunderbirds got their first taste of battle on 10 July 1943 when the U.S. Seventh Army under Patton and the British Eighth Army under Montgomery hit the southeast corner of Sicily with 181,000 troops.

under Lieutenant Colonel William O. Darby, both of which would hit the beach at Gela (Dime Force). To the 1st Division's right, the 45th's 180th and 179th Regiments (Cent Force) would land side by side north of the fishing village of Scoglitti. Eight miles south, the 157th would come ashore. Operating separately from, but in close coordination with, II Corps was Major General Lucien King Truscott's 3rd Infantry Division (Joss Force), on Seventh Army's far left flank, which would land near Licata and have the mission of securing the western third of the island. The 2nd Armored Division would form the floating reserve and support all three American divisions. The remainder of the 82nd Airborne Division would also wait in reserve in North Africa, along with the 9th Infantry Division, to be employed later. All of these divisions, with the exception of the 45th, had already seen combat in North Africa.[4]

Patton considered the 45th's landing to be vital, for within the Thunderbirds' zone were two key airfields. The 45th's battle orders called for the 180th to land south of the Acate River, capture the Biscari airfield along with the high ground about twelve miles inland, block the main north-south highway through the area, and make contact with the 1st Infantry Division on the 45th's left flank. The 179th was to land north of Scoglitti; capture that town, plus Vittoria; and take the Comiso airfield, some eleven miles from the coast, with the help of the 157th. The 157th Regiment would land just north of Capo Scaramia and seize Santa Croce Camerina, three miles inland, plus the high ground northeast of Comiso; assist the 179th Regiment in capturing the Comiso airfield; and link up with the Canadian 1st Division, which was on the task force's right flank. It was a large, complex, and essential mission to be entrusted to an untried division.[5]

On 8 July, while the convoy was steaming toward Sicily, the weather in the Mediterranean began to deteriorate. The wind shifted to the north and the water grew choppy, then turned into massive swells. Men unaccustomed to the ways of the sea became terribly seasick, and the task force commanders worried that the invasion, scheduled for the predawn hours of 10 July, would have to be postponed. But delay would only increase the likelihood of the task force being discovered by the enemy, and so Husky was kept to its timetable. One of the men in one of the ships was Second Lieutenant Trevor Evans, a mortar platoon leader with M Company, 157th, who recalled, "The ocean was very rough and almost everybody was seasick, including me. Down in the bottom of the ship where the men were, it was an inch deep in vomit."[6]

Eight miles from shore, Brigadier General Raymond McLain, commander of the 45th's Division Artillery, stood on the deck of his ship watching an airfield signal light somewhere in the direction of Scoglitti or Zafaglione make its regular sweeps, as though it were a sleepy sentry who had not yet spotted the enemy sneaking up on him. McLain saw a large fire burning on shore, perhaps near the Biscari airfield. Then flares began to pop and hang in the sky on their parachutes, and a large search light in the vicinity of Gela began traversing the armada, groping to see what was in the dark. The Navy's guns opened up against the light and other shore targets at 0330 hours, the tracers burning red arcs through the black sky.[7]

With the ships anchored at their stations offshore, the men quietly assembled on deck as they had done so many times before during practice landings. Only this time, it was different. This time, it was for real. The first landing on a hostile shore is always the easiest—and the most difficult. Easy because each soldier is a neophyte, a virgin to combat. The noise and confusion and horror of war are still incomprehensible, no more real than a training film. Although fear is running high, so is the excitement and elation of actually, *finally,* putting years of training to use. And difficult simply because the unknowns are overwhelming: How will I react to combat? How will my squad perform? my platoon? my company? my battalion? my regiment? my division? my army? Will I chicken out or will I hold my own? Will we land on the right beach? What happens if we don't? Do I have enough ammunition? What if my rifle jams? Where are my grenades, my bayonet, my cigarettes? What if I'm hit? Will I lose a leg? Will there be a medic nearby? Will I die? And so it went, private thoughts creasing each man's forehead as he looked toward land, watching the bright blossoms that flamed on shore with each round of naval fire, feeling the *crump* of the explosions against his eardrums several seconds after the visual display, waiting for the order to finally move from the comforting security of the mother ship into the bobbing landing craft several stories below. Nerves were stretched tight, mouths were too dry even to salivate, and many stomachs and intestines were in a state of distress.

Gone were the comfortable cotton khakis the men had worn on the voyage to North Africa. Each soldier was dressed for the occasion: steel helmet, olive-drab wool shirt and pants, waist-length cotton jacket, and ankle-high service shoes topped with canvas leggings. Around his waist, each combatant wore an ammunition belt with ten canvas pockets, each of which held an eight-round clip of ammunition, for a total of eighty rounds. Some men carried six additional eight-round clips in bandoliers looped over their shoulders. Over the ammunition belts were buckled inflatable life belts; should it become necessary, two CO_2 capsules would be activated, filling the tubelike belt with air. Attached to the ammo belts were haversacks—canvas packs that held everything a soldier would need to survive for a day or two on his own—rations, mess kit, eating utensils, wool blanket, poncho, shelter-half (half a pup tent; by "buddying up," two soldiers could build a complete tent that was barely large enough for one man), wooden tent pegs, collapsible tent poles, and extra socks and underwear plus personal articles such as toothbrush, shaving gear, comb, deck of playing cards, pictures of mom and dad, wife or sweetheart, and a small Bible. A 16-inch bayonet in a scabbard was attached to the pack, as well as a T-handle entrenching tool. Fragmentation grenades were either attached to D rings on the straps that connected the haversack to the belt or carried in a small canvas pouch.

Around his neck, each man wore a chain from which two identification disks—"dog tags"—dangled. These bore, in stamped letters and numbers, the soldier's name, serial number, religion, and blood type, to make it easier for frontline medics, rear-echelon doctors, and, should the unimaginable happen, the fellows from Graves Registration. The tags were taped together with black friction tape to keep them from rattling. Many men also had a small can opener, popularly known as a P-38, hanging from the chain as well. From the back of the ammunition belt hung two, sometimes three, canteens full of water. Also attached to the belt was a small pouch containing a wound dressing. No one wore a bullet-proof vest or body armor.

Slung over one shoulder was a large, bulky, canvas pouch that contained a gas mask; no one could be sure that the enemy wouldn't use poison gas against an invading force. Slung over the soldier's other shoulder was his most important piece of equipment: his weapon, usually a .30 caliber M-1 Garand semiautomatic rifle (manufactured by Springfield or Winchester); sometimes an older but more accurate bolt action M-1903 Springfield rifle with sniper scope; sometimes a lightweight .30 caliber M-1 carbine, which had a propensity to jam. Some men carried the heavy BAR—Browning Automatic Rifle. A small number of troops had the .45 caliber Thompson submachine gun, the weapon of choice of gangsters and G-men alike in the 1920s. Field-grade officers as well as regimental and battalion staff officers and some mortarmen and machine gunners wore .45 caliber M-1911 semiautomatic pistols. Some men lugged mortar tubes or mortar base plates or the mortar rounds themselves, strapped to their backs; others carried .30 caliber machine guns and tripods. Yet others manhandled the unwieldy anti-tank rocket launchers known as "bazookas." Every company, battalion, regiment, artillery battery, and forward observer required radio communication, and their heavy radios also had to be carried on the backs of human pack animals. Men assigned to the anti-tank companies would receive their weapons once they reached the beach: 37mm and 57mm anti-tank guns that would be brought ashore by landing craft. The 105mm and 155mm artillery pieces would also be towed in behind trucks, half-tracks, or tractors. Still, some men—the chaplains and medics—went into combat completely unarmed. Fully loaded, each fighting man carried at least fifty pounds of equipment, clothing, ammunition, and weapon. Many men worried, and rightly so, that they would drown if they jumped from the landing craft into water that was over their heads.

An hour past midnight came the order for the first unit, the 1st Battalion, 179th, to board its landing craft. This unit and many others were "rail-loaded," that is, the men climbed over the gunwales into landing craft that had been hoisted on davits to nearly deck level; once the craft had been loaded, it was lowered to the sea. On other transports, the empty landing craft were first lowered and then the men climbed down cargo nets to the boats. In total darkness, man by man, company by company, the number of men on deck diminished as each soldier struggled to boost himself and all he was carrying over the ship's gunwale, groped with nervous feet and fumbling fingers for the next handhold and foothold on the cargo nets that now doubled as ladders. They had practiced this many times—at Cape Cod and in Virginia—but this time a mixture of apprehension and excitement made their movements slow and awkward. Down the nets climbed the soldiers, like a swarm of olive-drab spiders, some wishing their precarious journey clinging to the side of the ship would end quickly, others wishing the descent would last an eternity—anything to delay the inevitable. Clouds of exhaust fumes from the idling landing craft drifted upward, choking those above. On one net-ladder, somebody lost a helmet; it clanged off the helmet of a cursing soldier below. On another, a soldier lost his grip and fell into the landing craft, injuring himself and several others on whom he landed.

At last all those going ashore in the first wave were packed tightly in the small assault craft that pitched and heaved with the waves. Soon many of the men were heaving, too, their breakfast meals lying in pools at their feet or on the man in front of them. The surf was so rough that in at least one case it took nearly three hours to load 748 men in the landing craft.[8] The command, "Shove off!" was shouted from above. The helmsmen gunned their engines, moved away from the larger ship, and began circling in the black, roiling waters, waiting for the signal destined to send them toward the dark island. At 0330 hours, parachute flares popped over the invasion beaches and the U.S. Navy destroyers *Tillman* and *Knight* opened up in support of the waterborne Thunderbirds.[9]

Brigadier General Raymond S. McLain, Division Artillery commander (pictured as a lieutenant general in postwar photo). (Courtesy of 45th Infantry Division Archives)

General McLain recorded the events in his diary:

> It seemed boats were circling everywhere. . . . Cox'ns were shouting orders from the deck to the boats, staff officers and radar experts were checking position by every known means. . . . We stood watching the boats form up and move off the line of departure. . . . H-Hour, which was two hours before daylight, would be about an hour late. . . . Destroyers moved in with assault waves. As they reached the line of departure, the destroyers moved to the flank and soon opened a terrific bombardment. . . . It was some time later when fire was opened . . . to the south in the direction of Camerina. The cruisers also opened at the same time and the *Abercrombie,* a British monitor. The shells of all these guns were plain red traveling lazily through the air. The *Abercrombie*'s guns' trajectory was nearly as high as it was long. It was an awe-inspiring sight. It was delivering death and destruction to a country that had not seen war for decades.[10]

Fire from Italian coastal batteries began splashing among the landing craft, forcing them to the right. At 0334 hours, shortly before H hour, the cruiser *Philadelphia* blasted back, with huge rings of smoke and flame issuing from the ship's big guns.[11] Around 0345 hours, the boats carrying the first wave of seasick 179th troops scraped the sand and the steel ramps dropped; the first Thunderbirds dashed ashore through the surf in a wildly confused melee.[12] Ten minutes later, according to the ensign in charge of the first wave, the first of the 157th's boats hit land and the men "walked out of the boats, quite surprised at the convenience of a bus ride. They seemed to stand rooted for a minute, not being able to realize the apparent lack of opposition."[13]

Glen K. Hanson, a platoon sergeant with L Company, 157th, recalled, "The water was kind of high and some of the less agile people had a little trouble getting ashore, but they got assistance from their buddies or their squad leaders. The water wasn't very deep—maybe two or three feet. We didn't get any enemy fire on our landing; the later waves did, though."[14]

It was not smooth going for all the boats. Tragically, two landing craft collided and swamped while trying to avoid a rocky outcropping, and thirty-eight men drowned.[15] At 0430 hours, a large enemy air assault was unleashed on the armada, its bombs coming close to the ships but causing only slight damage. Anti-aircraft fire and the arrival of a squadron of British Spitfires chased them off.[16] As it was the first assault landing for the division, as well as for the Navy boat drivers who brought them into shore—in a rough sea with ten-foot waves, no less—the result was more than a bit chaotic. Many units were separated or landed on the wrong beaches; others never made it in due to the landing craft getting hung up on rocks and sand bars. Still other boats dropped their ramps in too-deep water, and heavily laden men stepped off to drown without ever having fired a shot.[17] Lieutenant Eddie Speairs, C Company, 157th, recalled, "It was the weather that hurt us. And the Navy guys were scared to death; they had never done anything like this. They were under fire for the first time in their lives. The Navy had not trained their landing crews well enough—we were scattered all over. The waves were eight, ten, twelve feet high—where do you get that kind of training?"[18]

Tarzan Williams, K Company, 157th, remembered, "The sea was very rough and the Navy had a hard time landing us on the beach. Some boats made the landing, then got washed up on the beach. One or two turned over in the water. The boat I was on didn't land where it was supposed to, and we had to walk about a mile to get to our company. There wasn't much fight in us when we landed but, when the first man got wounded, it was shoot or be shot."[19]

Pete Conde, a corporal from Pueblo, Colorado, serving with E Company, 157th, heard that the 3rd Battalion suffered a number of accidentally self-inflicted casualties on the run in. "They had fixed bayonets to their rifles in the boats and when the boats got tossed around by the waves, a lot of the guys stuck themselves and each other with their bayonets."[20]

As the day wore on, more and more troops came ashore. Finally responding to the landings, coastal batteries and inland artillery opened up on the invaders. In the surf, some 200 landing craft lay abandoned, either

A confused jumble on the beach during the 45th's landing in Sicily. (Courtesy of 45th Infantry Division Archives)

knocked out by enemy fire, hung up on rocks, or immobilized because of mechanical problems.[21] Once on the beach, the Thunderbirds restored order to their ranks as best they could. Soldiers separated from their units hastily joined whatever unit was around. Some units were formed ad hoc, with the highest-ranking enlisted man in charge. The endless preinvasion briefings were paying off. Few soldiers sat idle in the sand, biding their time until an officer or NCO came along to tell them what to do. In various-sized groups, the men began pushing inland. Defensive positions on the beach, manned by Italian troops of dubious fighting ability, were quickly overrun by the men of the 157th and 179th. The 180th, dumped several miles west of its assigned beach and badly scattered on landing, ran into stiffer opposition while trying to take its objectives. Casualties were already being reported.[22]

Pete Conde recalled one of the first casualties his unit suffered while the men were dug in along a road:

> We were the last platoon in the battalion, the tail end. There was this young kid, an orphan, in our platoon. He was eighteen or nineteen years old. He had no family and was going to make the Army a career. He was laying there about five yards in front of me when a bullet came down the road and hit him in the shoulder. I ordered these two big guys to take him back to Dr. Atkinson, but by the time he got back to the aid station, he was dead. That bullet cut the vein that goes to the heart and he bled to death internally.[23]

Second Lieutenant (later Brigadier General) Felix Sparks, E Company, 157th Infantry Regiment, with his wife, Mary, in 1941. (Courtesy of F. Sparks)

General McLain recorded, "On the beach, an aid station was dressing many wounded men, both American and Italian. There were also about 200 Italian prisoners and a few Germans under guard there."[24] Meanwhile, the drowned bodies of soldiers, and a few sailors, were washing up on shore. Colonel Charles Ankcorn, the 157th commander, directed Felix Sparks, now a captain, to arrange for a collection and burial detail. The only available troops were sixty members of the regimental band. Pressing them into service, Sparks had the men collect the bodies, make identification wherever possible, and dig temporary graves in the stony soil about three miles inland from the beaches.[25]

Besides enemy action, the Thunderbirds also had to contend with a number of larcenous fellow Americans from an Army Engineer unit who were supposed to be performing shore party duties. Instead of helping bring vital supplies ashore, these thieves helped themselves to the contents of the officers' and enlisted men's bags that had been piled on the beach.[26]

That afternoon, McLain ran into General Middleton, whose jeep had been strafed by an enemy plane while he had been looking for one of his units on the road above Scoglitti. Middleton informed McLain that one of the battalion commanders—Lieutenant Colonel William H. "King Kong" Schaefer, the C.O. of the 180th's 1st Battalion—was missing. Schaefer, who had repeatedly drilled into his men the idea that they must do everything possible to avoid being captured, had himself been taken prisoner by the Germans in the early hours of the invasion.[27] According to Bill Whitman, a lieutenant with B Company, 180th, Schaefer received his nickname after his face had been burned early in life. Whitman wrote, "He was the ugliest-looking man in the U.S. Army, maybe the Navy and Marines as well. He referred to us in his battalion as his 'knotheads.' He was a brilliant tactician. He knew von Clausewitz from cover to cover." Another member of the 180th called Schaefer "one of the two greatest officers I have ever known." He went on to say, "What a man he was. Had he been C.O. of the 180th, he probably would have ended his military career as at least a major general instead of as a POW."[28]

Although still suffering from a leg injury sustained in a fall during the practice landing at Oran, Schaefer had led his battalion inland toward the Biscari airfield. Running into a company of Tiger tanks and two infantry battalions from the Hermann Göring Panzer Division, Schaefer tried to make a stand. Scattered and outnumbered, the 1st Battalion found itself in an untenable position, hammered by machine guns, tanks, mortars, and artillery and strafed by aircraft. A number of officers became casualties and the Germans forced the battalion to withdraw south of Highway 115. Schaefer and several officers took cover in a culvert and watched helplessly as German troops infiltrated the area. Schaefer was in bad shape. Supported by First Lieutenant Russell P. Blissman and First Sergeant Don E. Croft, the battalion commander left the protection of the culvert and tried to make it to friendly lines that had been set up in an olive grove. The trio never made it. Captured by the Germans, the three spent the duration of the war in POW camps.[29]

The 180th's battle for the Biscari airfield, situated on top of a plateau, was a difficult one that lasted a full day. Major Roger S. Denman had just taken over command of the regiment's 1st Battalion from the captured Schaefer when he was wounded and evacuated on the twelfth. Major Denman's replacement, Lieutenant Colonel Chester M. Cruikshank, lasted only a few hours; he fell into a hole and broke his ankle. On the fourteenth, the airport finally was secured by the 180th, but not before the Thunderbirds performed some considerable heroics.[30] The experience of Captain Ellis Ritchie of E Company, 180th, was typical. Ritchie was leading a platoon near the Biscari airfield when the crew of a German Mark IV tank spotted him and began firing their main gun at Ritchie from nearly point-blank range, blasting a tree in half just above his head. The captain coolly responded by directing his men to take out the tank with rifle grenades. They did.[31]

Bill Whitman recalled some harrowing times while leading B Company, 180th, to capture the Biscari airfield. His company was being raked by all manner of weapons as it climbed the slope of the plateau to the airfield. The enemy forces "would have been much better off if they hadn't used tracers. We could spot their machine guns and riflemen; killing the gun crews wasn't too difficult when they were manned by Italians. The Germans were something else again. Individual fights broke out all over the slopes, and it was all hand-to-hand in the semi-dark with the gun crews. One of my men beat a German officer to death with his helmet."

After digging up mines with his bare hands, Whitman and his men finally made it to the top. Ordered to sweep the supposedly deserted airfield for enemy, the lieutenant was shocked to discover the place crawling with Germans. "The planes contained snipers and the buildings concealed machine guns. Turrets on the planes swung around, opening fire with machine guns." The Americans blasted every German position they could find. "One of my men had a scare; he pulled the door open on a plane and was confronted with a dead German in a sitting position pointing a burp gun at him. He riddled the Kraut before he found out that he was already dead. The men kidded him about it for days."[32]

During the battle for the Biscari airfield, some of the troops captured an Italian Army finance officer. Relieving him of the Italian Army's payroll, one of the Americans, thinking the lira was as worthless as Confederate money, went on a spending spree with a pillowcase full of cash and even used some of the bills to light his cigarettes. Only later did he discover that he had burned, spent, or thrown away approximately $50,000 worth of still-valid currency.[33] Another odd occurrence took place when Lieutenant Colonel Ross H. Routh, the 45th's paymaster, was unexpectedly ordered ashore on D day with six field safes containing the division's $2 million payroll. When Routh reached the beach, he discovered that the safes, which were on another LCVP, had failed to make it to shore. During landing difficulties, the safes had been thrown overboard and were found underwater the next day. All of the money was recovered, but it took several days for Routh and his men to dry out the bills.[34]

Meanwhile, farther south, Scoglitti and Santa Croce Camerina fell quickly to the Americans, but Vittoria proved a tougher nut to crack. General McLain decided to take two jeeps and two half-tracks into sniper-infested Vittoria to reconnoiter the situation there. The town seemed to be in total confusion, with no city officials available with whom to negotiate a restoration of order. McLain and his men finally found a small group of minor police officials, along with a drunken American paratrooper who had been disarmed after dropping near the town. McLain had him, another drunken paratrooper, and two 45th men who had liberated some *vino* arrested. McLain also laid down the law with the police officials; either they pass the word that the sniping stop or the buildings from which firing came would be leveled.[35]

The adrenaline that had been pumping through the Thunderbirds during the buildup to the landings and the first hours of combat gradually gave way to the fear and weariness that comes with battle. Paul Cundiff, a member of Middleton's headquarters, wrote, "American soldiers had called the Sicilians dirty dogs and had intended to run their bayonets through them without mercy. When the dust of the first day of battle had settled, so had their mood of revenge. They gave the peasants their rations, their money, and chanted that the Italians were the real enemy."[36]

• • •

The battle for southern Sicily raged throughout 10 and 11 July, with the Germans taking over defensive positions from the Italians and staging several determined counterattacks and numerous air raids against the invaders. To the 45th's left, the Hermann Göring Panzer Division launched a fierce counterattack at the 1st Infantry Division at Gela but was beaten back.[37] Things also looked grim in the 180th's sector on the eleventh when tanks and infantry pushed the 180th off a ridge, ran unchecked through Colonel Forrest E. Cookson's regimental command post, and were finally stopped by artillery, tanks, naval gunfire, paratroops, and Thunderbirds a mere two miles from the seashore. That same day, the combined guns of four destroyers—the *Beatty, Laub, Cowie,* and *Tillman*—stopped several panzer attacks toward the 45th's beachhead.[38]

Tragedy struck the Allied effort late on the eleventh when 5,000 American anti-aircraft guns mistakenly opened up (along with some enemy guns) on the second airborne assault. Navy gunners shot down six of the 144 C-47s carrying members of the 82nd Airborne Division's 504th Regimental Combat Team who were about to parachute onto the island. Earlier that afternoon, a Liberty ship had blown up in a huge fireball during a German air raid, and less than an hour before the American transport planes appeared the Axis had bombarded the American fleet in another massive aerial assault; the Navy gunners, most of whom had never been under fire before, were more than a bit nervous and trigger happy when the American planes flew over in the dark. Rumors had also been circulating that the Germans were going to make a parachute drop against the beachhead that night.[39] In the wild melee, some 229 American parachutists were killed, wounded, or listed as missing in action and sixty planes were either destroyed or badly damaged by friendly fire.[40]

After a rough start, Colonel Cookson's 180th Regiment was finally getting its act together, and the Germans who stayed to fight around the town of Biscari suffered severely. Several large panzers and trucks were knocked out by the 45th's artillery and sat on the road, little more than blackened hulks. "In one vehicle," McLain wrote in his diary, "all that was left of the driver was his belt buckle with charred bits of the belt. One American soldier lay dead in the road, dead for a day or two. One American jeep was burnt out. It had some German papers in it and other German effects. It might have been the one captured [from] the ill-fated Schaefer's party."[41]

Lieutenant General Omar Bradley, commanding II Corps, recalled an unusual event that occurred on 11 July after the Comiso airfield had been captured by the 157th and 179th:

> Twenty-five enemy aircraft had been caught there on the ground and the wreckage of 100 more littered the revetments around it. I quickly rushed an AA battalion to Comiso to defend it against enemy air attack while it was being readied as a U.S. base. The first ship to land at Comiso after its capture was a twin-engined German bomber. As the JU-88 lowered its landing gear and banked into the pattern, our AA fired and missed. Just as soon as he had tax-

> ied to a stop, the pilot jumped out shaking his fist at the gunners. Not until then did he learn the field had been captured. Next two ME's [Messerschmitt fighter aircraft] swooped in but this time our gunners held their fire and two more pilots were captured.[42]

On the twelfth, General McLain had a close call with a German aircraft. Not far from the Comiso airfield, the general and a small party were doing reconnaissance work on a mountain road when American anti-aircraft fire opened up on an enemy plane high above them. The plane "started a dive from straight above us. We thought it was dive-bombing at the road we were on, but soon it burst into flames and came streaking by us about fifty yards out and landed about 300 yards down the mountainside." After running down the mountain toward the burning aircraft, the group pulled back because of the danger posed by exploding ammunition.[43]

At the Comiso airfield, a nickel-plated bicycle was captured along with a cache of weapons, other vehicles, and equipment. Some of the men presented the bike to Chaplain Leland L. Loy of the 157th, intending it to be a gag gift. "I had no other transportation at the time, so I put it to good use," he said. As the 157th's history reports, "The chaplain and his bike became a familiar figure on the roads and hills of Sicily and the cry of 'Hi-yo, Chappie' became part of regiment tradition."[44]

Second Lieutenant Trevor Evans, M Company, 157th, was maneuvering around the perimeter of the airfield when he spotted some movement ahead, near some camouflaged buildings. "I jumped up foolishly," he said, "and shouted and waved my carbine at them. They came out of the ground there, some thirty or forty Italian soldiers who gave up. A couple of my men took them to the rear."[45]

On the twelfth, after the fall of the Comiso airfield, the 157th was moving toward Charamonte when it was attacked by enemy aircraft. The next day, after Charamonte fell, the 157th took the towns of Elmo and Monterose after brief firefights. The regiment moved on to Licodia, where the Germans launched a fierce counterattack with artillery, flamethrowers, and murderous machine gun fire. The 3rd Battalion suffered sixty casualties but fought its way into the town and secured it.[46]

On the seizure of Vittoria on 12 August by the 179th, a detail from Division Quartermaster drove into town to pick up several trucks that had been captured by the regiment. After reaching the town, the drivers discovered looting, sniping, and a full-scale civilian riot going on. For seven hours the truck drivers attempted to quell the disturbance, clear out the snipers, and evacuate the wounded. Twelve Italian snipers were captured by the Quartermaster detail.[47]

Also on the twelfth, the British Eighth Army commander, Montgomery, pulled a "power play" that rankled nearly everyone in the 45th and caused some serious problems between the American and British high commands. Montgomery had been forced to abandon his costly attempts to break through the tough German defenses on the eastern coastal highway and unilaterally decided to skirt Catania by moving inland around Monte Etna's volcanic cone. Highway 124, which ran northwest from Vizzini to Caltagirone and then to Enna, was in the 45th's sector, and the division needed it to continue its push. Without waiting for approval from higher headquarters, and without informing Patton, Bradley, or Middleton, "Monty" decided to cut across the 45th Division's front and appropriate Highway 124 for use by his Eighth Army troops.[48]

Just after 1700 hours on 13 July, with the 157th preparing to assault Vizzini, Colonel Ankcorn was more than a little surprised to find a British unit, the 51st Highland Division, moving up the highway, clearly in the American sector, also on its way to attack the town. Late that night, with Montgomery's move already a fait accompli, General Sir Harold R.L.G. Alexander, who was Eisenhower's deputy commander, informed Patton that Highway 124, the Vizzini-Caltagirone road, now belonged to the British and was off limits to the Americans.[49] The next day, Patton gave Bradley the bad news: "We've received a directive from Army Group, Brad. Monty's to get the Vizzini-Caltagirone road in his drive to flank Catania and Mount Etna by going up through Enna. This means you'll have to sideslip to the west with your Forty-fifth Division."

Shocked, Bradley responded, "This will raise hell with us. I had counted heavily on that road. Now if we've got to shift over, it'll slow up our entire advance. May we at least use that road to shift Middleton over to the left of Terry Allen?"

Patton vetoed the request, stating that the change was to take effect immediately. "But that leaves us in a tough spot," protested Bradley. "Middleton is now within a thousand yards of that road. If I can't use it to move him over to the other side of Allen, I'll have to pull the Forty-fifth all the way back to the beaches and pass it around Terry's rear." But Alexander's directive was firm, and Bradley's protests fell on sympathetic but deaf ears. The 45th would have to pull out of the battle and perform an extraordinarily difficult maneuver.[50]

Brigadier General McLain recorded the Highway 124 incident in his diary: "We got orders to halt our advance short of the objective as two British divisions would march west on the road. We were not to fire or advance beyond two miles of the . . . road. So the observers of both the 171st FA Battalion and the 158th FA Battalion watched columns of enemy move back along the road as the British moved up, unable to fire on them. I phoned Corps, but orders were orders. So we sat tight."[51] The Thunderbirds, along with the 51st Highlanders, were holding their positions when along came the Canadian 1st Division, which had been ordered to pass through them for the purpose of attacking the fortresslike town, perched on top of a mountain. But the Canadians ran into trouble and asked for the nearby 157th's help.[52]

Lieutenant Colonel Charles Ankcorn, commanding the 157th, ripped a shipping ticket off the side of a nearby railroad boxcar and scribbled a terse order to Lieutenant Colonel Preston J.C. "Murph" Murphy, the 1st Battalion's C.O. "Murph, go help the British," the note read. The 1st Battalion, along with the 158th Field Artillery, ignored Montgomery's dictum and did as Ankcorn ordered, taking the high ground west of Vizzini and smashing resistance until the Canadians could enter and hold the town.[53] After the action, the Thunderbirds, loaded in trucks, were hauled back nearly to the beach and had to swing west behind the 1st Division before they could again resume their northward advance. Much precious time and gasoline had been wasted by this inter-Allied squabble and ninety-mile detour.[54]

The division soon found itself operating in the rough, rocky center of the island. Lieutenant Bill Whitman, B Company, 180th, recalled a bizarre and tragic incident while the 45th was moving through the Sicilian countryside. "An old, grey-haired, grandmotherly woman was in a small stone house with a knitting basket on her lap. One of our men went into the house to search it. He started to open a door leading into another room when the woman pulled a pistol from underneath her knitting basket and shot him in the back, killing him." The woman was taken prisoner.[55]

On 14 July, the fourth day of the 45th Division's introduction to savage combat, two unfortunate incidents occurred that reflected negatively on the Thunderbirds. Near the Biscari airfield, which was being assaulted by Captain John T. Compton's C Company, 180th, a fierce firefight erupted and a dozen of Compton's men were wounded. A group of thirty-six Italian snipers, some dressed in civilian clothing, surrendered. Remembering Patton's 27 June speech and apparently acting on an order from the general that enemy troops who fired upon medics and wounded soldiers or were dressed in civilian clothes were to be executed, Compton had the entire group shot.

On the same day near the same airfield, Sergeant Horace T. West of A Company, 180th, was directed to escort a group of prisoners of war to the rear for interrogation. After marching the group a short way, West inexplicably halted the prisoners and shot forty-five Italians with a machine gun. Compton and West were court-martialed for killing seventy-three POWs. Compton was cleared of the charges, but West was judged guilty and sentenced to life imprisonment. West served a year of his sentence, was reduced to private, and returned to duty. Captain Compton was reassigned to the 179th Regiment, distinguished himself with a number of heroic acts, and subsequently died in action in Italy in November 1943.[56]

During the first five days on the island, the 45th was credited with capturing or destroying more than 15,000 small arms, 10 million rounds of

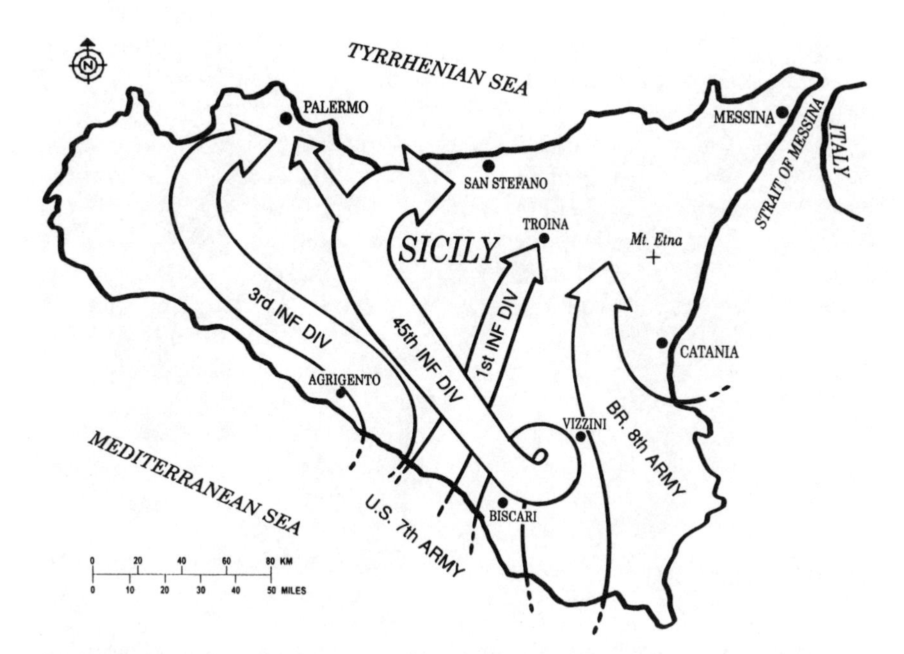

MAP 2.2 Slogging Across Sicily
The combined American-British operation squeezed the German and Italian defenders toward Messina. Squabbling between Montgomery and his American allies forced the 45th to perform a complex maneuver that required the Thunderbirds to pull out of the line, sweep behind the 1st Infantry Division, and head for the northern coast.

ammunition, 700 machine guns, 38 artillery pieces, 49 trucks, 160 aircraft at the Comiso and Biscari airfields, 44 tanks, and 220,000 gallons of fuel. Over 5,000 prisoners had been taken by the Thunderbirds and uncounted hundreds of the enemy had been killed or wounded.[57] These statistics would have been outstanding for a veteran division; for a green division in its first combat role, they are astounding. But the 45th was not allowed to rest on its laurels; the division still had many hard miles and hard battles ahead of it before it could relax. As Omar Bradley noted in his biography, *A Soldier's Story,* "For six days and nights, the Forty-fifth Division advanced across the center of the island in one of the most persistent nonstop battles of the Mediterranean war. Confined to a single northbound road, Middleton leapfrogged his regiments one through another to attack both day and night."[58]

At 1600 hours on 18 July, without much resistance, the division took Caltanissetta, an important railroad center and former hotbed of Fascism, with a population of 60,000. On the outskirts, General McLain saw an old man "carrying the mangled form of a boy about ten. The boy was still con-

Thunderbirds marching through the hot, dusty streets of Caltanissetta. (Courtesy of 45th Infantry Archives)

scious. . . . A doctor came by and I sent him to do what he could, but the boy was dying then. . . . Later I learned the child had picked up a German grenade left alongside the road and it had exploded. They left many little red grenades along the road. The Division chaplain said he had found two corpses with these grenades, with the pin pulled, pushed in the dead man's pocket so that, when removed, they exploded."

That night, McLain enjoyed a bath in the local palace that had been used by the Fascists as their headquarters and "slept in a fine bed with fine linen and soft covering, magnificent chandeliers, and drapes. I ate with Middleton, Patton, Bradley, and Teddy Roosevelt, Jr., who had come in, dust-covered from the First Division to coordinate a road we had to share with him the next day. . . . Cushman had found a smoked ham and it was sure good; reminded me of old Kentucky."[59]

Unlike the general, the GIs of the 45th had no time to luxuriate in the Fascist palaces of Caltanissetta, dine on smoked ham, or cleanse themselves in marble baths; they continued their footsore march through the city, moving up into the mountains toward Santa Caterina, their perspiring faces and sweat-soaked wool uniforms coated by the fine, white Sicilian dust. As they marched, they continued to meet, and overcome, German strongholds, mines, blown bridges, and harassing fire.[60] Charlie Dunham, a platoon sergeant with E Company, 157th Regiment, recalled, "We didn't have much transportation. We covered most of Sicily on foot. We were fortunate when we landed that most of the resistance was from the Italians; after we got up to the north coast, the fighting got more severe."[61]

Above Caltanissetta, the 180th took over the point from the 157th and smashed through a stout roadblock the enemy had erected at Portella di Reccativo on the evening of 19 July, then kept going. On the twentieth, the 180th had patrols on the outskirts of Palermo, Sicily's capital and largest city. Then the division got word it was being kicked off the highway again. This time, a Provisional Corps under Geoffrey Keyes, consisting of the 3rd Infantry and 2nd Armored Divisions plus two Ranger battalions, was given priority for the use of Highway 121 into Palermo, and the 45th found itself scrambling over rocks and boulders and donkey paths. Even this did not deter the Thunderbirds, who could almost smell the sea breezes ahead. On the morning of 23 July, thirteen days after landing on the southern coast, the 157th reached the northern coast, five miles east of Termini Imerese, and fanned out both east and west along the coast road.[62]

• • •

The Thunderbird's newspaper, the *Forty-fifth Division News,* began its overseas editions shortly after the unit landed on Sicily, publishing whenever it could find a press or a mimeograph machine. In its 22 July issue, the paper reported, "Lieutenant General George S. Patton, commander of the Seventh Army, has this to say about us: 'The Forty-fifth Division, a green outfit, went into combat with two veteran outfits, and asked for no favors, made no excuses. They kept up with the other outfits. I'm damned proud of every officer and man in the Division.'"[63]

About the only man in the 45th of whom Patton wasn't proud was Bill Mauldin, a young soldier and artist who graced the division's newspapers with cartoons of two grizzled soldiers named Willie and Joe who were always making humorously sardonic comments about the war in general, officers in particular, and the sorry state of affairs for the average dogface. Patton, who regularly fined unshaven or tieless soldiers, fumed over the fact that Mauldin "set such a damned bad example with his unsoldierly Willie and Joe." Once, Patton went so far as to directly order Middleton to get rid of Mauldin's cartoons. "Put your order in writing," Middleton responded. Patton never followed up.[64] Mauldin went on to greater fame with *The Stars and Stripes,* and Willie and Joe survived the war as two of the four most famous fictitious GIs of all time, the others being "Sad Sack" and "Kilroy," the latter a ubiquitous, long-nosed character whose visage always seemed to be chalked on every wall and fence throughout every city and village, along with the inscription, "Kilroy was here."

Patton himself was in considerable hot water. On 3 August, while checking on wounded soldiers at the 15th Evacuation Hospital, he came across a young, trembling soldier of the 1st Infantry Division who Patton thought was showing signs of "battle fatigue," a condition the general felt was only a euphemism for cowardice. He slapped the soldier across the face with his gloves in a misguided attempt to help the soldier "snap out of it." A few days later, it was discovered the soldier had been suffering from dysentery and malaria. On 10 August, Patton virtually repeated the same incident, slapping a quivering soldier from the 17th Field Artillery Regiment at the 93rd Evacuation Hospital. After shouting at the soldier, Patton waved his ivory-handled pistol in the man's face, threatened to shoot him, and then slapped him. On the sixteenth, Patton was chastised by Eisenhower. Soon after, the American media got wind of the incidents and some members of Congress began calling for Patton's head. Ike stood by Patton, but these incidents forever stained the career of one of America's greatest fighting generals.[65]

• • •

While Montgomery's forces were still battling for their lives trying to get around the heavily fortified slopes of Monte Etna, the 180th had a patrol on the outskirts of Palermo, but the 45th was then directed eastward along Highway 113 toward Messina. (Palermo was entered with little resistance by the 3rd Infantry and 2nd Armored Divisions on 22 July and, from the sea, by the 9th Infantry Division.)[66] The Thunderbirds took one coastal town after another, sweeping the less-than-determined Italian defenders from their path. The only time the drive slowed was to root out pockets of German troops, who fought with considerably more tenacity than their Italian Fascist partners. Seldom was a yard of ground yielded by the Germans without a determined fight. To the southeast of the 45th, the 1st Infantry Division was also having a hard time overcoming the rough terrain and German opposition.[67]

The 179th's historian paints a realistic picture of the northern coast of Sicily: "In northern Sicily, in contrast to the lowlands of the south, the country is rugged. Precipitous mountains, barren of vegetation to give cover to attacking troops, rise abruptly from sea level to a height of 3,500 feet. Towns dot the range, nestle precariously on the tips of peaks. These settlements are a throwback to ancient times, when inaccessibility was essential for safety and defense against brigands."[68] The 157th broke through stubborn defenses at Campofelice and took Cefalu. Further progress was temporarily hampered by a blown bridge and thickly sown minefields. While the 157th moved along Highway 113, to its south the 179th was protecting the 157th's right flank, traversing the rugged hills and mountains and overcoming opposition wherever it was found.[69]

Late on 24 July, the 180th passed through the 157th, crossed the Malpertugio River, and ran up against stiff German resistance at a 3,000-foot-high peak named Pizzo Spina. Cookson's men had to scale nearly sheer cliffs to

A lone 45th Division scout pictured heading out onto one of the smoldering Sicilian battlefields. (Courtesy of 45th Infantry Division Archives)

do battle with the Germans, who dealt out as much punishment as possible before pulling back.[70]

Acts of courage abounded on Sicily, one performed on 25 July by a Native American, Captain Otho Butler, commanding the 180th's G Company. Running a high fever from malaria, Captain Butler refused to be evacuated while his company withstood a sixty-minute artillery bombardment. Despite his illness, he led his men forward in an attack against strong German positions but was soon felled by the withering fire. Mortally wounded, he propped himself up on a boulder, telling his troops, "Boys, I'm hit. Take care of yourselves." After the battle, his men found his lifeless body on the rock. He, too, earned the Silver Star, awarded posthumously.[71]

The next day, the men of the 1st Battalion of the 180th, under the command of Lieutenant Colonel Charles H. Dewel, were approaching the western side of Castel di Tusa and contemplating the near-suicidal task before them. There were only two ways into the town. The first was along the coastal road, which was under direct observation by German gunners. First Lieutenant Bill Whitman found himself the point man for the entire Seventh Army as he led B Company, 180th, along the coastal highway. "We walked a quarter mile, a half mile, nothing! It was a beautiful morning. Each beautiful day was appreciated because we all knew that it might be our last." Rounding a curve, Whitman spotted a jeep with three men in it,

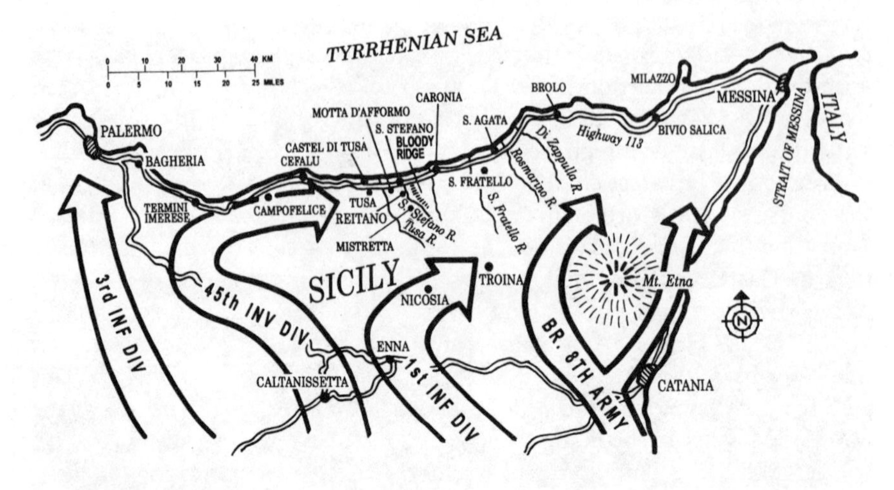

MAP 2.3 The Allied Sweep of Sicily
July 1943—The 45th, heading toward Palermo, was diverted eastward along Highway 113, Sicily's northern coast road. Heavy fighting lay ahead at "Bloody Ridge," just east of San Stefano.

stopped in the middle of the road. Cautiously, he approached the vehicle and discovered to his horror that all three were dead, shot in an ambush. He decided that a different route would be far healthier.[72]

The other way was to go up and over extremely steep terrain to the south of the town. Captain John T. Compton was directed to take his C Company and secure the high ground. This he did with a minimum of casualties, although suffering himself from the effects of malaria. Next, Dewel sent B Company, commanded by Captain James O. Smith, to reinforce Compton's men through a train tunnel that terminated near C Company's positions. With the high ground now in American hands, forward observers were able to bring accurate artillery and mortar fire down upon the Germans, who withdrew across the Tusa River and onto the high ground that would soon be known as "Bloody Ridge."[73] Here, General McLain "ran into artillery and machine-gun fire. The bullets would ricochet against the wall and on the road as I walked along. The artillery was going over. There was a lively fight with the Germans in the grove in the river and a mortar platoon, the artillery, and machine-gun bullets on our side. . . . I went down the road and found old Charlie Ankcorn standing in the road watching the fight."[74]

With the coast clear (or so higher headquarters thought), the rest of the 45th was ordered to drive east and take San Stefano di Camastra at the junction of Highways 113 and 117. It proved to be far easier said than done. A series of rocky ridges at the mouth of the Tusa River separated the two towns—ridges so steep that several pack mules carrying supplies to the 45th died of overexertion.[75] On the night of 26–27 July, the 157th passed through the 180th at Castel di Tusa and headed for the village of Motta D'Afformo when, at a high, rocky ridge west of San Stefano, the Thunderbirds met their greatest challenge on Sicily. The 180th's history states, "In the course of the entire Sicilian campaign, in so far as the Forty-fifth Infantry Division was concerned, there was not an action which surpassed that of Castel di Tusa in intensity of German fire."[76] Called "Bloody Ridge" by the Yanks, the rocky, thistle-covered area, also known on military maps as "Hill 335," bristled with strong fortifications, pillboxes, and other defensive works. It was here that the Germans were determined to stop the American drive long enough for the defenders to escape across the Strait of Messina to the mainland of Italy.

The 157th's 2nd Battalion, which had made a long march over forbidding terrain, moved up to Bloody Ridge and threatened it from the south while the 1st and 3rd Battalions pushed against the enemy stronghold from the northwest. The 1st Battalion was the first to run into tough opposition as it attempted to take Hill 335. It seemed that every rock and olive tree erupted with fire directed squarely at the Americans. Mortars and artillery poured down in a blizzard of steel, and chunks of metal and rock were flying everywhere with equal lethality. Murphy's 1st Battalion knocked out two pillboxes, but a vigorous counterattack forced the men back down the ridge.[77]

Sergeant Glen K. Hanson, L Company, 157th, said, "We had to call in the Chemical Mortar Battalion to help get the Germans off the ridge. They threw in high explosive and white phosphorus shells."[78] Captain Fred Thompson's D Company, 2nd Separate Chemical Battalion, moved its 4.2-inch chemical mortars through the railroad tunnel and laid down an intense barrage of white phosphorus shells. Of the WP, a German prisoner reportedly asked, "What the hell is that new weapon . . . that blew us out of our foxholes no matter where we were and burned our seats off at the same time?"[79]

Sergeant Henry J. Havlat, B Company, 157th, recalled the tough going at Bloody Ridge:

> My squad and I were on the point most of the way across Sicily. We had tough going at Bloody Ridge. One of my men, about ten feet from me, hit a trip wire. The last word he said was my name. Then a mine went off and his head came off. He didn't even fall over. When the explosion came, the Krauts knew we were there and they had their artillery set on that position. There was a dry creek bed there, and I wish I could have taken my men and jumped in that creek bed but we didn't have the time. That's when the artillery got us. The doggone first shell from the German barrage got me. I got hit in the right lung and got half my right shoe shot off and another chunk got me in the back. After the barrage lifted, I Company passed through us and one of the guys I knew in I Company said, 'I'll get the SOBs.'

> "There weren't enough medics to go around; if you could walk to the aid station, you had to. My ankle was bleeding—I must have bled a couple of cups right there—and I was afraid I was going to run out of blood. But I hobbled back about 300–400 yards to the ambulance before I passed out.

Havlat was evacuated to Oran, spent five months in Army hospitals in the States, and received a medical discharge from the service in December 1943. He still has a piece of shrapnel in his lung, about two inches from his heart.[80]

Corporal Robert "Doc Joe" Franklin, the ranking medic with I Company, 157th, said that the Germans

> started shelling the hell out of us. When those shells hit the rocks, they exploded in every direction, with shell fragments screaming all over the place. A shell landed on a rock close to me and I banged my chin on a rock and that knocked me out. I came to, but I was groggy. One of the fragments also cut the foot in half of one of our BAR men. It was just dangling by the skin. This man's wound was full of dirt and nobody had any water I could clean it with. So I took out my hunting knife and sliced off what was left of his foot, put some kind of awkward bandage on it, and loaded sulfa on it.[81]

The battle of 28 July lasted the entire day, with untold stories of heroism written in blood for every yard taken. Friend and foe were within yards of each other and grenades flew back and forth in profusion. Nightfall called a halt to aimed fire, but the enemy barrage never slackened. When dawn came, one GI found that he had spent the night sleeping in the same foxhole with a German. That morning, the Germans mounted several strong counterattacks designed to dislodge the GIs. Seeing his regiment in trouble, Colonel Ankcorn called for all the artillery support he could get. All four battalions of Division Artillery responded and pounded the Germans for a solid fifteen minutes. As the barrage lifted, the GIs emerged from cover and began ascending the ridge again. Shaking off the effects of the barrage, the Germans were waiting for the 157th as it advanced and opened up with every weapon in their arsenal. In places, the Germans again forced squads and platoons back. In an effort to cover their unit's withdrawal, four machine gunners, Privates first class William Olsen, George McGee, and Wesley Howe and Private Luis Blanco, stayed behind; all gave their lives so that their buddies might live. Each was recognized with the Distinguished Service Cross, awarded posthumously.[82]

Tarzan Williams recalled that after his unit came upon Bloody Ridge, "German artillery laid a barrage on us, so we dug in on a hillside in an olive grove. Every time somebody would get out of their foxhole, the Germans would shell us. The next day, the Navy sent a ship into the bay and a few salvos made the Germans move on." Williams also recalled that while his unit was awaiting further orders he saw a building on the hillside and decided to see who or what was in it. He and a buddy went to investigate and discovered a Sicilian woman hiding inside. "We told her we were American soldiers," he said. "She threw the door open and grabbed both of us and was kissing us when two more women came out and hugged and kissed us, too."[83]

After the battle for Bloody Ridge was over, "Doc Joe" Franklin tended the commanding officer of a neighboring unit, Captain Ralph Barker, L Company 157th.

> Barker asked me if I'd take a look at his feet. My God—on the balls of each foot, he had blisters that had broken on blisters that had broken on blisters. He had a half inch of raw flesh on each foot and he was walking on that. He belonged in the hospital. But I put one of my famous blister bandages on him—it was sulfa, then I rolled cotton and gauze to make a soft pad and taped that down solidly. He could walk on it and the sulfa took care of infection. Also, he had given away all his water to his men on Bloody Ridge. That whole day, charging up and down the ridge, he had no water. So I gave him some of my water and he said, "Boy, that's worth a hundred dollars!"[84]

As the twenty-ninth wore on, enemy resistance lessened; the Germans were pulling back toward Reitano. Late in the day, the 180th's 2nd Battalion moved up and took control of the coastal road leading to San Stefano. Again, it took bullets, bayonets, grenades, and guts—plus the guns of a Navy destroyer lying off shore—to dislodge the enemy. On the thirty-first, the 2nd Battalion was in control of San Stefano. The battle for Bloody Ridge was over, but at a heavy cost—163 Thunderbirds killed or wounded.[85] Every step of the way, though—every road and field and bridge and pathway—had been sown with deadly Teller and "Bouncing Betty" mines. Even German corpses had been booby-trapped by their retreating *Kameraden*. One soldier described his feelings: "You can't fire at a minefield—Jerry ain't there. But it sure gets you fighting mad for the next time."[86] Five days of fierce, hand-to-hand combat gave the Thunderbirds a taste of what they would experience for the next two years.

On 31 July, after twenty-one days of constant combat, the battered, bloodied, and bruised Thunderbirds were relieved from the front and given a period of rest near Cefalu to prepare for their upcoming role in the invasion of Italy. In those first twenty-one days, the 45th Division had lost 275 men killed, 573 wounded, and 141 missing in action. On the other side of the ledger, the 45th had accounted for 11,266 prisoners and inflicted hundreds of enemy casualties.[87]

Taking over for the 45th was Major General Lucian K. Truscott's 3rd Infantry Division, which had earned a nickname—"The Rock of the Marne"—during World War I. Patton wanted the Thunderbirds to know that he wasn't taking them out of the line because he was dissatisfied with their performance. Quite the contrary. Addressing one of the battalions, he said, "I hope you know how good you are, for everyone else does. You are magnificent."[88] Middleton, too, was satisfied with his division's accomplishments during the previous three weeks and placed much of its success on years of night combat training: "We took a great many prisoners after breaking through positions at night. . . . If our attack caused the enemy to try to withdraw under cover of darkness, the withdrawal would turn into a rout. In three weeks, my Division got to where it was doing well in night operations."[89]

As pleased as he was with the 45th, however, Patton was furious at the British. He had heard that Montgomery's Eighth Army was claiming undue credit for great and glorious victories on Sicily against overwhelming odds while his own American forces were characterized as enjoying a leisurely tour of the island while snacking on grapes. He was also frustrated that Terry Allen's 1st Infantry Division had allowed the Germans to execute a textbook example of a retrograde movement after a fierce battle at Troina. Therefore, Patton felt it was imperative for him and his American Seventh Army to restore national honor and take Messina before the British arrived. This burden would devolve to the 3rd Division.[90]

Held up by a strong rearguard force at San Fratello and the nearby mountain of the same name, a battalion of the 3rd Division was ordered to make an amphibious end run behind the German defensive line on 8 August, landing between Sant'Agata and the mouth of the Rosmarino River. Stiff fighting ensued, and the Germans were forced to pull back.[91] Patton then ordered Truscott to launch another amphibious assault on 11 August and land behind the Germans, who had set up another line of resistance at Brolo and the Di Zappulla River. Truscott complained that his men were not quite ready to make another assault, but an impatient Patton would not wait. A battalion from the 3rd's 30th Regiment landed at Brolo, some fifteen miles behind the German lines, and was nearly wiped out. The next day, the rest of the 3rd Division finally broke through and came to the decimated battalion's rescue, but only after paying a high price.

The battle for Sicily was reaching its climax. Just like toothpaste being squeezed from a tube, the Allies were squeezing the Germans toward their sole—and most advantageous—escape route, at the northeast corner of the island, where the gap between Sicily and Italy was a mere three miles wide. Wanting to put a cap on the tube before any more of the enemy could escape, Patton on 15 August ordered the 157th, along with the 158th Field Artillery Battalion, loaded onto ships at Termini Imerese to make an amphibious end run behind enemy lines to Bivio Salica, some twenty-five miles west of Messina. Apparently, Patton either did not know or care that the area was already in friendly hands; when the Thunderbirds hit the beach, they were greeted by members of the 3rd Division.[92] Even this unnecessary, unopposed landing was not without tragedy. Elements of C Company, 157th, had just rail-loaded into one of the landing craft when a davit

Thunderbirds trudging past a shattered Fascist monument in Messina, 17 August 1943. (Courtesy of 45th Infantry Archives)

broke, dumping the soldiers into the sea. Sixteen of the men in that LCVP were killed. "All of the men were fully loaded," said First Lieutenant Eddie Speairs, who was acting battalion S-4 (supply officer) at the time, "and they just never came up. I don't blame the Navy, but their boat people were poorly trained at that time."[93]

The division recovered from this incident to take part in the liberation of Messina. The 45th's official history claims that at 0430 hours on 17 August a patrol from the 1st Battalion, 157th, was the first Allied unit to enter the shattered ruins of Messina.[94] This honor, however, officially went to a patrol from the 3rd Division, which entered the city at 0200 hours the night before. Elements of the British Eighth Army arrived shortly thereafter. Sicily now belonged to the Allies.[95] The victory, however, was a hollow one. It had taken a combined force of some 450,000 troops, with an armada of warships and vastly superior air power, thirty-eight days to conquer the island and kill or capture some 32,000 Germans and 132,000 Italians. Allied casualties had been high—almost 20,000 Americans and British killed, wounded, or missing. Worse, the chance to slam the back door on the escaping Axis partners had evaporated; the last German transport left Messina for Italy at 0600 hours on 17 August. Nearly 60,000 Germans and 62,000 Italian troops were able to cross the Strait of Messina with much of their armor, artillery, and equipment intact and began to build a defense

Sergeant Nick Defonte fraternizing with a civilian in Palermo, Sicily, August 1943. (Courtesy of T. F. Bottinelli)

against the upcoming invasion of Italy. The Allies would soon be paying dearly for their failure to cut off the escape while they had the chance.[96]

To the average GI in the 45th Division, however, Operation Husky had been a roaring success. A green National Guard division had proven its worth, performing as well as the seasoned Regular Army divisions. Now it was time to rest and train for the next big push. Throughout the remainder of August, men and matériel piled up on Sicily, preparing for whatever the brass cooked up for them. The men of the 45th relaxed, enjoyed their first baths and clean clothes in weeks, and howled at Bob Hope's USO show in their bivouac near Cefalu. Some of the men even "forgot" the Seventh Army's rules against fraternization with the natives, especially when the natives turned out to be young, attractive, and female.[97]

Some men celebrated welcome news from home. One of them was Ray Williams, of the Ammunition and Pioneer Platoon, 1st Battalion, 179th. "My first son was born while we were in Sicily. He was two years old before I ever saw him. When I got the telegram telling me my wife had had the baby, I was the last guy in the outfit to see it."[98]

After Messina fell to the Americans but was still within artillery range of the Germans who had crossed to Italy, First Lieutenant Eddie Speairs and his driver were heading to the city. Speairs had his sights set on liberating some souvenir weapons he guessed were in the armory in Messina. He saw a war correspondent thumbing a ride by the side of the dusty road, so he stopped to pick up the journalist. "He asked where we were going," Speairs said, "and I said Messina. 'That's where I want to go,' said the newsman, and hopped into the back seat. I told him I wanted to find some souvenir pistols, since the war might be over tomorrow. He said he wanted to find a typewriter."

At the outskirts of Messina, a 3rd Division MP (military policeman) stopped the jeep and told the men the next stretch of road was a "shooting gallery" under enemy observation from across the bay, and advised the trio to "buckle our helmets and drive like hell." Speairs, his driver, and the passenger did as they were told. An 88mm round was fired at them but exploded harmlessly to their rear. Once he reached the armory, Speairs was disappointed to find nothing but some revolvers of World War I, or earlier, vintage. "But I took a piece of rope and strung about eighteen of 'em through the trigger guards. That's all I wanted to carry." When he emerged into the armory's courtyard, he found the journalist looking glumly at four ancient typewriters.

"I asked him if he found anything to suit him, but he said, 'These things are so old, they're worthless.' I gave him a ride back and we parted company. He didn't introduce himself and I didn't introduce myself."

About two weeks later, the 45th was back in Palermo, preparing for its next mission, when Speairs and a friend saw the journalist again. "This lieutenant said to me, 'Look over there—it's Ernie Pyle!' I said, 'Damn! That's the guy I gave a ride to!'"[99]

Ernie Pyle, the famed war correspondent, was one of the Thunderbirds' greatest supporters. In an August 1943 dispatch, he captured the fighting spirit of the 45th:

> It was flabbergasting to lie among a tentfull of wounded soldiers recently and hear them cuss and beg to be sent right back into the fight. . . . Of course not all of them do. It depends on the severity of their wounds, and on their individual personalities, just as it would in peace time. But I will say that at least a third of the moderately wounded men ask if they can't be returned to duty immediately.
>
> When I took sick I was with the Forty-fifth Division, made up largely of men from Oklahoma and West Texas [*sic*]. You don't realize how different certain parts of our country are from others until you see their men set off in a frame, as it were, in some strange faraway place like this. The men of Oklahoma are drawling and soft-spoken. They are not smart-alecks. Something of the purity of the soil seems to be in them. Even their cussing is simpler and more profound than the torrential obscenities of eastern city men. An Oklahoman of the plains is straight and direct. He is slow to criticize and hard to anger, but once he is convinced of the wrong of something, brother, watch out. These wounded men of Oklahoma have got madder about the war than anybody I have seen on this side of the ocean. They weren't so mad before they got into action, but now to them the Germans across the hill are all so-and-so's.
>
> And these quiet men of the Forty-fifth, the newest division over here, have already fought so well they have drawn the high praise of the commanding general of the corps of which the division is a part. . . . One big blonde Oklahoman had slight flesh wounds in the face and the back of his neck. He had a patch on his upper lip which prevented him from moving it, and it made him talk in a grave, straight-faced manner that was comical. I've never seen anybody so mad in my life. He went from one doctor to another trying to get somebody to sign his card returning him to duty. The doctors explained patiently that if he returned to the front his wounds would get infected and he would be a burden on his company. They tried to entice him by telling him there would be nurses back in the hospital. But he said, "To hell with the nurses, I want to get back to fightin'."[100]

The 45th was filled with men such as the ones Ernie Pyle described and for whom he had so much affection and admiration. Besides their obvious outward toughness, they had an inner strength that had been born in the hard days of the Great Depression and in the dust storms and fierce blizzards of the Southwest. Many of the GIs were expert marksmen, their shooting skills honed by years of hunting dinner—jackrabbits—with .22 caliber rifles. They were resilient men who knew how to trust their wits and live by them. In the coming days, months, and years, they would need every bit of that toughness and resilience to survive and to triumph in this war, for Salerno, Venafro, Anzio, Reipertswiller, and Dachau were still before them.

• • •

Even while the battle for Sicily was under way, the detailed planning for the next phase of the war went on. Back on 9 August, at the secret "Quadrant" conference between Roosevelt and Churchill in Quebec, the two leaders discussed post-Sicily plans. The American president had flatly rejected Churchill's scheme of going into the Balkans but looked favorably on taking at least the southern half of Italy, along with Sardinia and Corsica, as a prelude to attacking up through southern France.[101] Hitler, as it turned out, was absolutely convinced that the Balkans—and the route to the German-held oil fields in Romania—would be the Allies' next target, and had stationed large numbers of troops there.[102]

The next step had been arrived at after much wrangling and bickering among the Allies. The British had long campaigned for tying up the German forces in Italy—far from England's shore. Recalling the ghastly casualties suffered in the trenches of World War I, Churchill preferred to allow the British bulldog to nip at the ankles of Hitler's Reich rather than risk his limited manpower resources in a more direct confrontation. Besides, pinning down German divisions away from Normandy would further weaken the Germans' coastal defenses in France when the big blow did occur. In addition, the tremendous buildup of forces in the Mediterranean just begged for those forces to be used, and Churchill was the main advocate for pushing back the date of the invasion of continental Europe while continuing to expand operations in the Middle Sea.

On the other hand, Roosevelt, Marshall, and the rest of the American military establishment were pushing for Overlord, and the sooner the better, without the distractions and the draining of men and matériel (especially shipping) that a prolonged campaign in the Mediterranean would bring. The United States had hoped to invade southern France in 1943 (Operation Roundup), but the length of time it had taken to conquer Sicily adversely affected the timetable for Roundup, causing it to be shelved. In any event, the British and Americans had promised Stalin a true second front, that is, a campaign on the continent itself directed at the heart of Germany rather than more Mediterranean "sideshows." In the end, Operation Overlord was approved. But, since it would take another year for the American war machine to bring itself to full strength in England, the British plan to continue the war in the Mediterranean would be allowed to go forward, so long as its prosecution did not adversely affect the buildup for Overlord.[103] Still trying to influence the British, however, the Americans had been leaning toward an invasion of the islands of Sardinia (Operation Brimstone) and Corsica (Operation Fire-brand), as they were worried that a major land campaign in the rugged, mountainous spine of Italy would be too costly.

Global events ultimately played a role in the decision to invade Italy. On 5 July, the German Army in the east launched a heavy counteroffensive in the Soviet Union. An allied operation on the Italian peninsula, as Martin Blumenson states, "would tie down far more German forces than an invasion of Sardinia and Corsica," and could draw German forces away from the eastern front.[104] Had the Italian campaign gone smoothly, with the Germans pulling out and heading back to the Alps, historians would have been as lavish in their praise of the operation as they have been about Operation Overlord, which also owed much to luck. As it is, many historians, with twenty-twenty hindsight, have criticized the decision to invade Italy, pointing out that simply *threatening* an invasion would have tied down considerable Axis reserves, just as a vague threat to the Balkans was excuse enough for Hitler to maintain several divisions there. At the time the decision to invade Italy was made, however, no one could have foreseen the developments that would occur, the stubborn German resistance, the reverses on the battlefield, or the foul weather that continually plagued the theater. Had Overlord been subjected to the same run of bad luck, it, too, would have suffered the same stain of failure that has forever dogged the Italian campaign.

With the issue of Italy as the primary target finally settled, the Combined Chiefs of Staff and Allied Force Headquarters had to select one of several possible invasion sites. The coast close to Rome was considered briefly but discarded as being too far north and beyond fighter support from Sicily. Naples itself was also considered, but it was too heavily defended. The Gulf of Gaeta, north of Naples, offered attractive landing beaches but was also beyond fighter cover. The beaches of Salerno, forty miles to the south of Naples, seemed to hold the most promise. If the troops could land and then quickly move up and take the city, the Allies would have an excellent port to which vital supplies and reinforcements could be sent. Also, captured air bases south of Rome could be used to take the Allied bombing campaign heavily over southern Germany. The planners believed that a successful invasion at Salerno was indeed possible before the wet winter weather set in. They called it Operation Avalanche.

In addition, secret negotiations with the Italian government were under way to convince King Victor Emmanuel III to oust Mussolini and bring

Italy into the war on the Allied side. The planners expected that, if Italy were to capitulate, the Germans would withdraw to the north, possibly leaving Italy altogether.[105]

On 25 July, Il Duce was unceremoniously dumped as head of government, and he was arrested the next day.* Field Marshal Pietro Badoglio took over, publicly announcing that the war would go on while privately negotiating a way to end Italian involvement. An incensed Hitler, raging that Italy had stabbed Germany in the back, resolved to evacuate his troops from Sicily before they were cut off.[106] He also put into effect his plans for Operation Alaric, the German occupation of Italy drawn up in May when he suspected that Italy might not remain resolutely in the Axis camp. The result of Hitler's order also gave the Nazis "permission" to begin rounding up and deporting to the death camps the Italian Jews who had received protection from the worst forms of persecution during Mussolini's regime. The slaughter of the Italian Jews would begin on 16 September.[107]

In spite of the importance of Operation Avalanche, there were only enough landing craft to bring three divisions, plus American Rangers and British Commandos, onto the beach on D day, set for 9 September. Two corps—the American VI and British X Corps—would be committed to the battle, which was designed to quickly take Naples, just to the north of Salerno, and cause the Germans to retreat from the south.

A commander for VI Corps needed to be chosen; because both Bradley and Patton were still engaged in mopping up Sicily in late July, Major General Ernest J. Dawley was selected as the senior-ranking American ground commander. A West Point graduate, Dawley had commanded the 40th Infantry Division in 1941 and VI Corps when it arrived in North Africa in 1943. Marshall, Leslie McNair, and Clark all felt he was an aggressive and capable officer. Eisenhower had his doubts but acceded to the others' judgment.[108]

The British 46th and 56th Divisions, along with the American 36th Division, seeing its first combat action, would go in on D day. Due to the inadequacy of shipping, a decision had to be made as to which American division would form the floating reserve and follow up the initial landings. The choice came down to either the 3rd or the 45th. Eisenhower, the Supreme Allied Commander, selected the 45th.[109]

On 21 August, with the battle for Sicily over, Middleton and his staff flew back to Algiers to meet with General Mark Clark, who would head up

---

*Under the terms of the armistice, Mussolini was supposed to have been handed over to the Allies. For some reason, this was not done and Mussolini was held in arrest at a ski lodge atop the Gran Sasso, a mountain range to the east of Rome. To make a more flamboyant statement, Hitler had Mussolini rescued on 12 September by Otto Skorzeny's commandos, who dramatically whisked Il Duce off the mountaintop by plane and flew him to Germany via Rome (W.G.F. Jackson, *The Battle for Italy* [New York: Harper & Row, 1967], p. 118).

a new American army, the Fifth, and learn the 45th's role in the upcoming operation. Clark told Middleton that two-thirds of the 45th would be the floating reserve to be brought in if the invasion got bogged down or ran into serious trouble. The third regiment—the 180th—would be brought in as soon as shipping permitted.[110]

While the 45th prepared for its next test, considerable praise was bestowed on the division. In his memoirs, Major General Truscott, the 3rd Division commander, wrote, "The Forty-fifth Infantry Division had made a record of which any division could well be proud. This was its first campaign. The Division had planned and prepared under great disadvantages. For three weeks before the landing, while other divisions were training, this division had been at sea. Yet it had taken every objective and in the long drive across Sicily had kept pace with the veteran divisions."[111] Throughout the war, the 3rd and 45th would form a close attachment, fighting side by side in many campaigns.

Omar Bradley wrote to the division, "Now that the Sicilian Campaign has been brought to a successful conclusion, I desire to commend the Forty-fifth Division for its fine performance. . . . The whole campaign is one of which the members of the Division should feel proud. This contribution to the success of American arms is an indication of what the Division will do toward bringing the war to a successful conclusion."

George Patton, too, heaped his own special brand of praise on the 45th in an open-air address to the division in August near Bagheria: "The Forty-fifth Infantry Division is one of the best, if not *the* best division that the American Army has ever produced." The troops applauded wildly. He concluded his speech in typical, thundering, Pattonesque style:

> You are still up against a resourceful enemy, but you, as Americans, are his superior. When you meet him, as you will some day on the plains of Europe, you may expect him to throw large masses of armor at you. He will seek to drive through your center with a point of armor and, once through, will attempt to fan this point out, exploit it, and strike at your flanks and rear installations. But, by God, this point will not get through! When it strikes at you, you must be ready to strike it first!—blunt it!—hit it from both sides!—knock the hell out of it!—take the initiative!—hit and hit again until there is no point and nothing behind the point to oppose you. Drive forward!
>
> I love every bone in your heads, but be very careful. Do not go to sleep, or someone's liable to slip up behind you and hit you over the head with a sock full of shit, and that's a hell of an embarrassing way in which to die![112]

The men roared and cheered Patton, not realizing how prophetic were his words.

3

That Despondent Shore

9–14 September 1943

Thus we made our way down to the fourth ditch, to take in more of that despondent shore where all the universe's ill is stored.
—Dante Alighieri, *The Inferno,* Canto VII

THE GULF OF SALERNO is an almost-ideal site for an amphibious invasion—for both the invader and the defender. The beach—which stretches some thirty miles from the sheer cliffs of the Sorrento Peninsula and the city of Salerno in the north to Paestum, Agropoli, and the heights of Monte Soprano in the south—is wide and flat, making it easy to move inland. Once ashore, the invading troops would have a number of topographical features, such as dunes, gullies, foliage, and buildings, to use for cover and concealment. The troops, after moving inland a short distance, would find a coastal highway that links Salerno with Naples and Rome.

For the defender, the wide, flat beach also offers virtually unlimited fields of enfilading fire. From the mountains, hills, and high ground that form a background to the beach, the observation is excellent, and the attacker is faced with the disadvantage of having to attack uphill. The Allies couldn't have found a better place to land—and the Germans couldn't have found a better place to defend.

Slightly below the midpoint of the beach, the Sele River empties into the Gulf of Salerno. The British X Corps, consisting of the 46th ("North Midland") Division and 56th (known as both the "London" and "Black Cat") Division, along with a force of British Commandos, would hit the beach on the north side of the Sele, while Major General Fred L. Walker's 36th Infantry ("Texas") Division, as the first wave of Major General Ernest J. Dawley's VI Corps, would strike to the south near Paestum. Colonel William O. Darby's Ranger Battalions would assault the picture-postcard towns of Amalfi, Minori, and Maiori at the base of the rugged Sorrento Peninsula, which separates the Gulf of Salerno from the Bay of Naples.[1]

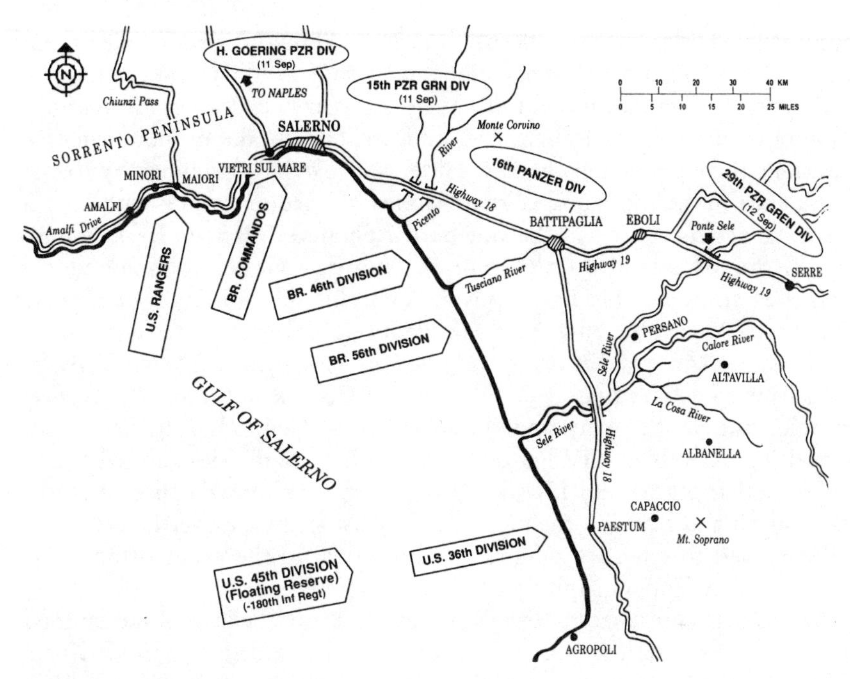

MAP 3.1 Operation Avalanche
9 September 1944—Mark Clark's combined British-American Fifth Army landed three infantry divisions, plus Ranger and Commando units, on the Salerno beachhead. Two regiments of the 45th waited offshore as the floating reserve. Although the beachhead area was manned by only one German division (16th Panzer Division) on D day, Kesselring swiftly brought in three additional divisions to stymie the Allied landings.

Optimism in the Allied camp was riding high. As the planners envisioned it, the force would land, move swiftly inland, take Naples, and drive on Rome from the south, sweeping any and all opposition from its path. Faced with the combined might of the British and American armies, the Germans would flee to the Alps. Everyone, it seems, had overlooked Napoleon's observation: "Italy is like a boot; you must, like Hannibal, enter it from the top."[2]

Prior to the Allied landings, the German force in Italy consisted of two armies commanded by bitter rivals—Army Group B, headed by *Generalfeldmarschall* Erwin Rommel, who was in charge of northern Italy and whose headquarters were at Lake Garda, and Army Group C, under *Generalfeldmarschall* Albert Kesselring, who commanded German forces in the south from his headquarters in Rome. Rommel had thirteen divisions, plus their support units, under his command; Kesselring had eight, mostly armored and motorized divisions.[3] Ever since Mussolini had gotten himself in trouble in Africa and Rommel's forces had been decimated trying to bail out Il Duce, Hitler had been deeply concerned about his shaky Axis partner and had drawn up contingency plans in case of an Italian capitulation. In the event, the German forces in Italy were to seize key Italian installations, capture or destroy the Italian fleet, and prepare to take up new defensive positions throughout the country. Hitler approved a plan whereby Kesselring's units in the south and German troops on Sardinia would withdraw to a strong defensive line in the northern Apennines manned by Rommel's men. Rommel would then become the supreme German commander in Italy. Kesselring so objected to this plan and his subordination to Rommel that on 14 August he tendered his resignation. Hitler promptly rejected it.

The successful evacuation of the bulk of German forces from Sicily led Kesselring to believe that he could manage a defense in the south, however. Forming the Tenth Army under *Generaloberst* Heinrich von Vietinghoff, Kesselring assembled XIV Panzer Corps with three divisions in the Gaeta-Naples-Salerno area and LXXVI Panzer Corps with nearly three divisions in Calabria and Apulia—the most likely invasion sites. Nevertheless, Hitler still planned to conduct a fighting withdrawal in the event of an Allied landing and an Italian capitulation.[4]

After Mussolini's arrest, Hitler's suspicions about the lack of Italian fortitude in prosecuting the war proved to be well founded. Despite Il Duce's thrust-jaw belligerence and boastful pronouncements about the strength of his nation's armed forces, the Italians' military resolve, when faced with anything more formidable than Ethiopian tribesmen, had been surprisingly nonexistent, even when defending their homeland in Sicily. Besides, the cost of the war was bleeding the country white in terms of both money and manpower. Among the general populace, support for the war was never very high, and now that the prospect of fighting on the Italian mainland was a near certainty, the people were panicked.

On the Allied side, preparations for the invasion were in full swing, Ike having made the final decision on 17 July to pursue the enemy onto the mainland.[5] Another mighty armada was being readied in North Africa and along the northern coast of Sicily. The invasion force was training and rehearsing, last-minute details were being reviewed, all possible problems were being considered and solutions drafted, and mountains of supplies were being loaded in their assigned cargo holds on their assigned ships in their assigned convoys. In the warm, calm days before the invasion, thousands of men were writing thousands of letters to wives, girlfriends, mothers, fathers, sons, daughters, sisters, brothers, uncles, and aunts, hoping—no, confident—that they would survive the coming battle. As Ray Williams, Ammunition and Pioneer Platoon, 1st Battalion, 179th, said, "The possibility of not making it back never crossed my mind. I guess I was young and not too intelligent. There was never a time when I thought I wouldn't be able to finish the job. It never dawned on me that I might get killed."[6]

• • •

To gain an idea of the tremendous logistical effort required for an operation of the magnitude of the Salerno landings, one need only look at the supplies that one division—the 45th—took with it to the beachhead: 791,200 rations (496,000 "five-in-one" meals, 186,000 K rations, and 109,200 C rations—representing just a one-month supply for *one* division). The K and C rations alone required sixteen trucks and trailers to haul them. In addition, thirty-two trucks and trailers were loaded with B rations—normally canned goods that required cooking by a unit's kitchen.

There were 800,000 gallons of gasoline in 160,000 five-gallon "jerry" cans, plus 150,000 gallons of fresh water in 30,000 five-gallon water cans. Another forty-two trucks and trailers were loaded with extra uniforms and clothing items; individual equipment; and essential organizational equipment such as tents, chairs, tables, field stoves, electric generators, lighting equipment, shovels, sandbags, stretchers, sterile bandages, splints, sulfa, scalpels, plasma, field desks, typewriters, boxes of preprinted government forms, and stacks of carbon paper to satisfy the Army's penchant for everything being recorded in triplicate.[7] In addition, the division's TO&E (Table of Organization and Equipment) authorized the unit to have 612 jeeps, 209 three-quarter-ton trucks, 30 ambulances, 356 two-and-a-half-ton trucks, 27 dump trucks, 18 four-ton trucks, and a number of other specialized vehicles.

To fight with, the division had 6,761 M-1 Garand rifles, 5,204 carbines, 1,157 .45 caliber pistols, 236 .50 caliber machine guns, 157 .30 caliber machine guns, and 90 .45 caliber Thompson submachine guns. There were 57 57mm anti-tank guns, 90 60mm mortars, 54 81mm mortars, 54 105mm howitzers, and 12 155mm howitzers.[8] And the above lists do not include the massive quantities of ammunition required to satisfy the insatiable appetites of the thousands of weapons. Multiply the above by the number of divisions scheduled to take part in the operation and one gains a new appreciation of the staggering effort it took to support an army in the field.[9] Yes, the 45th, like all other American infantry divisions, was supremely equipped to fight a war. And yet, with all of this food, ammunition, transportation, equipment, and weaponry—designed, engineered, produced, manufactured, sewn, molded, welded, cast, and stamped in thousands of mills, factories, and machine shops across America and purchased at great expense by the American taxpayer—the question of victory or defeat would depend solely on one simple, critical, unknown factor: the courage of the individual combat soldier.

• • •

Taking the spotlight in the center of the Italian stage for the upcoming drama were the two main protagonists—Clark and Kesselring.

Field Marshal Albert Kesselring, brilliant commanding officer of Army Group C. (Courtesy of 45th Infantry Division Archives)

Generalfeldmarschall Albert Kesselring was certainly one of the most charismatic, innovative, and effective commanders to serve the Third Reich and is regarded by many historians as one of the greatest German military commanders of the Second World War. Kesselring possessed an independent streak that often put him at odds with his Führer, yet his dogged defense of the Italian peninsula earned Hitler's grudging respect and admiration. In fact, of the entire German military leadership, only Rommel and Kesselring, and perhaps *Generaloberst* Heinz Guderian, stand out as brilliant, independent strategists.

Born in Marktsheet, Bavaria, on 20 November 1885, young Kesselring decided on a military career at an early age. As was the custom then, since his father was a schoolmaster in Bayreuth and not an officer, he was not automatically eligible to enter the Military Academy until he successfully completed a probationary period. He rapidly proved himself and was particularly outstanding in tactics. After graduation from the academy, Kesselring served in the artillery during the early years of World War I. His abilities caught the eyes of high-ranking officers and he was transferred to the General Staff in winter 1917. After the Armistice in 1918, he returned to Bavaria to find his home region in the throes of Marxist-inspired upheaval. So dismayed was he at Germany's defeat and the Communist revolution wracking his homeland that he seriously considered resigning his commission. Only his commanding officer's appeal to his sense of duty convinced him to remain in the service.

Between the wars, Kesselring, like most German officers, remained apolitical. He distrusted Hitler and his Nazi henchmen, but, having personally witnessed the Communist uprising, he decided to follow the Fascist course rather than a Bolshevik one, thinking it the lesser of two evils. In 1922, Kesselring was assigned to Berlin to help organize the drastically reduced Army (*Reichsheer*) mandated under the terms of the Versailles Treaty. Serving under Hans von Seeckt, Kesselring saw that Germany was pulling the wool over the eyes of the Allied Military Control Commission, which had the job of ensuring that Germany did not violate the principles of the treaty. Von Seeckt recruited the finest junior officers to form the core of a new, future army that would be better and stronger than the one that took the field in 1914. Kesselring quickly became von Seeckt's indispensable right-hand man and performed his staff roles with diligence and brilliance. While at von Seeckt's headquarters, Kesselring was made responsible for developing the staff structure necessary for the procurement of a new generation of weapons.

By the early 1930s, shortly after Hitler and the Nazi Party had come to power, Kesselring had left the staff work and was a colonel commanding an artillery regiment. He was unexpectedly informed that he would become the chief administrator of the *Luftwaffe,* the newly formed air force, under Hitler's crony, Hermann Göring. In this post, Kesselring's responsibility was to oversee the construction of air bases across Germany. In 1936, after the chief of the staff of the *Luftwaffe* died in an aircraft accident, Göring appointed Kesselring to the post. When Germany invaded Poland on 1 September 1939, touching off World War II, Kesselring, now forty-eight, was in command of *Luftflotte Nr. 1* (First Air Fleet), which provided bomber and fighter support to the invading German army.

In January 1940, Kesselring became commander of *Luftflotte Nr.* 2 and coordinated not only the bombing and air attacks on Holland and Belgium but also the airborne operation that would bring the all-important parachute troops into action. In the entire history of warfare, a coordinated air-and-ground assault on this scale had never before been attempted. So effective was the surprise attack that Kesselring was promoted to field marshal and went to work softening up the British Isles with his fighters and bombers for the planned invasion, code-named Operation Sea-Lion. No armchair commander, Kesselring personally flew several missions, including the infamous 14 November 1940 raid on Coventry. The Royal Air Force gave the Germans a pounding every time they crossed the Channel to bomb English cities, but it was obvious which side was eventually going to lose this war of attrition called the Battle of Britain. Down to a mere handful of planes and pilots, the British were suddenly given a reprieve when Hitler called off the invasion. Hitler's motives for canceling the cross-Channel assault have never been clear; more curious still was his decision, in the face of overwhelming advice to the contrary, to opt instead for his ultimately misguided attack on the Soviet Union. Kesselring's command was transferred to Poland to support the eastward blitz.

Again, the element of surprise was on Hitler's (and Kesselring's) side. The Soviet Army and its air forces suffered tremendous losses in the massive, surprise attack and, by November 1941, Leningrad was surrounded and German troops were in the suburbs of Moscow. It would be Germany's high-water mark. The brutal Russian winter, Hitler's insistence on attacking everywhere at once, and the lack of spare parts and maintenance for Kesselring's aircraft all combined to grind the German assault to a halt. Kesselring did not have long to brood about the turn of events for, in December 1941, he found himself transferred to Rome as head of all Axis forces in the Mediterranean, where the war was still going relatively well for Italy and Germany; his task was to secure the Reich's "southern flank" while the war on the eastern front wore on.

With his organizational skills and the talent to manage the Italian forces that got themselves into situations that were beyond their abilities or, alternately, failed to fight when they could have been victorious, Kesselring again proved himself more than capable. A natural diplomat, the genial Bavarian won over his Italian subordinates, who had initially felt hostile at the appointment of this foreign general to be their lord and master. Although he charmed the Italians, Kesselring never had a satisfactory personal or professional relationship with Rommel. Rommel, Hitler's favorite general, nominally under Kesselring's command, reported only to the Führer.

Despite the frostiness of his personal relationship with Rommel, Kesselring did everything in his power to aid the German cause. Realizing Malta was the key to supplying Rommel's Panzer Army Africa, Kesselring campaigned personally with Hitler for permission to assault the island with his paratroops, but even his considerable persuasive powers were insufficient; Hitler turned cautious and would not allow his field marshal to launch the attack. Had Malta been taken, it is possible that Rommel's forces could have been better supplied and possibly could have even defeated or stalled the Allied advance in North Africa. As it was, Panzer Army Africa, out of gas, ammunition, weapons, tanks, vehicles, spare parts, and reinforcements, was beaten, and some 250,000 German and Italian troops were dead or in captivity.

The five weeks of dogged fighting in Sicily had pushed the Axis forces to the northeast corner of the island, where the Allies could (and should) have finished them off. But a combination of Allied bungling and Kesselring's boldness allowed them to live to fight another day. Operating on his own, without any authorization for a withdrawal from Hitler (which he knew would never come), Kesselring organized what historian Shelford Bidwell has called "a German Dunkirk," managing to evacuate over 60,000 German troops across the Strait of Messina—*with* most of their heavy weapons and equipment.

An affable, optimistic man with a ready smile, Kesselring was known behind his back as "Smiling Albert." But he also possessed a cold-hearted streak, and subordinates—and the enemy—learned never to take him lightly. As Bidwell writes, "'Smiling Albert' he may have been, but no one disobeyed him twice." Blunt when he had to be, Kesselring is reported to have told Hitler, who was enraged at his field marshal's independently ordering a pullback of troops, "Of course your troops will always stand and fight to the death if you order them to, but consider whether having lost one army in Africa and another in Stalingrad you can afford to lose a third in Italy." Few officers could confront Hitler in such a manner and expect to retain their commands. Yet, Kesselring remained, to the very end, one of the few generals Hitler could trust.[10]

Kesselring's opposite number was Lieutenant General Mark Wayne Clark, commander of the U.S. Fifth Army. Born 1 May 1896 at Madison Barracks, New York, to Charles Carr Clark, an Army Infantry officer, and Rebecca Ezekiels Clark, daughter of European Jewish immigrants, he and his family moved with a frequency common to all military families. A tall, skinny, somewhat frail youth, prone to childhood illnesses, Clark was an ardent admirer of rough-riding Theodore Roosevelt and the dashing Second Lieutenant George Patton, who was stationed at Fort Sheridan, Illinois, along with Clark's father.

In 1913, standing six feet, three inches and weighing a slight 140 pounds, the seventeen-year-old Clark earned an appointment to the United States Military Academy at West Point, New York. At that time, the academy was filled with cadets who would one day become some of America's finest military officers, including Dwight Eisenhower, Matthew Ridgway, and Joe Collins. Never an especially strong student, Clark graduated 110th in his class, near the bottom, on 20 April 1917. He was commissioned a second lieutenant of Infantry and posted to the 11th Infantry Regiment in Georgia where he commanded a company. Although he drove his men hard, he was well liked and respected by them and earned high marks for efficiency and leadership.

Thanks to rapid promotions common in wartime, Clark was promoted to captain and, in April 1918, his regiment, now a part of the 5th Division, was sent to the trenches of the western front in France. When his battalion commander fell ill, Captain Clark suddenly found himself in charge of a thousand-man battalion. He and his unit were on the front lines for only a few days when he was seriously wounded by an artillery shell, and he spent six weeks recuperating from his injuries. His combat days were over, and Clark was transferred to the First Army Supply Section, where he quickly learned the intricacies of staff work.

In the postwar world, Captain Clark was transferred with numbing regularity from post to post, eventually winding up in Washington, where he was assigned to the office of the Assistant Secretary of War and given the task of helping the government dispose of war surplus real estate. Although the job was far from stimulating, Clark approached it with his usual enthusiasm and quickly won notice from his superiors. Following his stint in Washington, Clark was assigned to the Presidio in California, then to a post near Cheyenne, Wyoming. In 1929, just before the stock market crash brought on the Great Depression, he was posted to Indianapolis to instruct and advise the 38th Infantry Division, a National Guard unit. He was promoted to major in 1933. The same year that Franklin Roosevelt was sworn in as President, Japan conquered Manchuria, and Adolf Hitler became Chancellor of Germany, Clark was concentrating on his studies at the Army's Command and General Staff College at Fort Leavenworth, Kansas, and hoping for further promotions. More moves followed until, in 1937, Clark was assigned to Fort Lewis, Washington, and the 3rd Infantry Division, where he wore three hats: assistant chief of staff, G-2 (Intelligence), and G-3 (Operations). It was at Fort Lewis that he became good friends with Brigadier General George C. Marshall, destined to become the Army's Chief of Staff. Sought by Clark as a sounding board for his ideas on training and tactics, Marshall soon became impressed with the younger officer's sound judgment and innovative plans.

In 1939, with the war drums beating ever louder in Europe and Asia, Lieutenant Colonel Dwight Eisenhower, who had been serving on General Douglas MacArthur's staff in the Philippines, was assigned to Fort Lewis; the two men renewed their friendship, which had begun many years earlier at West Point. Clark pulled a few strings and had Eisenhower appointed to command a battalion in the 3rd Division.

Before Ike arrived on post, however, the course of history changed when Germany invaded Poland and the Second World War began. Suddenly, the understaffed, underequipped American Army was shaken out of its doldrums. The military expanded rapidly as young men rushed to recruiting stations. New weapons, equipment, and vehicles began to pour out of America's factories. Training programs took on a new and realistic urgency, and Clark devised a series of amphibious training exercises designed to improve Army-Navy cooperation. For months, he rehearsed practice landings involving some 14,000 troops of the 3rd Division, working out the logistical kinks and employing a variety of untried tactics and maneuvers. When the actual test took place near San Francisco, complete with Army Air Corps aircraft flying overhead cover, it was a smashing success. Marshall was impressed, and soon Clark, now a lieutenant colonel, found himself heading back to Washington for a position on the newly formed General Headquarters, close to the side of Marshall, who had become Army Chief of Staff as well as the commander of GHQ. Since each job was more than full time, Marshall appointed Brigadier General Leslie J. McNair to run the day-to-day operation of GHQ, which was charged with training the Army for overseas combat. Clark quickly became McNair's right-hand man. Within months, Clark so awed McNair that he was promoted from lieutenant colonel to brigadier general, bypassing the customary stop at full colonel.

Before the year 1941 was out, the United States was at war, not with one enemy, but with two, each half a world away. It would take a tremendous effort to defeat even one of the foes, let alone both, especially since America's Pacific Fleet had been all but destroyed and its land army was still trying to turn civilians into soldiers. The Army would need all the brilliant brains it could muster. One of those brains belonged to Eisenhower, whom Clark had recommended Marshall appoint as head of the War Plans Section. It would be a fateful appointment, for not only would Ike go on to gain fame as the organizer of the Allied invasion of continental Europe, but he would also gain considerable experience by first being in charge of the Allied landings of North Africa and Sicily.

As America mobilized, Clark's fortunes rose quickly. In 1942, he was given another star and command of II Corps, which was being formed in England, with Eisenhower, head of ETOUSA (European Theater of Operations, United States Army), as his superior. Embryonic plans were developed for an invasion of the continent in 1942 to relieve the German pressure on the Soviet front, but the lack of men, matériel and, most of all, landing craft made the invasion impossible. Instead, the decision, at Winston Churchill's insistence, was made to continue bombing the Reich while nibbling at its fringe in North Africa. Churchill, still haunted by visions of the ghastly slaughter of English soldiers on the battlefields of World War I and knowing that his country did not have America's unlimited resources, wanted to delay a full-scale confrontation with Hitler's armies for as long as possible. Marshall agreed that North Africa was also a good place for the unbloodied American Army to get its first taste of battle.

Eisenhower was picked to command the Allied force landing in North Africa, an operation named "Torch," and Clark was in charge of planning. The logistics of such an operation were overwhelming in their detail and complexity, yet Clark carried them out with his usual aplomb. The basic idea was for the Allies to land in Algiers and Morocco, which were held by the Vichy French. The Allies hoped the French would throw in their lot with the invaders rather than with the Germans, their masters. The Allies would then drive eastward into Tunisia and Libya to do battle with Rommel's Panzer Army Africa, which was at the end of a very long and tenuous supply line. But determining if the French would fight was of primary importance, and Clark was selected to find the answer.

In October 1942, at Eisenhower's behest, Clark took part in a mission of great personal danger and Byzantine complexity. Information suggested that General Henri Giraud, who had been hiding from the Germans in unoccupied southern France after escaping from a Nazi prison-castle, would be able to bring the French forces in North Africa into the war on the Allied side. Using all his diplomatic skills (and a few not-so-diplomatic tactics) on this secret mission, Clark logged many miles by plane and submarine between England, Gibraltar, and North Africa before he was able to wheel and deal with the many French personalities involved and gain their cooperation.

As Clark and Eisenhower had feared, the complex deal soured and, on 10 November, Italian and German troops poured into the areas of France previously under Vichy's control, occupying Corsica as well. Meanwhile, large numbers of Axis forces were rushed to Tunisia to do battle with the Allies, which had made their first amphibious landing of the European campaign. More negotiations—this time to bring the French forces in North Africa into the war on the Allied side—succeeded, and French units turned and fought the Germans. Clark was promoted and Ike personally pinned on his third star. Yet, in the United States and Britain, the "Darlan Deal" was denounced because Clark had negotiated with Vichy French Admiral Jean-Louis Darlan and representatives of a pro-Nazi government.[11]

While the American and British troops were giving Panzer Army Afrika a bloody nose, Eisenhower presented Clark with the Distinguished Service Medal for his efforts to swing the French to the Allied side. Ike told a subordinate, "Clark impresses men, as always, with his energy and intelligence. You cannot help but like him. He certainly is not afraid to take rather desperate chances which, after all, is the only way to win a war."[12] Command of the embryonic U.S. Fifth Army, which would be used to invade either France, Sicily, or Sardinia, was a toss-up between Clark and Patton. In the end, Eisenhower gave it to Clark—a promotion that took the sting out of the "Darlan Deal" criticism. For good or bad, it is the command with which he will be forever linked.[13]

• • •

The invasion of Italy was a two-pronged operation. On 1 September 1943, Montgomery's British Eighth Army crossed the Strait of Messina to the toe of the Italian boot in hopes of drawing German forces away from the Salerno beaches where the combined U.S.-British forces—Clark's Fifth Army—were scheduled to land on the ninth. Monty's men had not pushed very far northward when they ran into stiff opposition from *Generalleutnant* Smilo Freiherr von Lüttwitz's 26th Panzer Division. The slow drive by the ever-methodical Montgomery would get even slower, and Kesselring did not need to rush an inordinately large number of troops southward to contest him.[14]

With the exception of Darby's Ranger force, which would receive a supporting bombardment by British vessels five minutes after hitting the beach,[15] the predawn invasion of Salerno was planned with no preliminary bombardment to alert the enemy that the force was about to land. Dispensing with the bombardment would be a gamble, given the strength of the opposition, but Ike, Alexander, Clark, Dawley, U.S. Admiral H. Kent Hewitt, British Admiral Sir Andrew B. Cunningham, and the British X Corps commander, Lieutenant General Sir Brian G. Horrocks (who would be wounded during an air raid at Bizerte, Tunisia, the night before the task force sailed) felt the element of surprise was a gamble worth taking.[16]

Throughout the day and evening of 7 September, the GIs of the 157th (minus the 2nd Battalion) and 179th Regiments, plus artillery and other supporting units, loaded onto LSTs and LCIs in the harbor of Termini Imerese and sailed at 0200 hours on 8 September. From faraway Oran came the U.S. 36th Division; from Bizerte sailed the British 46th Division; and the British 56th Division set sail from Tripoli, Libya. The convoys would all converge north of Palermo and head directly toward the Gulf of Salerno.[17]

Because of *Luftwaffe* patrols over the sea lanes, Kesselring knew an invasion force was on the way and was preparing a hot welcome for them. Since 7 September, the Germans were fairly convinced that Salerno was the target. The Tenth Army commander, *Generaloberst* Heinrich von Vietinghoff, had *Generalmajor* Rudolf Sickenius's 16th Panzer Division, with 17,000 men and over a hundred tanks, as well as the Italian 222nd Coastal Division, cover the thirty-mile-long beachhead. Thick minefields were laid in the sand and in the water, strong points were reinforced, tank traps dug, and bridges and other key features rigged for demolition. The area bristled with machine gun positions as well as artillery and anti-aircraft guns.[18] Somehow, a copy of the Allied invasion plans had fallen into *Wehrmacht* hands; after the battle, it was discovered that the exact locations of the 45th's beaches were marked on German maps.[19]

At 1830 hours on the evening of the eighth, as the convoy steamed toward Italy, Ike's voice from Algiers crackled over the ships' loudspeakers with a startling announcement: "This is General Dwight D. Eisenhower, Commander in Chief of the Allied Forces. The Italian government has surrendered its armed forces unconditionally. As Allied Commander in Chief, I have granted a military armistice."[20] The behind-the-scenes maneuvering by the Allies had brought about the formal end of Italian participation in the war. On 25 July, with the Italian economy decimated and the Allies about to descend on his country in force and turn Italy into a wasteland, King Victor Emmanuel III had removed Benito Mussolini, who had held the reins of power for twenty-one years, and installed Field Marshal Pietro Badoglio as the new head of the government.[21] Men on the transports cheered deliriously, but this bit of good news gave most of the invasion troops a false sense of security—a sense that the war was as good as over. They thought there would be little, if any, opposition when they hit the beach. For others, the announcement merely reinforced their belief that it would be stupid to do anything risky and end up getting killed or maimed; caution would be their watchword.[22]

While the 500-ship armada, including a number of British aircraft carriers whose planes would provide air cover, steamed on under cover of darkness, the vessels were spotted and attacked by dive bombers but escaped with few casualties. The cat, however, was out of the proverbial bag; the

Germans knew the Americans were on the way. The 16th Panzer Division, although badly outnumbered, assembled in hidden emplacements above the landing beaches with a deadly array of infantry, tanks, self-propelled artillery, and the awesome, dual-purpose 88mm guns that the Germans called "*acht-acht.*"[23] Because of the heavily mined waters in the Gulf of Salerno, the British and American transports were forced to release their landing craft a considerable distance from shore—from nine to twelve miles out. It was a very long and a very tense run to the beach.[24] At 0200 hours on 9 September, the Germans opened up on the flotilla carrying the British X Corps, and a fierce land-sea duel commenced. The *Luftwaffe* also joined in and sank or badly damaged a number of vessels. In the dark and confusion, elements of the 46th and 56th Divisions were landed on the wrong beaches. Chaos reigned in the British sector throughout the day and into the evening of D day due to the ferocity of enemy fire.[25]

At 0335 hours, on the southern end of the beachhead, the first wave of Walker's green U.S. 36th Infantry Division—two reinforced regiments—landed without opposition just to the west of Paestum. Only the sounds of battle at the far north end of the landing area broke the stillness. The second wave of the 36th hit the beach seven minutes later—and the Germans opened up with everything they had. Parachute flares popped above the beaches, illuminating the stunned invaders, and the sands of Salerno became a killing ground as artillery and mortar rounds erupted and machine gun bullets tore into GIs caught in the open. Near the shore, deadly machine gun fire raked the beach from a fifty-foot-tall stone tower dating from medieval times. Combat virgins became veterans in minutes.

As anyone who has ever been in combat will testify, the battlefield is a terribly confused and chaotic place. At the higher levels of command, it is rare when a company, battalion, regiment, or division commander has anything more than the sketchiest idea of what those under his responsibility are doing or even where they are. Communications are often a shambles, with telephones and radio sets inoperable and messengers killed before they can relay a message. Units can be engaged and wiped out before their commanders even know they have met the enemy.

For the inexperienced foot soldier, the situation is even worse. To survive, an infantryman must hit the ground or find shelter in a hole or behind a wall. In so doing, his view of events occurring around him is severely restricted, limited to perhaps only a few feet or yards in any direction. The infantryman hugging the ground rarely sees the enemy, especially during a night battle, but is apt to expend considerable amounts of ammunition firing blindly in the enemy's general direction. Firing his weapon is the one activity that feels good to the soldier, as it is the only proactive thing he can do while being more or less inert. In most cases, he has no idea where the rest of his squad is, let alone the rest of his platoon, company, battalion, or regiment. Certainly, he has no concept of what is happening to the rest of the division; nor does he care very much. All that matters for the moment is staying alive, for, during a firefight, it seems that all of the enemy's weapons—and most of the "friendly" ones—are being directed solely at him. Ear-shattering noise is everywhere and the air is filled with flying shards of metal and snapping bullets. He is exhorted by his officers and NCOs to get up and move forward but knows that if he should move from his position of relative safety, he will become the target for every enemy gun in the area. Adding to the soldier's inertia are the screams and moans of wounded and dying men near him and the cries of "Medic!" The soldier on the battlefield, therefore, is continually torn between two polar opposites—to follow his instincts and stay where he is, in a place where he has experienced some temporary level of safety and comfort but which may in the next instant be the precise place where an artillery round or bullet will hit, or to summon every ounce of courage he possesses and move from that spot, exposing his fragile, vulnerable body to the risk of death or injury, even though a place where greater safety may be found may be only a few yards away. Such thoughts and dilemmas faced every man of the 36th Division that morning.

Above, in the predawn darkness of 9 September, the *Luftwaffe* swooped in over the beachhead and added to the terror and carnage. LSTs, loaded with tanks and personnel and moving toward shore, were set afire or sunk with horrifying consequences. Artillery rounds burst in the air above the landing craft, splintering the boats and shredding the men inside. Ramps on landing craft dropped open, only to invite murderous machine gun fire from shore. The men of the 36th, who, just hours before, had cheered the news that Italy was out of the war, were now fighting a desperate battle for their lives on Italian soil, and the sands where Italian sunbathers and picnickers once enjoyed themselves were now soaking up American blood. From inland, a loudspeaker blared in German-accented English, "Come on in and give up. We have you covered." Somehow, the invaders pulled themselves together, shook themselves out of their collective shock, formed into units, and began to fight back.[26]

Throughout the day, the battle for the beachhead raged. While the foot soldiers battled their way inland, more landing craft struggled to bring men, artillery, tanks, and supplies into shore. Dead soldiers and sailors, many without heads or limbs, floated in the oil-slicked water. Knocked out and burning landing craft bobbed helplessly in the surf, impeding the efforts of other landing craft to bring their human cargo and much-needed matériel to the beach. Tons of supplies piled up at the water's edge, preventing landing craft from dropping their ramps; due to the heavy fire, the Army's stevedore parties had been unable to keep the beaches clear. Overhead, the *Luftwaffe* and Allied air forces battled for control of the skies. But radio contact between the men on the beach and the men on the ships was virtually nonexistent, and the troops were unable to call for naval supporting fire for several crucial hours after landing. This deficiency was partially corrected by midmorning, and the Navy braved the intense artillery fire and enemy aircraft to draw close to shore and add its heavy guns in service to the infantry.

Also without adequate communications, Clark and Dawley, on ships offshore, did not know what was happening inland. The commanders could see the wrecked and burning landing craft and DUKWs* lying in the surf; could see the *Luftwaffe* skimming low over the beachhead and blasting the ships, men, and vehicles; could see and hear the tremendous fusillade that was being poured into the troops from the heights beyond the beach, but that was about all. There seemed to be the very real possibility that the landings had failed and that it would be necessary to somehow pull the survivors off the beach and abort the invasion altogether.[27]

At German Tenth Army Headquarters in Polla, some thirty-five miles southeast of Salerno, confusion also reigned. Commanding General Heinrich von Vietinghoff was trying to muster the troops needed to react to the invasion. The 16th Panzer was holding, but for how long? Two-thirds of the 16th's tanks had already been knocked out of action. Communications on land were as bad for the Germans as the land-sea communications were for the Allies. With Kesselring temporarily tied up in Rome, von Vietinghoff had to make his own decisions—and fast. He ordered XIV Panzer Corps to rush every unit it could spare to the Salerno area. The Hermann Göring Panzer Division and elements of the 15th Panzer Grenadier Division were dispatched from north of Naples, and the 19th and 29th Panzer Grenadier Divisions were on their way from the south to seal off the beachhead. Von Vietinghoff asked Kesselring for more troops and Kesselring requested that Hitler send two armored divisions being held in northern Italy, but, inexplicably, the Führer vetoed the request. Von Vietinghoff fretted; how large was the invasion force? Could he get enough troops to Salerno in time to throw the invaders back into the sea?[28]

Thanks to the heroic efforts of the Navy LST coxswains who braved the withering fire, American tanks and tank destroyers began to build up in sufficient numbers on the beaches about midafternoon and rumble inland, helping the infantry advance. In the sky, American and British fighters were keeping enemy aircraft at bay and hammering targets on the ground. Nothing,

---

*For troops involved in amphibious landings, the DUKWs (popularly called "ducks") were the workhorses that kept the vital supply lifeline between ship and shore operating. Basically a boat body on the Army's six-by-six truck chassis, the seven-ton DUKW had a propeller drive that enabled it to travel up to five knots in water while hauling 5,000 pounds of cargo or carrying up to fifty soldiers. On land, it could do fifty miles per hour (Eric Morris, *Salerno: A Military Fiasco* [New York: Stein & Day, 1983], p. 46).

however, could stop the newest of the Nazi wonder weapons: the glide bomb. These remote-controlled flying bombs, laden with 660 pounds of high explosive and guided by crews in high-flying bombers, took their toll of Allied warships lying offshore during the next few days. The British cruiser HMS *Uganda* and battleship HMS *Warspite* were both badly damaged, and the American light cruiser USS *Savannah* was put out of action by these flying menaces.[29] In addition, E-boats, the German equivalent of American PT boats, entered the harbor and sank the destroyer USS *Rowan* with torpedoes shortly after midnight. Over 200 men went down with the *Rowan*.[30]

Much credit must go to the Navy, for without its supporting fire, the invaders stood little chance. Time after time, British and American ships were called on to suppress an enemy artillery battery or break up a concentration of tanks that was threatening the beachhead. A naval historian has written, "The intensity and volume of naval gunfire delivered in direct support of troop operations here set a new high in that aspect of naval warfare; one that would not be exceeded in the Pacific until Iwo Jima and Okinawa. . . . On the basis of incomplete reports, it has been estimated that during the Salerno operation the ships delivered more than 11,000 tons of shell in direct support of troops ashore. This is the equivalent of 72,000 field artillery 105mm high-explosive projectiles."[31]

• • •

While the struggle continued on land and offshore throughout the ninth, the men of the 45th huddled in their landing craft, listening to the sounds of battle in the distance, contemplating the task before them and their chances of survival, and awaiting their cue. The wait lasted all day and through the night. In the early morning hours of 10 September, the LSTs and LCIs carrying the 157th and 179th in the Gulf of Salerno were illuminated by German flares that acted as beacons for swarms of attacking German fighters. Bombs straddled the ships and the guns of every ship in the harbor opened up on the aerial raiders. The *Luftwaffe* broke off the attack for a few hours, then came rushing back at 0420 hours. Again the bombs came down; again the guns of the ships filled the air with lead; again the ships carrying the 45th escaped destruction.[32] Far out in the bay, under the constant aerial attacks, Lieutenant Trevor Evans, a mortar platoon leader with M Company, 157th, was standing on the bridge beside the commander of the LCI. "He was a New Zealander who had taken part in the Dieppe raid," Evans said. "He was a very quiet individual. All of a sudden, he said, 'Excuse me,' and went below. He came up later and his arm was bandaged. Evidently, a piece of falling shrapnel had come down and hit him while he was standing there talking to me."[33]

Finally, reports from the beachhead began to reach Clark's command ship about 1700 hours and they painted a picture of a battle slowly being

Behind a screen of smoke, Thunderbirds hitting the Salerno beachhead, September 1943. (Courtesy of 45th Infantry Division Archives)

won. Despite stubborn enemy resistance, the 36th Division was advancing inland and taking key objectives. On the eleventh, the 36th's 142nd Regiment occupied Altavilla without opposition.[34] The main worry was a gap of some seven to ten miles between the 36th Division to the south and the British 56th Division to the north—a gap known as the Sele Corridor. The British had been expected to take the high ground around Battipaglia, west of Eboli, then link up with the Texans at the Ponte Sele—a vital bridge over the Sele on Highway 19, halfway between Eboli and Serre. But the Germans were offering unusually determined opposition at Battipaglia and the British had been unable to break through. The Germans then discovered the gap between the Allied forces and set about making plans to exploit it. The strategy was simple: smash through the gap to the sea with all the armor and infantry that could be mustered.[35] Meanwhile, Clark saw the same gap and realized it must be plugged. The order went out to bring in the floating reserve—the two regiments of the 45th Division.[36]

The 179th would be the first 45th Division unit to land, followed by the 1st and 3rd Battalions of the 157th (because of the shortage of transport, the 2nd Battalion was still in Sicily, along with the 180th), plus the 158th Field Artillery, A Company of the 120th Engineers, and A Company of the 120th Medical Battalion. At 1140 hours on 10 September, the transports carrying the 179th began their run in to shore. As the men waded through the surf and sprinted across the beach, all seemed much too quiet. Twenty minutes later the quiet was shattered as all hell broke loose and the *Luftwaffe* again pounced on the ships that were debarking men and vehicles. The men of the 179th moved quickly inland toward their regimental assembly area two miles south of Paestum, marching single file past discarded equipment, burning vehicles, empty brass cartridges, strands of communication wire, shattered trees, demolished buildings, and bloody bandages blowing in the soft breeze. From the east, beyond the coastal highway, the sounds of a terrific battle drifted in. The men sank into the sand, munched on K rations, and pondered their future.[37]

They did not have long to ponder. Placed under direct VI Corps control, the 179th was ordered by Dawley at 1500 hours to set out on a northeasterly course along the Sele River with its objective to secure the high ground near Serre, about seven miles east of Eboli, a distance of some seventeen miles inland as the crow—or Thunderbird—flies. The Ponte Sele would also need to be captured. To accomplish this mission, the regimental commander, Colonel Robert B. Hutchins, formed his unit into two columns. The first, or west, column was made up of the 1st and 3rd Battalions; the second, or east, column consisted of the 2nd Battalion, supported by the 160th Field Artillery.[38]

Early that afternoon, the 157th Regiment, minus the 2nd Battalion, came ashore. Due to the intense shelling he was receiving, the commander of the ships carrying the 157th dumped them on the wrong beach—south of the mouth of the Sele River instead of to the north. Clark was furious; he needed the 157th to rush up to the vicinity of Battipaglia, but the Ponte Alla Scafa bridge that carried Highway 18 over the Sele had been destroyed by the Germans and the 157th had no way to cross to the north side. The Engineers labored through the night to throw a pontoon bridge across the river.[39]

Meanwhile, after waiting for the cover of darkness, the 179th's two columns crossed Highway 18 and moved like twin bayonets pointed toward Serre. Throughout the night, the men of the 179th continued their advance, occasionally running into pockets of resistance, but by the time they reached the Sele, just south of La Cosa Creek, they found the only bridge there had been turned into a charred wreck by the Germans. The 179th's attached combat engineer unit began immediately to build a pontoon bridge downstream, which was finished within an hour, enabling the men and vehicles of the 179th to cross the river. Unknown to Hutchins and his men was the fact that while marching toward Serre they were on a collision course with a strong counterattack by elements of the 16th Panzer and 29th Panzer Grenadier Divisions on their way to split the beachhead in two. At dawn on the eleventh, after bypassing the town of Persano, located in the Y just above the confluence of the Sele and Calore Rivers, the tip of the regiment ran into massed enemy infantry and armor heading south, and the battle was on in earnest. The 16th Panzer crossed the Sele and took Persano, preventing a late-arriving American armored unit from coming to the 179th's aid. Heavy concentrations of German artillery slammed into the Thunderbirds, and German tanks were working their way around the 179th's rear, as well as hitting the Americans' positions on the north and west sides. Colonel Hutchins radioed the 157th, still several miles away, for assistance.

Realizing the infantry's plight, Lieutenant Colonel Jess Larson, commanding the 160th Artillery, ordered his batteries into action, and for hours the 105s dueled with the 88s. It was an unequal fight, but the American gunners held their own, beating off several panzer attacks with well-placed artillery barrages. For how long could the Americans hold back the German tide? The battle was growing in intensity and forward observers spotted a large force of some 200 enemy tanks massing near Serre. Cut off and surrounded in a small pocket, the 179th was being hammered from all sides and from above by aircraft, artillery, and mortar rounds.

The 1st Battalion, commanded by Lieutenant Colonel Wayne L. Johnson, hung on stubbornly, but the impact of the German assault caused Lieutenant Colonel William P. Grace, Jr.'s 2nd Battalion and Lieutenant Colonel Earl M. Taylor's 3rd Battalion to recoil from their positions, which uncovered the neighboring 36th Division's left flank.[40] Like sharks in a feeding frenzy, the men of *Generalmajor* Walter Fries's 29th Panzer Grenadier Division now launched another attack, this one from the vicinity of Serre; pushed past the momentarily dazed 2nd Battalion; and struck the exposed left shoulder of the 36th Division at Altavilla, driving it from the town.[41]

Grace's 2nd Battalion soon found itself cut off. Wounded men were dying for lack of medical treatment and Johnson asked for the engineers to construct a bridge across the Calore so he could evacuate his wounded and, he hoped, extricate his dwindling fighting force.[42] No immediate help was on the way. The British were hotly engaged eight miles to the north and the 36th Division was fighting for its own life around Altavilla.[43] At 1920 hours, Colonel Hutchins requested air support, but no planes were available. Hutchins then called for supporting tanks and tank destroyers, only to discover there were none; the armor was still several miles back, being held at bay by the Germans' heavy weapons. The 157th was moving, but running into strong opposition. Food and water were perilously low. Even the 160th Artillery was down to just five rounds per battery.[44]

As Mark Clark wrote in *Calculated Risk,* "The two fingers which the Forty-fifth Division had stuck out toward the Ponte Sele were being badly bruised, and it appeared they might be cut off."[45] Armed with nothing more than rifles, machine guns, hand grenades, and bayonets, the 179th fought back valiantly against the panzers. The night of the eleventh was ablaze with gunfire and tracers from both sides. The Germans closed in for the kill; the 179th Regimental Combat Team, it seemed, was doomed.[46]

Middleton, however, was determined not only to save the 179th, but to win the battle. He directed the 157th, 191st Tank Battalion, and 645th Tank Destroyer Battalion to come with all speed to the regiment's assistance.[47] Moving toward the battle himself, General Middleton encountered a motorized artillery battalion that was motoring to the rear, turned the men around, and directed them to fire in support of his division.[48]

Pete Conde, who had since been transferred to HQ Company, 1st Battalion, 157th, recalled that on the way to the 179th's aid, Colonel Ankcorn used a trick once employed by Alexander the Great several centuries earlier: "He ran the same battalion three times over a bridge under German observation to make them think his force was larger than it actually was."[49]

The 179th, meanwhile, was in a desperate fix. Ray Williams, a member of the Ammunition and Pioneer Platoon, 1st Battalion, 179th, recalled,

> That night, the whole battalion was in a circle. When you're gettin' tank fire from four directions, nobody has to tell you the enemy's behind you. We had a young major named Pete Donaldson. He was just a kid, maybe twenty-two years old, but he was a hell of a good Okie. He wanted everybody to know the situation. He went around and told everybody in that circle that the situation wasn't too good. His exact words were, "Tonight, you're not fightin' for your country, you're fighting for your ass, because they're behind us." We had only one artillery piece with us. A German shell had knocked the sights off the gun, so they were bore-sightin' that son-of-a-bitch, shootin' at tanks. They looked through the barrel and aimed it at a tank, then loaded and fired it. That's a desperate situation.[50]

The 157th's all-night march took it across the Sele to the north bank and on to a semicircle of five sturdy stone buildings that formed the Tabacchificio Fiocche—a tobacco factory—strategically located on a rise overlooking a crossroads west of Persano. Persano and the factory were both in German hands, and a tremendous fight broke out as the 157th came within range. Seven Shermans from the accompanying tank battalion were knocked out in an ambush and the Germans were poised to ram down the Sele-Calore corridor to the sea. Clark delivered an ultimatum to everyone on the beach: "You must not yield another inch. I call on every man to fight to the last round and the last breath."[51]

As darkness enveloped the battlefield, the men of the 179th grimly fixed bayonets and dug in to await what the night would bring. What the night brought was an anxious silence. The soldiers' minds played tricks on them; was that noise the sound of an infiltrating German patrol or just a rabbit rustling through the brush? That shadow—was it a rock or a German machine gun crew?

Dawn arrived, miraculously without further attack. As the 179th's regimental history reports, "Incredibly, impossibly, the Germans didn't realize

A postbattle photo of the strategic tobacco factory near Persano, scene of vicious fighting between the Wehrmacht and Thunderbirds. Whoever controlled the factory controlled access to several key roads. (Courtesy of 45th Infantry Archives)

the regiment's desperate plight, its shortage of everything a soldier needed to fight. They didn't realize how close they were to final, complete victory!"[52] Daniel Witts, Anti-Tank Company, 179th, said, "The Germans thought we had more than we did. That's why we didn't get wiped out. Had they known it, they could have pushed us right back into the water. It was just luck that they didn't finish us off."[53]

On the morning of the twelfth, Ankcorn's regiment, supported by armor from the 753rd Tank Battalion and 645th Tank Destroyer Battalion, fought its way into the tobacco factory's grounds, bringing some relief to the siege but getting bogged down itself in heavy fighting.[54] First Lieutenant Eddie Speairs, still the acting S-4 for the 1st Battalion, 157th, recalled an incident near the tobacco factory: "We were cut off. The whole battalion CP [command post] group was in a ditch up close to the factory. Lieutenant Colonel Murphy had put out a patrol and told us that as soon as the patrol comes in, we're going to send C Company out. While we waited, I went forward to the base of the hill." With Speairs was a fellow lieutenant, Albert W. Elmer.

> His family owned Elmer's Candy Company in New Orleans. We were lying up on this hill and I looked down and said, "There's a damn German down there." Elmer said, "Aw, hell, you can't see a German." I said, "He's right in

> the shade of that tree." He looked and said, "Damn, you're right." I was always kind of a sharpshooter and I got ready to shoot and he said, "Hey, wait a minute, that might be one of C Company's patrols." I said, "Nope, 'cause he doesn't have any leggings on." So I winged one at him and he took off running like a striped-ass ape; I didn't even scratch him. Later, he told everybody, "Never leave your leggings off if Ed's around—he's liable to shoot you."

But there was no levity during the next few minutes. The Germans were rushing men and tanks into the area. "I was on the far left end with Germans within sixty or seventy feet of us," Speairs said. "Why they didn't overrun us, I'll never know." A loaded half-track personnel carrier went to the 157th's rear, and a Tiger tank pulled up on the road. "The only thing between us and that Tiger tank was an eight-foot wall. Finally, Murphy said, 'If we stay here, we're going to get captured. Pass the word down; if we can get across the road in front of that tank, we'll make it.' The rest of the group moved out while Elmer and I covered them, then we crossed the road right in front of that tank. It was broad daylight, but they never saw us. We were just lucky. We got to the rear and held the line."[55]

While the desperate battle in the hills was going on, Clark, who had come ashore on the twelfth, was deeply concerned about the precarious situation on the beachhead and was questioning Dawley's capabilities in the face of the growing enemy threat. Clark felt Dawley was unaware of, or unimpressed by, the German pressure against the Sele Corridor gap being plugged by the 45th. In any event, Dawley could do little about it, since all of his forces had been committed and there was no Corps reserve. To salve Clark's fears, Dawley, on the night of 12–13 September, had the 2nd Battalion of the 36th Division's 143rd Regiment move into the 179th's positions. The 179th was then shifted into the gap between the British right flank at Battipaglia and the 157th's left flank at the tobacco factory.[56] That night, not knowing the 179th had been moved, the Germans charged the 157th at the tobacco factory, but in so doing, ran across the front of the repositioned 179th's 2nd and 3rd Battalions and were shot to pieces. Seven panzers were knocked out and the German infantry temporarily retreated.[57]

The victory celebration was short lived; the British 56th Division was taking a pounding at Battipaglia and exposing the 45th's left flank. Furthermore, Walker's 36th Division was ordered to retake Altavilla and Hill 424—a virtual impossibility given its battered, understrength state. On the thirteenth, the 36th inserted a company into the town but suffered heavy casualties while trying to take Hill 424. The lone company was then forced out of Altavilla.[58]

While scouting for a new mortar position, Lieutenant Trevor Evans, M Company, 157th, stumbled across the gruesome effluvium of war in a ravine: "It was quite a sight," he recalled:

There were bazookas and rifles hanging from the trees. The whole heavy-weapons company of a battalion from the 36th Division had been machine-gunned to death. Their faces had turned black and hard like an eggplant, and there were bright green maggots crawling out of the bullet holes. They evidently had started to dig foxholes, but they were only three or four inches deep, and there were C rations scattered around. My guess is that the battalion commander had felt sorry for them and failed to post security. Many had dug holes along the road where the digging was easier, but it was the wrong thing to do because the holes were all in a line. The German tanks had sprayed them with machine guns and then dropped their treads down off the road and just crushed them in a long line.

Evans also reported that an Italian cavalry school must have been nearby because, in a field not far away, there were twenty-five or thirty dead horses with their legs sticking up in the air.[59]

As the 45th Division's history states,

During these days of serious danger to the Allied position in the severe battle to maintain the narrow hold on the little piece of land, the fighting took on the character of individual combat. Although the superb teamwork between infantry and artillery, tanks, navy, air corps, tank destroyers all combined to bring about the final decision, it was the fortitude and persistence of the individual and his little squad or section that formed the foundation upon which the victory was built. Every man became an important block in the line of defense; every casualty was keenly felt.[60]

Brigadier General Raymond S. McLain, the 45th's artillery commander, led a convoy that broke through the German encirclement of the 179th's lines and delivered a vital resupply of artillery ammunition. Shortly thereafter, a squadron of tank destroyers arrived and the numerically superior panzers inexplicably withdrew. The siege of the 179th had been lifted, and McLain won the Silver Star for gallantry. Too often, high-ranking officers have received awards for little or no reason. Not so General McLain. As his citation reads,

Brigadier General McLain took charge of the efforts being made to re-establish contact with and bring relief to the threatened units. He directed the movement of these units and then proceeded in his vehicle past the leading elements through a fire-swept zone, thence by foot through mined areas for a distance of approximately two and one-half miles to reach the threatened combat team. Having ascertained by a personal reconnaissance the routes to and the situation in the combat team, he directed the re-establishment of contact and the bringing up of the necessary supplies and ammunition, and the evacuation of the wounded. Brigadier General McLain's disregard for his own safety and prompt action at a critical time contributed greatly to the success of the Division at the Salerno Beachhead.[61]

So close did the enemy come to breaking through the thin line held only by the two battered regiments of the 45th that artillerymen were ordered to leave their guns, grab rifles, and fight as infantry. Even cooks, clerks, and members of the regimental band were pressed into the fray. Unaccustomed to life behind a rifle, some of the troops hopped aboard a number of tanks and tank destroyers that were heading to the rear. McLain stopped the retreat and turned the men and vehicles around, saying, "The fight's up front, not back here."[62]

• • •

For some unknown reason, von Vietinghoff was convinced that the Allied invasion had failed and that the Americans were preparing to evacuate the beachhead. To finish them off, he ordered XIV Panzer Corps to launch another major attack between the 45th and 36th Divisions. At 1600 hours on the thirteenth, a dozen tanks from the 16th Panzer Division, plus infantry riding in armored personnel carriers, slammed into the 157th's right flank and another six tanks struck the left. Heavy artillery fire was added to the mixture until it seemed the entire earth was erupting. The 157th gave ground and then, about midnight, turned around and regained the lost real estate. The neighboring 36th Division was also being hit hard, and over 500 of the Texans were taken prisoner.[63] That evening, von Vietinghoff sent a telegram to Kesselring, declaring victory: "After a defensive battle lasting four days, enemy resistance is collapsing. Tenth Army pursuing on wide front. Heavy fighting still in progress near Salerno and Altavilla. Maneuver in process to cut off the retreating enemy from Paestum."

But, although bloody and bruised, the Allies were far from beaten.[64] Mark Clark noted, "The fighting was intense for a couple of hours, after which German tanks slipped down a draw, caught our men by surprise, temporarily trapped the battalion headquarters, and eventually forced our lines back enough to let the main German force cross the Sele River."[65]

Panzers again attempted to crack an opening through the Thunderbirds' lines and drive toward the confluence of the Sele and Calore Rivers with only two of the 45th Division's artillery battalions standing in the way.[66] The 189th Field Artillery, commanded by Lieutenant Colonel Hal L. Muldrow, and the 158th Field Artillery, under Lieutenant Colonel Russell D. Funk, dug in on the bank near where the two rivers meet, braved enemy tank fire, and replied with every weapon they had, firing thousands of rounds that day. As one historian noted, "The only troops who stood between the Germans and the sea were some supporting artillery of the Forty-fifth Infantry Division. These guns saved the day and quite possibly the battle."[67]

Clark later wrote,

> The ford beside the bridge and the road leading to it simply went up in dust. The fields and the woods in which the enemy tanks took cover were pulverized. When the Germans tried to fight their way across the ford, the fire laid down by everybody from the artillerymen to the piccolo player knocked them back on their heels. At one time the two battalions were firing eight rounds per minute per gun, and they acted as if they could keep it up all night if necessary and someone passed the ammunition. After several unsuccessful thrusts, the enemy column wavered and began to fall back. By sunset the two battalions had fired 3,650 rounds.[68]

Faced with such withering fire, the Germans gave up their attempt to cross the Calore and pulled back to Persano. It was the Germans who now found themselves besieged and low on critical supplies. Pete Conde recalled, "The Germans were almost out of 88mm ammunition. They were shooting smoke shells at us because they didn't have anything else to shoot."[69]

Since 10 September, the *Wehrmacht* had been hammering at the fragile gaps between the British and the 45th and between the 45th and 36th Divisions, each blow widening the gaps a little. The timely arrival of Montgomery's Eighth Army, like Blücher's Prussians coming to the aid of Wellington at Waterloo in the nick of time, could have made all the difference. But Montgomery was still one hundred miles south of Salerno, moving slowly and cautiously against token, rear-guard opposition. Incredibly, Monty even took a break of two days to allow his men to rest, build up supplies, and perform vehicle maintenance. He wouldn't reach the southern fringe of the Salerno area until 18 September.[70] At Clark's headquarters at Paestum, the Allies' hold on the beachhead seemed so tenuous that plans were made to evacuate his headquarters and the surviving VI Corps troops, à la Dunkirk, and deposit them in the British X Corps's sector in the event the Germans broke through. But Middleton would have none of it. "I told my staff that we weren't leaving," he said. Without informing his men of Clark's evacuation proposal, Middleton issued his own order that stiffened the resolve of every man on the beachhead: "Put food and ammunition behind the Forty-fifth. We are going to stay here."[71]

Eddie Speairs credits one man—First Lieutenant Kenneth P. "Kayo" Stemmons, leader of the Ammunition and Pioneer Platoon, 1st Battalion, 157th—for stopping the German effort to split the Thunderbirds and reach the sea. According to Speairs, on the night of 13–14 September, Stemmons's men laid all of the battalion's supply of anti-tank mines in the one avenue of approach he felt the Germans would use. "He picked a spot nobody believed would do any good," said Speairs. "He was as hard-headed as hell. He said, 'Goddamn it, I'm gonna put 'em there and you can all kiss my ass if you don't like it.'"[72]

Asked about this, Stemmons said, "In effect, that's about what happened." The battalion had a captain from the armor corps attached to it, and he and Stemmons and Lieutenant Colonel Murphy were arguing heat-

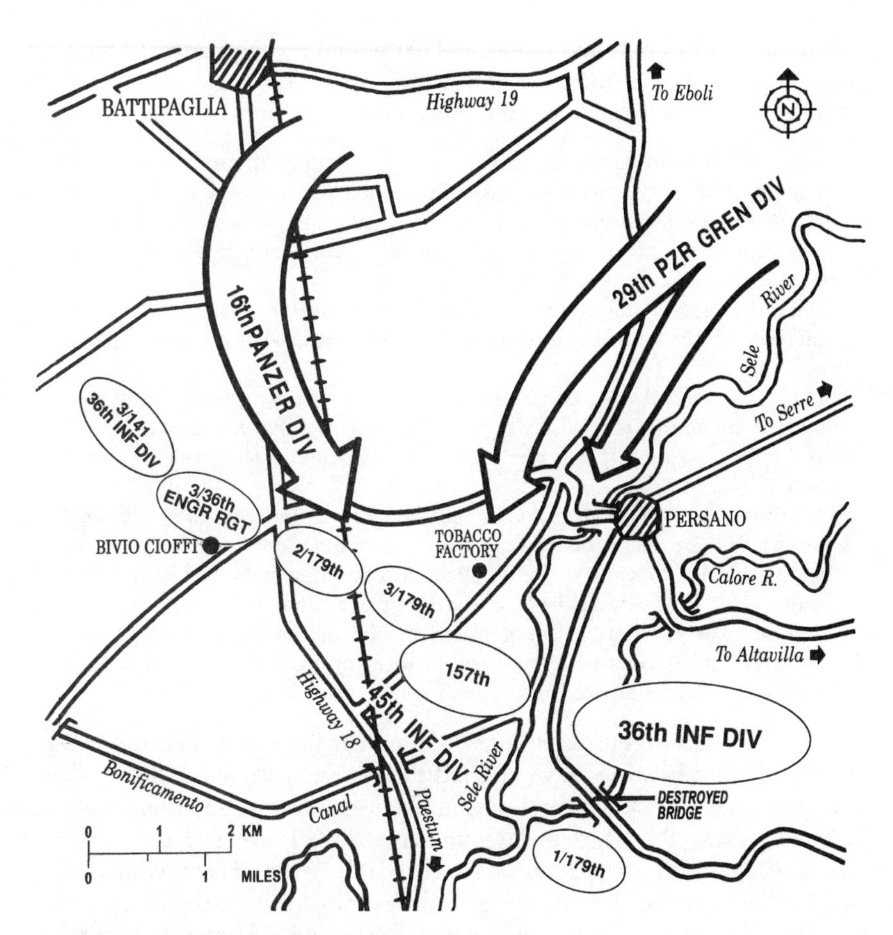

MAP 3.2 Stopping the Counterattack
14 September 1943—With the 45th Division forming a thin defensive line between Battipaglia and the confluence of the Sele and Calore Rivers, two German divisions launched a heavy counterattack in an attempt to smash through the Thunderbirds and drive to the sea.

edly about the best place to lay the mines. "To be frank," said Stemmons, "the Germans were about to push us off the beachhead—it's as simple as that. So when Murphy asked me, I said, 'Well, there's a big field with a knoll in it over there, and I'd put the mines clear across that whole field.'"

The armor captain objected. "No, no," he said, "We need to get 'em out on that road."

Stemmons retorted, "By God, if *you* were attacking, you wouldn't come straight up that road. You'd go behind that little valley up over the woods there."

"No, no, no," the captain replied. "That would bog you down. You'd be going too slow. Put the mines on the road."

"He was really adamant," Stemmons recalled:

> I said, "I've done looked at both places and I've walked the whole thing and I'm so damned tired now, but I know I'm gonna put 'em over there on that knoll, if it's all right with you, Colonel." Then the colonel said, "Well, if this armor man says his is the correct solution, if he really believes they should be someplace else, maybe we should talk this over."
>
> Then the captain started telling all his reasons why they should be on the road. When he was done, Murphy said, "Stemmons, what do you think of that?"
>
> I said, "I think that's just so much B.S. There's no way those krauts are gonna run up on that road. They're gonna come across that field and cut us off at the railroad tracks. If you were the armored commander, that's what *you* would do."
>
> Murphy said, "Well, yeah, you might be right. Tomorrow morning we'll know who's right. But right now, get those damn mines out." He turned to the captain and said, "My man's pretty much set on putting them over there." The captain said, "That sure the hell is the wrong place, Colonel."
>
> Colonel Murphy was a fine gentleman. He said to the captain, "Well, y'know, I'm going to go with the man I brung. I brought Stemmons this far—I'm going to take his advice."

Stemmons's platoon took all night to emplace the mines. Because it was pitch black, and because they expected the Germans to attack before daylight, the men didn't bother burying them—they just set them on the ground in a staggered pattern. Stemmons personally stepped out the pattern. Working with Stemmons was a corporal, Arthur Huey, who would take a mine from the men in the platoon as they brought the devices forward and place it where the lieutenant was standing. "After about an hour of doing this," Stemmons said,

> the guys stopped bringing the mines. We were out of mines and Huey and I were standing out there in the dark. Huey said, "Lieutenant, I'll run back and see." I said, "No, you stay right here. I'll see what's the matter." I went about fifty yards and I heard what sounded like a bunch of Germans. I hunkered down and said to myself, "God-dang it, they're already behind us." I stayed there for a few minutes and then I heard 'em going *thunk-thunk-thunk*. I couldn't figure out what they were doing. I finally got up enough nerve and moved a little closer, then I could tell they were talking English. It was the rest of my platoon. They had run into a watermelon patch and the dang guys had set the mines down and were thumping the watermelons, looking for ripe ones! Right in the middle of a war! You could get your dang head blowed off! So I got 'em back to work and we got all the mines laid out.

Stemmons's platoon set out its entire complement of mines, a total of more than 500 mines to cover an area some 200 yards wide.

As the lieutenant expected, before dawn the next morning, the German column came rumbling across the open field, straight for the thin American lines, and drove right into the minefield. Suddenly the ground erupted, and vehicle parts and bodies were flying everywhere. To add to the carnage, an artillery forward observer heard the vehicles detonating the mines and saturated the area with a barrage. The German attack was stopped cold.

At first light, Stemmons toured the battlefield. "I couldn't believe that a few anti-tank mines could do that much damage to a panzer unit," he said. The broken and burned hulks of eight tanks lay immobilized, along with two knocked-out personnel carriers. A large track lay on the ground, indicating that a larger tank had been destroyed, then retrieved. Two or three German corpses lay sprawled in the grass. "All the men's equipment was still there, and lots of evidence of wounded people that had been evacuated," he said.

> When they hit the first mine, I don't know why somebody didn't say, "Hold up, Fritz. Let's see what we need to do, or what we need to bypass." But they just ran pell-mell right down the line into the mine field. Those mines just devastated that outfit. They would have been right down in our flank, right down through our troops, so you think, boy, that really saved the day. Afterward, the colonel said, "I've got to give you credit, lieutenant—you had it figured right." And that armor captain—he never said a word. Not even "You were right, Stemmons," or "You lucked into that."[73]

"Stemmons got every one of them," Speairs said. "Afterward, we always bragged about Kayo's ability to pick out a minefield."[74]

Both sides were engaged in a desperate race to reinforce their positions. Bringing more troops to the beachhead before the Germans could seal it off was crucial for the Allies. The 45th Division's 180th Regiment and the British 7th Armoured Division were on the way but would not arrive until the fourteenth, and Alexander diverted some shipping to pick up the 3rd Division in Sicily and bring it to Salerno. Meanwhile, the Germans were rushing the 26th Panzer and 3rd and 15th Panzer Grenadier Divisions to the front.[75]

Because an immediate solution to his manpower problem was required, Clark called on his reserve force, the 82nd Airborne, which was on standby alert in Sicily. On the morning of the thirteenth, he directed Major General Matthew Ridgway to make a drop that night, with the drop zone close to the sea, between Agropoli and Paestum.[76] At 2326 hours on 13 September, men from the 2nd Battalion, 504th Parachute Infantry Regiment (PIR) of the 82nd Airborne, swooped low over the coast in C-47 Dakotas and jumped into the night. Another battalion dropped two hours later. Their objective: reinforce the 36th Division and retake Altavilla and the surrounding hills. By the seventeenth, they had accomplished their mission.[77] Another jump by the separate 509th PIR was scheduled to take Avellino, twenty-five miles north of Salerno in the British sector, on the night of 14 September. This operation went badly. There was little time to plan or rehearse; the transport planes became scattered; and the drop was made from too high an altitude, which dispersed the paratroopers over a wide area and units could not find one another in the dark hills and vineyards. For the next several days, this force was only able to carry out small, nuisance raids against the Germans.[78] (Decimated, the regiment was later reorganized as a battalion.)

At 0800 hours on the fourteenth, the *Wehrmacht* tried again to dislodge the 45th. The combined infantry-armor assault was aimed at the GIs near the tobacco factory; the Yanks cut the Germans to pieces. After falling back in shock, the enemy continued to mount strong counterattacks against the 157th and 179th, only to be driven back each time by the combined fury of American arms, including Navy ships in the harbor. Later that day, the 180th was brought ashore and the thin line held by the other two Thunderbird regiments finally had a reserve force behind it.[79] One of those landing with the reserve force was a new second lieutenant, Jack C. Montgomery, I Company, 180th. He had taken over command of his platoon after the platoon leader had been wounded two days after the Sicily landings. "I took charge of the platoon for the rest of the campaign in Sicily. When it was over, they recommended me for a battlefield commission. I got the commission the day before we went to Salerno."[80]

That afternoon, the crisis on the beachhead finally passed—the Germans had shot their bolt. Naval fire and aerial bombardment plastered German troop concentrations and the 36th Division stopped another German counterattack. The British 7th Armoured Division landed and assisted in reinforcing the gap between the British and the 45th.[81]

General Clark made a tour of the battlefield, stopping to visit with the 45th's troops in the Sele-Calore sector.[82] Of the men of the 157th and 179th Regiments he later wrote,

> These troops had been in the Sicilian campaign and were doing a fine job. They were well led by Major General Troy Middleton, the division commander. They had good liaison with their artillery and in the period of an hour that morning had knocked out thirteen enemy tanks. We were under artillery and small-arms fire most of the time we were talking to the men of these two regiments; but they went about their jobs in workmanlike fashion, and I had every confidence that they would stand their ground. They did.[83]

On the eighteenth, Eisenhower arrived at Salerno from his headquarters in Tunis and toured the battlefield. His presence there was more than just a sightseeing mission; the fact that the invasion had nearly failed concerned him deeply and he wanted to find out for himself just who had been at fault: Clark, Dawley, or Walker, the 36th's commanding general.[84]

Believing that strong German forces still remained around Persano, Clark directed the 45th to assault them on the eighteenth. But, "when morning came on September 18th, there was nothing in front of us," Middleton said.[85]

The 180th moved to the vicinity of Eboli, but by then most of the fighting was over. The gruesome remains of the battle that had just taken place, however, were everywhere. First Lieutenant Bill Whitman recalled, "There were knocked-out tanks all around with the dead tank crews still in them, and the hot summer air really made them smell to high heaven. We put handkerchiefs over our noses and made the best of it. The tanks were American."[86]

During the night, the Germans had quickly and quietly withdrawn to the north. But they had not given up or retreated very far, as the Thunderbirds would soon learn.

4

Heavy and Accursed Rain

19 September 1943–21 January 1944

> *I am in the third circle, filled with cold, unending, heavy, and accursed rain; its measure and its kind are never changed. Gross hailstones, water gray with filth, and snow come streaking across the shadowed air; the earth, as it receives that shower, stinks. Over the souls of those submerged beneath that mess, is an outlandish, vicious beast, his three throats barking, doglike: Cerberus.*
>
> **—Dante Alighieri, *The Inferno,* Canto VI**

NOW IT WAS THE TASK of the Allies to begin their northward march out of the Salerno beachhead. But there would be no headlong advance, no rapid dash up the "boot." To quote the 157th's history, "[The Germans'] withdrawal was as lethal as their attack, and there was no hurtling forward," as American newspapers had described the breakout from the beachhead.

On 19 September, on its way from Persano to Eboli, the 45th passed through a terrible wasteland, a grim battlescape littered with the detritus of war. It was obvious a great fight had taken place; wherever the eye looked, there were burned-out carcasses of tanks, trucks, and jeeps; bullet-riddled helmets; and punctured, blood-stained packs. Gas masks and full ammunition boxes lay scattered about. And everywhere there was the stench of rotting German corpses, lying unburied and bloating in the hot, September sun.[1]

An indication of the utter ferocity of the fighting is spelled out clearly in this undelivered letter written by a German soldier, dated 16 September and found by 45th Division troops:

> My dearest little wife—
>
> You will be amazed to read about our bitter fighting in the official *Wehrmacht* communiqués. We are fighting in the Eboli sector. Casualties are ever increasing. To add to the terror, the enemy air forces are bombing us relentlessly and

> atrociously. And with all that, an uncanny and perpetual artillery fire is scoring hits. Our fight against the Anglo-Americans requires more strength from us than our fight against the Russians. Many of us are longing to get back to Russia, even longing for the conditions as they were at Stalingrad.[2]

The Thunderbirds pushed up into the mountains that loom above Eboli and dug in to await whatever fate that Mars, the Roman god of war, had decreed for them. They didn't have long to wait: The Allies were directed to move northward to take Naples and push the enemy back beyond the Volturno River. It was an operation prosaically dubbed "Avalanche—Phase Two." The British X Corps, under Lieutenant General Richard L. McCreery, would spearhead the assault, with the U.S. VI Corps on its right. The 45th Division, on VI Corps's extreme right, would guard the flank of the Fifth Army advance and maintain contact with the British Eighth Army further to the east. In this way, the Allies hoped to roll up the entire length of the peninsula, pushing the Germans before them as they advanced.[3]

The Germans, however, refused to be easily pushed. They would withdraw, but they would do so at their pace, dictating when and where the battles would be fought. For the Allies, this was Sicily all over again, only on a larger scale. It was the worst kind of combat—nipping at the heels of a retreating foe who, on occasion, would choose to make a brief stand, lash out violently, and then continue to withdraw. The minefields the Germans left behind were thick and their artillery barrages frequent and deadly. Few bridges remained standing, and booby traps were everywhere. Glen K. Hanson, L Company, 157th, recalled the ferocity of the enemy fire: "We ran into some stiff opposition. The Germans shelled a little mountainside town we were in and I had to take cover under a bed to keep the roof from falling on me."[4]

The 45th advanced up and along either side of Highway 91 into mountainous territory, taking the shattered towns of Contursi and Oliveto, but only after much hard fighting. On their way to the Gustav Line, the Germans would exact a tremendous price for each foot of territory they relinquished.[5]

For the Allies, Rome was the prize, but it was a hundred miles away, over some of the most rugged terrain on earth. In addition, the Allies would discover to their dismay that the Germans had constructed a series of heavily fortified positions across the width of Italy. Closest to Naples was the "Barbara" Line, which ran along a ridge between the Volturno and Garigliano Rivers and then snaked over the southern Apennine peaks to the Trigno River. This line, in turn, was backed by the "Bernhard" Line, which took advantage of a narrow defile known as the Mignano Gap. Twelve miles further north was the "Gustav" Line, which began just north of the point where the Garigliano River empties into the Tyrrhenian Sea, and ran across

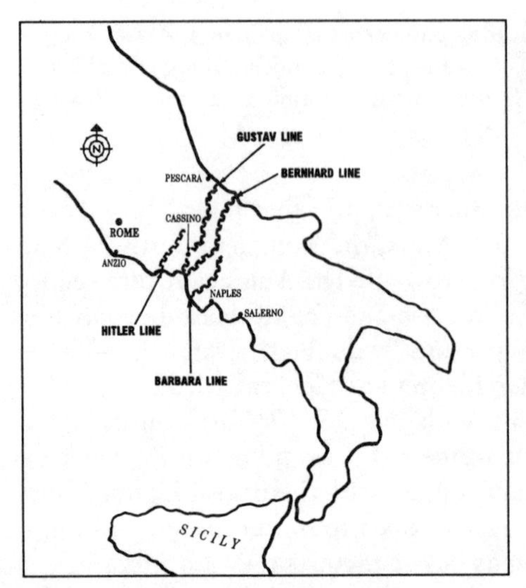

MAP 4.1 German Defensive Lines
The Germans constructed formidable barriers to thwart the Allied drive up the boot of Italy.

the mountains to the mouth of the Sangro River on the Adriatic side. The Gustav Line was the most formidable of all in southern Italy, made up of a series of bunkers, gun emplacements, and trench works constructed by Organization Todt, the German agency in charge of the design, engineering, and construction of fortifications.[6]

The Allies' most direct route to Rome was through the broad, flat Liri Valley, the entrance to which was barred by the Gustav Line. To reach the mouth of the valley, Clark's Fifth Army would be required to make combat crossings at three rain-swollen rivers—the Volturno, Garigliano, and Rapido—then take the impossible heights of Monte Cassino and Monte Majo that guarded the entrance to the valley with the same ferocity that Cerberus, the three-headed dog of Greek mythology, guarded the entrance to Hell. Like a seductive siren, the lure of the Liri Valley was more than Allied planners could resist. Through this plain, flanked by towering peaks that were a haven for the defender and a nightmare for the attacker, stretched Highway 6, the main north-south road to Rome. The Germans had fortified nearly every key point in the valley and were ready to make the Allies pay dearly, should they be so foolish as to try running the gauntlet.

But all that was still in the future. The most immediate problem facing the Allies now was breaking through the enemy defenses around Naples. Before that could happen, however, certain command changes needed to be made. On 20 September, the VI Corps commander got the ax. Eisenhower, Alexander, and Clark all thought the overworked Dawley had been too unsteady and lacking in sound judgment during the battle for the beachhead; Clark reluctantly relieved him. He wanted to install the 82nd Airborne's Matthew Ridgway as VI Corps commander, but Ike insisted on an old, reliable soldier, Major General John Porter Lucas, as Dawley's successor. Lucas had commanded the 3rd Infantry Division at Fort Lewis, Washington, had been an observer for the War Department during the North Africa operation, and had commanded III Corps in Georgia before being sent back to North Africa to act as Ike's unofficial deputy. After the fight for Sicily was over, Lucas briefly commanded II Corps before heading for Salerno.[7]

As part of the Fifth Army operation, the 45th was to swing northeast from Eboli to Oliveto, make contact with the British on the right flank, then head north up Highway 91 to take the high ground south of the Ofanto River near Teora. On the night of 20 September, the 180th ran into strong enemy resistance to the west of Oliveto. Artillery, mortar, and machine gun fire from the 64th Panzer Grenadier Regiment poured into the 180th's 2nd Battalion, commanded by Lieutenant Colonel Clarence B. Cochran, as it moved over the rugged ground toward Oliveto. The pounding continued for two days with the 180th able to make little progress. The 180th's 1st Battalion, under Major Charles W. Thomas of Denver, also ran into a hailstorm of machine gun fire from the ridges flanking both sides of the valley. Mortar and artillery fire were added to the fight but the 1st Battalion held fast.[8]

Many stories of heroism were written that day, but the saga of Second Lieutenant Ernest "Red Eagle" Childers, a Creek Indian from Broken Arrow, Oklahoma, stands out. Childers had joined the Oklahoma National Guard in 1937 and had graduated from the Chilocco Indian School. Standing six feet two inches and weighing under 150 pounds, the lanky Childers had been a first sergeant with C Company and received a battlefield commission shortly before the Salerno operation. The 180th was advancing through a valley on its way to Oliveto in the early morning darkness of 22 September. "We made contact with the enemy just before daylight," he said, "and to say the least, it was confusing." Moving silently to assault a German-held cemetery, Childers and a small patrol crossed a road that had been cratered by shellfire; he stumbled into a hole and broke his foot:

> I couldn't see the hole because it was dark. I guess the Germans heard me grunting when I fell in the hole and hit the ground, and they opened up on us with a machine gun. The gunner fired several blasts across my back. It didn't do my clothes any good, but I was lucky—he missed me. I began to roll until I rolled into the ditch on the far side of the road. I felt the pain severely in my foot, but I crawled up to where that machine gun was and, between me and the others, we eliminated that machine gun.
>
> After that, I was directed to go to the aid station that had been set up in a building a short distance away. I had to crawl up to the aid station and, about the time I got there, there was this large explosion, most likely from an artillery shell that hit the roof of that building. Of course, the blast came down through the building, where there were several wounded soldiers, and killed a doctor there.

Childers rounded up his eight-man patrol, reversed direction, and crawled up a hill toward the entrance of the cemetery, which was surrounded by a stone wall. "After going up about half of this incline," he said, "I encountered a group of Germans in a building. There were a couple of snipers in there, firing at me and other people, too. Back in my early days on the farm, as a means of survival, I learned to shoot rabbits—running, even—with a twenty-two. I'm not bragging, but I was a pretty good shot. Anyway, the two snipers were eliminated."

Childers spotted an enemy machine gun nest a short distance away. Still unable to walk on his painful broken foot, he continued crawling until he came to a small, ravinelike depression in the ground and continued on his hands and knees up this depression to a position behind the enemy gun. "First, a sniper started shooting at me from that machine gun nest and then he turned the machine gun around and opened up. Thank God he didn't qualify on the range. We exchanged a few shots, but neither of us hit each other. I could see the tops of their helmets. I picked up a rock and threw it. I thought that if I hit 'em on the head, at least I'd give 'em a headache. So I threw the rock and it went between them." Thinking the rock was a grenade, the two Germans bolted from their hole. Childers said, "As 'Granny' on the Beverly Hillbillies used to say, 'They hadn't oughtta done that.' When the first one jumped out, I was ready for him. I think he was still airborne when I knocked him off. There were a few shots exchanged with the next one, but I got him, too. I continued on to the next gun, which was about thirty-five yards away, and the same thing practically repeated itself. We exchanged a few shots there for a bit and I got one of them." The other one was eliminated by one of his eight men. Thinking he could lead his patrol to safety, Childers continued moving forward, but only succeeded in traveling deeper into enemy territory. "I got up to the top of the hill and there was a mortar observer in a stone house. He decided he was going to surrender." Out of ammunition, Childers directed one of the soldiers with him to take the man prisoner.

"I continued to crawl over the top of the hill and back down. Later in the afternoon, I was picked up and taken to the hospital. The battle went on for quite a while. They say the Germans always counterattacked, but there was no counterattack there, because there were no Germans left to counterattack." Childers was eventually evacuated to a hospital in North Africa. After recuperating from his broken foot, he was ordered to rejoin his unit. While waiting for transportation in Naples, he was informed Lieutenant General Jacob L. Devers, deputy commanding officer of the Mediterranean theater, wanted to speak with him. "My immediate thought was, 'What the hell have I done now?' Generals just don't go around talking to second lieutenants on a friendly basis." When he reported to Devers, a group of other recovering patients were lined up in formation and a military band was playing. "Somebody read the citation but I was so nervous, I didn't really understand what they were talking about. They put a medal around my neck and people came up and congratulated me. I asked one guy, 'What the hell is it?' and he said, 'It's the Medal of Honor.'"

Lieutenant General Jacob L. Devers (right) placing the Medal of Honor around the neck of Second Lieutenant Ernest Childers, C Company, 180th. Childers became the first member of the 45th—and the first Native American in history—to receive the nation's highest military decoration. (Courtesy of E. Childers)

Not only was Childers the 45th's first Medal of Honor recipient, but he was also the first Native American to be awarded the nation's highest military decoration. Childers never returned to the 45th; he was flown back to the States where he met with President Roosevelt and then went on a nationwide tour to promote the sale of war bonds. "Funny—one day I was a soldier and the next day I was a celebrity," he said, with a self-effacing laugh. He shrugged off the label of "hero." "'Hero' is just a term, a phrase. It's equal to calling me 'colonel' or 'mister.' It's just a title," he said, with genuine modesty.[9]

While the 180th and 179th were trying to drive the enemy out of the ruins of Oliveto on the twenty-third, a few miles to the northeast the 157th was battling to wrest control of Colliano from the Germans. Here, Corporal James D. Slaton of K Company, 157th, won the second of the two Medals of Honor awarded to 45th men that week. Acting as the point man for his squad as it moved up to assault an enemy force that had pinned down two attacking platoons, Slaton crept up to a German machine gun nest and ran his bayonet through the gunner. The bayonet stuck in the German's body and the gunner's comrade rushed to attack Slaton. Reacting instantly, Slaton detached the bayonet from his rifle and killed the other German with a single shot at point-blank range. On hearing the firing, a nearby German machine gun opened up on the corporal, who charged the gun across open ground and destroyed it with a well-placed grenade. A hundred yards away, another machine gun crew had him in its sights and began firing at him. Undaunted, Slaton leveled his M-1 and killed the crew. He survived without a scratch and enabled two pinned-down platoons to evacuate their wounded and regroup for another assault.[10]

The next day, the division assaulted well-entrenched German positions at Quaqlietta and Valva, capturing the towns only after hours of tough, bloody fighting. That afternoon, 24 September, contact with the enemy's rear guard was broken. About the only indication that "Jerry" was still in the vicinity was the continuous artillery shelling the division received during its drive northward.[11] On that same day, the 157th lost its commanding officer when Colonel Charles Ankcorn, who had done so much to build the fighting qualities of the regiment before the war, was severely wounded when his jeep detonated a mine near the front lines. Surgeons saved his life, but they were forced to amputate his right leg. Ankcorn had always set a tremendous example for his men, and the regiment felt his loss keenly. Taking command of the regiment was the division's chief of staff, Colonel John H. Church.[12]

On the morning of the twenty-seventh, the fine September weather suddenly gave way to days of torrential rain that drenched the men and turned fields and unpaved roads into viscous bogs. Adding to the division's misery was the tenacious enemy, which used every trick in the book to increase the 45th's casualty lists. Illness, too, took its toll. By the end of the month, the division was short 117 officers and over 2,500 enlisted men—many down with malaria they had contracted near Persano.[13]

Almost as heavy as the rain were the near-constant artillery and mortar barrages that fell from the sky. In addition, deadly German patrols infiltrated the Thunderbirds' lines under cover of darkness, and snipers took their toll of incautious GIs. Gone from American uniforms at the front were any outward signs of rank—officer insignia and noncom chevrons—as leaders so identified were prime targets for snipers. Mel Craven, a nineteen-year-old gunner with A Battery, 158th Field Artillery Battalion, recalled,

> We had a new second lieutenant assigned to the battery. Our battery commander, Captain Van Ness, brought him around to introduce him to everybody. Nobody wore any sign of rank, and we never called an officer "sir." This new second lieutenant was very upset at this so-called lack of military discipline, and no signs of rank. Our captain turned him over to the fellow who was acting more or less as the officers' orderly and he straightened him out. He said, "We're a fighting outfit and we don't go for that military crap around here." That's sort of a polite way of putting what he really said. It didn't take that second lieutenant long to assimilate, given the circumstances. He realized these measures were being taken for his own protection.[14]

Contact with the retreating Germans was again lost on 1 October, but the 45th didn't need Germans to suffer casualties. The 179th was strafed by American P-51s, resulting in one man killed, one wounded, and three trucks destroyed.[15] That same day, Naples fell to the British X Corps. The U.S. 34th "Red Bull" Division, another National Guard outfit (this one from North Dakota, South Dakota, Minnesota, and Iowa), grabbed a key bridge over the Calore River (a different river from the one with the same name near Salerno), and the 45th was ordered to expand the bridgehead and outflank the enemy facing the 3rd and 34th Divisions.[16]

• • •

No one could ever accuse the 45th's battalion commanders of avoiding danger. On 2 October, the division was ordered to make a long march of over fifty miles to the northwest and advance on the ancient city of Benevento—a movement that cost the life of the commander of the 180th's 3rd Battalion, Lieutenant Colonel John R. Patterson, of Phoenix. Colonel Patterson was loved and respected by the men of his regiment. His death, along with that of his operations sergeant, Norman Harris—the result of triggering a mine while walking into the battalion's bivouac area near Grottaminarda, close to the Calore River—was a bitter blow. Taking command of the battalion was Major Benjamin Bliss.[17]

The day following Patterson's death, VI Corps ordered the division to relieve the 34th in the vicinity of Benevento and move forward. Blown bridges over the Calore and rubble-strewn streets in the town delayed the relief effort, so the 120th Engineer Battalion was called on to build a temporary bridge southeast of town and bulldoze the debris from the streets. The work was not done in peace; heavy German artillery barrages saturated the area. To make conditions even more miserable, rain and sleet fell along with the shells. Another air raid by American planes added to the Thunderbirds' frustrations.[18] "It was bad enough that the Germans were shelling us," said Chaplain Leland Loy, 3rd Battalion, 157th, "but now we also had to contend with attacks by our own planes."[19]

In another unfortunate strafing incident during the push northward, Ray Williams of the Ammunition and Pioneer Platoon, 1st Battalion, 179th, lost a buddy to "friendly fire." "A British airplane came out of a dive and started strafing our convoy. My friend, Eddie Fisher, he got killed. The word we got later on was that the pilot had been wounded and blacked out, and when he came to, he saw our convoy down there and attacked it. Fisher got killed and we lost one of our two jeeps."[20]

In spite of the natural and man-made obstacles, the 45th Division pressed onward. For days, the men hunched their shoulders against the rain, their rifles slung upside down on their shoulders to keep water out of the barrels, their ears ever alert for the split-second warning whine of incoming shells. The GIs were a sorry sight, soaked to the skin and caked with mud from continually throwing themselves to the ground to avoid exploding ordnance. Wherever the Germans had taken out a bridge, the GIs huddled beneath shattered trees or on the lee side of demolished walls and waited while the engineers braved enemy fire and bolted Bailey bridges together. Moving on, the 45th continued to run into pockets of determined resistance dug into the rugged terrain.

On 7 October, the 180th lost another battalion commander when Lieutenant Colonel Clarence B. Cochran of Okemah, Oklahoma, commanding the 2nd Battalion, was wounded during a panzer attack against the battalion's positions near Fragneto Monforte, north of Benevento. Cochran's injuries proved to be so serious that he was evacuated back to the States. Captain Jean R. Reed took command of the battalion, only to become a casualty himself on the twelfth.[21]

The 180th took the town of Campolattaro on the eighth and held it despite a number of punishing counterattacks, but then lost its commanding officer, Colonel Forrest E. Cookson, who received orders for stateside duty. He was succeeded by Lieutenant Colonel Robert L. Dulaney, the 180th's executive officer, who had distinguished himself in the fight for Oliveto.[22]

The 180th finally occupied the city of Benevento, which once was the capital of the Samnites, a fierce tribe that had proven to be every bit as good as the Roman legions sent against it. Benevento is also where the marauding Greek king Pyrrhus, a cousin of Alexander the Great, was defeated by the Romans in 274 B.C. But the city had given up its warlike history; the Germans pulled out and the 45th moved in without a fight.[23]

Beyond Benevento, on the ninth, Second Lieutenant Jack C. Montgomery, a platoon commander with I Company, 180th Regiment, recalled, "I was supposed to set up this road block about two miles in front of where the rest of the battalion was. The last order was that the battalion and the regiment were going to move forward at daylight and the British were supposed to be on our right flank. When it got daylight, we saw the crossroads and the Germans that were holding it. We were up above them and we opened fire on them."

Opposing his platoon was a company of German infantrymen, at least four machine guns, mortars, two tanks, and a self-propelled artillery piece. In spite of the odds, Montgomery chose to attack. "We surprised them completely. For about fifteen or twenty minutes, we had a big firefight. We only had about two or three people wounded; they were able to walk out. We found out later from the Italians around there that there were about 200 German troops in the area, and we were almost completely surrounded. I didn't know that then. But we surprised them so much that they took off and we did, too." Before breaking off the brief fight, his men killed at least fifteen and wounded another twenty of the enemy. The skirmish, as it turned out, was unnecessary; the orders were changed—the battalion and regiment weren't going to move yet, and the British weren't on the right flank. In spite of this, Montgomery's courage and leadership earned him a Silver Star. His demonstration of bravery, however, would not be a onetime event.[24]

While the 45th occupied positions in and around Benevento, plans were finalized for the Allies to begin their large-scale attempt to cross the first of the three major rivers, the Volturno. The British X Corps, on the far left of

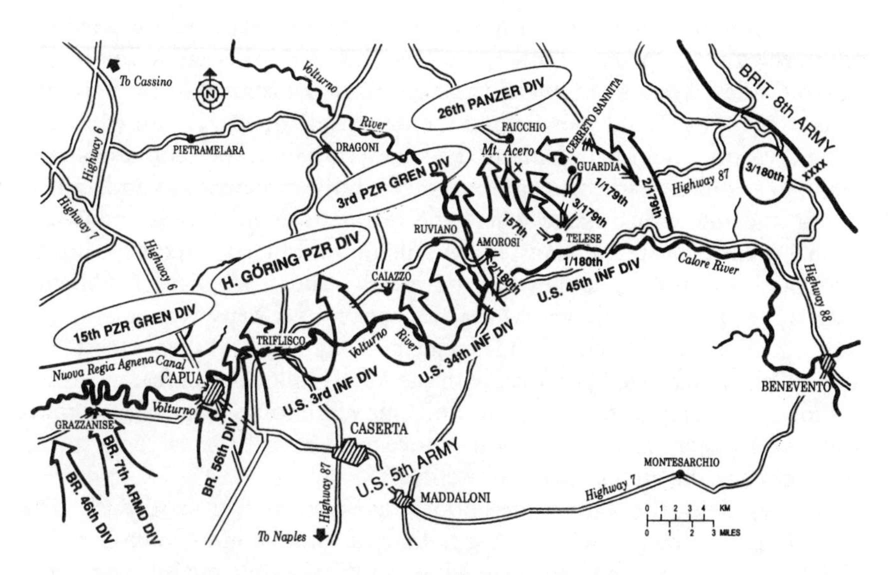

MAP 4.2 The Volturno/Calore River Assaults
12–14 October 1943—Mark Clark launched a massive six-division crossing of both the Volturno and Calore Rivers. The 45th Division, operating in the mountains on the Fifth Army's right flank, was assigned the difficult task of capturing Monte Acero and the towns of Amorosi, Telese, and Faicchio. (Positions approximate)

the Allied line above Naples, held a front of about twenty miles with the 46th and 56th Infantry Divisions and the 7th Armoured Division. To X Corps's right was the U.S. VI Corps, under Lucas, consisting of the 3rd, 34th, and 45th Infantry Divisions. Approximately thirty-five miles above the Volturno, the heights of Monte Cassino and the entrance to the Liri Valley beckoned to Clark and Alexander, almost daring the Allied commanders to attempt a drive to Rome.

Confronting the Allies at the Volturno was von Vietinghoff's Tenth Army, with elements of four divisions: the 3rd and 15th Panzer Grenadiers and the Hermann Göring and 26th Panzer Divisions—all part of XIV Panzer Corps. Although the Allies had numerical superiority, they were faced with the daunting task of crossing a river in front of a well-entrenched enemy.[25]

The Volturno was running fast and full, swollen by October's rains. Not wanting to waste time and allow the Germans to further reinforce their side of the river, Clark directed X Corps to begin its assault crossing before VI Corps was fully ready. But swampy ground, enemy action, and heavy downpours slowed McCreery's progress. Clark then turned to Lucas to see if he could make a crossing. Lucas assigned the 3rd and 34th to the task, with the 45th to guard the flank.[26]

On 9 October, Lucas visited Middleton's headquarters and outlined the 45th's role in the upcoming offensive. The Thunderbirds were to follow the Calore Valley westward toward the Volturno—a distance of over twenty miles. The 45th would move along the north side of the Calore while the 34th Division would march along the southern bank. The ground was exceedingly rough, with deep gullies, steep hills, washed-out and mined roads, and numerous places where the Germans could spring ambushes. Realizing his men were exhausted, Middleton told Lucas he could advance but could not guarantee it would be speedy. Lucas promised Middleton that the 45th would have a long rest once VI Corps was across the Volturno. The division commander reluctantly agreed, and the weary 179th and 180th were alerted to move, with the 157th following in reserve.[27] Delay followed delay as the VI Corps units moved into position. Heavy rains and heavy enemy fire on the 34th's movement from Montesarchio to the river set back the attack until the twelfth.[28]

For two days, the 45th made good progress in its westward push. The fiercest fight developed while trying to take the mountain town of Guardia. The 179th fought up a steep ridge while being raked by intense enemy fire, and the Americans replied with their big guns, keeping the Germans pinned down until the bayonet-brandishing regiment came close. The supporting fire then lifted and it took hand-to-hand combat to root the enemy forces from their bunkers. With the high ground above the town lost, the Germans abandoned Guardia but, once the 179th took up residence, sent a bill for the real estate in the form of punishing artillery fire from positions in the mountains to the north and west.[29]

On 12 October, the town of Cerreto Sannita was taken by the 2nd Battalion, 179th, and the 180th made contact with the British Eighth Army on the right flank. A day and night of bitter fighting followed. Pushing beyond Cerreto Sannita toward Titerno Creek, the division was again plagued by demolished bridges, random mortar and artillery attacks, and strafing runs—this time by the *Luftwaffe*. The 45th's objective was Monte Acero, which overlooked the upper Volturno. Capturing this feature, and the nearby town of Faicchio to its northwest, was essential if the 3rd and 34th Divisions were to have their right flank protected during the river crossing.[30] The Germans, too, knew that Monte Acero was a key feature and were determined to withhold it from the 45th. A battalion of the 26th Panzer Division was dug in on its slopes and blasted away with mortars and machine guns as soon as the 179th made its move against the height.

The 2nd Battalion of the 180th pushed its way into the village of Telese while the 1st Battalion drove against enemy positions in San Salvatore Telesino, to the northwest. The air was alive with flying metal and the sounds of battle as the 180th came under fire and was hit by an infantry counterattack. All four battalions of Division Artillery put a quick end to the German assault.[31] While the 180th was engaged to the north, the 179th climbed Monte Acero. The latter's K Company ran into heavy opposition on the southeast side of the mountain and withdrew under pressure. The Germans, thinking the Yanks were still in place, launched a counterattack at the company's abandoned positions. Thus exposed, the Germans were cut to pieces by the 179th's supporting artillery. Dawn on the thirteenth was heralded by the shaking of the ground and a low, thunderlike rumble off to the west; it was the long-awaited artillery preparation that signaled the assault crossing of the Volturno.[32] The other portentous event that day was that Badoglio's government, headquartered in Brindisi, declared war on its onetime Axis partner, Germany.[33]

First Lieutenant Bill Whitman's war came to a temporary halt on the thirteenth when, while reconnoitering a strong German armored force with a patrol, he was hit in the head by fragments from a tank round. Several other officers nearby were also wounded and a sergeant was killed. Eventually evacuated back to Oran, Whitman would recover from his injury and hitch a ride back to his outfit at Venafro in November.[34]

Shortly after midnight on 14 October, the 1st and 3rd Battalions of the 179th mounted a night attack against the Germans holed up at Faicchio. It was here that the Germans first used their multibarrel mortar—the *Nebelwerfer,* nicknamed the "Screaming Meemie" due to its bansheelike, bloodcurdling roar. Some GIs referred to the *Nebelwerfer* as that "six-barrel organ playing the Purple Heart blues."[35] Ray Williams, 1st Battalion, 179th, recalled that his initial encounter with a *Nebelwerfer* was particularly memorable. "The first time I heard that son of a bitch, I ran around a haystack seven or eight times. No matter which side I was on, it sounded like I was on the wrong side. It could damn near make your blood turn solid."[36]

Even in the face of *Nebelwerfer* barrages and raids by the *Luftwaffe,* Lieutenant Colonel Taylor's 3rd Battalion, in a bloody, twenty-four-hour engagement fought in a constant downpour, valiantly managed to penetrate German positions on the southern slopes of Monte Acero. As the 179th's history recounts, "As sergeants fell, privates assumed command until, one by one, the German machine-gun nests and pillboxes had been demolished."[37] By sundown on the fifteenth, the 3rd Battalion was in control of Monte Acero.

Also on the morning of the fourteenth, the 1st Battalion of the 157th passed through the 179th to attack Faicchio from the west. Simultaneously, K Company of the 157th hit Amorosi, near the confluence of the Volturno and Calore, and took the town. The 157th's 1st and 3rd Battalions forded Titerno Creek and wiped out enemy positions on the opposite side. In spite of German efforts to deny each geographic feature in the area from the Thunderbirds, Middleton's men were slowly but surely prevailing.[38] For the next four days, the 45th advanced against determined opposition at every hill, every village, every turn of the road. After pushing eight miles from

Faicchio to Piedimonte di Alife and taking the latter town, the 45th's drive was halted by Lucas. On 21 October, most of the division was relieved by the 34th Division and placed in Corps reserve for the well-deserved rest that Lucas had promised them. The 34th's 133rd Infantry Regiment would make little progress trying to advance farther in the coming days.[39] Also on the twenty-first, the 179th lost its fine commanding officer, Colonel Robert B. Hutchins. Suffering from illness, Hutchins was forced to relinquish his command to Colonel Malcolm R. "Bert" Kammerer.[40]

• • •

During the nine days of rest, the men enjoyed their first showers since leaving Sicily, exchanged torn and filthy uniforms for clean ones, listened to the reports on the Fifth Army's efforts to cross the Volturno (the assault was a success), worked on weapons and vehicles, received replacements, added up their successes, and counted their losses.[41] The Thunderbirds had been in continuous combat for forty days, which, up to that point of the war, was the longest an entire American division had been under fire in Europe without relief. In those forty days, the division had advanced some 200 miles, liberated 274 towns and villages, and paid for each mile and town in blood and blisters.

It was obvious that the Germans were able to hold off the division with small groups of highly-trained fighters, for, during the drive, the Thunderbirds had captured only 365 prisoners. In return, the enemy had inflicted a large number of casualties as it skillfully withdrew. The 45th had lost 30 percent of its strength from enemy action, illness, and injuries. The cold, wet, and weary GIs wondered if every single foot of Italy was going to be as ruthlessly contested as what they had met thus far.[42]

The rest period over much too soon, the 45th began relieving the 34th Division in late October in preparation for a Corpswide assault against the elaborate fortifications of the Bernhard Line, also known as the *Winterstellung*, or "Winter Line," which included the town of Venafro, some fifteen miles northwest. It was here, a few miles in front of the heart of the Gustav Line, that the Germans ended their northward retreat, took up strong defensive positions, and prepared to finally stop the Allied pursuit. According to the 179th's history, the Winter Line was "like the Siegfried Line, a series of strong points extending across the natural mountain barrier in great depth. It began at Venafro, San Pietro, Monte Rotunda, and Mignano. Each strong point was tied in to the next by a system of interlocking pillboxes dominating every peak and ravine. Each position was so placed that even when it fell, the Germans could withdraw to other prepared defenses which, on even higher knolls, commanded the heights just abandoned."[43]

If the 45th could attack and penetrate the defenses, the 3rd Division would be able to make another crossing of the Volturno as it looped further

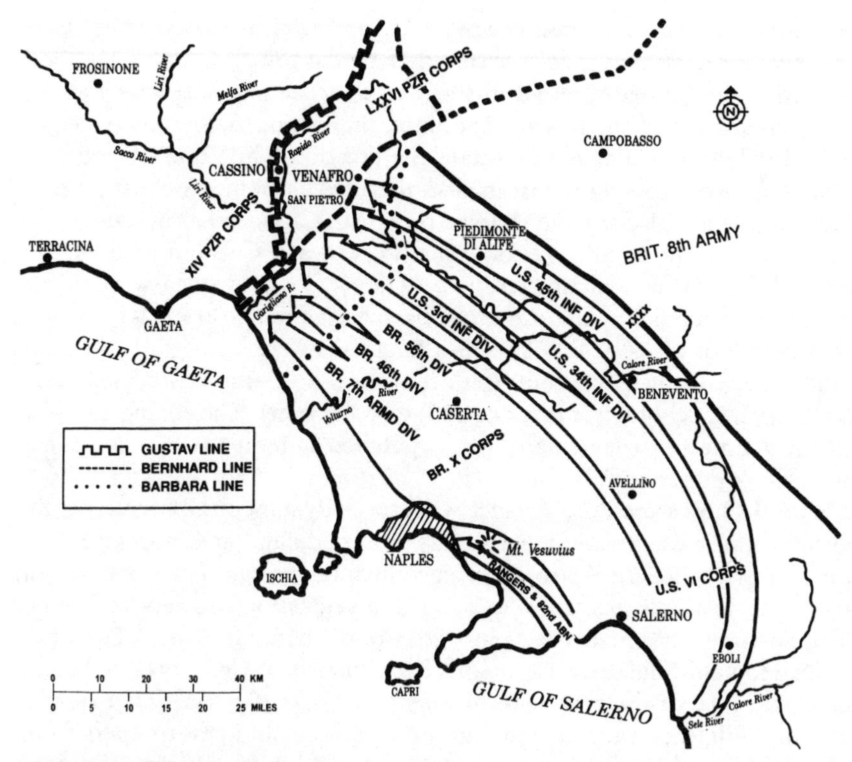

MAP 4.3 Fifth Army's Crawl up the Boot
Battling through the rugged Apennine mountains, the 45th, along with the rest of the Fifth Army, slowly advanced toward the entrance to the Liri Valley, guarded by the heights of Monte Cassino. (Positions approximate)

north and, it was hoped, advance into the Mignano Gap and then to Cassino and the Liri Valley.[44] On 1 November, the 45th took up attack positions on the eastern bank of the Volturno, northwest of Benevento, with the 3rd and 34th Divisions on its left. In front of the 45th were extensive minefields and booby traps, just waiting for the unwary. Enemy artillery was zeroed in on all the likely crossing points. The cold, rainy weather was also no friend of the Yanks as they contemplated the awesome task ahead of them.

The next day, patrols from the 180th crossed the Volturno and, on the third, G Company of the 179th followed, only to be hit by intense enemy fire and driven back to the eastern bank. That night, F Company, 180th, crossed but met no opposition.[45] At midnight on the fourth, the 179th's entire 3rd Battalion, now under the command of Major Merlin O. Tryon, waded across the icy, swiftly moving river and made it to the outskirts of Venafro. For nearly six hours, all was quiet; then, shortly before dawn, the battalion came under intense enemy fire. Fighting their way through German positions, Tryon's men moved closer to the town. K Company took Venafro single-handedly, moved through it, then ran into stiff resistance on the heights north of the town. That night, the rest of the battalion caught up and helped K Company maintain the position while the 1st and 2nd Battalions were crossing the river. Also that night, engineers constructed a bridge over the Volturno that enabled the 179th's attached armor and vehicles to cross. The 179th was now moving toward German-held Monte Santa Croce.[46] Ray Williams recalled, "The river was swollen with all the rain and was running real fast. It must have been about 200 yards wide and it was way out of its banks. The 36th Engineers were trying to put a pontoon bridge over it so we could get across but the German Air Force kept bombing the anchor ends, first one end, then the other. The engineers had a hell of a time but they finally got it patched together so we could get enough troops across."[47]

In the 180th's sector, the advance was especially difficult. Extremely stubborn resistance was encountered shortly after midnight on 4 November at a town known as Rocca Pipirozzi, perched high on a ridge. The slope was so steep that men had to grab onto rocks and vegetation to keep from tumbling down the mountainside.[48] Just prior to the battle for Rocca Pipirozzi, Major Howard Shinaberger, the 2nd Battalion's new C.O., was making a reconnaissance of the area with members of his staff when, just over the crest of a hill, they encountered a group of officers and paratroopers from the German 6th *Fallshirmjäger* Regiment. Thinking quickly, Captain Howard Crye, the battalion's executive officer, casually waved at the Germans, who waved back. The Americans then nonchalantly strolled away and jumped over a rock wall when the Germans were out of sight.

The battle for the tiny, picturesque village lasted most of the day, with the German paratroopers holed up in sturdy stone buildings and the Americans required to flush them out, one house at a time. Instrumental in the eventual victory was First Lieutenant Roderic C. Morere of New Orleans, a platoon commander with E Company. Although this was his first day in command of a rifle platoon, his displays of bravery rallied his men. Personally killing or wounding thirty of the enemy with his rifle, he directed his men in beating back seven counterattacks. While throwing a grenade, he was hit in the head and the live grenade fell to his feet. He kicked it away but was further wounded when it exploded. Refusing to be evacuated, Morere remained with his men and continued to fire on the Germans with his rifle. Two enlisted men—Sergeant Earl F. Bienvenu and Corporal Michael C. Urishko—finally reached him and, with Urishko carrying the wounded lieutenant on his back, made it back to friendly lines despite the enemy's best efforts to stop them. The Germans launched five more counterattacks at Morere's men but the platoon held. Morere spent five months in hospitals;

he received the Distinguished Service Cross and Bienvenu and Urishko were awarded Silver Stars.[49]

At daylight on the sixth, a patrol climbed Monte Santa Croce's slopes to root out the defenders, only to come across Brigadier General McLain, the Division Artillery commander, waging his own personal battle with a sniper. Taking over for the general, the patrol spent the rest of the day routing the enemy from its foxholes.

Below the heights, Lieutenant Colonel Wayne Johnson's 1st Battalion, 179th, took the abandoned town of Pozzilli, moved through it, and established defensive positions west of town. The 2nd Battalion had it a bit rougher. Moving up a slope south of Filignano, Grace's men were suddenly hit by a steel curtain of rifle, machine gun, and mortar fire. Calling on its own artillery and mortars, the 2nd Battalion took on each bunker, killing or capturing its defenders, then moving on to repeat the grim work at the next one. There seemed to be no end to the German strong points. Corporal Earvin Craddock of G Company, 179th, came across one particularly stubborn bunker that was spitting machine gun bullets, crawled within twenty-five yards of it, then charged the position, throwing grenades and firing his Thompson. The enemy gun crew died under Craddock's one-man assault. Not content with knocking out one German position, he repeated his heroics at another nearby position, destroying it also. The Germans on the hill pulled back and up to escape Craddock's relentless assault.[50]

First Lieutenant Eddie Speairs, now the executive officer of C Company, 157th, remembered that the 1st Battalion was relieving the 179th on a big, rocky hill near Venafro on 9 November: "Frank Affley was the C.O. and was one of the best officers you could ever ask for," he said.

> We threw our packs down with the company stuff because we had a lot of reconnaissance to do. We had two raincoats, though. By the time we got up the hill, it was dark, so we put my raincoat on the ground and pulled his over us and spent the night there behind a couple of rocks.
>
> Next morning, Captain Affley said, "You take the left side of the line and I'll take the right and we'll check this thing out and see how our line looks." While I was on the left side, I heard this machine gun fire and the word just spread like wild fire—Affley's been killed. So I hot-footed it over to the right side and I saw him lying down the hill. He had exposed himself too much and he had been hit and had fallen over the face of the hill. I don't remember who got his body, but we got him back. I called battalion to tell them what had happened and Murphy said to take command. So I became the new C.O.

At 2100 hours that night, battalion informed Speairs that C Company would attack the next day. "Murphy gave me two hills to take—Hill 759 was one and I don't remember the other. I thought, 'God damn! *Two* hills! Hah! It's gonna be a dinger!'"

A Thunderbird watching an Italian soldier and pack mule bring rations through an olive grove near Venafro, December 1943. (Courtesy of U.S. Military History Institute)

Speairs oriented the platoon leaders and told them what the company was assigned to do. C Company jumped off at 0530 hours by the light of the moon. Going down the hill, they ran into a group of Italian civilians who were getting out of the way of the coming fight. "They scared the hell out of us, 'cause we didn't know if there were Germans behind 'em, or with 'em, or what. We took a chance and passed 'em through the line of the company and we went ahead. About 0715, we started drawing fire." Speairs's artillery forward observer, Robby Roberts, called for fire on the enemy position and plastered it.

Shortly thereafter, a machine gun opened up on the company.

I crawled up on top of a rock to try and find that machine gun, and a sniper got me through the groin. The bullet went through the carbine clips on my belt and knocked me clear to the ground. There was an aid man right close—his two nicknames were "Doc" and "Shorty"—and he came over and cut my pants and shirt down and put a bandage on the wound and called the litter bearers over. To tell you the truth, I thought I was dead. Shorty said, "Lieu-

> tenant, you're gonna make it—don't worry." He gave me a shot of morphine, then they took me back. That was 7:30 in the morning and at 3:30 that afternoon I got to the aid station.

It was there that Speairs discovered that, instead of just a groin wound, the bullet had tumbled as it ripped through his body and had removed most of his right buttock. C Company finally took one of the two assigned hills—at 2230 hours that night, with the help of E Company. By then, C Company had no officers left and had lost a great number of enlisted men. It was, as Speairs had predicted, a "dinger." Speairs himself spent seventy days recuperating in Army hospitals before rejoining his outfit.[51]

Ray Williams, 1st Battalion, 179th, said, "Venafro wasn't miserable; it was a son of a bitch. Any time you're fighting a war and you're going uphill all the time and it's raining and cold, it's a son of a bitch. No matter what hill you run 'em off of, they run across a valley and onto another hill a little higher and wait for you. It was damn rough."[52]

Daniel Witts, with the Anti-Tank Platoon, 179th, echoed Williams's sentiments. "We couldn't use our anti-tank guns in the mountains, so we went on patrols constantly. The Germans were looking down our throats all the way. It was rainy and wet. You get dirty, you stink, you don't get a bath. It was so bad, I got lice on me. I get itchy just talking about it. They couldn't get clean clothes up to us, only food and ammunition."[53]

For day after cold, rainy day, the Americans and Germans battled for control of the rugged, unnamed hills around Venafro. Fighting fanatically for every yard of Italian soil as if it were the courtyard of the Reich's chancellery, the Germans battled to the last man, the last bullet. Even the paratroopers and members of the 1st Ranger Battalion brought in to help the 45th crack the Nazi line could make no significant headway.[54]

Meanwhile, in the German camp, a rift between Kesselring and von Vietinghoff developed, the latter upset because Kesselring had expressed displeasure at what he thought had been a too-quick withdrawal from the Barbara Line. Miffed, von Vietinghoff requested, and received, a leave of absence. From 5 November until 28 December, the Tenth Army would be under the temporary command of *General der Panzertruppen* Joachim Lemelsen.[55]

On 13 November, in the face of stiffening enemy opposition, worsening weather, and mounting casualties, Clark recommended to Alexander that the Fifth Army's monthlong offensive be halted. Alexander agreed and, on the fifteenth, all units ceased offensive operations for what was planned to be a two-week period that would allow the exhausted units to rest, wait for reinforcements, and prepare for yet another attempt to break into the Liri Valley. The period of relative inactivity would grow from two weeks to nearly two months.[56] It was obvious that the Fifth Army's worn-out divi-

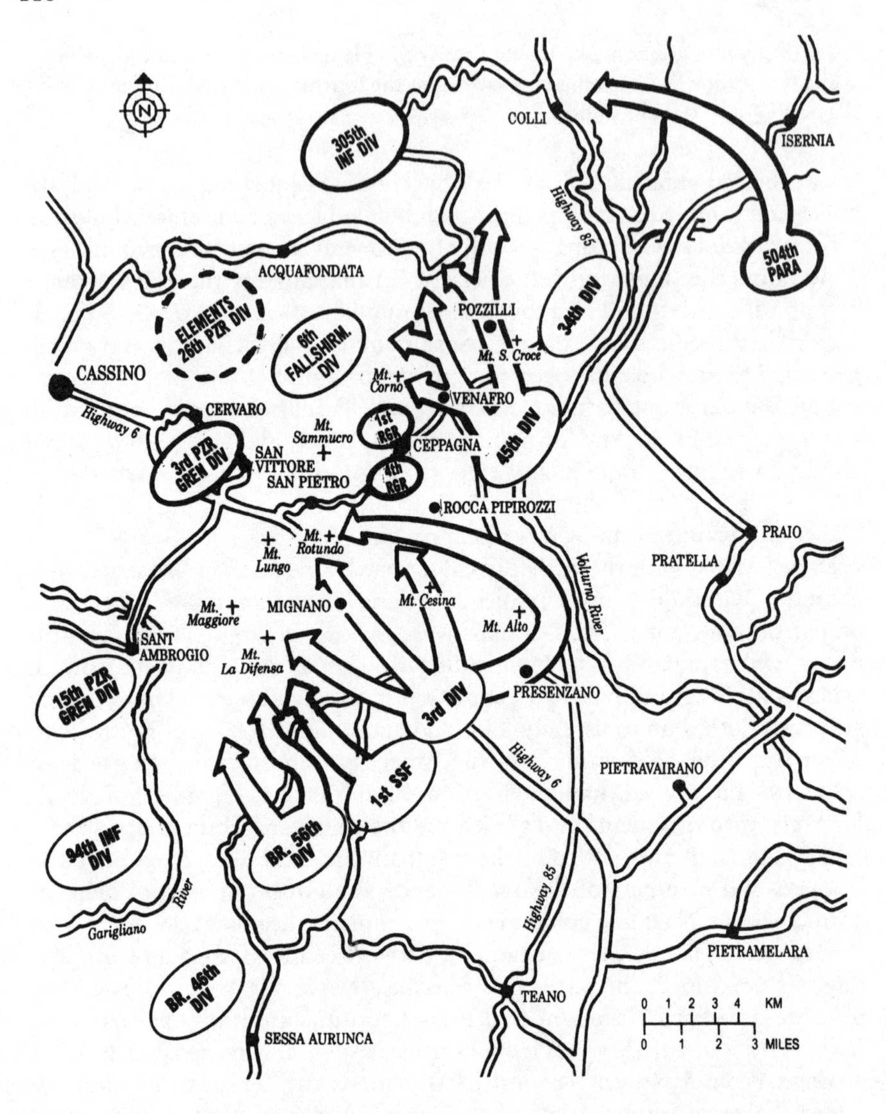

MAP 4.4 The Winter Line
5–15 November 1943—Following Highway 6 northward, Fifth Army approached the entrance to the Liri Valley. The 45th battled for Venafro and the surrounding mountains, but the formidable terrain, stiffening enemy resistance, and worsening weather combined to exhaust the Allied drive. The entire operation was halted on 15 November, and it was this stalemate that gave birth to the Anzio operation. (Positions approximate)

sions needed to be bolstered with some fresh troops. In late November, Clark received a 5,500-man Italian unit, the 1st Motorized Brigade. The token gesture helped somewhat, but it was not nearly enough.

Also in November, Clark received another unit, the 1st Special Service Force—a combined U.S.-Canadian commando outfit that would earn its sobriquet, "The Devil's Brigade," after a few clashes with the enemy. Utterly fearless, under superb leadership by Colonel Robert T. Frederick, and viewing the war as nothing more than a bar brawl, the 1st SSF would carve a lasting legend into the mountains around Venafro and later at Anzio.[57] Two French colonial divisions—the 2nd Moroccan and 3rd Algerian—arrived in December. A request went out to bring in the 85th and 88th Divisions, but they would not arrive until early 1944. Could the Allies hold the line until then?[58]

• • •

For the next few weeks, intermittent attacks by German aircraft and artillery and nearly constant rain with occasional snow flurries were the norm in the 45th's sector and along the entire front. Patrols continually probed the enemy's positions. Between patrols, the men of the 45th tried to stay safe and dry by bivouacking in Venafro's bombed-out buildings or under shelter-halves and ponchos stretched over foxholes. Many men came down with colds, the flu, and trench foot. It was a cold, dirty, thoroughly rotten experience. But it accomplished one thing: It gave the Thunderbirds another valuable lesson in endurance.[59]

In peacetime, Venafro is a pleasant and picturesque place. Monte Santa Croce looms spectacularly over the town, and groves of olive trees grace its terraced hillsides. A medieval castle and an old cathedral add charm to the scene. But this was war and no one noticed the town's amenities. The Yanks spoke instead of "Purple Heart Alley" and "Dead Man's Corner," where unwary GIs could be picked off by snipers or artillery. They complained of numb hands and frostbitten feet while on guard. There was Thanksgiving dinner punctuated by shell fire, and hours of standing in ankle-deep, freezing mud. Venafro, just fifteen miles due east of Cassino, would be remembered by every Thunderbird who survived the war as being a place of unremitting misery.

Sergeant Tarzan Williams, K Company, 157th, recalled that the ground was so hard and rocky that he and his men had to use picks to break the earth loose before they could begin to dig. One day, after moving to a new position and spending an hour digging foxholes, Williams and his men were standing around, "having a B.S. session, probably about girls, when the Germans laid in an artillery barrage on us." Williams and his men dived into their foxholes. A shell—either a dud or an armor-piercing round—landed beside Williams's foxhole and failed to detonate. It did, however, cave in the sides of his foxhole on top of him. "I couldn't move with all that dirt on top of me," he said. "When the shelling stopped, the men got out of their foxholes and looked around and said, 'Well, Vere got it.' I managed to call out to them, 'You SOBs—get this dirt off me so I can get out of here.' They got the dirt off me. Later, they said that if they knew I was going to be so mean to them, they would have shoveled more dirt on top of me."[60]

"At Venafro," said Ray Williams, 1st Battalion, 179th, "the ground was too hard to dig foxholes, so you took boulders and built one around you."[61]

The division instituted a policy of eight days on, four days off. A soldier would spend eight days exposed to the elements and the enemy in a position high up in the hills and four days off the line, supposedly recovering from his time on the line. The only problem, some GIs said, was that it took a full day to get down from positions in the hills, two days to thaw out, and another day to return to the line.[62]

Keeping the fighting man on the front lines supplied with the essentials was the job of the men and mules assigned to the service companies. Captain Minor Shirk, commanding officer of the 157th's Service Company, recalled, "All the supplies at Venafro went up by mule, and we often brought casualties down by mule. The government paid five dollars a day to the Italians for the use of their mules, and a hundred dollars if the mule got killed. That was more than *we* were paid. I remember there was this one soldier who refused to take a white mule up with the mule train. I don't blame him—you could see that white mule for a hundred miles."[63]

Operating the mule trains was a dangerous job. Daniel Witts said, "A friend of mine was a mule skinner. He and his mule got killed trying to get supplies up to us in the mountains."[64]

Sudden and violent death was always lurking at Venafro, even in the most bucolic settings. Sergeant Jack McMillion, platoon sergeant of L Company, 157th Regiment, remembered a night when a friend was out of his foxhole. "A random tank round went right through his neck and blew his head off," McMillion said.[65]

Charlie Dunham, E Company, 157th, recalled that his unit came off the hill on Christmas Day 1943 to enjoy a holiday meal in the relative safety of the rear. "We were eating our dinner and in comes three or four artillery rounds. They killed a couple of guys and wounded a chaplain. We thought we were safe back there. It was such a surprise; it really unnerved me more than a lot of other things did."[66]

George Nalley, K Company, 157th, also recalled that miserable Christmas. He had brought his squad down from the mountains to pick up large cans full of a special turkey dinner the cooks had prepared. "We started to go back up the mountains with the rations when it started rainin'. It rained so hard that the creek we had to cross was too high—we couldn't get back 'til the next morning. By that time, the turkey was all cold." Nalley also remembered another time, when the sun was out, enemy activity had subsided, and a few members of his platoon decided to have a card game. "I was on guard duty with a machine gun watching them get out of their foxholes, spread out a blanket, and start to play cards. All at once, everybody scattered. One guy come up by me—he couldn't say nothin'. All he could say was 'Uh, uh, uh, uh.' A German mortar shell had hit right between these guys on the blanket and never went off. It went plumb through the blanket and stuck in the earth with the fins sticking up. I got a couple of tent ropes and lassoed it and throwed it over the edge of a cliff."[67]

Morty Carr, HQ Company, 1st Battalion, 157th, was one of numerous soldiers to feel the effects of the terribly cold mountain weather, coming down with a case of immersion foot; he and the other soldiers routinely called the condition by its World War I name: trench foot. "Trench foot is when your feet are continuously cold and wet. The circulation stops. Gangrene sets in. Some boys lost toes and even feet. I was sent back to a hospital near Naples. I was fortunate—I didn't lose anything."[68]

"Doc Joe" Franklin, the ranking medic with I Company, 157th, also became an immersion foot casualty. "At Venafro," Franklin said, "the whole division froze its feet. I was hobbling around but I didn't know how bad it was." He was sent down to Naples for a three-day rest. On the night before he was supposed to return to the front, Franklin woke up screaming in the middle of the night. "My feet had thawed out and the pain was horrendous." The authorities put him in a local hospital for a day until they could get him on a plane to North Africa. There he stayed through December and January with a number of other trench foot casualties. "They had to move the hospital so they sent us all to a replacement depot to get us ready to be sent back to the front, but our feet hadn't healed. Hell, we could barely walk, but they sent us on five-mile hikes. I and a buddy of mine who also had frozen feet came in from the march about three hours after everyone else. There was some lieutenant there who was bawling us out and calling us chickenshit; he thought we were goofing off. We all volunteered to go back to the front rather than go on any more five-mile hikes."[69]

While the struggle in the mountains continued, one old campaigner was out of it. Major General Troy H. Middleton, who had led the 45th since October 1942, reluctantly stepped down as its commander. An old football knee injury had been aggravated by the cold, wet conditions and the constant climbing over the snowy, rocky ground at Venafro, and the knee had become so arthritic the general could barely walk. Deemed medically unfit to continue leading his troops, Middleton was ordered to seek medical attention at the Army hospital in Naples. On 22 November, in a driving rainstorm, he quietly and without ceremony turned over command of the 45th to the 3rd Infantry Division's assistant commander, William W. Eagles. After a stint in Naples, Middleton spent some time in North Africa conferring with Eisenhower about the proposed Anzio invasion (his verdict: The Allies didn't have enough ships or manpower available to make a success out of the invasion), then underwent further tests at Walter Reed Army Hospital. Attempts to muster him out with a medical discharge failed; he refused to go. Finally, Ike requested General Marshall send Middleton to him to become commander of VIII Corps, which would be going into France after the initial wave of Operation Overlord.[70]

Shortly after Middleton's departure, another well-liked, long-time officer—Brigadier General Raymond McLain, the Division Artillery commander—was also transferred out of the 45th. In August 1944, he would gain a second star and take command of the 90th Division, which was fighting in France.[71]

Now it was the turn of the forty-eight-year-old, Indiana-born William Willis Eagles to become the Thunderbirds' commanding general. Eagles had graduated from West Point in 1917 and held a variety of Army school and staff jobs before becoming assistant division commander of the 3rd Infantry Division in June 1943. Later referred to by Major General John P. Lucas as a "quiet, determined soldier, with broad experience,"[72] unassuming in appearance, Eagles ruffled some Thunderbird feathers shortly after taking command of the 45th. The 179th had just finished a bloody fight for a hilltop when Eagles appeared on the scene. Instead of playing the role of the concerned commander to the troops who had just come out of combat, he immediately chewed out two junior officers for being unshaven and having no leggings.[73] Although a George Patton might get away with this type of behavior, the incident left a sour taste in the mouths of many of the men who witnessed it. It would take time, but eventually most of the men of the 45th would come to respect Eagles's leadership qualities.

Command changes were also made on the German side. In November 1943, Rommel and his Army Group B were shifted from northern Italy to northern France to prepare for the anticipated cross-Channel invasion. Kesselring was put in sole command of the ground forces in Italy and given the title of Commander-in-Chief, Southwest. In addition to the Tenth Army, which consisted of two armored corps and ten divisions and had responsibility for southern Italy, Kesselring formed an additional army, the Fourteenth, under *Generaloberst* Eberhardt von Mackensen, which consisted of an Army corps and a mountain corps, overseeing nine divisions.

Despite the formidable force on paper, the truth was that the German forces in Italy at the end of 1943 were relatively weak. Of the nine divisions in von Mackensen's Fourteenth Army, only two were qualified for combat. The other divisions were a hodgepodge of battered units that had been withdrawn from the front to rest and reconstitute themselves, divisions that were in the process of being activated or reactivated, training and replacement units, fortress battalions, security battalions, and the like. As soon as a division in the Fourteenth Army reached full strength, it was shipped south to take the place of a battle-weary Tenth Army division in the Gustav Line. That tired unit would then be transferred to the Fourteenth Army and built up again. The Fourteenth Army was no rest camp, however. Besides being a manpower reservoir that constantly needed to be refilled, the Fourteenth also had the responsibility of guarding Italy's impossibly long coastlines and acting as an occupation force, trying to deal with the partisans, who were very active in the northern part of the country. The German situation in November and December, then, with the constant exchanging of exhausted divisions from the front for understrength but relatively rested formations around Rome, was precarious and ripe for exploitation by the Americans and British. Even though the Allies were also tired, they were in far better shape than their opponents, although they did not know it, and this lack of knowledge would prove to be most detrimental to the Allied cause.[74]

• • •

While the Germans worried over a possible Allied offensive, Prime Minister Winston Churchill looked at the static lines on the situation maps and worried that the chance for a swift end to the fighting in Italy was slipping away. Battling in the mountains north of Naples had proven unprofitable and costly to the Allies. There had to be a better way to defeat the Germans than by continually thrusting against their solid front, and there was. For centuries, military strategy has dictated that if the frontal assault does not work, one must attack from the flanks or the rear. The long, narrow peninsula of Italy was ideal for a flanking attack—but only by amphibious maneuver. The Allies must, declared Churchill, resort to an attack by sea. Thus was the seaborne invasion that would ultimately be directed at the resort city of Anzio conceived. In spite of the many obstacles to success, Churchill demanded victory, and no one was willing to deny him what he wanted. Perhaps he saw that the war was soon going to focus on American victories in France and he very much wanted his share of glorious British victories in Italy. After all, the GIs impressive showing in Sicily proved that the Yanks had learned much since their early reverses in North Africa; fighting on the continent was bound to result in even greater successes by the Johnny-come-lately Americans.

Plans for a seaborne flanking maneuver had been in the works since October, when it became clear that the dash for Rome was not going to be a swift one. Clark's first choice for a landing area was Formia, with the Gulf of Gaeta as a backup. Allied planners saw such an operation as offering two chances to end the stalemate in Italy: If Kesselring pulled troops out of the Gustav Line to deal with the threat to his rear, then the Allied forces facing the line would be more easily able to break through and roll the Germans up the peninsula. Should the enemy fail to employ Gustav Line units to counter the seaborne move, then the invasion forces likely would be able to capture Rome and cut off any German retreat from the south. Also, by taking Rome, the Allies would be far enough north in Italy to make an invasion of southern France, timed to coincide with the invasion from England in the north, a reality.

The rosy Allied scenario rested on several incorrect assumptions. First, it presupposed that the Germans were stretched to the limit in Italy and on other fronts and that no further manpower was available. Even if extra enemy troops *were* found and started to move toward the beachhead, the planners felt the superior Allied air power would be able to destroy the troop trains or truck convoys. At the very least, Alexander's staff felt the operation would tie up a large enemy force in Italy, where it could not be used to assist Hitler's other beleaguered armies on either the crumbling eastern front or the beaches of Normandy when the invasion of France finally began.

It all seemed so simple, scripting how the enemy would react to this threat from the rear. But the Germans had their own script in case of an Allied landing above the Gustav Line. In fact, Kesselring had been expecting just such an amphibious operation and had already drawn up contingency plans for dealing with it.

As the initial date for launching the invasion—1 November—drew closer, the shortage of shipping and a few other questions began to weigh on Allied optimism. First, the Navy told Clark that both Formia and Gaeta were unsuited for a large-scale amphibious operation. Next, no one had a good answer for what would happen if the main Allied force were to get bogged down on the Gustav Line, unable to help support the seaborne operation. Finally, if the Allies suffered heavy losses while trying to break through the Bernhard and Gustav Lines, would they be too depleted and exhausted to be of any value, even if they made the linkup?

One of the main problems with the operation was the fluidity of objectives, which seemed to change from week to week. If the objective was to seize Rome, that was one thing. But the invasion force was much too small to take Rome while holding the rear door shut if the Tenth Army troops decided to move against it from the southern front. If, on the other hand, the objective was to dislodge the Tenth Army from the Gustav Line, then the landing—now aimed at Anzio—was simply too far away to constitute much of a threat. Unfortunately, the objective was to do both and, in the end, the landing would accomplish neither.

To threaten the Gustav Line, a better solution would have been to land the invasion force to the immediate rear of the line, say, near Terracina, instead of seventy miles away. But the Italian geography made this idea impractical. The Gulf of Gaeta has very few beaches suitable for landing a sizeable army, and in many places mountains near the coast give the defender a definite advantage. Between the Gulf of Gaeta and Anzio lay the vast Pontine Marshes, a broad area unsuitable for tanks, vehicles, or, for that matter, infantry.

Added to these considerations was the fact that the Germans had fortified the coastline close to the western terminus of the Gustav Line to prevent just such a raid from taking place. And landing any further north of Anzio meant that the Allies would be beyond the range of fighter support. Anzio kept cropping up as the best in a long list of bad alternatives.

While the planners agonized over their decision, the calendar worked against them. Several proposed D days came and went due to the lack of shipping. The key to the Anzio operation was shipping, specifically LSTs—Landing Ship, Tank. Without them, the operation could not be mounted. And LSTs in the Mediterranean were in short supply. There simply were not enough ships to make, supply, and reinforce the landing. The reason was simple: The planned invasion of France was absorbing all available ships and landing craft, a situation some historians have called "the tyranny of Overlord." Although the Normandy invasion was still nearly half a year away, all the landing craft not absolutely necessary for day-to-day operations in the Mediterranean were ordered to England so that the Army and Navy personnel involved in Overlord could rehearse their roles.

On 8 November, after approval by the Combined Chiefs of Staff, Eisenhower directed Alexander to designate Anzio the landing site for an operation named "Shingle," scheduled to take place before 15 January 1944, the date the landing craft were to be released to Overlord.[75] On 18 December, however, Shingle was reluctantly abandoned. There simply was not enough time to work out the thousands of details necessary before 15 January.[76] But Churchill would not let his baby die so easily. While in Tunis and recovering from pneumonia, he pressured the British chiefs of staff to break the stalemate in Italy and Operation Shingle was resurrected on the twenty-third. But landing craft remained an insurmountable problem. There were only enough LSTs to transport one division and Churchill wanted a British division added.[77]

After conferring with his Italy commanders in Tunis on Christmas Day 1943, Churchill cabled Roosevelt to plead for the retention of fifty-six of the eighty-four LSTs in Italy until 5 February. In his cable, Churchill said, "Having kept [the LSTs] so long, it would seem irrational to remove them for the very week when they can render decisive service. What, also, could be more dangerous than to let the Italian battle stagnate and fester on for another three months?"[78] Roosevelt concurred, with the stipulation that Shingle must not hinder preparations for Overlord or Anvil, the latter being the invasion of southern France. A new release deadline of 3 February for the landing craft was imposed. Although he had private doubts that the operation could proceed, Clark went ahead with plans while keeping his fingers crossed for more LSTs.

Shortly before he departed for England on 8 January 1944, Eisenhower directed Alexander to carry out the Shingle plans, which called for the Allies to hit the beach at Anzio with a small, mobile force, overcoming the local German defenses, then driving twenty miles inland to secure the Alban Hills—the remnants of a long-dead volcano and the last natural barrier south of Rome. While this was taking place, the Allied troops in the south would break through the Gustav Line and drive northward. The combined forces would then head for Rome. Given the good beaches, flat terrain, and highway network around Anzio, Alexander's staff saw no reason why the Allies should not be able to land at Anzio and quickly capture Rome.[79]

With the invasion of France imminent and about to become an "American show" under Eisenhower's command, the Mediterranean became a "British show." Following Ike's departure for England to take the reins as the Supreme Allied Commander of Operation Overlord, General Sir Henry Maitland "Jumbo" Wilson had ascended to the post of Supreme Allied Commander in the Mediterranean. Field Marshal Sir Harold Alexander, who had been Ike's deputy in this theater, was elevated to Fifteenth Army Group commander and, as such, had control of all Allied air, naval, and ground forces in Italy. Churchill and General Sir Alan Brooke, Chief of the Imperial General Staff, were now the major architects of strategy in Italy, and Churchill was particularly keen on capturing Rome at the earliest possible moment.

At a meeting in Marrakech on 7 January, called by the Prime Minister and attended by the top Mediterranean commanders (except for Clark), the tremendous logistical problems that loomed over Shingle—mostly centering on shipping—were brushed aside and Churchill, who had just received the okay from Roosevelt and U.S. Army Chief of Staff George C. Marshall to delay sending the landing craft to England, put his enthusiastic stamp of approval on the invasion, promising to obtain additional craft for the critical days after the landings took place. Instead of being considered merely supplementary to Fifth Army actions along the Gustav Line, Shingle was elevated to the status of a major operation, as important as the invasions of Sicily and Salerno had been. Twenty-five additional LSTs were authorized by Churchill, bringing the total to eighty-eight. The operation was on.

One factor, however, was crucial: Because of the shortage of shipping, the Anzio force would not be self-sustaining. It was therefore vital that the southern force break through the Gustav Line and be north of Frosinone by the time the invasion was launched. Some were skeptical that such a breakthrough and advance were possible, given the Germans' history of strong defense, but Churchill's ebullient nature won over most of the doubters. The historian Martin Blumenson writes that optimism flooded Fifth Army headquarters:

> The deadlock in southern Italy seemed about to be split wide open. A successful landing at Anzio would dissolve the Gustav Line defenses and enable General

> Clark to move quickly into Rome and pursue the Germans into northern Italy and beyond. General Eisenhower would ensure victory with the cross-Channel attack that was then scheduled for May. Anvil, the invasion of southern France, would be unnecessary. The war would be over by autumn at the latest.[80]

A commander was selected for Shingle as well as the forces that would make the initial and follow-up landings. Major General John P. Lucas, who had taken over command of VI Corps from Dawley after the near debacle at Salerno, was selected to lead the invasion force. Truscott's trusty U.S. 3rd Division and the British 1st Division, under Major General W.R.C. Penney, were chosen to go in on the first day, along with two British Commando battalions and three battalions of American Rangers. The 45th Division would arrive shortly after the initial landings. The battered U.S. II Corps and British X Corps would remain to assault the Gustav Line in hopes of drawing all available German reserves to it, thus weakening the Anzio area defenses. Meanwhile, the British Eighth Army, under Lieutenant General Sir Oliver Leese now that Montgomery had departed for England, would keep the Germans on the Adriatic side of Italy pinned down with artillery and vigorous feints.[81]

As the days wore on, the number of available LSTs rose, but not by any appreciable number, and Clark was faced with the prospect of having to land troops without the requisite number of vehicles. Some of the troops, as well as tons of food, ammunition, and other supplies, would have to be shuttled in piecemeal after the initial landings. Furthermore, Clark would have to conduct all the seaborne resupply and reinforcements within two days of the initial landings, as the landing craft were scheduled to be sent to England forty-eight hours after the Allies hit the shore.[82]

Major General John P. Lucas, VI Corps commander and the scapegoat of Anzio. (Courtesy of 45th Division Archives)

Despite these monumental, unsolved problems, Operation Shingle was set to begin in the early hours of 20 January 1944. Lucas requested a postponement to the twenty-fifth; a compromise of the twenty-second was reached.[83] Everyone felt that to guarantee the success of Shingle breaking through the Gustav Line into the

Liri Valley was essential. But the terrain could not have been more favorable for the defender. Besides the strong German defenses, the Allies would first have to overcome the natural barrier of the Rapido and Garigliano Rivers, which were guarded by a number of formidable German positions on strategic heights.

In November and December, the Fifth Army managed to batter its way into the Mignano Gap, taking heavy casualties in so doing. The British X Corps had made excellent progress, but Major General Geoffrey Keyes's U.S. II Corps ran into difficulties as a steady rain turned the roads into quagmires and bogged down supporting vehicles. The 36th Division, still recovering from its mauling at Salerno, was given the weightiest role and sustained severe losses in the battles for Monte la Difensa, Monte Maggiore, Monte Lungo (with help from the 1st Italian Motorized Brigade), Monte Sammucro, and the town of San Pietro Infine, the latter just a few miles from Venafro. At the end of December, the 34th ("Red Bull") Division was brought up to relieve the exhausted 36th. The Mignano Gap had been cracked, but just barely, as there were no reserves to exploit the gains. Furthermore, the imposing heights of Cassino still overlooked the entrance to the Liri Valley, and the Germans were well prepared to make the Allies pay for any attempt to enter.[84]

While the situation at the Gustav Line remained worrisome, the prospects for the Anzio invasion were equally gloomy. Mulling over the possible fate of the invasion force once the shipping was withdrawn, "Jumbo" Wilson sounded his own note of warning: "Should maintenance not be possible, the force would have to be withdrawn with total loss of equipment, some loss of personnel, and serious risk to landing craft needed for the later assault against the south of France. However, the prize to be gained was high enough to warrant the risk."[85] Although the prize—Rome—was deemed great, the means to win it were slim. In effect, Clark was handed a faulty plan with unattainable objectives and an inadequate number of troops and ships and was told to make the plan work. In his diary, Clark confided that he felt he was being directed to perform the impossible and that the operation would leave the British 1st and U.S. 3rd Divisions "out on a very long limb." Clark, ever the obedient soldier, also noted, with frustration, "I am trying to find ways to do it, not ways in which we can not do it."[86]

• • •

In early January, in the rocky hills around Venafro, the average soldier of the 45th Division was completely ignorant of the high-level machinations that would soon involve him. The only thing he cared about was the fact that, for whatever reason, the division was being pulled out of the line. To say the Thunderbirds were glad to be out of the mountains would be a monumental understatement. "Overjoyed" might be a better term. After months of continuous combat in the rocky hills, mountains, valleys, and villages of the Apennines, in some of the worst weather conditions imaginable, the men of the 45th turned over responsibility for this sector of the front lines to the French Expeditionary Corps's (FEC) 3rd Algerian Division and began moving back, regiment by regiment, to various concentration areas near Naples to prepare for their third amphibious combat assault, although few of them at the time knew the nature of their next mission.[87]

Lieutenant Colonel Ralph Krieger, commanding the 157th Regiment's 1st Battalion, remembered, "The Anzio landings were kept secret from the men for quite a while. I only found out about it when we moved down to Salerno to practice the landings. The men found out about the invasion a couple or three weeks before it happened."[88]

The lower ranks had heard various stories about why they were being removed from the mountains. Captain Felix Sparks, C.O. of E Company, 157th, said, "We were told we were going to land at Anzio and advance to Rome."[89]

"The rumor was we were going to be used as paratroops to go into southern France," recalled Lieutenant Robert LaDu, then a platoon commander with F Company, 179th. "None of us had ever jumped before, but nobody cared. What difference did it make, anyway? We were off the line and that was all that mattered."[90]

Glen K. Hanson, L Company, 157th, said, "I'm not sure if we were even informed where we were going. I think we knew it was going to be an amphibious landing, but I'm not sure if we knew where. There weren't a whole lot of people who knew about it for fear that the information might leak out."[91]

Morty Carr, HQ Company, 1st Battalion, 157th, was glad to be leaving the mountains. "It was snowing and raining and cold at Venafro. It was miserable, but we endured. At least we got hot food and clean clothes there."[92]

Pete Conde, with the 157th's Anti-Tank Company, recalled that he didn't much care for the hills around Venafro. "I thought Anzio was a good idea because we were at a disadvantage trying to get up those hills; there were so many of them. I'd seen Cassino through binoculars, and I much preferred the end run idea."[93]

The 45th began quietly pulling out of its positions and infiltrating to the rear, in order to not raise the suspicions of the enemy. On 2 January the 179th withdrew after sixty-six straight days on the line. The leading elements of the regiment were trucked forty-one miles back to a rest area near San Potito; the last units to leave did so on the fifth.[94] On 3 January, the 180th Regiment began its pullback. On the tenth, however, the 1st and 2nd Battalions were attached to the FEC, trucked back into the hills, and assigned to help the 3rd Algerian Infantry Division win a hard-fought victory at Acquafondata. (In recognition of the 180th's role in assisting the FEC's entry into the front lines, the 45th was awarded the Croix de Guerre citation, signed by General Charles de Gaulle, from the Provisional Government of the French Republic.)[95] On 15 January, the two battalions rejoined the rest of the regiment near Faicchio.[96]

The 157th, too, left the line. Oliver R. Birkner, F Company, 157th, remembered, "I guided the French Moroccan troops in to Hill 1010 on 9 January to take over our position, so we could catch a boat to Anzio. Churchill wanted us to be in Rome and Hitler wanted us back in the sea. Both were badly disappointed with the outcome, which can be summed up with one word: 'meatgrinder.'"[97]

According to the 157th's Operations Summary, the nine days between 11 and 20 January "marked the first time in over four months that the 157th had not been engaged in attacking the enemy. Over 500 replacements were received and the Regiment was brought almost to T/O [Table of Organization] strength with the addition of these new men." Also during this period, the troops were twice trucked to Piedimonte to take advantage of the Quartermaster shower trucks.[98] The Thunderbirds encamped in an area called the King's Hunting Grounds north of Naples and used this period of respite to think about comrades who were lost and wonder about what was to come. In the 121 days of fighting since the Salerno landings, the 45th had been in actual combat for 110 of them. Casualty figures for the 45th after Salerno graphically show the savagery of the fighting; the division lost 651 men killed in action, 2,550 wounded, 256 missing, and 61 known captured. Another 119 died from wounds and 9,492 came down sick or were hospitalized with nonbattle injuries. On the other side of the ledger, however, since landing at Salerno, the 45th had captured 992 of the enemy, with unknown numbers killed or wounded.[99]

To give the men some much-needed diversion from combat, the Special Services Section showed movies nightly, the Red Cross provided its Mobile Doughnut Unit (along with several attractive American women with whom the soldiers could chat), and the USO brought in rubber-faced comedian Joe E. Brown and actor Humphrey Bogart, who entertained them at an open-air theater in Faicchio.[100] Morale was still high and some men went to extraordinary lengths to not miss the coming fight. First Lieutenant Eddie Speairs gave a striking example of just what serving with the 45th meant. Wounded the previous November at Venafro, Speairs was in a hospital in Naples when "the battalion surgeon came through the hospital one day and mentioned we were going to make another amphibious landing. I said, 'Let me get my clothes; I'm going with you.' That's the way we all were. I had men come back to the company on crutches. The esprit in that division was something nobody would believe. We loved that outfit. No Marine has more love for the corps than we have for the 45th."

When Speairs got back to the battalion, however, he found he had no strength. "I couldn't even lift my own bedroll. I was just hanging around battalion headquarters when the first sergeant went to the colonel and asked if I could go back and take over C Company. So that's how I got back to C Company." Speairs added,

> When you come out of the line and then go back in, you have some feelings of being scared, but when you're there and a few shells have landed close by, it doesn't bother you. You have to get rebaptised every time you go back into the line. It was far better, psychologically, to know you were there for the duration and the only way you're going home is in a body bag or if you get wounded. One time they told a forward observer with us that they were going to send him back to Fort Sill for some training and he bugged out on us. He got immediately scared. You ruin a man when you tell him he's going home; he wants to be damn sure he lives long enough to get there.[101]

Beneath the welcome break from combat, there was an undercurrent of anxiety, the certainty that the war would go on and that the 45th would once again be thrown into the cauldron. The division was reintroduced to close order drill, marksmanship, and small-unit tactical problems, many of them at night. Men spent hours cleaning their weapons, performing long-overdue maintenance on vehicles, and getting their gear squared away for the next fight. The mail caught up with the GIs and everyone found time to write home. A new batch of replacements—most just barely out of the thirteen-week basic training course—were assigned to regiments, battalions, companies, platoons, and squads. Each one replaced a man who had been a vital cog in the unit's machinery, a man who had acquired the veteran's sixth sense of knowing when to duck, a man who would rather die than let his buddies down. Each of the replacements would need to acquire years of experience within a very short period of time if he wanted to survive.[102]

One of the new replacements was eighteen-year-old draftee Edward "Don" Amzibel from Ashtabula, Ohio. Assigned to L Company, 157th, Amzibel recalled, "When I joined the 45th, they had just come down from the mountains for a rest. All of the soldiers were veterans and had been with the 45th Division for years. We were bivouacked on the side of a mountain town called Piedimonte. I only got to visit the town once. It wasn't much of a town, just a place to go. We were there for a week when we got orders to get ready to move out for the invasion of Anzio."[103]

• • •

The subject of sex is a topic that does not frequently appear in military histories, yet its exclusion seems curious since the quest for sex is a frequent obsession among virile young males. During interviews for this book, several ex-soldiers spoke of the need to assuage the fear of having a shortened existence and to relieve the stress and tension of battle through sex. As one of the men put it, "When I went overseas and started fighting, I realized that any day or any minute I could be pushing up daisies, so I thought I'd better start living it up."

Despite frequent lectures by division chaplains, admonitions by medical personnel, and showings of films alluding to the dangers of casual, unprotected sex, it appears that when the Thunderbirds weren't dodging bullets a goodly number of them—both married and single—were seeking female companionship, and that companionship was not hard to come by. A former Thunderbird remembered, "My squad and I had been billeted in a family's farm house. They had a daughter about nineteen or twenty years old that really liked me. One night I went out for guard duty at a bridge and this girl came with me. Needless to say, I didn't do much guarding that night."

Group encounters with a single willing female were not uncommon. One veteran recalled,

> We were moving down a road. We were the reserve company and were sent to a village about ten miles to the left of the rest of the battalion. We saw the Germans moving out of the village so we moved in. The rest of the company was scouting around the village and I was looking around, too. I looked up a staircase and a woman was standing there, motioning me to come up. I went up and asked her if there were any Germans around. She said no, and then invited me to spend some "horizontal fatigue" with her. Then she asked me to send up some of my comrades. Well, she serviced the whole platoon twice.

Another former soldier spoke of the time he met an Italian girl in Naples who "wanted an American *bambino* from me. I did my best to oblige, but two days later I was sent back to the front lines."

Not all the sexual encounters were provided gratis. Although prostitutes expected and demanded monetary compensation, C rations and chocolates were frequently used in exchange for sexual favors. One soldier was horny but broke; his solution was to earn ten dollars by donating blood. Seeing the poverty and near starvation among the civilians all around them (even young girls and elderly women worked the streets in order to live), many of the soldiers felt obliged to leave food or money for even willing amateurs.

• • •

In early January, German spies reported unusually large concentrations of ships in and around Naples harbor, indicating a major amphibious operation was in the works. Efforts to fortify the most likely landing sites went into high gear and units were shifted from the Adriatic coast and the Gustav Line to the vicinity of Rome in anticipation of a blow being struck somewhere near Rome. Compounding Kesselring's worries were reports of Allied troops massing at the Garigliano River. Was it possible that the Americans and British could launch both a major river assault to force a breach in the Liri Valley defenses *and* a major amphibious assault somewhere up the coast?[104]

Since hiding the growing armada from the many spies in Naples would have been about as easy as hiding an elephant in a parlor, a diversionary plan was instituted to mislead the Germans into thinking a landing would take place at Livorno, with dummy radio traffic and dummy ships constructed in Corsica. More false information was leaked that the British would launch a major offensive on the Adriatic side in late January. Even plans for a naval bombardment of Civitavecchia and Terracina were drawn up. Everything was designed to keep Kesselring guessing.[105]

The troops picked for the initial landing were hastily rehearsed, and this haste led inevitably to disaster. The British 1st Division's practice landing, six miles south of Salerno, went reasonably well, but not the U.S. 3rd Division's.[106] On 17–18 January, while attempting a night landing in a downpour, everything that could have gone wrong did. A navigational error caused the Navy to release the landing craft miles from the beach. Much equipment—including forty-three DUKWs, nineteen 105mm howitzers, and nine anti-tank guns—was lost at sea, and a number of 3rd Division men drowned.[107]

General Truscott, whose men would be in the first wave, ticked off a litany of problems: "Of thirty-seven LCTs assigned for the operation, only eleven went on the exercise. . . . No single battalion landed on time or in formation. . . . Transports were so far off shore that assault craft required three to four-and-a-half hours to reach the beach. . . . No single element was landed on its correct beach. . . . The rehearsal provided no test for communications, particularly with reference to naval gunfire."

Rear Admiral Frank J. Lowry, commanding the naval task force that would bring the troops to Anzio, commented, "The accidents were so many, that it appeared impractical on the face of it to make an assault without further training." To replace the lost equipment, matériel was taken from the British X Corps and from the 36th and 45th Divisions.[108]

Dismayed at the calamitous rehearsal, Truscott requested time to stage another and work out the many kinks, but Clark knew that that was impossible. "You won't get another rehearsal," he told the 3rd Division commander. "The date has been set at the very highest level. There is no possibility of delaying it even for a day. You've got to do it."[109]

Lucas, too, was quite alarmed by all the things that had gone wrong. In an attempt to buoy Lucas's flagging spirits, Admiral Sir John Cunningham, the cousin of Admiral Sir Andrew Cunningham, told Lucas not to worry. "The chances are seventy to thirty that by the time you reach Anzio, the Germans will be north of Rome," he optimistically declared.[110] Such cheery assurances did not help Lucas; in fact, he fretted that perhaps some vital intelligence was being kept from him—which it was. The Allies possessed a system called "Ultra" that enabled them to intercept and decode the enemy's fiendishly difficult encrypted radio messages. It was like having a hidden microphone in the opposing team's huddle.[111] Recent intercepts had disclosed the fact that the battle-hardened 29th and 90th Panzer Grenadier Divisions, located near Rome, were ready to be moved south to counter any Allied breakthrough along the Garigliano. It was also known that Hitler intended to pull his troops to positions in the northern Apennines in the event the Allies broke through the Gustav Line. The Allies, however, had decided months earlier to withhold information from field commanders to preclude someone who had knowledge of the top secret system from divulging information about Ultra.[112] One of the great and tragic ironies of the war was that the Allies possessed a marvelous system capable of intercepting and decoding enemy messages, yet its use had to be restricted for fear of tipping off the enemy and causing it to alter its encryption methods. Thus the men at the top knew what the Germans were thinking and doing; their subordinate commanders and the troops on the line were kept in the dark, often with disastrous results.

The first part of the one-two punch the Allies were about to deliver in Italy was aimed at the Gustav Line. Augmenting the Fifth Army on the Cassino front was the French Expeditionary Corps, made up of the 2nd Moroccan and 3rd Algerian Divisions, which was assigned to capture the flanks of the Liri Valley. The FEC would begin its attack on 12 January. Three days later, II Corps was to attack Monte Trocchio (a mere three miles southeast of Monte Cassino) with two National Guard infantry divisions, the 34th and 36th, along with the 1st Armored Division, with the intention of taking this key terrain feature overlooking the Rapido River. Once these two attacks were successful (on 17 January, the planners hoped), the British X Corps, consisting of the British 5th, 46th, and 56th Infantry Divisions, along with the 23rd Armoured Brigade, would drive through the center and smash the German defenses. Following this assault, II Corps would cross the Rapido south of Highway 6, establish a bridgehead near Sant'Angelo, and thrust northward with its armored columns leading the way to link up with the Anzio force.

The FEC jumped off right on schedule at 0630 hours on 12 January. That was about the last thing that went according to plan. For four days, the Moroccans and Algerians battled bravely at close range but could gain no headway against the well-entrenched German defenders. Elements of the 34th and 36th Divisions found easier going on Monte Trocchio, which the Germans had abandoned in favor of better positions on the far side of the Rapido.

Next, it was the British X Corps's turn. McCreery's X Corps was required to make two crossings over the Garigliano, one at Minturno and the other at Sant'Ambrogio, beginning on the night of 17 January. With the bridges blown and the Garigliano too deep to ford, the assault parties were forced to cross in boats. At first, surprise was achieved and the movement proceeded well. But then, troops reaching the far bank became immobilized by horrendous minefields and heavy artillery concentrations that rained down upon them. To make matters worse, fresh German reinforcements were about to arrive on the scene. To reinforce the newly formed and untested German 94th Division, which alone was containing the X Corps's assault, von Vietinghoff requested Kesselring send him the 29th and 90th Panzer Grenadier Divisions. On the eighteenth, the two divisions were on their way south. Hitler approved of Kesselring's action, insisting that the Gustav Line be held at all costs. Although elements of X Corps managed to establish a bridgehead about three miles beyond the Garigliano, the Germans struck back hard.[113]

On 20 January, as the Anzio force was leaving Naples harbor, the British 46th Division, on X Corps's right flank, ran into swift water at the confluence of the Liri and Gari Rivers and elements of the newly arrived enemy divisions while trying to take Sant'Ambrogio and was forced to retreat back across the river; another cause for the failure of the assault was blamed on the shortage of amphibious vehicles—the DUKWs that had been taken from the 46th to replace the ones lost during the Anzio rehearsal on the eighteenth.[114] Despite the setback to the British, Clark pressed the Americans to proceed with their crossing of the Rapido near Cassino. If what happened to the British X Corps was a setback, what happened to Keyes's U.S. II Corps, and especially to Major General Fred Walker's 36th "Texas" Division, was an unmitigated disaster. Walker's men had already suffered heavily at Salerno in September and on the Bernhard Line in December and had not been brought up to full strength. The 34th Division, on the 36th's right, was to feint and draw German attention away from the Texans' crossing at Sant'Angelo. Following a successful crossing by the 36th, Combat Command B of the 1st Armored was to drive through, followed by the 34th.[115]

The 36th's crossing was to take place on the night of 20 January to escape the all-seeing German eyes atop Monte Cassino. But excellent German positions, extensive minefields, and an icy, swiftly flowing river would combine to wreak havoc on the Texans.[116] Waiting for the 36th on the opposite side of the river was one of the *Wehrmacht*'s veteran units, *Generalmajor* Eberhardt Rodt's 15th Panzer Grenadier Division, which had seen heavy fighting in France, Libya, and Sicily.[117] The men of the 36th were hammered by artillery both before and after they reached the crossing site. Boats were blown out of the water, and the 36th's assault was raked with murderous fire from automatic weapons; in spite of the Texans' bravery, the attack never stood a chance. Only a handful of soldiers made it to the far bank, where the Germans blasted them with small arms, artillery, mortar, and tank fire, nearly annihilating the stranded, helpless force. Brave but futile acts followed each other in rapid succession. While delay followed delay in bringing up reinforcements, the men on the far bank were cut to pieces. On 22 January, what few men remained on the German-held side were captured or withdrawn. The first attempt to cross the Rapido had failed with terrible casualties to the 36th.[118]

Clark was shaken by the failure at the Rapido but resolved to put a good face on the disaster. In his diary, he wrote, "In deciding upon that attack some time ago, I knew it would be costly but was impelled to go ahead with the attack in order that I could draw to this front all possible German reserves in order to clear the way for [Operation] Shingle. This was accomplished in a magnificent manner. Some blood had to be spilled on either land or the Shingle front, and I greatly preferred that it be on the Rapido, where we were secure, rather than at Anzio, with the sea at our back."*[119]

Clark faced an agonizing decision: Should Shingle proceed or be canceled? His main force on the Gustav Line was stalemated, decimated, and demoralized and no closer to Anzio than when the offensive had begun. If he launched the invasion now, did it stand a chance—or would it, too, become bogged down? As the plans unraveled around him, it is valuable to consider what Mark Clark must have been thinking and feeling in the days and weeks before Shingle was launched. Although Clark left no introspective papers full of the kind of self-doubt expressed in Lucas's diary, we can make several assumptions as to his mental state based on what he did write and also on his character, which has been commented on by a number of historians. Clark has been severely criticized in some quarters for callously throwing away men's lives in pursuit of personal aggrandizement. Many of the 45th veterans interviewed for this book feel little sympathy for him, but this judgment may be too harsh. Vain and ambitious Clark may have been, but those closest to him knew he was seldom uncaring. Cast from the same mold as Eisenhower, Clark did not send men into combat lightly. He knew that battle casualties were the inevitable downside of his chosen profession and wanted to achieve victory at the lowest possible cost in human lives.

Clark faced what has been called the "loneliness of command"—the sense that every decision he made, no matter how mundane, could have profound consequences. At this crucial point of his military career, he would walk a personal tightrope; at one end was the glory of victory, but

*The blood that "had to be spilled" once coursed through the veins of nearly 1,700 men of the 36th Division, who were now either dead, wounded, or missing in action, and the 36th ceased, at least temporarily, to be an effective fighting force. The men of the "Texas" Division never forgave Mark Clark for what they believed he had done to them. After the war, the veterans of the division adopted a resolution calling for a congressional investigation into the fiasco on the Rapido. The Texas state senate endorsed the resolution and committees in both the U.S. House and Senate held hearings and studied the matter before the request to conduct a full investigation was defeated (Martin Blumenson, *Salerno to Cassino,* vol. 3 in the "U.S. Army in World War II; The Mediterranean Theater of Operations" series [Washington, DC: Center of Military History, 1969], pp. 346–351).

the abyss of defeat waited for him to make one wrong step, one wrong decision. Men's lives—even the question of ultimate victory—hung in the balance. It may be speculation, but Clark undoubtedly felt the same gnawing, gut-wrenching feeling that Eisenhower would experience in a few short months when the fate of the Normandy invasion and the battle for the continent would hinge on his decision to launch the massive Operation Overlord in the teeth of a gale. If Operation Shingle went forward and failed, Clark would be held accountable and probably would lose his command. If he chose to cancel Shingle after Churchill had fought so hard to make it succeed, he would be seen as being too cautious—and probably would also lose his command. Despite his optimistic predictions, Clark, a realist, knew there seemed only a slim chance of success, and much of that chance hinged on pure luck. Given the Hobson's choice that faced him and all the things that he knew could go wrong, Clark made the most momentous decision of his life: He chose to proceed with Shingle.

• • •

The two Allied divisions destined to make the initial Anzio landing were superb, battle-tested forces. The British 1st Division commander, Penney, was known to be a smart, fearless general in the mold of Montgomery, under whom he had studied at the British Staff College. The 3rd Division's Major General Lucien K. Truscott, forty-nine years old, also was an exemplary leader. His gruff, bulldog personality was enhanced by a childhood poisoning incident that had left his voice with a raspy, growling quality. Unafraid to expose himself to the same dangers his men faced, Truscott, wearing his trademark varnished helmet and leather bomber jacket, was frequently found at the front. Wynford Vaughn-Thomas, a British journalist who spent much time at Anzio, described Truscott thus: "In General Truscott, his British comrades-in-arms saw hints of the tough, hard-hitting cavalry leaders of the American Civil War plus an attractive dash of Teddy Roosevelt and his Rough Riders. This was how they hoped all American generals would be!"[120]

Vaughn-Thomas (and, for that matter, Churchill and Alexander) would have preferred Truscott to lead VI Corps ashore, but that role belonged to Lucas. Although the Americans generally liked Lucas and found him competent, he did not project the dynamism many felt the Anzio landings would require. True, he had led VI Corps on a successful, if methodical and unspectacular, advance northward following the Salerno landings, but he had not gained the confidence of his British superiors or subordinates, and the mistrust was mutual.

Looking a decade older than his fifty-four years, Lucas was a quiet, cautious, introspective general who was fond of puffing on a corncob pipe and asking for advice from his staff rather than issuing direct orders. Vaughn-Thomas has written that Lucas conveyed the "feeling of puzzled indecision to his immediate subordinates. His juniors knew him, somewhat disrespectfully, as 'Foxy Grandpa' and he tended to evolve his operational proposals in conferences which often resembled debating societies." The journalist concludes, "There was a need at Anzio of a man of steely resolution and resilience." Lucas, he felt, was not that man.[121] At first elated at being selected to command this daring and vital mission, Lucas soon felt misgivings and they rapidly got the better of him. Seeing that the American commander needed to have his self-esteem boosted, General Alexander told him on 10 January, "We have every confidence in you. That is why you were picked."[122] Later, Lucas would confide to Admiral Sir John Cunningham, "This is going to be worse than Gallipoli." Cunningham's response was blunt: "If that's how you feel, you had better resign." Lucas did not take the advice.[123]

Adding to Lucas's pessimistic feelings about his assignment were three signal events. On 12 January, General Donald Brann, the Fifth Army's operations officer, visited Lucas with the final order for Shingle. Brann also wanted to personally discuss with Lucas the wording in the order that directed him to advance on the Alban Hills. The primary mission, Brann told him, was to seize and secure a beachhead; Clark did not want him engaging in risky operations that might lead to the destruction of the task force. If conditions warranted an advance all the way to the Alban Hills, some twenty miles inland, however, Clark gave Lucas the freedom to pursue that possibility. But Brann emphasized that holding the beachhead was more important than marching inland and risking defeat.[124]

The second event that solidified Lucas's cautious approach and would dissuade him from attempting a more daring tack was a change in the mission of the airborne troops. Originally, the 504th Parachute Infantry Regiment was to drop about ten miles north of Anzio to hold the main highway and be in a position to advance on the Alban Hills. This portion of the final plan was deleted, and the airborne would be seaborne, arriving in the second wave. This change of plans said to Lucas that aggressively pushing inland and taking the Alban Hills was not something he was expected to do.[125]

The third event was perhaps the most telling of all in explaining Lucas's reluctance to act boldly. "Don't stick your neck out as I did at Salerno," Clark warned Lucas. Lucas took this last bit of advice to heart.[126]

With the large-scale Allied attacks along the Gustav Line holding the Germans' attention, the VI Corps's amphibious task force set sail for Anzio on 20 January. Lucas's diary entry for that day reflected his continued ambivalence: "I have many misgivings, but I am optimistic." He also wished that "the higher levels were not so over-optimistic."[127]

By the Americans, the maneuver up the coast behind enemy lines was called an "end run"; to the British, it was a "cat's claw." And, in the end, the latter description seems more appropriate, for the Allies would soon find themselves desperately hanging on to the beachhead by their fingernails.

5

Dangerous Waters

22 January—2 February 1944

> *And just as he who, with exhausted breath, having escaped from sea to shore, turns back to watch the dangerous waters he has quit, so did my spirit, still a fugitive, turn back to look intently at the pass that never has let any man survive.*
>
> —Dante Alighieri, *The Inferno,* Canto I

IN THE EARLY MORNING DARKNESS of 22 January 1944, Major General John P. Lucas, reluctant commander of the U.S. VI Corps, stood on the deck of his flagship, the destroyer-sized seaplane tender USS *Biscayne,*[1] three and a half miles off the coast of Anzio. Around him was spread an impressive, 354-vessel armada.* Packed into the vessels were approximately 40,000 tense, eager American and British soldiers, along with 5,200 vehicles. Overhead droned aircraft from the U.S. XII Air Support Command and elements of the British Desert Air Force. Ahead, the towns of Anzio and Nettuno were dark and silent, unaware that they were about to be thrust into the world's spotlight.[2]

At 0150 hours, two British landing craft, converted into rocket-launching ships and carrying 798 five-inch rockets, unleashed a five-minute salvo, sending shells screaming into the coast to detonate any minefields on the beaches.[3] Heavy German opposition of the magnitude encountered five months earlier at Salerno was anticipated, but the shore was strangely silent; the only sound was that of Allied ordnance exploding inland. Everything was

*The armada consisted of two command ships, five cruisers, twenty-four destroyers and destroyer escorts, twenty-three mine sweepers, thirty-two submarine chasers, two anti-aircraft ships, two gunboats, six repair ships, four Liberty ships, eight Landing Ship, Infantries (LSIs), eighty-four LSTs, ninety-six Landing Craft, Infantry (LCIs), fifty LCTs, and sixteen landing craft equipped with guns, AA weapons, and rockets (Martin Blumenson, *Salerno to Cassino,* vol. 3 in the "U.S. Army in World War II; The Mediterranean Theater of Operations" series [Washington, DC: Center of Military History, 1969], p. 356).

going perfectly, even better than planned—a fact that did not elate Lucas. Indeed, the lack of enemy response merely fed his worries that he was walking into a trap. Lucas tried to peer through the blackness, not only at the shoreline but also at the days and weeks immediately ahead. He was not at all sure that this operation would not end in a bloody debacle for him and the Allies.

Lucas had enjoyed a reputation as a solid, able officer, rarely given to panic. A West Pointer and World War I battalion commander, he had been one of Ike's right-hand men in the North Africa and Sicily campaigns; most of his superiors were confident that "Old Luke," as he was known, could handle the job of leading the forces ashore at Anzio. Old Luke, however, continued to view his assignment with private pessimism. A few days before Operation Shingle was launched, he confided to his diary, "Unless we can get what we want [in men and matériel], the operation becomes such a desperate undertaking that it should not, in my opinion, be attempted." The entire operation, Lucas fretted in his diary, "had a strong odor of Gallipoli and apparently the same amateur was still on the coach's bench," a not-so-veiled reference to Churchill's enthusiastic support, as First Lord of the Admiralty in 1915, of the disastrous Allied attempt to take the Dardanelles.

Lucas continued to agonize about the task force's objectives, which remained vague. He knew that a military operation without clear-cut objectives is inevitably doomed to failure. Was he to swiftly capture Rome? Or was he to siphon German forces away from the Gustav Line, allowing the Fifth Army forces there to finally break through and join his beachhead? Or was he and his invasion force merely to play the role of sacrificial lamb? Unfortunately, no one at the time could give him a definitive answer and in the intervening decades none has been forthcoming. He worried that if the invasion force managed to reach Rome (which was, at that time, guarded only by a couple of understrength German battalions), the salient created would be cut off and destroyed by the enemy. He also didn't believe that the enemy would weaken its defenses in the south to react to his incursion at Anzio; he thought it entirely possible that Kesselring could bolster his Gustav Line defenses *and* find enough troops to seal off the beachhead. To Lucas, the possibilities of a permanent stalemate along the Gustav Line *plus* an Allied disaster in the Anzio-Rome area were very real.[4] Despite the misgivings and second-guessing, it was too late to call off the operation; never before in World War II had such a large-scale endeavor taken place with so many involved in its planning and execution so divided over its objectives and so pessimistic about its outcome.

At H hour—0200 hours—the first wave of infantry-carrying craft, which had been circling in the darkness for nearly two hours, straightened their lines and began their run in to shore. Everyone was expecting to catch hell at any moment. Except for a few of the craft that ran into mines in the Anzio port, there was virtually no opposition.

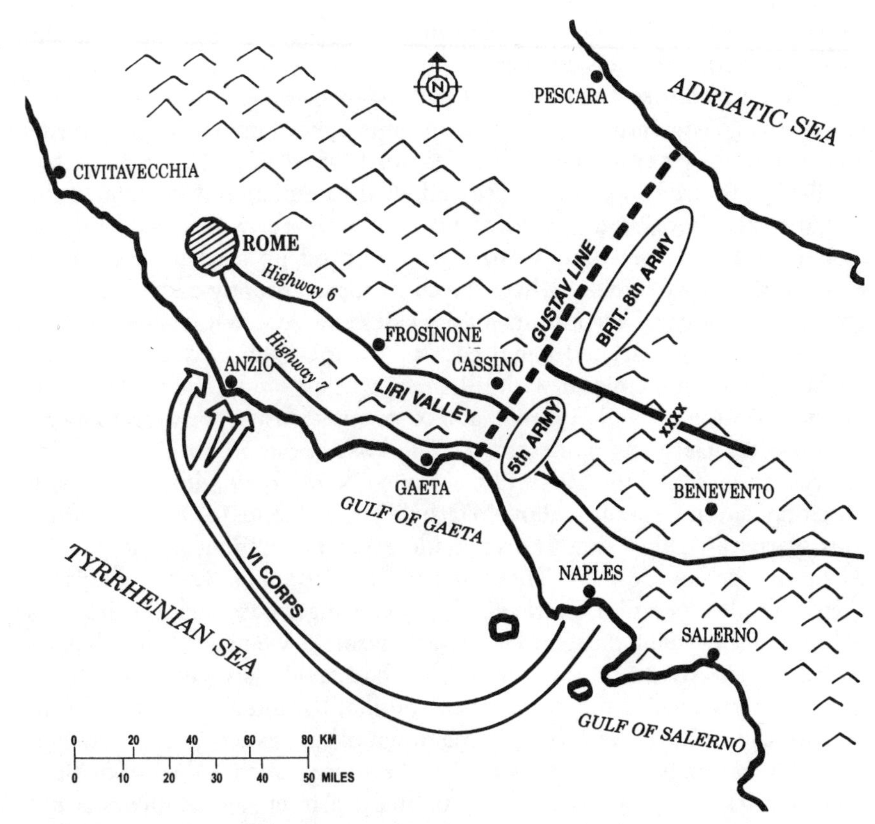

MAP 5.1 Operation Shingle—The End Run
January 1944—With the Allied Advance stymied all along the Gustav Line, VI Corps made an amphibious landing at Anzio, hoping to draw German forces away from the Cassino front and allow a penetration toward Rome through the Liri Valley.

Different sources have listed different German units in the area. According to German sources, just a handful of units guarded the potential invasion area that stretched along the coast from the Tiber to the Astura River: one panzer grenadier battalion and a company of engineers from the 29th Panzer Grenadier Division and two engineer companies from the 4th *Fallshirmjäger* Division, which was undergoing formation, plus forty-one pieces of various calibers of coastal artillery. Farther inland, in the Rome–Alban Hills area, were an Italian assault gun company, a company of panzers, a light anti-aircraft battery, and understrength, untrained elements of the 4th *Fallshirmjäger* and Hermann Göring Panzer Divisions. Only the headquarters of Army Group C, at Frascati, were available to organize a defense. The majority of other units were seventy miles to the south, bolstering the Gustav Line.[5]

As landing craft scraped the sand and the troops piled onto the shore, a few enemy coast guard and anti-aircraft units opened fire but were immediately silenced by naval guns.[6] Six miles north of Anzio, on "Peter Beach," the British 1st Division and the 9th and 43rd Commando Battalions of the 2nd Special Service Brigade landed and swiftly moved two miles inland; the Commandos cut the Albano-Anzio road and set up a roadblock.[7] Four miles to the east of Anzio, where the coast turns abruptly eastward, Truscott's 3rd Infantry Division hit an area designated "X-Ray Beach" near Nettuno and experienced equal ease in getting ashore. Truscott's men pushed three miles inland with all their artillery and armor, blew four bridges over the Mussolini Canal, and took up defensive positions to await the expected German counterattack. The boat-borne 509th Parachute Infantry Battalion and the 504th PIR occupied Nettuno by midmorning with little opposition.[8] Finally, Colonel Darby's 1st, 3rd, and 4th Ranger Battalions of the 6615th Ranger Force made a perfect landing in the port of Anzio at "Yellow Beach." (The 2nd and 5th Battalions were in England, preparing for Operation Overlord. The final Ranger Battalion, the 6th, was fighting in the Pacific theater.) Darby later wrote, "We had insisted that we be landed exactly on the correct beach. I had laughingly said that when I got out of my boat in the center of the flotilla, I wanted to be at the front door of the casino. The Navy put me down on the exact spot."[9] Few amphibious landings in World War II encountered such light opposition. Shortly after dawn, six Messerschmitts made a brief raid on the port but barely slowed unloading operations. A few hours later, another air raid sank an LCI. Other than these nuisance raids and a few desultory artillery barrages from guns located far inland, enemy response seemed slight.[10]

Throughout that first day, Allied troops and supplies continued to pour in. By midnight on the twenty-second, approximately 90 percent of the men and equipment on the ships—some 36,000 troops and 3,000 vehicles—had landed. The American and British casualty list for the first day was thirteen killed, ninety-seven wounded, and forty-four captured or missing. Two ships had been sunk. Over 200 Germans had been captured. Up to this point, the operation was a smashing success.[11]

Not only had the initial landings caught the Germans completely by surprise, but their daring had also captured the world's imagination. "Anzio will astonish the world," declared Churchill, with some justification. With its proximity to the capital of one of the three Axis powers (albeit one that had already capitulated), Anzio gave the free world hope that the end of this terrible war was in sight. The Germans, as usual, had other ideas.[12] Initially caught off guard, the enemy began to react. About 0300 hours, Kesselring was awakened with news of the landings. Without wasting a minute, he began marshaling his forces, using the code name Plan Richard as his clarion call to action.* Guessing correctly that the Allies expected him to denude the Cassino front to react to the threat to his rear, the wily Kesselring performed a masterful juggling act that enabled him to create a force strong enough to check the Allies on both fronts, plus do something that the Allied planners had thought impossible: bring in fresh troops from elsewhere.

At 0500 hours, he ordered the 4th *Fallschirmjäger* Division, which was in the process of being created, along with replacement units of the Hermann Göring Panzer Division, to take up blocking positions across the roads that led from Anzio to the Alban Hills. He then requested that OKW (*Oberkommando der Wehrmacht,* the German Army's supreme command in Berlin) send whatever additional units it could spare from southern France, Yugoslavia, and southern Germany. These would initially include the 715th Infantry Division, the 998th Artillery Battalion, a battalion of the 4th Panzer Regiment, and the 301st Panzer Battalion, with Hitler's newest "wonder weapon"—the remote-controlled, explosive-packed miniature tanks known as "Goliaths."

Also transferred to Italy from the Southeast Command were *Generalleutnant* Karl Eglseer's 114th *Jäger* (Light Infantry) Division and two battalions of artillery. The immediate activation of a new infantry division—the 92nd—was also ordered, but such an activation would take time. OKW quickly made units from the Replacement Army in Germany, including the headquarters of LXXVI Panzer Corps; three infantry, grenadier, and panzer grenadier regiments; rocket and artillery units; two battalions of Russian "volunteers"; six construction battalions; and a battalion of Tiger tanks, available to Kesselring.

Closer to the danger, *Generaloberst* Eberhard von Mackensen's Fourteenth Army in northern Italy provided the 65th Infantry Division (less one regiment) from Genoa, the 362nd Infantry Division (less one regiment) from Rimini, and two regiments of the 16th SS Panzer Grenadier Division from Livorno and Lubiana. Responding quickly, these units left for Anzio on 22 and 23 January. Next, Kesselring ordered von Vietinghoff to call off a planned counterattack on the Garigliano River and rush him the headquarters of I *Fallschirm* Corps along with as many combat troops as the Tenth

*In anticipating possible Allied amphibious movements above the Gustav Line, Kesselring and his staff had already established defensive zones and made plans to counter any attacks. Besides Plan Richard, Plan Gustav would respond to a threat to Genoa, Plan Ludwig to Livorno/Pisa, Plan Viktor to Ravenna, and Plan Ida to Istria on the Baltic side of the Adriatic (*The German Operation at Anzio; German Military Document Section; A Study of the German Operations at Anzio Beachhead from 22 Jan. 44 to 31 May 44*. War Department, Military Intelligence Division, Camp Ritchie, MD, 1946. 45th Infantry Division Archives, p. 5).

Army could spare. These included the bulk of the *Generalmajor* Wilhelm Raapke's 71st Infantry, *Generalleutnant* Fritz Gräser's 3rd Panzer Grenadier Division, and *Generalleutnant* Smilo Freiherr von Lüttwitz's 26th Panzer Division. Various other artillery, anti-aircraft, anti-tank, and support units were also transferred from the southern front. More would soon follow.

Kesselring established three divisional sectors in the defensive wall he was building around the beachhead. The fledgling 4th *Fallschirmjäger* Division, under *Generalleutnant* H. Trettner, would be responsible for the western sector and the 3rd Panzer Grenadier Division would control the center sector, while Conrath's understrength Hermann Göring Panzer Division would be in charge of defending the eastern sector. At 1700 hours on the twenty-second, the headquarters of I *Fallschirm* Corps, under *General der Flieger* Alfred Schlemm, became operational and assumed command of the beachhead defense forces. Determining that the Allies, for the time being, had insufficient strength to mount a major push toward either Rome or the Alban Hills, Kesselring sought to construct a solid barrier that would effectively contain the beachhead until he could build up sufficient forces to destroy it.[13] The stage had been set for one of World War II's most titanic struggles.

As news reports of the landings hit the air waves and newspapers, the eyes of the world suddenly turned toward a small, seemingly insignificant Italian coastal resort town. For over 2,000 years, Anzio, less than forty miles south of Rome, has been steeped in history. The Emperor Nero was born there (when it was known as Antium) on 15 December 37 A.D. and supposedly returned to his palace there to strum his lyre while Rome burned. The great Roman orator Cicero lived in Antium, and the mad Emperor Caligula once proposed moving the capital from Rome to the seaside resort. In 445 A.D., the Vandal king Genserico landed in Antium's port and passed through the town on his way to sack the Imperial City. To this day, ancient ruins abound in Anzio. Nettuno was born several centuries later, after Antium had been destroyed by the Saracens.

Over a hundred years ago, the area began to attract an upper-class clientele. Spacious villas appeared along the seacoast, and on a prominent hill between the two towns the gardens of the Villa Borghese were laid out. North of Anzio and Nettuno, on the outskirts of the nearby farm village of Carano, stood a national shrine—the simple tomb of General Menotti Garibaldi, the Brazilian-born son of Giuseppe Garibaldi, the nineteenth-century patriot who did so much to unify Italy. Fighting under the generalship of his famous father, Menotti Garibaldi earned Italy's highest military decoration during the war for Italian unity in the 1860s. He later earned the devotion of the people of the Anzio region by dedicating himself to political and agricultural reforms. He died in 1903 at Carano. His tomb would soon become a focal point of the fighting.[14]

Aerial view of the Anzio-Nettuno area. (Courtesy of U.S. Army Military History Institute

Although wealthy Italians such as the Borghese family had built luxurious homes at Anzio and used the town as a resort, it was never a particularly pleasant place to spend time, especially when one moved inland, away from the cooling sea breezes. The heat and humidity were oppressive, and the mosquitoes that infested the nearby Pontine Marshes carried malaria. Attempts to drain the swamps had been undertaken for centuries. In 443 B.C., Consul Appius Claudius embarked on a massive effort, only to see it drain the Roman treasury instead of the marshes. Further attempts were undertaken and once again abandoned during the reign of Julius Caesar. The land lay unused until Benito Mussolini came to power. In 1928, in one of his administration's most ambitious public works projects, Il Duce had a large drainage ditch constructed, running from the town of Padiglione to the sea. Numerous creeks, ditches, and smaller canals fed into the main canal, which, it turned out, also served as an excellent tank trap because of its width, depth, and steeply sloping sides.[15]

Arriving in Anzio a few weeks after the landings, the war correspondent Ernie Pyle used his characteristically blunt prose to paint a word picture of the area:

> I didn't waste any time getting off the boat, for I had been feeling pretty much like a clay pidgeon [*sic*] in a shooting gallery. But after a few hours in Anzio, I wished I was back aboard. No one could have described Anzio as any haven of peacefulness. Anzio and Nettuno run together along the coast of our beachhead, practically forming one city. There is really only one main street, which runs along the low bluff just back of the first row of waterfront buildings. . . .
>
> For these two towns are now (or rather, were until the war) high-class seaside resorts. . . . At one point, the towns extend two hundred yards from the water's edge, forming a solid flank of fine stone buildings four and five stories high. Most of these are apartment houses, business buildings, and rich people's villas. Today there is no civilian life in Anzio-Nettuno. . . . The Germans had evacuated everybody before we came, and we found the place deserted. . . . When our troops first landed, they found things intact and undamaged, but the Germans changed that. Little by little, day by day, these cities were reduced to destruction by the shells and bombs of the enemy. It happened slowly. The Germans shelled spasmodically. Hours would go by without a single shell coming in, and then all of a sudden a couple of shells would smack the water just offshore. A few buildings would go down, or the corners would fly off some of them. One day's damage was almost negligible. But the cumulative effect after a couple of weeks was heart-breaking. You couldn't walk half a block without finding a building half crumpled to the ground. The sidewalks had shell holes in them. Engineers repaired new holes in the streets. Military police who directed auto traffic were occasionally killed at their posts. Broken steel girders lay across the sidewalks. Marble statues fell in littered patios. Trees were uprooted, and the splattered mud upon them dried and turned gray. Wreckage was washed up on shore. Everywhere there were rubble and mud and broken wire.
>
> You've heard how flat the land of the Anzio beachhead is. You've heard how strange and naked our soldiers feel with no rocks to take cover behind, no mountains to provide slopes for protection. This is a new kind of warfare for us. Here distances are short, and space is confined. The whole beachhead is the front line. . . . Every inch of our territory was under German artillery fire. There was no rear area that was immune, as in most battle zones. They could reach us with their 88s, and they used everything from that on up. . . . A man was just as liable to get hit standing in the doorway of the villa where he slept at night as he was in a command post five miles out in the field. . . . Hospitals were not immune from shellfire and bombing. There are a lot of little places where a few individuals can take cover from fire. The point is that the generalized flatness forbids whole armies taking cover. . . . Space was at a premium. Never had I seen a war zone so crowded. Of course, men weren't standing shoulder to shoulder, but I suppose the most indiscriminate shell dropped at any point on the beachhead would have landed not more than two hundred yards from somebody.[16]

An English writer, describing the battlefield of Waterloo, called it "a small theatre for such a tragedy."[17] The same could be said of Anzio.

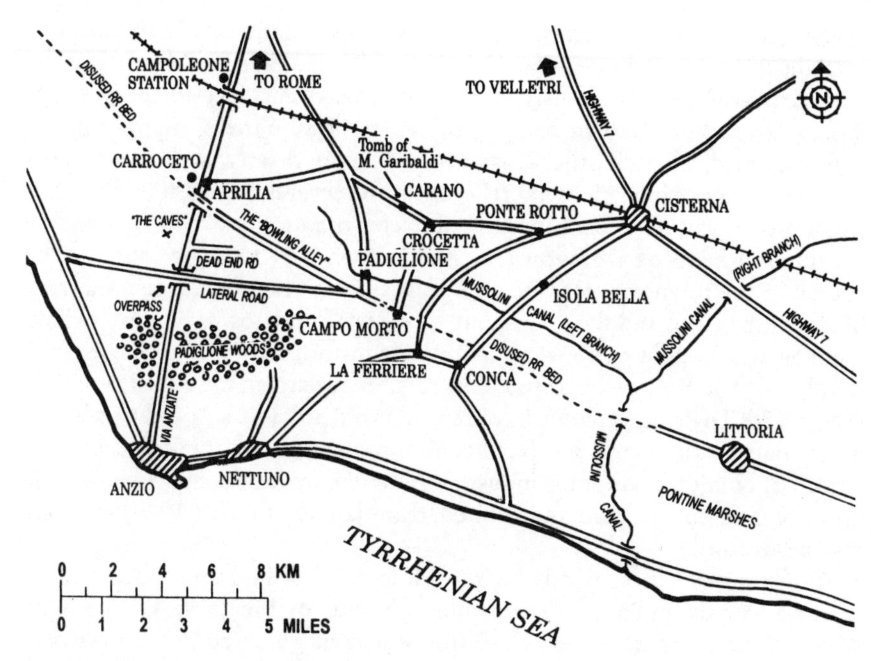

MAP 5.2 Anzio-Nettuno Area

Had the mythical Thunderbird been able to spread its wings and soar above the beachhead, looking toward Rome, this is what it would have seen: a wooded area of tall umbrella pines behind Anzio and Nettuno, known as the Bosco di Padiglione, or Padiglione Woods (called "The Pines" by the troops), running east-west across the upper boundary of the beachhead. Just beyond the edge of the woods, the land was as flat and featureless as a table, except for an unfinished highway bridge (which the Americans called the "Overpass" and the British dubbed the "Flyover") that crossed both the Anzio-Rome railroad tracks and the Anzio-Rome Highway (the Via Anziate), which ran parallel to each other. A handsome villa stood not more than a hundred yards north of the Overpass, and other farm houses dotted the landscape.

Less than two miles beyond the Overpass was another structure—a bridge to support a railroad track that had yet to be laid. This feature was called the "Embankment" and a road that led to it at an angle from the southeast was dubbed the "Bowling Alley" because it was so straight and level. Just beyond the Embankment was a small collection of buildings known as Carroceto Station, and, a half mile to the east, the newly created city of Aprilia, one of five model "Fascist towns" built in the region under Mussolini's orders in the 1930s (the others being Littoria, Pomezia, Sabaudia, and Pontinia). Aprilia opened in 1937 as a settlement for a projected population of 3,000 peasants brought in to work the new farms in the reclaimed Pontine Marshes. In its first eight years, Aprilia consisted only of some twenty-five to thirty buildings: a large church, town hall, Fascist Party headquarters, military police barracks, medical clinic, shops, wine store, movie theater, and a few apartment buildings. About the only relief from the severely modern architecture was a bronze statue of San Michele, complete with drawn sword, holding the decapitated head of a dragon and standing on a pedestal in front of the church in the town square. Due to Aprilia's geometric architecture and red-brick construction and the tall, square, smokestacklike tower on the city hall, the men who fought there, along with later historians, referred to the town simply as "The Factory" because of its resemblance to an industrial complex. (Some 45th Division veterans have referred to Aprilia as a "peanut factory" or a "soap factory," and it is possible that some men still think that the collection of buildings had some industrial function, but this is not the case. The only thing the town ever manufactured, from January to May 1944, was misery and death.)[18]

To the west of these towns lay the Moletta River and an eroded area of drainage canals, gullies, and streambeds known as the "wadis," the Arab word for the dry washes the British troops had encountered in North Africa. Here, however, the bramble-choked wadis were anything but dry. The gullies were, in some places, fifty feet deep, six feet wide, and hip deep in water.[19] Due west of Carroceto lay an area named Collina le Buon Riposo—or Buon Riposo Ridge, "The Place of Good Rest." Just to the south of the ridge and west of the Via Anziate lay a feature known as Cava di Pozzolana or, as the soldiers simply called it, "the caves," which the Irish Guards briefly occupied in early February. Four miles north of Carroceto Station and Aprilia was a small whistle-stop on the railroad to Rome known as Campoleone Station. The town of Campoleone lay a short distance farther north. Some thirteen miles southeast of Campoleone Station is the city of Cisterna, sitting astride Highway 7—the main north-south road that leads from Rome, past the southern flank of the Alban Hills, through Cisterna and Terracina, and on to Naples. Highway 6 paralleled Highway 7 much of the way, but led from Rome through Valmonte and Frosinone to Cassino and beyond.

This was farm country, Italian style. Here melons, grapes, tomatoes, and corn grew. Longhorn cattle roamed the fields, and more than one is said to have "committed suicide" by stepping on a mine (or catching a bullet in the brain), thus providing the Allies with a break from the boring GI rations—and a set of fancy horns to adorn the hood of an Army truck. Spread out across the flat, open farm fields were a few windmills and bright blue farmhouses (known as *poderi,* which were Mussolini's gift to Italy's World War I veterans as a way of buying their votes), sturdily built of stone and as strong as any pillbox or other military fortification. Some two miles north of Aprilia was a farm dubbed "Smelly Farm" by the British due to its large manure pile and, later, the putrid odor of dead and decaying livestock.[20]

On the far right of the beachhead area, the Canale di Mussolini—the Mussolini Canal—emptied into the Tyrrhenian Sea. The canal headed toward Cisterna for about five miles, then branched widely, one branch heading northeast, toward the hills known as the Colli Lepini, the other branch turning northwest toward the town of Padiglione. Straight north of Anzio, and about fourteen miles inland, lay the humped shape of the 3,100-foot-high Colli Laziali (the Alban Hills), which guarded the southern approaches to the Imperial City.[21]

The area seemed permeated with images of death. Here there was a town known as Campo Morto ("Field of Death"), another known as Femmina Morte ("Dead Woman"), and still another called Cavallo Morte ("Dead Horse"). The pastureland around the Overpass is called Campo di Carne ("Field of Meat").

• • •

No one, least of all Lucas, seemed to know how far the invasion force could push inland before running into heavy enemy opposition. In the first hours and days of the invasion, had fear and caution not overtaken the VI Corps commander, the Allies most assuredly could have captured the small railroad station at Campoleone, which was the key to taking Albano, which sits astride Highway 7 on the southwestern slopes of the Alban Hills, plus the town of Cisterna, which guarded the approaches to Velletri, farther east on Highway 7. Such a thrust would not have unduly extended the lines of communication that so worried Lucas and would have given the Allies a wider, deeper, and much more secure beachhead. The fact that these two lightly guarded key positions were not taken initially would result in months of terrible fighting, heavy casualties, and the legacy of failure on the entire Anzio operation.[22]

The recently arrived Allies, who thought they would be taking part in a bold gamble to capture Rome, sat around with nothing to do and couldn't understand why. The men of the 24th Guards Brigade bided their time beneath the tall umbrella pines of the Padiglione Woods, brewing tea, playing bridge, and wondering when orders to move would arrive.

German artillery began to increase in volume and deadliness and, at dusk on the twenty-third, the *Luftwaffe* mounted a raid with fifty-five aircraft on the idle invaders. With aerial torpedoes and radio-guided bombs, the *Luftwaffe* managed to damage the British destroyer *Jervis* and send its mate, HMS *Janus*, to the bottom of the sea with a loss of 159 men. Everyone on the beach wanted to know why they weren't moving.[23] The reason was simple: Lucas was afraid to move; intelligence reports were gnawing at him. In this early stage he thought more German units were in the Anzio area than were actually present, the result of fragments of larger units being thrown hurriedly into the line. So, if a battalion or regiment of a certain German division was known to be present, G-2 officers wrongly assumed the entire division was there.[24]

Cables flew back and forth from the beachhead to Clark's and Alexander's headquarters and to Number Ten, Downing Street, where Churchill demanded to know why the invasion was stuck and what was being done about it. (Once, when informed that the Allies now had 18,000 vehicles on the beachhead, the Prime Minister sarcastically remarked, "We must have a great superiority of chauffeurs.")[25] And so, while Lucas fretted and Churchill fumed, the Germans poured more men and guns into their ring around Anzio. Furthermore, the bold German pilots ignored the intense anti-aircraft fire and Allied air cover to take their toll of the vessels in Anzio harbor. Several craft were put out of action and a clearly marked British hospital ship, HMS *St. David,* was sunk.[26]

Had there been enough ships available initially to bring three or four divisions ashore on the first day, the story of Operation Shingle might have had a happier ending—or at least a quicker resolution. But the Allied effort lacked the ships needed to ensure a swift, stunning victory, and so the buildup went along slowly and methodically. It would take over a week before all of the 45th Division could be shuttled from Naples to the beachhead.

Morty Carr, a demolitions expert with the 1st Battalion, 157th's Ammunition and Pioneer Platoon, went in before the rest of the division in case there were any underwater obstacles that had to be cleared; otherwise the LCVPs couldn't land. He recalled, "We would have had to blow 'em up. But there was nothing there."[27]

Another early arrival from the 45th Division at Anzio was Nicholas Defonte, a member of the prisoner of war interrogation team. He was of Italian heritage and had studied Italian in high school and at Brooklyn College. He was attached to the British 1st Division as an interrogator/interpreter when it landed at Anzio. Unlike his buddies in the 45th, Defonte found himself with very little to do. "We lived in a foxhole for three months and didn't do a damn thing," he commented. "But the British were a terrific bunch. The only thing I didn't like was the British chow. It was horrible—hard tack and bully beef and so forth." But Defonte got lucky. Once his British unit was in a valley and nearby was an American ammunition dump. "I got to know the fellows there pretty fast and got to know that captain that was in charge. I asked the captain if he could put me on for chow line. He said, 'C'mon over any time.' So I'd go over there and have American chow." (After several months at Anzio, Defonte saw four Italian officers come into division headquarters. "I went over and began talking to them. One said the British wanted some Italian interpreters and interrogators. I said, 'That's what *we're* here for!' There were three of us. We'd been

German long-range artillery round splashing into Anzio harbor as DUKWs bring supplies ashore. (Courtesy of 45th Infantry Division Archives)

sitting there for three months, not doing a damn thing. That's the way the Army works, I guess.")[28]

The 179th was the first 45th Division unit to be pulled out of the line at Venafro; on 20 January, the regiment was attached to the U.S. 1st Armored Division and trucked sixty miles to Staging Area Number Three at Pozzuoli, a small port just north of Naples. On 23 January, the 179th boarded nine LSTs and nine LCIs for the hundred-mile trip to Anzio. The voyage north was uneventful except for two aerial torpedoes dropped by German planes that narrowly missed the British LST that was carrying the regiment's Command Group. The 179th arrived at Anzio on D+2—24 January.[29]

Unlike the hot reception that had welcomed the men at Salerno, the scene here, except for some random geysers being blasted skyward by sporadic enemy artillery rounds, was fairly normal. A number of ships were bustling to and fro, and the amphibious DUKWs were ferrying supplies in from other ships moored a safe distance from shore. Up ahead, lining the shore, were some attractive, whitewashed buildings, gleaming like palaces in the sun. From out in the bay, the damage wasn't too obvious.

Yes, Anzio looked quite peaceful and intact, especially when compared to all the bombed-out towns and villages the 45th had marched or fought through since Salerno. As the LSTs and LCIs reached their berths, the Thunderbirds grabbed their weapons and equipment, marched down the gangways to the dock, and then kept marching right through the city. Now they noticed the missing windows and pockmarks in the stuccoed walls made by bomb, bullet, and shell. There had been a fight here, all right, but it hadn't destroyed the place. Then the men of the 179th noticed one other thing. There were no civilians around. Here and there along their march, a mongrel dog or two barked at them or a mangy alley cat scooted out of sight at their approach. Although it was January, it was warm, especially with the thick wool shirts and pants, the field jackets, the haversacks, the ammo belts. Some men had M-1s slung over their shoulders; others lugged the heavy BARs and machine guns and the mortars. Others sweated under the weight of radios or ammo boxes, and the equipment carried by the whole olive-drab parade clanked dully as the men marched. Some of the officers rode by in jeeps, telling the men to watch their interval.

The 179th marched through the town, past a thick forest of umbrella pines, and under a highway overpass. Up ahead was a flat, treeless landscape that reminded some of the men of the billiard table smoothness of parts of Oklahoma. Only a few farm houses—and the mangled, burned-out wrecks of British vehicles—relieved the monotonous flatness of the scenery. Off on the horizon were some purple mounds—the Alban Hills, somebody called them. Then the GIs reached the place the Army had decreed for them to be and the sergeants cried out, "Dig in." Entrenching tools were produced and the men began to dig, only to hit water about a foot below the surface.

Ray Williams, of HQ Company, 1st Battalion, 179th, remembered the trip northward and the landing:

> I was on a ship with maybe thirty or thirty-five other soldiers. We didn't have any information about the landing at Anzio but, seeing as how this was our third amphibious landing, it was old hat. Anything to get out of those mountains had to be a better deal. We landed at about nine that morning. There was an awful lot of movement on the beach, trucks going everywhere, supplies being unloaded, stuff like that. The damage in Anzio at that time wasn't too bad. Most of the destruction was in the other town, Nettuno.[30]

Robert LaDu, executive officer of F Company, 179th, recalled,

> The water was choppy, and we had to circle in the harbor for about five hours. When we finally got to make our run in to shore, we were all seasick. Fortunately, the landing was virtually unopposed. There were shells coming in but no small-arms fire. That night, the Germans sent seven aircraft in. It was just beginning to turn a little dark and they came in and strafed and used anti-personnel bombs. All seven got shot down by our small-arms fire—rifles and machine guns and pistols—anything that could fire. That was really amazing. Back in the mountains, they'd strafe us every morning at eight, every noon, and every afternoon at four. So we had a lot of practice firing at aircraft. Everybody cheered when that seventh one went down.[31]

• • •

Early on 24 January, Lucas told Penney to send a patrol up the Via Anziate toward Campoleone Station and ordered Truscott to reconnoiter the road to Cisterna. A patrol from the 24th Guards Brigade, riding in small, tracked vehicles known as Bren carriers, rattled up the sapling-lined highway toward Carroceto. Except for a few peasants working in the fields, the Guards saw no one and encountered no opposition. It was only when the patrol reached the outskirts of Aprilia that it came under fire from rifles, machine guns, and a self-propelled artillery piece. The British hastily reversed course and reported the incident to Penney, who asked Lucas for permission to attack Aprilia. Inexplicably, Lucas hesitated for a day before giving his consent. By then it was too late. On the twenty-fifth, the Guards battled their way into the settlement, became ensnared in bitter, hand-to-hand fighting, and suffered extensive casualties in evicting the occupants. No sooner had they pushed out the enemy than they found themselves battling for their lives when hit by a strong counterattack by the 29th Panzer Grenadiers. The Guards held on, but just barely.[32]

Farther east, the 3rd Division ran into similar trouble trying to take Cisterna. Truscott asked Lucas to attach the newly arrived 179th Regiment to bolster his division's attack on Cisterna, but the Corps commander turned him down.[33] Now, *Generalleutnant* Paul Conrath's Hermann Göring Panzer Division, which had been badly mauled in Sicily, was exacting revenge on 3rd Division men. The American attack bogged down. To the 3rd's right, a thrust by the 504th Parachute Infantry Regiment toward Littoria was also blunted by strong German opposition. Beyond and between Aprilia and Cisterna, more men, tanks, and trucks were rolling in to reinforce the German line. The slim chance for a quick and stunning Allied victory at Anzio had evaporated.[34]

The men of the 179th barely had time to settle in at Anzio when, on the twenty-fifth, Clark met with Lucas, diplomatically expressed general satisfaction with the buildup, and suggested that the Corps commander should send his force out to take Campoleone and Cisterna, two towns that would be valuable as anchors for the Allied defensive line. Feeling confident that he would have sufficient troops on hand within a week to begin his march toward Rome, a cautiously optimistic Clark returned to his headquarters at Caserta.[35] On that same day, Lucas wrote in his diary, "I am doing my best but it seems terribly slow." The next day, he added, "This waiting is terrible. I want an all-out Corps effort but the time hasn't come yet and the weather will not help matters. Bad for tanks. I might be able to move soon," he wrote, hoping that the arrival of the rest of the 45th Division would give him the edge in men and matériel he thought was necessary before launching his offensive.[36]

On the twenty-sixth, bad weather struck again. Allied air operations were grounded, but the weather did not dissuade the *Luftwaffe* from pounding the beachhead. Alexander was growing impatient with the sluggishness of the operation and was being prodded by Churchill, who felt likewise. On 27 January, Alexander suggested by cable (Alexander, the quintessential British gentleman, rarely *ordered* anyone to do anything) to Mark Clark that Clark inspire Lucas to "press the advance with the utmost energy before the enemy reinforcements could arrive," and further suggested that "all efforts should now be concentrated on full-scale coordinated attacks to capture Cisterna and Campoleone followed by a rapid attack on Velletri."[37] Perhaps anticipating the unhappiness at higher headquarters, Lucas met with his division commanders that day to outline plans for pushing out of the beachhead.[38]

On the twenty-eighth, Clark headed, via PT boat, from the mouth of the Volturno River back to Anzio where he would, as he said, "remain until the attack got well started." The trip nearly cost Clark his life. As PT 201 approached within seven miles of Anzio, it was fired on in the dim morning twilight by an American minesweeper, AM 120, which had been on the lookout for German motor torpedo boats. Misreading or not seeing the PT boat's blinker signal, the nervous gunners on AM 120 splintered the plywood boat with 40mm and 5-inch shells, destroying the stool on which Clark had been sitting just seconds earlier and seriously wounding five men on board, including the skipper. None too soon, the situation was straightened out, the wounded taken aboard another ship, and Clark and his party continued on to Anzio, just in time to dodge a German air raid on the harbor.[39] Understandably, Clark was not in a patient mood when he reached Lucas's headquarters in Nettuno. He let Lucas know in no uncertain terms that the time had come for rapid movement. Lucas, for his part, rolled out his plans for enlarging the beachhead, plans that he said were to be set into motion on the twenty-ninth.[40]

If Lucas's lack of initiative and aggressive action was worrisome to both Clark and Alexander, it made Churchill livid. He thundered, "I had hoped we were hurling a wildcat into the shore, but all we got was a stranded whale."[41] In his diary, Lucas noted, "Apparently some of the higher levels think I have not advanced with maximum speed. I think more has been accomplished than anyone has a right to expect. This venture was always a desperate one and I could never see much chance for it to succeed, if success means driving the Germans north of Rome."[42]

• • •

The 179th assembled northeast of Nettuno; one of its first duties was to relieve the 504th Parachute Infantry Regiment on the twenty-ninth. The paratroopers had been holding defensive positions south of the Mussolini

Canal near Campo Morto—the town ominously named "Field of Death." Everyone's nerves were on edge.[43] Robert LaDu recalled, "We were spread so thin, we put the guys in one-man foxholes. One night, a German fell into one of our foxholes on top of one of our guys. Our guy screamed and yelled but there wasn't a shot fired. That German jumped out and high-tailed it for home. Our guy just about died from fright. We put our guys in two-man foxholes from then on. It just spread us out that much thinner."[44]

To the south, the rest of the 45th was preparing to move up the coast to reinforce the invasion, and farewell parties were commonplace. Mel Craven, of A Battery, 158th Field Artillery, recalled, "Our officers, at least in our battery, were an exceptional bunch. They threw a party for the enlisted men in a theater in Naples. They arranged for an Air Force band to play, there were several nurses there, and we had a dance. There were steaks, pork chops—a meal that you only dream of. When it was over, the officers did the KP. All through the war, there was that kind of relationship between the men and officers, at least in our unit."[45]

The 157th Regiment and the 158th Field Artillery Battalion boarded ships on 28 January and steamed northward. Tarzan Williams, K Company, 157th, recalled that the men were crowded into the forward areas below decks on tiers four bunks high. During the night, the ship Williams was on collided with an American minesweeper that had cut through the convoy. Both ships survived with minimal damage, but the men in the bunks were tossed about. "Every man on the left side of the aisle was thrown out," Williams said. "We hit the sides of the bunks on our right and fell to the floor. The man on the bottom bunk got the worst of it as the three men above him fell on top of him. The lights went out momentarily and there was a mad scramble with us trying to stand up and get our equipment back on our bunks."[46]

On 29 January, the 157th Regiment and 158th FA Battalion reached Anzio. To welcome them, the Germans staged one of their customary air raids, strafing the ships in the harbor at 1600 hours (and losing three planes in the process).[47] Bud McMillan, a nineteen-year-old sniper with K Company, 157th Regiment, on the same LST with Williams, recalled, "German planes were coming over and German artillery was falling among the ships and along the docks."[48]

The *Luftwaffe* raiders returned at 2000 hours for more. This time they managed to kill nine and wound thirty men of Battery B, 158th FA Battalion.[49] Mel Craven recalled the strafing run: "We were straddled by bombs. B Battery had already been hit pretty severely, with thirty or thirty-five either killed or wounded in the strafing attack. This was a horrendous casualty rate for an artillery battalion."[50]

Henry Kaufman, H Company, 157th Regiment, remembered that his unit "set sail on several fast PT boats with full combat gear. I don't recall how long it took to get to Anzio from Naples because, other than the officers, no one seemed to be aware of the time."[51]

First Lieutenant Eddie Speairs of C Company, 157th, recalled that "Anzio was the easiest landing you could possibly imagine. We walked in like we were going into New York City."[52]

Don Amzibel, L Company, 157th, said, "We had no trouble landing at Anzio. We didn't even get our feet wet!"[53]

The 157th marched a few miles inland to its bivouac area along the western coast of the beachhead and stopped, with the sea on its left flank and the U.S. 36th Engineer Combat Regiment (which spent much of the war operating as infantry) and British 2nd Battalion North Staffordshire Regiment on its right.[54] Bud McMillan said, "After we landed, we went up the left-hand part of the beach. We were committed right away; we marched right up there and dug in about three or four miles from the beach. We were evidently setting up a defensive line. We were picking up mortar and artillery fire and then we started doing patrol work and running into German units."[55]

With two-thirds of the 45th Division now ashore, the beleaguered Lucas felt that he had now accumulated sufficient strength to strike out from the beachhead in force and take, as Clark had directed, the key towns of Campoleone and Cisterna. He now had some 61,300 men, 237 tanks, over 500 artillery pieces, 27,000 tons of supplies, enormous air support (when the weather was favorable), and the firepower of the combined American and British fleets lying offshore. What he did not know was that Kesselring had thrown a virtually impregnable iron ring, with some 71,500 troops, around the beachhead.[56]

While the Germans were gearing up for the ultimate battle, Lucas was mobilizing his forces to push farther inland. On the right flank, the 3rd Division was to renew its efforts to take Cisterna, with the help of the 504th PIR and Darby's Ranger Force. The British force—consisting of the 1st Battalion, Scots Guards, 1st Battalion, Irish Guards, 2nd Battalion, Sherwood Foresters, 1st Battalion, King's Shropshire Light Infantry, and 1st Battalion, Duke of Wellington's Regiment—was to drive toward Albano, supported by Combat Command A of Major General Ernest Harmon's U.S. 1st Armored Division* (Combat Command B was still on the Gustav Line), which had arrived piecemeal between 24 and 28 January. The attack was

---

*The 1st Armored force was a sizeable one, consisting of Headquarters, Combat Command A; B Company, 81st Reconnaissance Battalion; 1st Battalion, 6th Armored Infantry Regiment; 1st and 3rd Battalions (one company) of the 1st Armored Infantry Regiment; a company from the 16th Armored Engineer Battalion; 91st Armored Field Artillery Battalion; an anti-aircraft battalion; and a platoon of Military Police to guard any prisoners (George F. Howe, *The Battle History of the 1st Armored Division* [Washington DC: Combat Forces Press, 1954], pp. 283–284).

planned to punch through the Germans' thin defensive positions along the railroad line that connected Campoleone Station and Cisterna. The 1st Armored was directed to stay off the highway, which was in the British zone, and operate in the muddy, ravine-laced "wadi" terrain west of the Via Anziate—a tremendous tactical blunder.[57]

Worse, the attack was compromised when three company commanders from the 24th Guards Brigade, with the plans for the assault on them, took a wrong turn and were ambushed by the Germans. The attack was postponed for twenty-four hours, but the objectives were not altered.[58] When the Allied assault finally began on 29 January, it ran headlong into the Germans. The British phase of the attack, spearheaded by the Scots Guards and Irish Guards, started out promisingly but fell back when hit by German tanks and self-propelled guns. The British then tried attacking up the Via Anziate with the Canadians' 46th Battalion, Royal Tank Regiment, only to have it, too, checked by fierce enemy resistance. Moreover, the 1st Armored's wide flanking attack to the west in support of the British quickly ran into trouble as the Shermans got bogged down in the gullies and soggy ground off the roads and were systematically picked off by German artillery, mortars, and anti-tank weapons; thick, low clouds kept the force from receiving promised air support.[59]

On the VI Corps's right flank, the 3rd Division's 30 January attack against Cisterna also ran into serious problems. Truscott wanted Darby's Rangers to infiltrate into the town by way of the Pantano Ditch to pave the way for his larger division force. But, just northeast of a group of farm buildings known as Isola Bella ("Beautiful Island"), the Rangers walked into a devastating ambush. Darby's lightly armed men fought valiantly but were no match for the panzers that rumbled through their ranks, crushing some men into the mud and literally tearing others to pieces at point-blank range with their main guns. The carnage and courage were stupendous. The few survivors, out of ammunition and facing annihilation, gave themselves up. Of the 767 Rangers who took part in the abortive operation, only six made it back to friendly lines. At his CP, Darby wept.[60] Forty-three men from the 3rd Recon (Reconnaissance) Troop, following behind the Rangers, were also trapped. Only one made it back.[61]

The 3rd Division managed to eke out a small gain but was still two miles from its objective. Stronger-than-expected German resistance had taken its toll on Truscott's troops. The 3rd consolidated its positions and prepared to renew the offensive against Cisterna on the thirty-first. Aided by a heavy aerial bombardment, the 3rd, along with the 4th Ranger Battalion, attempted again to storm the strong German positions, manned by the Hermann Göring Panzer and 26th Panzer Divisions. A sizeable tank duel broke out, and artillery from both sides saturated the area. The brutal battle lasted for another two days with neither side asking for or giving quarter.

The 3rd had closed to within 1,500 yards of Cisterna but in its depleted state in the face of mounting German reinforcements could go no further. Realizing his troops were near exhaustion, Truscott called off the assault, straightened his lines, and told his men to dig in and await the expected counterattack.[62] It was not an auspicious beginning to the Allies' attempt to break the stalemate in Italy.

In London, Churchill fumed over the lack of offensive success. In a message to one of his field marshals a few weeks later, the Prime Minister expressed his concerns, saying that Lucas at Salerno had

> distinguished himself in command of a corps [but at Anzio] seems to have had the idea in his mind that at all costs he must be prepared for a counter-attack. As a result, although directly I learnt the landing was successful, I sent Alexander injunctions that he should peg out claims rather than consolidate bridgeheads, the whole operation became stagnant. . . . Naturally I am very disappointed at what has appeared to be the frittering away of a brilliant opening in which both fortune and design had played their part.

The one bright spot, Churchill further reflected, was that the Anzio operation had caused Hitler to transfer eight additional divisions to the south of Rome, far from the planned Overlord invasion area in northern France.[63]

The Allies had suffered 6,487 casualties since hitting the Anzio shores just eleven days earlier. In spite of the casualty figures, luck played a role in the VI Corps operations; Clark's abortive 29 January–1 February offensive had disrupted von Mackensen's plans for a 30 January offensive of his own. Had the Allies not attacked when they did, there was a very real possibility that the German thrust would have driven a wedge between the units on the beach and chopped up the invaders.[64]

It quickly became obvious that the Allies lacked the strength to break through the German defenses and would need to wait until more reinforcements arrived. With the British 1st Division holding its positions on the front, the 1st Armored retired to the Padiglione Woods to dig its vehicles into the spongy soil and await further orders.[65] Alexander paid Lucas's headquarters a visit on 1 February. In his diary, Lucas noted, "He was kind enough, but I am afraid is not pleased. My head will probably fall in the basket, but I have done my best." Lucas, if nothing else, was very perceptive.[66]

• • •

With the 157th and 179th Regiments ashore, the naval shuttle service returned south to pick up the 180th. First Lieutenant Bill Whitman, commanding B Company, 180th, recalled that on 29 January his outfit was trucked to Pozzuoli, where they boarded an LCI just large enough to hold the 200 men in his company. The craft, along with scores more, pulled away from the docks that morning and headed northward.[67]

The 180th Regiment set foot in Anzio around noon on the thirtieth and by 2000 hours that night the entire regiment was in place near Nettuno. Rumors of an expected German paratroop landing were rife, and much of the 45th was on alert for *Fallschirmjägern* dropping from the sky. The rumors proved to be unfounded.[68]

On the thirty-first, the British, with the help of American armor, managed to push as far inland as Campoleone Station before being stopped. It would be the farthest Allied advance toward Rome for the next four months.[69]

The entire 45th Division was now on the beachhead but scattered in defensive positions, with the 157th Regiment initially on the left; the 180th in the center, south of Aprilia; and the 179th on the right. Company C of the 120th Engineers held positions to the rear of the 504th Parachute Regiment near Campo Morto. To the 45th's right was the 3rd Division. For the most part, the 45th had been spared the hard fighting that had produced long casualty lists for Penney's, Truscott's, and Harmon's divisions. But the Thunderbirds' respite from hell would not last much longer.[70]

As the men of the 45th reached their assigned positions, they automatically began the common activity of all infantrymen who move to a new location: digging in. Instead of being able to dig deep, safe holes, however, the men quickly struck water. "We had to bail 'em out with our helmets," recalled Tarzan Williams. Water-filled foxholes would plague everyone in Anzio for the next several months. It was just one of many nasty conditions the invaders would be forced to endure. The worst, of course, was the unceasing artillery fire.[71] John P. Griffin, a jeep driver with Headquarters, 3rd Battalion, 157th, had his jeep become a casualty at Anzio. "The first night at Anzio, I lost my jeep. We found a hole where there had been a German squad tent and about eight of us went in the hole to get some sleep. I had parked my jeep next to the hole, woke up next morning and my buddy said, 'Have you looked at your jeep yet?' I said no. He said, 'Well, you don't want to.' A shell had come in during the night and just made a sieve out of it. It was a total wreck. The guys from Division Ordnance came in and hauled it away."[72]

Being at the end of a long supply chain often meant deprivations for the frontline troops. Chester Powell, M Company, 180th, said, "The living conditions were terrible, and we grew hard-hearted. The Army sent some warm clothes to Anzio—parkas and coveralls—but the people in the rear echelon got most of it. I was a little bitter about that. We had combat shoes and leggings and a few had combat boots. I had a pair of overshoes, but not everybody had them. We lost a lot of men from trench foot. We had very little to eat—K rations and C rations and sometimes not anything. Anzio. . . . I still wake up dreaming about it."[73]

Morty Carr, HQ Company, 1st Battalion, 157th, vividly remembered details of life at the front:

> Some of us got shoe-pacs [a waterproof combination rubber-leather boot that was arguably the Army's best footwear for cold, wet climates] with an extra pair of innersoles. We'd put the extra pair of innersoles under our belts to dry 'em out. The next morning we'd insert 'em into the shoe-pacs and take out the old ones to dry 'em out. On the front lines, we'd get K rations. Three fellows would get boxes marked breakfast, supper, and dinner. They'd open up one of each and mix it all together and share it to change the taste. We all had Coleman stoves and we'd put the rations in our mess kits and warm it up on the stoves. If we were lucky, we'd find some potatoes and get some grease from rear echelon and we'd make French-fried potatoes. We also had what were called five-in-one rations. There were bacon and eggs and a fig bar for fiber and George Washington instant coffee in a tin. There were four or five cigarettes—Chelseas, Wings, and some other brands you never heard of. We had olive-drab toilet tissue. We also had some square-shaped lemon tablets that you could make juice out of.

Carr shared his foxhole with the unit mail clerk and a couple of other soldiers. "I probably shouldn't tell you this," he said, "but when one of the guys in the outfit was hit and was taken to the hospital, the mail clerk would open any package that might come for the wounded man, and if it was food, we'd have a snack that night. We didn't want it to go to waste."[74]

Italy, that February, was a far cry from the sun-splashed scenes of the tourist postcards. Cold, wet weather plagued everyone on the beachhead. The rain fell in unrelenting sheets, and men who thought they couldn't get any wetter, colder, or more miserable, did. Dry socks were always a prized commodity in the water-logged foxholes at Anzio. The problem was the socks only stayed dry for a few seconds. Ernie Pyle observed, "The boys learned to change socks very quickly, and get their shoes back on, because once feet were freed of shoes, they swelled up so much in five minutes a man couldn't get his shoes on."[75]

Ralph Fink recalled that the GI's wool shirt, pants, and overcoat "soaked up water like a sponge. We struggled along in our leather shoes through most of the winter of 1943–44 by putting dubbin [a water-proofing compound] on them."[76]

Bud McMillan, K Company, 157th, also recalled the soggy living conditions at the front: "We lived in slit trenches and we put tops on them, but when you're firing a lot, you've got to get out of those things. We had holes to hide in and we had holes we got in to do our shooting—slit trenches, mostly. You couldn't dig down too deep, because of the water. We had a lot of rain, so we put tops on 'em. Some of the tops were three or four feet high, especially when we were in company reserve, maybe just a few hundred yards behind the front. It wasn't too conducive to good living."[77]

Ray Williams, HQ Company, 179th Regiment, didn't mind the water. "Anzio was a little better than the rest of Italy," he said, "because at least you could dig a foxhole, even if it was wet and shallow. At Anzio, if you wanted to live, you stayed in your hole during the day. The Germans had a bird's-eye view of us."[78]

For several days, the Thunderbirds busied themselves with the housekeeping duties of war: improving defensive positions, laying mines and communication wire, establishing fields of fire, plotting artillery concentrations, and stringing barbed wire. The 45th's engineers, the 120th Engineer Combat Battalion, commanded by Colonel Louis G. Franze, also tried to improve the roads and unpaved trails, which owing to the heavy rains and the heavy volume of military vehicle traffic were nothing more than quagmires.[79] The mud of Italy was especially nasty. The *Forty-fifth Division News* cartoonist Bill Mauldin described the viscous mess: "Mud . . . is a curse which seems to save itself for war. I'm sure Europe never got this muddy during peacetime. I'm equally sure that no mud in the world is so deep and sticky or wet as European mud."[80]

"The roads were a muddy mess, and trucks, tanks, and tractors were stuck everywhere," recalled Tarzan Williams. "Once, when we were in reserve, they took the company out and we cut down trees to repair the mud holes so the trucks wouldn't get stuck. Later, they got wooden planks to build roads for the trucks to run on."[81]

Typical of American battlefield humor was a sign posted by the Engineers: "Pontine Marshes Development Co., Inc. Lots and Trees For Sale."[82]

None of this activity occurred during periods of peaceful bliss. The Germans were fond of interrupting the 45th's labors, as well as shipping in the harbor, with frequent artillery barrages and nightly aerial raids by the *Luftwaffe*. Mel Craven, of A Battery, 158th Field Artillery, remembered his first encounter with an enemy barrage:

> We were on top of our six-by-six trucks that pulled the howitzers and were right next to a canal that was wider than I could have broad-jumped with a running start. I looked up just in time for a concussion to peel my helmet off. Somebody said, "Let's get the hell out of here." Somebody else said, "But there's water down there." Somebody else said, "What the hell do you care? Get down here!" I went off the side of the truck and took off running. I evidently jumped off the truck and over the canal. To this day, I have no idea how I did that. Anyway, we were next to a vineyard and there were these wires strung between stakes to train the vines. I hit the first wire and got knocked on my tail. I crawled underneath that first bank of wires and got up and started running again, and it was just *ping, ping, ping*—those wires would not stop me. As I was running through this vineyard, somebody went past me on his hands and knees; he was crawling faster than I was running. That was my baptism into combat.[83]

Over in the 179th Regiment's sector near the Mussolini Canal, the medic George Ecker recalled that his unit had occupied a farmhouse. "We had a lieutenant who was in charge of our outpost who had recently come in from the Pacific. We were attacked early one morning by a German reconnaissance group. They threw a 'potato masher' grenade in the front door but never attempted to enter the house. In fact, they took off. But this lieutenant must have thought we were about to get captured, so he jumped out the window and left. He went back to headquarters and told them we got captured. Obviously, we weren't."[84]

Things were beginning to heat up for the Thunderbirds. As darkness fell on 2 February, a sixty-man German patrol was sent to probe the positions held by A Company, 157th Regiment, on the beachhead's left flank. The enemy stumbled into A Company's lines and was slaughtered at close range. It was obvious that the Germans were getting ready for something big.[85]

That same day, the Allies reluctantly decided that farther advance was impossible for the time being and that it would be necessary for VI Corps to go on the defensive. The 45th's trial by fire was about to begin.[86]

6

The Stream of Blood

2–15 February 1944

But fix your eyes below, upon the valley, for now we near the stream of blood, where those who injure others violently boil.
—Dante Alighieri, *The Inferno*, Canto XXII

THE DAY AFTER THE ALLIES called a halt to their attempts to break out of the beachhead and went on the defensive, the Germans made preparations to launch a massive counterattack designed to split the beachhead forces. On 2 February, behind a heavy artillery barrage, von Mackensen's troops moved toward Aprilia. The Allies countered with a barrage of their own and added an air bombardment, which destroyed the German artillery communication net and fire-direction charts. Because of this disruption, the main thrust of the German attack, now without effective artillery support, was postponed for twenty-four hours. Von Mackensen had another worry. It appeared that the Allies might be preparing another amphibious invasion in the vicinity of Civitavecchia, some sixty miles up the coast from Anzio. In its Operations Report of 2 February, German intelligence noted, "An enemy air reconnaissance unit, which always has only been encountered where invasions occurred, has made its appearance there."

With the situation around Anzio more or less stabilized, Kesselring directed some Fourteenth Army troops be diverted to Civitavecchia to keep an eye out for any possible Allied landing. The situation around Cassino, meanwhile, was not quite as stable, and Kesselring reorganized some of his forces to make the transfer of a machine gun battalion and an artillery company to the southern front possible.

But like a thorn in his foot, it was still Anzio that held Kesselring's attention. He directed the staff of LXXVI Panzer Corps, which had been with von Vietinghoff's Tenth Army, be transferred to Fourteenth Army to assume command of the sector that had been the responsibility of I

Fallschirm Corps. The staff, while directing the defense to prevent an Allied breakthrough, was also charged with making "preparations for the decisive attack, which will annihilate the beachhead." Combat Group "Gräser" (consisting of the 3rd Panzer Grenadier Division and 715th Infantry Division), Combat Group "Raapke" (the reinforced 71st Division), and Combat Group "Konrad" (the reinforced Hermann Göring Panzer and 26th Panzer Divisions) were placed under LXXVI Panzer Corps headquarters' control. In addition, I *Fallschirm* Corps, commanding the 4th *Fallschirmjäger* Division and the 65th Infantry Division, was given the responsibility of defending the coastline from Aprilia to the mouth of the Tiber. Three battalions of Italian parachute troops would also reinforce Axis lines in the Moletta River sector.[1]

On the evening of 2 February, after touring the front lines west of Cisterna, von Mackensen met with Kesselring to give him his impression of the situation: "In the battle to enlarge the beachhead, the enemy has suffered heavy losses in men and tanks, which was confirmed by prisoners. However, neither his will to attack nor his endurance to resist has been broken. The enemy strength is based in his accurate and strong artillery, which is abundantly supplied with ammunition, and on the supporting naval artillery, as well as his superior air force. The mental and physical strain is great on our fresh troops." Von Mackensen reported that the Hermann Göring Panzer Division and the 71st Infantry Division had been particularly hard hit by Allied artillery during their maneuver and that the artillery bombardments "demoralize many young soldiers and the older men often lose their courage." Von Mackensen concluded his report by promising attacks with limited objectives: "When the enemy is weakened by these attacks, an all-out counteroffensive will be launched."[2]

Kesselring was skeptical. Despite (or, perhaps, because of) von Mackensen's Prussian ancestry (his father, August, had commanded XVII Corps in World War I)[3] and his recent experience leading a panzer corps on the eastern front, Kesselring did not hold von Mackensen in high regard. Furthermore, von Mackensen had only been in the Anzio area since 25 January, and Kesselring thought him too pessimistic and cautious for an operation he knew would require spirit, imagination, and audacity. For his part, von Mackensen viewed Kesselring as an incurable optimist, with no firm idea of the enormity of the task he was assigning to the exhausted troops of the Fourteenth Army. So poorly did the two commanders get along that von Mackensen twice submitted requests for transfer; Kesselring twice turned him down flat.

In spite of their differences, the two men did agree that a massive German counteroffensive to dislodge the Allies from the beachhead was essential. Although their 29 January counterattack had been stillborn, the two officers devised a new offensive designed to regain control of the beachhead.[4] In Germany, Hitler saw the Allies' invasion, and its subsequent inertia, as offering a unique opportunity to end the string of recent defeats of his forces. He sent the following message to Kesselring, which was read to the troops:

> Within the next few days, the "Battle for Rome" will commence. . . . This battle has a special significance because the landing at Nettuno marks the beginning of the invasion of Europe planned for 1944. Strong German forces are to be tied down in areas as far as possible from the bases in Britain where the majority of the invasion troops are still stationed. The object of the Allies is to gain experience for future operations.
>
> Every soldier must therefore be aware of the importance of the battle which the 14th Army must fight. It must be fought with bitter hatred against an enemy who wages a ruthless war of annihilation against the German people and who, without any higher ethical aims, strives for the destruction of Germany and European culture.

With their Führer's edict firmly in mind, Kesselring, von Mackensen, and their key generals and staff officers began planning to lance what Hitler called "the abscess south of Rome." The next German counterattack was scheduled for the night of 3–4 February.[5]

Using the rainy night of 3–4 February as cover, the two divisions of Combat Group Gräser struck against the exposed flanks of the British line—a salient that has been referred to as a "thumb"—to regain the lost ground around Aprilia, smashing into the British at several points: at the Duke of Wellington Regiment and King's Shropshire Light Infantry dug in south of Campoleone Station; at the Irish Guards north of the Vallelata Ridge; at the 6th Gordons around Smelly Farm; and at the Grenadier Guards holding the Embankment south of Campoleone Station. The British tried bringing up a relief column, supported by British tanks, but it was repulsed. In a cold rain, the battles continued without letup throughout the day and night of the fourth.[6] At the end of the day, the Germans totaled their successes: twelve British tanks destroyed, four aircraft shot down, and some 900 men captured in a pocket north of Aprilia.[7]

At midnight on the fourth, the Germans launched another attack against Aprilia, now occupied by the 168th Brigade of British Major General Gerald W.R. Templer's already-weary 56th ("London") Division, which had just arrived a few hours earlier from the Cassino front. The British gave as good as they got for several days, but it was clear they could not maintain their position for long.[8] The Factory was caught in a strong German vise, with powerful forces converging on the shattered village from both east and west. While the infantry, tanks, and self-propelled 88mm assault guns (called "Hornets" by the Germans) closed in from the sides, artillery, rocket, and mortar fire pasted the 168th Brigade from above.[9]

The British journalist Wynford Vaughn-Thomas has referred to the British as "specialists in triumphant retreats," and they certainly needed every bit of that skill as they pulled back from the dangerous salient that their drive to Campoleone had created.[10] On the night of 4–5 February, von Mackensen ordered a feint against the U.S. 3rd Infantry Division south of Cisterna. Thinking an all-out assault was under way, the 3rd fell back a mile and a half, learned it was all a ruse, then gradually retook its old positions.[11] Although a shortage of ammunition was becoming a problem due to Allied air forces interdicting their supply lines, the Germans estimated they had superiority in artillery, with more than ninety-four batteries—372 guns—around Anzio, as opposed to fifty-nine batteries (not counting naval guns and self-propelled artillery pieces on the Allied side).[12]

Except for artillery and air attacks, 5 February was relatively quiet. On the sixth, the *Luftwaffe* flew over the 157th's positions and dropped antipersonnel "butterfly" bombs,* prompting a renewed flurry of construction activity among the hole-bound Thunderbirds. In short order, the foxholes were covered with stout timbers, heavy logs, cardboard from ration boxes, and thick layers of dirt.[13] On 6 February, additional reinforcements poured into the German lines, and OKW ordered that the 92nd Infantry Division, being activated in the Civitavecchia area, be ready for action by 15 April. In addition, von Mackensen directed that a new assault to capture Aprilia would take place during the night of 7–8 February, with diversionary attacks to take place all along the front. *Generalleutnant* Helmuth Pfeiffer's 65th Infantry Division was to attack Carroceto and the Factory from the west while the main attacking force, made up of elements under the control of LXXVI Panzer Corps, and supported by *Generalmajor* Wilhelm Raapke's 71st Infantry Division, would hit the two towns simultaneously from the east. The *Luftwaffe* was charged with keeping the skies clear of Allied aircraft.[14]

For two days, tension built all along the Allied front. Patrol activity on both sides increased, and the expectations of a major German attack loomed large. The only questions were where and when. The answers would be provided very quickly. The enemy's assault began on schedule at 2100 hours on

---

*The container holding the "butterfly" bombs was as tall as a man, hollow, and contained 6 to 108 explosive devices that were twice the size of the American hand grenade and four times as heavy. When released from an aircraft, the container opened, scattering the smaller bombs, which had small "wings" to slow their descent, over a wide area. Many would explode in the air, above entrenched soldiers. From a distance, the sound of the detonations reminded some soldiers of popcorn. The German pilot and his plane were soon dubbed "Popcorn Pete" (John Bowditch III, ed., *Anzio Beachhead*, vol. 14 in the "American Forces in Action" series [Washington, DC: Department of the Army Historical Division, 1947], p. 53; and Warren P. Munsell, Jr., *The Story of a Regiment: A History of the 179th Regimental Combat Team* [privately published, 1946], p. 60).

the seventh and spread like a wind-whipped prairie fire all along the line around Carroceto and Aprilia. Heavy artillery saturated the British 1st Division positions, and then the 2nd Battalion, North Staffordshire Regiment, on the right flank of the 157th's 3rd Battalion, was hit hard by tanks and infantry. Next, the 24th Guards Brigade felt the weight of the enemy's heavy attack. Pfeiffer's division, using the cover of darkness and the deep ravines west of Carroceto, managed to infiltrate deeply into British positions.

At the same time the Germans launched their assault against the British, the 157th's 3rd Battalion's positions near Buon Riposo Ridge were suddenly jolted by a heavy artillery and mortar barrage, followed by a large, combined attack of German tanks and two battalions of infantry directed at the seam between L Company on the 157th's right flank and the British North Staffordshire Regiment to its right.[15] Allied artillery added its voice to the fray and, for over two hours, American and British troops battled the Germans by the light of exploding munitions, parachute flares, and a cold moon. The 3rd Battalion's commander, Major John Boyd, was killed during the bloody engagement. Captain Merle Mitchell, the battalion executive officer, took command and shifted the companies to meet the expected renewed assaults. A raiding party from K Company captured a German machine gun crew that had infiltrated inside L Company's lines and was cutting down unsuspecting Thunderbirds. Positions were lost, won, then lost again.[16]

One of the Yanks in the 157th's 3rd Battalion, Sergeant Glen Hanson, of L Company, recalled, "We were right in front of a dairy. The dairy farm had a reinforced battalion of Germans headquartered there and, on the night of the seventh and eighth of February, they tried to split our front with tanks and artillery."[17] At 0300 hours on the eighth, the Germans thrust deeply into the 2nd North Staffs' positions, turned west, and hit the 157th's 3rd Battalion with tank and small-arms fire from the right rear. Now down to less than seventy men and out of ammunition, the North Staffs requested permission to attach themselves to Hanson's L Company. But the 3rd was in no better shape. To save the battalion, Captain Mitchell withdrew L Company to a stream south of Buon Riposo Ridge and bent the battalion's right flank to the southeast to better counter the German threat. Somehow, when the 3rd Battalion pulled back, the British soldiers who had attached themselves to L Company failed to follow and were taken prisoner. Before long, the ridge was in the hands of the German 65th Division.[18]

One of the Thunderbirds remembered that another British unit moved up during the battle. "We were having a real sharp firefight," said Jack McMillion, a platoon sergeant with L Company, 157th.

> The night of the attack, the terrain was better so we could bring tanks around on the Germans. We had kind of a gully the Germans couldn't come through. During the night, the Irish Guards came stumbling through. Our officers told

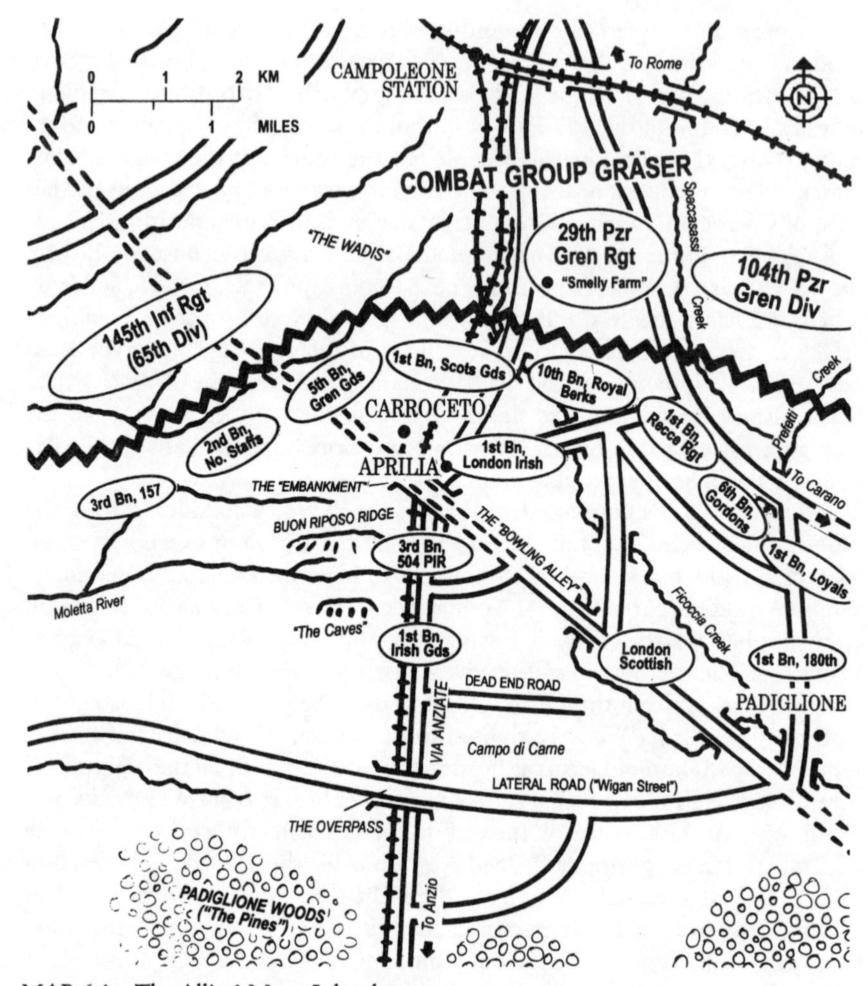

MAP 6.1 The Allies' Move Inland
7–9 February 1944—The British 1st Division moved northward, above Carroceto and Aprilia (also known as "The Factory"), but all was in vain, as German resistance stiffened and the British were pushed back. The drive inland would be the farthest Allied advance for the next four months. (Positions approximate)

them we were being surrounded by Germans and that maybe the Brits should stay there with us. But the British C.O. said the orders were to move from this point to that point, and so they moved out. We don't know how they fared, but everything was so dark and confused, they probably made it.[19]

Don Amzibel, another member of L Company, 157th, recalled the battle very clearly:

Aerial view of the ruins of Aprilia. This view looks north, with the Alban Hills in the distance. (Courtesy of the 45th Infantry Division Archives)

> The British were right next to my foxhole. They ran out of ammunition and had to make three or four bayonet attacks. A British soldier I got acquainted with got killed that day. We got knocked out of there, too. They brought up some tanks. Before you knew it, the Germans were right down in our area and we had to pull out. Tanks and infantry—we were running alongside of them and they didn't even notice us. They must have been on dope, that's all I can say. Before we knew it, they were right in our CP. They even stole all our mail! Jack McMillion was our platoon leader and we just played follow the leader. It was dark, but he got us back to some higher ground.[20]

By dawn on the eighth, I Company, 157th, had counterattacked and regained its former position, although the Germans were still in possession of the ground once held by L Company and the North Staffs.[21]

The intensity of the artillery employed during the one-night battle was astounding. In the battle for Fort Vaux at Verdun in 1916, it was considered remarkable that 1,500 to 2,000 German shells per hour fell on the French fortress.[22] Yet, during the 157th's fight on 7–8 February, over 24,000 rounds were fired by the 157th's supporting gun batteries—a tremendous amount, especially given the relatively brief duration of the battle. The 3rd Battalion alone used up an entire three days' worth of machine gun ammunition, along with over 9,200 60mm and 81mm mortar rounds. Following this brief-but-bloody battle, the 45th's positions went ominously quiet for two days while the Germans shifted their attention to other Allied units.[23] Under cover of darkness late on 8 February, von Mackensen again threw his legions into the effort to regain Aprilia. Heavy artillery rained down on the British 1st Division, and the German 65th Infantry Division drove the 5th Grenadier Guards back to the railroad station and Embankment in Carroceto.[24]

To the right of the 157th, Combat Group Gräser was rolling like a gigantic killing machine, slowly chewing up the forward companies of the 1st Battalion Recce (Reconnaissance) Regiment, 10th Royal Berkshires, and 1st London Irish. Again, by infiltrating behind British lines, the Germans caused panic and inflicted casualties on units that suddenly found themselves surrounded. But the deeper the Germans penetrated into British-held territory, the harder it became for them to sustain their momentum. A small German force made it all the way to the Factory, only to be cut to pieces by a band of determined defenders, including some American tank destroyers.* The few Germans who survived were taken prisoner.

To the east of Aprilia, however, other elements of Combat Group Gräser battled the British 168th Brigade before both sides dug in and hammered away at each other for hours at near point-blank range. General Penney, the British 1st Division commander, moved his reserves into these two critical areas to forestall any German breakthrough. On the right, the 6th Gordons were moved up to fill the gap between the 1st Loyals and 10th Royal Berks. Taking the Gordons' place in reserve near Padiglione was the 1st Battalion, 180th.[25]

Despite the pounding they had received, the Germans now renewed their efforts to drive the British away from Carroceto and Aprilia. During the night, the German attack consisted of small units infiltrating into British positions. Dawn on the ninth brought no better news. The 24th Guards Brigade and 504th PIR, along with the 1st Scots Guards, all of which were dug in north of Carroceto, came under heavy attack. Two companies of the 1st Scots were surrounded and the rest of the battalion was forced to pull back. Combat Group Gräser also renewed its assault on the 168th Brigade to the east of Aprilia with a four-regiment attack. The 29th Panzer Grenadier Regiment split the seam between the 1st London Irish and 10th Royal Berks and knifed 2,000 yards to the south.[26]

Penney messaged Lucas that his 1st Division was at less than half strength and could no longer hold its portion of the front. The British were being systematically wiped out.[27] But no matter how desperately Penney appealed, Lucas did not seem to grasp the urgency of the 1st Division's situation and continued to reject Penney's requests to throw the Corps reserve—the 45th

---

*The M-10 tank destroyer was a modified Sherman tank with an open, less heavily armored turret, a high-velocity 3-inch gun, and a crew of five.

Division—into the battle. All he would offer was the support of the 180th and a few of Harmon's tanks, which was not nearly enough.[28]

That morning, the German 735th Infantry Regiment battled its way into Aprilia and kicked out the few remaining British defenders. By afternoon, both the Factory and Lateral Road were back in German hands.[29] Penney then tried to regain his division's lost positions on Buon Riposo Ridge, but the attack was stymied. In the end, the valiant British merely added to their growing casualty list.[30]

The battle continued into the next day. The 1st Armored Division now rejoined the fight, attempting to take Buon Riposo Ridge from the west, but the mud again quickly bogged down the Shermans. Harmon then shifted his objective to the Factory, but here, too, the American tankers became easy prey to German mines, 88s, and anti-tank guns. Immobilized, seven tanks were picked off by German gunners, and the rest were forced to withdraw. All day on the tenth, battles raged around Buon Riposo Ridge, Carroceto, and the Factory, but the Allies could gain no headway.[31] From above, Allied bombers disrupted von Mackensen's plans to bring fresh troops into the fight, blanketing the area with high explosives. As smoke and darkness enveloped the battlefield, it became obvious that another hard day of fighting had been endured by both sides, but that the Germans had gained the upper hand.[32]

On 10 February, Churchill, still trying to light a fire under the operation, sent a cable to Alexander, which read in part, "I have a feeling that you may have hesitated to assert your authority because you were dealing so largely with Americans and therefore *urged* an advance instead of *ordering* it. You are however quite entitled to give them orders, and I have it from the highest American authorities that it is their wish that their troops should receive direct orders. . . . The Americans are very good to work with, and quite prepared to take the rough with the smooth."[33] Things, however, were not going smoothly at Lucas's headquarters. After a long, acrimonious meeting on the morning of the tenth, attended by Lucas, Penney, some of his officers, and Major General William W. Eagles, the 45th's commander, a plan was worked out: The 1st Battalion of the 179th, along with two companies of the 191st Tank Battalion, would relieve the British and strike at the enemy around Carroceto and Aprilia. H hour for the attack would be at dawn on the eleventh. "Old Luke" then turned to Eagles, said, "Okay, Bill, you give 'em the works," and abruptly left the meeting.[34]

The 45th, scattered about the beachhead, was finally being reformed into a cohesive unit. The reorganization also called for the division's 180th Regiment to take over for the battered British 2nd Brigade north of Padiglione. The 157th, which had already seen considerable fighting on the left shoulder of the beachhead, was relieved south of Buon Riposo Ridge by the 36th Engineer Combat Regiment and assigned to Corps reserve, then moved astride the Via Anziate.[35] The 180th was shifted to the right, and the 179th was placed between the 157th and the 180th.[36]

Eddie Speairs, now a captain in command of C Company, 157th, recalled that he was directed to make a one-company assault against German-held Aprilia: "I don't know who canceled it, but they did. I probably wouldn't be here today if we had made the attack."[37] Instead, the task of assaulting Aprilia fell to Lieutenant Colonel Wayne L. Johnson's 1st Battalion, 179th, and Major Merlin Tryon's 3rd Battalion, 179th, supported by two companies of the 191st Tank Battalion. Unfortunately for the Yanks, the Germans had intercepted a radio message and knew the Americans were coming. The results were predictable.[38]

The attack on 10–11 February was presaged with a heavy artillery saturation and aerial bombardment by hundreds of Corsica-based bombers. The ground shook beneath the GIs' feet as though the earth were being throttled by an enraged giant. Chester Powell, M Company, 180th, recalled that the sky that morning was filled with Allied aircraft. "There were more airplanes than I ever saw in my life. Flying Fortresses, B-24s, and a little of everything else was up there. A lot of 'em got shot down. There were bodies coming out with 'chutes and without 'chutes and planes disintegrating over us."[39]

Robert Rogers, a member of the 180th's Service Company, also remembered the battle in the skies: "The B-17 and British Lancaster bombers always came in the daytime, made their turns in groups of six planes, and dropped their bombs along the side of the Alban Hills. We could see the German ack-ack explode and occasionally a plane got hit and crashed. One day, a B-17 got hit, the autopilot was set, and the men in the plane started bailing out one by one. A nineteen-year-old came down in our company area and he was naturally thrilled not to have gotten killed."[40]

At 0630 hours on the eleventh, Johnson's 1st Battalion left its line of departure and moved against Aprilia, but without the promised armored support; the tanks failed to arrive on time. By 1000 hours, the infantrymen had battled their way to the road south of Aprilia but soon expended their ammunition. They fell back, replenished their load, and returned to the road. As A and B Companies approached the Factory across the barren terrain, murderous fire from every building and foxhole in the area hit them, but the men of B Company managed to fight their way into a few buildings at the southeast corner of the village.[41] One of those there was George Ecker, a medic with the 179th. "When it appeared that we might be driven back into the sea, our men fixed bayonets and charged the enemy," he said.[42]

Even the sight of cold steel had little effect on the Germans, for then came the sound that foot soldiers have learned to fear—the sound of tanks. From their hiding places in Carroceto rumbled the panzers, followed by deep ranks of gray-coated infantry. The Thunderbirds, hopelessly outnumbered and outgunned, had no choice but to fall back.[43] Ray Williams, HQ

Company, 1st Battalion, 179th, recalled that the headquarters men were filling sandbags and passing them up to the upper floor of a building being used as an observation post just outside of the Factory. "The next morning at daylight, the German tanks attacked, and in three minutes' time they had that whole building knocked to the ground. The Germans just beat the holy hell out of us. We had to retreat or, as the Army calls it, we 'withdrew.' Our battalion moved back a thousand yards and there was less than a company left in the whole 1st Battalion. Less than 200 men. I was one of only three in our platoon who wasn't killed or wounded."[44]

All day long, Wayne Johnson's 1st Battalion struggled for its life, fighting off one German counterattack after another. By nightfall, all of A Company's officers were dead, wounded, or missing, and the enlisted ranks were reduced by 50 percent. The 191st Tank Battalion, which showed up two hours late, lost eight of its Shermans, and several others were badly damaged. During the night, German artillery fell in unceasing numbers on the stalled attackers.[45] Ray Williams also remembered,

> The largest tank battle we had was right out in front of us. Through binoculars, you could see them really mixing it up. Of course, when somebody missed, we got the receiving end of the shell. It was all part of the game. I remember there were some brick buildings out there, two or three stories high. Our tanks were mixing it up with the Germans and one of our tanks ran behind one of the buildings for protection and a German tank started shooting at the building, knocking off a layer at a time until there was no building for that tank of ours to hide behind. The Germans finally hit it. It was a hell of a show.[46]

At 0353 hours on the twelfth, what was left of Johnson's battalion, aided by I Company on its right flank and the tardy tanks, tried again to force an entry into the Factory. Once again they made it to the walls, and once again they were thrown back by panzers and infantry. Once again the 1st Battalion retreated to its line of departure—torn, bloody, and exhausted. The attempt to take Aprilia and Carroceto had to be temporarily abandoned.[47]

• • •

To Captain Clay Barnes, commanding the 157th's Anti-Tank Company, the fact that the Germans held the high ground beyond the beachhead robbed the Allies of any opportunity to maneuver during daylight hours. "During the day, we couldn't move because the Germans were up in the hills and had all the observation. We did everything at night and tried to get back in our holes before daylight in order to survive. There wasn't anything we did the Germans couldn't observe."[48]

Besides the enemy fire, the high water table at Anzio made living below ground a particularly unpleasant experience. Ralph Fink, D Company, 157th, said,

> We lived like a bunch of rats in the mud. We were near an irrigation ditch—there were a lot of them in this section of the beachhead. They were about four feet deep, eight feet wide at the top, and there was a stream at the bottom, not too deep. We got into these ditches and dug into the bank. During daylight hours, we could not get out of our foxholes. As soon as it got dark, everybody was waiting to get out. But you had to slouch to stay under the ground level in this ditch. If you straightened up, your head and shoulders would be above ground level and the Germans would see that and start popping away. That's where the term, the 'Anzio Slouch,' came from [a reference to the infantryman's acquired ability to walk without standing up].[49]

Tarzan Williams, K Company, 157th, recalled that the men would dig foxholes and "the water would run in off the sides of the foxholes. We had to dig a ditch inside the foxholes to catch the water and we had to bail the water out with our helmets. One man was sleeping in his foxhole and water was filling it up; if an artillery barrage hadn't come in and woke him up, he might have drowned."[50]

Vincent Mainente, a sergeant in the 179th, told Ernie Pyle about a unique way he had devised to stay dry in his foxhole. "The sergeant saved up empty wooden C-ration boxes, and one night he nailed them together and made a raft to float on top of the water in his foxhole. I gathered that it wasn't a hundred percent successful in keeping him dry, but at least there wasn't any harm in trying," Pyle wrote.[51]

Bill Rolen was an eighteen-year-old replacement who joined I Company, 180th Regiment, shortly after the initial landings, and Anzio made a lasting impression on the youngster: "I had just come out of basic training in Florida and it was unbelievable to go from a nice, quiet place in the States to that. Anzio was a terrible place where a lot of people died. All these guns going off and planes going over every night. They'd drop flares and it would be as bright as day and you felt the enemy was looking right at you."[52]

To protect themselves from enemy bombardments, the men of B Company, 157th, pulled a road over themselves. The company commander, Captain Kenneth P. Stemmons, recalled, "We dug from the ditch back underneath the pavement. We would get hits on top of the road and it would cave dirt in on us, but it was like we were in a concrete bunker. There had been a big wooden fence along the back side of that road; when we left, it was nothing but matchsticks."[53]

Medic "Doc Joe" Franklin, I Company, 157th, was knocked unconscious several times by the constant concussions of the artillery and temporarily deafened by the blasts on several other occasions. "I remember one time when a shell had exploded four or five yards from me. One of my corporals was yelling to me but I thought the poor guy had gone crazy. He was flapping his mouth but I couldn't hear anything. I thought something had happened to *him*. I didn't realize I was deaf. My ears rang like crazy for about a day."[54]

It was not only shot and shell that assaulted the men on the front lines; the rich assortment of odors was a constant assault on the olfactory nerves as well. There was the ever-present acrid smell of burned powder from exploding tank, artillery, and mortar rounds as well as from rifles and machine guns. There was the rancid odor of wet, manure-rich earth, torn up by munitions. There was the overpowering, choking smell of burning vehicles, sometimes intermingled with the sweet smell of burning flesh. There was the nauseating foulness of feces and urine-soaked mud in the bottom of the foxholes. Since the men could not clean themselves or change clothes, there was the constant stink of perspiration-drenched wool uniforms. And when the wind was wrong, there was the sickening stench of decaying flesh, both human and animal, that drifted in from no-man's land.

Captain Kenneth P. Stemmons in his defensive position dug under an Anzio roadway. After the battle, a fence behind the position had been reduced to toothpicks. (Courtesy of K. P. Stemmons)

• • •

Orders came down for the Thunderbirds to move forward. In the predawn darkness of 15 February, the wet, cold, and exhausted members of the 157th's 2nd Battalion climbed out of their soggy foxholes, strapped on their packs, shouldered their weapons, and trudged off into the night toward enemy lines.[55] Lieutenant Colonel Lawrence Brown, the 2nd Battalion commander, set up his CP in a feature known as "the caves," which the Irish Guards had occupied in early February.[56] The caves were an elaborate labyrinth of tunnels southwest of Carroceto and just south of Buon Riposo Ridge. ("Ridge" is a misnomer, implying a steep geographical feature. In reality, Buon Riposo is a slight swelling in the ground. To the men in and around the caves, however, it loomed as ominous as any mountain.) The caves, large enough for trucks to drive through, extended underground in all directions for hundreds of yards, making them either an ideal place to defend or a death trap. In addition to the battalion CP, the medical aid sec-

View of some of the remaining caves in 1996. (Author photo)

tion and artillery radio crew also set up shop in the caves; the infantry companies were arrayed in a line in front of the caves. Captain Felix Sparks's E Company, on the 2nd Battalion's right flank, straddled the Via Anziate and railroad track. Company G was on E's left flank, and F Company, in battalion reserve, backed up the gap between E and G. The men silently took over previously prepared positions, loaded their weapons, and looked into the blackness in front of them, wondering what might come.[57]

On the right side of the 45th's line, near Padiglione, Staff Sergeant Howard Thomas, an artillery forward observer with I Company, 180th Regiment, distinguished himself with an act of almost unbelievable bravery. On the night of 11 February, Thomas was on the receiving end of an intense German artillery barrage. A huge explosion ripped through I Company's ammunition dump, about fifty yards south of the house where he was located, and the bursting shells were silhouetting GIs and giving away I Company's position. Despite the grave danger to himself from enemy artillery and his company's own detonating ammunition, Thomas dashed into the ammo dump and pulled cases of mortar shells away from the rest of the burning and exploding munitions. When he encountered wooden cases of shells on fire, he buried them with handfuls of dirt and mud. For his act of courage, Thomas was awarded the Bronze Star.

The next night, Staff Sergeant John Gann, a Native American from Stilwell, Oklahoma, and also a member of I Company, took command of his platoon when the platoon leader was wounded and the platoon sergeant was stricken with illness. Directing the rifle and machine gun fire of his platoon and working with Sergeant Thomas to call in accurate artillery fire, Gann broke up a heavy German assault against I Company's positions.

One of the foot soldier's very least favorite tasks, yet one of the most vital if contact with the enemy was to be maintained and intelligence gathered from prisoners, was patrol activity behind enemy lines. Such patrols were mainly carried out at night by small bands of brave men, and the hazards were enormous. One such patrol occurred on the night of 13 February. A patrol from F Company, 180th Regiment, under the command of Staff Sergeant Herman Rhodes of Savanna, Oklahoma, set out to explore enemy positions northwest of Padiglione. The squad-sized patrol had only gone a few hundred yards when it was attacked by a company-sized German force. Initially holding its ground and fighting off the attack, the patrol realized it was in danger of being surrounded. The tiny group tried to withdraw, but the Nazi noose was being drawn tighter and tighter. It was then that Sergeant Rhodes began blasting the encircling enemy with his Thompson submachine gun. For thirty minutes, he held the Germans at bay while his men slipped out of the trap and headed back to friendly lines. A German machine gun crew spotted the escaping Americans and began spraying the area with lead. Private first class Edward Pagen crawled through the cold, wet mud and silenced the gun with a well-aimed toss of a grenade. During this action, Sergeant Bill Rush crawled across open ground to reach a wounded comrade, pulling him several hundred yards to safety. Tech Sergeant Claude Carpenter joined Rhodes to keep the escape gap open, and the patrol eventually made it back intact. Rhodes, Carpenter, Rush, and Pagen all received the Bronze Star for valor, and Rhodes later received a battlefield commission to second lieutenant.[58]

Often interspersed between acts of valor were acts of kindness. Don Amzibel, L Company, 157th, recalled the day when some GIs in his platoon talked two Germans into surrendering. "A couple of men in our platoon spoke very good German and they would talk to the Germans who were only fifty yards or so away. They were very dirty and hadn't eaten for days. My squad was in direct support of our frontline troops so I had to keep the German POWs in my foxhole until it got dark. I had a box of 'D' bars which I gave them. They ate most of them. After it got dark, the POWs were taken away and, for them, the war was over."[59]

At about this time, several of the Thunderbirds received incredible news—they were going home! One of the lucky ones was Sergeant Charlie Dunham, E Company, 157th, who had been with the unit since the late 1930s. "I had enough points, so I came home on rotation. The Army would rotate about one percent of the company every month, or something like that. I didn't bother to figure it out; I just came home. I went back with two of the lieutenants who were in the company, and also with a sergeant from the mortar section. I was back in Naples when I got word that my company had been pretty well wiped out."[60]

In the 180th Regiment's sector, enemy activity was increasing. On 14 February, E Company took the brunt of an assault by the Germans. Staff Sergeant James Boggs was one of a handful of men guarding the remnants of a blown bridge over one of the innumerable streams that ran through the area. The Germans closed in on Boggs and his men, threatening to surround and annihilate the group. Despite the 10 to 1 odds against him, Boggs refused an invitation to surrender, and his men picked off one German after another as the enemy crept closer. Some 300 yards away, Staff Sergeant Jeremiah Dunne learned of Boggs's predicament and took a detail of six men to attempt a relief of the outpost. Just as the Germans were closing in for the kill, Dunne and his men charged the Germans, catching them by surprise. Momentarily diverted from their attack on Boggs's position, the Germans directed their attention toward Dunne's small group, which skillfully withdrew. In the confusion, Boggs and his men were also able to make it safely back to I Company's lines, and both Boggs and Dunne later received Silver Stars for their courageous actions.[61]

Captain Joseph Bosa of the 171st FA Battalion wrote in his diary on 14 February:

> There have been several German fighters over today, one very low over our position. Our planes are not maintaining the constant watch they originally put over us. About 50% of the time the planes are Jerries. The greatest damage so far as the daylight raiders are concerned in this part of the bridgehead is that it stops our batteries from firing. Of course, in case of a counter-attack or anything of that nature they would have to continue. Our old AA [anti-aircraft] that was with us at Venafro is back with us again.[62]

The "old AA" units were soon to be very busy. Shortly after midnight on the fifteenth, the vastly outnumbered pilots of the *Luftwaffe* began two days of daring bombing and strafing raids against the beachhead.[63] That morning, the Germans unleashed eight air raids against the beachhead. Bill Rolen, I Company, 180th, remembered, "There was this German plane that came over. Everybody yelled 'hit the ground!' This plane dropped something—some sort of miniature gadget that just glided along. As it glided, it pitched out little bombs, a little bigger than hand grenades, every second or so. This gadget must have gone along for five hundred yards with these little bombs jumping out of it and exploding. I'm not sure if anybody got hurt. It was strange. I never saw anything like it again."[64] (Rolen apparently saw one of the "butterfly bombs" in action.)

Keeping the men on the front lines supplied with water, food, and ammunition was a task filled with great danger and difficulty. Ralph Fink, D Company, 157th, remembered,

> Our drivers in D Company were really good. Much of the time, they were in decent places getting hot meals. After dark, they had to come up and find us to deliver our rations. We were eating mostly K rations and carried several Hershey D ration chocolate bars in our packs. They had the nutrients of one meal. There were times when our drivers couldn't find us in the dark, with all the shelling going on. That's when we fell back on those chocolate bars. We also had a problem with water. Sometimes we had to fill our canteens from a stream. We'd drop in two halazone tablets to disinfect it, but it tasted like the dickens.[65]

Captain Minor Shirk, commanding Service Company, 157th, recalled, "We were attacked by German fighters on a daily basis. Our forward observers had these Piper Cub planes they used for observation; they were basically the eyes of the artillery. I've actually seen a Piper draw a Messerschmitt down and then flip aside and the fighter would go right into the ground. They were pretty good at that, those Piper Cub pilots."[66]

• • •

The morning of 15 February saw a general increase in German pressure all along the Thunderbirds' line. More and more German patrols attempted to infiltrate the American defenses, and the mortar and artillery shellings grew more frequent and intense. To make matters worse, large shells from railroad guns in the hills crashed into the beachhead with alarming regularity. The British and Americans answered back with their own artillery along with salvos from warships lying off the coast. It was clear that something big—very big—was about to happen. But, again, the questions were where and when.[67] One thing became obvious: When the major counterattack came, it would no doubt come down the Via Anziate, the straight-line shot from Carroceto and the Factory to Anzio. As the only north-south paved road, it was sure to be heavily used by the German panzers, as the ground off the roads was too soft and muddy. Straddling this road were the twelve 57mm anti-tank guns under the command of Captain Clay Barnes, the C.O. of the 157th's Anti-Tank Company. "Our 57mm guns were not too effective against those Tiger tanks," Barnes said, with understatement. "We hadn't gotten the better anti-tank guns at that time. After the battle for Anzio was over, I don't think we had a single gun left."[68]

Captain Shirk was never very impressed with the stopping power of the American anti-tank guns, especially against the thick armor of the panzers, but had the utmost respect for the Germans' 88mm dual-purpose gun:

> The most vicious gun the Germans had was that 88. We never had a thing that came close. We had those 37mm and 57mm "BB guns." The velocity of that 88 was terrific. I remember one time when the Germans were shooting 88s down the road and we pulled our trucks off the side of the road and dug them in. We'd dig the whole nose of the truck down so we could get the truck underground. The shells started coming in and one of my men said, "I've got to

get out of here." I said, "Grady, you stay in that hole or I'm going to hit you in the damn head with my helmet," and I would have, 'cause all you had to do was stand up and you'd have had it. While we were there, the British came up with a convoy of trucks. They stopped about where we were dug in, got out, walked in front of their trucks and built fires in order to make tea. Those British would fight like hell, but they just had to have their tea. About the time they built their fires, the Germans cut loose with their 88s and just raked that column. It was terrible.[69]

On 15 February, Captain Bosa made the following entries in his diary:

Today the skies have been full of vapor trails as German planes at high altitude approach our positions. About twenty-five have been over twice today. A group of five have dive-bombed north of Anzio at least three times. Some of them then just go on over, evidently from the southern area.

Over 60 of our bombers went over this morning headed north. Also our A36A's have been busy on the enemy's front lines. We have been firing considerably at long range targets using our reinforcing artillery.

Last night for the first time in several nights there was no attempt to break through in our sector. Night before last a heavy patrol got in several hundred yards. Our artillery assisted materially in getting them out. Our troops last night occupied the cemetery which we used as a base point. That represents a gain of about 1,000 yards in that part of the sector. They may not be able to stay but if they do it will give us a good outpost there.[70]

Since the landings three weeks earlier, the world had been watching the Anzio beachhead, but on 15 February that attention suddenly shifted to a point some seventy miles to the south at the entrance to the Liri Valley—to a Benedictine monastery built high atop a strategic hill known as Monte Cassino in A.D. 529. At 0930 hours that morning, 254 heavy and medium Allied bombers droned high above the ancient abbey and unleashed their deadly cargo. Nearly 600 tons of high explosives, followed by an intense artillery barrage, reduced the hallowed building to heaps of rubble. Many around the world were outraged, because the Allies had promised to respect this medieval monument. But the pronouncements of diplomats and generals were insufficient in the face of prolonged military stalemate. Unfounded rumors had convinced the Allies that the Germans were using the monastery as an observation post and they felt justified in destroying it in order to finally break into the Liri Valley. As it turned out, the Germans had *not* been using the monastery, but did have OPs around it. Once the building was destroyed, the rubble created excellent bunkers, and the Germans moved in. The New Zealand forces that had campaigned for the abbey's elimination still could not take the hill, and the entrance to the Liri Valley remained tightly sealed.[71] The controversy swirling around the destruction of the abbey was of little concern to the men on the Anzio beachhead; they were too busy trying to stay alive to worry about the ethical implications of the destruction of a fourteen hundred-year-old cloister.

The fifteenth was also a memorable day for Tarzan Williams, K Company, 157th. His unit was preparing to move to a new position and he and two buddies were carrying their bedrolls to a drop area when a German shell screamed in, wounding one man. "Two men ran to him when another shell came in and wounded *them*. When we started back to our area, another shell came in and hit a big tree. There were nineteen men hit by that last shell, including me. I remember seeing my helmet rolling slow in front of me. The next thing I knew, I was running as hard as I could the other direction when I came to my senses. I stopped running and tried to figure out what happened." Somebody asked Williams where he was hurt, but he replied that he wasn't wounded, that he had only been knocked senseless. Then Williams saw blood all over the front of his mustard-colored wool shirt. "My shoulder and neck were bleeding. The doctors patched me up and later that night I got to the field hospital. For four days, they took X rays of my shoulder; they thought my collarbone was broken. My shoulder, neck, and chest were all black and blue." During the course of the war, Williams would be wounded six times.[72]

The war-movie cliché showing soldiers dying in the arms of their comrades was all too real for the men of the 45th. Al Bedard, a corporal with HQ Company, 157th Regiment, remembered a buddy named George S. Viereck, Jr., a Harvard graduate. (Viereck's father, George, Sr., was a notorious member of the German-American Bund, a pro-Nazi group that tried to keep the United States out of the war.)[73] Of his buddy, Bedard said,

> He was very intelligent, loved to play chess, and could debate on any subject. As far as his appearance went, he looked like Sad Sack. Otherwise, he was a very conscientious soldier. At Anzio, George and I and two other men were on an observation post when, all of a sudden, the Germans started to shell us. The OP [observation post] was nothing more than a sandbag revetment at the edge of a tree line. One of the soldiers yelled out that he had been hit. I went up and saw he had caught a piece of shrapnel. It just missed a vein but shattered his leg. While I was attending to him, George ran back to the CP and got a couple of guys with a litter and came back to where I was. We got this fellow on the litter and the four of us carried him. On the way back from the CP, the Germans lobbed in a couple of mortar shells. George got hit with a fragment across the temple. He died in our arms; he just bled to death. He kept asking us, "Please help me, please help me." There wasn't a thing we could do for him.[74]

First Lieutenant Bill Whitman, executive officer with B Company, 180th, went on a reconnaissance late in the afternoon of 15 February. B Company was scheduled to relieve a company of the 179th and Whitman's job was to make the necessary arrangements with the other company commander. His journey interrupted by heavy enemy barrages, Whitman finally found the company and was talking with another soldier when the area came under fire. "They kept shelling for the next ten minutes or so," Whitman wrote, "and then ceased fire. I looked over at the man I had been talking to and saw that the pack on his back was smoking. I grabbed him and he slipped down into the ditch. He was dead. A hot shell fragment had gone into his back and killed him."

Whitman found the company commander, made arrangements for the relief, and then, as it was growing dark, started to return to B Company. Three German planes came in fast and low, strafing the area. As he hit the ground, Whitman's foot stepped in something soft and squishy; it was the mangled face of a dead American lieutenant. "I think at that moment, my morale was at about bottom. As I stood there alone in the evening, looking down at that dead man, I wondered if I might end up the same way before this thing was over. I sure hated to bring the company up to this hot spot."[75]

On that same night of 15 February, Captain Clay Barnes was racing northward in a jeep on the Via Anziate to check on one of his anti-tank gun squads, which was covering the main north-south highway. He, his driver, and the X.O. (executive officer) of the 2nd Battalion zipped under the Overpass when a German tank up ahead began firing down the road, straight at them. "We had a burst so close, I don't know why we weren't all killed," Barnes said. "We jumped out of the jeep and went on foot to my gun squad. They had the gun in an old Italian house that was just about blown down. I took the squad leader and my driver and we went up to see how close the Krauts might be. We saw a couple of Krauts digging a shallow trench, silhouetted against the sky. We captured 'em and took 'em back in my jeep and turned 'em in at Regimental Headquarters."[76]

The heavy German shellings, the air raids, the vicious patrol activity, and the strong local attacks were merely a prelude to the tremendous onslaught that would begin the next morning. Under the cover of darkness, and beyond the knowledge of VI Corps, the roads north of Aprilia were choked with scores of tanks and thousands of men of *Generalleutnant* H. G. Hildebrandt's 715th Infantry and *Generalleutnant* Fritz Gräser's 3rd Panzer Grenadier Divisions moving to their jump-off positions. The next German counterattack was about to be unleashed.[77]

The German Army was infamous for its counterattacks. Almost without exception, every attack was met with a violent counterattack. If the first counterattack was unsuccessful in throwing the enemy back, then a second counterattack, and a third, and a fourth, and so on was mounted until the lost ground was either regained or the German forces were so depleted that further assault was impossible. Much of this often-suicidal response sprang from Hitler's doctrine that any ground taken from the enemy was sacred German soil, to be defended to the last man. Naturally, then, the Allied landing to the rear of the Gustav Line was an impertinence that had to be dealt with harshly. Kesselring now had assembled elements of nine German divisions around the Anzio beachhead, ready to launch Operation *Fischfang* ("Fish Hook"). These included the Hermann Göring Panzer, 26th Panzer, 4th *Fallschirmjäger*, and 114th *Jäger* Divisions; the 65th, 362nd, and 715th Infantry Divisions from the Fourteenth Army; the 29th and 3rd Panzer Grenadier Divisions (the latter veterans of Stalingrad); the Infantry *Lehr* (Demonstration) Regiment; the Artillery *Lehr* Regiment; the 1027th and 1028th Panzer Grenadier Regiments; the Tiger Battalion; and an assortment of other combat and support units. Also thrown into the battle would be two Italian SS battalions, maintaining their loyalty to Mussolini. Overall, the Germans had an assembled force of some 125,000 troops against 100,000 of the Allies.[78]

After the war, Kesselring wrote,

> I myself was convinced, even taking their powerful naval guns and overwhelming air superiority into consideration, that with the means available we must succeed in throwing the Allies back into the sea. I constantly kept in mind the psychological effect of their situation on the staff and troops of the American VI Corps. Penned in as they were on the low-lying, notoriously unhealthy coast, it must have been damned unpleasant; our artillery and the *Luftwaffe* with its numerous flak batteries and bombers alone saw to it that even when "resting," their soldiers had no rest.[79]

Although the Allies were certainly restricted, so, too, was the enemy. A flanking attack was impossible, given the restrictions formed by the sea; and, unlike the Allies, the *Wehrmacht* had no amphibious capability. And an attack on either flank would have brought the attackers perilously close to the awesome array of Allied naval guns. They, therefore, had no choice but to attack frontally the area manned only by the 45th.[80]

Some 45th veterans have felt that the reason Kesselring and von Mackensen decided to hit the center of the 45th's line was because the Germans' excellent intelligence service had identified the Thunderbirds as "only" a National Guard outfit and therefore of supposed lesser quality than the Regular Army units formed in a semicircle around the beachhead. In actual fact, however, the reason was more practical; the 45th was positioned along the Via Anziate—the only hard surface capable of supporting tanks on their drive directly into the heart of the Anzio waterfront and the Allied encampment. Besides, the Germans were well aware of the 45th's capabilities, having received a firsthand education in Sicily and at Salerno.

With Aprilia, Carroceto, and Buon Riposo Ridge in German hands, von Mackensen thought it would be a relatively simple matter for his forces to cross the three miles of open ground and smash through the Allies' final beachhead line. It would be Dunkirk all over again. Von Mackensen's plan was brutally simple. In the early, gray hours of Wednesday, 16 February, the onslaught would begin with diversionary attacks on either end of the Allied line. On the right, elements of LXXVI Panzer Corps and the Hermann Göring Panzer Division would strike at Lucien Truscott's 3rd Division while, on the extreme left flank, most of Trettner's 4th *Fallschirmjäger* Division and Pfeiffer's 65th Infantry Division would attack the battered British 56th Division's positions.

Then, following a pulverizing artillery bombardment, the strength of the German attack—all or parts of six divisions (the 65th and 715th Infantry Divisions, 114th *Jäger* Division, 3rd Panzer Grenadier Division, and elements of the Hermann Göring Panzer and 4th *Fallschirmjäger* Divisions)—would apply their combined weight on a four-mile front, from Buon Riposo Ridge to Spaccasassi Creek. Behind these units, von Lüttwitz's 26th Panzer and Fries's 29th Panzer Grenadier Divisions would stand ready to barrel down the Via Anziate with their armored vehicles and punch through the thin center of the Allied line—a thin center manned only by the 45th Infantry Division. The tenuous seam between the 157th and 179th Regiments was the *Schwerpunkt*—the point where the German strength would be concentrated.[81]

7

The Rush of Jousts

16 February 1944

Before this I've seen horsemen start to march and open the assault and muster ranks and seen them, too, at times beat their retreat; and on your land, o Aretines, I've seen rangers and raiding parties galloping, the clash of tournaments, the rush of jousts, now done with trumpets, now with bells, and now with drums.

—Dante Alighieri, *The Inferno*, Canto XXII

BEFORE FIRST LIGHT on 16 February, the soaked, freezing soldiers of the 45th Division lay shivering in their muddy foxholes, in ravines, or in the scant shelter of half-demolished buildings, wondering what the dawn would bring. For many of them, it would bring their last day on earth.

The Thunderbirds had spent another cold, miserable night enduring the intermittent *crump-crump-crump* of harassing mortar and artillery fire. As the eastern horizon grew lighter, revealing a cold, foggy morning, few of the Thunderbirds had yet been able to stretch the cold out of their aching limbs and joints. Fewer still had been able to relieve their bladders. And none had yet cracked open a breakfast repast of cold K or C rations. The harassing fire abruptly ceased and, for a few minutes, there was a total and unnerving silence. Even the frogs stopped croaking—a bad omen.

Then, from off in the distance, it began—the deep-throated barking of heavy guns, the coughing of mortars, the screaming of rockets from the barrels of the *Nebelwerfers*. Within seconds, the shells came whistling in, more fearsome than anything the Thunderbirds had yet experienced, falling among the American dugouts all along the 45th's line, smashing into the wet earth, burying some men alive in their holes or vaporizing them completely with direct hits.[1]

Being on the receiving end of an artillery or mortar barrage is one experience for which nothing can adequately prepare a soldier. Basic trainees get a mild taste of what it is like to be under small-arms fire by being required to low-crawl under barbed wire while machine gun bullets crack like whips a foot or two above their heads, but no army has ever been able to devise a way for men to safely experience what it is like for high-explosive shells to rain down on them randomly for hours or days at a time. Soldiers in training can observe from a safe distance the rather spectacular effects of a barrage, but the closest trainees ever get to being near a large explosion is on combat training courses where they are required to crawl through a landscape where pits, the perimeters of which are rimmed with sandbags, periodically erupt with quarter-pound sticks of TNT. Comparing the explosive power of a quarter-pound stick of TNT with a large-caliber shell, however, is like comparing a peashooter to an elephant gun.

Although the devastating effects on human tissue of red-hot chunks of jagged steel spun and hurled through the air at terrific velocities are well known and easily imagined, rarely does one hear about the other, major effect of an artillery explosion: concussion. When a steel container packed with several pounds of explosives detonates within yards of a human being who otherwise may be shielded from the blast and fragments by being below ground or behind a stout wall, the effect of the concussion is liable to cause the person's lungs to literally burst inside the chest. Even if a way *were* found to adequately protect trainees from the flying steel shards and the concussive effect of the shells, it is doubtful that the military would want to give young recruits the slightest hint of the terrifying emotional scars with which even the briefest bombardment would leave them. Being shelled is not something most soldiers ever become comfortable with or accustomed to.

Daniel Witts, of the 179th's Anti-Tank Platoon, survived more than his fair share of barrages and bombardments. "You're nervous, you're sweating, but you put up with it," he said. "I saw two guys get hit when we first went to Sicily. They came back to the front but they were always cautious after that. We called them 'turtles'—they didn't want to get out of their holes. I didn't understand it until I was wounded later in France. They shouldn't send a man back to the front once he's been hit."[2]

The 16 February bombardment to which the 45th was subjected lasted, on some parts of the line, from 0630 to 0745 hours—one hour and fifteen minutes of unremitting agony, and each soldier who survived the ordeal has the details of that morning burned indelibly into his memory. All of them described it as hell. Lieutenant Colonel Ralph Krieger, commanding the 1st Battalion, 157th Regiment, recalled, "It was hell, I'll tell you for sure. I lost quite a few people, including my orderly. We were in an advanced CP in a ditch and the Germans started shelling us. He got hit by a direct hit on his foxhole; I was right alongside of him. How I missed getting hit, I don't know. My S-2 [intelligence officer] was wounded at the same time."[3]

The constant thumping of the German guns suddenly ceased, replaced by the roar of tank engines coming to life, the shrill whistles of officers and noncoms, the courage-building shouts of men launching themselves into combat and perhaps toward their deaths. The soldiers of the 157th who dared to lift their heads above the rims of their foxholes were greeted by an astonishing sight: scores of gray, mud-caked Mark IV and Mark VI panzers, accompanied by thousands of men from the 3rd Panzer Grenadier and 715th Infantry Divisions, rushing at them in their ankle-length overcoats, spilling across Anzio's soggy, cratered landscape, falling into shell holes, emerging, firing from the hip, yelling, singing.

Just to the east of the 157th, the men of the 179th were equally surprised to see, barreling through the fog, thousands more of the enemy, preceded by tanks too numerous to count.[4] "Here come the bastards," somebody shouted. Stiff, frozen men who could barely move a muscle a moment earlier were now galvanized into action, emptying clip after clip of rifle ammunition or pouring steady streams of machine gun fire into the massed ranks of the enemy until the barrels were too hot to touch. What bullets did not stop, the big guns did. Artillery forward observers grabbed their radio handsets and called in coordinates to the gun crews farther back. Within seconds, thousands of shells were raining down on the brave but hapless Germans, caught in the open. It was a turkey shoot. There simply was no way to miss hitting the exposed enemy. Heavy ordnance was pumped into the onrushing enemy by American and British artillery, mortars, three tank companies, four anti-aircraft batteries, two Royal Navy cruisers sitting offshore, and the considerable resources of the 12th Air Support Command and Desert Air Force.[5]

The fields in front of the American positions sprouted with dirty mushrooms as the shells burst, hurling German soldiers to the ground or catapulting them in the air like rag dolls and tearing huge gaps in the onrushing ranks. Whole units simply vanished behind curtains of erupting earth, never to be seen again. Yet, more came on, a seemingly ceaseless wave of Teutonic warriors determined to "lance the abscess" and throw the Allies back into the sea. During the night of the fifteenth, the ground had frozen enough to give the panzers a firm surface on which to operate. But the next morning, the mud thawed, turning the fields into quagmires. The panzers were therefore restricted to the roads, where they became easy targets for American gunners, just as Harmon's 1st Armored Division tanks had been sitting ducks for German gun crews three weeks earlier.[6]

Also on the night of the fifteenth, Lieutenant Colonel Lawrence Brown's 2nd Battalion, 157th, had moved about three kilometers forward of the Overpass and settled into positions astride the Via Anziate previously occupied by the British, with G Company on the left at Buon Riposo Ridge, E Company to the right with a couple of tank destroyers guarding the highway, F Company between them, and H Company in reserve. South of the ridge, the 2nd Battalion set up its CP in an extensive labyrinth of caves. No sooner had the Thunderbirds settled in than, according to the 45th's official history, "The full brunt of the enemy assault struck Company E head on."[7]

In the foggy, half-light of dawn, E Company's commander, Captain Felix Sparks, saw some forms moving. Thinking they might be members of the neighboring 179th, Sparks radioed back to battalion headquarters and asked, "Are the 179th wearing overcoats?" Told they weren't, Sparks said, "Then those are Krauts coming after us." Sparks also remembered, "We knew we were in for trouble because we could hear tanks moving right up close to us." Then the Germans zeroed in with an extremely accurate artillery preparation on E Company's position. "They really laid it into us for about ten minutes," Sparks said. "They turned the whole earth over. But we had hardly any casualties because we were well dug in. The barrage was more of a nuisance than anything else. Just as soon as the barrage lifted, they sent three tanks through us. They were over on my left; they didn't come down the main road, which was where my 3rd Platoon was. They came so fast I couldn't believe it. But there was no infantry with them, which was dumb."

Sparks immediately yelled to the tank destroyers, "Get 'em!"

The T-D commander hesitated. With his head sticking out of the M-10's hatch, he asked, "Are those British tanks?"

"Hell, no—they're German tanks!" Sparks yelled back. The tank destroyers immediately went into action, blasting away at the panzers at near point-blank range, and blew the first two to pieces. "It was like they disintegrated," Sparks recalled. "Parts were flying everywhere." The commander of the third tank saw what had happened to his comrades and beat a hasty retreat.

"Right after this," Sparks said, "one of the tank destroyers moved a little off to the left, maybe fifty to seventy-five feet off the highway. I don't know why. Maybe he was trying to find a position where he'd have a longer field of fire. That was a mistake. There was a German tank waiting there and it knocked him out. He went up in flames and burned me out of my foxhole." Five minutes later, however, came a wave of German infantry, running awkwardly across the muddy ground in their long, gray overcoats. "I don't know if they were drunk or what," said Sparks, "but they were yelling and screaming—what they were saying I don't know. But we cut them down. Some got in with us but we killed every damn one of them. Over on our right, the Germans were hitting the 179th at the same time. I couldn't see what was going on but I could hear the firing. The Germans botched up the attack but good," Sparks said. "The first time they had tanks but no infantry. The second time they had infantry but no tanks. About thirty minutes later, they came again. This time, they had tanks *and* infantry. That's what killed us. The tanks went right up to our foxholes and blew my men right out of them."

During the furious struggle for E Company's positions, a crewman of one of the tank destroyers did something that Sparks will never forget:

> He strapped himself to the .50 caliber machine gun that normally was used as an anti-aircraft weapon. It was mounted awkwardly on the side of the tank destroyer, and the gunner would always put a big leather strap around himself so he could lean back while firing up in the air. This sergeant strapped himself on and was firing the gun down into the attacking waves of German infantrymen. But they got him with what we call a burp gun. I watched the dust spurt out the back of his jacket as the bullets hit him. He was killed, but he stopped the Germans right at the edge of my foxhole.

Sadly, Sparks never learned the name of the soldier who sacrificed his life trying to save E Company.

By now, the situation at E Company's position had become critical as the Germans sent battalion after battalion against Sparks's men. "Around noon, I had only one tank destroyer left and he was just about out of ammunition," Sparks recalled. "I decided he couldn't do us much good any more, so I told him to get out while he could, and he took off. Those tank destroyers are pretty fast, compared to a tank. They could do thirty or thirty-five miles per hour. The Germans were firing at him all the way. Later that afternoon, the Germans came in and that's when I ordered our artillery to fire on our positions. That broke up their attack. Most people don't realize that it isn't rifles or machine guns that cause most of the casualties," Sparks said. "It's the artillery. If you're in the open, artillery fire is *deadly*. If you're in a foxhole, it doesn't bother you unless it drops *into* your foxhole. But if you're attacking in the open, artillery fire is very, very deadly, and they had to attack in the open to get to us. I just called in the artillery and that stopped them."[8] It was not, however, the end of E Company's ordeal. If anything, it was merely a prelude.

• • •

After overrunning units of the 157th along the Via Anziate, three regiments of panzers and infantry slammed into the left flank of Major Merlin O. Tryon's 3rd Battalion, 179th. F and G Companies had the misfortune of being the farthest forward and thus the German juggernaut slammed first into their ranks. Casualties were staggering. Men and machines swirled around in a dance of death. Men yelled, screamed, moaned. Rifles, pistols, and automatic weapons added their staccato punctuation to the overall cacophony. Hand grenades exploded with dull thuds, muffled by mud. Positions were abandoned, then retaken. Radio messages crackled back and forth to and from headquarters and the fighting units. K Company reported that one of its platoons was cut off; L Company attempted to come to the rescue, but panzers forced it back. I Company found itself surrounded but managed to fight its way out of the encirclement. Heroism beyond measure was the order of the day on both sides as soldiers sacrificed themselves to save their buddies, their guns, their foxholes, their tanks, their units.[9]

The carnage continued unabated for hours. Daniel Witts, Anti-Tank Company, 179th, recalled, "A shell dropped into a hole about two or three holes over from me and killed two guys. One guy was named Francis Clark—we called him 'Brookie' because he was from Brooklyn. The other guy was from Virginia. It just blew the hell out of them."[10]

William H. Gordon, also of the 179th's A-T Company, remembered "The Germans practically ran us over. In fact, several of our positions had to pull back to where I was. Everybody was scared. We thought about running, but we didn't run."[11]

Now a crisis erupted to the left of the 45th. Although the Germans' diversionary attack against the 3rd Division near Cisterna gained no ground, elements of the 4th *Fallschirmjäger* and 65th Divisions west of Buon Riposo Ridge directed their assault through the deep ravines of "wadi country" at the 167th Brigade of the British 56th Division, which had been on the 157th's left flank. The British reacted to the diversion by unexpectedly pulling back, and E Company suddenly found itself alone and exposed on the left side of the 45th's line.[12]

"The damn fool Germans finally discovered we had nobody on our flank," Felix Sparks said. "I don't know why they didn't figure it out earlier, but they didn't. The Germans would fight like hell but sometimes they were utterly stupid."[13] Stupid or not, the enemy wiped out Sparks's platoon, which had been the only E Company unit on the west side of the road.

Pete Conde, a member of the 157th's Anti-Tank Company, said, "After the British withdrew, our flank was open. The Germans came in and really surprised the mortars behind the hill, where I was. Many of our fellows were captured."[14]

Bud McMillan, K Company, 157th, vividly remembered the morning of the sixteenth:

> As soon as it got light, they started the artillery barrage all around us and then they started running across the open land right there in front of us. With my sniper's rifle, I was able to shoot the ones I thought were officers or NCOs. You pretty well had your choice of what you were going to shoot at. Up to 400 or 500 yards, you could really pick 'em off. The enemy used fire and movement, where they'd run forward, hit the ground, roll, come up and run some more. Of course, we weren't just sittin' there. There was mortars fallin' all around us and they had machine gun cover, too. I was in the slit trench, just shootin' at them, and a piece of shrapnel came down and hit me in the right thigh. I took off my belt and tied a tourniquet around my leg and I kept on fightin'. There really wasn't but about nine or ten of us doin' any shootin'—the rest were either gone or in hidin'. Just to our immediate front there must have been a hundred or more Germans running right at us."[15]

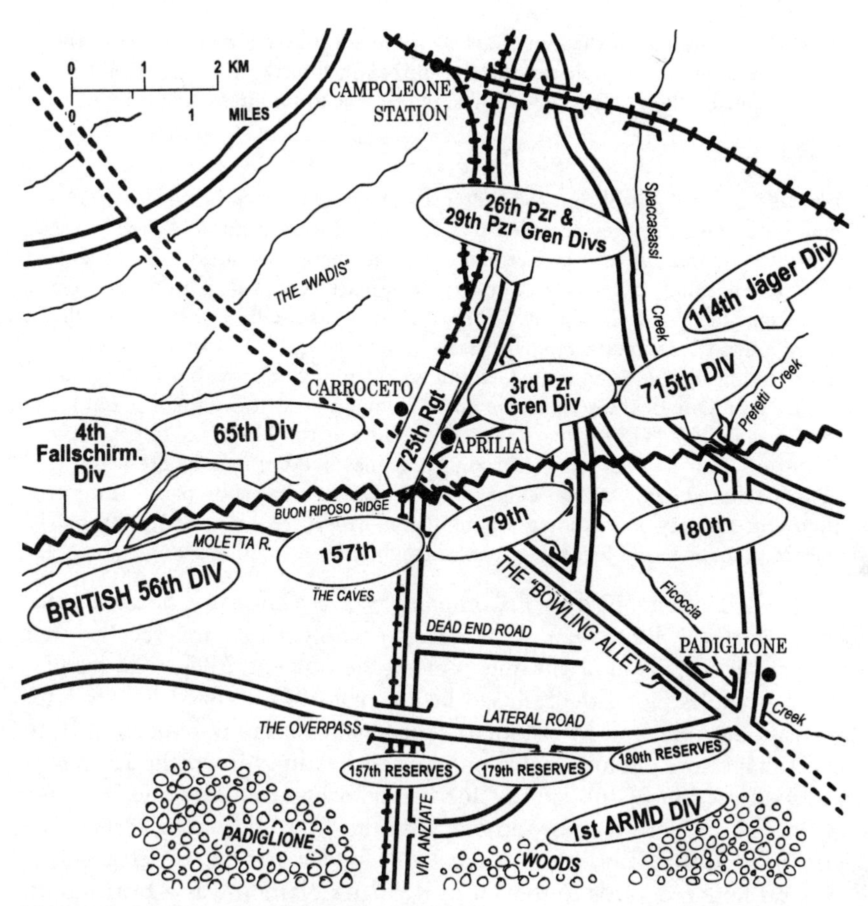

MAP 7.1 The Major German Counterattack
16 February 1944—The Germans struck back hard all along the front line, but the main effort fell to the 725th Regiment of the 715th Division, which employed massed tank and infantry charges against E Company, 157th Regiment, which straddled the all-important north-south highway. (Positions approximate)

Robert LaDu, the executive officer of F Company, 179th, recalled that instead of feeling fear, he was fascinated by an unusual phenomenon:

> I could see something like a speck go in front of my eyes. It happened several times—there were several minutes in between and I got to wondering—am I cracking up? I raised my head up and about a quarter of a mile down the road was a German tank. It fired and you could see the projectile come out. There was a ring of smoke and something that looked like lead coming out of a lead pencil and all of a sudden there was that black speck in front of my eyes. That tank must have been firing about three feet over my head. I thought that if I could see

the shell coming out of the gun, maybe I could see it going the other way. The tank fired again and I could see the end of that shell just quivering. Then it hit and exploded. I didn't think anybody would be able to see anything like that.

LaDu added,

We were at the point of that road. Before daylight, you could hear those German tanks moving; they sounded like so many coffee grinders. When it got light, we counted twenty-six German tanks out there. We called for anti-tank help, but nothing came. Our company headquarters was in a house and we were right next to E Company. When the Germans finally ran us out of the house, our C.O., Captain Homer Ness—he was from Brush, Colorado—came out right ahead of me and some German was standing there with his rifle up to shoot Ness. One of the sergeants from E Company shot from the hip and hit the German. For the next five days, all we did was run like crazy to get away from those tanks. They broke through our lines like nothing. There were so many of those Germans; they came in almost like in a battalion parade formation. Our artillery was landing among them—you'd see a rifle flying through the air, or an arm or a leg. It was just a slaughter.[16]

To the left of the 179th's F Company was G Company. Second Lieutenant Charles R. Reiman, a platoon leader with G Company, recalled that on the sixteenth, his unit was dug in along the Bowling Alley, with his platoon in foxholes along the railroad bed in front of the road. Shortly after daybreak, an American M-5 "Stuart" reconnaissance tank pulled out from some foliage to Reiman's right and started heading down the road in a westerly direction at full speed "for maybe a hundred feet and then got zapped. It burst into flames—no one got out. We could not tell where the Germans fired from since there was a lot of hidden area to our left front."

Several hundred yards to the left of Reiman's platoon was a British unit. Reiman watched as the Germans launched an attack against them. "There was an opening in the trees that enabled us to see the Germans running, rifles at the port, and it seemed to me that they had fixed bayonets, but of this I am not certain." Reiman tried to help the British. "There was a .50-caliber machine gun to our right along the railroad bed. I had the machine gun brought up to our position but discovered that it had a ruptured cartridge in the chamber." He then witnessed a group of Americans taken prisoner by a lightly armed German reconnaissance vehicle. "I don't believe a shot was fired. That vehicle was moving rapidly south on the road from the Factory. It pointed its little cannon down in the direction of the foxholes and everybody stood up with their hands up. I don't think that there were any foot soldiers with the vehicle—it was moving too fast."

Later that day, Reiman's own position came under attack:

Out of the hidden ground to our left front, there appeared an armored vehicle. It was not a tank, but more like a rectangular box with an 88 sticking out the

> front. Possibly there were machine guns, too—I'm not sure. This vehicle stopped near the ravine and fired between five and ten rounds at the G Company CP and hit it every time. I started to unlimber our bazooka but my men got very nervous, so I didn't use it. I wasn't sure that I could hit it at 200–300 yards, anyway. We did not fire at the vehicle. It withdrew back around the hill it had come from. Possibly this was the source of the shell that got the light tank early that morning.
>
> Things quieted down after it got dark. During the night, whoever was on guard began to fire—at what I don't know—but within a matter of seconds, every man in the 2nd Platoon was firing.

Reiman picked up a flare gun and began illuminating the area. "As far as I know, no one was shooting at us."

After the firing stopped, the lieutenant decided to check out his platoon's left flank along the railroad bed. Suddenly he heard hobnailed boots running nearby. He fired wildly in the darkness in the direction of the sound. "I couldn't see a thing, so it was pure luck. I heard some yelling—I had hit two men, one in the guts and one in the leg." His platoon came running to see what was going on and managed to capture another German, unwounded. All the prisoners were sent to the rear.

The next morning began badly. The frightening roar of tanks was off to Reiman's left and getting louder. "Then, to our front, out of a ditch about 150–200 yards away, there appeared maybe 100 Germans stretching, yawning, and posturing as if daring us to shoot. Anyway, they didn't worry me nearly so much as that tank that I could hear coming down the railroad bed. I could not raise Captain Mallory [G Company C.O.] on my radio." Small-arms fire was crackling overhead from the unit that had, just moments before, been yawning and stretching. Reiman was able to contact the lieutenant in charge of the heavy machine guns that were supporting his platoon and told him he was planning to pull back to the blacktop road with the rest of the company. Reiman advised the other lieutenant to pull back first.

> Of all the mistakes I probably made, the biggest one was my decision to be the last one out of that position. *I* should have led them back to the road, but I didn't. I was the last one out—we didn't lose a man. The last thing I saw when I left that position was the top of a tank turret up the railroad bed to our left. Five seconds more and it would have been in position to fire right down our position. As I raced up the various ditches toward the black top to rejoin my platoon, I decided that I was going to start acting like an officer instead of a rifleman, so I threw away my M-1. I thought we'd be making a stand and that I would need to be free to direct my platoon.

When he reached the road, he could not find his platoon. He did find the CP, however, and the company commander told Reiman he had directed the platoon to keep falling back. But Reiman wasn't satisfied with the captain's answer and so struck out on his own to locate his men. Under fire, he headed west along the road's ditch. "This time I went further west, thinking that maybe my men were scattered out in the countless foxholes that had been dug along that road. I glanced to the east just in time to see a German half-track recon vehicle, with infantry crouched behind it, stop at the road junction and all of G Company stand up with hands high." After briefly considering going back to rejoin the company, Reiman decided to jump in a nearby foxhole and play dead. "I laid there all day. German tanks stopped and fired from right close to where I was. Our own artillery, firing at the German tanks, threw enough dirt on me to make my 'death' look very realistic. That night, I made my way back to the American lines."[17]

Everett W. Easley, E Company, 179th, remembered looking out of his foxhole as the assault began:

> There was this white flash from artillery or a tank. They laid three shells on my hole within arm's reach and didn't hurt a thing. Blew our rifles all to hell, but didn't hurt us. It was a hell of a mess, though, I'll tell you. That night, we got orders to withdraw and some withdrew and others didn't. We were all disorganized then. I stayed with my friends. The Germans came running down this ditch and we just kept shooting them as fast as they came. There were three German tanks that came down the road. About every two minutes, they'd fire their machine guns about a foot and a half high off the road. I scrambled across the road and there were Germans all over the place. In the dark, they must have thought I was one of them.[18]

Daniel Ficco, the acting first sergeant with C Company, 157th, remembered the morning of the sixteenth: "I told my men to hold their fire until there was a couple hundred Germans coming across an open area. Then I gave the order and we fired. We had some mortars and the ground was almost black with the Germans coming at us. I was firing an M-1 and it got so hot, I could hardly touch it; I don't know how many rounds I put through it."[19]

Kenneth P. Stemmons, commanding B Company, 157th, said, "When the Germans finally broke through on the left and ran behind us with infantry and tanks and a little bit of mechanized stuff, it got so bad that I had to call for artillery on our position. I had asked for quite a bit of it and they replied, 'Let us give you a little bit to see if that's what you really want.' But we were all in our holes and the Germans were running around in the open. We got the artillery and the Germans suffered terrible casualties."

To Stemmons's right, the Germans punched through with an armor-led thrust and began firing at B Company's flank, right down the ditch that they occupied. With B Company being hard hit and pinned down, the infantry poured through. But Stemmons's men reacted as they had been trained to do. "Our riflemen felt they accounted for as many Germans as our artillery or machine gun fire. You get a couple hundred men firing in the same general area, it gets brutal." Stemmons had a standing operating procedure in his company: If a man fired, he fired an entire eight-round clip, then reloaded. A few random rounds seldom stopped the enemy; only a full-fledged fusillade, approaching the intensity of automatic weapons fire, had the desired effect. "It was hard on ammunition, but when your life is on the line, you couldn't care less," he said.[20]

Don Amzibel, L Company, 157th, remembered, "A buddy of mine from Chicago and I were on an outpost when all hell broke loose. All kinds of flares lit up the area and tanks were rolling down the hill towards us. German soldiers were running by us as if we weren't there. Of course, it was dark and maybe they were doped up." Amzibel and his buddy left their outpost and pulled back to L Company's main defensive line. "When we reached our lines, I shouted out the password and our lieutenant yelled out, 'Let them in. They're our boys!' We were completely surrounded but somehow we managed to work our way out of it. It was the first retreat I had been in. I guess we were lucky—all of us could have been captured. The attack came as a complete surprise. Only a few of our men were left alive at the conclusion of the battle."[21]

In the 180th's sector, First Lieutenant Donald Knowlton, a forward observer with the 160th FA Battalion, had set up his OP in a house southeast of Aprilia. When the infantry around him was forced back, Knowlton refused to leave his position and continued to call in fire on the attacking waves. The Germans decided that he would have to be eliminated and assaulted the house. After shooting three of the enemy with his carbine, he was hit in the head with a slug from a Schmeisser machine pistol and taken prisoner. His last order was to bring fire down on his own position, and the Germans were forced to flee, leaving the badly wounded lieutenant for dead. Later that day, counterattacking Thunderbirds retook the house, found him still alive, and got him back to an aid station. Knowlton survived and was awarded the Distinguished Service Cross.[22]

In his book *Scouts Out,* First Lieutenant Bill Whitman, the executive officer of B Company, 180th, wrote that he was

> brewing a cup of coffee over one of the small Coleman stoves when a tank shell came screeching in and went . . . right through the hole I had just gotten out of. Everyone got quite a kick out of it except me. The sky was suddenly filled with artillery, tank, and mortar shells. The tank fire was the worst. The German tanks stood off and fired direct cannon fire into us. Men were hit all around within a few minutes. The pounding kept up. We all hugged the sod. Shouts attracted our attention and we turned and looked over the flats and what a sight! Everywhere you looked there were hundreds of troops wearing long gray overcoats flapping in the morning breeze, the light glinting off the

naked steel of their bayonets. Brother, if you don't get religion at a time like that, you never will![23]

Chester A. Powell, a squad leader in M Company, 180th Regiment, recalled that his unit was dug in forward of the Mussolini Canal when the Germans

> charged us across an open field and we were cut off for four days. There was a house there with three Italian girls and an old man. That old man was our communication line, carrying messages to the rear for us. My squad had the only machine gun left in action—the rest had been knocked out. I got on the gun myself and when the attack came, we stopped the infantry pretty well and then the artillery got them. The Germans had those small, remote-controlled tanks that probably didn't weigh over 400 pounds.* They started to come at us but the artillery got them. We held on 'til night, then it was every man for himself to get back to the Mussolini Canal.[24]

One of the attacking units was the highly touted but inexperienced Infantry *Lehr* Regiment, normally stationed at the Infantry School at Döberitz, and sent to the fighting personally by Hitler. The unit had considerable experience in testing new infantry weapons and showcasing battle tactics for generals and diplomats far from the front, but only half of the soldiers had any experience under the Sturm und Drang of actual combat. Because it knew nothing about the terrain, Kesselring and von Mackensen attached this unit to the 3rd Panzer Grenadier Division, but did not commit it until late in the day, at about 1830 hours.[25] When the unit finally began to cross the open field, the withering fire from the Americans hit the Infantry *Lehr*'s officer corps particularly hard and brought its advance to a halt. Leaderless, the green troops broke and ran.[26]

Although the Infantry *Lehr* proved useless in its first test, the rest of the German units attacked with incredible tenacity, heedless of the cascade of red-hot steel being poured into their ranks. A few made it to the 45th's lines, where they dove into foxholes and battled hand to hand with the surprised occupants. Grenades flew back and forth, and the gunfire from the entrenched Thunderbirds was murderous. German tanks rattled along the battle line, pumping their high-explosive shells and machine gun bullets into the American positions, but soon these steel monsters were either

---

*The remote-controlled miniature tanks, called "Goliaths," were packed with 200 pounds of explosives. Steered by trailing wires, the Goliaths had a range of nearly a half mile. Although the Germans hoped to be able to pilot them undetected into Allied lines and then detonate them, they were easily spotted—and just as easily knocked out by small-arms fire. The Germans used thirteen Goliaths against the Allies at Anzio, with little effect (Christopher Hibbert, *Anzio: The Bid for Rome* [New York: Ballantine, 1970], p. 128).

German armor preparing for battle at Anzio. Even heavier armor was employed to dislodge the 45th from its critical position—to no avail. (Courtesy of Bundesarchiv, Koblenz)

aflame or retreating to the relative safety of the rear. The men of the 45th, who thought they had seen it all, had never seen anything like *this*.

Artillery again saved the day. The 45th's supporting guns were firing as fast as the gunners could slam shells into the breaches. Mel Craven, A Battery, 158th Field Artillery, said, "In basic training, I had been taught that the maximum rate of fire of a 105mm howitzer was four rounds per minute. When the attack came, I and another man were on a two-man gun watch; the rest of the crew was asleep. When the Germans hit, we didn't have enough time to call and wake them. By the time the rest of the crew got out of their foxholes and down into the gun pit, we had almost expended thirty rounds of ammunition." Craven and his crew were firing as quickly as they could. "We estimated we fired between ten and twelve rounds per minute. After a captured German soldier came back through our lines, he had one request—he wanted to see our 'automatic artillery.' That gave us an indication what rate of fire we were putting out."[27]

James Bird, a corporal with A Battery, 160th Field Artillery, said, "At Anzio, we had stacks of shells prepared with four, five, six, and seven propellant charges. When firing reduced charges [three, four, or five], we often used a lanyard attached to the trigger and could get as many as five shells fired without having to wait for the tube to return to the battery position."

Bird also related, "Lieutenant Colonel Russell D. Funk's [C.O. of the 158th Field Artillery Battalion] personal records show his battalion fired 26,448 rounds [2,200 per gun] in support of the 157th Infantry Regiment, roughly one-third of the total fired by Division Artillery between 16 and 22 February."[28]

• • •

On the front line, Captain Felix Sparks was trying to save what was left of E Company, 157th, which had taken the brunt of the initial German assault. "On that first morning," Sparks said, "E Company and the Germans had both taken some pretty heavy casualties. At about 11 or 11:30, I saw this German half-track with a white flag on it coming down the main highway." When the vehicle stopped, Sparks climbed out of his foxhole and walked over to it. A German officer emerged and opened the conversation.

"Captain," said the officer in excellent English, "you have a great number of wounded here and we have a number of wounded. Would you agree to a truce of thirty minutes so we can each evacuate our wounded?"

Sparks didn't have to think twice. "Yes, that would be all right. Let's get busy."

Sparks shouted to his men that a short truce was in effect so both sides could gather up all their casualties. "I had one truck left that, miraculously, hadn't been knocked out," he said.

> It was a one-and-a-half-ton truck that was a prime mover for a 57mm antitank gun. The gun had already been knocked out and the truck was behind a farmhouse that had been hit a number of times. We loaded about twenty or twenty-five wounded onto the truck and I sent them to the rear. We did not try to carry out the dead, of which we had quite a number. This all took about twenty minutes. The Germans had litter bearers picking up their people and putting a lot of them into their half-track.
>
> As soon as our truck got out of sight, I figured the battle was on again, and it was. That's when I called in the artillery fire on our own positions. Sometimes an artillery barrage will completely disorient some soldiers. They completely lose control. You hear this crash, crash, crash that goes on for five or ten minutes. I've seen soldiers go insane from a barrage. I even had one of my officers go insane—took off running as fast as he could go, right in the middle of the barrage. He got out all right, and they put him in the hospital. I never heard of him again.

Sparks's men stayed low in their holes as the American guns put shell after shell into their positions, ripping the exposed enemy to shreds. For the moment, E Company was safe.[29]

A few miles behind Sparks's position, Captain Merle Mitchell's 3rd Battalion, 157th, was catching hell around the Overpass, just a few short hours after it had moved to this location. The structure was functionally useless, for the road that was supposed to cross it had yet to be built. Its sole raison d'être, it seemed to Mitchell's men, was to act as a magnet for German shells. As the 157th's official history states, "Third Battalion's position was one of the most strategic on the entire beach. An enemy break-through at the cross-roads would have paved the way for a German assault straight through to Anzio and would have split the beachhead forces in two. That such was the purpose of the enemy, there could be little doubt."[30]

While the GIs of the 3rd Battalion curled themselves tightly in their water-filled holes, a terrific barrage saturated the area. Nearly everything in the German arsenal—from heavy artillery, mortars, tanks, aircraft, "Screaming Meemies" (the dreaded, multibarreled *Nebelwerfer* rocket launchers), and the huge "Ferdinand" self-propelled guns to the distant railroad guns—hammered Mitchell's men unceasingly for hours. The aid station was especially hard hit and the battalion CP had to pull back 600 yards under constant bombardment. Casualties were appalling. Some men went mad and rushed from the relative safety of their holes, only to be cut down or torn apart by flying metal. It did not seem possible that human beings could survive such punishment.[31]

To Tarzan Williams, K Company, 157th, the electrically fired *Nebelwerfer* was a particularly unpleasant weapon:

> The shells flew through the air with a high-pitched scream. I don't know if the shells done much damage when they landed, but when they were flying through the air, they put everyone's nerves on edge. One night the moon was shining bright. I seen a German truck about 800 yards to the right-front of me. It turned around and I seen it was pulling one of these things on a trailer. The truck stopped and two or three men got out to fire the thing. Then here comes the screaming shells over us. When the last shell was fired, they jumped in the truck and got out of there. They didn't wait to be introduced to our artillery.[32]

Over on the left flank of the 157th's position, Lieutenant Joe Robertson's G Company was being hard hit by tanks and infantry, but here American artillery was turning the panzers into scrap metal, and some 200 gray-clad corpses were piled up in front of G Company's right flank. On Robertson's left flank, however, one of his platoons had been wiped out and the enemy was drawing dangerously close to the company CP. Realizing the moment called for desperate measures, the lieutenant got on the radio and directed artillery fire down on his own positions. The result was only partially effective; although many of the enemy were torn to pieces, the survivors jumped into G Company's foxholes and battled men with knives, bayonets, entrenching tools, and bare hands. The Americans were forced to give ground. That afternoon, another tank-supported wave hit G Company's right platoon, knocking out two anti-tank guns and blasting the Thunderbirds in their foxholes at point-blank range. Many Americans died or were taken prisoner.[33]

The 179th, dug in just south of Aprilia, also was forced to pull back as the weight of the German assault became too great to bear. Heading for Padiglione, the panzers managed to break through a defensive line of anti-tank guns and blasted the GIs with flanking fire. But as day wore into evening, the German drive began to lose steam. The farther it stabbed into American lines, the more it was subjected to withering fire from every weapon within range.[34]

A member of the 179th's Anti-Tank Company was William H. Gordon. He recalled, "There were three platoons of three guns each in the Anti-Tank Company, along with a mine platoon. Each gun platoon was assigned to support an infantry battalion. During an advance, the mine platoon went in front of the infantry with mine detectors and would clean the mines out so the infantry could go through." Gordon also remembered,

> The 57mm gun was very heavy and it was hard to move it around. So they would put us in a position guarding a crossroads in case something did come that way. We had armor-piercing shells, but we often had to fire at trucks and personnel. We could not elevate our guns; it was strictly a flat-trajectory weapon—straight through. At Anzio, they put us in the best possible place in case there was a tank attack. When the Germans came and tried to push us off the beachhead, there was quite a bit of wild firing, with tanks and everything.[35]

• • •

For the wounded, receiving timely medical treatment was always a life-or-death ordeal. If a man was wounded outside his hole during the day, it was almost impossible for the medics to reach him, for the Germans shot at anyone who moved during daylight hours. In these cases, the wounded man usually was left in the open until darkness, when the medics could retrieve him and get him to an aid station in the rear. Often, the trucks bringing up food, water, and ammunition during the night did double duty and took the wounded back with them. One medic, George Ecker, 179th, recalled that he once rescued a soldier who had been blinded when a mortar round hit him on top of the helmet. Escorting the soldier across Anzio's flat, unforgiving terrain during the day while under intense fire earned him a Bronze Star for gallantry. Ecker said, "I never gave the danger of being a medic a great deal of thought. I had a responsibility to do and I hopefully responded to the best of my ability."

Another time, Ecker picked up a casualty under cover of darkness in a jeep modified to carry a stretcher across the hood and another across the back. This night, while Ecker negotiated his way across the darkened battlefield, the jeep lurched into an irrigation ditch and dumped the wounded soldier off the hood and in the ditch. "Fortunately, the casualty wasn't that badly wounded, and we were able to get him back into the jeep and out of there," Ecker said.[36]

Chaplains were usually where the men needed them most. "The chaplain's station was always with the forward aid station," said Chaplain Leland Loy.

> We did everything from digging foxholes for the medics to binding minor wounds to giving last rites. I even went on some litter hauls when we ran out of litter bearers. In the forward aid station, you were never out of artillery or mortar range. I've been sniped at by rifles, I've been sniped at by 88s and by Anzio Annie, and I received eight battle stars in Italy and Europe. About every six weeks, some of us chaplains would take an LCI and go down to Naples and visit the wounded. We'd stay there a week and then come back. Actually, I was glad to get back to the front because the guys in the rear area were more scared than the guys at the front. Back in the rear, you imagine things—at the front, you're where reality is.[37]

On the night of the sixteenth, Daniel Ficco, of C Company, 157th, went out on a three-man patrol to capture a prisoner:

> There were two Indians in our group, named Valdez and Chavez. We didn't wear helmets; we wore those knit jeep caps and we turned 'em so you couldn't see the bill on 'em. Also, my hands had been hit by shrapnel earlier and they were all bandaged up. At night, the white bandages were pretty obvious, so I took some mud and covered 'em up so I could get by. We went up to a bridge that went over the canal. There were German troops all up and down this bank as far as I could see. We walked down into a ditch with Germans all around. On the other side of the bank, there were three tanks and some armored vehicles; they looked like they were getting ready for an attack. So we worked our way over to the road along the bank to a big bush and we saw a guard walking back and forth on that bridge. I told Valdez and Chavez that I was going to go down the road a ways and then come back up the road and have this guard stop me. Valdez and Chavez would be behind him and then they could take him. Well, we took him prisoner and made it back to our lines. I gave my report and our artillery and tanks put down a pretty good field of fire right where the enemy was.[38]

At 2030 hours on the sixteenth, reports were received that thirteen German tanks were rolling down the main highway after having knocked out a section of 57mm A-T guns.[39] The panzers were now grinding forward, pumping shell after shell into the flanks of the 3rd Battalion, 179th, forcing it to withdraw farther. A mass of Germans had slipped behind G Company—which was now cut off from the rest of the battalion—and was causing panic.[40] As the regiment's official history states,

> For the first time in its history, the 179th's companies and battalions were disorganized, scattered. Communications cut, the C.O. [Colonel Malcolm R.

> Kammerer] got only vague reports as to the location and situation of his forces. The M.P.s had to establish straggler lines along all roads to direct those who had escaped the enemy's clutches and were wandering around behind the lines, shaken, lost. . . . Men did trickle back in twos and threes, but they couldn't be employed to buttress the sagging line; they came back crying, hysterical. Even veteran section leaders, ashen-grey and quaking, broke under the strain: sleepless for days and pinned in their holes by artillery, they had come out only to find Brobdingnagian steel monsters charging at them from all sides, pouring out a deadly fire as they came. These men had looked down the muzzles of cannons twenty-five yards away! Those who lived were only half alive. One haggard, ragged squad leader who came back without a squad, squatted on his haunches outside the S-1 tent. For two hours he sat unmoving, eyes glazed and wide open, staring into space. Not a sound escaped his lips, but for two hours tears rolled down his cheeks unchecked.[41]

Yes, the 179th's 2nd and 3rd Battalions—both reduced to little more than company strength—had been routed and defeated, but only temporarily. Here and there, officers and noncoms were pulling together the shattered remnants of their units, reorganizing them, exhorting them, calming them, preparing them to go back into the battle.

Pausing to regroup and wait for reinforcements, the Germans gave the nearly beaten 179th Regiment the breathing room it needed. Lieutenant Colonel Wayne L. Johnson, commanding the 1st Battalion, ordered A Company to shore up the battered 2nd Battalion in front of the Lateral Road on exposed ground two and a half kilometers south of Aprilia.[42] "They brought up cooks and cook's helpers and clerks and anybody else who could carry a rifle," said Robert LaDu, F Company, 179th.

Kammerer ordered a counterattack at 2300 hours that night. Hastily assembling a force from what remained of A, E, and F Companies, the 179th attempted to throw the enemy back. LaDu recalled being startled at the attack order:

> We were going to attack! Colonel Weigand said to me, "You take the point—we're going back across that road." The German tanks just drove up and down that road and shot up everything. I had just spotted a German and I figured if I don't get him, he's going to get us if we tried to walk across that open field. So I started to skirt that field and the colonel yelled at me, "Not that way—right across here!" I held my finger up and tried to hush him. Well, I got the German and told him to walk right straight to the colonel. I took one prisoner, but he wasn't normal. I don't know if he was doped up or what, but he was just dazed. We had a bunch of our guys captured, too. We went back across that road into a little streambed and held it that night. The next day, they told us to fall back to a wooded area, the Pines [the Padiglione Woods]. Colonel Weigand was being relieved—he had had diarrhea for two months, and battle fatigue. They sent up Colonel Darby, who had been in charge of the Rangers, and he took over the battalion temporarily.[43]

Helping the 179th to stem the gray tide rushing at it was Lieutenant James M. Sherrick, a forward observer with the 160th Field Artillery. Informed by another officer that the 179th was pulling back and the infantry could no longer provide covering fire for Sherrick's OP, which was rapidly being surrounded, the artillery lieutenant made a fateful decision: He told his enlisted men to pull out—he would stay and continue to call in fire coordinates. Alone in the building, which was being blasted by enemy artillery, Sherrick continued to shorten the range on the American shells and drop them among the German soldiers, who were nearly at the door. His last transmission was to shell the very house he was in, then his radio went silent. Given up for dead, it was learned later that he had been taken prisoner. For his courage, Sherrick was awarded the Distinguished Service Cross.[44]

Everett Easley of E Company, 179th, also recalled the desperate nature of the counterattack:

> Things were really screwed up, with people from all different outfits mixed up together. Then we got orders to attack! Jesus Christ! We hadn't had any sleep for two or three days! But we got together and took off. There were burning tanks all over the place—it smelled like roasting meat. We found them ready to attack us. We were lucky; we had a rolling barrage. It was unbelievable the mess our artillery created. The Germans must have been concentrated and got the full force of a whole bunch of artillery. There were heads, arms, and legs scattered from hell to breakfast.[45]

The 179th's brave but pitifully small counterattack was soon thrown back when the Germans counter-counterattacked with a flanking maneuver by their panzers. E Company was hard hit, A Company had 30 men reported as missing in action and was nearly annihilated, and F Company was battling for its life. The 179th had no option other than to call off the attack and retire as best it could.[46]

Meanwhile, in the 157th's sector, the *Wehrmacht* now attempted to hit Lieutenant Joe Robertson's G Company near the caves by using the wadis to its advantage. Seeing the advancing enemy, G Company's machine gunners and BAR men, situated atop Buon Riposo Ridge, raked the area with deadly fire each time the Germans tried moving toward their position. Soon the wadis were choked with scores of German dead and the enemy was forced to temporarily break off the attack.[47]

Although wounded in the leg, Bud McMillan, K Company, 157th, was still at his post, firing at targets. "Just before dark, here comes a whole bunch of British guys," he said.

> They came right up to where we were and stood up and fixed bayonets and started blowing whistles and they attacked right through us. I remember thinking, "Oh Lord, them mortars are gonna come in here now." I just took off,

holdin' on to the belt around my leg and hobblin' and jumpin' ditches and barbed wire fences and dodgin' bullets. I ran on back a pretty good ways and I had lost right much blood during the day and I had my leg all bandaged up. I got back there pretty far and there was this British tank firing near the Flyover right straight down the road. I got down along the bottom of that road. I remember the German anti-tank shells comin' over and they'd hit the ground and go *tuh-weee* and go on off. And those British guys were walkin' around that tank up there and firin'. Finally, I crawled out and one of them saw me and came down and saw that I was wounded. He took my canteen cup and went back up and got me a cup of tea. They cooked it right on the back of the tank. I took a swallow of that and it burned my tongue and that hurt worse than the damn leg wound did.

In a little while, a shell came in and hit the tank and blew it up. It might've killed a couple of the Brits, I don't know. After a while, another vehicle came along and some British guys helped me up the hill and put me in a vehicle with a British tanker named Doolittle. His ears were all burned off, and his nose and hands were burned up. They evacuated us back to the hospital area at Anzio.[48]

McMillan was sent back to Naples, where he stayed for about a month, and then rejoined his outfit on the beachhead in April.

That night, Captain Felix Sparks made his way back to the rear and picked up what was supposed to be a platoon of Sherman tanks, only to find just two tanks available to him. "The rest supposedly had mechanical problems," he said, with some skepticism. Nevertheless, he brought the two Shermans up to the front under cover of darkness and positioned them where the two tank destroyers had been earlier in the day.

When the Germans started coming after us the next morning, the tanks kept them off of us. So the Germans went way around our left flank and had broken through the 179th on our right, so they didn't bother us very much. Sometimes the German replacements would make a mistake and get lost and barge right through our positions, so we'd shoot them. Moving at night is very difficult. But they didn't make any concentrated attack on my position after the first day. They didn't even shell us. But they were all around us and in back of us. They had already learned that if they did attack, we'd bring in artillery fire. So they gave our position a wide berth.

Sparks's company, which once numbered nearly 200 men, was down to less than 50 by this time. As the gray river of German infantry and tanks streamed by on the left and right, heading for the sea, the two tanks with E Company took them under fire. The Germans tried knocking out the American armor, but without success. Although temporarily safe, the remnants of E Company were merely a small island in a sea of enemy troops. And this island would soon be engulfed by a tidal wave.[49]

Elements of I Company, 157th, were sent forward to reinforce the 2nd Battalion but were soon turned around. "We took two platoons and weapons out to help 2nd Battalion at the caves," recalled "Doc Joe" Franklin, a medic with I Company.

> The scouts went forward from where we stopped, then they came back and said we weren't needed. We should have been there. Anyway, we went back to our original bivouac area, about 300–400 yards behind the underpass, and then it hit the fan for the 2nd Battalion. Our company was butterfly-bombed that night and I had casualties all over the place. I was taking care of a British soldier whose jaw was blown away when our first sergeant, Willard Cody, came by with the company. He called out to me to stay with the wounded and he'd send someone back for me.

(Cody would later be awarded both the Silver Star and Legion of Merit and receive a battlefield commission.)

A nearby explosion later that day caused Franklin to brave flying metal to see if any wounded needed his help. It was too late; one of the lieutenants in the company had been examining an unexploded butterfly bomb when it went off, removing his arms and legs and literally blowing his brain out of his skull. Three other men who had been watching the lieutenant also lay dead. Sickened by the sight—and the stupidity of playing with unexploded ordnance—Franklin stayed with some mortarmen for the rest of the night until someone came to guide him to I Company's new positions a few hundred yards in front of the Overpass. The company had just survived another artillery barrage and attack by infantry. There were plenty of casualties around—both living and dead—so he set up his aid station in a lean-to shed of a nearby farmhouse. The battle raged all around Franklin's makeshift hospital. At one point, the Germans even blew up a clearly marked ambulance.[50]

• • •

Although the main weight of the German thrust fell on the 157th and 179th Regiments, the 180th, farther to the right, was not spared. Lieutenant Bill Whitman, executive officer of B Company, 180th, described the incredible human-wave attacks:

> There were no let-ups in the German attacks. They were like animals as they leaped over their own dead and continued to come on. Some were firing from the hip with their submachine guns and some were using captured American BARs. Some screamed encouragement to others as their lines wavered under our intense small-arms fire. I had given the men orders not to fire until they came within 300 yards of us and then to pour the fire into them. This range almost guaranteed no misses as there were so many of them coming at us. Our company 60mm mortars took them under fire before they came within 300 yards of us. Meanwhile, the artillery was swish, swish, swishing the shells over our heads and into their midst and air bursts over their heads. . . .

> The deep irrigation ditches to our front played a large part in stopping their tanks. Even so, the German tanks advanced as far as they could and then supported their infantry with direct cannon fire on our positions. Their fire was murderous. The ranges were so short that when they fired, it sounded like "Slam-Bang"; the shells seemed to explode as they were fired from the guns. . . . We held because we knew that if we didn't we would die. It was just that simple. Everywhere to our front were dead and dying Germans. Their gray heaps and bundles that were bodies were strewn across the open ground. We were shooting them to pieces. Wave after wave, in groups and singly, they kept coming. As men fell dead or wounded behind our machine guns, others sprang into their places and kept the guns firing. I remember when one attack was starting, one of our corporals yelled to his men, "Here they come. All right, you sons-of-bitches, start earning your pay!"[51]

Many men not only earned their pay but lost their lives in service to their units. Private first class Max Lowing, a member of the 180th's Anti-Tank Company, aimed his 57mm anti-tank gun, virtually worthless against the Germans' heavy armor, and fired away, his shots pinging harmlessly off the thick-skinned enemy tanks. Lowing did slow the panzers momentarily, however, before they cranked their turrets in his direction and destroyed him and his piece with a direct hit before rumbling on.[52]

Lucas tried to restore the 45th's dented lines. He ordered Ernest Harmon, the stocky firebrand commanding the 1st Armored Division, to send a battalion of tanks cross-country to aid the 45th's efforts at rebuilding the human dike that had earlier been burst by the German waves. But the tank support failed when the Shermans got bogged down in the mud and were picked off by German gunners. Late that day, the 1st Armored sent a company of Shermans up the Via Anziate from under the Overpass to duel with the onrushing panzers. The fight lasted for several hours, and when the smoke cleared, the enemy armored thrust had been halted. As darkness fell, Harmon's tanks withdrew to the protection of the Padiglione Woods to be available in case they were needed again.[53]

The 45th Infantry Division, which only a short while ago appeared to be on the verge of disintegrating, was restoring itself. L Company, the 180th Regiment's reserve company, filled the gap between E and F companies. Other units and stragglers were pushed toward the gaping holes that had been torn in the defense.[54] At midnight on the sixteenth, the left flank of the 157th managed to make contact with a British unit—the 7th Battalion of the Oxford and Buckinghamshire Regiment—and hoped that the flank had been secured.[55] After dark, food, water, and ammunition were distributed to the men all along the front, and the dead and wounded were brought out, often under continual harassing enemy fire. Of indispensable help again to the 45th was the artillery, which broke up massed assaults of armor and infantry. In fact, on the sixteenth, the division's four artillery battalions fired a total of 8,616 105mm and 155mm rounds, 3,633 by the 160th FA Battalion alone.[56]

But E Company, 157th, was being systematically ground into oblivion. Shortly before midnight, a company from the 715th Division's 725th Grenadier Regiment infiltrated into Captain Sparks's positions and killed or captured the men in the outposts.[57] One of Sparks's men taken prisoner was Second Lieutenant Jeremiah W. Moher, a platoon leader. His platoon was dug in on the west side of the highway.

> A small detachment of Germans came down a ditch by the highway and captured me and two of my men. We started back up the road and I got shot with a machine pistol by some German in another group going the opposite direction toward our CP. They hit me and the sergeant with me. I had a bullet hole in the top of my left arm and one at the elbow. They took us back about a thousand yards to their CP and held us there for about a day, then they took us away. There were about five of us from E Company. They also patched me up. But they only saw the wound at my elbow; the other one was still bleeding. We walked about a day and I said, "Hey, I'm still bleeding." They said, "Oh, we missed that hole." It was worse than the one they patched.[58]

• • •

The situation was also tense in the 180th's sector. First Lieutenant Bill Whitman, B Company, 180th, recalled, "I heard the 'clicks' close around me as the soldiers fixed their bayonets. I remember a flush of pride surging through me as I laid my tommy gun magazines out side by side; if I was to die, it would be with my men, the bravest of the brave."[59]

Captain Joseph Bosa, of the 171st Field Artillery Battalion, recorded some of the events of the day in his diary:

> Our artillery fired almost continuously until nearly noon. During the p.m., things slacked up a bit, but there were many targets until well into the night.
>
> Last night and today the German planes have been over and around us in almost continuous sorties. The bombers circle low at night and, in spite of the 90mm AA fire, are able to drop their bombs at will. At times it seems that our superior air force is almost a myth. The Jerries hit our ammo dump near the beach and have depleted our supply somewhat.
>
> The Forty-fifth Div. units took most of the blow and our artillery was instrumental in knocking out several tanks as well as holding the foot troops of the enemy down.[60]

The mud-caked Thunderbirds huddled, shivering, in their watery foxholes—holes that the men feared might soon become their graves. With darkness descending over the battlefield, it was easy to let one's mind flow, to endlessly rerun the incredible events of the day, to remember wounded comrades, missing comrades, dead comrades and wonder if one would soon join them. Many of their officers were gone, and their sergeants as well. The heavy mantle of leadership would soon pass to inexperienced corporals and privates first class. Each man felt utterly alone, yet connected by some strange, mysterious force to his brethren in arms huddling in holes to his right and to his left. What would morning bring—renewed attacks or a respite from the awful fighting?

As terrible as the German onslaught of 16 February had been, worse—much worse—was still to come.

8

Abandon Every Hope

17–18 February 1944

Through me the way into the suffering city, through me the way to eternal pain, through me the way that runs among the lost. Justice urged on my high artificer; my maker was divine authority, the highest wisdom, and the primal love. Before me nothing but eternal things were made, and I endure eternally. Abandon every hope, who enter here.

—Dante Alighieri, *The Inferno,* Canto III

DURING THE BRIEF LULL THAT FOLLOWED the massive initial German counterattack on 16 February, Kesselring drove to von Mackensen's headquarters in Genzano, south of the Alban Hills, in his big field marshal's staff car. Gone was Kesselring's genial, "Smiling Albert" nature. He had little faith in the general to begin with; now he was livid over the inability of von Mackensen's Fourteenth Army to win the field on the sixteenth. Did von Mackensen not realize that by not splitting the 45th Division and driving through to the sea, the entire German effort in Italy was in grave danger—that both of their military careers were in jeopardy?

True, von Mackensen had thrown everything he had at the Allied line and gained considerable ground, inflicted heavy casualties on the Americans and British, and appeared, for all intents and purposes, to be within an arm's length of a major victory. But by not gaining that victory, the all-out effort was, clear and simple, a failure of disastrous proportions. Morale in the Fourteenth Army was at its lowest ebb, the result of the relentless Allied shelling and the fact that the 45th refused to break. The day's effort had expended many lives, used up many precious rounds of ammunition, and burned up many liters of scarce fuel but had not resulted in the one thing that Hitler demanded: victory. Now an even greater effort would be required. And that effort must come immediately.[1]

The effort, however, would have to come mostly from decimated units. In the first two days of the counterattack, the Germans had lost 2,569 men killed, wounded, or captured, and the average infantry battalion was down to 120–150 men—about the authorized strength of a German infantry company.

One German soldier of the 715th Division wrote home: "It's really a wonder I am still alive. What I have seen is probably more than many saw in Russia. I've been lying night and day under artillery barrages like the world has never seen."[2]

Von Mackensen issued orders that the infantry-armor attack would continue without letup against the Thunderbird positions during the night of 16–17 February. Then, shortly after dawn on the seventeenth, the *Luftwaffe* would bomb and strafe the 45th. Following this, elements of the German 65th and 715th Infantry and 114th *Jäger* Divisions would emerge from their hiding places in and around Aprilia and Carroceto and strike the 157th and 179th Regiments while two additional divisions—the 26th Panzer and 29th Panzer Grenadier Divisions, augmented by two tank battalions—would move into position and stand poised to exploit any cracks in the American line. Over 450 artillery pieces, railroad guns, rocket launchers, and anti-aircraft guns would support the German attack. With his superior's angry words still ringing in his ears, von Mackensen knew that, this time, the attack *must* succeed.[3]

The second major attempt to split the 45th began on schedule in the predawn hours of the seventeenth with another bone-jarring barrage that went on and on and on. The GIs of the 45th hunched over deeply in their holes, gritted their teeth, said their prayers, and did the only thing they could do—they took it. After what seemed to be an eternity, the fearsome German artillery barrage finally slackened. But the Thunderbirds knew all too well that the lessening of artillery did not signal a respite; instead, it heralded the fact that the enemy infantry and armor were about to join the clash. Like some sort of superhuman monster that would not die, the undeterred German Army threw fourteen infantry battalions, plus the *Lehr* Regiment, which was attempting to regain its self-respect, into yet another all-out assault across the muddy, pockmarked fields against the American positions.

At about 0430 hours on the seventeenth, Private first class Lloyd C. "Blackie" Greer of Lindsay, Oklahoma, a machine gunner with I Company, 180th, was sleeping fitfully in his water-filled foxhole when he awakened to the sounds of the enemy drawing near. Jumping to his gun, he saw enemy infantry heading toward his position and the positions of nearby F Company, which his gun was supporting. His .30 caliber gun immediately began chattering, scything men down as though they were stalks of wheat. The Germans brought up a 40mm anti-tank gun in an attempt to silence Greer. At a range of one hundred yards, the piece shattered Greer's machine gun.

Stunned but unhurt, Greer abandoned his position, found another machine gun, and resumed firing, wiping out the gun crew that had wrecked his first weapon and once again stopping the attacking lines. Greer kept up his fire all day, pausing only to reload. That night, while back at the company CP to pick up supplies, he saw his company commander, who praised his work with the machine gun and said, "I'll see you tomorrow night." Greer replied, "I don't think you will, sir," convinced that his luck had run out and that within another twenty-four hours, he would be either dead or captured. He was right on one of those counts.[4]

Guns cracked on both sides, tracers spun through the air, men shouted and screamed, and munitions exploded underfoot and in the air; the earth was in convulsive upheaval. Wave after wave of steel and flesh flung itself at the American positions, was cut down, only to be replaced by countless more waves. Two cruisers offshore and hundreds of American artillery pieces joined the battle and, from the skies above, the Allied air forces added their bombs and rockets to the carnage below. At 0900 hours, a massive Allied air armada appeared in the sky, dropping 1,100 tons of explosives onto the onrushing lines of Germans—to date the greatest tonnage of bombs dropped in support of ground troops.[5] Captain Joseph Bosa recorded the air assault in his diary: "This morning, hundreds of bombers have gone over—they are British mostly, with some B-17s. The British [planes] may be Lancasters. . . . We can stand up on the rise above our FDC [Fire Direction Center] and see the flashes of the German AA fire from the ground. The bombers are really pounding."[6]

No sooner had the Allied planes disappeared, their work done, than the outnumbered, audacious *Luftwaffe* came roaring in with forty-five Stuka dive bombers, swooping down on the American defenders, and knocking out the 3rd Battalion, 179th's communications. Although the Allies claimed air superiority (in fact, the Allies had some 2,000 aircraft to the Germans' 350),[7] to the soldier on the ground it seemed more like fifty-fifty. A grim joke of the day went: "We get thirty-six hours of air cover every day—twelve of ours and twenty-four of theirs."[8]

Having been pummeled for hours by nearly every weapon in the German arsenal, the 179th's 2nd and 3rd Battalions seemed on the verge of destruction. In the fragile seam between the 157th and 179th, south of Aprilia, the Germans kept hammering away to force an opening.[9] At Buon Riposo Ridge, where H Company, 157th, was in support, the bombardment by the Germans' railroad guns finally eased up and Corporal Henry Kaufman, who had turned twenty-three just two days earlier, crawled out of his slit trench to look for a safer position. He was devastated by the scene outside his foxhole—dead Americans, many ripped limb from limb, lay scattered in grotesque poses about the torn-up landscape. Shaken, Kaufman moved back to a ten-foot-high cliff where he found a buddy, Private first class Fred

White. Suddenly, a German tank appeared and began blasting the area with its 88mm gun. The two soldiers frantically dug into the side of the cliff (one never went anywhere at Anzio without one's entrenching tool) as shells screamed overhead. White slipped into his horizontal foxhole, but all Kaufman had time to do was hit the dirt. The panzer finally backed off and Kaufman looked up to see that the shelling had caved in the cliff on top of White. Kaufman frantically used his hands to dig out his comrade, who was unhurt except for some cuts and scratches on his face.[10]

• • •

Just as the continued blows of a hammer push a nail, little by little, into a board, so too did the continual German pounding manage, by noon, to push the scattered and disorganized remnants of the 45th back about a mile down the Via Anziate to the intersection of Dead End Road. Two panzers accompanying the *Lehr* Regiment rushed forward and rumbled through the pockets of defenders. One tank was knocked out before it reached the Overpass, but the other continued on, passed through the opening, and became the target for every Allied gun in range. Within seconds, it was nothing more than a shattered, smoldering wreck.

Although the center of the division sagged under the unrelenting pressure, the left shoulder, held by the 157th's 2nd and 3rd Battalions and buttressed by the British 56th Division, and the right shoulder, manned by the 180th, bent their flanks to resemble the sloping sides of a bowl and held. But for how long?[11]

Throughout the seventeenth, the Thunderbirds absorbed every blow the Germans aimed at them, bending but not breaking. Tons of German shells slammed into the 45th's positions with seemingly no effect. It was obvious, however, that the battle for the beachhead had reached a critical stage. No unit could be expected to withstand indefinitely the pounding that the 45th was receiving. It also became obvious that Lucas's days as VI Corps commander were numbered. The pressure from Alexander and Churchill on Clark to dump Lucas and put a more dynamic, offense-minded leader in his place became irresistible. Clark looked at the choices available to him—the other division commanders—and realized Truscott would be the best. Clark sent a message to Truscott that relieved him from command of the 3rd Division and installed him as deputy VI Corps commander, with the expectation he would soon take over from Lucas. Major General John "Iron Mike" O'Daniel assumed command of the 3rd.

Arriving that afternoon at VI Corps's headquarters, which were spread out between a former Italian Army artillery barracks and a maze of underground wine cellars in Nettuno, Truscott discovered an atmosphere of gloom and doom pervading the command post. He also learned that Lucas had just ordered a counterattack. The acetate-covered situation map in headquarters graphically showed what was happening on the battlefield: arrows drawn with red grease pencils indicated enemy movements stabbing toward the Allied positions, drawn in blue. The smudge marks on the acetate made it clear that the lines had been drawn and redrawn many times, each time closer to the Lateral Road, VI Corps's final defensive line.[12] On the map, where the caves were indicated, a blue circle had been drawn, with the military symbol for the 2nd Battalion, 157th, lettered inside. Brown's command post had become the broken-off tip of a salient as the Germans either wiped out or pushed back the units that were on either side of it. Essentially, the 2nd Battalion was surrounded. As the battalion's perimeter continued to shrink due to the pounding it was receiving from all sides, what few of Brown's men who had not been killed or captured gravitated toward the relative safety of the caves.

No one could say for certain why the caves—a vast series of tunnels carved into a large hill mass—were built, but they seem to have been constructed during World War I and may have been used to store gunpowder, which had been manufactured in Anzio. Carved out of soft sandstone, the walls had turned granite-hard due to exposure to the air over the years.[13] Henry Kaufman provided a detailed description of the caves:

> There were some six caves in all, about a thousand or so yards apart. . . . These particular caves were very large, about a normal city block long and a half a block wide and about fifteen feet high. Each cave contained maybe fifteen ten-by-twelve rooms. The cave I was in sheltered me and five other members of my company, as well as at least fifty Italian women of assorted ages, some with babies. They were all refugees from nearby Aprilia, trying to survive the bombing and shelling of both sides and so they were actually living in these caves.[14]

On the night of the seventeenth, a soldier from E Company dashed breathlessly into the 2nd Battalion CP in the caves; a force of about a hundred Germans was right behind him. Warned of the impending attack, the defenders took up positions at the mouths of the caves and let loose with a hail of bullets and grenades. Forward observers brought down artillery fire—high explosive and white phosphorus—on themselves and the enemy in an hour-long barrage. Most of the attacking force was killed or wounded and the men, women, and children inside the caves were safe, at least for the time being.[15] Outside, however, the panzers were now behind the lines of Lieutenant Joe Robertson's G Company, creating havoc and panic. G Company was virtually cut off.

Things were no better in E Company, which had been nearly overrun by the 725th Grenadier Regiment of the 715th Infantry Division and was left stranded in its forward position.[16] Sparks's company was saved from total annihilation only by the bravery of its men and that of the two tank crews, commanded by First Lieutenant Tommy L. Cobb, Jr., from the 191st Tank

Battalion, that he had brought forward. The Shermans' 75mm main guns and .50 caliber machine guns worked overtime, keeping the Germans from getting too close. Sparks's men—fourteen from E Company and four from H Company who had attached themselves to E—were in a precarious spot and nearly out of ammunition. Four panzers were closing in on the tiny enclave when, at 0500 hours, Sparks received orders to retire what was left of his company to the caves, several hundred yards to the rear.[17] He said,

> I got orders to pull back and form a line that was more or less on a line with other parts of the battalion. The other two companies, F and G, were to my left rear, 300–400 yards away. They were in an area called the caves. The other two companies were not *in* the caves; they were on top of a flat ridge [Buon Riposo Ridge], with the ravine and caves behind them. It was a weird position. The caves were cut into the side of a ravine, and you could get a hundred men in there without any problem. The entrance was maybe ten feet wide and it got bigger inside the chamber. I had never seen it before; I didn't even know it was there.
>
> I first thought of moving the night before, but if you try to make a retrograde movement at night, you lose control of your people; they're liable to disappear on you. So I decided to make it in daylight. I gave orders to my men to dig in on a little hill that was about fifteen or twenty feet high and adjacent to the main highway. When we got to that little hill and started digging in, we started to get fired upon by tanks. But we were already pretty well dug in. And we had German troops going by us on both sides. We were the right flank of the battalion, which had not existed prior to the time we got there. We had excellent observation and were dug in in a circle. The Germans just went by us and left us alone. But what the damn fools didn't know was that I had an artillery radio and every time I saw a group, I brought in artillery fire on them.[18]

Cobb's tanks knocked out two of the enemy panzers while the 158th FA Battalion dropped smoke shells to screen E Company's retrograde movement.[19]

Within the labyrinth, the battalion staff had set up its command post. Here, too, the medical detachment, under Captain Peter Graffagnino, the 2nd Battalion surgeon, had set up shop. Wounded Germans and Americans alike were cared for by Dr. Graffagnino and his medics, with the help of German doctors and aid men who had been captured. In other parts of the caves, German POWs were kept under guard.[20] Pete Conde made several hazardous trips to the caves, bringing up jerry cans full of precious water, and was struck by an oddity. "I remember seeing this German doctor in there who had been captured," he said. "The German doctors had pistols and wore them all the time—nobody took his away from him. This doctor still had a pistol in a holster on his belt. He was taking care of the German wounded."[21]

Every man in the caves had an assignment. First Lieutenant Jean Unterberger, the battalion S-2 (intelligence officer), had the thankless job of crawling out to the battlefield and searching German corpses for anything that might yield information. "After one of the hardest battles," he said, "I went down in the field and found a dead German, about twenty years old." In the German's pocket was an unfinished letter to his mother: "Shortly after you get this, I will be dead. Our officers have lied to us. We are low on ammunition and low on food. The war is lost. Germany is lost." Unterberger later turned the letter over to the Red Cross in hopes that it would find its way to the dead soldier's mother.[22]

Corporal Al Bedard, one of Unterberger's men, said, "My job was to set up observation posts and accompany patrols behind enemy lines. Anything we saw that should be reported to the CP, we reported. Most of us were picked from each line company—I was originally in G Company—so every time G Company would go into action, I'd go with them. We were more or less the liaison between the company commanders and the battalion CP."[23]

• • •

At dusk on the eighteenth, the Germans were again dangerously close to the caves, infiltrating up to the openings singly and in pairs. The men inside poured an unceasing stream of fire into the enemy, cutting the Germans down whenever one or more tried to enter the caves. A company of German troops crept close enough to the entrances to engage in a small-arms-and-grenade duel with those inside. The 157th's G and H Companies, occupying the high ground near the caves, raked the attackers while, inside, Captain George Hubbert, an artillery liaison officer from the 158th Field Artillery Battalion, called friendly fire down on the position. For two hours, the murderous bombardment continued, until the last German was dead, wounded, or had withdrawn. The next morning revealed scenes of gruesome horror, as scores of dead Germans, or parts of Germans, covered the ground in front of the caves.[24]

Henry Kaufman reported,

> From February 17th to the 18th, we were trapped by the Germans and unable to move more than fifteen or twenty feet outside of the cave. On the 18th, we were attacked by the enemy, in very close hand-to-hand combat, with fixed bayonets, right outside the entrance to our cave. Using the mouth of the cave whenever we could for protective cover, we somehow managed to kill several Germans outside the cave; in the ensuing battle, we captured an entire German machine gun nest consisting of three Germans and their machine gun. We brought the Germans and their machine gun into the cave and kept them there as our prisoners of war.[25]

Al Bedard said that in the caves,

> We had perfect cover there, but there wasn't a hell of a lot we could see. In the entrances to the caves, we set up fields of machine gun fire. The Germans attacked us night after night with one outfit after another, and we broke up their

> attacks for at least seven days. Every morning I'd look out and there'd be German machine gun crews lying dead behind their guns where our interdicting fire had cut them down during the night. They had us surrounded and we couldn't get out, but we kept breaking up the center of their attack every time they tried to hit us. Finally, they threw everything they had at us. The last couple of nights we called down our own artillery on our positions to break up the attacks. They were swarming all over the tops of these caves out in the open.[26]

Meanwhile, Henry Kaufman, unaware that the 2nd Battalion was in a nearby cave, had left his portion of the caves to find an officer—any officer—who would take the responsibility of leading the men to the rear (a rumor going around was that anyone who retreated from the caves without an officer present would be court-martialed for desertion). Kaufman took off to find the cave that held the 2nd Battalion CP. Unable to locate it, Kaufman found a few men in foxholes, farther to the front, near a two-story building. They were the remnants of E Company, still holding out and fighting for their lives. He was told there were no officers left in E Company; they thought Captain Sparks had been killed. Kaufman managed to make it back to the caves, where the situation was becoming worrisome but not yet desperate.[27] After dark, wounded soldiers were slipped out the back entrances and guided 1,000 yards to the rear where jeeps and ambulances were waiting to evacuate them to the hospital. Supplies were brought up under armed guard and details crawled out to obtain water from nearby streams.[28] As precarious as the 2nd Battalion's position was, it was vital for Brown's men to hold it, for it formed a solid shoulder on the left flank and was truly an irritant in the side of the attacking Germans. But no one knew how long the 2nd Battalion would be able to remain.

The men isolated on the front lines and in the caves were in serious need of resupply; water and rations were nearly exhausted and the Germans had cut off the routes used by the supply parties. So desperately thirsty were the men that, according to the 157th's history, "Near one company sector trickled a stream in which lay several dead Germans, who had been cut down by machine-gun fire. The water ran blood red but the thirsty men filled their canteens, boiled and drank it."[29] Philip Burke, the executive officer of B Company, 157th, remembered his time at the caves. "We were hit by a German attack, but they couldn't get us because the apertures and openings to the caves were easily defended. We were pretty secure there, but there was a hell of a lot going on around us. The part of the caves I was in had two or three openings from which we were defending. We couldn't move out except at night, when we'd go down to the creek to get the dirtiest water I ever drank. It was drainage from the farms in the area."[30]

The Germans encircling the 2nd Battalion began saturating the area with their six-barreled *Nebelwerfer* rocket launchers. "When the shelling subsided a little," Henry Kaufman reported, "we heard one of the women in the rear of the cave screaming hysterically." The woman's baby, its face purple, was

View of the "Gate of Hell," the battered Overpass that became the Germans' objective—and obsession—from 16 to 19 February 1944. (Courtesy of 45th Infantry Division Archives)

dead in her arms, having suffocated from a lack of oxygen. "Evidently, the women were cooking in the rear of the cave using charcoal as fuel." The charcoal had used up the oxygen at the rear of the cave, which had no ventilation.[31] For the moment, the 2nd Battalion was relatively safe, but supplies were rapidly dwindling, enemy pressure was growing, and Brown knew that he and his men could not hold out in the caves indefinitely.

• • •

Besides the surrounded 2nd Battalion, one other crucial feature was plainly obvious on the situation map in Lucas's command post. At the point where the Via Anziate bisected the Lateral Road, there was a symbol for a highway overpass, or, as the British called it, the Flyover.

If anything at Anzio was the literal embodiment of Dante's allegorical Gate of Hell, it was the Overpass. The only paved road that ran straight from the German lines at Carroceto to the sea passed through the Overpass. A high, sturdy embankment ran for more than a hundred yards on either side of the Overpass, channeling all attempts to reach the sea toward its gaping maw. To achieve their objective, the Germans would have to cross flat, open ground and pass through this small archway, no more than twenty yards wide. To stop them, the Allies would have to defend this opening with everything they had.

With the 2nd Battalion of the 157th shunted off to the side and surrounded and the 179th pushed back and in disarray, there now seemed to be little to stop von Mackensen's troops from driving all the way to the beach. There was only one banged-up unit left in their path: the 157th's I Company, commanded by Captain James C. Evans, which had formed a thin, semicircular defensive position in front of the Overpass and was prepared to hold to the last man. Here, and all along the 45th's line, everyone knew the crucial moment was about to come.[32] Now the years of experience gained in the monthly drills in the National Guard armories of Oklahoma City and Denver and Albuquerque, the annual summer encampments at Camp Maximilliano Luna and Camp George West, and the large-scale maneuvers at Fort Bliss and Fort Polk were about to pay off. Whatever fighting spirit was carried in the blood of the sons of those who moved the American frontier westward—or who valiantly resisted that westward expansion—was about to be called on. The hard steel of character that was forged on the parched rock of Sicily, the flaming cauldron of Salerno, and the icy heights of Venafro was now to be put to the ultimate test.

General Eagles ordered the 157th's K and L Companies to shore up I Company guarding the gateway to the beachhead. Behind the Overpass and Lateral Road were four "stop lines" manned only by clerks, cooks, and anyone else capable of firing a rifle. No one gave much hope of these stop lines stopping anyone should the Germans break through at the Overpass.[33] William C. Pullum, first sergeant of K Company, 157th, recalled that his company had been recently moved up to the Overpass. "We were in a blocking position with I Company. We were on one side of the road and I Company was on the other. We were in front of the Overpass and were in a very tenuous position. We had an awful lot of folks wounded there. We were actually supposed to attack and relieve the men at the caves, then realized we couldn't. Daylight caught us and we started to get casualties like it was going out of style."

The company commander was wounded, and two lieutenants who had gone out on missions failed to return, so Pullum went to one of the lieutenants and told him he was going to have to take over the company. "While we were talking, he got shot. Then I went to another one and told him he was the last officer and that he would have to take over and darned if *he* didn't get shot! So I took over and for the first time, the radio worked. It hadn't worked up until then and it didn't work after that." But Pullum got a message to the battalion commander and told him the company was in an exposed position and requested permission to pull back. Captain Mitchell, the battalion commander, granted permission and Pullum managed to get the company back to the position they had occupied the night before.[34]

At dusk on the seventeenth, the expected German attempt to breach the Overpass began. A concentrated force of German troops charged I Company's position but became hung up on the rolls of concertina wire strung in front of the position and were cut to pieces by intense machine gun fire. During the night, the Germans tried infiltrating the position from the right flank, blasting the area with three well-concealed tanks and directing another fearsome artillery barrage at the Overpass's defenders. Captain Evans's company was hanging on, but just barely. During the night, it received a vital resupply of ammunition but no food or water.[35]

• • •

The German side was equally in crisis. Faced with a dwindling supply of ordnance for his big guns, Kesselring issued the following directive to his subordinates:

> On the first day of attack [16 February], our artillery expended much ammunition. This large expenditure is not in proportion to our supply. The ammunition must be utilized to clear the way for our infantry by destroying enemy pockets of resistance. The infantry must make use of our artillery fire and the fire of its own heavy weapons [i.e., mortars and machine guns] in order to gain ground. It appears that fighting on the beachhead will last for several more days and we cannot expend ammunition on secondary targets.[36]

As punishing as its attacks against the Allies had been, the Fourteenth Army was exhausted and nearly incapable of mounting another serious offensive. Its finest combat units had been reduced to tattered remnants of their former selves, and morale was running perilously low. The 715th Division, southeast of Aprilia, had been especially hard hit and was placed in corps reserve. Mackensen desperately requested *Luftwaffe* support to aid the ground troops.[37] Still, the Germans' relentless attacks had pushed the Allied line back a mile. Victory seemed close enough to grasp. And dawn brought with it a solid overcast and heavy rain; no worry about Allied air attacks. Von Mackensen wrestled with the uncomfortable gambler's dilemma of deciding whether to cut his losses and back away from the table or risk everything on one roll of the dice. He decided to gamble, demanding one more maximum effort from his troops. He was determined finally to break through the battered, bent, and bloody Thunderbird Division that was causing him so much trouble.[38]

Von Mackensen directed *General der Infanterie* Traugott Herr, commander of LXXVI Panzer Corps, and *General der Flieger* Alfred Schlemm, commander of I *Fallschirm* Corps, to keep up the assault throughout the night of 17–18 February. On Friday the eighteenth, the main thrust would be concentrated against the small patch of land bordered by Dead End Road as the start line, the Via Anziate as the right flank, and the place where the Bowling Alley intersects with the Lateral Road as the left. Into this small area the Fourteenth Army commander would throw the best of what he had left—the 721st, 741st, and 735th Infantry Regiments and the 29th and 309th Panzer Grenadier Regiments. This mighty force would be aimed primarily at the 157th's 3rd Battalion and the 179th, which first would be "softened up" with a devastating barrage of artillery, mortar, tank, and rocket fire. If the Germans could break through there, they could at last pour everything into the gap, split the beachhead, and push all the way to the sea, just as they had nearly done at Salerno before the 45th had held the line. The moment had come for the final, all-out assault.[39]

"Although the Third Panzer Grenadier Division and the 715th Infantry Division were able to penetrate deeply the enemy's battle positions [on the sixteenth]," von Mackensen stated, "our attacks have not produced the anticipated results. Our task is to commit the second wave," which consisted of the 26th Panzer and 29th Panzer Grenadier Divisions. The Hermann Göring Panzer Division would also be employed to pin down the 3rd Division and other Allied units on the eastern flank. The I *Fallschirm* Corps units would do the same to the British on the western flank. "All commanders are advised that the battle of the Nettuno beachhead [the Germans referred to the campaign as the battle of Nettuno; the Allies called it the battle of Anzio] has reached its critical stage, that our troops must advance and pursue the enemy under all circumstances. Only a complete elimination of the beachhead ends our mission."[40]

On the night of 17–18 February, while the Germans moved into their assembly areas and prepared to drive south against the Thunderbirds, General Eagles began implementing Lucas's order to attack to the north. Neither side knew the other was about to attack across the same ground, and a head-on collision—known as a "meeting engagement"—between the two forces was inevitable. The German attack began, as usual, in darkness, while a cold, driving rain kept Allied sentries huddled in their water-filled foxholes. German soldiers crawled silently through the muddy ravines, infiltrating between the British 167th Brigade and Lieutenant Colonel Brown's 2nd Battalion, 157th. On the 45th's right, German tanks and a reinforced battalion struck the positions of the 180th's G Company, which was holding the regiment's left flank along Ficoccia Creek. Heavy artillery saturated nearly the entire beachhead area.[41] While this was taking place, the relatively unscathed 3rd Battalion of the 157th, along with the 2nd and 3rd Battalions of the 179th and tanks from the 1st Armored, moved out from the area of the Overpass and Lateral Road to relieve Brown's men at the caves, and restore the division's lines. Not surprisingly, the Allied counterattack went badly. Running into von Mackensen's divisions massing for their assault, Harmon's tanks were stopped by mud and by enemy gunners, and K and L Companies of the 157th's 3rd Battalion were turned back by heavy fire after managing a thousand-yard advance almost to the Dead End Road. L Company and machine gun crews from M Company, the heavy-weapons company, fell in with I Company in front of the Overpass.[42]

Jack McMillion, L Company, 157th, remembered this trying time.

We had been the secondary line of defense. We suddenly became the front line. We were astride the highway leading to Rome, and the Germans had tanks that were shooting right down on us, and they had a hell of a lot of artillery. They came with planes and dropped those butterfly bombs on us. They were quite determined to push us off that beachhead.

When the Germans started to break through, L Company was in reserve. We were supposed to go up and plug the gap between the 179th Regiment and our own 2nd Battalion. We went up there, stumbled around—it was a miserable night, with lightning and shelling and every other damn thing. We got up there and we knew things weren't like what we thought they were supposed to be. We could hear friendly fire to the right and friendly fire to the left. This was supposed to be a small gap, but it must have been a half mile wide and there were just a few of us people up there.

We didn't realize that the line had broken so far, that the Germans had driven such a wedge between our units. We could see men over there; they should have been ours, but our patrol never came back. It was dark and they stumbled into the Germans. Our officers were trying to decide what to do when a big Tiger tank—silhouetted there, it looked as big as a locomotive—cranked up and went behind a house and was going further down. Behind it was this whole string of German soldiers, and here we were, sitting in this little drainage ditch, outnumbered and outgunned. Off to our front and to the right came one of these German rocket launchers—*Nebelwerfers,* I think they're called. The rockets screamed up and over us, heading for the Overpass behind us. Our chief felt that he who runs away lives to fight another day, so we beat it back to where we were among friends. The German column was marching down the road behind the big tank, so we followed a little drainage ditch that veered off to the left to get away from them. The Germans didn't know who we were. They hollered out but nobody answered back. When we got back close to our lines, it was just beginning to get light. From the second house from the Overpass, we saw guys in overcoats and they hollered at us in English, "What outfit is this?" I happened to be at the tail end of the column and somebody up front answered back who we were. About that time, they started shooting at us—they were Germans! Fortunately, we only had a man or two wounded.[43]

Glen K. Hanson, a communications sergeant with L Company, also recalled the incident. "The Germans started shooting at us—you could see the bullets hitting the building that we were going by. One of our people got hit right in the fleshy part of the rear end, but everybody made it back to the Overpass."[44]

The 179th's failed counterattack on the night of 17–18 February left the regiment's 2nd and 3rd Battalions in a dangerously exposed position at the terminus of the Dead End Road. With the Germans fighting back savagely, the commanders of K and L Companies were taken prisoner and most of their men routed.[45] The 2nd Battalion, hard hit by panzer fire, pulled back and tucked itself behind A Company's outpost line. There was no safety here, however, as the enemy sent swarms of tanks and infantry against the outnumbered A Company. Most of the company was taken prisoner, with only fourteen members able to withdraw to friendly lines.

The GIs of the 179th's 3rd Battalion, too, were helpless against the overwhelming odds and pulled back without authorization from their officers or noncoms, most of whom were already dead, wounded, or captured. In near panic, Kammerer's regiment withdrew to the Lateral Road, making contact with the 180th on its right. Many of the men were completely unable to function, fearing for their lives and tormented by the horror of seeing friends blasted to pieces or crushed in the mud under the steel tracks of the panzers. As the morning sky of 18 February grew lighter, Kammerer requested air support. His request was turned down due to the rain and low ceiling, but tanks from the 1st Armored were sent up to help hold the line.[46]

• • •

The scene in von Mackensen's command post was one of weary satisfaction; all of the sacrifices were about to pay off with grand dividends. Reports poured in indicating that the American lines were broken and that the enemy was fleeing. Now the final blow must be struck—the blow that would split the Allies once and for all and win the beachhead. Everything must be thrown into the widening breach. The moment had arrived for the decisive battle of the Overpass. The Germans were about to storm the Gate of Hell.

Truscott, at VI Corps headquarters, evidently realized the imminent danger of the German counterattack and scrambled to bolster the defenses at the Overpass. Before a dawn cloaked in rain and fog, with the chill of death heavy in the air, General Penney sent the 1st Battalion of the full-strength Loyals (North Lancashire) Regiment to help reinforce the 3rd Battalion, 157th, at the Overpass; their sector of responsibility ran from I Company's positions in front of the Overpass about a mile to the east along the Lateral Road (which the British called "Wigan Street"), where it merged with the 179th, trying to reorganize. No sooner had the British arrived and settled in than the earth around the Overpass began to shudder and erupt; mud and men were flung skyward as the German heavy artillery dropped their huge shells on target. The Overpass was again obliterated by unrelenting barrages, one of which lasted three hours. Then, through the rain and smoke that obscured the Dead End Road, ghostly forms began moving.[47]

Just as Pickett's men had marched across desolate ground into the mouths of the Union guns at Gettysburg some eighty years earlier, so von Mackensen's men marched—or, rather, ran—into the massed Allied weapons waiting for them at the Lateral Road. Across the thousand yards of featureless mud that separated the Dead End Road from the Lateral Road came the gray lines of yelling men and fume-spewing panzers, heading straight for I, L, and M Companies of the 157th and the Loyals, whose ears were still ringing from the fierce barrage. Now it was the Loyals' turn

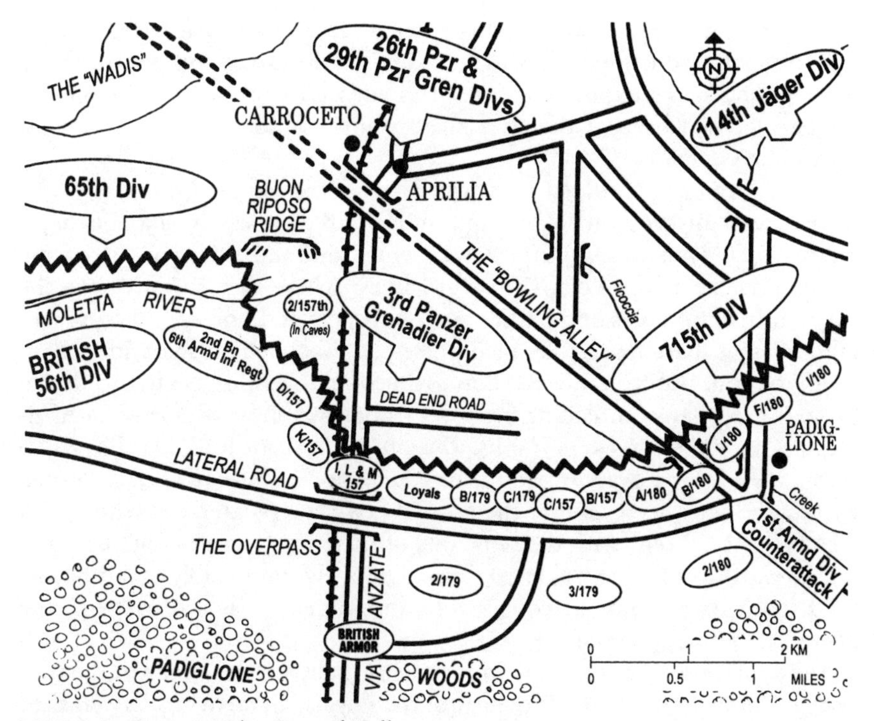

MAP 8.1 Storming the Gate of Hell
18 February 1944—Roaring down the Via Anziate, the Germans pushed the 45th back to the Lateral Road and aimed their strongest thrust at the Overpass—the "Gate of Hell"—in an all-out effort to split the beachhead forces. The 2nd Battalion, 157th, was cut off and surrounded in the caves south of Buon Riposo Ridge. (Positions approximate)

to face the full fury of the German assault. The North Lancashire men clutched their Enfields and Sten guns and PIATs (Projector, Infantry, Anti-Tank—the British bazooka) and braced themselves for battle. As the first wave of Germans—the *Lehr* Regiment—came within range, the British let fly a terrific fusillade. The attackers fell hard, toppling face first into the blood-soaked muck or jerked backward by the force of the bullets like dogs that had run unknowingly to the ends of their leashes. Artillery tore through bodies as if they were made of tissue paper. The screams of men who were sliced open or ripped apart by the cascade of steel carried above the din of weapons, and the enemy continued its charge. How could they find the courage to keep coming after us? wondered the defenders from the relative safety of their watery foxholes.[48]

Shortly before noon on the eighteenth, Captain William H. McKay, observing for the 45th's artillery in a Piper Cub high above the battlefield, spotted some 2,500 Germans and numerous panzers on the move from the vicinity of Carroceto down the Via Anziate. British and American guns—224 of them—were quickly brought to bear on the target and, for nearly an hour, pounded the exposed and helpless enemy force. But as fearsome as the barrage had been, it barely seemed to make a dent in the numbers of onrushing Germans.[49]

Hitler's legions continued to swarm across the open field, even as whole companies vanished in the flame and smoke of the pitiless artillery bursts. A platoon of Loyals on an outpost was wiped out and a few of the enemy made it as far as the Loyals' forward lines, where they jumped into the soggy British foxholes and battled with bayonets and knives and entrenching tools and bare hands like men possessed, like men crazed with the insanity of war, until they were shot, stabbed, clubbed, or beaten to death. From the left flank, enfilading fire from troops dug in west of the Via Anziate tore into the attackers' ranks. Despite the hail of lead, the Loyals' B Company CP was overrun, and it took a major counterattack, supported by British tanks, to recapture the ground. Two hours later, the whole mad scene repeated itself, with the remnants of the *Lehr* Regiment again plunging forward, leading the charge. Once again, the impossibly small battlefield, with its absence of cover and concealment, was strewn with the flower of Germany's youth.[50]

The scenario was played out with equal brutality in the sector of the I, L, and M Companies, 157th, to the left of the Loyals. German artillery crashed into the GIs' positions and the massed attacks came right up to the Thunderbirds' foxholes. So high was the mound of German corpses piled in front of the Americans, the riflemen had a hard time seeing additional targets.[51] "Doc Joe" Franklin, I Company, 157th, recalled that he and First Sergeant Willard Cody were in a dugout covered by timbers, sandbags, and a haystack. Then the German long-range artillery began again. "The Anzio Express came in—we heard it almost all the way. It took off the top of the haystack and landed about ten feet behind us. It went off like it was the end of the world. It was so hot, it set the haystack on fire—and that was *wet* hay, because it was raining! After that shell went off, every sandbag was shredded. There was so much dust inside our hole, we could hardly breathe."*[52]

*The veterans of the 45th have often talked about being on the receiving end of two large railroad guns, "Anzio Annie" and the "Anzio Express," yet there is some discrepancy as to the date these guns were first employed against the beachhead. Some sources claim the guns were fired as early as 7 February whereas others say that these two guns were not used at Anzio until 24 March. The 45th Division history records that they were first employed on 4 and 5 April (Ennio Silvestri, *The Long Road to Rome* [Latina, Italy: Etic Grafica, 1994], p. 168; and John Bowditch III, ed., *Anzio Beachhead*, vol. 14 in the "American Forces in Action" series [Washington, DC: Department of the Army Historical Division, 1947], p. 113; and Leo V. Bishop, George A. Fisher, and Frank J. Glasgow, *The Fighting Forty-Fifth: The Combat Report of an Infantry Division* [Baton Rouge, La.: Army-Navy Publishing Co., 1946], p. 83).

Jack McMillion of L Company, 157th, said,

> We got back and fell in with I Company at the Overpass, and the first and second platoons stayed to help I Company. Our third platoon went back to our weapons platoon. As I understand it, orders said that the Overpass was as far as we could back up. We were at the end of our rope at that particular point. Behind us, we had tank destroyers that had their noses over the embankment and were firing at the Germans and the Germans were firing at them, and we infantry were hugging the mud in between. You'd dig a hole and there'd be water in the bottom. You'd stick your head up and they'd shoot at you. It was so miserable, you wouldn't believe it. Later on, they sent our mortar section up to help 2nd Battalion; we never got a man back out of that.[53]

Don Amzibel, a member of McMillion's platoon, also recalled the day:

> We had gone up to fill a gap between two units the night before. In the morning, we found the outfit we were supposed to replace had pulled out, leaving us behind German lines. We were trying to work our way to the I Company position at the Overpass when we were spotted by the Germans. I guess we interrupted their breakfast, because they started hollering at us and chasing us, waving their mess kits. Our top sergeant, Jack McMillion, fired a few shots at them and they retreated back to their lines. We did manage to finally get over to the I Company position, where we were told to dig in. The shelling was awful. Tanks fired a few feet over our heads trying to knock the Overpass out of commission. Every time a mortar shell landed near us, we were buried with dirt and mud. If the Germans had broken through, they'd have cut the beachhead in two.[54]

Twenty-year-old Hubert L. Berry had just arrived at Anzio as a replacement for I Company, 157th, and immediately found himself engulfed in the hellish fighting for the Overpass.

> We had walked through a creek, and the water was knee deep or a little deeper. There was quite a bit of shelling and we went under the Overpass at night and dug in there on flat ground. We were pretty well pinned down there. Digging in was difficult. You'd dig down about six inches and hit water, so I dug around the edges and built kind of an island to lay on. I remember the British asking the night they came up, "Why don't you dig your holes deeper?" We said, "You'll find out."
>
> The Germans had perfect observation from the high ground. If we had to crawl back to the CP for some reason, the Germans would see that and they'd know where the officers were, and they'd shell the area. They killed or wounded nearly all our officers.
>
> The Germans came in on us two or three times and we used small-arms fire on them. Every time one of our tanks went up the road, the Germans would knock it out right quick. We never did advance from that spot. We got word we were going to, but I guess it got a little too hot. The Germans got about

> seventy-five or a hundred yards away. It was about sundown and we opened fire on 'em. I saw several of 'em fall. Later that night, we got word they wanted us to hold our fire while they removed their dead. At the Overpass, my buddy, Cordle, from Nebraska, got wounded by artillery and I heard him holler, "They hit me." A medic come and got him. Then there was a Polish fellow in our outfit that was just the other side of Cordle. This Polish fellow got killed and several other people around me got killed. The closest artillery round that hit near me was about six feet away. They were hitting all over the place, especially back where the CP was.

Berry soon came down with a case of trench foot. "We had to stay in our hole all day long. Our feet got cold and just stayed cold and we didn't have a change of socks. After the battle, we had to walk six miles back to the wooded area with no feeling in our feet."[55]

Bernard Fleming, a sergeant with the Anti-Tank Company, 3rd Battalion, 157th, told of his experience with artillery barrages at the Overpass.

> We came under a mortar and artillery attack. We had relieved another outfit that had been there and they had had good dugouts in the side of the Overpass, so you had a roof over you. You could hear the shrapnel singing through the air all the time. During this one barrage, everybody dived into their holes and a mortar shell landed, oh, I'd say a foot from ours. If it had been an artillery shell, or if we hadn't had a roof, we'd have all been killed. Being under a barrage, all you can do is huddle down and get as small as you can and sweat it out. Two of the fellows that joined the division with me died in an artillery barrage. They were in the same foxhole together at the Overpass. A big shell landed near their hole and they died from the concussion—there wasn't a mark on their bodies. One of them had just come back from the hospital, too. He hadn't been back for more than a week when he was killed.[56]

Many men distinguished themselves at the battle for the Overpass. "Doc Joe" Franklin had high praise for one of the men in I Company—a former cattle rancher named Jackson "Cowboy" Wisecarver. "In my opinion, Cowboy was probably the greatest soldier in the war. He was a light machine gunner in our company. I saw him in action. During the battle for the Underpass," as Franklin called it, "he killed over thirty Germans in one day." Wisecarver also carried a .45 caliber pistol. "He's the only guy I knew who could shoot the eye out of a fly with a .45; I couldn't hit a *wall* with a .45." Another soldier who earned Franklin's praise was Kenneth Kindig, a sniper with I Company, whom Franklin called "a one-man army."[57]

Kindig recalled that he and his buddies tried digging foxholes near the Overpass but

> you'd dig down about a foot and hit water, so we never had much protection. The company command post was on a little higher ground so they could dig down about three feet. We were in front of the Overpass and about five to ten

yards apart. We were scattered pretty good so that if an artillery shell came in, it wouldn't get all of us. I was in a foxhole near the company command post when the Germans let loose with an artillery barrage. One of their shells landed right next to my foxhole and caved it in on me. The shell didn't go off; it was a dud. If it *had* gone off, it would have blown me right out of there.

Kindig had been issued a brand-new rifle with a telescopic sight and was performing sniper duties. "We had barbed wire out there and the Germans were trying to get over it and under it and around it. I was on the outskirts with that sniper rifle and they were coming up through some drainage ditches at us. I picked them off before they could get around to us." Kindig was credited with killing or wounding twenty-five of the enemy. He was soon put out of action himself during a brief lull in the fighting.

I was sitting up and had my rifle laying across in front of me. I was eating a little can of pimiento cheese and some crackers when a mortar round came in. I got hit in the head with a piece of shrapnel. I didn't even hear it go off—they say you don't hear the one that gets you. A piece of shrapnel went through the front of my helmet and lodged in the back, between the helmet and helmet liner. I guess it knocked me out for a little bit. When I woke up, I was still sitting up and my can of cheese was running over with blood. The shell also blew the stock and telescopic sight off my brand-new sniper rifle.

Somebody in the next foxhole hollered for a medic and a medic ran over and put a compress on my head and put me in a foxhole near the company CP to wait until dark. We couldn't move in the daytime so they had to wait until dark to get me back to a hospital ship.

Kindig was in the hospital for about a month, rejoining his unit in April. He more than deserved the Bronze Star he was awarded.[58]

Although it is axiomatic that most soldiers never know the importance of a battle until it is long over, many of the men at the Overpass were keenly aware of the strategic importance of their position and what was expected of them. Tarzan Williams, K Company, 157th, said, "We knew we were the main line of defense. We knew we'd have to hold to the last man if necessary. You had to have the attitude of kill or be killed."[59]

Bernard Fleming recalled some of the emotions that take place during a battle. "Before a firefight, you're nervous, but during it, you're so busy, you're not even thinking about it. Two minutes seems like twelve hours—you think it will never stop. After it's over, you're nervous again. You look around to see who's left, who got hit. It's unreal—like watching yourself in a movie. Nobody can really describe it."[60]

George Nalley, K Company, 157th, echoed Fleming's sentiments.

You were scared, but when you got into it, you found out you weren't as scared as you thought you were. You were too busy trying to stay alive and

> help your buddies. In combat, we took care of one another. I thought more about my buddy than I did about myself. After the battle was over, then you'd get to thinkin' back. Every time you went up to the front, you thought your time was next. That worked on your mind. After a time, some guys couldn't take it. One night this other guy and I were on guard duty. He had been in combat for a long time and he was gettin' like he couldn't hardly take it no more. I laid down to get me some sleep and I heard him click the safety off his rifle. I said, "What's the matter?" and he said, "There they come, there they come." I looked up and it was actually Captain Neil Quick. He was just going around, making his rounds, checkin' our positions. I said, "Hold it, hold it." After that, this kid went all to pieces. We sent him back. He just had more than he could take. After that, I was in the hole all by myself for six days and nights.[61]

Jack McMillion said, "We stayed there, about 100–150 yards in front of the Overpass, for maybe three days and nights. We were mixed in with the British. When our platoon went in, we were practically at full strength, maybe thirty-eight in our platoon. When we got relieved and pulled out, there were ten of us still walking."[62]

"Doc Joe" Franklin said, "We had a radio message that said, 'You hold 'em one more day and we'll have 'em licked.' I thought, what's this *we* stuff? But we held 'em through the barrages and daily assaults until they finally gave up." Later wounded himself, Franklin had the opportunity to talk with a British soldier in the hospital who had fought at the Overpass. "He said they ran out of ammunition, lost ground, then they fixed bayonets and retook the ground just with bayonets. They did this three times until they didn't have enough men to do it any more. He said the only honorable way out of there was to throw your rifle away, pick up a wounded man, and run off the battlefield with him."[63]

• • •

Try as von Mackensen's men might, the German assault on the eighteenth could no longer sustain itself in the face of overwhelming Allied fire. The ground was virtually covered with dead and dying soldiers and the burning wrecks of German tanks. The exposed troops simply could advance no farther; those who could still walk or crawl retreated to their start line and beyond, many of them crying and exhausted. Although the infantry was, at least temporarily, stalled, the German artillery was still very much alive and continued to punish the Allies.

At 1415 hours on 18 February, while enemy artillery crashed around his CP, the 179th's commander, Colonel Malcolm R. "Bert" Kammerer, came to the end of his rope. He, like most of his men, had not slept for days and was unable to function effectively. Additionally, General Eagles had ordered Kammerer to use all his rear echelon personnel to stop any troops who retreated and establish defensive lines along Carroceto Creek. Instead, Kammerer sent a member of his staff to find a new regimental command post farther to the rear. The displeased Eagles relieved the colonel on the spot, replacing him with Colonel William Orlando Darby, whose Ranger battalions had been destroyed just eighteen days earlier in their ill-fated attempt to take Cisterna.[64] Darby, who had been slightly wounded on the fifteenth, reported for duty at the 179th's CP. Martin Blumenson writes, "Darby . . . found the headquarters dispirited. His contagious confidence, energy, and enthusiasm invigorated the headquarters."[65]

Major Merlin Tryon, whose 3rd Battalion had been all but annihilated earlier in the day, came to Darby with a confession: "Sir, I guess you will relieve me for losing my battalion?"

The usually aloof Darby patted Tryon on the shoulder, smiled wearily, and said, "I just lost three of them, but the war must go on."[66]

Although Darby's appointment brought an immediate infusion of hope and lifted the morale of the men of the battered 179th, he was appalled at the condition of the regiment he had just inherited; one battalion had but a handful of effectives remaining, another was at less than half strength, and the third was seriously under strength. Communications were in tatters. At 1748 hours that evening, Darby requested that the 179th be pulled out of the line long enough to rest and refit. "We are getting attacked all along the line," he told Colonel Martin, the division's operations officer. "We will have to get out of here. We can't keep this CP here any longer and still function. . . . These people are pretty shaken. There's men streaming back from all directions and it's going to be a job to get them organized."[67] Not unexpectedly, Eagles denied the request; he simply had no other unit that could fill the hole in the line that the 179th's departure would create. To help, however, he did attach the 157th's 1st Battalion to the 179th's right flank where it linked up with the 180th and allowed Darby to shorten his regiment's front.

Darby then set about the critical task of reorganizing the battered 2nd and 3rd Battalions to withstand the next expected German assault. He reorganized the remnants of the two units and ordered rear echelon troops—clerks and cooks—to grab their weapons and take up frontline positions along the Lateral Road. He then moved up Lieutenant Colonel Wayne L. Johnson's 1st Battalion from regimental reserve. No sooner had the 1st Battalion dropped into place than the Germans came again with their seemingly inexhaustible waves of tanks and infantry, smashing into Lieutenant James H. Cruikshank's B Company and Captain Hurd L. Reeves's C Company, determined to achieve the final breakthrough.[68]

Never shy about calling for artillery when the situation demanded it, Darby helped preserve his regiment by radioing for some of the heaviest barrages that Division Artillery had yet unleashed (on 18 February alone,

Division Artillery fired 12,557 rounds in support of the ground troops).[69] Stunned by the fury of the defense, the Germans fell back, retired from the corpse-littered field or took cover in shell holes or ruined houses, gathered their courage, then renewed the assault minutes later, only to receive the same deadly greeting. Darby's infusion of hope must have done the trick, for the 179th held fast against both assaults.*[70]

Not realizing how close they were to breaking through Darby's regiment, the Germans shifted their attacks to the units on either side of the 179th while elements of the 1st Armored Division moved through the 179th to reinforce its portion of the lines. Darby now had the breathing room he needed to bring his nearly extinct regiment back to life. Soon he would be training his regiment in the same skills and tactics that had made the Rangers such an elite and feared fighting force. Darby even devised a number of innovations—such as a grenade-throwing slingshot that made use of trees and jeep tire inner tubes—that he hoped would reduce casualties among his men.[71]

Replacements joined the division at Anzio, only to become casualties themselves within hours of arrival. "One afternoon, we got two brand-new people assigned to us," said Ralph Fink of D Company, 157th. "By midnight, both of them had been wounded and taken off to the hospital. We never saw them again. Here were two guys who came in, got hit, and none of us even knew their names."[72]

Lieutenant Charles Reiman, G Company, 179th, had a similar experience. Badly mauled on the seventeenth, G Company was pulled back to the Padiglione Woods to be restocked with fresh troops. He recalled, "Late one afternoon, we received our new company C.O. I invited him to share my foxhole, which was about four feet deep and just wide enough for two. He was with us maybe six hours. That night, the enemy dropped a pod of butterfly bombs and he was the only one hit—two fragments in the spine. I had better luck with the next two C.O.s. Captain Bill Morrison was the next one to take over G Company. He was okay. And Fred Snyder, the next C.O., was a good one, too."[73]

---

*Darby would remain with the 45th until April, when he was reassigned to the Operations Division of the War Department General Staff in Washington, D.C. It was a desk job, and the action-minded Darby disliked it intensely. He spent several months touring Army bases and using his combat experiences to make training more realistic. In March 1945, Darby returned to Europe to evaluate air support of ground troops. Having once served under General George P. Hays, commanding general of the 10th Mountain Division, which had arrived in Italy in January, Darby got himself assigned to the mountain troops and became assistant division commander of the 10th. On 30 April, in the town of Torbole on the northern end of Lake Garda, a random round from an 88 exploded near where Darby and a group of officers were standing. Darby was hit by shrapnel and died within minutes—just two days before the war in Italy ended. He was promoted to brigadier general posthumously (Michael J. King, *William Orlando Darby: A Military Biography* [Hamden, Conn.: Archon, 1981], pp. 160–175).

The awful anonymity of death at Anzio also struck Alex Dryden, a nineteen-year-old replacement who had joined the 45th Cavalry Reconnaissance Troop at Venafro. Recalling the jeeps that would bring food and ammunition to the hole-bound troops, he said, "They'd take the wounded back, and the dead, too, if they could. You'd see five or six bodies piled on each jeep. Often, on the same night a new soldier came up to face combat, he was killed. His lieutenant wouldn't know him—he never even got to speak to him."[74]

Although the 157th and 179th Regiments suffered the brunt of the enemy attack, the Germans did not spare the 180th, on the 45th's right flank. They threw another full-scale tank-and-infantry assault, supported by a heavy artillery barrage, at the 180th. With their fanatical charges across exposed ground, reminiscent of the tactics of World War I, the Germans became nothing more than cannon fodder, falling by the score. But more came on to take their places. After Lieutenant Colonel Weigand's 2nd Battalion, 179th, unexpectedly was forced to pull out of the line, Lieutenant Colonel Daniel Ahern, commanding the 180th's 1st Battalion, kept his unit from crumbling in the face of the unrelenting assault. The Germans were close, very close, to widening the gap between the 179th and 180th and rolling down to the sea.[75]

At 1000 hours on the eighteenth, Sergeant Woodrow Riggs and Private first class George Zeck of HQ Company, 2nd Battalion, 180th, situated near Padiglione, distinguished themselves when they learned of a wounded man lying in Ficoccia Creek. Crossing 500 yards of flat, open ground that was being ripped by fire from both sides, Riggs and Zeck reached the wounded man and because they had no stretcher, alternated carrying the casualty on their backs, running in short bursts, hitting the ground, then dashing for a few more yards before repeating the dangerous activity. Miraculously, all three made it back to the battalion aid station, where the surgeons saved the wounded man's life. Both rescuers received Bronze Stars.[76]

Earlier on the eighteenth, the 2nd Battalion, 180th, was being attacked from three sides by tanks east of Aprilia. At 0625 hours, Major Howard L. Shinaberger, the battalion C.O., ordered Companies F and G, dug in near Padiglione, to withdraw to the east; somehow, First Lieutenant Benjamin Blackmer, who had just taken command of G Company the day before, never got the word. When Captain Robert Guenther's F Company pulled out, Blackmer's men stayed behind and found themselves completely surrounded and in imminent danger of being overrun. One of the men in Blackmer's company, Private first class William J. Johnston, G Company, 180th, from Colchester, Connecticut, was manning a machine gun post. Johnston was a crack shot and he took on an attacking force of some eighty enemy troops, killing or wounding twenty-five of them. Despite being pounded by artillery, mortar, and small-arms fire all day long, he remained at his gun, blasting away whenever a German soldier foolishly showed himself. Two Germans managed to crawl so near to him that he could not depress his gun to hit them, so, grabbing a pistol and a rifle, he picked them off just yards from his position.

G Company's position was tenuous, and Lieutenant Blackmer decided that a fighting withdrawal through the encircling forces was the company's only chance. Johnston covered the withdrawal while Blackmer extricated the rest of the company. Artillery fire—whether American or German has never been determined—plastered the area and Johnston was hit just above the heart with a chunk of shrapnel. Deemed by a medic fatally wounded, Johnston elected to remain behind. A passing soldier helped Johnston reposition his machine gun and engage the enemy alone. As Blackmer's men pulled back, the sound of Johnston's gun could be heard above the din of battle for another ten minutes. Then the position fell quiet as the Germans overran it. Everyone in his outfit gave silent thanks to the brave soldier who had sacrificed his life so that they might live. By the time they made it back to friendly lines, G Company had lost 75 percent of its men.[77]

Captain Joseph Bosa's diary entry for Friday, 18 February, reads:

> This morning and afternoon beginning at about 4:00 a.m., the Germans have been throwing everything they have at us. Our front line troops have been under constant shelling by tanks and self-propelled guns, and our batteries have been getting fire—lots of it—all day. Last night the 179th on our left fell back—rather earlier, perhaps night before last—leaving our [180th's] left flank exposed.
>
> About 9:30 this morning Lt. Conley and Sgt. Ayers were killed. Lt. Conley was out as F.O. [forward observer]. Ayers was with him. They had been firing on troops from a house OP [observation post]. . . . A direct hit must have got them.
>
> We have been strafed and our front lines bombed several times today. Our air superiority seems to be questionable at such times.
>
> Last night, the report is that the 179th lost about one company killed or captured. They made an attack to restore their lines but failed to do so. The 180th has given some ground to straighten the lines.[78]

Small units found themselves isolated, with Germans swarming around them. Sometimes, surrender was the only sensible thing to do. Private first class "Blackie" Greer had kept the attacking hordes at bay since the sixteenth. Now, on the eighteenth, F Company, which Greer was supporting, was forced to pull back and Greer had to make a choice: withdraw or continue to fire in aid of a small group of F Company men who were in danger of being overrun. He chose to stay, fighting off the Germans and allowing the remainder of his company to make it safely to the rear. Finally, Greer's ammunition ran out and the Germans charged his position, taking him and a few others prisoner. "There were thirteen of us," he reported later. "Five from H and eight from F Company, in a group which a score of Jerries escorted to the rear through our own artillery barrage. A German colonel told us, 'For you the war is finished. In three days the others will be swimming in the sea.' We were then lined up, faces to the wall, with hands over heads, and forced to stand that way for forty-five minutes. The Jerries didn't bother with the wounded who couldn't walk; they killed them on the spot. I was five yards away from the spot when two Jerries machine-pistoled an American soldier." Greer would eventually escape from his captors and make it back to the division. For his deeds, he was awarded the Distinguished Service Cross.[79]

• • •

Although it was not yet obvious, the German tidal surge at the Overpass was Hitler's last major thrust in Italy. As dusk settled over the bloody battlefield on the eighteenth, the fearsome artillery barrages lessened, and the small-arms fire withered away. Off in the distance, the crack of rifle and machine gun fire sounded like so many puny firecrackers. There was no sense of victory in the Allied line in front of the Gate of Hell, no cheering, no exultation—only a weariness, a feeling of relief that each man who had survived had done so for another minute, another hour, another day. Indeed, the collective thought was that the Germans would soon come again in their nearly overwhelming numbers, their seemingly endless supply of fanatical troops who would throw down their lives for the Führer and for Germany.

As one historian has written, "The Germans had been told that the Forty-fifth Infantry was a National Guard outfit manned largely by Red Indians, racially inferior people who had no love of the white man and probably wouldn't fight. How wrong they were."[80]

The weary Thunderbirds—both white and Indian—and their brave British counterparts in the Loyals, raised their heads slightly above the rims of their foxholes to scan the battlefield. Panzers and self-propelled 88s lay broken and scattered in the mud and atop the Via Anziate, like the discarded toys of some giant child who had grown bored with them. The crumbled remains of farmhouses and barns relieved the flatness of the horizon and smoke drifted across the churned-up, once-bucolic farm fields. And everywhere, the still-smoldering field was covered with the lifeless gray bundles of what had, until recently, been some of Germany's finest, bravest soldiers. Some bundles twitched, and German voices calling for their sergeants, their comrades, and their mothers could be faintly heard. Here and there, German aid men moved among the bundles, checking for signs of life.

The 45th had held and the Allies had won, yet the enormity of their accomplishment had yet to sink in. And although victory had been achieved, the battle, as events would shortly prove, was far from over.

9

The City of Flaming Red

19–23 February 1944

But tell me: those the dense marsh holds, or those driven before the wind, or those on whom rain falls, or those who clash with such harsh tongues, why are they not all punished in the city of flaming red if God is angry with them? And if He's not, why then are they tormented?
—Dante Alighieri, *The Inferno,* Canto XI

ANZIO HAD CEASED TO BE merely a battle; it was now an immense test of wills. For the commanders on both sides—as well as for the politicians in the United States, Great Britain, and Germany—Anzio was a gigantic showdown in which the loser would be the first one to blink. Like Verdun a generation earlier, Anzio was a self-perpetuating meat grinder that sucked men into it simply because it was there.

The fact that the Anzio invasion force had not lived up to the expectations to which it was held was causing consternation and embarrassment far beyond the battlefield and forcing the politicians to put a good face on the problem. Churchill had already received a cable from the U.S. Joint Chiefs of Staff, expressing their growing disillusionment with events in Italy. In an address to the House of Commons on 22 February 1944, Churchill said,

> It was certainly no light matter to launch this considerable army upon the seas—forty thousand or fifty thousand men in the first instance—with all the uncertainty of winter weather and all the unknowable strength of enemy fortifications. The operation itself was a model of combined work. The landing was virtually unopposed. Subsequent events did not however take the course which had been hoped or planned. In the upshot, we got a great army ashore, equipped with masses of artillery, tanks, and very many thousands of vehicles, and our troops moving inland came into contact with the enemy.

> The German reactions to this descent have been remarkable. Hitler has apparently resolved to defend Rome with the same obstinacy which he showed at Stalingrad, in Tunisia, and, recently, in the Dnieper Bend. No fewer than seven extra German divisions were brought rapidly down from France, Northern Italy, and Yugoslavia, and a determined attempt has been made to destroy the bridgehead and drive us into the sea. Battles of prolonged and intense fierceness and fury have been fought. At the same time the American and British Fifth Army to the southward is pressing forward with all its strength. Another battle is raging there. On broad grounds of strategy, Hitler's decision to send into the south of Italy as many as eighteen divisions, involving, with their maintenance troops, probably something like a half a million Germans, and to make a large secondary front in Italy, is not unwelcome to the Allies. We must fight the Germans somewhere, unless we are to stand still and watch the Russians. This wearing battle in Italy occupies troops who could not be employed in other greater operations, and it is an effective prelude to them.

These fine words masked the fact that Churchill and "Jumbo" Wilson were frustrated by the double stalemates—and blamed Lucas for the intolerable situation on the Anzio front.[1]

In Germany, too, the Anzio operation was under intense scrutiny. In early March, Kesselring's chief of staff, *Generalmajor* Siegfried Westphal, had the thankless task telling Hitler that Army Group South no longer had the strength to lance the abscess. As Westphal wrote after the war,

> The top political and military leaders had to be informed of the true state of affairs at the front. The soldiers had accepted every hardship and suffering that the fighting in the Pontine marshes and the hellish war of attrition had imposed, but it had all been in vain. What value was sacrifice if the success remained unobtainable? The situation in the Italian war theatre made it necessary to make an end to the fighting there as soon as possible. The duty of the Army Group was to tell the unvarnished truth. A written report would have been useless, because it would have made no impression on Hitler. The only way was to speak to him in person.

Westphal was sent to Hitler's alpine retreat at the Obersalzberg near Berchtesgaden to inform the Führer of the gravity of the situation in Italy.

> At first, Jodl [*Generaloberst* Alfred Jodl, chief of the *Wehrmacht* Army General Staff] would not admit me, saying it was better that he should speak to Hitler himself. He did so and provoked an outburst of rage. Hitler demanded to see the man 'who had been slandering his troops.' At the same time he ordered, for the first and last time during the war, that twenty officers of all arms and ranks should be fetched from Italy, so that he could question them about the conditions under which they were fighting. He would have done still better to visit the front and convince himself of our aerial and artillery inferiority on the spot.

> I made my report to Hitler on the Obersalzberg during the evening of March 6. For more than three hours I unfolded the reasons which had made it impossible to throw the enemy back into the sea, despite all our reinforcements. After five years of war, the troops had become exhausted to a frightening degree. The heavy losses had seriously handicapped the commanders of all ranks. . . . Hitler made frequent interruptions, but I was able to keep him to the subject.

Westphal went into detail about the main reasons the German Army was unable to push the Allies back into the sea: the narrow front along which Fourteenth Army was required to operate, the coastal geography that dictated suicidal frontal assaults and prevented the army from employing large-scale flanking maneuvers, the muddy fields that restricted the panzers to the lone north-south road where they were easily picked off, the inadequate supplies of artillery ammunition, and the Allied air superiority. Westphal could have added to the list the tenacity of the British and American troops, especially those of the 45th Infantry Division.

Westphal said that Hitler

> knew well how great was the war-weariness which afflicted the people and also the *Wehrmacht*. He would have to see how he could bring about a speedy solution. To do so, however, he needed a victory. A victory on a large scale, for instance on the Eastern Front, was impossible for we had not the strength. That was why he had hoped that success would attend the Nettuno assault. I left the room with the feeling of having met with understanding. Keitel [*Generalfeldmarschall* Wilhelm Keitel, Chief of Staff, OKW] later bade me farewell with the words: 'You were lucky. If we old fools had said even half as much, the *Führer* would have had us hanged.' Hitler did indeed appear to be in a depressed mood that evening. But, looking back, it seems possible that he deliberately showed sympathy for our difficulties in Italy in order to put our minds at rest. On the two following days, he questioned the officers from the front, who could only confirm what I had already said. The hoped-for consequences, however, were not forthcoming.[2]

Lucas, meanwhile, was still on the hot seat, just as he had been ever since VI Corps landed nearly a month earlier. At a noon meeting at his Nettuno headquarters on the eighteenth, he was pressured by Clark, Truscott, and Harmon to launch another counterattack at the Germans with 1st Armored tanks, a regiment of the 3rd Division, and the 169th Brigade of the British 56th Division, which was at that moment in the process of debarking. Reluctantly, Lucas gave in. He really had no other choice, for to keep his units static and allow them to be destroyed piecemeal by continuous German attacks would satisfy no one. Plans were swiftly drawn up for a combined armor-infantry counterattack to smash into the Germans, who had unceasingly hammered the thin line of Thunderbirds and Loyals in front of the Overpass for days. The plans called for a two-pronged approach by both U.S. and British units to relieve the pressure on the embattled defenders. It was hoped that Task Force H (for Harmon) and Task Force T (for Templer, who had taken command of the British 1st Division in addition to his own 56th Division after Penney was wounded on 17 February) would hit the flanks of the salient and catch the Germans, focused on their attacks at the Gate of Hell, by surprise. H hour was set for early on the morning of the nineteenth. Harmon's force was to travel up the Bowling Alley toward Carroceto while Templer's force was to strike out from the Overpass, travel up the Via Anziate, and head for the Dead End Road. The 30th Infantry Regiment of the 3rd Infantry Division also would join in the assault. Thus the Allies hoped to pinch off the German salient and capture or destroy the bulk of the enemy forces within it.

In the black, rainy, predawn hours of the nineteenth, the Allied counterattack got under way as elements of the 1st Armored Division's 6th Armored Infantry Regiment, draped in their glistening ponchos, moved through the 180th's lines on their way to hit the eastern flank of the enemy salient. Rain-slicked tanks roared and clanked in the darkness and slithered on the muddy roads. The men of the 180th, crouching in ditches and water-filled holes, waved to the passing troops, called out "good luck" and "give 'em hell," and flashed the thumbs up, or V-for-victory sign, but troubles soon manifested themselves. The British got a late start because the 169th Brigade, which had been pulled out of the fighting along the Gustav Line the day before, had had its unloading operations at Anzio delayed by mines in the harbor dropped by the *Luftwaffe*. Templer's force could only mount an attack with tanks but no infantry. It did not progress very far before enemy fire turned it back. Furthermore, the 3rd Division infantrymen had to slog eight miles in the rain and mud and darkness to reach their assembly area near Padiglione. Then it was learned that an unknown force—either a platoon or a battalion—from the 45th Division was in the area scheduled to be saturated by a heavy barrage just prior to the start of the counterattack; should this friendly force be sacrificed for the sake of the assault? After considerable agonizing on Harmon's part, the barrage went ahead as planned; to his relief, it was learned later that the Thunderbird unit—a platoon—had pulled out of the impact area just in time.[3] A large enemy force, moving down the Bowling Alley, was caught by the subsequent barrage and torn to pieces. After advancing toward Carroceto, however, Harmon's task force was met by strong German resistance and the advance came to a halt.[4]

Bill Whitman recalled watching the troops and tanks moving through on their way to the counterattack: "We were all elated! Now, the Germans were going to get a taste of their own medicine!" Unfortunately, the assault quickly ran into trouble.

> It was a fiasco plus! The Germans waited until they got within good rifle and machine-gun range, and then let them have it. The Germans chopped them to bits. Captain McGough and I helped a wounded armored force sergeant back

> through our lines. He was carrying an M-1 rifle and the barrel was twisted almost back on itself. . . . There were so many casualties that it was almost unbelievable to us. All these men killed and wounded and they had not gained a half inch of ground. We learned later that the attack by the regiment of the Third Division had fared no better. Our hopes and morale went down. We must have been thinking—if two regiments can't make a dent in the Germans, we are really up against it.[5]

Harmon's men eventually recovered their composure, overcame the resistance with a determined assault, and rounded up hundreds of demoralized German prisoners—handing them over to the 180th for processing, but not before some of the surrendering Germans were shot down by their own men. In spite of the efforts of their countrymen to prevent them from going over to the Americans, some 700 prisoners were taken on the nineteenth—many of whom were bitter that their leaders had misled them into thinking the Allies were on the verge of defeat.[6]

In his diary entry for 19 February, Captain Joseph Bosa wrote:

> Yesterday and last night were the hardest 24 hours we have had. The Germans pushed us back in the 179th sector so far that C Battery had to move back to their alternate position. A Battery was shelled every time they opened up and B received several rounds. So far only a few men in the batteries have been hurt and not one killed in the positions. They are well dug in. This morning over 50 rounds fell within 100 yards of our FDC. A battery of the 41st FA which has moved in within 150 or 200 yards of us is partially responsible. They are practically in the open. . . .
>
> This morning we fired a preparation for an attack by the 1st Armored Div. who went through the 179th to reinforce them and reestablish the lines. So far the attack has been successful and our tanks are taking more of a part than usual. Up to now the tanks and TD's have remained more as defensive weapons.
>
> This afternoon our bombers hit again. This time only a few, but dive bombers gave a great deal of assistance along the front. . . . The 30th Infantry have gone in today in the critical "factory area." They have advanced enough to stabilize our lines. The 180th is still standing firm like a rock.[7]

In front of the Overpass, meanwhile, the Germans continued to throw themselves at the Thunderbirds and Loyals, with no slackening in the ferocity of their attacks. Lieutenant Colonel Wayne L. Johnson, commanding the 1st Battalion, 179th, was seriously wounded by a German shell while in a forward observation post; the battalion's operations officer, Captain Gail C. McLain, standing next to Johnson, was killed. Although both legs were shattered and he was bleeding profusely and in excruciating pain, Johnson continued to direct his battalion's defense against the German onslaught until Darby ordered him evacuated.

All day on the nineteenth and well into the night, the Germans continued to strike against the 179th, but it was clear that the attempt was beginning to lose steam. At 1700 hours, in the fading light, the Germans hurled one last, desperate attempt to dislodge the regiment. In a scenario that had repeated itself like an unending loop of movie film for the past four days, gray-clad soldiers rushed the American positions only to end up as torn and bleeding pieces of meat in the mud of Campo di Carne. Firefights lit up the night with tracer bullets crisscrossing the landscape like some giant, luminescent cat's cradle, with bullets occasionally angling off into the sky after ricocheting off a tank or a rock or someone's helmet. After hours of fierce fighting, the smoldering ground was covered with dead German soldiers, but the 1st Battalion had not been moved. The artillery continued to pound suspected enemy positions well into the night.[8] Pete Conde commented, "In one day, our artillery fired more shells than Napoleon fired in his lifetime."[9] Charles Reiman put it even more succinctly: "What saved our butts was the artillery."[10] In just four days—from the sixteenth through the nineteenth—Division Artillery unleashed 48,311 shells at the enemy.[11]

On the nineteenth, a soldier no one expected to see alive again returned to the 180th. Private first class William J. Johnston, the G Company machine gunner who had been seriously wounded and left for dead at his gun, had proved to be too tough to kill. Although in great pain and bleeding profusely, he remained at his gun without sleep during the night of 18–19 February, killing or wounding seven more of the enemy the next morning. In spite of his wounds, he had crawled—bare-footed—back to the regiment. (The passing Germans assumed he was dead and had taken his boots.) He was even able to pass on vital information to G-2 about the enemy's positions. Amazingly, he recovered from his wounds, and his incredible bravery and gutty determination earned for him the Medal of Honor. He lived to the age of seventy-one.[12]

Also on the nineteenth, Joseph Bosa recorded in his diary: "A news flash came through this afternoon that our troops have broken through at Cassino."[13] But the news flash was merely a false rumor. The day before, a Fifth Army offensive to break through on the Garigliano had gotten off to a promising start but soon bogged down due to heavy German resistance. Kesselring rushed the 90th Panzer Grenadier Division, along with the bulk of the 29th, south to hold the line. No Allied troops broke through. The Gustav Line was as solid as ever.[14]

As it seemed that the war might drag on for yet a while longer, Captain Bosa and another officer on his staff spent a few hours working on their dugout and putting a roof over it. Bosa added to his diary the following:

> Now we'll both feel a little safer from fragmentation from our own AA at least. Sometimes it falls like hail. Several tents are full of holes from it. Also

> there was a daylight raid this afternoon during which about five Heinies dropped bombs from ME 109s, or similar ships, equipped for dive bombing. Our bombers gave them a good going over again. Fifty or 75 medium bombers and several dive bombing missions were carried out. One plane dropped its load back of our lines but reports are that no one was killed although several were buried and had to be dug out.[15]

The men of the 180th Regiment continued to be pounded, along with their brethren in the 157th and 179th. On the nineteenth, Staff Sergeant Joe Plese of A Company, 180th, ignored heavy enemy fire to go from one position to another to restore order and repulse the enemy's attack. When his platoon leader was hit, Technical Sergeant Billie Wilson, also of A Company, took charge of the weapons platoon, directed murderous mortar fire on the attacking Germans, and also personally repaired the telephone lines to his OP each time enemy shells cut them. For their deeds, Plese was awarded the Silver Star and Wilson the Bronze Star.

In F Company's sector, Staff Sergeant Louis P. Ferro took command of his company's mortar section, directing the fire of 350 shells. At one point, the accurate mortar fire knocked out a German tank and an accompanying platoon of infantry. When the tank was hit, the infantrymen tried to run but were cut down by F Company's riflemen. Ferro was later awarded the Bronze Star.

Private first class Homer C. Rhodes, of H Company, a crewman on a .30 caliber machine gun, watched as members of his and a neighboring crew were picked off by enemy sharpshooters. Heedless of the danger, Rhodes served as assistant gunner and ammunition bearer for both his gun and the neighboring one. His gun barrel too hot for him to continue using the weapon, Rhodes volunteered to cross open ground that was being saturated with mortar fire to obtain a replacement weapon, and he repeatedly exposed himself to enemy fire to get ammunition for himself and for the other gunners. His bravery under fire earned him the Bronze Star.[16]

Casualties among the Thunderbirds continued to mount. First Lieutenant Bill Whitman, commanding B Company, 180th, recalled, "The fighting was so bad that I refused any more replacements who were not battle trained; the new soldier was either killed, wounded, or went out of his mind under the conditions that existed."[17]

The 179th's history records that 1,291 replacements joined the regiment near the end of February.

> Yet still the reinforcements came inadequately trained. Many had received their basic training, shipped overseas, got their combat initiation, and died in the line of duty—all within seventeen weeks of their induction into the Army! And because of the psychopathic unbalance induced by heavy losses and the resultant images conjured up by impressionable, unseasoned youngsters,

> among the novitiates were many cases of AWOL, desertion, and self-inflicted wounds. More court-martial offenses occurred in February in the regiment than had occurred in the previous eight months combined, yet court-martial had no effect. When the fear psychology seizes a man, he goes over the hill regardless of threats and consequences. Nor can he be frightened or shamed. He is beyond any feeling but the impelling need to get away, to get out of it.[18]

Robert LaDu, F Company, 179th, related an incident in which he was having a problem with one of his men who had reached the breaking point.

> He had gone berserk. He jumped out of his foxhole and ran over to me and said he had to see the medics.
>
> "What's the matter?" I asked him.
>
> "I'm wet and I'm cold," he replied.
>
> "All of us are," I said. "Now get back in your hole and stay there." He did this about three times and the Germans would shell us every time he'd get up. The third time he did it, I said, "If you get out again, *I'm* going to shoot you." Whether or not I really would have, I don't know. But he stayed in his hole.[19]

Similarly, Ernie Pyle reported a conversation he had with Sergeant Michael Adams of the 179th:

> Adams seemed a little older than the others; his hair was beginning to slip back in front, and I could tell by his manner of speech that he thought deeply about things. He got to talking about soldiers who cracked up in battle or before; the ones who hung back or who thought they were sick and reported in as exhaustion cases. . . . Sergeant Adams told me how some of the replacements, after only a few hours under fire, would go to the company commander and say, "Captain, I can't take it. I just can't take it."
>
> That made Sergeant Adams's blood boil. He said to me, "They can't take it? Well, what the hell do they think the rest of us stay here for?—because we like it?" And it's that spirit, I guess, that wins wars.[20]

Although the living conditions under fire at Anzio were terrible, and death was always tugging at a soldier's sleeve, it was often the small irritants that got under a man's skin. "There were a lot of little things that made me mad at Anzio," said Captain Kenneth P. Stemmons, B Company, 157th—things like a shortage of wristwatches, winter clothing, and telescopic sights.

> We had damn few telescopic scopes. The Krauts would start firing on us, 300–350 yards away. They could do that effectively because they had scopes. Supply acted like you needed an act of Congress to get one. The same thing was true with watches. You'd tell your men, "At five o'clock, we're going to go." Maybe there's three guys in the whole company that have a watch. We'd keep asking Supply, "We need one for every squad." They'd say, "We gave you one last Friday." But, hey, that guy's gone. You can't go out and rummage

around on the battlefield to see if you can find one, you know. But Supply never figured that out.[21]

• • •

On 22 February, Captain Joseph Bosa noted,

> Yesterday evening and last night the Germans made their strongest bid in our sector so far. They started out with a time barrage from 88s. Some way or another our G-2 had received word of it and we were set to give them all we had. Their time barrage lasted about 30 minutes and when that was over their tanks had moved in close. We were able to put enough artillery in front of them though to "sew them up." They didn't get through or in, but it looked bad for a while. About ten last night during the bombing raid, they hit one of our main ammo dumps on the beach, or wherever it was. It burned for hours and after midnight ammunition was still exploding. They also dropped more personnel bombs. Of course, they're looking for our batteries.
>
> This morning they hit again on the right of the 180th. The 180th is still sticking out and taking the brunt of all the attacks. The 179th has pulled back and our left flank is considerably exposed. The Jerries hit at first one side and then another. They walk on into our barrages unless we use time fire. When that starts, they move out or break and run. They have plenty of nerve or are driven to it. Their attack today lasted until around noon when things began to get quieter.[22]

On the left flank of the 45th's line, von Mackensen was determined to wipe out the pockets of resistance in and around the caves and so sent in the 65th Infantry Division to finish off the stubborn Thunderbirds. Kenneth Kerfoot, commander of H Company, 157th, who was holed up in the caves, remembered the night of 19 February as one of his lowest points. "We tried to get out that night. It was midnight and the darkest night I ever saw in my life. We had seventy or eighty men left out of a hundred, but forty or fifty were 'walking wounded.' German machine guns pinned us down. We would have been slaughtered, so we surrendered at the crack of dawn." About his only satisfaction came when, while being marched to the rear as a prisoner of war, he saw stacks of German dead, "piled up chest high and a city block long, waiting for burial."[23]

Despite the Germans' most fanatical efforts, the 157th's 2nd Battalion was still holding out. On the twentieth, a German tank rolled up to the entrance to Henry Kaufman's cave with one of the most feared of all weapons: a flamethrower. The tank poured a stream of liquid fire into the opening and burned Kaufman's upper right arm. But he and the rest of the men inside drove off the enemy with hand grenades and armor-piercing machine gun bullets.

Two days later, the Germans launched another full-scale attack at the men in the caves, this time using tear gas. Coughing and gasping for air,

Artist's rendition of the 2nd Battalion, 157th's desperate Battle of the Caves. (Courtesy of U.S. Army Center of Military History)

their eyes burning, Kaufman and his five H Company buddies (who had all discarded their gas masks when they landed at Anzio) gave themselves up, and the three Germans who had been taken prisoner a few days earlier were reunited with their *Kameraden*. A less-happy fate was in store for some of the women. "When the Italian women started coming out of the cave," Kaufman wrote, "coughing and rubbing their eyes, the Germans machine-gunned the first few who came out of the cave, calling them collaborators. The German officer in charge ordered them to cease firing. Although my vision wasn't too clear, I noticed a lot of dead Germans around the outside of the entrance to the cave. I knew we had killed some of them, but I didn't think we had killed as many as I saw, about twenty-five or thirty dead bodies."

Suddenly, Allied artillery began crashing near the group. Kaufman and a buddy were ordered by a German to pick up one of the corpses and carry it to a casualty collecting point about fifty yards away. The German who gave the order said that the body they were carrying was that of his brother. After the body was placed in an area with about a hundred other dead Germans, the Americans were directed to climb an incline, on top of which was a railroad bed. "As we came down the incline, we were amazed to see thousands of Germans lying there behind the railroad tracks, using the rise in the terrain as protective cover. All their weapons were pointing in the direction we had just come from," Kaufman noted. Soon, he and his H Company buddies joined a mass of Allied soldiers—Americans, British, and New Zealanders—being moved northward to Rome. As the group of prisoners was marching under guard along the road, more Allied shells hit the area. The gunners "were not aware," Kaufman stated, "that they were killing and wounding more Allied prisoners of war than Germans. . . . One of the British soldiers, running alongside me, was hit directly in the face with shrapnel. I couldn't see his facial features, I only saw a mass of blood. His entire face seemed to have been blown off." Kaufman believed the soldier died shortly thereafter. As the group double-timed away from the area, Kaufman saw a great many young Americans lying dead alongside the road. "I can't really say whether or not these dead Americans had been killed by American artillery fire or American planes. It is possible the Germans shot them to avoid the burden of holding them as prisoners of war."*[24]

For Robert LaDu, F Company, 179th's executive officer, the war was over on 21 February. He had been with a group of officers at the rest area in the Pines when they were introduced to the 179th's new commanding officer, Colonel Darby. Shortly afterward, LaDu was handing out V-mail forms† to a group of newly arrived replacements so they could write a letter home when a large shell—possibly from Anzio Annie—exploded in a tree, sending a chunk of shrapnel through LaDu's hip and killing or wounding five of the soldiers. He was hospitalized for the next three and a half months, then returned to the States and given a medical discharge.[25]

• • •

From his isolated position on a slight hill, Captain Felix Sparks sent one of his sergeants out to find battalion headquarters. The noncom discovered it in the caves south of Buon Riposo Ridge and returned with the word that a British unit was going to relieve the battalion on the night of 21 February. Sparks said, "That was about the stupidest thing I'd ever heard in my life; we were completely surrounded and cut off, but the British were going to relieve us and we were supposed to go to the caves and consolidate all the

---

*Kaufman spent time in several POW internment camps, including five days in the Dachau concentration camp (which would be liberated by the 45th more than a year later; he was one of only a handful of American prisoners of war to have been held at Dachau). He eventually escaped from another POW camp and made it back to American lines.

†V-mail was the military's special form of correspondence. To save space on the ships and planes heading to and from the European theater, a serviceman's friends and relatives were allowed to write him on a single sheet of paper, which was then photographically reduced before being sent overseas. The servicemen in Europe also used the forms, which were then photographed and the film developed in theater. The negatives were flown to the United States, where the letters were photographically enlarged from the negatives and then mailed to the recipients.

men we had left in the battalion. The British were then going to take over our positions and the following night we would withdraw. The only problem with that grand scheme was that the British were almost annihilated trying to get up to us."[26]

The relief turned out to be just another unmitigated disaster on a battlefield that had already seen far too many of them. The 7th Battalion, Queen's Own Royal Regiment of the 56th Division, heroically battled its way to the caves, losing seventy-six men to shelling, small-arms fire, mines, and an aerial attack. By the time they reached the caves, the survivors had lost most of their supplies, ammunition, and supporting weapons. With resupply so tenuous, Lieutenant Colonel Brown decided to wait another twenty-four hours before pulling his men out.[27]

Sparks said, "When their battalion commander finally got up to us, he only had a handful of men left—he'd lost over half of them trying to get to my position. He didn't even have a machine gun, so I gave him ours." Sparks told the British officer he would need the gun back when the 2nd Battalion started to break out the next day and said that he would return for it. "The British made the relief and my sergeant guided us back to the caves," Sparks said. "We were down to about sixteen men by that time. We spent the night in the caves. There were maybe three or four hundred men left in the battalion, out of around a thousand. The wounded were all in there, too. When the Germans attacked, we brought in artillery fire right in that ravine in front of the caves. I don't think we had any casualties that night."[28]

In trying to root out the Yanks from the caves, the Germans took a pounding. But despite their high casualties and the tremendous volume of artillery fire being dropped on them, the Germans managed to force an entry into a portion of the caves on the twenty-second, free a number of their men who had been taken prisoner, and capture a platoon from the 157th's F Company.[29]

On the opposite side of the line from the caves, a Cherokee officer from Oklahoma was about to earn the fourth of the eight Medals of Honor awarded to men of the 45th in World War II. Before dawn on 22 February, near Padiglione, a large force of German infantry had positioned itself in three echelons, at 50, 100, and 300 yards, in front of the platoon commanded by Second Lieutenant Jack C. Montgomery, I Company, 180th Regiment, who had received a battlefield commission the previous September. "The terrain there was kind of flat," Montgomery recalled.

> It was a little after daylight. My platoon was supposed to have about forty people, but we were down to about twenty. We were on I Company's left flank, and there was a road between us and the company to our left. There were one or two houses there that hadn't been all knocked down yet, but nobody was living in them. The Germans were around one of those houses and

> they just got closer to us than they should have. I was looking to see where they were and what they were doing—I had no intention of doing what the Army said I did.

The nearest enemy position, consisting of four machine guns and a mortar, began hammering I Company's positions. The wiry Montgomery crawled through a muddy ditch in the darkness to within grenade range of the nearest German position. "I just told my platoon to cover me and I went out there. When you did that, you never looked back. You knew that as long as they're alive, they'll be looking out for you," he said. Easing himself onto a small mound, Montgomery began lobbing grenades and firing away with his M-1 until eight Germans were dead; four others surrendered. After bringing his prisoners back to his own lines, he spotted a group of the enemy near another house and called for artillery. While the barrage was still going on, Montgomery, armed only with a carbine, again crawled out into "no-man's land," where he assaulted the second line of enemy with the fury of a man possessed. Ignoring the tremendous volume of rifle and machine gun fire being directed at him by the Germans, he killed three, knocked out two machine gun nests, and captured seven more of the enemy, then single-handedly went after a group of German troops in and around the house, some 300 yards away. American artillery was still exploding around the building as he closed in on it. The Germans decided to make a run for it, but Montgomery cut them off and took another twenty-one prisoners. His total for the morning was eleven dead, thirty-two captured, and an unknown number wounded.

That night, while helping an adjacent unit fight off a German assault, he was seriously wounded by mortar fragments. "I was always going somewhere I didn't have any business going," he said. "I went over to a different company—K or L—to see how they were doing. I was coming back alone through a big ditch when a shell hit. I don't remember much about it. I was hit in the left leg and right arm and right chest. It wasn't very long before my medic found me. I don't remember his first name but his last name was Beadle. Your medic was one person that you had to have confidence in. I knew Beadle would find me." Beadle did, and Montgomery was evacuated back to the hospital on the beachhead, stayed a few days, and then was scheduled to head to Naples on a hospital ship. The ship was being targeted by German gunners, however, and was forced to depart without him. For several weeks, Montgomery was laid up at the beachhead hospital—an experience that unnerved the courageous lieutenant more than combat did. "The hospital was just tents, and the tents had holes in them from all the enemy artillery and mortar fire. I'd roll off the cot and lie on the floor and tell them, 'Dig me a hole here.' It wasn't long before they dug holes for everyone. They finally sent me back to Naples on an LST. When I got back to the States, it was a year and a day since I had left."

Second Lieutenant Jack Montgomery, I Company, 180th Infantry Regiment, recipient of the Medal of Honor. (Courtesy of 45th Infantry Division Archives)

Montgomery eventually recovered, returned to active duty, and was stationed at Camp Wolters, Texas, late in 1944, when he received a letter from his company clerk, asking if he had received the Medal of Honor yet. This puzzled him, but he gave it little thought. In January 1945, Montgomery received orders to report to the White House, where President Roosevelt presented him with the nation's highest military decoration while his two brothers, two of his three sisters, and his mother looked on proudly.[30]

• • •

Time was running out for the 2nd Battalion men in the caves. Al Bedard remembered a brave lieutenant:

> He volunteered to go up on top of the caves in a foxhole and zero in our artillery on the Germans, which he did. All he was armed with was a trench knife. He did that for about an hour and we blasted the hell out of the Germans. There were dead Germans lying everywhere. After the barrage was over, this lieutenant came in and sat down inside the cave with us. We got orders to move out and fight our way back because they couldn't supply us any longer. We went around waking up everybody. Totally exhausted people were falling asleep—we had been in this damn place practically without sleep for a week. I looked at this lieutenant. He had a cigarette hanging out of his mouth—I thought he was asleep. But he was dead. He evidently died of concussion—his heart stopped. To this day, I don't know his name.[31]

At 0200 hours on the morning of 23 February, now that the British had taken up positions at the northern openings to the caves, Lieutenant Colonel Lawrence Brown's 2nd Battalion made its breakout from the southern openings, which faced the beach. But by that time, the caves were almost completely surrounded by the enemy. Brown knew an orderly withdrawal, rather than a mad dash back to friendly lines, was essential and made up a schedule indicating when each unit would leave. At 0130 hours, the battalion began slipping out of the caves in single file. G Company went first, followed by the remnants of F Company, Headquarters, Heavy Weapons, Sparks's E Company, and the walking wounded.[32]

Felix Sparks remembered, "We didn't have the faintest idea what was going on in back of us. All we knew was that there was a hell of a lot of fighting going on because we could hear it." Sparks told Lieutenant Colonel Brown that he'd been on the flank earlier and thought he could figure out a route to get back to friendly lines—after he went back to his old position and got the machine gun he had lent to the British. "I'll meet you at the bridge across one of the ravines," Sparks told Brown.

The captain took off and made it back to his company's previous position on the small hill near the highway, which was some 200–300 yards from the caves. "There wasn't a soul there," Sparks recalled. "Not a soul. You talk about being spooked—I was spooked. My machine gun was gone—the British had just disappeared. They obviously had been captured." Sparks went to the bridge and met the retreating column. Taking the point, Sparks led the single file of men stumbling through the dark toward the beach, roughly parallel to the main highway but a few hundred yards to the west. The group reached a narrow bridge over one of the ravines, where the men promptly bunched up. Five minutes after crossing, Sparks volunteered to go back to the bridge to make sure everyone crossed it safely.

After the last man had passed, Sparks found a British water can and some British biscuits. "I was starved to death; I crammed my mouth full." He stood there for a few moments, just listening, and then started forward to rejoin the column. Suddenly, from the direction of the head of the column, the sound of a German machine gun ripped through the chill night—the column had run into the enemy. "The Germans had established a line and we had wandered into it," Sparks said. "The firing didn't break out until about half of our column had passed through their outpost—they probably thought we were German replacements. The bullets were really flying and I was yelling, 'Fire back, fire back.' I could see the flashes from the machine gun that was giving us fits. Then I yelled, 'Everybody follow me!'"

Avoiding the bullets, Sparks crawled to where the column had parted and came across several men who had been either killed or wounded. Again exhorting the men to follow him, Sparks headed toward a nearby canal, but only a few of the men followed. "We got to the canal; the sides were pretty steep and all covered with vines and vegetation," he recalled. "We sort of fell all the way down to the bottom, which was about eight or ten feet deep, and the water was maybe a foot and a half deep. When we got down there, I took a head count. There should have been at least forty men with me, but I discovered I only had about twelve men, including a wounded operations officer from the battalion. I figured everybody who was coming was there, and that everybody else was either dead or had given up."

Sparks told the small band that they would have to infiltrate through enemy lines and to hold their fire if the Germans fired at them. "We started off and got to their lines and the Germans yelled at us. They heard us—we couldn't move without making some noise. Finally, they threw a few grenades but didn't hit anybody. We got through them before they knew what was happening and they didn't fire at us because they couldn't really see us." His group continued on for about another half mile and emerged from the canal into a British-held position. "Scared the hell out of them, I'll tell you that," Sparks said. "We came out into a British artillery unit and when these British gunners saw me crawl out of the canal, they took off running into the woods like crazy. I hollered, 'We're Americans!' so they wouldn't shoot at us." Sparks later learned that the first half of the column had made it back to friendly lines.

Reflecting on the fate of E Company, Sparks said, "When we started out from the caves, I had fourteen or sixteen men left. We were never able to evacuate any wounded after the first morning. We had to leave the wounded in the cave with the doctor and the medical team. They were all taken prisoner after we pulled out. The doctor volunteered to stay—in fact, he refused to leave. He told the battalion commander, 'Colonel, I'm not going to leave these men.' The battalion commander didn't argue with him."[33]

The doctor—Captain Peter C. Graffagnino—said,

> We had thirty wounded on litters and about nine men stayed behind with them. Those who got out were supposed to send up litter bearers. On February 24th, they sent up an ambulance with ten men, but they had to stop about a mile away and walk in. We made a truce with the Germans to evacuate the wounded. About six p.m., we started through the German lines. We had twenty-four men on litters and used other wounded to help carry them. The regimental dentist was in front and I was in the middle of the column. We were both waving Red Cross flags like crazy. About halfway through to the ambulance, a German major in a tank at a farmhouse stopped us. He had a sergeant who spoke English. I really think the major did, too. He insisted that we be captured. We argued for half an hour about the truce, but they took us all prisoner.

Dr. Graffagnino spent the rest of the war in a POW camp.[34]

Lieutenant Philip Burke was wounded during his escape from the caves. "There were all these ravines dug by high water from the mountains," he said. "I was trying to get through them back to our lines and the Germans were up above, firing down on us. I happened to have a submachine gun with me and managed to take care of a couple of them up on the high walls." Burke was wounded in the side and back of the head. Although bleeding and in pain, he could still walk. "We were able to make it back to the British lines and they aimed us back to the American lines." Once back to friendly positions, Burke was evacuated to the 300th General Hospital in Naples, recuperated, and rejoined the 45th a few weeks later, still at Anzio.[35]

Pete Conde recalled a soldier who died during the 2nd Battalion's withdrawal. "Johnny McCorkle was from Lamar, Colorado, and he loved war," he said. "He played it to the hilt. He was a gutsy crapshooter and a gutsy soldier—unbelievable. Leon Siehr and Johnny McCorkle headed toward the English lines and Johnny McCorkle got hit with an 88 that tore off his arm and they couldn't stop the blood and he died."[36]

Not surprising, the British who had relieved the 157th's 2nd Battalion in the caves met with disaster. Nearly out of food, water, and ammunition, the men of the 7th Battalion, Queens Own, soon found themselves surrounded with no means of defending themselves. The 2nd Battalion, 6th Queens, attempted to bring up supplies to the trapped battalion but was turned back, and a planned airdrop was scrapped due to poor weather. On the twenty-third, the German 65th Infantry Division overran two of the British companies in outpost positions and forced the third to take cover in the caves. That night, the remaining troops of the 2nd Battalion, 7th Queens, attempted to infiltrate back to friendly lines in small groups, but most were either captured or killed. The Germans took control of the area that had been so valiantly held by the 2nd Battalion, 157th Regiment.[37]

• • •

Once he had made it back to the beach, Sparks received 150 new recruits and was told to mold them into a new E Company. "I only had a few days to whip them into shape, form new platoons, and pick new platoon leaders. I had lost all of my officers and NCOs." (A few days later, T-4 Leon Siehr of Burlington, Colorado, the only other member of E Company to escape death or capture, made it back to friendly lines. He would be killed in action three months later.)

Even in the relative security of the rear area, there was no safety. Sparks recalled that his unit was unable to do much training "because we were under fire all the time. We had more casualties in the rear than I ever had on the front lines."

The Germans also mounted air attacks almost every night with one or two bombers. They didn't do much damage but one night eight of Sparks's men were killed by a single bomb. "They were all recruits who had just come up to the company," he said. "I sent them over to dig foxholes and the bomb dropped before they could dig."[38]

On the twenty-third, Joseph Bosa noted in his diary, "We at last have had one quiet night and morning. Only one air raid last night—it was too cloudy. Rain this morning. This afternoon has seen a little activity in front of the 179th on Dead End Road down which the Germans run tanks to fire on our troops."[39]

During the five bloody days from 16 to 20 February, VI Corps suffered 3,400 battle casualties, most of them from the 45th Division. In those five days, some 400 men of the 45th Division had been killed, 2,000 were wounded, and a thousand were listed as missing in action. Many of the missing were now prisoners, but others had simply been obliterated by the nearly constant artillery and mortar bombardments or buried forever under the mud of Anzio. Another 2,500 Thunderbirds had been evacuated for nonbattle causes—immersion foot, exhaustion, and exposure.[40] The 2nd Battalion, 157th, was especially hard hit. When the battle of the caves began, Brown's battalion had 38 officers and 713 enlisted men; when they returned to the beachhead, there were only 15 officers and 162 men left.[41]

Yes, the Thunderbirds had suffered, but they had also held against the best the enemy could throw at them. And by holding, they had saved the beachhead from annihilation. Unfortunately, the 45th Division has never been credited for its part in saving the Anzio beachhead in the same way that, say, the 101st Airborne Division was credited with the defense of the American line at Bastogne. Although other units played a significant role in the battle of Anzio, and a few have claimed or been given credit for "saving the beachhead" (most notably the U.S. 3rd Division—which, in addition to its "Rock of the Marne" sobriquet also laid claim to the title, "The Rock of Anzio" in its division history),[42] it should be obvious that to the 45th Division belongs the lion's share of the credit.

The 157th regimental history pulls no punches: "There remains little doubt but that in the five days that followed [16–22 February], Second and Third Battalions saved the beachhead."[43] The 179th's history says, "In stopping the German offensive, the Forty-fifth Division had borne the brunt of the four-day, six-divisional attack."[44]

Other historians infer the 45th's contribution. Martin Blumenson, in *Anzio: The Gamble That Failed,* writes, "The Germans struck the Forty-fifth Division once more. For four hours confusion and desperation characterized the fighting. . . . And when the noise ceased and the smoke lifted, it was plain for everyone to see—the Germans had failed to achieve their breakthrough."[45]

A war correspondent's story began, "Of all the American units engaged in the Italian Campaign, none has fought with more valor or suffered more sanguinary ordeals than the Forty-fifth Infantry Division now fighting at Anzio. It was this Division which bore the brunt of the main enemy blow during Major General Eberhard von Mackensen's second and strongest attempt to annihilate the bridgehead." And an article in the Mediterranean *Stars and Stripes* states, "For four days the Forty-fifth fought stubbornly against a drive which, if successful, would have cut the beachhead in half from north to south."[46]

Even if these words had never been written, every Thunderbird knows in his heart that one division saved the beachhead: the 45th.

• • •

There was one more Allied casualty at Anzio. On the twenty-second, Major General John P. Lucas, the embattled VI Corps commander, was given the ax. Replacing him was Clark's selection, Major General Lucian K.

Truscott. In actuality, it was not Clark who relieved Lucas but Alexander, under pressure from Churchill, who saw him as "defeated." Alexander had told Clark, "I am very much dissatisfied with General Lucas. I have no confidence in him and his ability to control the situation. I very much fear that there might be a disaster at Anzio with Lucas in command and you know what will happen to you and me if there is a disaster at Anzio."[47]

Clark, to his credit, was concerned about his friend's emotional state and wanted to let him down gently, without hurting him. Clark really could find no fault with Lucas, for he had done exactly what Clark had ordered him to do: establish a beachhead at Anzio. Although Lucas subsequently has been criticized for not dashing inland to take the Alban Hills and perhaps even Rome, the fact is he was never given that task by Clark, even if Churchill thought otherwise. To Lucas, his "firing" did not come as any great surprise. He knew his job had been on the line since the operation began a month earlier and knew that Alexander and Churchill had been displeased with the invasion's progress—or lack thereof. But Lucas always felt that he had been dealt a bad hand and had been expected to accomplish the impossible with too few resources.

Clark tried to assure Lucas that he had not lost confidence in him, that Lucas had been right not to plunge recklessly ahead to the Alban Hills, that he had been correct to build up the beachhead (and especially the vast stocks of artillery ammunition that proved to be invaluable) to withstand the inevitable German counterattacks). All this was true, yet the dismissal—in spite of his promotion to commander of the Fourth Army in the States—was still a bitter blow. "I thought I was winning something of a victory," he confided to his diary.[48]

Lucas was gone, but the rest of the Allies were still there, and more punishment was in store for them—especially for the men of the 45th.

10

Any Respite Seemed Unsuited

24 February–22 May 1944

And I, looking more closely, saw a banner that, as it wheeled about, raced on—so quick that any respite seemed unsuited to it. Behind that banner trailed so long a file of people—I should never have believed that death could have unmade so many souls.

—Dante Alighieri, *The Inferno,* Canto III

LIKE A PALL OF SMOKE following a barrage, an uneasy tension drifted over the beachhead. The Germans had, for all intents and purposes, lost the battle for Anzio. Kesselring, von Mackensen, and even Hitler now knew their decimated ranks had neither the strength nor the will to break through the Allied line, but the Allies did not. For all the British and Americans knew, the Germans were continuing to receive reinforcements in preparation for yet another massive, all-out charge against their fragile defensive formations.

Unable to achieve the final penetration in the center, which had been held by the 45th against some of the most intense and sustained attacks on any battlefield in the whole of the war, von Mackensen turned his attention to the eastern flank—where the 3rd Infantry Division, 504th Parachute Infantry Regiment, and 4th Ranger Battalion were arrayed in a line from Carano to Isola Bella, south of Cisterna. Perhaps a more favorable outcome could be found there. Von Mackensen's plan called for his troops to attack down the banks of Spaccasassi Creek, break through the American lines, and drive all the way to the west branch of the Mussolini Canal. Since the battle for the Overpass had depleted and demoralized his main forces, von Mackensen had worked feverishly, with limited resources, to rebuild and reorganize his Fourteenth Army. Fresh troops were added to the patchwork quilt of German units, which consisted of the 114th *Jäger* Division (reinforced with the 1028th Panzer Grenadier Regiment of the 715th Infantry Division), the still incomplete 4th *Fallschirmjäger* Division (which had roughed up the British 56th Division on 16 February), the 362nd Infantry Division (a relatively inexperienced unit that had been relieved from its coast-watching duties), and remnants of the 26th Panzer and Hermann Göring Panzer Divisions. The battered 29th Panzer Grenadier Division was placed in reserve but would stay ready to exploit any penetrations. In all, the five German divisions about to launch themselves against the Yanks totaled roughly the same number of men as their American foes.

On the afternoon of the twenty-eighth, the Germans blanketed the movement of their troops with smoke shells and shifted the bulk of their artillery from the British front to the village of Carano. Thus tipped off to the Germans' likely objective, Truscott transferred two artillery battalions to beef up the guns already in the 3rd Division's sector and had them sited to cover the enemy's most likely assembly areas and avenues of approach, which had already been thickly sown with mines. At 0430 hours on the twenty-ninth, the first of some 66,000 rounds of Yankee artillery that day was fired—more than double the number of rounds fired on any day during the main German counterattacks from 16 to 20 February. The effect on the massed German formations, preparing for their predawn attack, was devastating. Great gaps were torn in the enemy's ranks by the combined firepower of the 105s and 155s. Tanks, guns, and men were catapulted into the air. It did not seem that anything could live through the deluge of American steel. Yet, out of the smoke came wave after wave of Germans, screaming their *Heil Hitler*s and *Gott mit uns,* and singing their patriotic songs with their last breaths. No Japanese kamikaze warriors were ever more fanatical than the Germans who threw themselves against the Allies at Anzio.

The heaviest of the initial attacks hit the 509th Parachute Infantry Battalion in the vicinity of Carano. The 1028th Panzer Grenadier Regiment and elements of the 362nd Infantry Division slammed into B Company of the paratroopers, which was dug in about a mile northeast of the village. The force of the assault pushed B Company 700 yards to the rear; only one officer and twenty-two men made it back. Now having burst through the outer defenses of the American line, the 1st Battalion of the 1028th turned southwest across the open farm fields, heading for the half-strength A Company, 509th Parachute Infantry Battalion. A massed salvo of artillery and mortar fire greeted the Germans, but still they came on, until the fire became so intense—and their casualties so heavy—that they were forced to take cover in a ditch.

To the west of Carano, the 2nd Battalion of the 1028th, trying to outflank the defenders, became hung up on barbed wire and was cut to pieces by machine gun fire from the 3rd Division's I Company, 30th Infantry Regiment. Nearby, the crew of a disabled Sherman from the 751st Tank Battalion knocked out three enemy panzers and undoubtedly helped to save the day.

Earlier on the twenty-ninth, considerable hard fighting between the Hermann Göring Panzer Division and the 3rd Division's 15th Infantry Regiment surged back and forth around the tiny farm settlement known as Isola Bella. When the battle finally ended, seven panzers had been turned into immobile wrecks and nine others were damaged. More important, the American line had held.

To the east of Carano, the 362nd Infantry Division repeatedly tried to crack the American lines with combined tank-and-infantry attacks—and were repeatedly stopped by artillery, mortar, tank, and anti-tank fire. When Allied planes joined in the action in midafternoon, shattering the German formations and scattering the survivors, the danger of a German breakthrough around Carano had come to an end. That evening, the 3rd Division and the paratroopers counterattacked and regained much of the lost ground. The Germans had no better luck farther east, where a hodgepodge of units tried to assault the well-prepared positions held by the 4th Ranger Battalion, the 1st Special Service Force, elements of the 509th Parachute Infantry Battalion, and O'Daniel's 3rd Division.[1]

On the twenty-ninth, Captain Bosa recorded the following in his diary:

> This morning I went on duty at four a.m. in FDC. We fired Corps' targets for about an hour and then had to pull our batteries off to put them on defensive fires on our own front. A large patrol of Germans had worked in and captured a machine gun and personnel. After this threat, we received word that 509th Paratroopers had been attacked and had been forced back 500 yards and possibly were being flanked. We shifted our fire and that of the 189th to this sector and fired on roads and draws and reported troop locations.[2]

On the far right of the American line, the German attacks were finally showing some success. On the rainy night of 29 February–1 March, K Company, 7th Infantry Regiment, was blasted out of its foxholes by a panzer attack. The company's anti-tank weapons gone, the GIs fought back with Molotov cocktails until artillery fire could be brought to bear. Here the 3rd Division received a bloody nose but held its ground. West of Ponte Rotto, however, tanks and infantry from the 26th Panzer Division rumbled down the road between Cisterna and Campo Morto, pushing Americans out of the way as it continued on. As day turned to night, *Nebelwerfern* added their screeching voices to the surrealistic symphony. The German drive, subjected to withering fire, eventually stalled.

The next day, 1 March, the Germans again tried attacking the American line near Ponte Rotto in a driving rainstorm, but their own diminishing strength and the growing power of Allied artillery made their assaults suicidal. Now it was time for the momentum to swing to the Allied side. On 2 March, a clear day, the Allied air forces worked over the enemy troop concentrations with unerring accuracy. The air armada, which consisted of 100

B-17s and 241 B-24s, escorted by 63 P-47s and 113 P-38s, pulverized the triangle between Carroceto, Velletri, and Cisterna. The enemy was unable to mount any serious assault that day.

On the western side of the Via Anziate, where the British 56th Division held sway, 660 men of the 9th and 40th Royal Marine Commandos were used to great effect in silent, deadly raids against the enemy's forward positions. The well-worn 56th Division received a much-deserved break in the second week of March, when it was relieved by the British 5th Division and was shipped south to take up a reserve position on the Cassino front. Gradually, the Allies were gathering strength—strength that could not be matched by the other side. Kesselring directed von Mackensen to break off the attacks against the 3rd Division; he was convinced that they would accomplish nothing but the complete destruction of the Fourteenth Army. In spite of Kesselring's orders, the 26th Panzer Division somehow found the courage to try again on 3 March, hitting the 3rd Division's 3rd Battalion, 7th Infantry Regiment, at a small bridge southwest of Ponte Rotto. The Americans launched a counterattack to regain control of the bridge, only to be thrown back with heavy casualties.[3]

During this period, while attention was focused on the attacks against the right side of the Allied line, the Germans did not completely forget about the 45th. Things stayed hot on the Thunderbirds' front for the first two weeks of March. On the first, in the 180th's sector near Padiglione, the Germans struck at F, G, and I Companies' positions. The small-but-sharp attacks, including attempts to infiltrate the Thunderbirds' lines under cover of night, were to continue for a week.[4] The Germans kept up pressure on the 179th and 180th with small-scale ground attacks, accompanied by heavy artillery concentrations, and it appeared that the Germans were preparing for another counteroffensive.[5] A patrol brought back information from a captured German that the enemy would attack the 179th on 6 March. A well-placed artillery concentration on the assembly areas and avenues of approach put an end to that plan.

The next night, a battalion of the 6th Armored Infantry Regiment relieved the 1st Battalion, 179th, for several days of well-deserved rest. On the eighth, the 2nd Battalion was given a respite from the rigors of the front line. But on the same day, the 180th was pummeled by heavy artillery barrages, followed by a ground attack with tanks and infantry. Allied artillery beat off these attacks. Enemy artillery barrages and small, aggressive patrols against the division's front lines for the next two weeks certainly gave no indication that the Germans were beaten.[6]

In spite of the continual enemy action, a semblance of normalcy began to pervade the front. On 5 March, the unit paymaster doled out the Thunderbirds' pay for the past two months. "We have plenty of money and no place to spend it," lamented Joseph Bosa, who had been promoted to major and moved up to battalion executive officer on 2 March.[7]

• • •

For most of the rest of the month, the Anzio battlefield was relatively quiet. There were, of course, the "normal" harassing artillery barrages by both sides, along with aerial dogfights. (Major Bosa reported that on the seventh, the troops on the ground were entertained by two pilots in the sky: "We heard a burst of machine-gun fire, then a plane plummeted straight to the ground. Not long after, we could see a parachute floating lazily to earth. The 180th picked up the pilot, a German, who had been wounded in the back. They rushed him to the hospital.")[8]

On 11 March, the 45th was alerted for a new offensive operation called Plan Panther that was set for the nineteenth. Then the name was changed to Plan Centipede. Then, on the night of 18 March, Centipede was canceled altogether, due mostly to insufficient air support.[9] Although the attack was called off, nature staged her own display of power. On the nineteenth, in an event that seemed as if Italy itself was venting the agony of war raging across its surface, the great volcano Vesuvius, just south of Naples, erupted with a roar that drowned out all of man's weapons, belching a huge, gray, mushroom cloud of smoke and ash some seven miles into the atmosphere.[10]

On the twentieth, a one-platoon assault by the 179th, supported by tanks, artillery, and mortars, attempted to remove enemy forces that were uncomfortably close to the unit's positions along Spaccasassi Creek. The next night, combat patrols engaged in equally savage fighting. Many of the GIs, dodging bullets and shrapnel, wondered why some people were referring to this period as a "lull."[11] Patrols from both sides continued to probe each other's defenses, capture prisoners, or become prisoners—or casualties—themselves. Daniel Witts, Anti-Tank Company, 179th, recalled the deadly mission of some of the patrols: "You'd go out on patrol and try to draw enemy fire to see if anybody was around." He also remembered the ghastly reality of no-man's land: "There was barbed wire and mines and dead men lying out there on the wire, men who had gone on patrols and were shot. Just skeletons in clothes. Some had been lying there for three months. Nobody could go out there and get 'em."[12]

Ralph Fink, D Company, 157th, remembered a very spooky incident that occurred while he was on guard duty one night along the front lines. "My buddy, Jim Tobin, and I were in a foxhole about midnight. It was an overcast night, and we saw something there that was really creepy." One of the men glanced back at a shattered house that was about a hundred yards to their right and set back a short distance from the ditch. All the windows had been knocked out and the roof was gone except for the very top beam. This night, there seemed to be something formless and shapeless moving back and forth across that beam. "Jim and I watched this for a minute or two. It made the hair stand up on the backs of our necks. Maybe it was a flare in the distance that might have reflected off a low cloud. But to this day, I'm not sure that we did *not* see a real ghost on the peak of that roof."[13]

The mystery of the "ghost" may have been solved by V. I. Minahan, a platoon commander in C Company, 157th. He said, "It wasn't a ghost; it was a dog. The almost-destroyed house contained the headquarters of Company C at that time. I often visited the company headquarters (at night, of course) to pick up supplies, talk with the company commander, etc. I distinctly remember the dog pacing back and forth along the roof beam, night after night. I cannot remember whether some GIs finally got the dog down, or whether he was still up there when we left the position."[14]

Bill Rolen, I Company, 180th, recalled a nightmarish incident during a night patrol. He was in no-man's land when the group came under mortar fire. It was pitch black and Rolen jumped for what looked like a big, dark hole in the ground. It turned out to be the maggoty, rotting carcass of a cow or horse. "I jumped right out of that thing—I was in terrible shape," he said. "I can laugh about it now, but it wasn't so funny then."[15]

During this time, Alvin "Bud" McMillan returned to K Company, 157th, following his recuperation from a leg wound. Not long after, an American fighter crash-landed atop the foxhole of two of his buddies, Alex McBryde and Joe Perry, of B Battery, 158th Field Artillery. "I heard at the time that our boys shot it down by accident," McMillan said, "but I don't know if that's true or not. The pilot got out of the plane all right. Alex wasn't in his foxhole but Joe Perry was. Alex had just gotten out of the hole and the plane skidded in there and stopped on top of it. Nobody on the ground got hurt. They couldn't get the plane out of there, of course, so they just put one of those camouflage nets over it. But the Jerries used it as a firing point and kept zeroing in on it with their guns."

McMillan said that he had a Springfield .03 sniper's rifle with a four-power scope on it. "During the lull, I did right much snipin'," he said. "One morning I came across a Kraut shaking out his blanket and I shot him. I crawled down to where he was and he had a sniper's rifle, too—a real good one, so I used *it* for quite a while." Shortly thereafter, McMillan went out on a patrol and entered a house.

> I went down to the wine cellar and there were these three huge wine kegs. The Germans had shot holes in 'em, and the wine had all poured out, and it was about knee deep in the cellar. We took some hay and straw and wiped out the wine in a couple of those kegs, then we crawled in 'em and spent the night. The next morning, I found a jar and filled it up with some of the wine and came up out of the cellar. As I walked around the corner of one of the farmhouses, there was about a seven-foot Kraut standing there with a machine pistol, less than a hundred feet away. We both started shooting at each other at about the same time. One bullet hit me in the right thigh, about three inches from where I had got hit by the shrapnel, and about eight or ten bullets went

Sniper Alvin "Bud" McMillan (left) and Alex McBryde, K Company, 157th Infantry Regiment, sitting on a P-40 that crash-landed on McBryde's foxhole at Anzio. (Courtesy of A. McMillan)

> between my legs, and one hit my left shinbone and knocked me down. I had a Thompson [submachine gun] and my bullets were all hitting him in the chest, and the bullets just kind of picked him up and carried him back a long ways. It killed him.
>
> There was some more Krauts around and we got in a little firefight. We threw a grenade and killed another Kraut in a foxhole and then one raised his hands up and I hobbled over there and got him out and we carried him back. So we captured a German on that patrol.

McMillan was taken back to one of the large tent hospitals on the beach. While he was there, the hospital was hit by long-range German artillery fire and several of the medical personnel were killed and wounded. McMillan remained at the hospital for ten or twelve more days, receiving penicillin, but no one removed the slug from his leg. Finally, he hobbled over to a nearby motor pool and "borrowed" a weapons carrier loaded with rations. He followed signs to the 158th Field Artillery, where he had a friend from his hometown of Fayetteville, North Carolina. Leaving the vehicle at the battery, he finally got directions back to K Company. "I went back and rejoined my outfit," he says. "They never did officially discharge me from the hospital."[16]

Things finally quieted down as the Germans went onto the defensive and abandoned—at least for the near term—any plans to continue the offensive. Both sides dug in, improved their positions, called for reinforcements, and waited for the day when they would either begin a new offensive—or try to stop the enemy's efforts to annihilate them. From time to time, Allied units were rotated off the front lines and given a few days away from staring death in the face. Tarzan Williams, K Company, 157th, recalled, "We got relieved for three days and the next morning the supply sergeant had barber tools. We got a set and cut the men's beards for them so they could shave easy. We had a thirty-two-day growth of beard."[17]

When they weren't dropping artillery shells or aerial bombs on the Allies, the Germans were dropping propaganda flyers over the Allies on the beach. One leaflet displayed a grinning skull with the headline, "Beach-head Death's head." Another, directed at British troops, showed a seminude woman and an American sergeant getting dressed after a bout of sex; the headline said, "While you are away . . . "—a not-too-subtle attempt to foment anger and distrust between the Allies. Another, also aimed at the British, read, "General Clark certainly played you a dirty Yankee trick! And who has got to bear the consequences?" There is no evidence that these psychological weapons had much effect on their intended targets, but many of the dug-in Allied soldiers appreciated the extra ration of "toilet paper" the Germans generously provided them.[18]

• • •

Von Mackensen's last-gasp attempt to push the Allies back into the sea had ended with the loss of more men and equipment than he could afford. It has been estimated that in the brief period from 29 February to 4 March, the Germans lost 30 percent of their tanks and over 3,500 men killed, wounded, or taken prisoner. The Allies had also been seriously weakened. In *Fatal Decision,* the historian Carlo D'Este cites figures indicating that, from 22 January to the breakout in May, the Allies at Anzio had some 7,000 men killed in action; 36,000 wounded or missing; and 44,000 evacuated due to injuries, accidents, and illness. Casualties were not confined to the ground forces. The British Royal Navy lost two light cruisers, three destroyers, a hospital ship, three LSTs, and an LCI; the Germans sank two American Liberty ships, two minesweepers, one LST, and five landing craft.[19]

Like a pair of utterly exhausted pugilists, the two armies leaned shoulder to shoulder against each other, too physically and mentally tired to raise their gloves and throw the decisive punch. As one historian has written, "Fortunately, the Third Division, which bore the brunt of the last enemy offensive, had been given an opportunity to prepare for the final German attack. The weeks when the enemy was concentrating his assaults along the axis of the Albano road had been used to absorb and train replacements and to strengthen defenses. . . . When the enemy attack lost its momentum,

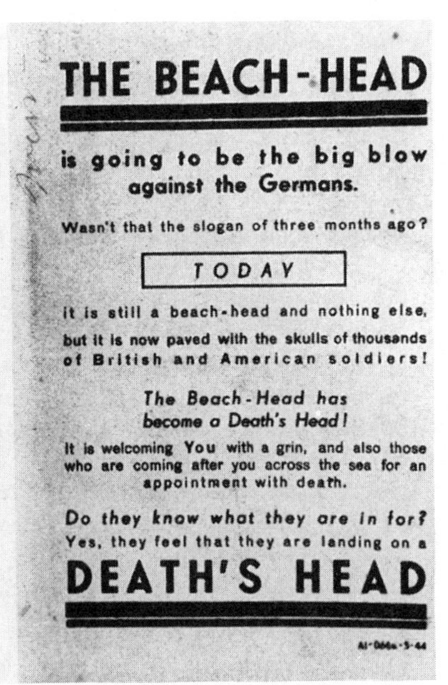

THE BEACH-HEAD

is going to be the big blow
against the Germans.

Wasn't that the slogan of three months ago?

TODAY

it is still a beach-head and nothing else,
but it is now paved with the skulls of thousands
of British and American soldiers!

The Beach-Head has
become a Death's Head!

It is welcoming You with a grin, and also those
who are coming after you across the sea for an
appointment with death.

Do they know what they are in for?
Yes, they feel that they are landing on a

DEATH'S HEAD

Front and back of a German propaganda leaflet. (Courtesy of 45th Infantry Division Archives)

the Third Division, although weakened, was still capable of sustained fighting and its positions were almost intact."[20]

On 24 March, the Thunderbirds' brief respite from the front lines came to an end as the 157th, as patched up and retrained as possible, relieved a regiment of the 3rd Division and it was back again to the dangerous, deadly job of patrolling behind enemy lines, fighting off small-scale attacks, and enduring the intermittent shellings.[21]

On 10 April, with the front more or less stagnant, the war-weary 45th, in which nearly every man resembled Bill Mauldin's scruffy Willie and Joe characters, began pulling back to the wooded area known as the Pines to rest and refit.[22] Besides being a break from the rigors of life at the front, this brief period off the line meant that the GIs could finally enjoy hot meals; exchange their dirty uniforms for clean ones; and get a chance to cleanse their filthy, stinking bodies. Morty Carr, a member of the Ammunition and Pioneer Platoon, HQ Company, 1st Battalion, 157th, remembered that personal hygiene had been virtually impossible on the front lines. "When the shower truck came, we'd get a change of clothing. That happened about once a month. Otherwise, we'd take a bath out of our helmets."[23]

In spite of the occasional artillery bursts and air raids and training regimen, life a few miles behind the front lines settled into a boring routine. Recreational activities began to be organized for the war-weary soldiers. Sporting events were staged and underground movie theaters, scooped out of the sand by bulldozers, provided entertainment, as did the division band.[24] In the British sector, soldiers wagered their pay on the outcome of beetle races and soccer matches,[25] and the GIs were equally creative when it came to devising ways of relieving the ennui. Mel Craven, A Battery, 158th Field Artillery, recalled,

> We'd get horses, donkeys, anything that would run, and have a race. We had baseball games that would, at times, go all the way through to completion. At other times, they'd be cut short by an artillery barrage. We speculated that the German artillery observer might have a bet on the losing team, so he'd break up the game with a barrage. These were things the fellows would do to retain their sanity, to relieve the strain. There was no place on the beach that was out of artillery range [or wasn't] essentially under direct observation.[26]

Ralph Fink remembered some relatively good times off the front lines. "We had hot meals and could relax and maybe play a little softball. We'd throw down some T-shirts for bases and somebody'd bring out a couple of bats and a couple of balls and we felt like we were playing in the World Series—even in those clodhopper combat boots."[27]

Felix Sparks recalled that, during this time, the division was rotated in and out of the front lines—six days on and three days off.[28] But although the pitched battles that had marked the middle of February had subsided, deadly activity still continued. German artillery still crashed into all parts of the Allied-held ground at odd intervals, German patrols still tried to infiltrate into Allied lines, and German aircraft still made deadly sorties over American and British positions, often targeting the large hospital area with its clearly marked tents.[29]

Don Amzibel, L Company, 157th, learned firsthand that the hospital was not a safe haven. He had developed an eye problem and was in one of the large hospital tents. "One night, the pilot of a German plane that had been shot down unloaded his incendiary bomb on the way down. The bomb landed on the hospital. I spent most of the night helping to carry litters of patients and helping to clean up the mess."[30]

"Doc Joe" Franklin, a medic with I Company, 157th, remembered, "One day in the Pines, some officer put everyone on close order drill to exercise them. The Germans threw some 88mm fire in there while they were drilling and just slaughtered them. That ended the exercises."[31]

Nowhere on the beachhead were the Allies out of range of the German gunners, who did not need pinpoint accuracy to keep everyone's nerves on edge. Ernie Pyle wrote,

> In my wartime life, I've had a good many stray shells in my vicinity, but not until I went to that beachhead was I ever under an actual artillery barrage. The Germans shelled us at intervals throughout the day and night, but usually there were just one or two shells at a time, with long quiet periods between.

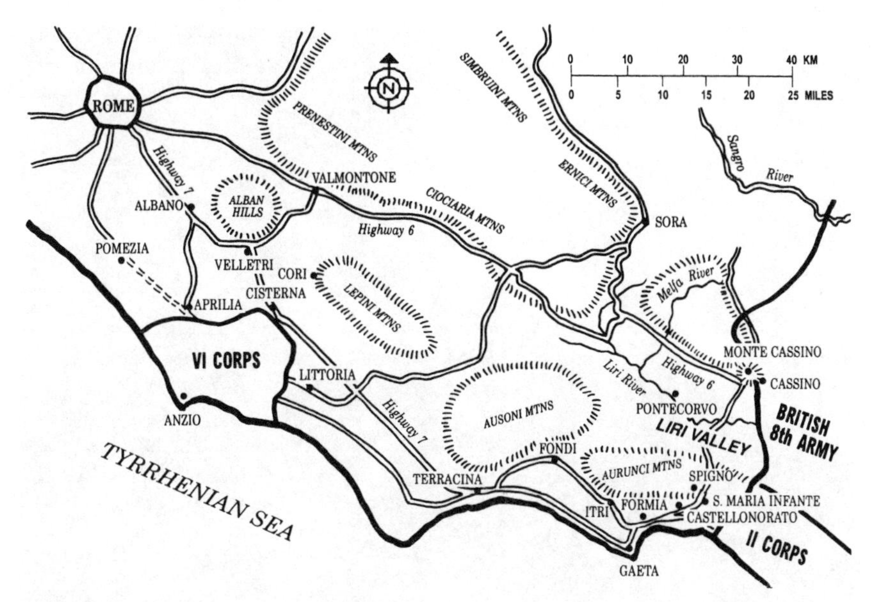

MAP 10.1 Stalemate on Two Fronts
With VI Corps pinned down around Anzio and II Corps and the British Eighth Army stymied along the Gustav Line, a quick resolution to the situation in Italy appeared impossible.

> One night, however, they threw a real barrage at us. It was short but, boy, was it hot. Shells were coming faster than we could count them. One guess was as good as another, but I estimated that in two minutes they put a hundred fifty shells into our area.[32]

The two biggest guns were a pair of huge, 280mm guns mounted on railroad carriages and hidden in tunnels in the Alban Hills. The Germans had named one of the guns "Leopold" and the other "Robert," but the GIs on the beachhead simply referred to them as "Anzio Annie" and the "Anzio Express," the latter because the sound of the shells flying overhead caused some soldiers to imagine a runaway train roaring through the sky.

Direct descendants of the 240mm railroad guns the Germans had used with such devastating effect on the western front in World War I, these two Krupp-made monsters could hurl shells packed with 550 pounds of high explosive up to thirty-eight miles. It took the German crew six to ten hours to haul the guns out of their hiding places—one was in a tunnel near Castel Gandolfo, the Pope's summer residence—and prepare them for firing. (In spite of this, the Allied air forces were never able to find them outside their tunnels and knock them out; both survived the war.) As soon as a few shells were fired, the guns were returned to their tunnels. Although the shells

Anzio Annie, one of the Germans' huge railroad guns, after it was found abandoned in Civitavecchia. (Courtesy of Hubert Berry)

rarely landed among the troops packed tightly into the small, congested beachhead, they scared the devil out of nearly everyone.[33] According to one 45th Division veteran, when one of the shells roared overhead, "It felt like it was going to suck you out of your foxhole."[34]

Everyone who survived Anzio, it seems, has a story about these guns. Ralph Fink, D Company, 157th, said, "The incessant shelling was the nasty part. That Anzio Annie—I think it was a psychological weapon. They were trying to hit ships in the harbor but we could hear that shell going overhead. It made sort of a roaring sound. Some guys claimed they could see the shell going over. Maybe they did; it had a slow speed. But it was more of a psychological thing than a danger to us personally. They weren't going to waste those big shells on troops that were dug into foxholes."[35]

Bill Rolen recalled that he would hear one of the big guns fire somewhere up in the mountains and then, "When the shell got over us, a booster would go off. It would scare the hell out of you. Of course, if you heard the booster, you were safe, 'cause it was already past you on its way to the harbor."[36]

Leland Loy, a chaplain with the 3rd Battalion, 157th Regiment, said, "I will never forget one incident with Anzio Annie. I was standing in front of my foxhole one day when Annie lobbed a shell over. It exploded about 150 yards beyond me and a piece of that shrapnel hit within fifteen feet of me. That was a close one."[37]

George Ecker, a medic in the 179th Regiment, said, "I saw some of the craters that the Anzio Express made and you could have put several box cars in them."[38]

The boxcar analogy also cropped up in Minor Shirk's recollection of the big guns. "Can you imagine what a boxcar would sound like flying through the air?" he said. "That's what the Anzio Express sounded like."[39]

In his book, *Vertrauensmann: Man of Confidence*, Henry Kaufman, H Company, 157th, wrote,

> Between the 15th and 16th of February, these two guns never stopped firing. I clearly remember lying in my slit trench on the side of a hill while the Germans used "searching and traversing" fire. First, a shell would burst about fifty yards in front of me and about thirty yards to my right. Then the next shell would burst about forty yards in front of me and about twenty-five yards to my right. They kept "searching and traversing" with each shell always coming closer and closer to me. I noticed a lot of little birds falling out of the trees nearby. They were all dead and I thought, if a little bird doesn't have a chance, what kind of chance have I got?[40]

Food, too, became an obsession with some of the men who were sick and tired of nothing but K and C rations. Even Spam would have seemed a delicacy. Tarzan Williams decided to take the food problem into his own hands.

> When we come back for three days' rest, I asked the cooks what rations they had. They said just C rations. I asked them what they would do if a cow got killed by artillery fire. They said they would cut it up into steaks and cook it for us. I went back to the machine gun section and told the boys what I was going to do and they were ready to go with me. We cut two poles and got enough ropes and knives for the job and went out in the field where the cows were when an artillery barrage came in. I shot a young-looking cow and we cleaned it out, cut off its head, and tied it to the poles to take to the kitchen. The next day, the cooks cut it up into steaks. The next time we came in for three days, the cook said all they had was C rations so I started out to get another cow and half the company wanted to go with me. I was afraid too many men would draw too much attention but we got ourselves another cow.

Williams declined to say if some equally hungry forward observer might have called in the artillery on the bovine targets.[41]

Although the British had their traditional rum ration, many of the men of the 45th had gone months without drinking anything stronger than Coca Cola or instant coffee. To remedy the situation, Daniel Witts, Anti-Tank Company, 179th, recalled, some of the men built a moonshine still. "They made it out of copper tubing they got from old cars and whatever else they could find. One night they were getting drunk and one guy had been eating spaghetti from the ten-in-one rations and he threw up and thought he was bleeding. He goes over to the aid station and finds out he's just drunk and throwing up spaghetti instead of blood."[42]

Now that they were no longer subjected to continuous fire, many of the GIs used this period to improve their foxholes. Soon the underground entrenchments became as elaborate as those of the previous world war—and even included little touches of home. Scroungers gathered doors, mirrors, and even furniture from the ruined houses to make their little holes in the ground more livable. Shelves appeared to hold the soldiers' personal items, and wooden floors—some with carpets—began to replace the mud variety. Floor and table lamps, hooked up to jeep batteries, provided lighting, purloined stoves heated the premises, and pinup photos from *Yank* magazine commonly graced the walls.[43]

Ralph Fink, D Company, 157th, recalled, "When Jim Tobin and I dug our machine gun emplacement, we got some boards and things and built a little hut behind the gun emplacement. We had enough space where we could fire the gun and our heads would only be about an inch above ground level. One morning I stuck my head up just a few inches to scan the front and immediately a bullet crashed into the board beside my head. I later dug the bullet out with my pocket knife. I still have it. It's sort of my lucky bullet."[44]

Morty Carr said, "I shared a foxhole with three or four other guys. We put logs or boards over the top of our foxhole. Then we'd put a shelter-half—that's half a pup tent that each of us carried—over the logs and then put some dirt on top. We used to run a wire from a jeep and attach an incandescent bulb so we had lights in our foxhole. We could play cards and play the radio. Those foxholes were like forts."[45]

Tarzan Williams recalled, "When we were in the rest area, we put roofs over our foxholes, as the night bombers would fly over and drop anti-personnel bombs on us. They were small bombs but they would cover a large area. One night I left my pack on the top side of the foxhole. The next morning it was riddled with holes and on the roof of our foxhole we seen three bomb marks on it. The men were on guard duty in their foxholes and nobody got hurt."[46]

A source of entertainment and information for the men at Anzio was a radio personality everyone called "Axis Sally," who broadcast her nightly propaganda program from Nazi-run studios in Rome. Sally's signature tune was "Between the Devil and the Deep Blue Sea," and she always signed on with "Hello, suckers!" Then she would play popular American records (especially those with a nostalgic quality, such as "I'll Be Seeing You," "Moonlight Serenade," and "It's Been a Long, Long Time") interspersed with blatant propaganda and pleas for the Yanks and Tommies to give themselves up and spend the duration in a nice, safe POW camp.[47]

James Bird, of A Battery, 160th Field Artillery, recalled that he and his buddies listened to her and her English sidekick, named George, over the radio. "We knew they were a lot of crap, but we tuned 'em in for diversion. Sometimes they came off with some sickening sweet things and sometimes they had information on people who had been captured. We did enjoy some of the music they played, though."[48]

Morty Carr also has memories of Axis Sally's broadcasts. "She'd come on the radio at night and say things like, 'We know you're there, men of the 45th Division, especially this company and that company,' because a lot of men were taken prisoner and I guess they told 'em what company they were from."[49]

A few days before he was wounded and evacuated on 21 February, Robert LaDu, F Company, 179th, learned from Sally that a friend had been taken prisoner. "Captain Carpenter—everybody called him 'Hot Damn,' because that was his favorite expression—had been our company commander before he was transferred to B Company. He got captured at Aprilia and Sally came over the radio and our kitchen crew heard it. She said maybe you other guys from the 179th ought to come over and join Captain Carpenter and spend the rest of the war in Berlin."[50]

"She'd come on at night about seven," recalled Pete Conde, of the 157th Regiment's Anti-Tank Platoon, "and people would try to get near a radio to listen so we'd know what was going on. She would even give us the password for the day. *I* didn't even know the password, but *she* did! After our dentist got captured at the caves, she came on the radio a night or two later and said that doctor so-and-so wanted to give a message to his wife in Chicago: 'I'm going to Berlin a little ahead of schedule, dear.'"[51]

On occasion, Sally could be very perceptive. One night she told her audience that Anzio was "the world's largest self-sustaining prisoner of war camp." Few GIs could argue with her point.[52] She was also a good prognosticator; she once informed the 1st Armored Division that they would receive a nasty surprise. The next night the division was subjected to a particularly heavy shelling.[53]

At least one member of the 45th actually met Axis Sally: Private first class Lloyd C. "Blackie" Greer, who had been taken prisoner during the German counteroffensive in February. While at a prisoner of war camp in Rome in April, Greer was visited by Sally and her broadcasting cohort. Greer described Sally as

> a six-footer, about forty years old, with light red hair. She is homely and quite stout. She could speak fluently several languages and she conversed with many of the men in the prison. George was dressed in a First Lieutenant's uniform and looked neat and handsome. He is about thirty-two, six feet two inches tall, and speaks fluent English with a British accent. They asked us our names and addresses and that night they broadcast them. Then we had a radio for the first and only time and heard the two of them broadcast. I understand men of the 180th heard them, too. They had with them both times an American sol-

dier out of the 179th Regiment who had been captured on February 17th. He used to do radio work in civilian life, so they impressed him into service.*[54]

During the lull, the artillery became the chief protagonist. James Bird, a gunner and corporal with A Battery, 160th Field Artillery, had been wounded earlier in the Italian campaign and rejoined his outfit in April at Anzio. He talked about an unauthorized practice in which his gun crew would sometimes engage to hit targets beyond their normal range:

> We had prearranged shells ready to fire in a particular direction—a Charge Three or Four or Five. At other azimuths, you might have a Charge Six or Seven. Charge Seven was used for targets at the greatest range, and sometimes the gunners would add more than the authorized amount of powder to give the round an extra boost. We'd put the powder in that shell case and tamp it around so the propellant would pack down in the case. Then we'd put the projectile in and set the elevation at 778, which was the maximum range. Then we'd set the azimuth toward an 88 battery that was setting up to hit us. With our ordinary Charge Seven, we couldn't hit them. With that extra Charge Seven and a long lanyard—you would never fire it right up next to the gun 'cause you never knew what's going to happen—we'd get behind a bunker and pull the lanyard and that thing would go off with a hell of a bang. The next thing you know, we'd wake up that 88 battery and they'd be firing back and everybody on the beach is wondering what the hell is happening. A couple of times we got hit pretty hard with counterbattery fire and our bunkers were caved in and we'd have to dig our guys out. Fortunately, our battery was never knocked out.[55]

Charles Keffler, a medic with the 3rd Battalion, 179th Regiment, found time to write a sardonically humorous letter to the utility company in Ohio that had employed him before the war:

---

*There were two "Axis Sallies," one broadcasting from Berlin and the other from Rome. The Axis Sally to whom those in the Mediterranean theater listened was Rita Luisa Zucca, the American-born daughter of a New York restaurateur. She had been visiting Italy when Mussolini embroiled his country in the conflict in June 1940. She renounced her U.S. citizenship and stayed to lend her aural talents to the Axis powers. After the war, she was convicted by an Italian court on collaboration charges and served nine months of a four-and-a-half-year sentence (William G. Schofield, *Treason Trail* [Chicago: Rand McNally, 1964], pp. 24–25). The Berlin Axis Sally was Mildred Gillars, who had been born in Portland, Maine. An aspiring actress, Gillars moved to Berlin in 1935 to teach English at the Berlitz School of Languages. She later took a job with Radio Berlin and eventually hosted her own music and pro-Nazi propaganda show. Although she called herself "Midge at the Mike," everyone called her "Axis Sally." She was arrested and tried for treason after the war and spent twelve years in prison. She died in 1988 (Dale P. Harper, "American-Born Axis Sally Made Propaganda Broadcasts for Radio Berlin in Hitler's Germany," *World War II Magazine*, Nov. 1995).

As you no doubt have heard over that very famous grapevine, I am in the Medics. . . . which isn't such a bad break for me, because I don't draw guard duty or any of the details or have any combat duty to do as my only weapon is the Red Cross arm band.

Right now I am an Aid Man with one of the companies, my office is my home which is a very comfortable place consisting of living room, bedroom, kitchen, bathroom and office. I am a little cramped as my house is only about 6 ft. long, 4 ft. deep and 4 ft. wide, which I built myself by digging into the side of a mound. The entrance or porch is made of bags of sand and mud over which I placed logs, fence posts, or any other pieces of wood I could find or steal, cardboard from ration boxes and dirt anywhere from 6 to 12 inches deep with a shelter-half over this to prevent the rain from soaking my carpets which are used as my bed, in other words blankets. The door is always open because it is a small opening just large enough to dive through. . . . The only inconvenience I have is the bathroom. . . . I have to use my bathtub to wash and shave with as it is the only thing that holds water. Of course it is rather small as it is my steel helmet. This inconvenience is overcome at times after a continuous rain for several days, at which time I have running water inside my palatial quarters. . . .

My office hours are from daylight to dark during which I give out pills for aches and pains, also GI's [gastrointestinal disorders], bandage cuts, wounds, etc., providing the men can get to me without being seen by the enemy. The calls I make are usually from dark to dawn and are to foxholes which are very easily reached on foot or hands and knees through sand and mud several inches deep and under a barrage of artillery, mortar, machine gun and rifle fire, falling shrapnel from anti-aircraft guns and strafing by planes. The light I need is furnished by flares which the enemy is very kind to supply. The rest of the time I have to myself to roam around at will inside my house. It isn't very healthy to roam around outside. . . .

So you see I don't have it too bad, my cost of living is very low, I only need one suit and one pair of shoes, I have no need for a car and my food comes in boxes. I am not worried about rent or income taxes. . . . Well, Pat, take care of things and encourage the donating of blood because it really means a lot to the men here. I know because I see what it does for them. Give my regards to all the fellows. You can expect me back just as soon as we have this mess cleaned up. I hope that won't take too long.[56]

• • •

Major Bosa's diary reflects the inactivity of much of March: "All quiet. . . . We had no air activity during the night. . . . Rained practically all day; not much activity of any kind."[57]

Things, however, were not so quiet seventy miles south along the Cassino front. Every attempt by the Allies to overcome the German observers on Monte Cassino and break into the Liri Valley had ended in bloody failure. To remedy the situation, Alexander began to take greater control over the forces there. Apparently unhappy with Clark and his Fifth Army's inability to crack the Gustav Line, he stripped the British and Commonwealth units from Clark and brought the bulk of Leese's Eighth Army across the spine of the Apennines, extending its area of operations to include Cassino and the mouth of the Liri Valley. The new offensive was given the code name "Diadem."

The II Corps, under Keyes, had lost its experienced combat divisions to build up the Anzio front. These were replaced by two inexperienced infantry divisions fresh from the States—the 85th and 88th.[58] Subsequently, II Corps and the French Expeditionary Corps were compressed into a narrow strip along the coast. Before the major offensive was launched, however, the provisional New Zealand Corps would give the capture of Monte Cassino one more shot. Few commanders in the Mediterranean theater were as "gung ho" as Lieutenant General Sir Bernard Freyberg, a winner of the Victoria Cross in World War I and commander of the New Zealand Corps. He exuded every confidence that the attack by his Kiwis finally would be successful.

The plan was a complex one, requiring close cooperation between ground and air forces. Following a heavy aerial bombardment, the 2nd NZ Division, along with the 4th Indian Division, would attack and secure the town of Cassino (which was in the hands of the 1st *Fallschirmjäger* Division), at the base of Monte Cassino and then climb the slopes of the mountain to root the German defenders from the ruins of the abbey. While this was taking place, the British 78th Division and Combat Command B of the 1st Armored Division would advance into the Liri Valley and push toward Valmontone. The key to the operation, Freyberg was convinced, centered on a massive bombing of the town of Cassino. This, in turn, required three days of clear weather. D day for the assault was made contingent on a favorable weather forecast. Although Freyberg felt confident his tanks and infantry would be able to push through the town and be in position to assault the mountain within six to twelve hours, others were skeptical, feeling that the rubble from the bombing would make the streets of Cassino impassable. Freyberg brushed aside their concerns and enlisted General Henry H. "Hap" Arnold, commander of the U.S. Army Air Forces, to his side. Arnold believed fervently in the value of strategic bombing and felt that Allied air power could break the stalemate in Italy. Although his superiors remained doubtful, they gave Freyberg the green light and, on 15 March, following a forecast of good weather for several days, the mighty air armada of some 200 medium and 360 heavy bombers—the largest air attack against a target in the Mediterranean—was unleashed on the unsuspecting Germans holed up in the town of Cassino.

At first there was the low drone of airplane engines far off in the distance. At 0830 hours, the first wave of medium bombers (consisting of 72 B-25s and 101 B-26s) approached the target and released its cargo of deadly eggs. The town simply vanished beneath a curtain of dust and flying dirt. Fifteen minutes later, a stream of 262 B-17s and B-24s, accompanied by dive bombers, worked over the ruins of the town, shaking the ground like an earthquake for miles around. The bombing by the "heavies" continued until noon, the sorties interspersed with artillery fire. Over 1,000 tons of bombs rained down on the defenseless town, utterly destroying every home, apartment, shop, school, and church. When the last plane dropped the last bomb and headed back to its base, the combined guns of the Allied force—746 of them—opened up and plastered what was left of Cassino with a forty-minute saturation barrage. To all observers, it seemed impossible that anyone—even the tough German paratroopers—could survive such an onslaught. But apart from being dazed and deafened by the horrific bombardment, much of the German 1st *Fallschirmjäger* Division was still intact and waiting in the rubble for the ground assault. The Allies discovered this fact when the New Zealand and Indian troops started to move toward the remains of Cassino; they were met by a blizzard of mortar and machine gun fire. The tanks supporting the infantry also ran into problems; there were so many collapsed buildings that streets were virtually unrecognizable, not to mention impassable. On those streets that weren't completely obstructed by rubble, huge craters blocked the way. Engineers trying to clear the obstacles or fill in the craters fell victim to German snipers.

That afternoon, another heavy raid by 120 B-17s and 140 B-24s was mounted over the town, but clouds had moved in, preventing the bombardiers from seeing their targets. Thus thwarted, the aircraft turned around with the bombs still in their racks. Dive bombers, however, were able to drop their ordnance on targets on and around Monte Cassino, but this did not materially aid the infantry and tanks trying to overcome German resistance in the town. To add to the misery, the predicted clear weather turned into heavy rain at dusk, soaking the attackers. The bomb craters filled with water, further hampering Allied progress. The next day saw few positive developments. The air force returned but its 266 tons of bombs did nothing to affect the outcome. The Germans were still well entrenched in the ruins and their fire kept the New Zealanders and Indians from taking what was once a town.

From the seventeenth to the twenty-first, very little progress by the Allies was reported. The Germans still held the upper hand. The dropping of over 1,200 tons of bombs and the firing of nearly 600,000 artillery shells had flattened Cassino but had barely made a dent in the German defense or determination. On the Allied side, the loss of nearly 300 killed, over 1,500 wounded, and almost 250 missing New Zealand and Indian troops was a bitter pill to swallow. The commanders—Alexander, Clark, and Leese—directed Freyberg, whose own enthusiasm for the contest had been seriously shaken, to break off the attack. The next attempt by the Allies to break through along the Cassino front and into the Liri would have to wait for warmer, drier weather.[59]

With the Gustav Line as impenetrable as ever, the order for a breakout at Anzio also seemed unlikely to be issued. The closest thing resembling movement on the beachhead was some shuffling of Allied units near the end of March. The 45th, just north of the Lateral Road, took responsibility for about a three-mile front that ran from about a mile east of the Overpass, then in a northeasterly direction to Carano. The 179th held the westernmost portion of the division's line while the 157th was pushed out into a bulge beyond Carano. The 180th was placed in reserve.[60]

To the 45th's right was the 34th Infantry Division, under Major General Charles W. Ryder, recently arrived from the Cassino front, and to its right, O'Daniel's 3rd Division. South of the 3rd, along the Mussolini Canal where it emptied into the sea, Frederick's 1st Special Service Force stood guard. Although its ten-mile front was more than the 2,400-man force could realistically be expected to handle, the 1st SSF made up for this shortcoming with its jolly ruthlessness and by the fact that it was backed up by the 1st Armored Division. To the 45th's left was the British 1st Division, with Penney back in command. Occupying the front from the 1st's left flank to the sea was Lieutenant General Philip Gregson-Ellis's British 5th Division, which, like the 34th, recently had been moved up from the south, replacing the 56th Division. The 504th PIR and the remaining Ranger battalion were withdrawn from Italy and sent to England to prepare for Operation Overlord.[61]

Personnel changes in the 45th were also made. On 28 March, Lieutenant Colonel Ashton H. Manhart was assigned as the new executive officer for the 180th, and Lieutenant Colonel Chester G. Cruikshank, who had been with the 180th before being wounded at Biscari, Sicily, on 13 July 1943, became the new commander of the 2nd Battalion, 179th. And 2 May would see a new commander for the 179th; Colonel Henry J. D. Meyer succeeded Colonel William Darby.[62]

In March, Ernie Pyle visited the beachhead and spent time with the Thunderbirds. He wrote,

> There's nothing that suits me better than a breathing spell, so I stayed and passed the time of day. My hosts were a company of the 179th Infantry. They had just come out of the lines that morning and had dug back of the perimeter. . . . Every few minutes a shell would smack a few hundred yards away. Our own heavy artillery made such a booming that once in a while we had to wait a few seconds to be heard. Planes were high overhead constantly, and now and then we could hear the ratta-tat-tat-tat of machine-gunning up out of sight in the blue. . . . That scene may sound very warlike to you, but so great is the contrast between the actual lines and even a short way back that it was actually a setting of great calm.[63]

Some soldiers discovered that being off the line had its own special disadvantages, such as certain "chickenshit" annoyances. First Lieutenant Bill Whitman, I Company, 180th, provided an excellent example:

> We were put in Regimental Reserve. Six or seven men and myself were put on pass to Naples and Sorrento. We proceeded back to our kitchen area to obtain clean uniforms, and to clean up prior to going to the dock. . . . We took no weapons. We had no sooner arrived at our company kitchen when, lo and behold, the assistant division commander arrived with our Regimental Supply Officer, Major Bill Brogan. The general was supposed to be inspecting the battalion kitchens. . . . He got out of his command car and walked over to the six or seven of us and shouted, "Fall in, with weapons." We had no weapons since we were going on pass. We turned to our mess sergeant who excitedly pointed and said, "Over there." We went over to a pile of weapons that had been sent back from the front line for repair, having belonged to men who had either been killed or wounded. They were muddy, rusty, and almost inoperable, and were awaiting pickup for return to Ordnance for overhaul. We grabbed the first weapons that came to hand . . . and fell in line for inspection by the general. The general came to the first man; the bolt of his M-1 rifle was rusted solid! He couldn't even retract it! The little general jumped up and down with rage. One man got the bolt on his carbine open by extra-human effort, and the mud flew out, or rather, squelched out. I thought the general was going to have a heart attack. His face turned scarlet. Meanwhile, Major Brogan kept trying to tell him that these were not our own weapons, and that we were only here to go on pass after coming off the front line. . . . Major Brogan finally was able to get the general calmed down and back in his car. The general stood up and shouted, "Rotten, rotten," as they drove off.

Whitman also reported that, later, eleven of his men went to Naples on three-day passes. All eleven were immediately arrested by the Military Police as soon as they set foot in the port city and jailed for the duration of their passes. Their heinous crimes: pockets unbuttoned, no neckties, sleeves rolled up, and caps worn incorrectly.[64]

• • •

It has been said that war consists of long periods of boredom interspersed with moments of intense terror and that every soldier knows the law of reciprocity: The good times must eventually be balanced with the bad. The GIs knew the lull couldn't last and it didn't. From 29 to 31 March, heavy artillery fire fell in the 157th's sector. Like all the Allied troops at Anzio, the Thunderbirds were again looking death and danger squarely in the face and waiting for either the inevitable breakout or a resumption of the German onslaught.[65]

In April, Captain Eddie Speairs's C Company, 157th, left the relative safety of the Pines area and relieved a company from the 3rd Division on the outskirts of Carano. The position was adjacent to Captain Kenneth Stemmons's B Company, which was holed up in the tomb of Menotti Garibaldi. Speairs described his experiences at this position:

Our CP was a hole dug under the ruins of a two-story farmhouse. To its left was a similar house, which was a platoon CP. I believe the entire company was on line, so there was no reserve platoon. The relief was accomplished without incident and we were settled in shortly before dawn. The CP "hole" held four men—First Sergeant Joe Alle; Lieutenant Don Waugh, exec officer; my runner, whose name I can't recall; and me. After a short nap, we decided to get some fresh air and eat a K ration. The sun was shining and we hugged the back wall of the house and checked out our surrounding territory. The first thing that met my eye was a huge, white sow, flat on her back and deader than a hammer. I cursed the 3rd Division collectively and individually, with the choicest words saved for the company we had relieved. I knew we faced a burial party that night and it was going to take a hell of a hole.

We were just starting to eat our rations when two shells landed very close. Before we could scramble into our hole, several more came in and then they ceased. I said that it was just an accident, for there was no way they could have seen us up against the back of the house, so we went out again. This time we got about two minutes of sunshine before the first round arrived and we set a new record for entering the hole. Two rounds hit the house and that made believers out of us for the rest of the day. After dark, I headed back for the battalion CP, and the shovel detail went to work on the sow. At battalion, I took one look at the situation map and discovered my problem: Company C was on a salient that stuck out far enough to allow a German forward observer a clear view of our "backyard." There would be no more sunshine for us or anyone else in "Charlie." I returned to the company and we all started settling into a routine which we followed for the next thirty-two days. All movement was from dark to daylight. We resupplied water, rations, and ammo, evacuated the sick and wounded, put out patrols, and every man was checked by an officer or NCO. We also had to haul out or bury our trash, for too much litter would draw fire come daylight. Some of today's ecologists would probably approve of this system!

There were no baths or clean clothes. We lived on K rations. If you urinated in daylight hours, you rolled on your side, used a waxed K ration box or an old C ration can and threw it over the side. Defecation was strictly nocturnal. Our days were even more of a pattern, for when you can't leave your foxhole, monotony really sets in. We had accumulated extra sound power phones and all were put to use. All were on one line, so a couple of cranks would get someone on every phone and jokes or information would be disseminated. Any little incident was welcomed, such as a new lieutenant who tidied up his hole one day and carelessly put most of his belongings on the berm around his hole. A machine gun made a clean sweep of it and educated the lieutenant at the same time. Depths of the foxholes varied, and the primary control was the water table. You dug down 'til it started getting muddy and you had to quit. The company CP under the house was dry but noisy. The Germans obviously knew it was a CP (maps captured after the breakout proved this) and, when they had nothing else to do, would drop in a few rounds. We counted eighteen hits on the house one day, but the more they knocked it down, the better we liked it!

During the thirty-three days we were in this position, those of us who moved around the area at night ran into some odd things. The first night after the relief, I found four turkeys roosting in what was left of a hen house. They went to the rear that night and returned, roasted, two nights later. Sergeant Hughes (mess sergeant) did a good job on them and they were divided up to the best of our ability. We saw a hen with about ten baby chicks the first day, but they disappeared. About the third night, I headed out to a forward position, and on the way I saw a man crawling down a shallow ditch and I hit the ground, for there was no reason for a GI to be crawling in that area. The light was dim but I could see the top of the man's body and it was not moving. I challenged him very quietly, and after a bit, when there was no movement or reply to another challenge, I crawled toward him. To make a long story short, it was a very dead German who died on his hands and knees and was leaning against the side of the ditch. Between the dim light and my imagination, I would have sworn he was crawling when I first saw him! Later, I mentioned to Sergeant Marsh (it was in his platoon area) and he grinned and admitted it had startled him, also. Later on I heard that Marsh was playing poker with some very smelly lira and I think I know where it came from.

One night, someone in the rear got a brilliant idea and decided to run a tank down a path in our area just after dark, stop and fire a number of rounds in the direction of the Germans, and then hightail for the rear. Obviously, this drew artillery fire on only one group—*us!* I protested to battalion but to no avail. The tank was back the next night and we had a repeat performance. This time when I called battalion, I said to tell the tanker we had found some scattered mines and they had better sweep the area. No one enjoys sweeping for mines in the dark, and that ended *that* idea.

C Company was finally relieved by another unit and Speairs stood watching his mud-encrusted men trudge back to the rear area.

Everyone was tired and dirty (all water had come up in five-gallon cans and it wasn't wasted on washing), but all were smiling. Finally, our medics came along in a group and they were all carrying something in their hands. I said, "What do you have there?"

One of them grinned and said, "Captain, do you remember the hen and little chicks at the farmhouse?" I said, "Yes, but they disappeared." He said, "We caught them the first night, dug a hole and fed and watered them." I said, "What the hell did you feed them?" And he said, "K ration crackers." They fried them a couple of days later and I got a drumstick that looked like a pigeon leg!

We finally reached the rest area and the cooks and supply personnel had everyone's personal belongings in platoon stacks and served us a hot breakfast and coffee. As we finished eating, Lieutenant Slade walked up with a camera and shot a picture of Don Waugh, Joe Alle, and me. Joe was killed a few weeks later during the breakout and Don was killed about three months later at Rians, France. I could write a book-length eulogy to these two men, but it would boil down to—"the two best soldiers I've ever known."[66]

Shown in April 1944 after their first hot meal in a month, Captain Anse H. "Eddie" Speairs (left), C.O. of C Company, 157th Infantry Regiment, enjoyed a moment with executive officer Lieutenant Don Waugh (right) and First Sergeant Joe Alle (front). Both Waugh and Alle were later killed in action. (Courtesy of A. H. Speairs)

On 6 May, the Germans again attempted a thrust at the Thunderbirds, attacking B Company, 179th, dug in along Spaccasassi Creek, with tanks, mortars, and artillery. Although some of the troops managed a deep penetration, counterattacks by other elements of the 1st Battalion quickly eliminated the threat.[67]

The beach grew more quiet with each passing day while the level of tension rose commensurately. As the Yanks and Tommies improved their defensive positions, raced beetles, and played softball, the stocks of ammunition, gasoline, and other war supplies grew to enormous proportions just beyond Anzio's battered port. Each day and night, scores of DUKWs made the trip from the shore to the supply ships anchored a few miles out to sea, and back again, bringing with them the tons of matériel essential to mount a new offensive. The moment for the Allied breakout was drawing very near.[68]

11

Leave This Savage Wilderness

22 May–30 June 1944

You see the beast that made me turn aside; help me, o famous sage, to stand against her, for she has made my blood and pulses shudder. "It is another path that you must take," he answered when he saw my tearfulness, "if you would leave this savage wilderness; that beast that is the cause of your outcry allows no man to pass along her track, but blocks him even to the point of death."

—Dante Alighieri, *The Inferno,* Canto I

FOR THE NEXT SEVERAL WEEKS, the two sides at Anzio were content to improve their defensive positions, batter each other with artillery barrages and aerial assaults, and prepare for the eventual resolution of the stalemate. For the Americans and British, this period was spent building up the vast quantities of supplies, ammunition, and extra troops necessary to finally overcome the Germans' "iron ring." For the Germans, it meant forgetting about offense and concentrating solely on how to prevent the Allies from breaking out. Kesselring and von Mackensen, knowing the eventual offensive would come, frantically shuffled their forces to prepare for any of four possibilities: an Allied breakout attempt at Anzio, another offensive along the Cassino front, a new landing somewhere north of Anzio, or any combination of the above.

To this end, the Hermann Göring Panzer Division was withdrawn from the Anzio area and sent to Livorno for rest and refitting (and to be closer to Civitavecchia in case the Allies landed there); the 114th *Jäger* Division was moved to the Adriatic front; and the 90th Panzer Grenadier Division was transferred to Frosinone, between Rome and Cassino. The 26th Panzer and 29th Panzer Grenadier Divisions were designated Army reserves and pulled back to the south of Rome, where their precious panzers would be safer than on either front, but could still be employed in case of a breakthrough. Smaller units continued to be added to the encirclement, and the number of combat troops increased from 65,800 on 14 March to 70,400 on 10 April, along with an additional 70,000 support troops. At the Gustav Line, Kesselring also added more men, many of whom were Russian "volunteers." Between Monte Cassino and Monte Petrella, over 400 artillery pieces, heavy mortars, and *Nebelwerfers* were the teeth that guarded the mouth of the Liri Valley.

In March, Kesselring ordered the construction of another "stop line," this one called the "C" (for Caesar) Line. It ran from the Anzio beachhead in a northeasterly direction over the mountains, through Avezzano, to Pescara on the Adriatic coast. The Hitler Line, backing up the Gustav Line, was also improved with the addition of miles of barbed wire, thousands of mines and tank traps, and concrete pillboxes sited to cover likely avenues of approach. Unfortunately for Kesselring, he could only guess at Allied intentions and troop dispositions at Anzio and along the Gustav Line, for the virtually nonexistent *Luftwaffe* was unable to perform any meaningful reconnaissance.

On the Allied side at Anzio, by the end of March, there were approximately 90,000 combat troops on the beachhead, with tens of thousands more in supporting roles. The British 1st Division remained on the line, although the 24th Guards Brigade was replaced by the 18th Brigade. Combat Command B of the 1st Armored Division arrived from the Cassino front in April to bring the division to full strength.[1]

Similar preparations by the Allies along the Gustav Line had been going on for months as the Americans and British readied themselves for one final stab at breaking into the Liri Valley. Operation Diadem would begin by deceiving the Germans that another amphibious assault, this one aimed at Civitavecchia, was about the begin. To this end, Allied naval units practiced beach landings at Salerno, and signs indicating a fictitious Canadian Corps appeared near the beach, with the expectation that Axis spies would see and report on them. Dummy radio traffic was carried out to make any eavesdroppers think nonexistent units were actually in place and preparing for a new landing. Beach recon parties and stepped-up Allied aerial surveillance of the Civitavecchia area also added to the illusion.

While the campaign of disinformation was taking place, elaborate steps were also taken to deny the enemy the truth about what was happening. When an armored unit was pulled out of the line during the night, dummy tanks made of wood and canvas stood in for the real things come the next morning. On a road beneath the Abbey of Monte Cassino, a mile-long screen was erected to shield the view of troop and vehicle movements from the Germans. Whenever possible, unit movements were conducted under the cover of darkness. Concentrations of troops, vehicles, and supplies gathered for the final assault on Monte Cassino were covered with vast acres of camouflage netting. All of this deception worked beautifully, for as late as 11 May, Kesselring believed only six Allied divisions faced his forces at the opening of the Liri Valley when, in actuality, eleven divisions were present.

The Fifth Army front on the Gustav Line, consisting of Keyes's II Corps (composed of the 85th and 88th Infantry Divisions, which had arrived in April), was squeezed into about a twelve-mile front just above the Garigliano River from the coast to the western edge of the opening of the Liri Valley; the British Eighth Army had responsibility for a much longer front, along which was positioned X and XIII Corps and II Polish Corps, with I Canadian Corps in reserve. The French Expeditionary Corps, with its Algerian and Moroccan divisions, along with some 12,000 *Goumiers*—Berber mountain warriors with a reputation for pitiless ferocity and little regard for the rules of warfare—held the gap between the Fifth and Eighth Armies. On the Adriatic side of the Apennines was the British V Corps. All told, the two Allied armies on the Cassino front had over 600,000 men awaiting the order to go.[2] A simultaneous air operation, known as "Strangle," would disrupt the flow of men and matériel by road and rail to the German-held areas. Once the offensive began, this heavy pounding from the air would, it was hoped, prove invaluable.[3]

The biggest secret of the European campaign was when and where the Allies would invade France. In April, Clark flew back to Washington to meet with George C. Marshall, who wanted to discuss the situation in Italy as it pertained to Operation Overlord. Clark was informed that Overlord would probably take place in late May or early June and that Marshall wanted Rome to be in Allied hands before that date. Alexander was similarly informed, and it was decided that the Allied offensive against the Gustav Line would begin at 2300 hours on 11 May. Once it was successfully under way, the Allies at Anzio would begin their attempt to break out—an operation named "Buffalo." Alexander ordered Truscott's VI Corps to attack in a northeasterly direction toward Cori, drive to Valmontone, and either cut off German supplies to the Tenth Army or prevent the Tenth Army's withdrawal up Highway 6. That accomplished, the two Allied forces would meet and head for Rome. The Americans were to be given the honor of entering the Imperial City.[4]

Alexander spoke of the upcoming spring offensive in boxing terms—a "one-two punch." The first blow would be struck along the Gustav Line, with the second punch—a left hook—being delivered by VI Corps at Anzio. Besides capturing Rome, the other objective of the twin assault was to tie up as many German divisions as possible in Italy, where they could not be used against the invasion forces in Normandy. In these regards, Diadem and Buffalo did not differ much from Shingle's original objectives. The difference now, the Allies felt, was that they were considerably stronger and the enemy was considerably weaker than had been the case in January and February.

Supremely unhappy with Alexander's ideas, Clark set about devising his own plan for VI Corps—or, rather, four plans—which he presented to Truscott. Besides the drive on Valmontone, he drew up two plans that had VI Corps heading directly for Rome and another that envisioned a push due east to Sezzi. When Alexander visited the beachhead on 5 May, Truscott, somewhat naïvely, told the Fifteenth Army Group commander about these alternative plans. According to Truscott, "General Alexander, charming gentleman and magnificent soldier that he was, let me know very quietly and firmly that there was only one direction in which the attack should or would be launched, and that was from Cisterna to cut Highway 6 in the vicinity of Valmontone in the rear of the German main forces." Truscott reported his conversation to Clark, who viewed Alexander's statement as meddling in the affairs of his army. Clark then got on the phone and blistered his superior for trying to take control of Fifth Army.[5]

In his diary, Clark noted, "We not only wanted the honor of capturing Rome, but we felt that we more than deserved it. . . . My own feeling was that nothing was going to stop us on our push toward the Italian capital. Not only did we intend to become the first army in fifteen centuries to seize Rome from the south, but we intended to see that the people back home knew that it was the Fifth Army that did the job and knew the price that had to be paid for it."[6]

And, indeed, Clark's Fifth Army had paid a stiff price. As mentioned earlier, the casualties for VI Corps during the four months of fighting at Anzio totaled almost 90,000 men, including 7,000 killed and 36,000 wounded or missing, with 44,000 evacuated due to illness, injury, trench foot, and other nonbattle causes. At the beachhead hospitals alone, some 92 medical personnel were killed and another 387 wounded. A number of wounded patients were also killed or wounded again by German artillery and air raids. These terrible statistics, Clark believed, more than justified his determination to have Fifth Army obtain Rome by any means necessary.[7]

• • •

While both sides waited for the start of the next offensive, things were not altogether quiet along the 45th's front. On 2 May, in the 179th's sector north of Padiglione, Staff Sergeant Harry H. Dunbar of C Company went out on a patrol through enemy artillery fire and brought back two prisoners. The next day, he went back out again, this time armed with a submachine gun and grenades, and wiped out a particularly troublesome machine gun nest. That night, with his platoon arrayed in front of a house serving as the battalion CP, a company-sized German attack hit Dunbar's lines. Between bursts from his Thompson, the sergeant used up an entire box of grenades against the attackers. A shell burst within a yard of his foxhole, dazing him, and a bullet hit him in the shoulder, but Dunbar's one-man war against the German Army never slackened. All night long, Dunbar stayed with his men, directing their fire as wave after wave of the enemy rushed their lines, and he called in artillery fire that knocked out two panzers. At dawn on the fourth, with the enemy still to his front, the wounded sergeant crawled out into no-man's land with a supply of grenades, which he used to drive the Germans away. Only after he had exhausted his arsenal did he return to his platoon and was evacuated to the rear. He was awarded the Distinguished Service Cross for his gallantry.

On the fifth, B Company, 179th, was struck by a German force that was driven back after a sharp fight. To let the enemy know that the Thunderbirds were still very much on their guard, Division Artillery dropped 9,000 rounds on suspected enemy targets the next day.[8]

On about the ninth or tenth of May, Sergeant Jack McMillion, L Company, 157th, and his platoon were dug in about 200–250 yards from a German unit occupying a drainage ditch. He said,

> We had some guys from the Oklahoma regiment in front of us and when we relieved them one night, they said, "Don't make any noise, because these Germans will jump up and spray the area and somebody might get hurt." Sure enough, our 2nd Platoon was moving in and the Germans opened up and some of our guys got killed. About the third day we were there, we finally located this German with a machine pistol. One of our fellows said, "I'm going to go out there and get that SOB. Every time I get up at night to take a crap, this guy tries to shoot me." It was broad daylight and he didn't have to do it, but he was just tired of this guy bothering us. Since we knew the German's location, we put fire across his head while a few of our guys crawled up. The German must have heard them coming because he threw a potato-masher grenade and just missed them. They dropped a grenade into his hole. I guess it didn't kill him. He must have been wired in to his buddies because pretty soon a Red Cross flag appeared. Some of our fellows spoke German and they began hollering back and forth and it turned out they wanted to pick up the wounded. So they came out with a litter about fifty yards in front of me and picked him up. That put a stop to the harassing.[9]

All along the front, both in the forward foxholes and back in the Pines area where men relaxed and pretended their baseball games were the World Series, the sense that the "lull" was about over was very palpable. But no breakout at Anzio could be contemplated without a tremendous reserve of supplies to feed, equip, fuel, and arm the force, propelling it all the way to Rome and beyond. To this end, half a million tons of supplies of all description had been brought ashore and hidden in scattered equipment, fuel, and ammunition dumps throughout the beachhead, along with vast inventories of tanks, half-tracks, self-propelled artillery, trucks, jeeps, and various other types of specialized vehicles.[10] "I had never seen so many tanks in my life," recalled Daniel Witts, Anti-Tank Company, 179th. "There were hundreds of them they kept bringing ashore."[11]

• • •

With a fearsome drumroll of artillery all along the front, Operation Diadem, the great Allied offensive against the Gustav Line, began exactly on schedule at 2300 hours on 11 May 1944. Some 1,060 guns behind Eighth Army and 600 more behind II Corps and the FEC opened up. At the same moment, the 4th Moroccan Mountain Division left its line of departure to attack Castelforte while the 2nd Moroccan Infantry Division set off to seize Monte Majo. The 3rd Algerian Division was in support. The U.S. 85th Infantry Division, under Major General John B. Coulter, and 88th Infantry Division, commanded by Major General John F. Sloan, also set off for their objectives: the high ground overlooking the Ausonia corridor on II Corps's left flank and the village of Santa Maria Infante, respectively.

Just as Operation Overlord would enjoy the lucky stroke of several key German commanders being away from their posts when the invasion was launched, the start of Diadem also benefited from the absence of several critical decisionmakers; von Vietinghoff was on leave, as were *Generalleutnant* Fridolin von Senger und Etterlin, commander of XIV Panzer Corps, and von Senger's chief of staff. In addition, Siegfried Westphal, Kesselring's chief of staff, was ill and on convalescent leave in Germany. The timing could not have been more fortuitous for the Allies. To add to the confusion in the German camp, on the night of 11–12 May, the headquarters staff of the German 44th Infantry Division was in the midst of taking control of five battalions on Monte Cassino when the Allied barrage lit up the night.

Dawn on the twelfth found the Moroccans and the Italian 1st Motorized Infantry Brigade attacking along the banks of the Garigliano River toward La Guardia. The *Goumiers,* backed by a Moroccan mountain regiment and a regiment of mountain artillery, stood ready to exploit any breakthrough. The battles raged throughout the twelfth. After a day of bitter fighting against the 15th Panzer Grenadier Division, Major General Andre Dody's 2nd Moroccan Division managed to reach the summits of Monte Feuci, Monte Girafano, and Monte Majo on the thirteenth. German counterattacks were stopped cold, and the first crack in the formidable Gustav Line appeared. Once Monte Girafano was in Allied hands, the Italian 1st Motorized made swift progress up the Garigliano to San Apollinare.[12] Alarmed at these developments, Kesselring rushed the 90th Panzer Grenadier Division to the south to shore up Raapke's splintered 71st Infantry Division while simultaneously looking over his shoulder for the amphibious landing he expected to hit Civitavecchia. The German intelligence services were telling him, as late as 14 May, that a force of three Allied divisions was gathering around Naples, with another four divisions on Corsica, preparing for an amphibious landing somewhere north of Anzio. Because of this threat, Kesselring had been unwilling to release his reserves to stem the Allied breakthrough on the Cassino front.[13]

The American 85th and 88th Divisions did less well than the French in their first full-scale combat engagement. Both divisions came up against especially stiff resistance and took considerable casualties.[14] On the night of 12–13 May, in the Eighth Army sector, the British XIII Corps managed to establish a bridgehead over the Rapido River southeast of Cassino. Meanwhile, the Polish troops gathering northeast of Monte Cassino were preparing to assault the massif. On the thirteenth, the II Corps commander, Geoffrey Keyes, met with the commanders of the 85th and 88th Divisions to indicate that Clark wanted a renewed offensive that day; the British, French, and Poles were *not* to outshine the Yanks.

Shortly after the attacks began, the *Luftwaffe* made one of its rare appearances over Allied lines and strafed Coulter's men. Little progress was made in the 88th's sector as well, as the attack by several units was badly coordinated, and this unsynchronized assault also caused problems for the neighboring 85th, which was hit by strong counterattacks. Both divisions suffered extensive casualties before discovering that the Germans had pulled out after their lines had become unhinged by the success of the FEC's assault. On the fourteenth, the 88th Division pushed a small German rearguard unit out of Santa Maria Infante and secured the totally destroyed village, then took Spigno the following day. Watching the FEC's dramatic progress as it speared deeply into the Liri Valley, Clark ordered Keyes to send the 88th on to Itri, nine miles beyond Spigno, while the 85th was to push up the coast on the heels of the retreating 94th Division. On the fourteenth, the 85th ran into a wall of resistance at Castellonorato, the last major stronghold on the western side of the Gustav Line, but managed to prevail. With II Corps and the FEC bulldozing the Germans out of their way, the western flank of the once-impregnable Gustav Line was beginning to crumble.[15]

As the Germans abandoned their positions, Allied troops all along the line occupied them. Hills and mountains and villages which, for months, had been the scene of bitter dispute were suddenly available for anyone who cared to claim them. To the Allied brass, it seemed almost too good to be true. Could the drive actually break into the Liri Valley? Monte Cassino was still the key, and the Germans had not yet abandoned it. Another assault against the omnipresent mountain would have to be launched, and this time the task fell to the Polish 3rd Carpathian and 5th Kresowa Divisions, which would advance from the north while the British 4th and 78th Divisions would apply pressure from the south. Although at half strength due to the heavy casualties they had taken in the Apennines, the Poles were eager for the challenge, thirsting for the opportunity to pay back the Germans for what Hitler had done to their country for nearly five years. The 1st *Fallschirmjäger* Division held tenaciously to Monte Cassino's rocky heights, thwarting the Poles' best efforts. The fighting went on for hours; when they finally ran out of ammunition, the frustrated Poles simply threw rocks at the Germans and sang the Polish national anthem.[16]

On the fifteenth, Kesselring learned that the Canadian 1st Infantry Division and the South African 6th Armoured Division, which he had been fooled into thinking were about to take part in a new amphibious operation, were actually at the entrance to the Liri Valley. Realizing that the anticipated seaborne landing at Civitavecchia was all a ruse, he ordered the 26th Panzer Division, in reserve near Rome, to rush to the south the next day. Hitler aided the cause by authorizing the transfer of the 16th SS Panzer Grenadier Division from Germany to northern Italy.[17] Also on the sixteenth, under constant prodding by von Vietinghoff, Kesselring reluctantly allowed the Tenth Army to pull back from Cassino to the Hitler Line; to delay any longer would risk the annihilation of his forces in the south. *Generalmajor* Richard Heidrich, commander of the 1st *Fallschirmjäger* Division, refused to withdraw until personally ordered to do so by Kesselring, however. Once the personal directive was received, the parachutists reluctantly and quietly abandoned the rubble of the abbey, the shattered town below, and other fighting positions on Monte Cassino's slopes and headed for the next line of resistance.

On the morning of 18 May, a unit from the 12th Podolski Lancers and a handful of men from the British 4th Division met atop the mountain amid the empty ruins of the monastery. The fourth and final battle for Cassino was over.

Where once the Germans had been cruel occupiers, it now became the turn of some of the Allies to be seen as inhuman. Rumors that the Poles shot a number of wounded Germans in the cellar of the ruined monastery surfaced after the war. The *Goumiers,* too, came in for their share of criticism after reports circulated that the North African troops had robbed and murdered civilians and had even taken part in gang rapes of Italian women.[18] Of the *Goumiers,* one Italian wrote,

> We have suffered more during the twenty-four hours we have been in contact with the Moroccans than under the eight-month-long German domination. The latter robbed us of our goats, sheep, and provisions during their raids but they always respected women and our poor savings; how bloody and violent the former, who raped and threatened to kill children, women, youngsters, and raided and plundered everything they found. The few German soldiers who were found guilty of cruel crimes like these were immediately shot. Not even the [French] officers managed to prevent the Moroccans from being so pitiless. . . . During the occupation of the little village of San Michele where many of the families from Cassino had sought refuge, the American-Japanese parties [442nd Regimental Combat Team] were extremely generous and proper, out

> of consideration for the inhabitants. But things took a turn for the worse when they were replaced by the French-Algerian troops who plundered everything, raped women and girls, and stole the few heads of livestock. The wife and sister of Tancredi Grossi (who would be the mayor of Cassino) were only saved by the prompt help of the American soldiers.[19]

From mountain peaks that had been the scene of brutal fighting for months, the enemy forces were now pulling out and heading for the next defensive line—the Hitler Line, a few miles behind the Gustav, where they hoped to slow the Allied advance. (When it later appeared the Hitler Line would fall, the Germans changed the name to the Senger Line, so that a feature named for the Führer would not be associated with defeat.)[20] But the casualty reports pouring into Kesselring's headquarters were alarming. The 71st Infantry Division, for example, was down to only a hundred men still capable of carrying a rifle. Kesselring also dispatched the 29th Panzer Grenadier Division from its reserve position near Rome on the nineteenth, but it was too late. The Allied drive, although moving at a crawl, was unstoppable. If von Vietinghoff didn't quickly withdraw what remained of his Tenth Army, there would be no Tenth Army left.

• • •

Amid an air of rancor and tension, Alexander and Clark conferred again on 17 May to go over the details of Operation Buffalo—the actions that VI Corps would take once it broke out from Anzio. Clark's heart was set on achieving the place in history that would accrue to the Liberator of Rome. But, even though the Americans were officially slated to occupy the city, Alexander wanted no side excursions that might allow German units to escape from the south of Italy; for him, the Allies must concentrate on taking the more militarily important city of Valmontone, which controlled Highway 6. In Clark's mind was Marshall's dictum that the Allies should be in Rome before Overlord was launched—something that might not happen if VI Corps was forced to go to Valmontone. The honor of taking Rome was supposed to be reserved for Fifth Army, but Clark wondered what might happen if his army got bogged down fighting in Valmontone and Eighth Army "just happened" to bypass the action and dash for the city on the Tiber. Chafing at the bit Alexander had thrust into his mouth, Clark began scheming for a way that he could have Rome without technically disobeying Alexander's directive. He found it. On the eighteenth, Clark told Truscott that once the Allies broke out of the Anzio encirclement and headed for Cisterna, he wanted Frederick's 1st Special Service Force to be the only unit to head for Valmontone—the rest would make a left turn when they reached Cisterna and take off for the Imperial City.[21]

But first, the situation on the southern front would need to be resolved. On the western flank, II Corps's 85th and 88th Divisions had finally over-

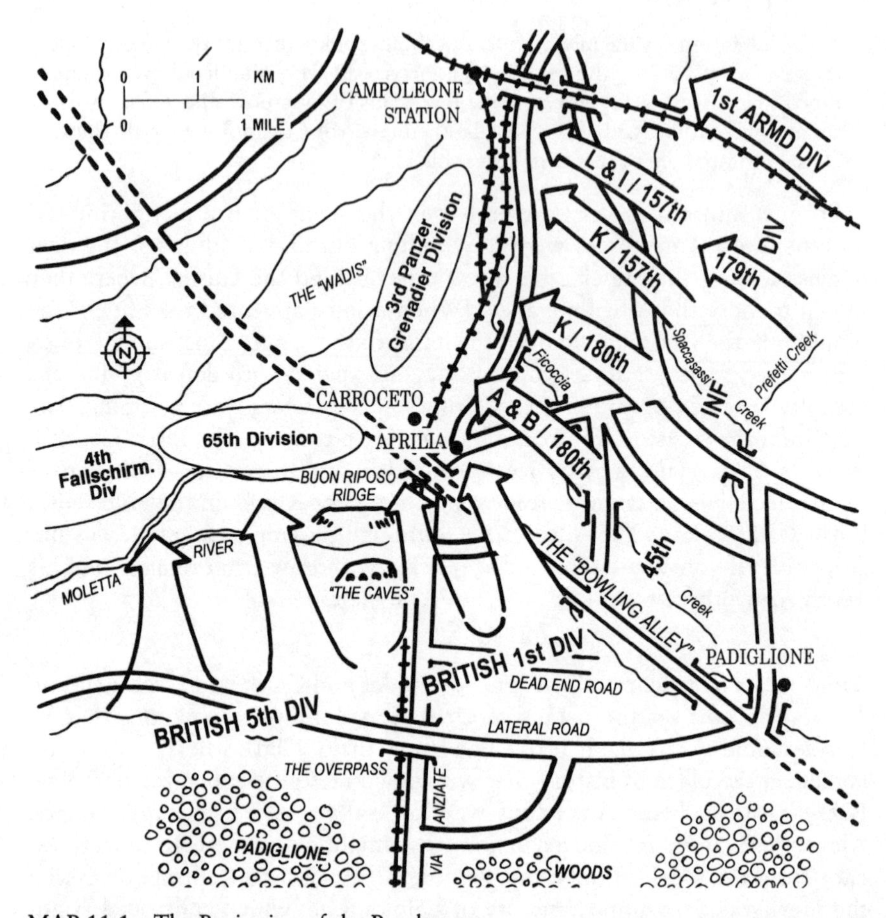

MAP 11.1 The Beginning of the Breakout
17–28 May 1944—With the British on its left and the 1st Armored Division on its right, the 45th Infantry Division broke through the encircling enemy ring as the Allies dashed for Rome. (Positions approximate)

come the jitters that accompanied their introduction to combat and were now driving like two well-oiled fighting machines. In fact, they were far outpacing the Eighth Army's units, which were slowed by determined resistance along the Hitler Line. Ignoring a suggestion from Alexander that Clark might have to send II Corps and the FEC to help the British, the American urged Keyes to go full speed up the coast and break through the last vestiges of resistance on the Hitler Line between Fondi and Terracina; Clark wanted the two American divisions to be in a position to link up with the Anzio forces when the beachhead breakout came.[22]

It was now time for the stalemate at Anzio to end, time for the Allies to burst from the beachhead like bats out of hell. Ever since the word had

Thunderbirds and tanks dug in along the Mussolini Canal awaiting the signal to begin the breakout from the beachhead, May 1944. (Photo courtesy of 45th Infantry Division Archives)

been passed down that the Allies soon would launch a massive attempt to escape from their "self-sustaining POW camp," the Thunderbirds had been preparing for the moment. Training was stepped up, marksmanship was emphasized, and physical conditioning activities began to turn soft bodies back into muscular ones. Weapons were disassembled, cleaned, and put back together a dozen times a day. Equipment was checked and double-checked. Seasoned veterans tried to cram a year of combat experience into nervous replacements. Many of the GIs who had seen more than their fair share of deadly battle and had observed what had happened to the Germans' human-wave attacks, worried about crossing the flat ground between them and the enemy line, but resigned themselves to it. Others saw the breakout as a chance to pay back the Germans for the months of misery they had been forced to endure and were eagerly looking forward to the decisive, upcoming battle.

The long-awaited end of the siege that had lasted at Anzio for 125 days began at 0630 hours on a cool and cloudy Tuesday, 23 May. Two nights earlier, engineer units had advanced into no-man's land to clear paths with "snakes"—lengths of pipe filled with explosives—through both Allied and German minefields, and the assault forces that had moved up to their assembly areas took great care to hide themselves from the inquisitive eyes of the enemy, lest the Germans launch a counterattack and disrupt the breakout plans.

The key to the success of the offensive was the swift capture of Cisterna, followed by the taking of the town of Cori, on the slopes of the Lepini Mountains. By achieving those objectives, VI Corps would be able to control the roads leading to Valmontone and cut the Tenth Army's line of communications. Operation Buffalo would be led by the 1st Armored and 3rd Infantry Divisions pushing toward Cisterna. The 45th would play a key role—driving between Aprilia and Carano and protecting the 1st Armored's left flank until Cisterna was taken, then making a left turn and heading toward Rome, along with the rest of VI Corps. The 1st Special Service Force would screen the main attack's right flank while the 34th Infantry Division, recently brought up from the south, would be intermingled with the 1st Armored Division and help protect Harmon's tanks.[23]

Nearly a year of bitter fighting in Italy, however, weighed on the minds of the Allied brass. Nothing ever seemed to go according to plan; would this latest attempt to gain ground turn into just another bloody disaster, ending in another stalemate? Had the Germans reinforced their lines enough to stop the drive before it could get started? Would the attacking Allies meet the same terrible fate that had befallen the Germans when *they* tried to charge across open ground?

One of the problems the Americans faced was concealing large numbers of tanks moving into their jump-off positions close to the front lines. The Americans solved this by tying in feints by the tanks with artillery bombardments. From the middle of May onward, the 1st Armored used a ploy whereby while artillery was hitting the enemy's positions, a number of Shermans would rush forward as if they were about to attack, stop, fire a few rounds, then pull back. During each retreat, a few of the tanks would pull off the roads and take cover in previously prepared hiding places near the front. Truscott hoped that the Germans didn't notice that when twenty tanks made their dash to the front, only fifteen or so went all the way back to the rear.[24]

On the night of 22 May, the British 1st and 5th Divisions launched a diversionary attack (Operation Hippo) from their positions on the left side of the Allied line, designed to divert German attention away from the American assault on the right flank.[25] That same night, officers of every unit in VI Corps gathered their men around them and read to them the following message from Major General Truscott:

> For more than four months, you have occupied the most dangerous and important post of any Allied force. You have stopped and defeated more than ten divisions which Hitler had ordered to drive us into the sea. You have contained on your front divisions which the enemy sorely needed elsewhere. You have neglected no opportunity to harass and injure the enemy. Arduous conditions you have accepted willingly and cheerfully, and you have not failed to improve

in discipline and training and in condition. You have set a standard that has won the admiration and respect of our United Nations. For your services during these trying times, I congratulate you.

Now, after four months, we attack. Our comrades of the Fifth and Eighth Armies—Britons, Poles, French, Americans, Italians—have achieved a great victory on the southern front. They are driving the enemy to the north. They have set the trap—it is for us to spring that trap and complete the destruction of the German Tenth Army. I need not tell you that the battle will be hard and difficult. But we are superior in strength. Our pilots control the skies under which we fight. Our equipment, our weapons are the best the world has ever seen. Our plans have been carefully prepared and in great detail. Every officer and man knows the part he is to play. No preparation has been neglected. You are free men, against whom no slaves of a tyrant nation can ever stand. Our comrades in the south are fighting their way toward us. The eyes of the world will be upon us. Be alert, be vicious, destroy the hated enemy. Victory will be ours.[26]

Worship services that night were full to overflowing as men made their peace with their Maker. "Not only are there no atheists in foxholes, there are also none on the eve of battle," commented Chaplain Leland Loy.[27]

• • •

The Thunderbirds awoke early on the twenty-third; those who could keep food down ate a few bites of C and K rations, but most mouths were too dry to swallow. Keyed up for the moment, filled with a mixture of excited anticipation and dread, the men took up their places on the line of departure. Platoon leaders looked at their watches over and over again, awaiting the moment to begin the great offensive. At H hour, 0545 hours, the artillery opened up a short distance behind the troops waiting for the jump-off. Salvos of shells whistled menacingly overhead; seconds later bright flashes appeared a mile or more ahead, followed by the sharp concussion and noise of the explosions. Soon the sound of the guns firing and the shells detonating blended together so that it was impossible to distinguish one from the other. Allied aircraft roared through the sky, dropping bombs into enemy positions. The green replacements believed and hoped and prayed that the tremendous bombardment that was grinding the German lines into dust would enable them to advance safely across the open ground; the veterans knew better.

Captain Felix Sparks, now the executive officer with the 2nd Battalion, 157th, recalled,

VI Corps had brought in two or three new divisions and we had a staggering amount of artillery. We had ninety-six artillery pieces firing in direct support of our regiment, which is a staggering amount. Normally, we had eighteen. We knew it was going to be a bloody operation—the Germans had had about three months to prepare their defensive positions. The other units on our right and our left had the same type of support—not as much as we did, because we

> had the central sector, but they all had plenty of artillery support. It's hard to imagine the roar and the din. We had concentrations laid on—we'd shell the hell out of an area and then we'd raise it a hundred yards, a walking barrage. The earth was shaking and the German guns were replying. Both sides were firing like crazy. The whole earth was shuddering and trembling, and the sound was deafening. It was like the world was coming to an end. Then our troops advanced.[28]

Above the unceasing blasts of the guns, officers and noncoms shouted for their men to move out, thrusting their arms in a forward motion. Somebody yelled out, "Let's kill the dirty bastards!" To the right of the 45th, the engines of hundreds of tanks of the 1st Armored Division, as well as those of the 191st Tank Battalion in the 45th's midst, roared to life, filling the air with clouds of blue exhaust. The entire olive-drab mass of men and machines—ten miles wide—started toward no-man's land, toward the ravaged landscape that was being torn apart by American and British munitions. Even at a trot, the advance across the open terrain seemed to take an eternity. Here and there were scattered bits of the once-mighty German Army—splintered rifles, spilled ammunition cans, tank parts, punctured helmets, shredded uniforms, decomposing body parts, and an occasional skeleton still clad in field gray. The rough ground, deeply cratered by artillery and scarred by tank treads, was still muddy and slippery, and some men lost their footing as they ran. Occasionally, a frightened soldier would take cover in a water-filled shell crater, only to be hauled out by a noncom or an officer and told to keep moving. Sixty fighter-bombers from 12th Air Force roared overhead. The cacophony of guns and shells and tank engines and shouted commands swelled into an ear-splitting, mind-destroying crescendo.

Then the Germans recovered from the shock and surprise of the Allied charge. Shells exploded among the advancing GIs, flinging men into the air like dolls, while a hail of bullets from MG-42s and MG-34s and Schmeisser machine pistols and K-98 rifles smacked into unprotected bodies, spinning men to the ground. The Thunderbirds who had been here since February gained a new appreciation for what the German soldiers had endured during their suicidal charges against the Allied lines. The GIs—all three regiments of the 45th—kept going, running across wheat fields and through ravines and past shattered houses and beyond a small cemetery that had changed ownership frequently during the past four months. Past the cemetery, L Company, 157th, wandered into an uncleared minefield and the devices began exploding like deadly popcorn, blowing off the feet of unsuspecting Thunderbirds. Scores of wounded men were required to lie unattended in the field until dark fell, when the mines were cleared and litter teams could reach them. The pitiful moans and cries of the wounded, many of whom were without food or water all day, were drowned out by the roar of battle.[29]

A German self-propelled 88 and an American medic jeep (note Red Cross flag) lay destroyed during the first day of the breakout from the Anzio beachhead. (Courtesy of K. P. Stemmons)

Up ahead, the Thunderbirds could see their first objective—the slight rise of the railroad bed, exploding in great plumes of dirt and flame. Suddenly, in a rush, the Americans were there. Some Germans, their fear-filled faces caked with dust, emerged from their emplacements with hands held high as the Thunderbirds closed in. The GIs kicked out the Germans and sent them to the rear as the tanks crossed the tracks and took up firing positions. "Doc Joe" Franklin, I Company, 157th, remembered one of the Germans his unit captured. "He spoke English and said he had been on the Russian front but had never experienced anything as vicious as our breakout from Anzio. He said it was the most vicious thing he had ever seen."[30]

During the morning of the breakout, near Carano, Platoon Sergeant Van T. Barfoot, L Company, 157th, a Choctaw from Mississippi, became part of the legend of the 45th. Barfoot recalled, "From the end of the battle for the Overpass, up until the breakout, we were moving in and out of positions from time to time all over the beachhead to relieve other units. About the first of May, we moved in along the Carano Creek on the extreme right flank of the division, overlooking the cemetery. We stayed there for a while and then moved back. Just before the jump-off, we moved forward to the same positions." Barfoot had made several patrols—more than anyone else in the platoon—into no-man's land nearly every night.

I felt that this time I knew what was out in front of me because I'd been patrolling out there. I'd been out to the corner of the cemetery several times and knew the Germans were dug in. I got to within twenty-five or fifty yards of the cemetery and could see their gun positions there. We found trails through the minefields because, at night when I was out there, I could watch the Germans patrolling, so I also knew where the minefields were. We had talked about getting out of that beachhead for a long time and the people in my platoon were ready to go. I felt absolute confidence that we were going to make it. Finally, the word came that we were going to make the move. It was just a normal, routine operation. I feel there was nothing I did on that first day of the breakout that wasn't normal for being in the attack. We were in a frontline position in Carano Creek on the extreme left flank of the 157th. It was like being in a big gully; the creek bed just barely had water running in it. The next unit to our left was a unit of the 180th. We were to take a little hill that went to the railroad that ran diagonally across the front. To reach our objective, we had to move across a relatively flat part of the ground. Our company attacked through the cemetery with the right flank platoon and the left flank platoon. Mine was the third platoon, and we went west of the cemetery, going north across a wheat field. When we advanced about to the cemetery, that's when the firing began."

An estimated sixty Germans, supported by three machine guns, in a series of interconnected zigzag trenches, blocked the route of advance of Barfoot's platoon. "We had advanced probably 800 or 900 yards before the Germans began firing. They opened fire and it was obvious that they had us in a cross fire and that we were going to get cut down if we continued to move across the open ground. So I suggested to our platoon leader that I move over to the left flank so that I could maneuver part of the platoon. He agreed and I went around to that side of the platoon. I told them to cover me and I'd go around to the left to see if I could get the gun position."

Barfoot crawled to within twenty-five yards of the first machine gun position and lobbed a grenade that killed two, wounded three, and destroyed the gun. He then leaped into the trench and began hunting more of the enemy. Continuing on, he attacked the second gun with a storm of fire from his Thompson, killing two more and wounding another three.

As I moved around the corner, there were several people in the trench—I think they were eager to give up—and I took the third position. As I did, firing ceased in that area and our platoon began to move forward. How many people came out of there—ten or fifteen or twenty—I don't know; I didn't stop to count 'em. I made 'em get out of the ditch and stand up and our troops moved in. We moved up and took our objectives and we were in the Germans' defensive positions in the zigzag trenches. We could not contact the platoon that was supposed to be on our right, so I went out with three or four people to try and contact them. We went down the ditch and up the edge of the hill to try and see them, but we didn't make contact with them. Several hundred yards to our front was a small railroad trestle over the ravine we were following. There was an underpass alongside the stream where vehicles could go under the railroad. On our way up, we ran into an abandoned German field piece, an antitank gun. We tried to turn the thing around so we could use it for our own defensive purposes but it was so large we couldn't move it around. I put some German potato-masher grenades in the breach and muzzle, pulled the cord, and got in the ditch. That destroyed the gun.

Then I heard armored vehicles on the other side of the railroad tracks and we started to withdraw back to the rest of the platoon's position. On our way back, I saw one of the tanks come under the trestle and it started toward our platoon's position. I took a rocket launcher we had with our group over to where I could get a good look at the tank. He didn't see me and continued to come. I didn't have but two rounds. Fortunately, the first round hit the front of the track and broke it and the tank just started turning in a circle. Then it tilted over in a little ditch and people started to get out. Of course, this gave me a good opportunity to get them. Then I saw the other tanks veer to the left and they went up across the hill. The artillery started firing. Thinking we had withdrawn when the platoon on our right had withdrawn, somebody apparently called for artillery on our position, because it began to hit around us.

When I got back to the platoon, I learned our platoon leader, Lieutenant Robert Nation, had orders to withdraw the platoon. While he was withdrawing the rest of the platoon, I went around checking the troops. I found one chap, Corporal Gimberling, one of our assistant squad leaders, who had been wounded. He had been hit in the hip with shrapnel and his hip was torn up pretty badly. Then I found Sergeant Armstrong, who had been hit in the arm and wasn't able to negotiate very well. Everybody else withdrew with Lieutenant Nation and I took these two people back to an aid station about 1,500 yards to the rear. I had to carry Gimberling on my back because he couldn't walk. Armstrong could walk, but only with extreme difficulty. So he leaned on me when he had to be assisted across some of the ditches. I managed to get them back to the aid station. The second or third day was pretty bad. Our company C.O., Captain [Clifford R.] Austin, was killed on the twenty-fifth going across an open field. It was a German barrage—an air burst—that got him.

For his actions on 23 May, Barfoot would be awarded the Medal of Honor.[31]

Many of the advancing Thunderbirds weren't as lucky as Barfoot. On the day of the breakout, Glen Hanson, L Company, 157th, was wounded. "We were in front of the ditches that drained the Pontine Marshes and we were alongside a railroad that split the beachhead. A German machine gunner was sitting on the railroad tracks and was cutting up our troops as they came up over the hill. I was one of them that he hit—I got it in the leg."[32]

Jack McMillion, L Company, 157th, was also severely wounded on the first day of the breakout. "I never knew what actually got me," he said.

Sergeant Van Barfoot, later promoted to second lieutenant, earned the Medal of Honor while serving with L Company, 157th Infantry Regiment. (Courtesy of 45th Infantry Division Archives)

I've always thought it was probably a mortar, because there was a mortar concentration going on, but I might have stepped on a mine, because there were mines all around. I had moved some guys out of a minefield and I bandaged up some guys who had stepped on mines. I wasn't a medic and we didn't have a medic with our unit that day, but I was kind of handy wrapping people up and putting a few patches on guys. I had a big aid pack, which infantry people usually didn't carry, and I had given a few guys some morphine shots and bandaged them up. I had just done all I could and was moving up to join the company when I either stepped on a mine or got hit with a mortar. Finally, an aid man got to me. My leg was broken in two about ten inches above the foot. The shoe and the foot were intact but it was torn up so bad that he just took his big scissors and cut it off. I had tried to stop the blood as much as I could. He said I was in kind of a bad situation. He couldn't stay—he had to move on and help others. He said, "If I put a tourniquet on you and you can't loosen it, you'll wind up with gangrene. If I don't put one on, you'll bleed to death." About that time, two guys were coming back with German prisoners and they made the Germans carry me back.[33]

It was during the breakout that Don Amzibel, L Company, 157th, also suffered grievous wounds.

My buddy, Herb Schimbeck, and I had been manning an outpost all night long near Carano, close to the German lines. We came back to our outfit at ten a.m. and got in our foxhole to get some sleep. An enemy mortar shell landed in our foxhole and exploded. Herb got killed and I got hit. Another friend, Martin Kraus, gave me water and sulfadiazine and got the medics. They pulled me out of the hole and we went up a draw, when the Germans dropped a couple of shells in and the medics set me down. I hollered at them, "I ain't dead yet—let's get the hell out of here!" Then I caught a piece of shrapnel the size of a .45 bullet in my right shoulder; it's still in there. I didn't realize I had been seriously wounded—I kept telling my friends that I'd be back. They just shook their heads and said, "No, you won't."

I woke up the next day in the hospital and I was in a body cast. My right leg was gone. I still had my left leg for about eight more days. Gangrene had set in

> and the veins had popped. They treated me real good there at the hospital and at Anzio.

The only thing Amzibel was bitter about was the way he received his Purple Heart, the medal awarded to soldiers wounded in combat.

> The doctors had built a tent over my remaining legs and had twelve-pound weights hanging over the edge of the bed pulling the skin over the exposed ends of my legs. Some sergeant walked into the room and said, "Are you Corporal Amzibel?" I said yes. He said, "Congratulations, here's your Purple Heart," then he turned and walked out. When I had been stationed at Camp Shelby, Mississippi, they had our whole division turn out on the parade ground and watch as they awarded the Purple Heart to some guy that had been wounded in the Pacific. I always think about that.[34]

• • •

To the right of the 45th, Combat Command A's tanks, with infantry from the 34th Division riding on them, roared into the gaps on either side of Formal del Bove Creek, overrunning opposition and taking stunned prisoners by the score. By 1300 hours, the leading company of tanks and the accompanying infantry battalion had crossed the railroad and held the high ground some 500 yards north of the tracks.[35] Their first objective reached, the GIs paused for a breather. Canteens were pulled out and packs of cigarettes were passed around. Everything was going much better than they had expected. The survivors smiled and grinned at each other and congratulated one another on their good fortune and then sank down into the enemy's bunkers and trenches and foxholes to think about their buddies who hadn't made it across the field and to think about what was to come.

Sparks said,

> The biggest problem we had initially was that the Germans had put out thousands of anti-personnel mines. They had a little mine called a *Schu* mine. It looked like a little box made out of wood, but it had a quarter pound of TNT in it. They would bury this just a few inches under the ground and when you stepped on it, it had a device that forced the lid down and ignited the charge. They had thousands and thousands of those. Unfortunately, we could not detect them because they were made out of wood and our mine detectors could only detect mines made out of metal. We lost several hundred men from those mines. Usually, the men weren't killed, but their feet were very neatly severed at the ankle. I had people lose a foot who were standing five feet away from me. When the troops were running forward, they didn't have the chance to look for mines. Many times, I could spot the mines easily because I wasn't doing any firing. In some cases, you could spot them because the dirt would be a little higher at that point. I was following behind one of our companies and I had the tank destroyers drive ahead to detonate the mines. A tank destroyer could run over them and explode them; it had no effect on the tank destroyer.

> So I had them run back and forth to clear a path while they were firing at German tanks.[36]

Daniel Witts, Anti-Tank Company, 179th, recalled seeing several Sherman tanks equipped with flails that detonated the unseen mines. "When we pushed off, there weren't enough engineers to sweep these mines, so they brought these tanks up that had big rollers with chains on the front, and they'd roll the roller and the chains would beat the mines and explode 'em." The flail tanks would also be employed at Normandy.[37]

Extremely tough going was encountered as the 180th moved up Spaccasassi Creek and along the Aprilia-Carano road, where Germans, holed up in fortified houses, hammered the Americans. Tanks from the 191st Tank Battalion, with their .50 caliber machine guns and 75mm cannons, were brought forward to silence the opposition. During the operation, Lieutenant Colonel Daniel K. Ahern, commanding the 180th's 1st Battalion, was wounded in the arm by a sniper. Lieutenant Colonel Martin H. Otto assumed command after Ahern was evacuated.

In every battalion, company, platoon, and squad of the 45th Division, Thunderbirds wrote new definitions of the word "courage." First Lieutenant Adam Michalkovich, a platoon leader with E Company, 180th, was hit in the shoulder by a German bullet shortly after his unit began moving forward. Refusing aid, he continued to lead his platoon despite being subjected to small-arms, artillery, and mortar fire and enemy counterattacks. At the head of his platoon, Michalkovich continued to rush at the enemy troops and engage them, despite his obvious pain and loss of blood. Only at 2100 hours that night, after his platoon had taken every objective to which it had been assigned, did Michalkovich finally allow himself to be evacuated to the aid station. Tragically, he later died. For his unselfish actions, he was awarded the Silver Star, posthumously.

In G Company, 180th, Second Lieutenant Charles A. Brandt and Tech Sergeant John P. Sessions, both Oklahomans, aggressively led their platoon through an Allied artillery barrage and a German minefield to attack heavily defended German positions. Within thirty minutes, their platoon had killed or wounded sixty-five of the enemy and taken another ninety-five prisoner. Continuing on, the unit captured a battery of German mortars while Sessions personally accounted for fifteen of the enemy killed or wounded. Although hit by mortar fragments, Brandt grabbed a BAR and led his men to the next objective before permitting his wounds to be cared for. That first day, Brandt's platoon was credited with wiping out an entire enemy company and six mortars.

First Lieutenant Roderic C. Morere, who had been seriously wounded but earned a Distinguished Service Cross the previous November at Rocca Pipirozzi near Venafro, again proved his mettle under fire when he led F

Company, 180th, on the first day of the breakout. Moving in the open from one of his company's machine guns to another while being shelled and sniped at by the enemy, Morere was able to position his automatic weapons to effectively support the 2nd Battalion's advancing troops.

During the afternoon of the twenty-third, the 2nd Battalion, 180th, commanded by Lieutenant Colonel Howard Crye, attacking from the area around Carano, overwhelmed a battalion of the 29th Panzer Grenadier Regiment, captured the battalion commander, and held the ground about a mile northwest of the village. Crye's men, however, soon ran into strong resistance. Near Carano, L Company was counterattacked by a force of some fifteen or twenty panzers, fell back, and then called for artillery fire, which knocked out ten of the enemy tanks. The 3rd Battalion made good progress, but three of the tanks accompanying it were disabled by mines, two suffered mechanical breakdowns, and four others became immobilized by mud.[38]

Bill Rolen, a replacement with I Company, 180th, vividly remembered the morning of the breakout.

> We took off across an open field and had gone a couple hundred yards when the Germans suddenly opened up on us with a machine gun and pinned us down. They just let us get right up to them. There were little gullies there, just big enough for your body to fit in. We all hit the ground. You'd look up and could see the bullets coming and you'd see the grass being cut by the bullets. The guy I came up from Naples to Anzio with died there. His name was Wheatley. He was from around Chicago, a real nice man, had a wife and two little girls. He died there in those first fifteen minutes of the breakout. He was next to me, within fifteen, twenty feet. It was a machine gun that got him. All of a sudden that machine gun stopped and somebody yelled and off we went again. We overran them. They were in a big ditch and we were able to eliminate them. But they also killed a bunch of our people. That ditch was big; you could have put a four- or six-story house in there. A lot of dead Germans were there. That ditch was as far as we went that day. We stayed in it that night and their planes came over and dropped flares and lit up the ditch and here's all these dead Germans down there. That's a bad experience for an eighteen-year-old.[39]

By sundown on the first day, the 45th Division and Combat Command A's tanks had reached all their objectives. But the 1st Armored's Combat Command B, farther to the right, had tougher going as it ran into thick anti-tank minefields. Some twenty-three Shermans and seven tank destroyers were put out of action by the buried explosives. Unable to drive through, the armored attack stalled until snakes, which had been inadvisedly held in reserve, were brought forward to blow paths through the mines. Several hours were lost due to this problem. By the time evening fell, CCB had only reached the railroad line. In spite of the difficulties, the armor-infantry attack had cracked the line held by the 362nd Division and stabbed a mile beyond.

The 3rd Infantry Division had less success attempting to battle its way to Cisterna, just as it had had since January. Arrayed around Cisterna were elements of the 362nd and 715th Divisions, plus a regiment of panzer grenadiers and thousands of unseen mines. Trying a flanking movement to the right with tanks and T-Ds, the 3rd Infantry Division employed a bayonet charge and took key positions southeast of Cisterna. The 3rd also suffered 995 battle casualties on the twenty-third, the largest number of casualties incurred by an American division in World War II in a single day.[40]

As the twenty-third came to a close, Kesselring assessed the situation. Cisterna was still in his grasp, but the 45th and 1st Armored Divisions had made serious incursions to the west of Cisterna. If the Fourteenth Army were to collapse, the fate of the retreating Tenth Army would also be jeopardized. Kesselring again advised von Vietinghoff to hasten his withdrawal from the Cassino front.[41]

• • •

On the twenty-fourth, the assault resumed. The 45th Division, still supporting the armor's flank, was making excellent headway. Late that day, the Germans struck back hard against the Thunderbirds. A reinforced infantry battalion, supported by armor, hit Companies E and G of the 180th's 2nd Battalion. Fierce fighting ensued, with the 2nd Battalion giving up some ground. A counterattack later by the rest of the battalion restored the lines.[42]

In the 179th's sector along Spaccasassi Creek, the enemy also struck on the twenty-fourth, only to be turned back by deadly artillery fire and white phosphorus mortar shells from the 83rd Chemical Mortar Battalion.[43] The Thunderbirds' penetration of the outer defenses of the Caesar Line threatened the left flank and rear of the 3rd Panzer Grenadier Division, to which the Germans responded by sending a force of fifteen Tiger tanks against the 180th and even more against the 157th. Heavy fighting broke out and the tanks appeared to be gaining the upper hand when a barrage of American shells shattered the German attack, forcing the surviving panzers to retreat.[44]

Sparks recalled,

> The Germans counterattacked with Mark V and Mark VI tanks and disrupted our attack for a while. What saved us were those tank destroyers. Their 90mm guns with a high muzzle velocity were a match for those German tanks; our own Shermans were certainly no match. The Sherman was a rotten tank. It had an air-cooled airplane engine and used high-octane gas, and when you hit one, flames would shoot a hundred feet high. We called 'em "Ronson lighters." It would make cinders out of the crew. And they were too noisy; when one cranked up, you could hear it for a mile. The other problem was it had a very poor gun—a 75mm that just didn't have the velocity. It could hit a German tank with an armor-piercing shell and the round would just bounce off. As lousy as they were, they still did a lot of good. The Germans' Mark IV tank wasn't much better. But their tanks were heavier than ours. The Shermans

> were absolutely, 100 percent helpless. Some of our troops came running back when those German tanks broke through and I thought we were going to have a rout on our hands. We had a hard time restoring order there for a while. I was yelling at everybody that they couldn't go back, and when I found any stragglers, I just assigned them to the nearest company I could find. The tank destroyers were then able to knock out a number of German tanks and they finally broke off the counterattack.[45]

The breakout also seared itself into the memories of other Thunderbirds. Sid Pollock, C Company, 157th, said,

> The breakout was something else. I think every American gun on the beachhead went off before we started our push. We were pushing up the canals and the Germans were shelling us like hell until we broke out. The shells were just raining down on us. The Germans had good dugouts, with railroad ties on top of them. You could never knock them out. I saw a lot of American tanks blown up—the light tanks with the 37mm guns. They were setting off Teller mines and blowing up. The 1st Armored Division took a hell of a beating.[46]

"Doc Joe" Franklin, I Company, 157th, remembered that his company's commanding officer, Captain James G. Evans, was captured during the breakout.

> I was at regimental headquarters, which was set up in a big cavern. There was a German tank that had been knocked out on the road above it that was blocking the entrance to the cavern, and dead Germans in the tank. Evans had orders to take a hill and he called in on his radio to Colonel Church, who was in the cavern. I heard the conversation. Evans said to Church, "If I take that hill, we're going to be cut off and captured, because I have no flank protection anywhere." And Church said, "I don't give a damn—go up and take that hill." So Evans took that hill and, sure enough, he got captured. Later, in Germany, one of the outfits liberated a prisoner of war camp where Evans was and he came back. He was in pretty bad shape so they sent him back to a hospital in the States.

Franklin will also never forget a serious injury to Captain Ralph Barker, C.O. of L Company. "He stepped on a mine and lost a foot. Somebody visited him later in the hospital and said, 'I'm sorry you lost your foot, Captain.' Barker said, 'That's all right—that's the one that was always getting cold anyway.' That's the kind of guy he was; he never let anything bother him."[47]

At the time of the breakout, B Company, 157th, was holding a very unusual position. The company commander, Captain Kenneth P. Stemmons, recalled,

> We set up our company CP in Garibaldi's tomb. The tomb was located out by itself. There was a big, ornate farmhouse with a big windmill about 300 yards away, and all of the grounds had a rail fence around it. I assumed it was like a national park. Inside the mausoleum itself, it was about ten feet wide by

The shell-marked tomb of Menotti Garibaldi at Carano, where units of the 45th held out against repeated German attacks. (Courtesy of K. P. Stemmons)

> twenty feet deep. It was about ten feet tall and had marble inside and had family members entombed in caskets in the walls. In the center there was a flat marble piece with Garibaldi's name on it, and there was a big, ornate brass rail around it. The Krauts knew we were in there and they were firing their tanks' guns at us. They were firing armor-piercing, high-explosive shells, and the shells would come in one side and go out the other before they would explode. It tore up everything inside. Somebody wised up and removed a marble slab and we discovered that his actual tomb was twenty feet below. He was entombed in a concrete bunkerlike thing down there. We hastily made a ladder and set up the CP down on his tomb. There were six or eight of us in there. We were so far down, somebody back at battalion called me the "submarine commander." We had candles going for light, and when the Krauts would fire and hit the building, the concussion of the explosions would suck out all the air and the candles would go out.

Although B Company's position was relatively secure, it caused some supporting units moments of insecurity. For example, the communications platoon from HQ Company had to string wire nightly from headquarters to the tomb while under fire because the shelling kept breaking the wires. "They hated to come to B Company," Stemmons related.

When B Company attacked out of the tomb a couple of days later, a soldier gave Stemmons a map he had found on a dead German. The map had

"*Hauptmann Stemons*" [*sic*] written next to Garibaldi's Tomb. "They knew *where* we were and *who* we were," he said.

> We had most of our casualties when we jumped off at Anzio. When the push came, we went from the Garibaldi Tomb position. B Company had been built back up to full strength—193 men at that time. We had some extra machine guns we had pilfered from somewhere. The first morning we didn't do too well. Then we tried to go out at night and got into a minefield. The next morning, there was only about thirty-eight of us left. We had a lot killed, wounded, missing, and captured. Then we get the attack order and we're supposed to cover a front of 400 yards from L Company to the 34th Division over there, and they act like we've got a full complement of 200 men!

Stemmons also remembered that his unit's front was located along a small canal in which dozens of dead soldiers—both German and American—lay.

> We got most of the American casualties out but there were some that were buried deep in the water, that were there when we took over the positions. But there were also quite a few dead Germans. When we broke out, we went through that little canal and everybody who got wounded ended up with gangrene because of all the filth in the water. There were little, half-inch, red, wiggly worms all over us when we came out of the canal. We all had to take our boots and britches off and wipe ourselves down. When we finally moved out, we went out with a bang. We really dealt the Krauts a blow. We shot 'em up, we cut a bunch off, and we took a bunch of prisoners. We captured a battalion CP, complete with their battalion commander. It must have been three or four days before we got any replacements at all. We fell in as reserve behind 3rd Battalion and they filled us up with more troops.[48]

Captain Eddie Speairs, in command of C Company, 157th, recalled that his company was in reserve the first day.

> We stayed in a creek bed and moved up a short ways. That afternoon, B Company got counterattacked and pushed back, and they committed C Company. We retook the terrain. B Company was reorganized and relieved us. I got hit later that day by an artillery fragment when we were moving C Company to act as reserve for another battalion. Then I got wounded by a land mine. Neither of these wounds was anything to talk about. Then, that night, we got into a hell of a fight. I gathered up what was left of 1st Battalion—C Company had only one platoon left; the other platoons had got cut off in the rear and I didn't know where they were. I had the only working radio and could communicate with the rear. They told me to gather everything I could and keep the line. The next day, they pushed another battalion in and relieved us.* Then the Germans

*With characteristic modesty, Speairs plays down this action, for which he won a Silver Star. One of his men, Sid Pollock, said, "We had a wonderful head man in Captain Speairs. If you wanted to find him, you had to go to the front, never the rear. He was always in the front, even when he became the X.O." (Sid Pollock, telephone interview with author, Mar. 14, 1995).

> pulled out and we started to move. But the German artillery had put little flags everywhere and they knew exactly what the coordinates were on each flag. If any Americans got close, the Germans had a ready-made target.[49]

Ken Vogt, a platoon sergeant with E Company, 157th, remembered, "The first day wasn't too bad because we caught 'em by surprise. I think our battalion took 1,800 prisoners that first day. The second day was when we really caught it. We started out with a full company and about thirty in reserve; by the end of the day, I think we had twenty-one men left." Many of the casualties occurred when E Company tried to advance across a wheat field. "The company began taking small-arms fire and everyone hit the ground, crawling forward," Vogt said. "When you mash wheat down, it stays mashed down." From the German positions on a slight rise, the enemy could see the trails being left in the wheat field by crawling men and began firing at the front end of each trail. Vogt said,

> I could hear my men getting hit. I backed up my trail a few feet and went just off to the side. I had no more backed up than fifty bullets hit right where I had been laying. The lieutenant said we couldn't go back, we had to go forward. I told him, "I'm ready. When you holler, we'll go." Well, he hollered and my platoon was the first one to come up and go. Out of my whole platoon, there were just three of us that got up. The rest had been killed or wounded. We ran sixty or seventy yards, and as soon as my platoon went into the ditch, the next platoon went, and so on. We got into the ditch and I got a glimpse of the Germans—they were pulling out. They didn't realize there was so few of us left. Fortunately, they didn't hit us with artillery.[50]

Morty Carr, HQ Company, 1st Battalion, 157th, recalled carrying a rocket launcher (commonly known as a "bazooka") during the breakout.

> Every so many feet, there was another German tank. With the bazooka, I blew the tracks off a few of them. We walked through a creek that was pretty deep. We were drenched but at least we had some protection because the Germans were right around the bend in the creek. I also remember, during the breakout, we were delivering food and ammunition to the guys on the front lines. It was hot and we were parched and we wanted a drink. We came across a watermelon patch in no-man's land and we were out there eating watermelons.[51]

Everett Easley, E Company, 179th, described the breakout as being "something else. We attacked up a creek and the Germans were raising hell and attacking us. We finally made it to the top of this hill." To his surprise, the German soldiers were "a bunch of kids—little bitty guys. But they could hold their fingers on the triggers as good as anybody else." Easley also recalled seeing, at the height of the battle, "one of the bravest men I've ever seen. He was a captain in the Medical Corps and he had his aid station right out in the open. A truckload of wounded guys came in and they were stacking them up like cordwood and that captain just worked around the clock."[52]

Another 45th veteran also had nothing but praise for the medical teams. Daniel Witts, a member of the Anti-Tank Company, 179th, summed up the feelings of everyone in the division: "You gotta hand it to the medics—God bless those guys—what they went through. They were probably the bravest guys out there."[53]

Felix Sparks said,

> It took us three or four days to break out of that beachhead. It was very bloody and we had heavy casualties because we were going right into the teeth of their defensive positions and mines and barbed wire. After we finally started to move, I was in a jeep with my communications officer and my driver; we were going forward to set up our new command post when a German tank spotted us. He was firing at about 300 yards' range and missed us by about 50 feet. We abandoned the jeep in a hurry. I had no idea there were any German tanks left in the area. The Germans fought back bitterly, but we were making substantial progress. We actually broke their main line of resistance the first day, but they kept making counterattacks and they had a lot of anti-tank guns that knocked out an awful lot of our tanks, maybe thirty or forty of them.[54]

Tarzan Williams, K Company, 157th, recalled, "We finally broke through the German lines and got up on the high ground. We looked down on Anzio beachhead and realized that the Germans could see everything the Americans had been doing on the beachhead. No wonder we were always getting shelled."[55]

• • •

The 45th found itself heavily engaged for the next several days as it bored its way through the Caesar Line defenses. On the morning of the twenty-fifth, the 3rd Battalion, 180th, was to lead the attack from positions west of Carano. First Lieutenant Bill Whitman recalled, "Each platoon leader blew a whistle at 11:00 a.m. and we started climbing up the bank of the ditch. The Second Battalion companies yelled encouragement. I looked to the right, and there, as far as the eye could see, were men walking forward. It was the U.S. Third Infantry Division. I looked to the left, and there were the men and bayonets of the First Battalion of our 180th Regiment moving forward. I thought to myself, 'You'll never see a sight like this again.'" Whitman's unit had gone only about a hundred yards when it began receiving machine gun and artillery fire. As the unit closed in on an enemy position, Whitman's first sergeant, a man named Casey, told him that four Germans were in a nearby ditch, ready to tear up anyone who tried to assault their position. Whitman and Casey worked out a plan. "I exposed myself above the ditch for a second and when they raised up," he said, "Casey emptied a clip from his M-1 rifle at them. I saw one German come tumbling out of a small tree and another one fall over backward. Casey reloaded his rifle and raised up again, too high; one of the Germans who was left shot him through the right thigh. At that time, I fired a burst from my old 1928 Thompson submachine gun into them and that was that."

Not quite. The area quickly came under enemy mortar fire and Whitman and Casey were forced to pull back. Reaching the company CP, Whitman found a wounded officer, but the company commander was gone. Whitman called for a couple of Shermans to knock out an anti-tank gun that was stalling the company attack. One of the tanks was knocked out before the other blew the German gun to pieces. Next, Whitman turned his attention to a German position in Prefetti Creek that had the company pinned down. Leading a charge against the position, Whitman directed the GIs to take out the enemy with grenades. A few of the Germans tried to fight back but were quickly silenced; the others surrendered. Whitman soon encountered his company commander, and the two of them, along with a major from the accompanying 191st Tank Battalion, discussed plans to fight off the expected counterattack. At this moment, a soldier rushed up and told the major that one of his tanks had been hit and was on fire.

"The tank major had gotten to his tank and had gotten inside with his crew to move it to some cover," Whitman wrote. "They took a direct hit from a German anti-tank gun some distance off and blew up. The major and his crew were all dead. They had given us good support during the attack."[56]

The situation was not going well for the Germans. The 29th Panzer Grenadier Division had arrived too late to plug the holes in the crumbling Gustav Line and, like the rest of the Tenth Army troops, was rapidly retreating up the Liri Valley. Von Mackensen was madly scrambling to reposition his I *Fallschirm* Corps troops to keep the dam from bursting around Cisterna. Kesselring, the eternal optimist, was uncharacteristically gloomy about his army's prospects.

Meanwhile, Clark and Truscott met in the latter's command post, which had been relocated to Conca, to discuss changing VI Corps's direction from the northeast—toward Valmontone—to the northwest—toward Rome. Truscott told his superior that he felt such a change of direction would be justified only if von Mackensen moved I *Fallschirm* Corps from the Caesar Line in the Alban Hills to Valmontone; otherwise, the risk of becoming embroiled in bitter fighting in the Alban Hills was too great. If, on the other hand, I *Fallschirm* Corps remained where it was, Valmontone would most likely be relatively easy to take and would give VI Corps a solid wall against which the retreating Tenth Army would have to smash.

To Clark, Truscott was merely parroting Alexander's words. Clark's argument was that if Alexander expected the Tenth Army to allow itself to be trapped at Valmontone, he was sorely mistaken, for the Germans could simply avoid Valmontone by using secondary roads. What Clark didn't say but was undoubtedly thinking was that the British were scheming to bog down VI Corps and Fifth Army so that they could be the first into Rome. Nevertheless, Truscott had his staff prepare an alternate plan that would involve a change of direction to Rome in case battlefield circumstances warranted.

The battle for Cisterna wore on. The inexperienced 362nd Division was putting up a fanatical defense (von Mackensen had ordered them to fight to the last man) that thwarted every effort by the 3rd Division to take the town, which was by now nothing more than a large heap of rubble. On the morning of the twenty-fifth, elements from Keyes's II Corps finally linked up with elements of VI Corps near Borgo Grappa. Intense fighting was still taking place along portions of the Hitler Line where the 1st *Fallschirmjäger* Division, which had escaped from Cassino, stopped the I Canadian Corps near Aquino on the Melfa River. The resistance did not last long; soon the Canadians were pouring over the river and thrusting farther up the Liri Valley. The rest of Eighth Army, however, beset by confusion and traffic jams, was unable to expand the bridgehead.

Finally, on the twenty-fifth, the 3rd Division took a pile of ruins that had once been the city of Cisterna. German resistance was rapidly evaporating. Truscott felt confident that his troops would soon be astride Highway 6, waiting for the retreating Tenth Army to fall into the trap.

Truscott's sense of satisfaction soon gave way to shocked surprise, for Brigadier General Donald Brann, Clark's operations officer, informed him that Clark wanted the 3rd Division and 1st Special Service Force to block Highway 6 while the bulk of VI Corps made a sharp left turn and headed for Rome. Dividing his forces, especially since there was no indication that I *Fallschirm* Corps had left the Alban Hills to reinforce Valmontone was, Truscott argued, a serious violation of military principles. Realizing his objections were falling on deaf ears, Truscott began preparations for the switch. Alexander was not consulted.

At 1115 hours on the twenty-sixth, VI Corps, minus the 3rd Division and the 1st SSF, made an abrupt turn and headed for Rome. Finally informed of the change of plans, Alexander hid his anger at his insubordinate subordinate, merely saying that Clark's plan to drive for Rome "is a good one." His memoirs reflected Alexander's true feelings, however: "Mark Clark switched his point of attack north to the Alban Hills. . . . I can only assume that the immediate lure of Rome for its publicity value persuaded him to switch the direction of his advance."

The Hermann Göring Panzer Division, now under the command of *Generalleutnant* Wilhelm Schmaltz, pulled out of its rest camp at Livorno and was moved to Valmontone to withhold the city from the Allies. But only one battalion had arrived there by 26 May. And the 3rd Division, along with Frederick's 1st SSF and a battalion from the 1st Armored, were on their way. After being held up by a mistaken attack by American aircraft* and a German barrage, the Allied force finally descended on Valmontone, only to discover the rest of the Hermann Göring Panzer Division had already arrived. A terrific fight broke out and, while the Americans were hotly engaged, the fleeing elements of Tenth Army sneaked past the action and continued northward toward Rome. The Tenth Army had been permitted to escape and join up with the Fourteenth Army—all because, some say, Clark had split his forces. In the meantime, I *Fallschirm* Corps had not budged from the Caesar Line that ran through the Alban Hills and, when the rest of VI Corps tried to plunge through it, on the twenty-sixth, the Americans were repulsed with heavy losses.

One solution to Clark's twin stalemate dilemma came from an unlikely source. Alphonse Juin and his French corps, being squeezed out by the British, came to Clark with a proposal: If they were permitted to move forward, their weight might tip the balance in the VI Corps's favor. Clark also saw the involvement of the French as being likely to obstruct the roads so that the British could not reach Rome ahead of the Fifth Army. Severe wrangling with Alexander over which army had the right to use which roads broke out; Clark resolved to be the first into Rome by hook or by crook.

A plan was advanced that would require the hard-luck 36th Division, which had been butting its head against the Caesar Line, to infiltrate the German defenses. It was a gamble; an infiltration operation on such a large scale had never been tried before. In the dead of night, the 36th penetrated the Hermann Göring Panzer Division's lines on top of Monte Artemisio and took the position. A determined counterattack could not dislodge it from the 36th's grasp. The door to Rome from the south was at last wide open.[57]

The roads leading to Rome had become the Italian Grand Prix, with every unit and every war correspondent racing to be the first to enter the Imperial City. Keyes's II Corps, barreling up the flat, straight Highway 6 from Valmontone, was hell-bent on beating Truscott's VI Corps, coming a shorter distance, but via a more twisting and easily defended road from the Alban Hills. Every parallel side road, and even flanking fields, were filled with olive-drab American jeeps, command cars, trucks of all sizes, tanks, and tank destroyers—all heading flat out for Rome. Hard on the heels of II Corps was a unit from the French Expeditionary Corps. To make sure his corps would win the race over Truscott's, Keyes sent a mobile patrol of

---

*Major General Harmon, when he learned that his 1st Armored Division had been mistakenly attacked by American aircraft, messaged Truscott: "Friendly planes have strafed our troops three times in the last two hours. Tell the Air Corps to get the hell out of the air, as we can get along better without the SOB's. If they don't stop strafing our troops, we are going to shoot the hell out of them" (Dan Kurzman, *The Race for Rome* [Garden City, NJ: Doubleday, 1975], p. 308).

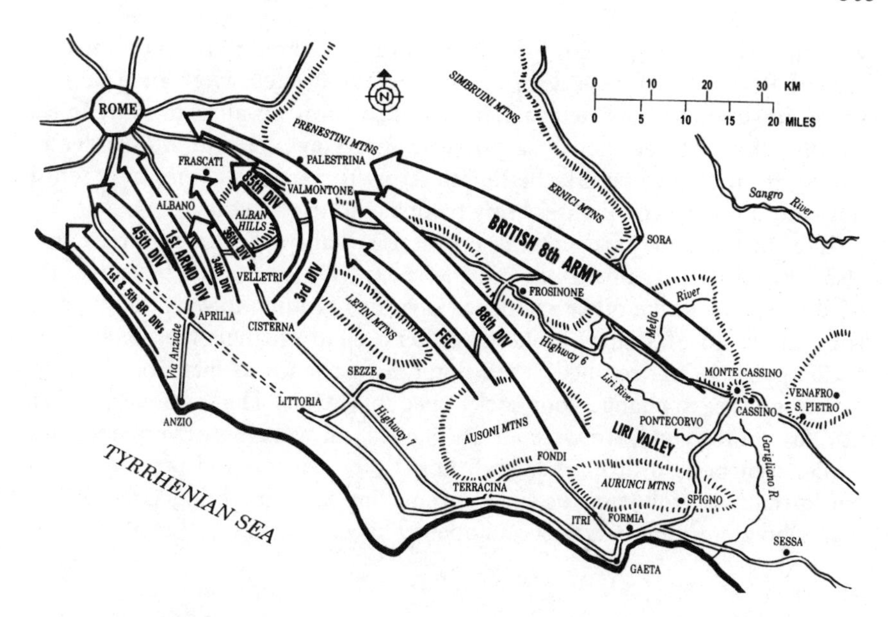

MAP 11.2 The Rush for Rome
15–25 May 1944—With the defenses of the Gustav and Hitler Lines finally breached, the Allies at the Anzio beachhead broke out and joined the mad dash to capture Rome before the Normandy invasion relegated the Italian campaign to secondary status. (Positions approximate)

sixty men in eighteen jeeps racing ahead, along with a group of newspaper and newsreel photographers to document II Corps's triumphal entry.

Wehrmacht rearguard units, however, were doing their best to slow the American advance. It seemed that every time a column of vehicles entered a town or rounded a curve, the lead vehicle would be raked by automatic weapons fire or hit by an 88mm shell or a *Panzerfaust* round. Compounding this problem was the fact that the pilots of American planes, thinking the vehicles below were escaping Germans, continued to accidentally strafe the American columns.

As VI Corps emerged from the Alban Hills, the 36th Infantry Division, moving up from the south, and the 1st Armored Division, driving from Anzio, nearly came to blows to see which division would take the lead. A compromise was worked out and both divisions traveled together down the same highway, with the infantry on the right side and the armor on the left. This chaotic situation became even more entangled when it appeared the 85th Division was about to cut in front of the 36th and 1st Armored. Threats were issued, including one that VI Corps troops might open fire on the men of the 85th if they got in their way![58] Clark, too, was adamant about which army would be the first to enter Rome. As one historian has written, "Even though both French and British wanted to be in on the capture of Rome, Clark was determined to make it exclusively an American show. So strong was his determination not to allow his allies to share in the capture that, he revealed in a postwar interview, he told Alexander he would, if ordered to permit the Eighth Army to participate, not only refuse but would fire on any Eighth Army troops who tried to do so."[59]

Like their counterparts coming up the Liri Valley, the Anzio forces were also driving hard against time and the enemy. On the march to Rome, the 45th was, like all the other exhausted divisions heading toward the Imperial City, made up of scruffy-looking soldiers, dead on their feet. Ken Vogt, E Company, 157th, recalled, "You don't get a chance to shave or clean up. You might get to change your socks once in a while. That's about all. That last day on the road, we were all bedraggled, all worn out. Every once in a while, somebody'd drop over and they'd pick 'em up and put 'em in the trucks that were following us, give 'em smelling salts, and bring 'em to. Every man who got put in that truck and opened his eyes, he'd say, 'Let me out!'"[60]

• • •

The end of the grinding war of attrition on two fronts in Italy was greeted with great relief by the people of the free world. Of the breakout, the 28 May 1944 edition of *Life* magazine crowed, "In a single week of determined attack, the Allied campaign in Italy, which not long ago was written off as a disappointing stalemate, became a heartening success."[61]

On 1 June, along with a host of other divisions, the 45th was driving toward Rome, battling its way through determined pockets of resistance. On that day, the 45th's Division Artillery fired an astonishing 16,956 rounds—more than double the amount it expended on 16 February, at the height of the massive German counterattack.[62] Unlike the rest of the Fifth Army, however, the 45th Division was required to take the slow route—moving cross-country south of the city and battling against stubborn rearguard forces. The 157th Regiment was directed to head in the opposite direction—toward Cisterna and Velletri. At 2100 hours, the 157th's 2nd and 3rd Battalions were temporarily attached to the 36th Division to bolster its attack against Germans entrenched on the high ground near Velletri. The town fell to the Yanks the next day and the grateful citizens poured out their hearts (and their wine) to their liberators. The celebrations were brief; the 157th was sent back to join the rest of the division for its push against Rome's southern suburbs.[63]

The first also saw the 179th heavily engaged in what has been called the battle of K-9, a hill to the southwest of Genzano. The Germans were barricaded behind solid concrete emplacements and were pouring bullets into the 179th as the men tried to come up the slope to root them out. The 3rd Battalion had already had two of its commanders, Lieutenant Colonel Edward E. Webber and Major Richard M. Strong, killed in rapid succession but kept hitting the enemy's flank while the 1st and 2nd Battalions tried to keep the defenders' heads down. The Germans fought back with a ferocity not seen since the first two days of the breakout. This was no small, rear-guard delaying force; these troops meant business. Fire from every weapon in the Germans' arsenal hit the 179th as it tried to advance, and casualties mounted sharply, especially among the officers and noncoms. The battle lasted without letup through the night.

At dawn, E Company rose to make the final assault behind a barrage of American artillery and mortar fire. But the high explosive hadn't dimmed the Germans' ardor for battle and E Company walked into a hail of bullets. Six tanks were called in to help, and E Company, following the armor, was at last able to make it to the summit and claim the hill. Naturally, the evicted enemy counterattacked almost immediately, with Mark VI tanks, self-propelled 88s, and infantry. A reinforced company, supported by Shermans, hit the attacking Germans with a flanking maneuver and drove the enemy back. On 3 June, the 179th was rolling again, but without facing the stiff resistance that had claimed so many Thunderbirds since the breakout. The Germans finally were on the run.[64]

Lieutenant Charles Reiman, a platoon commander in G Company, was one of the 179th men involved in the battle for K-9. He said,

> Hill K-9 was taken by E Company. Lieutenant Winters was the C.O. and he rode a tank—the only way we could get the tanks to fight. As I remember it, Winters got wounded in the finger. The trenches on top were deep and not inter-connected. The part that Winters took was secured by Second Platoon. At mid-morning on June 4th, G Company moved north on the west side of K-9. Elements of the Thirty-fourth Division had punched a small hole in the enemy's line. I am not aware of any support from our tanks. As G Company moved forward through a deep cut in the hill, elements of the Thirty-fourth were in sight and a lot of bullets were flying across the road just over their heads but too high to offer any threat to us. German artillery from the west, intended to interdict the road, was landing fifty yards to our right and really was no threat. We moved ahead unopposed. I had no map. Captain Fred Snyder, my C.O., had shown me, on his map, a point where a railroad crossed the road. I was supposed to turn to the east. However, no railroad showed up and the whole column stopped while Snyder came forward and we discussed the mystery of the missing railroad. It was decided to continue on the road.
>
> Further north, we descended into a wide valley. Just as the valley began, we came upon a house at a road junction that was occupied by a German anti-tank crew. We quickly occupied the house, taking four prisoners, one of whom got wounded in the process.

Noticing a steady stream of enemy, some wounded and on litters, moving past the house, Reiman and his men took about fifty Germans prisoner.

Those who tried to fight back were killed on the spot. "Snyder had us pull back down the road we had started on and we were led eastward, through the woods, until we came to another road. There we huddled in the ditch until daylight, at which time a convoy of trucks came and delivered us to a bivouac area outside of Rome."[65]

On the first, the 180th found itself in the fields to the west and northwest of Campoleone, attacking through the lines of the 6th Armored Infantry Regiment and the 179th's 1st Battalion toward a road junction and railroad near Genzano. Shortly after leaving the line of departure, 1st Battalion units began taking heavy small-arms fire and the Germans attempted to hit the battalion on the right flank. Headquarters Company, not normally a combat outfit, came to the rescue and, with the help of a single tank, tore into the attacking Germans and saved the day. A private, Peter Poggioli, recorded some of the actions involving A Company:

> The lieutenant [Second Lieutenant Paul B. De Tosky] told me that it would be plenty rough, as we had the roughest sector in that section of the line. We were to have C Company of the 179th as our right flank protection and our own first and third platoons as our left flank protection. We attacked at about six a.m. and went about 500 yards ahead before we ran into anything. The first obstacle was a bunch of riflemen and a couple of machine guns. These opened up on us, and we killed a few Jerries and captured six or seven of them. . . . We started to go further in, in the process of cleaning out machine-gun nests which infested the area and [continued in a line for] 100 or 150 yards further.

Thinking that some of the enemy were actually members of the 179th, the platoon commander pressed on, only to find the unit attacked on the right flank. "We could not get any reinforcements and just had to fight it out. The Germans killed nine of our boys before we could get started. Then four others were wounded right quickly. We were surrounded and fired everything we had at them, but there were just too many. . . . Finally they had us worn down by weight of numbers and there was nothing left to do but give up." Poggioli later escaped from his captors.

Despite this setback and other casualties inflicted by the enemy, the rest of the battalion continued toward its objectives. The 2nd Battalion, too, had been hard hit but was undeterred in its mission. At 0400 hours on the second, the 180th's 1st Battalion followed a barrage against enemy positions on high ground about a kilometer to the northwest. Again, German resistance was stiff and American casualties heavy. The Germans had excellent fields of fire from stone houses and were set up in a vineyard, where fighting took place at point-blank range. Only individual heroics by a number of men, including Private first class Wallace L. Richards and Technical Sergeant Joe A. Blair, who gave their lives to save their friends, enabled the battalion to overcome the enemy.[66]

First Lieutenant Bill Whitman recalled that enemy resistance seemed to increase exponentially as the Yanks got closer to Rome. As the 180th began another daily assault on 3 June, the regiment was hit by heavy artillery, mortar, and machine gun fire, practically stopping the assault in its tracks. Whitman positioned his men in ditches and set up the company CP in a farmhouse and was observing the area through binoculars when the enemy counterattacked. "All hell broke loose," Whitman said.

> A machine-gun burst shattered the window and frame, and stitched the wall behind us. Plaster, wood, and dust filled the room. We both [he and a Lieutenant Shires, artillery forward observer] crawled back to the window and looked out. There they were, as big as life; there must have been over a hundred of them screaming and running towards our ditches. Shires and I ran down and yelled for our radiomen. We then went upstairs and Shires started calling in his artillery fires and I informed the battalion commander of the counterattack. All was noise as our men opened up on the oncoming Germans. . . . I heard our two tanks open fire. They were behind the house. The Germans didn't know that they were there. Lieutenant Shires got them out from behind the house and . . . got them firing almost immediately. Point blank, they opened up on the Germans, and were the Krauts surprised, bless their black "Superman" Aryan hearts.

The German attack was broken; Whitman's company had suffered 17 casualties, but over 150 Germans covered the ground and another 15 or 20 were taken prisoner.

Shortly after the battle ended, a company of men from the 179th came marching up the road. Whitman told their captain,

> I didn't think it was safe letting his men walk in the ditches on each side of the road as they might be mined. I asked him where he was heading and he told me to Albano. I wished him luck, but personally I didn't think that he was going to make it if he continued on the way he was going. Sure enough, he and his company got up the road to the forward edge of our objective, where his road made a junction with the other paved road . . . and the Krauts plastered them with artillery and heavy mortar fire. His men were in the open, standing up, and received the full effects of the fire. I felt this was a needless waste of human lives and it was. They suffered enormous casualties for no purpose.[67]

• • •

On the night of 3–4 June, Keyes's mobile patrol reached the outskirts of Rome. Not wanting to enter the dark, unfamiliar metropolis that might be crawling with well-armed German units, the patrol bedded down on the lot of Cinecitta, Italy's major film studio. At dawn on the fourth, the patrol crossed an overpass that had been wired for demolition by the Germans and moved cautiously forward into the still-sleeping city. At 0600 hours, the lead jeep entered Rome through the Porta San Giovanni—and immediately came under enemy fire that halted it. Captain Taylor Radcliffe of the 1st Special Service Force, the patrol's commander, was the first Allied soldier to enter Rome.

For the next two or three hours, other advance elements of the 1st Armored and 3rd and 88th Infantry Divisions probed at Rome's various entrances, and all have claimed to have been the first to enter. In the initial communiqués from the scene, the 88th was credited as being the first unit to set foot in Rome, but that was because the war correspondents were unaware of Captain Radcliffe's earlier arrival. Also unknown to almost everyone was the fact that, at 0900 hours, a French patrol from the 3rd Algerian Division, under Captain Pierre Planès, was the first to reach the heart of the city, driving through empty streets past the Vatican and halting in the deserted Piazza di Venezia—the square in front of the huge, white "wedding cake" monument to King Victor Emmanuel II, under the same balcony where Mussolini once exhorted the Italian throngs with his Fascist boasts.

Meanwhile, outside the city, Frederick's task force was being held up on Highway 6 by a couple of self-propelled 88s. General Keyes drove up to Frederick, who was observing the battle, and informed the brigadier that Clark had to be in Rome by 1600 hours. When asked why, Keyes replied, "Because he has to have his photograph taken." Keyes knew that the Normandy invasion was only a day or two away and that it would soon crowd the Italian campaign off the front pages of the world's newspapers. Clark and his entourage, which included Keyes and Frederick and a phalanx of reporters and photographers, braved sniper fire long enough to be filmed in front of a large "ROMA" sign marking the city limits; then, with many parts of the city still under the control of the Hermann Göring Panzer Division, Clark drove out of Rome and spent the night outside its ancient walls. The next day, with most of the Germans in full retreat to the north and much of the city secured either by Allied troops or Italian partisans, Clark returned as the heroic conqueror. The Romans, who had peered through their shuttered windows at the sound of vehicles in their streets, now began appearing on the sidewalks, throwing flowers and shouting "*Benvenuto, Americani!*" to their liberators. Clark drove around for a while, allowing the adulation and gratitude of the citizens to wash over him, and eventually wound up in Saint Peter's Square, where he had to ask an American priest for directions to city hall.[68]

Elements of the 45th reached the southern outskirts of Rome on the afternoon of 4 June. The 1st Battalion, 180th, fought off a small group of Germans and secured a bridge over the Tiber about five miles southwest of the city at 1900 hours. At 0300 hours on the fifth, Lieutenant Colonel Howard C. Crye's 3rd Battalion, 180th, crossed the bridge and soon after met up with a detachment of British troops. After a few small, sharp engagements with the enemy on the far side of the river, a number of prison-

Lieutenant General Mark Clark (left front) touring the Imperial City. The French General Alphonse Juin is shown in the jeep behind him, with the Vatican in the background. (Courtesy of 45th Infantry Division Archives)

ers were taken and, on the morning of 5 June, the battle for Italy, as far as the 45th Division was concerned, was basically over.[69]

Captain Minor Shirk, commanding the 157th's Service Company, recalled, "We came to the Tiber River and started to cross it on a pontoon bridge. We got right out in the middle of the river and looked downstream and here came a Stuka dive-bomber. He let his bomb go and it went right over us and landed in the river and exploded. We were lucky."[70]

Rome was but a few kilometers away, but the division saw only the fringes of it. Felix Sparks remarked that the division was not there on a sight-seeing tour. "We were in hot pursuit of the Germans, so we didn't stop to celebrate. We went right through the city and set up camp on the other side. It took us several hours to get from one side of the city to the other, though, because the civilians were all over, throwing flowers at us. The rear echelon—Army headquarters—came in and *they* had the big party."[71]

The Thunderbirds moved through the southern sections of Rome to bivouac in the rolling terrain on the west side. Behind them, on the seven fabled hills, the city gleamed like a dusty jewel. Here, out of range of German snipers and artillery, the GIs pitched tents, pulled the boots off their blistered, aching feet, and fell into a deep sleep, undisturbed by the crash of guns or the danger of infiltrating patrols. On the morning of 6 June, as the 157th's history says,

> The artillery radios were tuned in to BBC and a few of the troops lay on the ground nearby, sunning themselves and listening to the music. Suddenly there came a blunt announcement: "Allied forces have crossed the channel and have landed on the coast of France."
>
> Morale went high with the knowledge that the all-out Allied assault had begun. Hope returned to the eyes of the weary infantry. The war in Italy was over. There wasn't a bit of doubt about it in the minds of the infantry as the tanks swept on to the north. As a matter of fact, with that beachhead in France, the whole war was about over. It had to be. These agreements were so unanimous that men failed to dig in when the regiment moved June 9 to an area about fifteen miles from Rome. That night, "Butterfly Bill" flew over and dropped some samples of his wares.[72]

Although the Germans had given up the city to the Allies, their dive-bombers made nightly passes over the Thunderbirds' encampment to drop deadly reminders that they were still in the neighborhood. One of the 180th's "old-timers," Lieutenant Colonel Howard C. Crye of Hugo, Oklahoma, who had been with the regiment since the 1930s and had risen to command the 3rd Battalion, was killed on the night of 9 June in one of these air raids. Crye had survived every battle in which the 180th had fought since Sicily without so much as a scratch; it was tragically ironic that he should be killed in his sleep after the fall of Rome.[73]

For its labors the past two years, the 45th was rewarded with a brief period of rest, relaxation, and recreation. Hot showers and hot chow appeared, along with fresh uniforms. Special Services broke out the bats, balls, gloves, and horseshoes. Men wrote long letters home. The Red Cross Clubmobile came around with doughnuts and pretty girls. Awards and decorations were handed out, including a Distinguished Unit Citation to the 2nd Battalion, 157th, for its stand during the battle of the caves at Anzio. Passes for Rome became plentiful.[74] "They trucked us into Rome," recalled Everett Easley, E Company, 179th, "and stopped right by the Coliseum. We walked over and went in and looked around. The Romans were glad to see us, and scared, too—they didn't know what was going on."[75]

Howard W. Walton, I Company, 157th, who joined the 45th as a replacement just before the breakout, remembered his brief stint in Rome: "We got to visit Rome for one day. I talked to a couple of nuns along the Tiber River, we went to the Vatican, and then we were sent back to Salerno for training."[76]

"I had a fantastic time in Rome," said Ray Williams, Anti-Tank Company, 179th.

> It was so good, they kicked us out the first night—we weren't allowed to stay. The next day my lieutenant came to me and told me and Jones to get a couple of jeeps with trailers and go into Rome and find some lumber to build some latrines for the officers. So we went in and went to MP headquarters and asked if they'd watch our trailers. They said okay, so we unhooked them and spent the whole day touring Rome in our jeeps. We didn't find no lumber—we didn't even look for any. That evening, we got back out to the outfit and I told the lieutenant we couldn't find any lumber so he said go back tomorrow and look again. We spent three days driving around Rome, supposedly looking for lumber. We never found a stick.[77]

Captain Kenneth P. Stemmons, B Company, 157th, said, "Most of us got a couple or three days in Rome. We were supposed to be reorganizing and getting new equipment and so forth, but everybody in our company took some time off. The men should have had a week in Rome, but the Army did not do that. I got to go through the Vatican and spent a night in the Grand Hotel. In fact, I've still got the room key as a souvenir."[78]

• • •

With Rome finally in Allied hands, it was time to reflect back on those who had sacrificed everything to make the victory a reality. The casualty toll at Anzio was, as one can well imagine, heavy for the battle's relatively brief duration. The combined Allied and Axis losses for the four months came to a total of some 94,400 men—the equivalent of nearly seven 14,000-man divisions! The ferocity of the fighting during the brief breakout period is clearly evident in the 45th Division's own casualty reports. From 23 May to 4 June, the division lost 442 men killed and over 3,200 wounded, missing, or sick or injured.[79] In the 275 days that had elapsed from the landings at Salerno to the fall of Rome, some 20,000 Allied soldiers had been killed—12,000 of whom were Americans. Over 100,000 American, British, Polish, and French Colonial troops had been wounded. That was the price of victory in Italy—and another eleven months of hard fighting were still ahead before the battle for Italy was truly and finally over.[80]

With the opening of the "second front" in Normandy, the world's attention suddenly shifted from Italy to northern France, just as Clark knew it would. The sacrifices of tens of thousands of men were quickly forgotten as the dispatches from France—reporting on the swift dashes of Bradley's and Patton's armies, which contrasted so starkly with the months of little or no progress in Italy—gave the free world hope that the war would soon be over; Italy never offered that hope. As the historian and 45th Division veteran Fred Sheehan put it, "It still seems incredible to those of us who were there that so much of the world's attention could be focused on so tiny a piece of the world's topography for so long, then pass into limbo so quickly and almost permanently."[81]

The 45th's job in Italy was finished. A new operation was in the works, an operation that would require the services of divisions experienced in the art and science of amphibious landings. In late June, the division was trucked to the Salerno Training Beach and began all over again to learn how to load into, and debark from, landing craft.[82]

12

Dreadful Minos Stands

1 July 1944–28 April 1945

There dreadful Minos stands, gnashing his teeth: examining the sins of those who enter, he judges and assigns as his tail twines. . . . Now notes of desperation have begun to overtake my hearing; now I come where mighty lamentation beats against me. I reached a place where every light is muted, which bellows like the sea beneath a tempest, when it is battered by opposing winds.

—Dante Alighieri, *The Inferno,* Canto V

IN A PERFECT WORLD, there would be no war. But if wars were required, the appropriate reward for what the 45th accomplished in Italy would be to bring the survivors home to a hero's welcome and allow them to live out the rest of their lives soaking up the Colorado or Oklahoma or New Mexico sun on their front porches, with one arm embracing their family members and the other arm engaged in hoisting a cold beer or lemonade, while they graciously accept the accolades and monetary tribute of a grateful nation.

Alas, such an idyllic, storybook ending for the 45th was not to be. To the victors do not always go the spoils. Sometimes, when one has been successful in battle, the reward is more battle; the weary troops must keep going and going and going, until ultimate victory is finally achieved or they are destroyed in the process. And so it was for the 45th. Less than two short weeks after arriving in the Imperial City, the 45th Division struck its tents, climbed into trucks, and headed south; the Army had a new assignment for the Thunderbirds: their fourth amphibious combat assault, this time against the southern coast of France as part of Operation Dragoon.

On 16 June, the 45th was the first division detached from VI Corps control, reverting to Fifth Army control. The 3rd and 36th Divisions would soon follow. By the twenty-third, all elements of the 45th had taken up residence near Battipaglia, the scene of considerable bloody fighting in the hills above the Salerno beaches. The next day, the Thunderbirds began again learning how to assault a beach from the sea.[1] For many of the thousands of replacements who had joined the division since the Anzio invasion, such training was a new experience. For some of the old hands, the upcoming offensive seemed to be pushing their luck just one time too many. Tarzan Williams, K Company, 157th, recalled feeling that he wouldn't be in France for very long. The persistent, ominous inner voice that many combat soldiers have heard kept nagging at him, whispering that something bad was going to happen. A buddy tried to talk Williams out of the premonition, but it persisted.[2]

The amphibious training lasted until 7 August, when the 45th, along with the other divisions taking part in the operation, were moved to Naples and combat-loaded on the transports and assault craft.[3] With the bulk of the German Army in France still engaged in a furious struggle with the Allies advancing toward Paris from the beaches of Normandy, to say that the enemy's guard was down along the southern coast would be a monumental understatement. On 15 August, the U.S. Seventh Army commander Lieutenant General Alexander M. Patch, with one French and three American divisions (the 3rd, 36th, and 45th), along with the 1st Special Service Force (which would take two islands off the coast), landed on the fabled Riviera coast between Saint-Tropez and Cannes with only light opposition. Instead of putting up a stiff fight as they had at Sicily, Salerno, and Anzio, the Germans mounted only token resistance and then quickly pulled back, hoping to make a stand farther inland. Indeed, throughout France, German Army Group B, now under the monocled *Generalfeldmarschall* Walter Model, a master of salvaging desperate situations, was in general retreat.[4]

Back under VI Corps control, with Truscott still at the helm, the 45th landed and encountered only light and disorganized opposition. But the nagging feeling that something was about to go wrong continued to wear on Tarzan Williams. He didn't have long to wait. "When we were on the Higgins boat, the same feeling come over me again," he said.

> I was in the second wave that hit the beach and went on this hillside to get the rest of the company. There were mortar shells landing on the side of the hill, getting closer to us. Then one landed about fifteen feet to my right. I felt something hit my leg and I looked down but didn't see anything. Then I seen the man in front of me and one in back of me bleeding. One had his face bleeding and the other had his hand hit. I looked at my leg again and seen a hole in the pants leg. I opened my pants and seen blood running down my knee, so I took off my pack. The other men were laying on the ground, calling for the medic.

The medic arrived and started working on the wounded men, but Williams had another premonition that told him to get out of the area. Feeling that the Germans had zeroed in on their position, he told the men

The 45th wading ashore from an LCI on the French Riviera, 15 August 1944. (Courtesy of the 45th Infantry Division Archives)

that the next round was going to land among them. They managed to move behind a large boulder—just as an enemy shell crashed into the very spot where they had been lying. Although Williams was one of only seven casualties in the 157th on D day, the "voice" had saved his life.

After being temporarily patched up, Williams was sent to the rear and evacuated by sea. On the boat that would take him and other wounded soldiers to a hospital on Corsica, a sailor produced a bottle of champagne. "I can't say that I like champagne all that much, but that really was good. The bottle was passed around twice for eleven men." Williams was checked out at the hospital and a decision was made to send him by C-47 cargo plane to Naples, where he was operated on and spent two weeks recuperating. While talking with one of the 157th's chaplains, he learned some disturbing news. "The Army sent a telegram to my folks, telling them I was missing in action. About a month later, the Army sent another telegram telling them I wasn't missing but I was wounded in action. By that time, I was back on the front lines in France again."[5]

The invading Thunderbirds drove inland and, with the rest of Patch's Seventh Army pushing up toward the heart of France, covered more ground in a day than they had in months in Italy. In fact, so swift was the advance that in seventeen days the division CP moved eleven times. The drive was exhilarating; town after town fell to the advancing 45th. Grateful civilians lined the roadsides, crying, waving to the Yanks, and throwing flowers. The only problem, the veterans knew, was that at some point the fleeing Germans would decide to make a stand, and then the real struggle would begin; Hitler's troops would never let the enemy enter the *Vaterland* without one hell of a fight. On the nineteenth, the 45th captured Barjols, thus opening the route into the lower Durance River Valley. The division crossed the swollen river and the 180th headed toward Avignon, the 179th headed toward Volonne, and the 157th crossed the Luberon Mountains and drove toward Apt, where it quickly overcame a small German delaying force from the 11th Panzer Division. The 179th was ordered to proceed on to Grenoble, where it was attached to the 36th Division, driving on that city.[6]

Not until they ran up against the 11th Panzer Division again in the vicinity of Le Puy on 21 August did the Thunderbirds slow down. But there was no heart left in the German defense, and the enemy was rapidly dispatched. Hundreds of Germans were marched off to the POW compounds. On 23 August, the 36th Division occupied Grenoble and was relieved by the 179th Infantry Regiment. The French Resistance was active in this area, helping to round up small bands of Germans or pointing out larger formations to be taken under fire by the Americans. East of Grenoble, a thousand Germans were taken prisoner.[7]

Meanwhile, Tarzan Williams was frantically trying to rejoin his outfit. After recuperating in Naples, he had been brought back to southern France by ship and caught a northbound train with a large group of fresh replacements. But the locomotive soon broke down and the troops on the train were told that a new engine wouldn't arrive until that evening. Williams and a few other soldiers received permission to temporarily leave the train, but while they were sight-seeing in town, another engine arrived, was coupled to the passenger cars, and pulled out, leaving Williams and four others behind. Realizing they were now absent without leave, a crime punishable by death by firing squad, the five Americans did everything possible to reach their unit. The group—Williams, a corporal from the 157th's 2nd Battalion who had also been in hospital, and three replacements—hopped aboard an ammunition train and rode with a load of 500-pound bombs as traveling companions. When the train stopped for the night, the group jumped on a freight train heading north until it, too, halted.

After being fed by a Transportation Corps unit and stuffing their pockets with American cigarettes and chocolate bars, Williams's group continued on. Flagging down a civilian bus, the quintet boarded, but the driver refused to let the men ride, for they had no French money. The French passengers came to their aid, protesting to the driver to relent. In gratitude, Williams's group paid their fare in cigarettes and chocolates. The bus ride proved to be a short one; the bus could not cross a bombed-out bridge, so the Americans dismounted and hiked to the railroad station, where they waited for the next

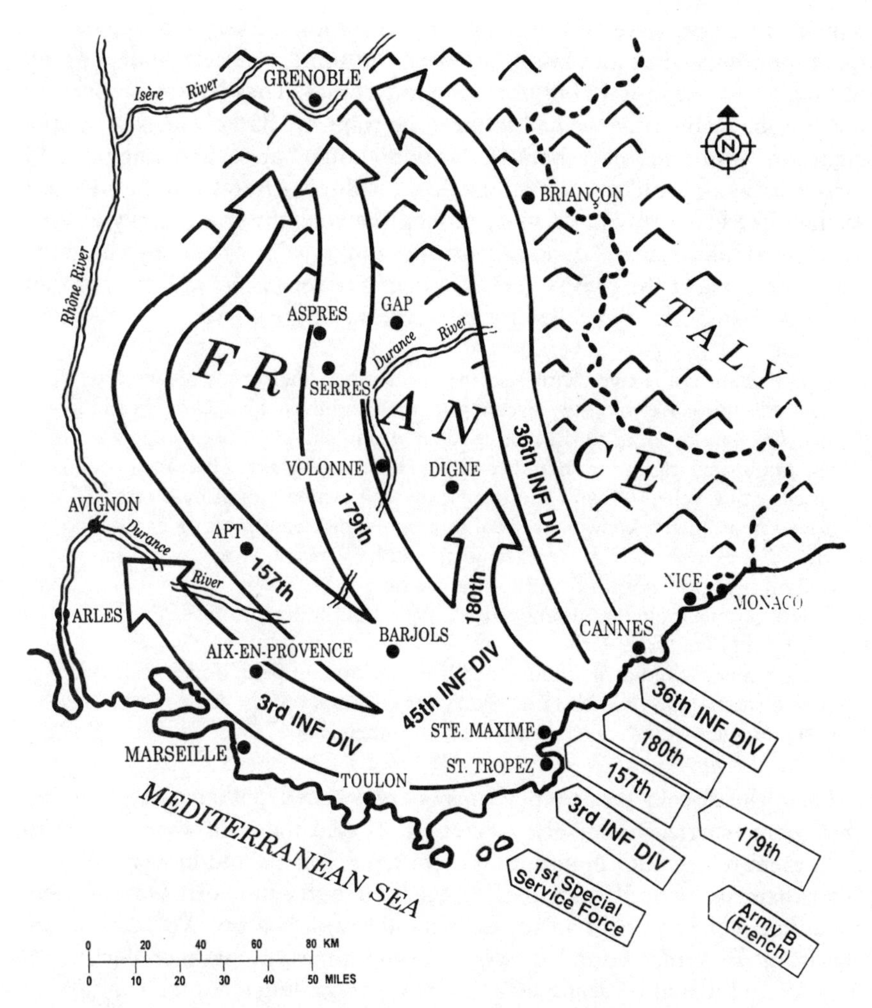

MAP 12.1 Operation Dragoon—The Invasion of Southern France
15 August 1944—Alexander Patch's U.S. Seventh Army, with the 45th Division in the center, landed on the French Riviera against weak opposition. The Army moved northward, making substantial progress against an enemy in disarray. (Positions approximate)

train north. While they were waiting, a French soldier struck up a conversation with them. Learning the Americans were trying to get to the front, he escorted the group to the French equivalent of a USO club.

"There were several FFI [*Forces Françaises de L'Intérieur,* the French resistance fighters] soldiers and women there," Williams remembered. "The soldier called attention and told everybody that two of us had been wounded and we were all going up to the front lines. Everybody shook our hands and hugged us and kissed us. Then the good wine come out. I drank my share of wine in Italy but none as good as that. They had food for us at lunch, too. By the time we had to meet the train, we had given away all the cigarettes and chocolate bars. Everyone shook hands and hugged and kissed us again, and we left to catch the train." After stopping at what seemed like every town and village along the way, the train finally arrived at its destination near Grenoble and the Yanks went off in search of the camp. Arriving at the camp's gate, Williams and the others told their stories to the MP on duty, who called for the sergeant of the guard.

> The sergeant come over with two men. They had their guns drawn like we were criminals. We told the sergeant our story and they called camp headquarters. We were brought to the colonel who was in charge of the camp. We told him about missing the train and catching rides to get there. He leaned back in his chair and yelled, "Don't you men know you can be shot as deserters?" The three replacements knew they were in trouble and were looking at the floor. The colonel looked at the replacements and he was really making an impression on them; the corporal and I were laughing.
>
> The colonel looked at us and yelled, "What outfit are you from?"
>
> We told him, "The 45th."
>
> He really looked at us funny, then told the captain behind us to take us to our division area. Then he said, "For your information, the 45th just got here two hours ago and the men just settled in to their tents."

Later, the three nervous replacements approached Williams and told him they were worried about being arrested. "I told them he wasn't going to send them to the guardhouse; they were replacements and he was going to send them up to the front lines to get their butts shot off. One of them asked me if the colonel had scared me and I said, hell no. We had been on the front lines and wounded two and three times, going back each time. The colonel would be doing us a favor by *not* sending us to the front."[8]

• • •

On the twenty-seventh, the 179th took Bourgoin, between Grenoble and Lyons, in an effort to cut off elements of five German divisions heading for Lyons and, from there, withdrawing farther eastward into Germany.[9] On 30 August, the 157th received a new regimental commander when Colonel Walter P. O'Brien replaced John H. Church, who had been promoted to brigadier general.[10]

While the division was in camp near Grenoble, close to the Swiss border, patrols from the 45th continually probed into the French Alps to test the enemy's strength and resolve. To slow the Thunderbirds' advance, the Germans destroyed every bridge behind them, mined the roads, and established

The joyous residents of Bourg, France, greeting their liberators on 4 September 1944. (Courtesy of the 45th Infantry Division Archives)

defensive strong points wherever the terrain was suitable. To add to the problems, days of steady rain drenched the division in its drive. Still, the 45th pushed on into the Meximieux area, northeast of Lyons.

On 1 September, with the 36th Division and French II Corps battling for Lyons, the 45th engaged an armor-and-infantry German force moving up from Lyons toward Bourg. Try as they might, the elements of two regiments of the 11th Panzer Division could not dislodge the 179th and the FFI units from their blocking positions. By that afternoon, the enemy had lost nearly 400 men, along with five tanks and three self-propelled guns. Allied casualties were light; eleven men of the 179th were killed or wounded in the action, and the Germans broke off contact as night fell. The next day, the 45th continued up Highway 75 and kicked the German defenders out of Pont d'Ain. Resistance seemed to be crumbling and the GIs gradually gained confidence that nothing could stop them now. On 4 September, elements of the division entered Bourg and captured nearly 5,000 Germans from eight different divisions, twelve *Luftwaffe* units, and twenty other battalions, along with vast quantities of weapons, vehicles, and other war matériel.

To a soldier, few moments are as sweet as those spent marching through a liberated town. Being cheered, applauded, and kissed by a grateful civilian population is an experience that no soldier ever forgets or dismisses lightly. For many soldiers, in fact, such moments are their raison d'être—

the single event that makes all the hardships worthwhile. The civilian populace of Bourg showed its gratitude by welcoming the triumphant 45th with flowers and wine and kisses as the Thunderbirds marched through the city.

But although the civilians could rejoice in their freedom, the soldiers knew that more hard fighting lay ahead. Patch was pushing the 45th to continue its drive in a northeastwardly direction, cross the Doubs River at Baume-les-Dames, and cut off the Germans heading for the Belfort Gap. At Baume-les-Dames, the Germans put up a determined defense, but the 180th made a flanking maneuver that threatened to encircle the enemy; on the eighth, the Germans pulled out. The 45th was unable to pursue quickly because of drenching autumn rains that washed out roads.[11] On 11 September, in another day of hit-and-run fighting, the 157th's 3rd Battalion ran into a hornet's nest of Germans after taking the town of Abbenans. During the fighting, Major Merle Mitchell, who had taken command of the battalion as a captain at Anzio on 7 February when the previous C.O. was killed, was himself killed. Mitchell, along with the S-3, Captain Henry Huggins, and a number of other men, died when they were ambushed while on a reconnaissance mission. Felix Sparks, promoted to major after becoming C.O. of the 1st Battalion, was transferred to take command of the 3rd.[12]

A German general, Walter Bosch, chief of staff of the Nineteenth Army, paid homage to the Thunderbirds after the war:

> The thrust of the 45th U.S. Division north from Baume-les-Dames on Villersexel was the most dangerous and most critical potentially for us of all the different attacks launched by the French and the Americans at that time in that region. . . . The thrust of the 45th U.S. Division was aimed at the backs of the LXIV Corps and the IV Air Force Field Corps. Against this it was possible to engage only scrapped together units, the Dehner battle group. However, this group, assisted by elements of the 11th Panzer Division, succeeded in parrying this dangerous thrust.[13]

In a rainstorm on the fourteenth, in action near Grammont, platoon leader Lieutenant Almond E. Fisher of E Company, 2nd Battalion, 157th, earned the division's sixth Medal of Honor. While leading his men in the predawn darkness, he was stopped by a well-arrayed line of enemy machine guns just twenty yards to his front. With total disregard for his own safety, Fisher crawled into the German-held hills and personally knocked out a gun position with just his carbine. Moving his platoon ahead, Fisher again went to the ground when another machine gun opened up. Crawling out alone, the lieutenant wiped out the enemy gun crew with grenades. The platoon continued on, only to be stopped an hour later by another fusillade of rifle and machine gun fire. Spotting an enemy soldier with an automatic weapon, Fisher and an enlisted man eliminated the threat. German fire intensified but Fisher was undeterred. When a German soldier attempted to engage a Thunderbird in hand-to-hand combat, the lieutenant killed him with a shot from his carbine. A half hour later, German machine guns had the platoon pinned down once more, and once more Fisher proved unstoppable. Moving across an open field to engage the enemy, he knocked out the position. His incredible night was not yet over, however. The platoon moved again, only to be hit once more by heavy machine gun fire. With just two grenades left in the entire platoon, Fisher took the explosives, crawled across an open field, threw both grenades, and destroyed the position. Other enemy troops tried counterattacking Fisher's platoon, but he organized the defense to hold them at bay. The battle reached a crucial stage, with hand-to-hand fighting taking place all along the platoon's perimeter. During the melee, Fisher was wounded in both feet but refused to be evacuated. Although unable to walk, he crawled from position to position, checking on his men and repositioning them when necessary. Once the enemy backed off, Fisher crawled 300 yards to the nearest aid station, from which he was then evacuated.[14]

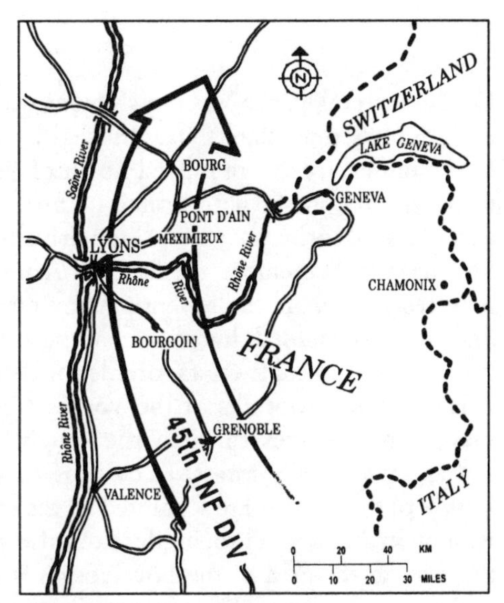

MAP 12.2 The Continuing March
Mountains, rivers, delaying tactics, and deteriorating weather greeted the Thunderbirds as they inexorably pursued the enemy toward Germany.

Patch's Seventh Army was moving rapidly northward in hopes of linking up with Patton's Third Army, driving eastward. If they could meet, they would trap a large part of the German First Army in a pocket. The Germans resisted furiously, but the two Allied armies managed to join forces on 12 September, near Chatillon-sur-Seine, and some 18,000 Germans were taken prisoner.[15]

As part of the Seventh Army drive, the 45th continued to press on toward the Vosges Mountains, clearing the enemy from one city, town, and village after another, towns with such names as Rougemont, Villersexel, Lure, and countless more, each one in peacetime beautiful and charming in its own, peculiar French way. And at each one, more and more young Americans, veterans and replacements alike, were killed or maimed for life. It was a dirty business but somebody—specifically the Yanks—had to do it.[16]

• • •

On 16 September, the VI Corps's front was realigned. The 45th, on the Seventh Army's right flank, was relieved by the French 1st Infantry Division; the Thunderbirds were moved north of Vesoul on the VI Corps's left flank to maintain contact with units of Third Army and establish a bridgehead across the Moselle once the Allied drive resumed on the twentieth.[17] In the final days of September, the Seventh Army encountered a stiffening of German resistance. As the Seventh Army history records, "The enemy supply lines were shortened; his ranks had been reinforced; and he occupied positions on terrain that was favorable for defensive action."

Here, in the foothills of the Vosges Mountains, the natural barriers are many, the passages through the rough country few. The two mountain ranges—the heavily forested Low Vosges to the north and the rugged High Vosges to the south—are separated by the easily defended Saverne Gap, northwest of Strasbourg. Through this area also runs the Moselle River. Situated on the river in the area of the Low Vosges is the city of Épinal, with two main routes running through the mountains: one that goes through Saint-Die and the Saales Pass leading to Strasbourg, and another that runs through Gerardmer and the Schlucht Pass, the gateway to Colmar and the Alsatian Plain. To reach Germany, Seventh Army would need to pass through this formidable country. Already intelligence reports were streaming in to Patch's headquarters indicating that a heavy buildup of enemy troops from Nineteenth Army was taking place in the Vosges area. The 45th was ordered to capture Épinal and cross the Moselle, proceed in a northeasterly direction to take Rambervillers and Baccarat, and be prepared to seize the Saverne Gap. Meanwhile, the 36th Division would cross the Moselle near Eloyes, then advance upon Saint-Die and the Saales Pass. The 3rd Division would simultaneously cross the river at Rupt-sur-Moselle and take Gerardmer en route to the Schlucht Pass.

The 36th Division began its portion of the operation on the night of 20–21 September. The Germans were waiting on the opposite bank and, for a few anxious hours, it appeared as if the 36th's debacle at the Rapido was about to be repeated as intense fighting broke out and men in the assault boats were slaughtered. By the twenty-second, however, the brave Texans had gained a foothold on the opposite bank and had overcome stubborn enemy resistance. Two days later, bridges had been thrown across the Moselle and the area was in the 36th's hands.

On the twentieth, the 3rd Division launched its attack to cross the Moselle near Rupt. As had the 36th, the 3rd ran into considerable German resistance. It took elements of the division three days just to reach Rupt, where it hurried across an intact bridge. By the twenty-fourth, Rupt had been cleared of snipers. But bad weather and heavy enemy fire prevented further progress, and the 3rd was replaced by a French division and directed to try another crossing, this time in the 36th's sector.

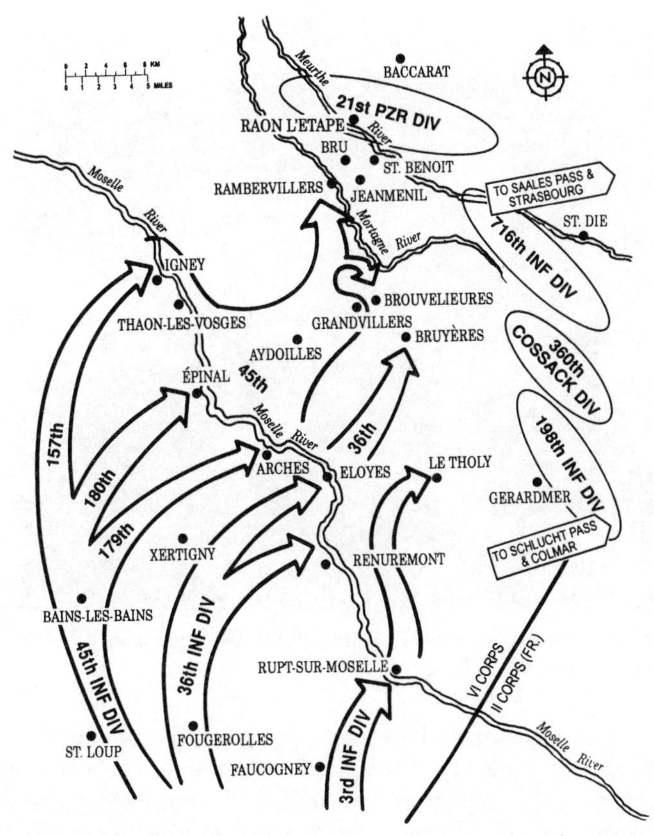

MAP 12.3 Crossing the Moselle
20–25 September 1944—To secure routes to Germany through the difficult Vosges Mountains, the 3rd, 36th, and 45th Divisions battled stubborn opposition to force a crossing over the important Moselle River. (Positions approximate)

The 45th began its attack against German troops holding the Épinal area on the night of 21–22 September. The 157th was to attack north of the city at Igney, the 180th would hit the center of Épinal, and the 179th would attack to the south, at Arches. The 45th's assault, although no cakewalk, was considerably easier than those launched by either the 3rd or 36th Divisions. Infantry from the 157th waded across the Moselle at Igney and an American-built bridge in the Third Army sector enabled armor and artillery to cross with relative ease. The 179th, too, was able to cross with little enemy harassment. The Germans recovered from their surprise, however, and fought back fiercely; it was all in vain, for by the twenty-fourth, both regiments were firmly established on the opposite bank. The 180th, assaulting the city of Épinal, which had a population of over 27,000, had a far tougher nut to crack. For over a month, the Germans had been strengthen-

Thunderbirds crossing the Moselle near Épinal, 24 September 1944. (Courtesy of 45th Infantry Division Archives)

ing the city's defenses, including conscripting French civilians to dig a series of trenches around the city. Three infantry battalions, plus a large number of mortars, rockets, artillery pieces, minefields, booby traps, and anti-aircraft guns stood ready to repel any invaders. On the twentieth, the 180th began its assault and was immediately hit with fierce, concentrated fire that brought its movement to a halt. It took two days for the regiment to crawl to the western edge of the city, where it engaged in clearing the buildings one by one. Tanks from the 191st Tank Battalion helped the GIs blast the defenders from their positions and destroy roadblocks and obstacles, and informants from the FFI reported that two bridges were still intact on the east side of town.

On the afternoon of the twenty-second, the Germans decided to abandon Épinal, and American artillery struck the enemy column as it moved across the river. To keep themselves from being followed, the Germans also blew the last two intact bridges. On the twenty-third, despite heavy fire coming from the opposite bank, the 180th crossed the river in three places before the 36th Engineers managed to erect a 140-foot Bailey bridge over the Moselle. On the opposite bank, on 25 September, the three regiments of the 45th linked up; the Seventh Army bridgehead across the Moselle was secure.[18]

It was at Épinal that Second Lieutenant Van T. Barfoot was pulled out of the fighting to receive the Medal of Honor—for his actions during the breakout from Anzio on 23 May. Barfoot said, "They took me out of combat and awarded it to me right then. In the meantime, I'd been promoted to second lieutenant and moved over to I Company and given a platoon. They called me back to regimental headquarters and held a ceremony just outside Épinal. Then they sent me back to the States—they wouldn't let me go back into combat."

During the course of the war, Barfoot was wounded three times—the first by concussion near a little town called Pozzilli, near Venafro. Reflecting back on that time, he said, "That was probably the worst day I saw in my life. We lost most of our 3rd platoon there. Then, when I went back up in November, I was hit in the leg by a mortar shell that, fortunately, was a dud. Finally, I was wounded when we invaded Southern France. A German just about got me—he shot off my lieutenant's bar. Part of it went down my back and ended up in my first-aid pack and the other part hit me in the top of the head and cut the scalp. A piece of the bullet went out the back of my helmet. I was fortunate," Barfoot concluded, with considerable understatement.[19]

With the 3rd, 36th, and 45th Divisions all across the river, the Seventh Army drive picked up steam. The 45th, especially, was having considerable success in moving from Épinal to Rambervillers over open ground. German roadblocks were smashed and town after town fell while most of the German units rapidly withdrew to the east. The towns of Domevre, Sercoeur, Padoux, Girecourt, Gugnecourt, Pierrepont, and Memenil, where resistance was reported as slight to nonexistent, were liberated by the 45th. Only when the 179th and 180th reached Grandvillers on 28 September was any serious opposition encountered. After two days of hard fighting, the town was under Thunderbird control.[20]

The bold VI Corps drive soon ground to a halt. Rain turned the unpaved mountain roads into quagmires, snow fell in the higher altitudes, and squabbles over supplies broke out between the Americans and the French. All this enabled the Germans to retreat to their prepared positions along the Meurthe River, and there was little movement on the Seventh Army side during the first two weeks of October. While the troops rested and resupplied themselves, plans were drawn up for the continuation of the offensive. By studying maps, it became clear to the Corps brass that the only routes through the forested mountains were through the towns of Bruyères and Brouvelieures, and then on to Saint-Die and the Saales Pass—an area well defended by the 16th and 716th Infantry Divisions, along with elements of the 21st Panzer Division. The plan called for the 3rd Division to stab into German lines toward Saint-Die with the 45th and 36th Divisions on its flanks.

The first phase of the assault required the 45th to take Brouvelieures, then swoop down on Bruyères from the north and northeast while the 36th, to which the Japanese American (Nisei) 442nd Regimental Combat

Team was attached, attacked the town from the west and southwest. The 179th seized Brouvelieures on 22 October, then helped the 36th take Bruyères. The 180th, north of the 179th, ran into considerable opposition while moving from the Fremifontaine area on its way to cross the Mortagne River. Despite the enemy fire, the 180th made it over the river on the twenty-second and by the thirtieth had occupied Saint-Benoit. The 157th was less fortunate in its attempt to break through enemy strongholds in the Bru and Jeanmenil areas. Only by totally destroying the towns was the 157th able to capture them.[21]

While the Thunderbirds mopped up and consolidated their gains, changes at the corps level were being made. On 25 October, Lucien Truscott turned command of VI Corps over to Major General Edward H. Brooks and departed France to assume command of Fifth Army in Italy, still slogging its way through the Apennines on its way to the Alps.[22]

On 31 October, near Jeanmenil, Tarzan Williams was wounded for the sixth and final time.

> The morning before, I had that feeling again that something was going to happen but I didn't know what, so I was really leery all that day. We got up on a mountain and just started digging in when the Germans counterattacked. I dropped my shovel, grabbed my rifle, sent my ammo carrier after more machine gun ammo, and got where I could see the Germans firing. My gunner could not see over the brush to see his targets. I told him where to shoot and counted twelve German machine guns that were firing over our heads. We stopped six or seven guns from firing. I looked back and seen the riflemen running back, so our machine gun section was all alone. To the right of us, M Company had two water-cooled machine guns and were firing at the Germans. The gun I was with run out of ammo so we fired our rifles and hand guns. Things quieted down so I went to the other gun, twenty-five yards to our left, to see how much ammo they had. A German seen the tree I crawled behind and shot me in the arm. It jolted every bone in my body and rolled me over on my back.

One of Williams's men then killed the German.

"I got set up and blood was running out of my sleeve. They said to get to the medics and get bandaged up. I went back to the company CP and told the captain that the riflemen had pulled back and the machine gun section was up there by themselves and out of ammo." While an aid man at the CP tended to Williams's wound, the captain directed the platoon sergeant to get his men back on the line and ordered more ammunition brought up to the machine guns. Rather than wait for the litter bearers to come up that night, Williams and another soldier who had been wounded in the head decided to walk down the mountain to the aid station. On the way down, and in spite of his injuries, Williams helped some tankers get a tank out of a ditch. Then it was on to the aid station, where surgeons set his broken arm in a cast. Later, at the hospital, Williams declined a general anesthesia so he could watch the doctors sew up his wound.[23]

• • •

In early November, plans for the Seventh Army's attempt to crack the German defenses at the Saverne Gap in the High Vosges and advance on Strasbourg and the Rhein were formulated. Here the Germans were numerically weaker, their morale low, and their defensive positions well constructed but too far apart to be mutually supporting. Brooks's VI Corps, which would initiate the Seventh Army attack on 12 November by hitting the German line in mountainous country along the Meurthe River between Baccarat and Raon L'Etape. The XV Corps, under Major General Wade H. Haislip, would lead the main assault the following day, driving for Sarrebourg and then farther on to Phalsbourg and Saverne, to the northwest of Strasbourg. It was hoped that the combined, two-corps thrust would drive a wedge between the German First and Nineteenth Armies and open the door to southwest Germany.[24]

On 8 November, the 45th was detached from VI Corps control, pulled out of the line, and given time to rest and recuperate at Bains-les-Bains for the upcoming fight in which it would surely play a major part. The 45th had been at the head of the Seventh Army drive for eighty-six continuous days, during which time it had bagged nearly 11,000 prisoners of war.[25]

The Seventh Army's assault went off like clockwork on 12 November, with VI Corps units, led by the 100th Infantry Division in its first major combat engagement, slicing through the German defenses like a well-honed rapier.[26]

The Thunderbirds' respite lasted only until the twenty-second, when the division was alerted for movement back to the front and assigned to Haislip's XV Corps to assault the enemy entrenched in strong positions in the Lower Vosges Mountains, an area that bristled with the guns and turrets of the Maginot Line—the extensive defensive positions that had been built by the French in the 1930s to keep the Germans out of Alsace-Lorraine but had been in German hands since 1940. The 45th was ordered to attack the Maginot forts at Mutzig and help the 3rd Division break through a mountain pass from Saint-Die to Schirmeck. For once, the 45th was not required to be the spear point of the advance, but the drive was anything but easy. Following behind the French 2nd Armored Division, the 45th assaulted the fortifications at Mutzig, taking them after three days of extremely heavy fighting. Grinding slowly forward against pockets of resistance in numerous mountain villages, the Thunderbirds continued to meet and overcome the enemy's best efforts to stop them.

In this, the Alsace region of France, most of the towns have German names: Mietesheim, Zinswiller, Gumbrechtshoffen, Rothbach, Bitschhof-

Major General Robert T. Frederick, who created and led the 1st Special Service Force ("The Devil's Brigade"), assumed command of the 45th Division in December 1944. (Courtesy of 45th Infantry Division Archives)

fen, and Oberbronn, to name but a few—reflecting a time when, following the Franco-Prussian War of 1870, it became German territory. Stripped from Germany following its defeat in the First World War, the provinces of Alsace and Lorraine were reannexed by Hitler in 1940. Most of the residents of the area spoke German as well as French and were subject to conscription into the Reich's armed forces. The enemy troops holed up in the villages, forests, and hills of Alsace fought back with all the fury and determination of men defending their homeland. German mortars, rockets, artillery, and small-arms and automatic weapons fire were poured on the GIs, and the men of the 45th—including the division's commander—continued to become casualties. On the thirtieth, Major General William Eagles was wounded when his jeep detonated a mine; on 3 December, the division's reins were taken over by one of World War II's most colorful and enigmatic individuals—Major General Robert T. Frederick who, at thirty-seven, also became the youngest division commander in the U.S. Army.[27]

With his mustache and slight build, the handsome, soft-spoken Frederick reminded some of a bank clerk and others of a movie star. But there was never any question about his ability to lead men in combat, for he had created one of World War II's toughest and most brazen commando units—the combined American-Canadian 1st Special Service Force known as "The Devil's Brigade." In the Force's secret Montana training camp, Frederick personally supervised a rigorous physical fitness program that made Airborne and Ranger training look soft by comparison. Every man in the Force became a parachutist, skier, expert marksman, and skilled knife fighter; even the chaplain was required to qualify on the pistol and carbine ranges. Frederick, a West Pointer (class of 1928), apparently did not know the meaning of the word "fear." Wounded nine times (the last two times on 4 June, on the outskirts of Rome), he was a charismatic leader who instantly inspired trust and respect in all who served under him. His ability to go without sleep was legendary, and he never asked his men to do anything that he himself would not do. While in charge of the Force, Frederick frequently led deadly patrols deep into enemy territory and shared every hardship and danger with his men. Churchill once called him "the greatest fighting general of all time," and he brought this same esprit de corps to the 45th.[28]

The split of the German First and Nineteenth Armies had been achieved, and Major General Jacques Le Clerc's French 2nd Armored Division, the first Allied division to enter Paris, rolled into Strasbourg on 23 November, securing the city after two days of brutal combat.[29] During the month of November, Seventh Army had captured 23,623 prisoners and showed no signs of stopping. But that was before Seventh Army reached the French-German border. [30]

The officers of the 45th looked at their maps and did not like what they saw in their assigned area of operations. Before them lay a nightmarish honeycomb of small villages, thickly wooded hills, snowy mountains, and swift, icy streams. If they ever made it through this maze, which gave all the advantages to the defender, they would then be faced with the concrete-and-steel German-held fortifications of both the Maginot and Siegfried Lines. It was a daunting challenge.

In late November, the division began what would be its biggest test of sheer courage and endurance since Anzio. With the 157th on the left, the 179th in the center, and the 180th on the right, the division moved forward into an area heavily infested with the compressed German army the Thunderbirds had been chasing since August. On 1 December, the men of the 157th, attempting to move from Ingwiller to their objective at Niederbronn-les-Bains, ran into determined enemy resistance at Zinswiller. It took three days to finally overcome the opposition. The 157th then moved on and attacked the German defenders inside Niederbronn but made little headway until the ninth, when the town finally fell to O'Brien's regiment.

While the 157th was heavily engaged, the other two Thunderbird regiments had crossed the Moder River and taken Ingwiller and Kindwiller after much hard fighting and many casualties. The 179th and 180th were then required to engage in more intense combat in the villages of Engwiller and Mietesheim. After a daylong battle, the 179th took Engwiller and crossed the Zintzel River, but the 180th was up to its collective neck in trouble at Mietesheim. After taking the lower half of the town house by house, the 3rd Battalion, 180th, was forced out by a counterattack of tanks and infantry on 1 December. The village fell to the 3rd Battalion the next day, but not before many young Americans had been killed or wounded. The battle for Mertzwiller on 5 December was even tougher; units from the nearby U.S. 103rd Division, on the night of 7–8 December, were called on to relieve the 180th, which was battered from days of nonstop fighting. Pausing to catch their breath, the men of the 45th steeled themselves for the ordeal to come.[31]

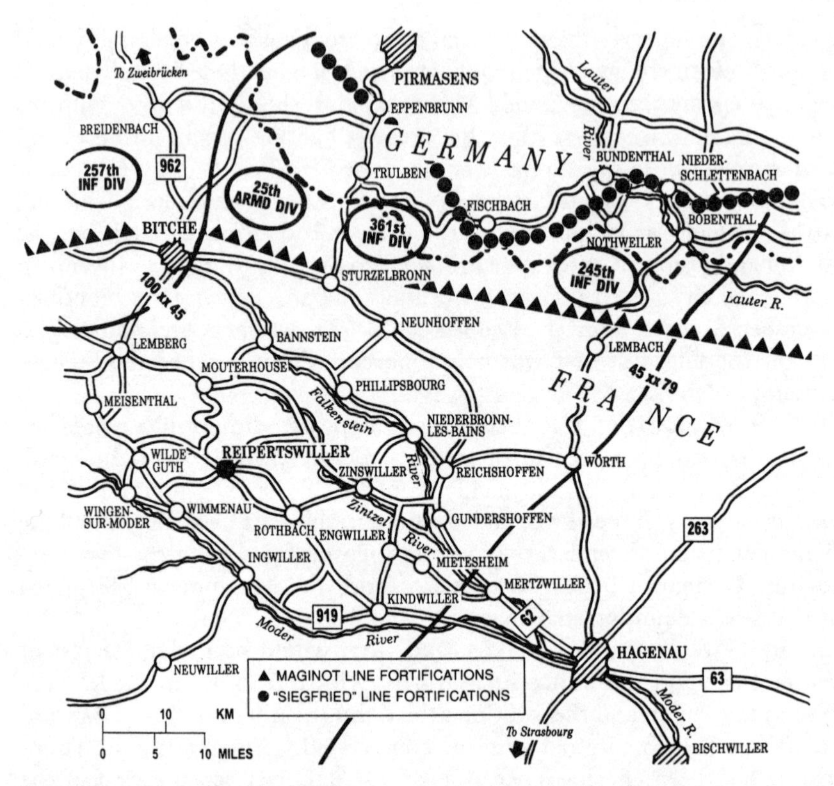

MAP 12.4 Reipertswiller Area
December 1944–January 1945—Rugged country northwest of Strasbourg where the Germans occupied the French Maginot Line as well as their own formidable Siegfried Line became the scene of much bloody fighting as the 6th SS-Gebirgs (Mountain) Division smashed into the Thunderbirds. (Positions approximate)

On 12 December, the 45th, along with the rest of Patch's Army, was on the doorstep of Hitler's Reich, at the towns of Lembach and Wingen in the heart of the Maginot Line's Lauter Fortified Region. The two towns quickly fell to the Thunderbirds and, on 15 December, the 45th became the first Seventh Army unit to set foot inside the German homeland. The next day, the 45th and 103rd Divisions together led XV Corps into Germany. Trailing, and to their right, were the 79th Infantry and 14th Armored Divisions. Although there was a weary exhilaration in the air, everyone knew that no matter how fanatical the enemy defense had been up to this point, it was nothing compared to what would happen once they entered the sacred *Vaterland*.[32]

At first probing the German defenses with strong patrols, the 45th soon discovered that the days of the German Army conducting fighting withdrawals were over. The Germans had fallen back to their border fortifications they called the *Westwall* (which the Yanks and Tommies called the Siegfried Line), which stretched like a concrete snake from the Swiss border, past France, Luxembourg, and Belgium, to terminate in Holland. The *Westwall* was to Germany what the Maginot Line was to France—a daunting defensive line that only the most daring or foolhardy would attempt to penetrate. The key to the Siegfried Line defenses was the bunker. Thousands of them—most of which were twenty-one feet wide, eighteen feet high, forty-two feet deep, with multiple levels, reinforced concrete walls, and ceilings up to nine feet thick—stretched north and south as far as the eye could see. Each bunker was placed in relatively close proximity to those on either side of it in order for them to be mutually supporting. Each bunker had well-sited embrasures, or firing ports, for machine guns or 37mm anti-tank guns to ensure interlocking fire with the neighboring bunker. Below ground, a network of storage rooms, sleeping quarters, and even kitchens and mess halls was designed to provide a safe, comfortable haven for the troops manning the miniforts. Outside, smaller pillboxes and a system of fighting trenches that connected one position with another were arranged behind vast fields of mines and barbed wire. Behind the fighting positions, additional bunkers existed for housing supplies, equipment, vehicles, and even reserve troops.

To keep armor and other vehicles at bay, miles of anti-tank ditches and squat, concrete pylons, known as "dragon's teeth," were constructed in front of the bunkers. For the attacker, the whole setup was designed to be fiendishly difficult and deadly. But the system was far from impregnable, provided the attackers were well-stocked with courage. Hundreds of miles to the north, the Siegfried Line had already been penetrated several times in several places. In September, the 28th Infantry Division had punched through above Luxembourg, followed shortly by the 4th Infantry Division. South of Aachen, in the Hürtgen Forest, American troops from the 9th Infantry Division had made a shallow penetration in October. At Saarlautern, in early December, the 95th Infantry Division poked through, as did the 90th Division nearby. Numerous other divisions—British as well as American—tried and failed. And each attempt to break through, whether successful or not, had cost the attackers hundreds, even thousands, of casualties.[33]

When it became the 45th's turn to attempt breaching the *Westwall,* the GIs did it in a remarkably simple, methodical manner. First, all the heavy firepower that could be mustered was hurled at a single bunker and its neighboring pillboxes and trenches. While this bombardment kept the defenders' heads down, the infantry crawled forward and took the communications trenches under mortar and rifle fire. Machine gun fire was also directed at the bunker embrasures to keep the enemy away from the openings. While all this was taking place, some brave soul, loaded down with white phosphorus grenades, would attempt to crawl on top of the bunker and drop a grenade down the ventilation shaft. This usually resulted in the survivors rushing outside, their uniforms aflame, where they were "hosed down" by American gunners. Once a single bunker fell to the Thunderbirds, the Yanks used it as a starting point to attack neighboring bunkers from the flank, enlarging the initial hole in the defensive line. In this manner, the 180th's 3rd Battalion, in December, managed to knock out seven bunkers along a front of 1,700 yards and had penetrated the *Westwall* to a depth of 1,200 yards.[34]

Once across the French-German border, the 157th and 180th Regiments headed for their assigned objectives: the towns of Bundenthal and Nieder-Schlettenbach and the high ground around them. To impede the Americans, the Germans dammed a small stream, known as the Lauter River, near Nieder-Schlettenbach. As the Thunderbirds approached their objectives, they were faced with a flooded area that stretched from just north of Nieder-Schlettenbach to just south of Bundenthal. The effort to cross this watery obstacle did not go well. Intense fire from pillboxes forced back an attempt by the 2nd Battalion, 157th, to cross with the aid of boats and by wading in freezing, chest-deep water. The 1st Battalion's move against Bundenthal, above the flooding, met with initial success but soon turned sour. On 18 December, only a single platoon from C Company managed to make it into the village via an anti-tank ditch and insert itself into a few houses on the far side of the Lauter. The platoon, however, was soon cut off from the rest of the company, which was driven to ground short of the stream by German fire.

G Company, 157th, attempting to outflank the resistance that had stopped the 2nd Battalion's previous effort, was unable to cross the Lauter. Two platoons from G Company, led by the company's executive officer, First Lieutenant Carl Byas, managed to reach the town and occupy two houses but were then cut off. Systematically attacking the stranded platoons, the Germans killed a number of men, including the two platoon commanders, First Lieutenant Hermes A. Clark, Jr., and Second Lieutenant William Sheard. When the 157th was ordered to pull back, the platoons in Bundenthal were given up for lost. Early on 23 December, Sergeant William Alter and Private Albert Guriel, from one of the cutoff G Company platoons, volunteered to attempt to infiltrate back to friendly lines; they were successful and reported personally to General Frederick that the trapped platoons were basically intact but unable to hold out much longer. The historian Hugh Foster wrote, "Under cover of a 1,000-round artillery barrage on the night of 23 December, a large patrol moved close to the town. Then a smaller patrol, consisting of Medic Corporal Raymond Dwyer, Privates first class Edgar Ingleton and Joseph Long and led by Technical Sergeant Warren Haynes of B Company, moved forward, contacted the trapped men, and led them to safety.". Haynes was awarded the Distinguished Service Cross for this action, and Alter and Guriel both earned Silver Stars.[35]

The bitter combat along the Siegfried Line took its toll, and the mid-December weather was predictably miserable. Only when they evicted the occupants of a bunker or fortified house were a privileged few GIs able to get in out of the elements; the vast majority were forced to exist in icy foxholes, with frostbite and immersion foot adding to their woes. For most of the 45th, as well as for the other infantry divisions along the eighty-four-mile front line, Christmas 1944 was spent in frozen holes in the ground with frequent deliveries of highly explosive gifts from the Germans.

Meanwhile, farther north, Model's Army Group B had launched Hitler's last-gasp offensive in the west through the "impenetrable" Ardennes Forest—a counteroffensive that later became known as the "Battle of the Bulge." Eisenhower ordered all Allied offensive actions to temporarily cease until the crisis of the "Bulge" could be dealt with. To counter the enemy threat, elements of XII Corps—the right flank of Patton's Third Army, which had been on XV Corps's left—were pulled out of the line and rushed up to the Ardennes to hit the southern flank of the German salient. To cover the gap left by the departure of XII Corps, Sixth Army Group moved the 103rd Infantry Division, which had been to the right of the 45th, to plug the hole to the 45th's left. The Thunderbirds were then directed to spread out and take over responsibility for the 103rd's former positions.

The units in the American Sixth Army Group were ordered to give ground in the event of strong enemy attacks. On the basis of this order, Truscott directed VI Corps, including the 45th, to pull back to more easily defended terrain, despite the fact that the division was systematically reducing the Siegfried Line fortifications. The Thunderbirds were incredulous when they found themselves ordered out of Germany and trucked back to France to a place that had been taken by the Americans weeks earlier. The reason for the order soon became clear. The German First Army had massed seven divisions in the Lower Vosges Mountains above Bitche and Bliesbrück for another major counteroffensive, code-named Operation *Nordwind,* against Seventh Army's extended front. German objectives were many: destroy American forces in the Lower Vosges, regain control of the Saverne Gap, and eventually link up with elements of Nineteenth Army, which was to drive westward from Gambsheim while other German forces, virtually encircled in the "Colmar Pocket," would attempt to break out to the north. One of the enemy forces above Bitche was the 12th *Gebirgsjäger* (Mountain) Regiment of SS *Gruppenführer* Karl Brenner's 6th SS *Gebirgs* Division. On 30 December 1944, after a long trip from northern Finland and Norway, which had begun a month and a half earlier, the first elements of the mountain regiment assembled in the wooded Pfalz region on the French-German border between Pirmasens and Eppenbrunn, where they were attached to the 361st *Volksgrenadier* Division.[36]

The mountain division was an excellent, battle-hardened unit with considerable skill and experience in harsh winter combat conditions.[37] The historian Keith Bonn called the 6th SS "undoubtedly the best German division in the upcoming fight for the Low Vosges; in fact, it was probably the best German infantry formation on the entire western front in early January 1945."[38] Felix Sparks would later call the enemy unit "the best men we ever ran into, extremely aggressive, and impossible to capture. There was no driving them out, for they fought 'til they were killed."[39]

To prepare for the expected German onslaught, the 45th was being beefed up. Four additional regiments—from the 70th, 79th, and 103rd Infantry Divisions along with the 14th Armored Division—plus supporting units from other divisions would be attached to the Thunderbirds, and General Frederick found himself in temporary command of twenty-six infantry and ten artillery battalions. The division would require all this added strength, for in its sector of responsibility, which stretched northeast from Rosteig to Nieder-Schlettenbach, the Germans were preparing to unleash against the Thunderbirds the ferocious attack of a desperate army with nothing left to lose.

The coordinated German assaults began on the last day of 1944 against the western side of the Seventh Army line, south and southeast of Sarreguemines. The German attacks did not go well, and *Generaloberst* Johannes Blaskowitz, commanding Army Group G, decided to shift the point of attack farther east, where some success was being reported at the seam between the 44th and 100th Infantry Divisions, southeast of Wingen-sur-Moder. Further probes explored the area between the 100th and 45th Divisions, an area held by a Corps unit known as Task Force Hudelson. The 275th Infantry Regiment of the 70th Infantry Division, attached to the 45th, was on that flank and was scheduled to relieve Task Force Hudelson. Before the relief could be effected, however, the Germans struck hard, virtually destroying the task force. On 2 January, the 45th faced an all-out German effort against its left flank. Unless they were stopped, the Germans could drive into the Alsatian Plain, where they could spread anywhere to cause havoc behind the lines of the American and French troops.

On 3 January, with fighting taking place along most of the Seventh Army front, the 12th SS-*Gebirgsjäger* Regiment hit the 179th and remnants of Task Force Hudelson at Wingen-sur-Moder, taking hundreds of prisoners and pushing the Yanks back to Zittersheim, some two miles to the rear.[40] This German advance, however, created a salient that enabled the 179th's 3rd Battalion and the 1st Battalion from the attached 313th Infantry Regiment, 79th Infantry Division, to nearly surround the enemy force. With the German mountain troops essentially trapped in a bag, the 70th Division's 276th Infantry Regiment moved up from the southwest to engage the enemy in Wingen-sur-Moder. Meanwhile, the 180th put a lid on the bag and held the line while the 12th SS-*Gebirgsjäger* Regiment, trapped in the village, fought for its life. During the night of 6–7 January, despite being surrounded on all sides, a number of the mountain troops managed to deflate the bag and infiltrated back to German-held territory.[41]

White phosphorus shells exploding on the fringes of Reipertswiller, France. (Courtesy of 45th Infantry Division Archives)

On 11 January, the Germans returned, crashing in force through the wooded hills of the Bitche and Bannstein Forests and launching a heavy attack against the Thunderbirds. The 2nd and 3rd Battalions of the 180th were forced to pull back 600 yards under the weight of the assault. Their unexpected withdrawal uncovered the left flank of the 1st Battalion, 314th Regiment, attached to the 45th from the 79th Division, and forced that battalion to abandon two strategic hills, numbers 343 and 388, above Reipertswiller. To fill the dangerous gap caused by the withdrawal of the 1st Battalion, 314th, Frederick ordered Lieutenant Colonel Lawrence Brown's 2nd Battalion, 157th, to leave its relatively undisturbed position on the division's right flank to the Reipertswiller area and launch an immediate counterattack and regain the two hills. Brown's men struck enemy positions on the night of the eleventh and the next day endured repeated heavy shellings and fought off continual attempts by the SS to push them off the hills. In spite of being completely frozen and exhausted, Brown's men were relieved that night by the 1st Battalion, 314th Regiment, and ordered to relieve the 2nd Battalion, 276th Regiment, northeast of town. Moving back to Reipertswiller before dawn, the worn-out Thunderbirds collapsed in barns, cellars, doorways, or wherever they could find space to sleep. Their rest was brief, however, as Brown, fearing the 2nd Battalion, 276th, had given its positions away by transmitting uncoded radio messages and was abandoning its defenses, awoke his battered battalion and rushed it back to the front along Hills 328 and

415, where they bolstered the line that was sporadically manned by a very disorganized 2nd Battalion, 276th.[42]

On the frigid morning of the fourteenth, the seriously depleted 1st and 3rd Battalions of the 157th crossed the line of departure in an attempt to take the snow-covered mountainous terrain north of Reipertswiller. The two battalions had not gone far when enemy artillery and mortar rounds began saturating the area, hitting the units with unusual ferocity. Machine gun fire from emplacements hidden in the thick woods ripped into the Thunderbirds, who had been moving through the woods in a column of companies rather than battalions abreast, and the cries of the wounded mingled with the concussion of exploding shells. Artillery, bursting high in the snow-blanketed trees, brought tree limbs and hot metal fragments down on men who huddled helplessly in their hastily dug holes. Whenever a man unwisely showed himself, the Germans cut him down with a burst of fire.[43] Felix Sparks, commanding the 3rd Battalion, 157th, vividly recalled the fury of the German fire: "It was the worst beating we ever took from terrific, concentrated artillery barrages, and that includes Anzio. Men were unable to get out of their holes, even without enemy infantry in front of them."[44] From 0830 that morning until well into the night, the enemy poured such sustained artillery fire into the 157th that it seemed the German gunners were bent on exhausting every ammunition dump in the Reich.

The next morning, Sparks's battalion was again ordered forward and assigned to take two hills. By noon on the fifteenth, I, K, and L Companies had reached their objectives without sustaining heavy casualties, but the successful drive had created a salient that stabbed 1,500 yards into the enemy's lines and the companies found themselves being hammered from three sides. B Company, from Ralph Krieger's 1st Battalion, trying to move up to protect the 3rd Battalion's right flank, took a ridgeline but was then forced back to its start line by heavy fire. Around 1700 hours that evening, the Germans came hard and they came in force. The Thunderbirds, defending the hills, took a terrible pounding. One sergeant in K Company, 157th, remarked, "It was the worst mess I ever saw. Dead and wounded Americans were lying all over the area. We had no way of evacuating the wounded, much less the dead, until night." The Germans also suffered; another soldier reported, "Enemy dead were piled up like cordwood in front of our positions."[45] On Sparks's left flank, the 1st Battalion of the 315th Regiment was ordered to break off its supporting attack and prepare to return to its parent division, the 79th. Sparks and his men found themselves in a dangerous position, with no relief in sight. It appeared no food or ammunition could be delivered to the 3rd Battalion, and very few of the wounded could be brought out. Late that night, however, resupply parties and medical evacuation teams managed to reach the battalion and perform their vital missions. A number of wounded were evacuated, but then the Germans tightened the noose around the Thunderbirds.[46]

With the arrival of the SS Mountain troops, pressure on the 3rd Battalion positions increased and remained heavy. Beginning early on the sixteenth, Sparks's battalion was hit continuously with infantry assaults, rockets, mortars, and long-range tank fire, but the Thunderbirds refused to yield. Indeed, in its virtually isolated state, the 3rd Battalion had nowhere to go and nothing to do except absorb the punishment. Later that afternoon and all through the night, SS mountain troops, with orders to take the American-held hills, moved into the high ground in front of and on both flanks of Sparks's men. Although the Germans began to send additional troops into the valley behind the hills in an effort to surround the 3rd Battalion, one company each from the 1st and 2nd Battalions managed to link up with the 3rd Battalion to reinforce the hilltop positions. Around midnight on 16–17 January, however, the Germans cut off the men on the hills from further physical contact with the rest of the regiment.

When the Germans sealed off the resupply and evacuation routes, seventeen gravely wounded soldiers remained on the hills. From midnight on the sixteenth through the twentieth, only the barest minimum of ammunition, rations, and medical supplies reached the stranded companies, and no wounded could be brought out. The less seriously wounded and those subsequently hit were left to fend for themselves. If hit, a man simply had to hunker down in his water-filled foxhole and perform his own first aid. The more seriously wounded men were gathered in other holes while the medics treated them with the ever-dwindling medical supplies.

The SS assault now turned its fury on G Company, 157th. According to Hugh Foster, "G Company was reinforced by one platoon of E Company and by at least one platoon of heavy machine guns from H Company. When G Company was overrun on the morning of 18 January, virtually everything was lost, including all the machine guns, the whole of the E Company platoon, and all but about twenty of the G Company men." Attempts by other 45th Division units to reach Sparks's entrapped men ended in failure.[47]

Bernard Fleming, a squad leader in the Anti-Tank Platoon, 3rd Battalion, 157th, tried to reach the cut-off companies.

> We were supposed to fight up the mountain and get to the troops who were trapped on top. Then the platoon got orders to pull back, but the orders never got to me because most of the fellows in between were either killed or wounded. When the others pulled back, it left us wide open all around and we were trapped up there in a little hole in the woods. I sent two men out to get help—one at a time. The first one I sent out was shot through the ankle. The next one went out and got killed. So I told the rest of the fellows to take care of the one who got hit in the ankle and I went out to get help. I made it back to our lines and told my platoon leader about the men who were trapped. He told me to tell Colonel Sparks, who then took a tank and went to get the wounded out.[48]

On the eighteenth, Sparks called for tank support from the 191st Tank Battalion. Only two Shermans responded. With the snow flying and bullets pinging off the tanks' steel skin, Sparks, firing the machine gun mounted on the tank commanded by Sergeant Virgil Zeek, directed the armor up a steep mountain trail in an attempt to relieve the encircled companies. The first tank slid sideways on the icy road and was knocked out. Sparks leaped from the second Sherman, dashed across the snow-covered ground, and dragged three wounded soldiers back to it, one at a time. The astonished Germans were so in awe of Sparks's act of bravery that they held their fire while he hauled the wounded men onto the tank, which reversed down the narrow trail to the aid station.[49] Sparks's valiant attempt to save the encircled companies failed, and even a follow-up attack the next day by the rest of the regiment, along with the 2nd Battalion, 179th, and all of the artillery firepower in the division, could not break the SS unit's iron grip.[50]

Early on 20 January, with shell, shot, and snow still filling the air, the 2nd Battalion of the 411th Infantry Regiment (a 103rd Division unit attached to the 45th specifically for the purpose of coming to the aid of the 3rd Battalion, 157th) attacked the Germans three times and were three times repulsed. Sparks's battalion appeared doomed. That night, the Americans tried to break out to the rear, but the enemy had completely surrounded the snowy hills. One of the trapped men, Private first class Benjamin Melton, reported, "We attacked toward the rear, trying to break through the German line that separated us from the rest of the regiment. Ammunition was scarce but we made progress until the enemy artillery zeroed in on us. Some of the men were blown to bits and I saw one officer get a direct hit and just disappear."

Seeing that escape was temporarily futile, Melton returned to his hole. The Germans demanded the Americans surrender, but Melton had already heard about the massacre at Malmedy (where, on 17 December, during the Germans' Ardennes offensive, over a hundred unarmed American POWs were lined up in a snowy field near this Belgian village and machine-gunned; only a handful survived). "I didn't want to stay there and be killed in cold blood. Together with Private Walter Bruce and another fellow whose name I don't remember, I set out to try to get back to our lines. The other man was killed by machine-gun fire but Bruce and I made it back to the battalion CP." Melton also reported that at least 75 percent of the 3rd Battalion had been killed, wounded, or taken prisoner.[51]

Melton and Bruce were the lucky ones. The 157th Regiment and the units attached to it during the battle suffered losses of 158 killed, 426 captured, and some 600 wounded or evacuated due to injuries and illness. Seven company commanders and some thirty platoon leaders were killed or captured during the weeklong struggle. Most of the losses were inflicted on the five surrounded rifle companies (C, G, I, K, and L), but every unit assigned or attached to the regiment lost men. Hugh Foster added, "Representatives of other units were also on those hills. Men from all three battalion heavy weapons companies (D, H, and M) were lost, too, including heavy machine gunners and heavy mortar forward observers. Also lost were forward observer parties from the 158th Field Artillery Battalion and the regimental Cannon Company, medics from the regimental Medical Detachment, one platoon of E Company, and three tank crews from the 191st Tank Battalion." The battle of Reipertswiller was the most devastating single loss in the history of the 157th Regiment.[52]

• • •

Despite the heavy casualties, the 45th held the line with steely determination and stopped one German assault after another. A captured German general later said, "The Forty-fifth Infantry Division beats any outfit that I have ever seen. We did not expect them to show up in front of our attack. . . . The Forty-fifth met our attacks not with counter-attacks but with *attacks*. In fact, we were never really able to get a big attack going again after we met the Forty-fifth north of Wildenguth, Wingen, and Reipertswiller. We were kept off balance all of the time."[53]

The battered 45th was relieved in late January by the recently arrived 42nd ("Rainbow") Division and withdrew from the front; it took more than 1,000 replacements to bring the division back up to a strength allowing it again to be considered combat ready. Ten days later, it moved back to the front near Wimmenau, but by then things had quieted down considerably. Like most lulls, this one wouldn't last. Patch's Seventh Army was ordered to make an all-out thrust into Germany in the vicinity of Saarbrücken. Training, especially in techniques of river crossing and "bunker busting," was stepped up. Once again, the division, resting in the vicinity of Sarreguemines, was directed to prepare to punch through a section of the Siegfried Line, this time east of the Blies River. H hour for the new offensive was at 0100 hours on 15 March 1945. The 45th, back under XV Corps control, was moved into the front line between elements of XII Corps on its left and the 3rd Division on its right.[54]

In the darkness of a cold, March morning, the Seventh Army attack began. Leading the assault, four companies of the 180th moved across the Blies in small boats, and shortly thereafter the 120th Engineers threw two footbridges over the river and the rest of the regiment followed. The 157th and 179th also crossed successfully.

A week earlier, farther north, the Yanks had captured a bridge over the Rhein at Remagen and were driving hard to the east; now it was Patch's turn and he hoped to be crossing Germany's most important waterway soon. As expected, the Germans put up a strong initial fight and then pulled back their outer defensive positions in front of the Siegfried Line fortifications. On the seventeenth, the Thunderbirds reached the bunkers and pillboxes and dragon's teeth, and just as they had done farther south in the closing weeks of 1944, they began systematically to eliminate them. As the 157th's history records,

> Then the men crawled out of their holes and attacked the world's greatest defensive fortification. Artillery was behind them, tanks were with them, planes were over them, but the riflemen felt naked before the fire of those concrete walls. They had flamethrowers, bazookas, demolitions, grenades, and every automatic weapon, but their main tools were speed, courage, and teamwork. Speed and courage in braving the fire to cross the anti-tank ditches, to crawl through the Dragon's Teeth and assault the pillboxes. Teamwork, beautiful in its precision, to work close enough to apertures to toss in grenades, bazooka fire, or the tongue of death from the flamethrowers. . . . If a man hesitates, if a man falters, if a tank pulls back, a lot of men die. But there was no faltering, no pulling back here. Men lost lives and limbs in that attack, but from its start there was never a doubt of its success, and the enemy must have realized that as he saw them come. No concrete ever poured could stop these men.[55]

On 18 March occurred one of the most extraordinary acts of heroism ever performed by any American soldier during the war. A complex of enemy bunkers and trenches blocked the 180th Regiment's advance, and every man knew it would be hell trying to break through the Siegfried Line at this point near the town of Nieder-Wurzbach. A hill, designated Hill 366, and six bunkers all afforded the enemy excellent fields of fire and a commanding view of the only approach route the 180th could take. The first crack in the line occurred early on the eighteenth when F Company managed to occupy one of the bunkers and establish its CP there. During the night of 17–18 March, the enemy tried several times to dislodge the GIs with fierce counterattacks, but all had been beaten back. But the GIs could not move forward because of the high volume of fire being directed at them by the Germans in the neighboring bunkers and trenches. Whenever a man showed himself, he became a magnet for lead. The company was pinned about as flat as a company could be pinned. F Company's commander, First Lieutenant Jack L. Treadwell, however, was determined that the situation was about to change.

Approaching Staff Sergeant Hewitt Wilson, Treadwell announced, "Get your platoon ready—the company is going to take that hill." But before Wilson could gather his men, Treadwell was gone. Shortly before 1700 hours, with darkness falling, the Alabama-born, Oklahoma-raised Treadwell, armed only with a Thompson submachine gun and some hand grenades, set out on a one-man mission to eliminate the enemy strongholds.

Sergeant Wilson later commented, "The Jerries were in pillboxes and trenches further up the hill and, because there was absolutely no cover, it was impossible to stick your head out of the trench without getting shot at." Near the CP, Treadwell found the commander of a Sherman tank. Treadwell's battalion commander, Lieutenant Colonel John W. Kaine, also observed the lieutenant's actions. He wrote, "I heard him yell to a tank driver near the CP, 'C'mon, let's go, tanker!' After much preparation, the tank crew did get started and followed him, but were never closer than fifty yards behind."

A member of Treadwell's company, First Lieutenant Oscar Rudner, said, "I noticed Lieutenant Treadwell leading a tank, making his way toward Pillbox E, which was about 100 yards from the company CP. He carried a Tommy gun. There was no cover or concealment available to him along his route of approach. Lieutenant Treadwell paid no attention to the rifle and machine-gun fire which was coming at him from the north and northwest. He kept walking into what seemed to be certain death, until he reached Pillbox E. Here he threw a grenade into the firing slit, and stuck his Tommy gun inside. After a couple of bursts, out came four Krauts with their hands up. One of these was the German officer who was in charge of the pillboxes on the hill."

Sending the German captives back to his lines with their hands held high, Treadwell started up the hill toward the next position, designated Pillbox D. The ground around him was churned up with the impact of bullets hitting as every enemy rifleman and machine gunner within range focused his attention on him. Incredibly, all missed. Spraying his Thompson around the landscape, Treadwell continued on and flushed the enemy out of Pillbox D, sending them down to the American lines.

Rudner continued, "Lieutenant Treadwell then cut right over the crest of the hill toward Pillbox F. This particular box had been giving my platoon the most trouble as we advanced toward our objective. Lieutenant Treadwell approached it from the flank, and was again the target of sniper and machine-gun fire from further up the hill. Without hesitating, he attacked this pillbox with his Tommy gun and hand grenades and took the pillbox with several more prisoners."

Sergeant Wilson noted, "He could have taken cover in a connecting trench and made his way slowly, but instead he chose to go straight toward the pillbox about fifty to seventy-five yards away. Again he was fired at from the front and both flanks. With all the lead that was flying, I don't see how he made it without being hit."

Treadwell noticed that his solo act was having a positive effect on the enemy—scores of them leaped from the trenches and disappeared over the hill. Despite enemy artillery now splattering around him, he headed for Pillboxes A, B, and C; overcame the resistance at each one; and motioned for the survivors to come out. In all, Lieutenant Treadwell took six concrete fortifications and captured eighteen to twenty prisoners single-handedly.

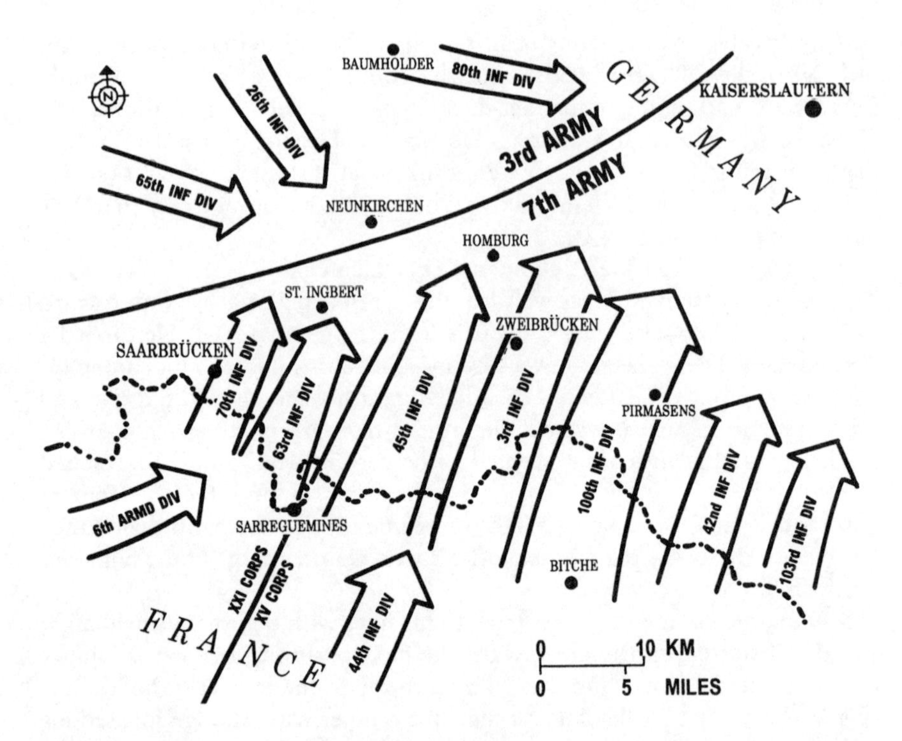

MAP 12.5 The Drive of XXI and XV Corps into Southwest Germany
15–21 March 1945—Patch's Seventh Army, on Patton's right flank, smashed through the Siegfried Line and knifed into the Pfalz (Palatinate) region of southwest Germany. The 45th formed the left flank of XV Corps. (Positions approximate)

And all without receiving a scratch. Treadwell's men now reacted to their leader's act of courage. They swarmed out of their trenches and began clearing the rest of the hill.

For his astounding act of bravery, Treadwell later received the Medal of Honor. The award, added to his Distinguished Service Cross, three awards of the Legion of Merit, the Silver Star medal, two Bronze Star medals for valor, four Purple Heart medals, and the French *Croix de Guerre,* made him the most decorated soldier in the 45th Division. More important, his one-man assault helped his company, and the division, break through the Siegfried Line.[56]

No less heroic was twenty-eight-year-old Corporal Edward G. Wilkin of C Company, 157th. On the same day that Lieutenant Treadwell was staging his one-man war, Wilkin was doing the same in the 157th's sector. With the rest of his platoon pinned down by the enemy firing from pillboxes, Wilkin rushed one pillbox after another despite the blizzard of bullets aimed at him, killing those inside with grenades and forcing those who wanted to live to surrender. Coming up against a thicket of barbed wire, Wilkin called for "snakes" and blasted a path through the wire. Like Treadwell, Wilkin became the focus of every rifleman, machine gunner, and mortarman in the area. It mattered not to him that the enemy was fighting from trenches or behind reinforced concrete walls—he went after any target of opportunity, even to the point of chasing German soldiers across an open field and into a trench.

When evening fell, the exhausted Thunderbird refused to rest, using his last bit of strength to distribute rations, water, and ammunition to the rest of his platoon. As Wilkin's citation reads,

> Hearing that a nearby company was suffering heavy casualties, he secured permission to guide litter bearers and assist them in evacuating the wounded. All that night he remained in the battle area on his mercy missions, and for the following two days he continued to remove casualties, venturing into enemy-held territory, scorning cover and braving devastating mortar and artillery bombardments. In three days he neutralized and captured six pillboxes single-handedly, killed at least nine Germans, took thirteen prisoners, aided in the capture of fourteen others, and saved many American lives by his fearless performance as a litter bearer.

Sadly, Wilkin did not live long enough to wear America's highest combat decoration; a month later, he was killed in action deep inside Germany. His was the only Medal of Honor awarded posthumously to a member of the division.[57]

• • •

By the nineteenth, after days of intense fighting and considerable casualties, Seventh Army was pouring into defenseless Germany, heading northeast toward Homburg, Zweibrücken, Kaiserslautern, Mannheim, and the Rhein, some one hundred miles away. On the twenty-third, the 45th, along with the 3rd Infantry Division, reached the west bank of the river north of the city of Worms and prepared to cross it. Early on the twenty-sixth, the 179th and 180th Regiments, in partnership with the 40th Engineer Combat Group, used the cover of darkness to make their crossing in small assault boats. At first, the crossing proceeded without incident, but then the Germans caught wind of what was happening and flayed the boat-bound Thunderbirds with everything they could muster. Casualties were heavy, but the two regiments established a beachhead on the far bank. The 157th crossed the Rhein later that day. The very heart of Germany was now open to the Allies.

Along with the entire American Army, the 45th Division dashed eastward across Germany, taking towns and prisoners as it rolled. White sur-

Men of the 180th Infantry Regiment marching through the ruins of a German city, oblivious to the shock of an elderly woman viewing her destroyed home. (Courtesy of U.S. Military History Institute)

render flags hung in profusion from windows where once the red, white, and black Nazi banners had proudly waved. The Germans in the path of the advancing armies knew the war was lost; there was little reason for further resistance. At least, that appeared to be the situation until the 45th reached the city of Aschaffenburg and its smaller neighbor, Schweinheim, located between Frankfurt and Würzburg. Here, a fanatical SS major named von Lambert decided to make a stand, and an officer's candidate school in Aschaffenburg gave the major a hard core of dedicated Nazis who would help stiffen the resistance.[58]

On the twenty-ninth, Sparks's 3rd Battalion, 157th, attacked Schweinheim and the battle was on. Street fighting is the bane of the infantryman's existence; each building becomes a bunker that must be knocked out by close-in fighting, streets and alleys become corridors of death, and each window hides a possible sniper. K and L Companies, stocked with new men after the debacle at Reipertswiller, were particularly hard hit by enemy counterattacks, which weren't conducted solely by military units; it was reported that even German women and children joined in the battle. As the

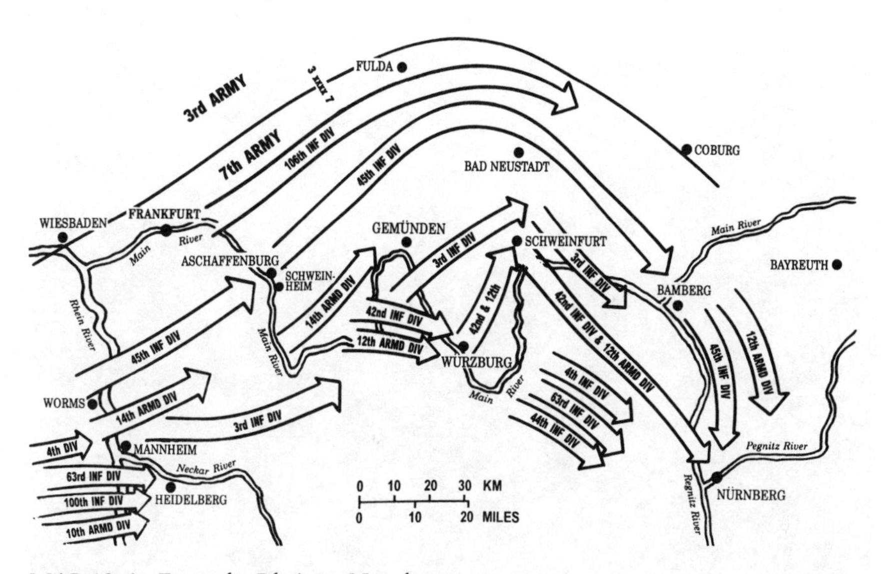

MAP 12.6 From the Rhein to Nürnberg
The Thunderbirds, moving rapidly on the Seventh Army's northern flank, crossed the Rhein on 26 March 1945, battled fiercely for Aschaffenburg and Schweinheim from 29 March to 6 April, captured Bamberg on 14 April, and attacked Nazidom's sacred city, Nürnberg, on 17 April. (Positions approximate)

45th Division history states, "Boys of sixteen and seventeen, thoroughly indoctrinated with the theory that it was glorious to seek death for the Fatherland, refused to surrender and had to be killed in their foxholes and entrenchments."[59] Only by pulverizing the city with artillery and aerial bombardment were the GIs able to advance. The battle continued throughout the thirtieth as men dashed through the rubble to wipe out pockets of immovable defenders. And Aschaffenburg still remained to be taken.

The defense of Aschaffenburg was unusually savage, even to Thunderbirds who thought they had witnessed about every brutish act imaginable. A number of civilians who tried to escape from the city were gunned down by their uniformed countrymen, and a German lieutenant who attempted to surrender to the Yanks was found hanging from a steel support above a shop, with a sign attached to his body that read, "Cowards and traitors hang!"[60] Captain Eddie Speairs, now the 157th's adjutant, flew over the city in an observation plane and dropped leaflets calling for the garrison's surrender—or else. The ultimatum was ignored and Aschaffenburg was reduced, over the next nine days, to a heap of rubble.[61] James Bird recalled one good thing that came out of the siege of Aschaffenburg: "We found a *Wehrmacht* warehouse filled with all kinds of wine, brandies, and liquors, and acquired a truck full, which lasted for months."[62]

Two American tanks blasting the stubborn defenders of Aschaffenburg, 27 March 1945. (Courtesy of 45th Infantry Division Archives)

The pursuit of the enemy continued—or rather, the drive into Germany's heartland, for there were few German units willing to be pursued or make a stand against the onrushing American Seventh Army, with the 45th Division on its left flank. The division continued in a northeasterly direction until, near Fulda, it abruptly changed direction and headed southeast toward Nürnberg. Town after town fell to the conquerors—Pfaffenhausen, Florsbach, Oberndorf, Mettgers, Schwarzenfels, and dozens more. The next major city encountered by the Thunderbirds was Bamberg, on the Main River, north of Nürnberg.

Bamberg was one of the most important population centers in this part of Germany. It had become a focal point for tens of thousands of wounded German soldiers, displaced civilians, and conscripted laborers. Vast food, ammunition, and supply dumps were located here, and the Thunderbirds even came across a trainload of some 1,500 Goliath miniature tanks in the marshaling yards. Most troubling of all were reports of another von Lambert–type of fanatical Nazi who had vowed to defend the city to the last man.

The 180th overcame stubborn resistance in Bamberg's northern suburbs and established a bridgehead over the Main on 12 April while the 3rd Infantry Division moved in from the south. German resistance stiffened, then faded. The GIs could be thankful that the promised fight to the last man did not materialize, but the 180th still killed or captured 2,100 enemy soldiers. On the twelfth, every American soldier was stunned to learn that his commander-in-chief, President Franklin D. Roosevelt, had died. But the war went on. By the fourteenth, Bamberg was declared secured. While the 180th mopped up, the 157th and 179th, along with the 3rd Division, prepared to swoop down on Nürnberg, Bavaria's second-largest city, which had a prewar population of 400,000.

At Nürnberg, in the 1930s, Hitler staged his huge Nazi party rallies. Hundreds of thousands of faithful supporters traveled from across Germany just to march in the parades, hear the speeches, and ride the wave of nationalism with which Hitler was raising Germany from the ashes of defeat in World War I, the ravages of a ruinous inflation, and the depths of the Great Depression. Here, in the ancient walled city that was once most famous as the home of the great artist Albrecht Dürer, Hitler, Göbbels, Hess, Streicher, and other high potentates of the Third Reich exhorted the masses to follow the swastika to glory and world domination. Now the seeds of hate and militarism that had been sown here a decade earlier had blossomed into a poisonous harvest that had doomed the evil regime.

Nürnberg was already a shambles by the time the 3rd and 45th arrived. Countless air raids had turned the once-beautiful medieval metropolis into a burned-out, unrecognizable charnel house. By 17 April, the Yanks had encircled the city and patrols entered it, again rooting out snipers and other pockets of resistance from each block, each ruined building, each cellar.

The Germans fought back fiercely with 88s, mortars, machine guns, and anti-aircraft weapons. American artillery and aircraft answered back, and every street was turned into a shooting gallery. The parts of Nürnberg that hadn't already been demolished by the months of Allied bombing were reduced to dust by the intense street fighting and the big guns from both sides that incessantly hammered each other at near point-blank range. The going was painfully slow for the 45th, but progress *was* being made. After five days of fighting, the Americans had gained the upper hand; the Thunderbirds had bagged nearly 10,000 prisoners and liberated an Allied POW camp that contained some 13,000 American and British soldiers. On the nineteenth, the 45th linked up with elements of the 3rd Division. The next day, Hitler's fifty-sixth birthday, organized resistance in Nürnberg came to an end. To celebrate, the dog-tired soldiers marched in a parade the next day in front of the Seventh Army commander, Alexander M. Patch, down the same streets where once Hitler's minions had proudly goose-stepped before their Führer.

The division hardly had time to savor its victory when new orders came down directing it on to Munich. On the twenty-second, the division mounted up in jeeps, trucks, tanks, tank destroyers, and any other vehicle that could carry troops and began a mad rush toward the enchanting city on the Isar River—the happy home of *Gemütlichkeit*—where Hitler and the Nazi Party got their start in 1923.

If the Thunderbirds thought their previous motorized dashes had been swift, nothing could compare with this one. Town after town flashed by, each festooned with white flags. Resistance was slight and half-hearted at best as thousands of demoralized German soldiers gave themselves up without a fight. The sense that the war was nearly over was very palpable. It was a great and glorious moment.

And then the 45th reached Dachau.[63]

13

To the Eternal Dark

29 April–7 May 1945

And here, advancing toward us, in a boat, an aged man—his hair was white with years—was shouting: "Woe to you, corrupted souls! Forget your hope of ever seeing Heaven: I come to lead you to the other shore, to the eternal dark, to fire and frost. And you approaching there, you living soul, keep well away from these—they are the dead."
—Dante Alighieri, *The Inferno,* Canto III

THE EXISTENCE OF German concentration camps was common knowledge among the Allied political and military establishments for years, and the one at Dachau, the Nazi regime's earliest such camp, was particularly notorious. Located in rolling, wooded hills some ten miles northwest of Munich, Dachau had been an ordinary, peaceful suburb of some 15,000 persons. Its main claim to fame was the special quality of the light found there, which had made it a haven for artists. This bucolic atmosphere changed forever in March 1933 when the Nazis converted a gunpowder factory on the city's northern outskirts into a prison camp to house their political opponents. At first, it was nothing more than a normal detention facility. But once the Nazi regime became more ruthless and realized that Europe's Jewish population could be manhandled without the world intervening, the *Konzentrationslager,* or KL, acquired a much more sinister persona. Hundreds of camps and subcamps based on the Dachau model were built, followed by the horrendous extermination camps.

In 1937, the gunpowder factory was virtually completely rebuilt into a modern penal colony. In addition to the internment camp itself (designed to hold over 30,000 prisoners in thirty-four single-story, wooden barracks), there was a huge SS complex, where guards were schooled in their brutal craft. Here, too, were the finance offices for the entire SS, an NCO school, training facilities, living quarters for the guards and officers, a military hospital, a camp headquarters building, detention facilities for wayward SS personnel, a variety of shops and factories that relied on the camp's slave labor, and storerooms bulging with clothing, shoes, and eyeglasses confiscated from the inmates. Outside and to the northwest of the prisoners' enclosure stood a crematorium, where the never-ending parade of corpses was consumed. Almost redundant within the prisoner enclosure was another building—a "punishment barracks" where pitiless scenes of torture and murder were carried out.

An electrified fence separated the prisoners' compound from the SS complex, as did a deep, dry moat with steep, concrete sides and a swiftly flowing canal—the Würm River. Seven watchtowers manned by armed guards were strategically placed around the enclosure, and guard dogs patrolled the fence line. A ten-foot masonry wall enclosed the entire complex, shielding the nefarious activities within from prying eyes. A sign on the gate of the *Jourhaus*—the camp's guardhouse, which enclosed the only entrance into the prisoners' compound—ingenuously proclaimed, "*Arbeit macht frei*"—"Work makes one free." As with all of the Nazis' concentration camps, the prisoners' food was meager and of poor quality, the hours of labor long and hard. Behind the high walls, unspeakable cruelties were carried out by the SS guards on the helpless inmate population.

After the defeat of Hitler's forces at Stalingrad in 1942–1943, able-bodied Germans employed in the war industries were conscripted into the armed services and a severe labor shortage ensued. This was partially ameliorated by the use of huge numbers of concentration camp inmates in the munitions and armament factories, as well as other industries.[1] The SS grew rich on this enterprise, for it received vast sums of reichsmarks from industries that employed the slave labor.[2]

A distinction should be made here between the Nazis' "concentration camps" and the "death camps." Concentration camps such as Dachau, Mauthausen, Natzweiler-Struthof, Gross-Rosen, Stutthof, Theresienstadt, Flossenbürg, Bergen-Belsen, Dora-Mittelbau, Buchenwald, Neuengamme, Ravensbrück, Sachsenhausen, Oranienburg, Plaszow, and many others—plus their thousands of subcamps—were built and primarily used as prison facilities and slave labor camps in which anti-Nazis, homosexuals, religious clergy of all denominations, common criminals, gypsies, and anyone else the corrupt regime thought posed a danger to it were locked up. Jews, too, were incarcerated in the KLs until, following the infamous Wannsee Conference of 1942, a more terrible fate was decreed for them—the "final solution." The death camps of Auschwitz, Auschwitz-Birkenau, Chelmno, Sobibor, Treblinka, Belzec, and Majdanek were built in Poland for the sole purpose of carrying out human exterminations on an unprecedented scale.

Although Dachau was never one of the Nazis' "death factories," over 30,000 prisoners nevertheless died there during its twelve years of existence. Many inmates died from being overworked and underfed. Many died at the hands of brutal guards; many died of disease; many died while being tortured; many died by firing squad; and many died as the result of being used as human "guinea pigs" for ghastly, pseudo-scientific experiments carried out by the camp's medical personnel.[3] Here, inmates were cruelly subjected to experiments in the effects of malaria, tuberculosis, hypothermia, and decompression at high altitudes through the use of a decompression chamber.[4] A small gas chamber existed at Dachau, and liberating soldiers learned from inmates that it had been used, despite claims to the contrary.[5]

In March, as the Allied armies were pushing into Germany from east and west, the Nazis were trying frantically to evacuate the concentration and death camps and hide the evidence, or were making last-ditch efforts to exterminate as many Jews as possible before ultimate defeat befell the Reich. Because of reports from escapees, Lieutenant General Wade H. Haislip's advancing XV Corps was prepared to deal with the conditions it expected to find at Dachau. Much also was learned about concentration camp conditions after Buchenwald, some 220 miles north of Dachau, was liberated by the U.S. 6th Armored Division on 11 April. Shortly thereafter, a special Dachau group was constituted of members of the Corps's G-5 (Civil Affairs) section; a displaced-persons detachment responsible for food, medical, and sanitation matters; and a military government unit, plus two batteries of the 601st Field Artillery Battalion, detailed to act as security guards.[6]

Colonel Kenneth E. Worthing, the XV Corps G-5, prepared a plan for dealing with the camp. In it, the G-5 demonstrated extreme prescience about Dachau:

> We will uncover concentration camp at Dachau, containing unknown number of prisoners (reports vary from 12,000 to 30,000). This camp is the most important concentration camp in Germany and many famous, important persons and much valuable information may be in the camp. The camp may also contain, in addition to the political prisoners and Jewish internees, large numbers of convicted criminals. Conditions at the camp will probably be bad, insofar as food, health, and sanitation are concerned. Prior to our occupation of the camp, the German guards may have left and many of the prisoners may have departed. . . . Danger from typhus and other diseases, and security measures, require that control be exercised over the large number of curiosity seekers who may be expected to flock to the camp.

About the only assumption Worthing made that turned out to be wrong was that he initially expected the 20th Armored Division, which was sandwiched between the 42nd and 45th Divisions, to be the first unit to reach the camp.[7]

The unanswered questions on everybody's mind were: How many—if any—of the camp's inmates would still be alive? and Who would liberate the camp? It would be the latter question that would fuel the flames of an interdivisional dispute between veterans of the 45th and 42nd Infantry Divisions for decades to come.

Near the end of April, officers at XV Corps headquarters, poring over maps, saw that the 45th was in the best position to reach the camp first. A call was made to Frederick's headquarters and the wheels were set in motion; only the 45th was selected to be involved in the liberation. At 1135 hours on 29 April, the XV Corps G-5 log reads: "Called Chief of Staff, 45th Division and Military Government Officer of 45th Division and told them of plans. Both stated they were pleased with plans and that teams should move at once [to take over control of camp once it was secured]." No mention was made of any role to be played by the 42nd Division, operating to the right of the 45th.[8]

Lieutenant Colonel Felix Sparks's 3rd Battalion, 157th, beefed up with tanks and artillery, was on the right flank of the 45th's drive on Munich. "My orders were to smash through resistance as rapidly as possible to get to Munich," Sparks recalled. "In my task force, I had the whole 191st Tank Battalion, two batteries of artillery, a company from the 120th Engineers, and some backup units from Corps. The infantry loaded onto the tanks; we could get about six men on one tank. The rest of the infantry followed behind on foot. I divided the task force into two columns; I commanded one column and Major [George] Kessler, my executive officer, commanded the other. We operated on parallel roads. That way, if one column got held up, the other could continue on."[9]

Besides the 45th and 42nd, a number of other American units were also pushing toward Munich from the northwest: the 3rd and 86th Infantry Divisions, along with the 20th Armored Division and 106th Cavalry Group. Prepared to resist them in the vicinity of Dachau were elements of the 2nd *Gebirgsjäger* Division and 212th *Volksgrenadier* Division, along with various and sundry other units.[10] Kenneth Wickham, the 45th's chief of staff, who, along with Frederick and Paul Adams, had come from the 1st Special Service Force, said, "We were pursuing the German army as we aimed toward Munich; that was our number one mission. Dachau was in the way."[11]

In his memoirs, the 45th's assistant division commander, Brigadier General Paul D. Adams, wrote,

> The previous night, I noticed Dachau would be in the Division zone that day and I talked to Frederick about it. I said, "I don't know what we are liable to see there, and I have heard all sorts of things about it but I don't know what we are liable to encounter, but I do think that you or I should be with the 157th Infantry tomorrow when it moves in." So he allowed as how he would go along with them and did. . . . The 42nd Division had a hand in it by getting

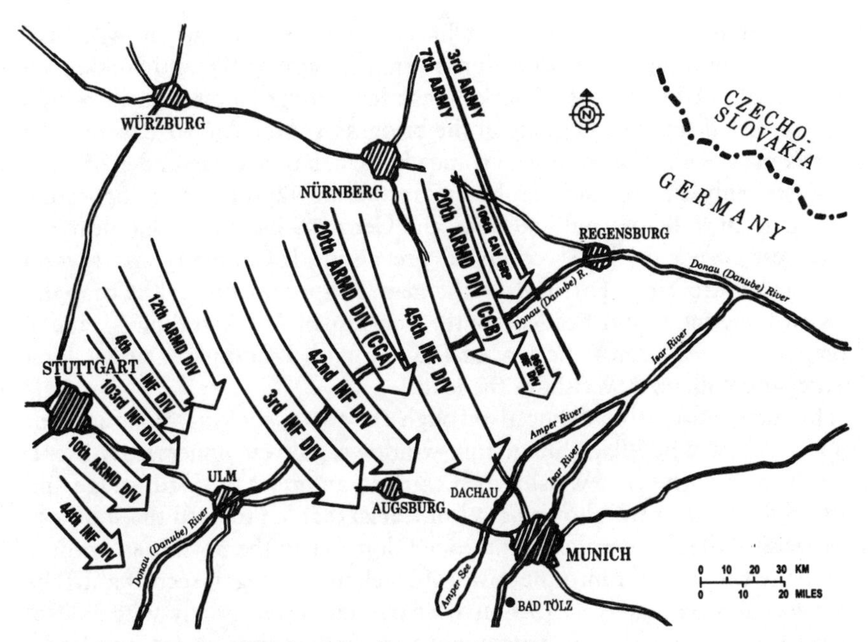

MAP 13.1 The Final Push—Nürnberg to Munich
After the fall of Nürnberg, the 45th dashed for Munich but received orders directing elements to liberate the Dachau concentration camp. (Positions approximate)

> out of zone and getting into the town of Dachau, but the Forty-fifth was the one that did the business of actually going in and clearing the place out of enemy and taking the place over.[12]

• • •

On 28 April, one day after the Russians and Americans had linked up at the Elbe, the 45th was directed to liberate the concentration camp at Dachau, and the 157th's S-3 radioed a message to Sparks and the other two battalion commanders: "Dachau may be very important, both militarily and politically. Be especially careful of operations in this sector."[13] Sparks received orders diverting him from his drive toward Munich. "I got orders by radio directing me to take the concentration camp," he said, but he wasn't happy about them. "The orders pissed me off no end because that would slow us down. I didn't consider the concentration camp a military objective."[14]

At 0922 hours on the twenty-ninth, Sparks received another message stating, "S-3 to all battalions—Upon capture of Dachau by any battalion, post air-tight guard and allow no one to enter or leave."[15] Sparks was also told that, once the camp was captured, nothing was to be disturbed. The evidence of atrocities was to be left for an international prisoners' committee to investigate. Most of the men of the 157th knew little about concentration camps and had no idea what these orders meant or what lay ahead.[16] They received an education on that unseasonably cold Sunday, 29 April. At about 1100 hours, Sparks's task force fought a brief battle with a rearguard element guarding one of the bridges over the Amper River.[17] The 157th's progress was also slowed somewhat when they came under friendly fire mistakenly directed at them by units from the 42nd Division, operating to their right.[18] Before pulling back, the Germans blew a bridge near the northwest corner of the SS complex, preventing L Company and several tanks from crossing. Farther north, near Ampermoching, K Company crossed the Amper and headed south. The rest of 3rd Battalion—I and L Companies—headed for the city of Dachau with I Company, under First Lieutenant William P. Walsh, in the lead.

The men cautiously advanced through the town, looking anxiously for snipers. A few white flags hung from windows. All was unnervingly silent. In the center of the city, Walsh's men came to an intact railroad bridge and crossed the river, then followed a set of tracks that led toward the southern perimeter of the SS complex, about one kilometer to the northeast, while L Company turned right into the town of Dachau and began securing it. The time was approximately 1215 hours. Sparks conferred briefly with Walsh. Sparks said, "I told him my orders said to seize the camp, seal it, and let no one in or out." Sparks also ordered M Company, the heavy-weapons company, to attach a machine gun platoon to I Company. "This was a platoon of .30 caliber, 'light' machine guns. While fighting in the Vosges, we had junked our heavy machine guns. They required a crew of four and were just too heavy to lug around."[19]

Walsh confirmed the conversation.

> Sparks came up to me and says, "I want you to go out these railroad tracks." There were a pair of railroad tracks heading out in the general direction of camp. You really couldn't see the camp from the village. . . . And Sparks said, "Don't let anybody out. It's a concentration camp." I didn't even know what a concentration camp was. I had seen a prisoner of war camp in upstate New York, up near [Camp] Shanks . . . where they had Germans in it. I'd seen them in there playing soccer and all that kind of stuff, and I kind of thought it was a compound for prisoners. And [Sparks] said, "Don't let them out. We got all kinds of food and medicine and what-have-you coming in here behind us, and we're going to take good care of them." I said okay and we start down these railroad tracks.[20]

Sparks and Walsh's I Company moved out, totally unprepared for what they were about to encounter. Between the town and the camp, Sparks's men saw a string of thirty-nine railroad cars standing on the track. Some were open-top gondola cars, others were enclosed boxcars, and a few more were old third-class passenger carriages. There was no engine.

If ever the American soldier needed confirmation of the reasons why he was in uniform, why he was at war, why he was required to put his life on the

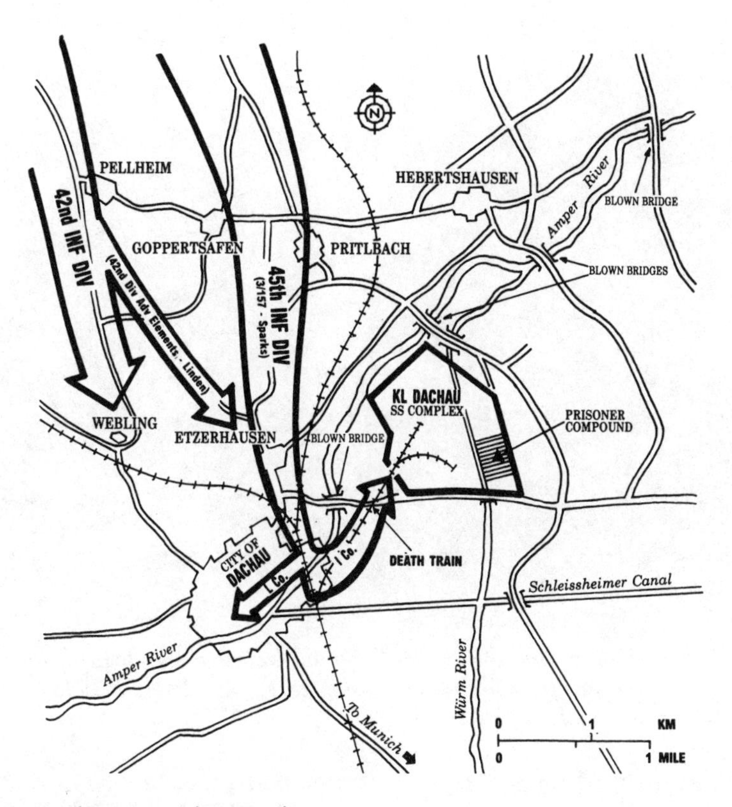

MAP 13.2 The Approach to Dachau
29 April 1945—Task Force Sparks approached Dachau from the north, not knowing what terrible scenes awaited. Also unknown to the Thunderbirds was the fact that the 42nd Division, without orders to do so, was also heading for the Dachau concentration camp. (Positions approximate)

line day after day, enduring all hardships and discomfort and danger, it was contained in these thirty-nine railroad cars. Here was the very embodiment of the evil Nazi regime that he had sworn to vanquish. As they cautiously approached, the familiar, sickening stench of death greeted them. An officer gave an order and a soldier moved forward in a running crouch toward the nearest car, looked in, covered his mouth and nose with his hand, then motioned the rest of the men forward. In each railroad car were piles of rotting human corpses—a total of 2,310 men, women, and children, to be exact—either totally naked or partially clad in blue-and-white-striped concentration camp uniforms. Mainly Poles, most of them had starved to death while being moved from Buchenwald in an effort to keep them from falling into the hands of the approaching Allies. Many others had been killed by their sadistic guards; still others had died while fighting among themselves during the trip. A few with enough strength to attempt escape had been shot down by

Ghastly cargo: 45th Division troops stumbled across a trainload of more than 2,000 corpses outside the concentration camp at Dachau, 29 April 1945. (Courtesy of 45th Infantry Division Archives)

the SS guards or brutally beaten with rifle butts, their brains oozing from shaved, emaciated skulls. An order from SS head Heinrich Himmler to destroy the evidence of atrocities had gone unfulfilled.[21]

Private first class John Lee was one of the first men on the scene. "These people were stuffed in these cars," he remembered. "The cars had bullet holes all over them, evidently from strafing on the way to Dachau. Most of the GIs just stood there in silence and disbelief. We had seen men in battle blown apart, burnt to death, and die many different ways, but we were never prepared for this. Several of the dead lay there with their eyes open, a picture I will never get out of my mind. It seems they were looking at us and saying, 'What took you so long?'"[22]

Besides the obvious horror, what sticks in the mind of everyone who was there was the awful smell. Peter J. Galary, a medic with I Company, said, "All my men were throwing up like mad. What a stench."[23] Ralph Fink, who arrived later on the twenty-ninth, recalled, "The odors inside these cars were unbelievable, with rotting bodies and feces. We learned later that these people had been underway for many days, locked in the cars with no food or water. Some of our men cursed, some wept, and most of us went into a state of almost total shock."[24] James Bird, a corporal with A Battery, 160th Field Artillery, who arrived a day later, remembered, "When we arrived at the main camp, we noticed a penetrating odor that I cannot now describe. I recall there was a railroad siding on which a train of 'forty-and-eight' type railroad freight cars was parked. These cars contained bodies clad in striped clothing. The side doors of the cars were open and piles of bodies also lay below the open doors alongside the track."[25]

Sidney Olson, a *Time* magazine correspondent, wrote, "The cars were filled with dead men. Most of them were naked. On their bony, emaciated backs and rumps were whip marks. . . . The smell was very heavy."[26] Another journalist, coming on the scene shortly after the camp had been liberated, reported, "The stench is like that of Belsen [which had been liberated by the British two weeks earlier]; it follows you even when you are back in the Press camp."[27]

Recalling the horror of the moment, Sparks said, "I saw two prisoners lying on the pavement with their brains squashed. We didn't do a detailed examination of the bodies in the cars. We looked in to see if anyone was alive and then continued on. I heard later that there might have been a couple of people still alive, but I doubt it very much."[28]

Paul Adams noted, "The encounter with the freight cars did excite our soldiers quite a lot. They got mad and they got angry and there was no monkeying around when they got through that compound gate."[29]

In James Strong's film documentary *The Liberation of KZ Dachau* (the abbreviations for *Konzentrationslager,* "KZ" and "KL," seem to have been used interchangeably), William Walsh said,

> We didn't go very far when the first Goddamn thing we saw was twenty or thirty boxcars—some open at the top, some closed in—and here are all these Goddamn people in it. And you kind of figure, well, maybe they're sleeping, maybe they're hungry, or maybe . . . you soon realize they're all dead. And you think, "What the hell is this?" We had never seen anything like that before. And don't forget, we had seen our own buddies shot—some mangled, some shot dead. . . . We had seen women and children in some areas that had died from artillery. . . . But, Jesus, here we are, and there was nobody in front of us. . . . I wasn't five miles behind the line; I wasn't ten miles behind it. . . . I was on the line and so were the men in my company and the other companies, and here's this Goddamn thing. I'll tell you, you get pretty shaken.[30]

As I Company neared the walled SS compound, probably somewhere between 1230 and 1300 hours* Sparks realized the camp was much larger

*Questions have arisen regarding exactly when Sparks and I Company reached the camp, because the 157th S-3 logged a radio message from I Company at 1430 hours indicating that Walsh's men had reached the outskirts of the camp. The time in the log is probably inaccurate, as I Company was in the town of Dachau at 1215 hours and it is unlikely it took the unit another two and a quarter hours to travel the one kilometer from the center of Dachau to the camp, especially since the company was not engaged with the enemy. Furthermore, Sparks told the author that no one that day was paying much attention to the time and that he had been out of radio contact with the S-3 for "several hours."

Medics inspecting one of the railroad cars discovered by Sparks's men outside the Dachau concentration camp. (Courtesy of U.S. Army Military History Institute)

than he had first suspected. "We went along the south side of the camp and I saw the main entrance and decided to avoid it; if the Germans were going to defend it [the camp], I figured that's where they'd do it."[31] Sparks then directed Walsh to take the bulk of I Company through the railroad gate at the southwest corner of the camp.[32] Sparks's decision to avoid approaching the main gate would result in much confusion and controversy for decades to come for, inside that gate, the Germans were ready to surrender, not fight. A small "surrender party," complete with white flag, was waiting inside the main gate, where they expected the Americans to arrive.

To a man, I Company was seething with anger at what they had discovered on the railroad tracks. John Lee remembered, "Tears were in everyone's eyes from the sight and smell. Suddenly, GIs started swearing and crying with such rage: 'Let's kill every one of these bastards,' and 'Don't take any SS alive!' Never had I seen men so fighting mad willing to throw caution to the wind."[33] Walsh said,

> There's a big gate, and this German guy comes out of there. He must have been about six-four or six-five, and he's got beautiful blond hair. He's a hand-

> some-looking bastard, and he's got more Goddamn Red Cross shields on and white flags. . . . My first reaction is, "You son of a bitch, where in the hell were you five minutes ago before we got here, taking care of all these people?" . . . Well, everybody was very upset. Every guy in that company, including myself, was very upset over this thing, and then seeing this big, handsome, son of a bitch coming out with all this Red Cross shit on him.[34]

Walsh kept the German with the unit at the head of the column. As they started through the camp, he suddenly made a break and one of Walsh's men shot him down.[35]

I Company continued grimly on, many of the men stunned and sickened at what they had encountered, others bent on avenging the mass deaths of people they did not know. After entering the camp, the company split into several smaller groups. Suddenly, four SS men, their hands up, emerged from their hiding place and surrendered to Walsh's party. But Walsh was not having any of it. He had heard stories of the notorious SS and had just seen firsthand the awful fruits of their labor. Beside himself with rage, Walsh herded the four men into one of the railroad cars and emptied his pistol into them. They lay there moaning when Private Albert Pruitt came up and finished them off with his rifle.[36] The killing of unarmed German POWs did not trouble many of the men in I Company that day, for to them the SS guards did not deserve the same protected status as enemy soldiers who have been captured after a valiant fight. To many of the men in I Company, the SS were nothing more than wild, vicious animals whose role in this war was to starve, brutalize, torment, torture, and murder helpless civilians. Lieutenant Harold Moyer, a platoon commander in I Company, later commented, "I heard every man, or a lot of men, who said we should take no prisoners. I felt the same way myself. I believe every man in the outfit who saw those boxcars prior to the entrance to Dachau felt, and was justified, in meting out death as a punishment to the Germans who were responsible."[37]

Walsh's company moved on, suppressing sporadic enemy fire that came from the many buildings that filled the complex and rounding up prisoners as they went. On a railroad spur farther inside the complex, another patrol encountered a second string of railroad cars. Empty now, the blood and feces still caked on the wooden floors and walls left the men of I Company with no doubt as to the fate of its human cargo.[38]

• • •

While most of Walsh's men entered the camp through the railroad gate, Sparks led a small group to a point a few hundred yards farther east along the southern perimeter and climbed over the high wall, ending up in the backyard of one of a group of incongruous, attractive, well-kept homes. "We went in the back door of this house into the kitchen," Sparks said.

I told my men to be careful of booby traps. We looked around; there were three or four bedrooms and I walked into a child's room with toys scattered on the floor. These were definitely SS officers' quarters. We went out the front door into the street. It was just like a suburban town, with a street and well-kept lawns and roses, lots of roses. Off to my left I heard some sporadic firing, but I couldn't see where it was coming from. We advanced down the street very cautiously; when you're clearing out buildings, you have to be very methodical.

Sparks eventually reached a large building he assumed was the camp headquarters. "It had a big lobby," he said.

At one end were some glass cases with some antique firearms in them. I heard some more firing and immediately left the building. I still couldn't see the confinement area because of all the trees and buildings. As I was going along, Lieutenant Walsh, the I Company commander, came out from between two buildings, chasing a German, and he was screaming, "You sons of bitches, you sons of bitches, you sons of bitches." I struck Walsh and knocked him down. He was sitting on the ground, hysterical. I told him, "I'm taking over command of your company."[39]

Walsh, of course, was not a green lieutenant or a neophyte to the brutality of war. He had joined the division in November 1944 and had participated in the fighting at the Maginot and Siegfried Lines and at the brutal battles for Aschaffenburg, Bamberg, and Nürnberg.[40] But every man, no matter how inured to combat he has become, has his breaking point, and Dachau was Walsh's. One of Walsh's men, Sidney C. Horn, recalled, "It took seven men to take Lieutenant Walsh into a room and get him quieted down. He really lost it there."[41]

Walsh confessed,

I'll be honest with you. I broke down. I started crying. I just . . . the whole thing was getting to me. This was the culmination of something that I had never been trained for, that nobody had ever said this goes on. . . . My feeling at that time was, when I saw all these people, their families don't know this. I mean, their fathers, their mothers, their sisters, their brothers, their children, don't know they're here, and they're going to be suddenly gone and nobody will ever know what happened to them.[42]

A short time later, Walsh pulled himself together, but his ordeal was not yet over.

Walsh and the rest of I Company were clearing buildings of Germans as they moved through the camp. Coming on the SS camp infirmary, Walsh ordered all outside, regardless of their condition. John Lee recalled,

Our platoon entered the hospital and searched room to room to clear everyone out. Several were in hospital beds with bandages on their arms and legs. Some

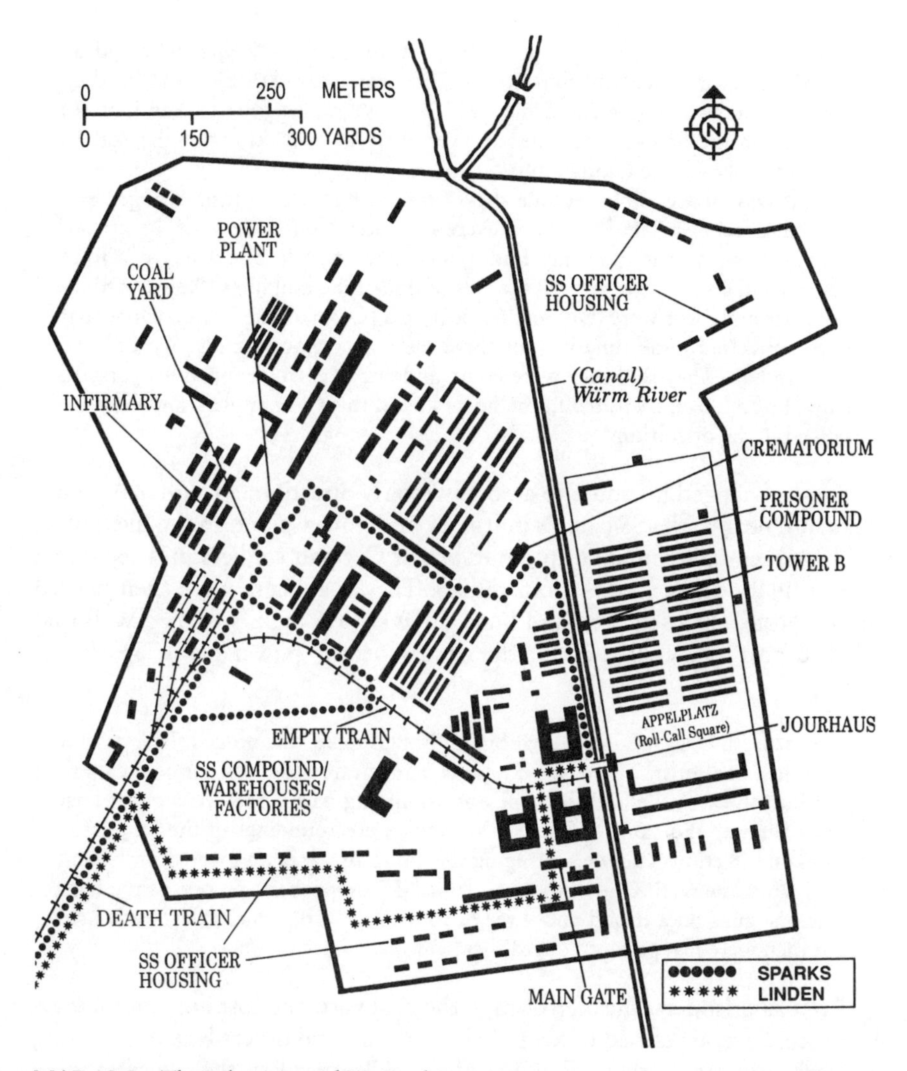

MAP 13.3 The Liberation of KL Dachau

Entering the concentration camp some 60–90 minutes before the 42nd Division, Lieutenant Colonel Felix Sparks's 3rd Battalion, 157th, took a longer route through the camp to the prisoner compound. The advance party from the 42nd, under Brigadier General Henning Linden, went directly to the main gate, where those in charge were waiting to surrender.

were on crutches, feigning injury. These were German Wehrmacht and SS guards, dressed as Wehrmacht soldiers. They were moved outside and lined up with the doctors, nurses, and medics. There were also four or five inmates working in the hospital who became very helpful in picking out the real SS men, as well as those faking injury.

This was all accomplished in a short time, with much confusion, anger, and sickening feelings. The SS troopers were separated from the rest of the prisoners. Just about that time, my buddy, Bob McDonnell, and I heard a loud scream and commotion around the side of one of the buildings. We went to investigate and there were two inmates beating a [German] medic in a white coat with shovels. By the time we got there, he was a bloody mess. We ordered them to halt. They said they were Poles, and one of them dropped his pants to show he had been castrated in the hospital and this German was somehow involved in the operation.[43]

Sparks changed his route to a northwesterly direction, a route that would take him near to the SS camp's infirmary and power plant. In the meantime, Walsh's men had rounded up a number of German soldiers and separated the ordinary army troops from the SS. The SS soldiers were then herded into a large, enclosed area and lined up against a high, stuccoed wall that formed part of a coal yard for the camp's nearby power plant. Sparks related,

It must have been used as a coal bin, although there was no coal in it at that time, just coal dust. There was a narrow gauge railroad track for coal cars to run into the area. Behind the wall was a building with a red cross on it; I assumed it was the camp infirmary. My men were rounding up the SS guards from all directions and were bringing them into this area and were lining them up against the wall. One of the men from M Company set up one of the light machine guns on a tripod and three or four of the others had rifles. I assumed our men were just going to guard these guards.[44]

Even as prisoners, the SS troops in the coal yard had lost none of their arrogance. Several refused to keep their hands up and others began muttering to each other in German. The handful of GIs guarding them were getting nervous and wondering what they should do if the Germans decided to escape or rush them. John Lee recalled that the GIs

shouted for the SS 'to keep their Goddamned hands up and stay back.' Lieutenant Walsh called for the M Company machine gun to set up facing the prisoners and to fire at them if they didn't stay back. The gunner loaded the belt in the machine gun and pulled back the lever to cock the gun to ready it for firing, if needed. The SS troopers, seeing the machine gun cocked, thought they would be shot, panicked and started toward us. That's when someone yelled to fire and the machine gun opened up a short burst of fire and three riflemen and myself [Lee carried a BAR] responded.[45]

Just before the firing began, Sparks was distracted by another soldier approaching him. "He said, 'Colonel, you should see what we found,' so I started to go off with him. I hadn't gotten more than ten yards away when all of a sudden the machine gun opened up. I wheeled around. The gunner had fired one burst—maybe ten or twelve shots—at the guards."* The SS guards dove for the ground but, in the hail of gunfire, seventeen of them were killed. Sparks said,

> I ran back and kicked the gunner in the back and knocked him forward onto the gun, then grabbed him by the collar and yelled, "What the hell are you doing?" He said they were trying to get away, and then he started crying. I pulled out my .45 and fired several shots into the air and said there would be no more firing unless I gave the order. I told them I was taking over command of the company, and I ordered them to get the wounded into the infirmary. A lieutenant from M Company [Lieutenant Daniel F. Drain] was there; I don't recall seeing Walsh and Busheyhead there at that time. That lieutenant was pretty shaken up. I told him, "Lieutenant, let's not have any more firing here."[46]

The medic Peter Galary, whose brother Walter had died at Anzio while serving with the 179th, witnessed the scene. "There was one SS who hollered in German, 'Drop to the ground,' and that's what they all did. When the shooting started, I even grabbed one guy's gun and said, 'Fire it over here,' but he was still holding it tight. I wanted him to kill that one SS, 'cause he seemed to be the leader. He survived. Our guy shot, but at random. I refused to patch up the Germans we shot."[47]

Sparks said,

> I never like to see people killed unnecessarily, no matter what their stripe is or what they have done. We did kill some people there that I consider unnecessarily. However, given the circumstances, well, I'm sorry about it. It was just one of those things that no one could control. Actually, the people that we killed died a much easier death than the people that they tortured and killed, as we subsequently found out. Torture and hangings and execution in various manners was a daily occurrence. So, in a way, we were kinder to them than they were to the people that they murdered. But, at the same time, I never countenanced any unnecessary killing at any time during the war. We tried to take

---

*Charges of mistreatment of German guards at Dachau were investigated by Lieutenant Colonel Joseph Whitaker, the Seventh Army's Assistant Inspector General. During the I.G.'s investigation, the machine gunner, Private William C. Curtin, said he fired three long bursts with a total of thirty to fifty rounds expended (Joseph M. Whitaker, "Investigation of Alleged Mistreatment of German Guards at Dachau," May-June 1945 [*I.G. Report*], William Curtin testimony, p. 40, National Archives). On further investigation, Whitaker found fourteen empty .30 caliber brass casings on the ground along with fifteen spent .45 caliber casings and an undetermined number of empty carbine shells, indicating considerably more firing had taken place (Whitaker, *I.G. Report,* Exhibit F, National Archives).

Three defiant SS soldiers remained standing after Private William C. Curtin (kneeling) fired a burst of machine gun fire into their ranks near the Dachau power plant. Many of the sixty Germans on the ground feigned death, but seventeen were dead. (Courtesy of U.S. Army Military History Institute)

> prisoners and treat them honorably. But that was one situation that I was just unable to control for a short time.[48]

Inwardly boiling at what had just taken place, but understanding the motivation behind it, Sparks remembered the enlisted man who had wanted to show him what new horrors I Company had uncovered. Departing the coal yard, Sparks followed the soldier toward the crematorium. What he discovered there was beyond imagining. In a small building next to the ovens, Sparks saw piles of emaciated corpses, stacked nearly to the ceiling. A later count revealed approximately two hundred bodies. The crematorium had run out of fuel and the corpses had been left unburned.[49] (The corpses here and throughout the camp, including the SS bodies in the coal yard, were left undisturbed for several days while investigators took a full accounting and photographers recorded the scene. A stunned James Bird later came upon the crematorium, where his mind was forever etched with nightmarish images. "I recall seeing the ovens used to burn bodies and recollect there were still some partly consumed bodies in some of them," Bird said. "One of my buddies photographed many scenes there and later provided us with

Corpses piled in grotesque poses in a room next to Dachau's crematorium. (Courtesy of U.S. Army Military History Institute)

copies. I do not have them now because I think my mother destroyed them, since they were beyond her belief.")[50]

Henry "Hank" Mills, an acting corporal and a member of the 3rd Battalion's Intelligence and Reconnaissance Platoon, recalled discovering a pond behind the crematorium and noticing something unusual in the scum-covered water. "I couldn't figure out what I was seeing, so I got myself a little forked branch and I reached into this pond and pulled out a piece of human bone from a body that had been burned. I couldn't believe it."[51]

Karl Mann, a twenty-year-old member of the 3rd Battalion's Headquarters Company and Sparks's German interpreter, remembered that he had picked up an inmate in striped prison garb along the way. "I guess he must have been a trustee or something, with special privileges, because he was outside the prisoner compound. I brought him along with us because he could explain things to us. When we got to the crematorium, I remember seeing a number of pottery containers, like red clay flower pots. There were a few dozen of them. Somebody, maybe the trustee, told me that they put the ashes in there and sent them back home to their families."[52]

Near the crematorium was a group of dog kennels. By the time Sparks got there, the occupants, mostly Dobermans, had been shot dead by 3rd Battalion men. "My men killed a bunch of guard dogs, twenty-five or thirty of them, that the Germans had used to patrol with and track down escaped prisoners," Sparks said. It was later learned from the inmates that prisoners were sometimes tied to nearby metal poles while the guards delighted in provoking the dogs to maul the prisoners.[53]

By now, I Company was only a few yards from the northwest corner of the prison compound, where nearly 32,000 inmates were huddled in their barracks, not knowing if the next few minutes would bring their liberation or their death. Many feared that as the Americans approached the camp, the SS would carry out Himmler's orders to dispose of them all in one final outburst of hatred.

• • •

Unknown to Sparks, after I Company had discovered the trainload of corpses, had entered the camp at its southwest corner, had carefully searched scores of buildings, had rooted out and killed some German soldiers, and was generally moving from west to east across the northern portion of the camp, a small advance party from the 42nd ("Rainbow") Division was rapidly closing in on the camp.

The 42nd had a long and proud tradition. One of the American divisions to have seen combat in the First World War, the 42nd was reactivated at Camp Gruber, Oklahoma, in July 1943 and trained for eighteen months before receiving its overseas assignment. The Rainbowmen, so named for the rainbow patch they wore on their left sleeve, landed in France in early December 1944, and elements of the division, as part of Task Force Linden, saw their first combat near Strasbourg on the day before Christmas. The rest of the division closed with Task Force Linden in February and, on 16 February, relieved the Thunderbirds in the Vosges Mountains. As part of Seventh Army, the 42nd participated in the thrust into Germany and the battles for Wertheim, Würzburg, Schweinfurt, Fürth, and Nürnberg.[54]

In the early hours of 29 April, the 42nd, with its CP at Osterzhausen, a small village nearly fifty kilometers to the northwest of Dachau, began pushing southward. As with all of the other American units dashing through Bavaria, the prize was Munich. In fact, at 0220 hours that morning, the 42nd's commander, Major General Harry J. Collins, sent a message to his 222nd Infantry Regimental Combat Team: "Combat battalion to be moved as soon as possible, regiment to follow thereafter as desired. Case of champagne to first battalion to enter Munich." Collins made no mention of Dachau.

At 1000 hours that morning, the 222nd's 2nd Battalion commander, Lieutenant Colonel Donald E. Downard, radioed that his unit had fought a skirmish at a roadblock and captured an unspecified number of prisoners, who were sent back to G-2 for interrogation. At 1115 hours, Downard's troops encountered another roadblock, which was quickly overrun.[55]

About noon, another battle took place at the tiny hamlet of Webling, two kilometers northwest of Dachau, on the Aichach-Dachau road. Here, a detachment of some forty SS troops were dug in on a slight rise, forming a blocking position. Tanks from the 20th Armored Division and another unit from the 222nd Regiment of the 42nd Division, approaching Webling, were fired on by the SS. One American was killed as the Rainbow Division men stormed the German positions. A group of SS troops then surrendered and were herded into the yard of a farmhouse, where the SS officer who had surrendered his unit was killed by a blow to his head with an entrenching tool. Searching the buildings, the Yanks shot and killed a German, thinking him to be a soldier; he turned out to be the owner of the farm. A number of French POWs were also flushed from their hiding places. While the rest of the American unit battled against isolated pockets of resistance near the farm, the others lined up their seventeen captives in front of a copse of trees and shot them down. According to one source, a total of forty-three SS men died that day at Webling.[56]

Major General Collins knew his division had not been authorized by the Seventh Army to attempt entering KL Dachau; that was the 45th's assignment. But a contingent of American and foreign war correspondents had heard the 42nd was close to the camp and were evidently pressing the division to move toward it—and take them along. There were also the humanitarian concerns. How could he say no? He gave orders to Brigadier General Henning Linden, the assistant division commander, to move into the camp.[57] According to Linden's testimony to the inspector general, at approximately 1530 hours,[58]* the 42nd's advance party, following on the heels of the 45th, came upon the ghastly scene at the railroad siding. Technician Fifth Grade John R. Veitch, driving one of the jeeps, recalled, "I had no idea where we were going or what we were going to see. Then we encountered the train with all the bodies. It was terrible."[59]

The advance party entered the camp at the railroad gate, then turned east, drove past the empty SS officers' homes, and continued toward the main gate. Leading the group were two generals—Linden and Brigadier General Charles Y. Banfill, deputy commander for operations, U.S. Eighth Air Force, who was accompanying the 42nd to observe the effects of sup-

*The 42nd's G-3 Periodic Report has sometimes been quoted to indicate an earlier arrival (1300 hours) for the Rainbowmen, but that time indicates when elements of the division entered the town, not the camp. It should also be noted that in the Periodic Report the map coordinates of Y7469 are given. These coordinates are for the town; the camp's coordinates are Y7670 (*42nd Division G-3 Periodic Report,* Apr. 30, 1945, p. 1, National Archives).

porting aerial operations. Others in the entourage, which was mounted in five jeeps, included Major Herman L. Avery, the 222nd Regiment's supply officer, Captain John E. McLaughlin, commander of the regiment's Headquarters Company, First Lieutenant William Cowling, and a number of enlisted drivers and bodyguards. Two jeeps carrying members of the press also tagged along, with the Belgian reporter Paul Levy and a photographer, a Mr. R. Algoet, in one and Sergeant Peter Furst, a photographer with *Stars and Stripes,* and the war correspondent Marguerite Higgins in the other.[60]

"We got to the outskirts of the camp and heard a lot of small-arms fire," Veitch said. Not knowing if enemy fire was being directed at them,* Linden's party spilled from the jeeps and took cover in a drainage ditch near the camp's main gate. "I looked up and all I could see in front of me was the posterior of someone peering around the front wheel of my jeep," said Veitch. "General Linden said, 'Get that person back here under cover—go up and get him.' So I crawled up and hit him in the butt and it was that lady reporter, Marguerite Higgins. When she turned around, I said, 'Oh my God,' then I told her the general wanted her back there with the rest of us. That was my only encounter with her. I'm not even sure how she got there. She wasn't with our group; she must have been tagging along somewhere behind us."[61]

Marguerite Higgins was a twenty-five-year-old fledgling war correspondent from the *New York Herald Tribune* who had been in Europe only since March but was determined to make a name for herself. Two weeks earlier, at Buchenwald, she had received a quick introduction to the horrors of the camps. But Buchenwald was yesterday's news; what she wanted was to be in on the liberation of a camp. While at Buchenwald, she teamed up with German-born Sergeant Peter Furst. Furst had a jeep, so the two of them pressed forward toward Dachau along the same general route that was being taken by the 45th and 42nd Divisions.[62]

Earlier that day, Higgins had arrived at the 222nd's headquarters (a fact that was noted in the regimental journal: "A few moments after General Linden and group arrived, they were joined by two representatives of the *Stars and Stripes,* Miss Peggy [*sic*] Higgins, a representative of a Chicago [*sic*] newspaper, and a photographer [Algoet] from the Belgium government."[63] Although the evidence is sketchy, one can surmise that she informed the officers there that she had learned that the 222nd was close to the infamous Dachau concentration camp and would they be so kind as to allow her to tag along with Task Force Linden so that she could get the biggest scoop of her journalistic life. Furst and Higgins, her femininity disguised beneath a heavy German army coat and winter hat with the earflaps pulled down, attached themselves to the tail end of Linden's party.

*This firing apparently was being done by I Company, 157th, already inside the camp.

Veitch added,

> The small-arms fire let up and then, out of the gate area, came this SS officer. I think there was another man with him. I ended up going up to this SS officer and stuck my .45 in his ribs and told him to put his hands on his head. I'm hitting him in the ribs, trying to get his hands up, but he saw I was just a grunt and he was an officer. I brought him back to the general and Linden said to me, "Tell him to put his hands up." I said, "Sir, he won't do it." Well, General Linden always carried a little stick, kind of hickory stick with a knob on the end, and he hauled off and hit this guy up the side of the head and said, "Put your hands up," and he immediately did. He saw that Linden was a general officer.[64]

The 222nd's narrative in its Report of Operations for April 1945, states that when Linden's party entered the camp, they "were met by the Red Cross representative [Victor Maurer] from Geneva, Switzerland, who was at the camp to object to the Nazis' treatment of the prisoners, and who officially turned the camp over to this small group." The narrative continues: "All but a few of the SS guards were turned over to General Linden and his group by a young German Lieutenant [a *Leutnant* Wickert], who was brought to the camp from the Eastern Front only two days before for the sole purpose of turn- [*sic*] the camp over to the Americans when they arrived."[65] A brief "ceremony" took place near the main gate, with the German detachment under the protection of a white flag on a broomstick held by Victor Maurer. As acting commandant, Lieutenant Wickert turned over the camp to the 42nd.

In his testimony to Lieutenant Colonel Whitaker, the Seventh Army assistant inspector general, Linden recounted the event, which differs somewhat from Veitch's recollections:

> When we were about one hundred yards from the southwest corner of the camp, three persons, one bearing a white flag, approached us from the gate house. We dismounted some seventy-five yards from the gate house and found that these three were Swiss Red Cross representatives or, rather, one was and the other two were SS officers. The interpreter stated that he and the SS troopers and one or two others had been sent into the camp the night before to take over and surrender the camp to the American forces, and asked me if I was an American officer. I replied, "I am assistant division commander of the Forty-second Division." He said, "Take forty or fifty guards to take over the camp." I immediately dispatched one of the guard vehicles with the message to Colonel Buldoc, about a kilometer back in Dachau.[66]

William P. Donahue, a bodyguard for General Linden, recalled that while they were at the main gate, Linden sent him back to the town of Dachau to find Lieutenant Colonel Lucien E. Buldoc, the executive officer of the 222nd Regiment, and request that he move the rest of the 222nd Regiment to the camp. Obviously, for Donahue to drive to the town, find the colonel, and bring him back to the camp gate would have required a not-inconsiderable amount of time—probably between fifteen and thirty minutes. After he returned with the officer, Donahue said, "They [General Linden's party] hadn't moved from where they were [at the main gate]."[67]

Linden testified to the I.G., "At this time, small-arms fire broke out to the west of us in the camp area. I sent the aide [Lieutenant Cowling] to the enclosure to determine the cause of the shooting. He sent word back in a few minutes to come in and see the situation."[68]

According to the historian Hugh Foster, who has spent many years researching the events surrounding the liberation of Dachau, it may not have been Cowling who was the first to reach the prisoner compound, but rather Lieutenant William Walsh of the 157th.[69] Indeed, in the documentary *The Liberation of KZ Dachau*, Bill Walsh told his story:

> We finally get up to the main gate. This is the gate that says, "Work makes you free."... And when I get to the gate, I asked if anybody spoke English, and there was an Englishman there [Albert Guerisse, also known as Patrick O'Leary]. I think he was a naval officer ... and I said to him, "Are there any Americans in there?" And he says, "I don't know.... I think so, but there may be only one or two." And then I said, "... I can't open the gates, but I want you to know there's all kinds of medical supplies and doctors and food and stuff like this coming behind us, and they're going to take care of you." And he said, "I want you to come in here first.... I want you to see what was going on." And then he finally prevailed on me. I said, "Okay, I'll go in." And I went in with Busheyhead and a sergeant. Of course, we had to squeeze through the gate because they're all inside, screaming and hollering.

Following Guerisse toward some buildings, Walsh was astounded by the *Inferno*-like scenes unfolding before him.

> There's two or three guys in uniform that are being hammered to death with shovels ... by the inmates. They're the kapos or the ... trustees, or whatever. They have them in every camp, and there they are, they're being beaten to death. [Guerisse] takes us up into an area where they had been experimenting on high-altitude stuff.... There were a lot of bodies on this boardwalk outside this building. But he shoved me inside this building where they used to take these high-altitude tests ... used to put these guys in this thing and drain the air out.... Went into a couple of other [buildings], and I'd swear there was women in there and a couple of children, but we were making a real fast tour. I get to another barracks and [the bunks] are roughly four high, and they're all full of straw. There's no mattresses or anything.... There's an old guy in the second bunk and he's reached out and he's got a cigarette in his hand.... It's a German cigarette, I think, and it's water-stained, a little yellow color on it, and he's offering it to me. The Englishman's right behind me and, of course, everybody is staring out of their bunks at us ... and I say, "Oh, no, *you* keep it."

As an inmate himself, Guerisse understood the significance of the simple gesture—that by giving away his only worldly possession, the prisoner was showing his eternal gratitude for the arrival of the Americans, his liberators, his saviors. Practically whispering in Walsh's ear, Guerisse said, "Take it. That's the only thing that guy owns in this whole world. That's his everything . . . a cigarette. Take it."[70]

• • •

At the main gate, Linden and the small knot of Rainbowmen were champing nervously at the bit, hearing sporadic gunshots and waiting to enter the camp. At last, Donahue's jeep, with Lieutenant Colonel Buldoc in the passenger seat, roared into view. A decision was made to send Lieutenant Cowling, Linden's aide, on a scouting mission inside the camp. Cowling, possibly accompanied by an enlisted man, moved in cautiously, went about two blocks north, turned east, and saw the *Jourhaus* gate 150 yards ahead of him. Cowling's exploits were chronicled in an article in the *New York Times,* written by Howard Cowan:

> When Lieutenant Colonel [*sic*] Will Cowling of Leavenworth, Kan., slipped the lock in the main gate, there was still no sign of life inside this area. He looked around for a few seconds and then a tremendous human cry roared forth. A flood of humanity poured across the flat yard—which would hold a half dozen baseball fields—and Colonel Cowling was mobbed. He was hoisted to the shoulders of the seething, swaying crowd of Russians, Poles, Frenchmen, Czechs, and Austrians, cheering the Americans in their native tongues. The American colonel was rescued but the din kept up.[71]

(This news report is curious in that it calls into question whether the war correspondent, Howard Cowan, was even present—he is not mentioned in the initial group of Linden's party—or whether he was only repeating what he was told later or was simply inventing a thrilling story. Most war correspondents would know the difference between a lieutenant and a lieutenant colonel. Plus, according to eyewitness statements, Cowling was not "rescued," but returned to Linden's group at the main gate by himself.)

Donahue recalled, "We then went to the prison camp in our jeeps. Seven or eight German soldiers came out of [the *Jourhaus*] and dropped their rifles. I lined 'em up and told 'em to stay put. About that time, Tinkham and Oddi came up and, a minute or so later, the general came up."[72]

In his testimony to the I.G., Linden said,

> I moved in with my guards into the [military part of the camp], and I found that the inmates—having seen the American uniform of my guards there, and those of the Forty-fifth Division—approaching the main stockade [i.e., the *Jourhaus* and the western side of the prisoner enclosure] from the east, had stormed to the

fence in riotous joy. This seething mass increased in intensity until the surge against the steel barbed wire fence was such that it broke in several places, and inmates poured out into the roadway between the fence and the moat [canal]. In this process, several were electrocuted on the charged fence.[73]

Veitch also recalled the mad scene. "At the gate, one of the inmates tried crawling over the wire—these people were half-crazed—and he died, electrocuted."[74]

Guido Oddi, one of Linden's bodyguards, remembered, "Our group was the first party of people to go in there [to the prisoner enclosure]. When they saw us, they knew right away we were Americans and they started shouting and waving tiny American flags. I don't know where they got the flags—I imagine the women who were there made them out of swatches of cloth."[75]

While Walsh was still learning firsthand about conditions inside the camp, the advance party from the 42nd Division arrived at the *Jourhaus,* where a group of SS guards surrendered to Linden's men without incident. In his testimony to the I.G., Lieutenant Colonel Walter Fellenz said,

> In company with General Linden, Colonel Buldoc and bodyguards of each of these two officers, we entered the camp after having been told by the general's aide that apparently the SS troopers had deserted it. After entering the camp gate, we moved along the road about 150 yards and there to our right about 150 yards down the road was the prison enclosure itself. As we advanced toward the enclosure, thousands of the inmates were standing around the gate yelling, crying, and waving their hands. Some of the bodyguard of the general who entered the camp prior to our party's entering were in the process of removing approximately eight German soldiers from the room on the right half of the gate of the stockade [the *Jourhaus*].

Once they reached the *Jourhaus,* Linden's group found a number of prisoners attacking several German guards who had surrendered. To safeguard the Germans, Fellenz directed Sergeant Robert Killiam to take them to the main gate to join the others who had surrendered. A new problem then presented itself. Fellenz said,

> As we drew near to the gate, we were warned by the inmates that there were other German troops manning one of the towers to the left of us [Tower B]. This tower was approximately 200 yards away from us at this time. On the ground in front of the door to the tower, I saw a man who appeared to be in German uniform. With my field glasses, I identified him as a German soldier and I also saw several other German soldiers in the tower itself. By this time, bodyguards of the above-mentioned officers also saw the German soldiers. Part of the soldiers immediately rushed toward the tower going by the trail near the barbed wire fence. Others of the bodyguards moved by the road opposite the fence. . . . As we approached the tower, several weapons were fired, including some automatic weapons.

Joining the group rushing the tower along the west side of the canal, Fellenz observed that the firing was coming both from the tower and from the American troops approaching it. "As I approached the tower," he told the I.G., "I could see an American soldier there and a German soldier struggling within the tower. Several bruised and beaten soldiers were coming out of the door at the same time under guard of our troops."*

Fellenz said that after crossing a small bridge that spanned the canal he went in the tower and started up the stairs. Then gunfire broke out. "Several more shots were fired inside the tower and when these shots were fired, the men guarding the prisoners outside the tower shot through the windows of the tower and apparently the German soldiers outside the tower attempted to free themselves from the custody of our troops and were shot in the struggle." When asked to identify the American soldiers involved in the shooting, Fellenz replied he didn't know, but he added, "In addition to the bodyguards which I have mentioned above, there were elements of the Forty-fifth Division in the area at that time. I am not positive but there is a possibility that some of these troops were intermingled with the bodyguards that I have mentioned above."[76]

The shooting began some minutes after Technician third grade Henry J. Wells, the interpreter accompanying the 42nd's party, proceeded to the tower and fired a burst at the door with his .45 caliber M-3 "grease gun." A number of German soldiers emerged, some with their hands up and others not. Someone indicated there were more inside, so Wells called for the rest to come out. Once all the guards had been flushed from the tower, Wells formed the group, numbering sixteen men, into two ranks with their backs to the canal. A group of Americans, possibly including Lieutenant Colonel Fellenz, along with some I Company, 157th men, held the captives under armed guard, and one of the Americans began disarming the Germans. Whether one of the SS men provoked the action by making a move for a weapon has never been conclusively established, but suddenly the Americans fired into the group. With bullets flying, Wells hit the ground, began firing wildly, and narrowly escaped being hit himself.[77]

An inmate's view of the incident was provided to Whitaker by Marion Okrutnik, a Pole, who had been inside the compound near Tower B when the shooting began. He said through an interpreter,

> I could not tell exactly from where the Americans came because we were compelled to stay in our block, and then doors were closed, but they came from

---

* The source of this firing, and even Fellenz's testimony, has been under question, as other eyewitnesses have testified that no enemy fire came from the tower. Fellenz first wrote a highly imaginative account of the "storming of Tower B," in which he claimed that he and a handful of 42nd Division officers braved a hailstorm of automatic weapons fire to rout the enemy from the tower. Under questioning by Lieutenant Colonel Whitaker, Fellenz recanted that story.

the direction of the woods. [Presumably, Okrutnik saw men from the 45th, as the area around the crematorium is wooded whereas the area near the *Jourhaus,* in 1945, was not.] When we saw the American soldiers, nobody could keep the doors closed. They were broken open and we ran out. When the soldiers got to the tower, they began to shoot. I was not more than five meters from the wire. The Germans did not shoot. When the Americans got to the tower, they ordered, "Get out." The Germans came down out of the tower one at a time with their hands over their heads, but one German remained in the tower. The Germans were lined up side by side with their hands up with the canal behind them, generally facing the tower. They were all supposed to be out of the tower but the Americans believed not, and one of the Americans broke open the door of the tower which had been closed and made the last German come out. The other soldier was guarding the Germans who had already surrendered. As the one American brought the last German out of the tower, they moved over to the line where the other Germans were, and this last German also was lined up with his hands above his head. The American soldier started to search him and as he did, the German also jerked his hand toward the place under his left armpit as if he were reaching for a gun. As he did that, the American soldier who had brought him from the tower stepped back and the other soldier who had been guarding the soldiers with his gun went "B-r-r-r-r-r-r-t!!!," and it was finished.[78]

Another member of the 42nd, Technician fifth grade John G. Bauerlein, testified to the I.G.,

These other prisoners were lined up alongside that little canal, and the last one was sort of slow in coming down, and as he came down, one of the GIs pushed him to the rear of the other prisoners. As he got closer, he still kept pushing him and pushed him right into the water. I guess as he went in, he grabbed and pulled some more in. That must have been about two men, and after they fell in, the GIs on the other side opened up. At the same time, GIs on this side opened up on them, too. They shot them all down. I moved out of the way because I was afraid of getting hit.[79]

Lieutenant Colonel Fellenz, on the other hand, testified that he saw no Germans being pushed into the water or anyone shot while in the canal. He did, however, recount that he saw American troops venting their rage by firing into the dead bodies of the fallen guards.[80]

John Veitch has a different recollection of this scenario:

Shortly after we got to the gate, there was a group of guys—I think they were from the 45th. They grabbed about ten or a dozen of these guys and threw them in the moat [canal]. They were standing in water more than waist high, then the soldiers proceeded to shoot them. The moat turned the color of port wine. I saw that and, frankly, I went over and laid down behind a rock, scared to death. I was sick. I did see a 42nd Division guy with a grease gun, but the rest of them were people from the 45th.[81]

When the firing stopped, seven SS guards lay dead on the bank of the Würm River canal. If the count of sixteen Germans rousted from the tower is correct, the bodies of nine other guards fell into the canal and were washed downstream, for only seven bodies were accounted for in the I.G.'s report. Linden's men then apparently withdrew from Tower B and the *Jourhaus* and returned to the main gate.

Shortly after the shooting, Sparks, along with a number of I Company men, arrived at Tower B from the crematorium. Seeing only 45th Division men in the area, with no 42nd Division personnel around, Sparks assumed the I Company men had killed the Germans who were lying in a neat row at the base of Tower B. Continuing on to the *Jourhaus,* Sparks still saw no one from the Rainbow Division and did not even realize that members of the 42nd were inside the camp. It was only decades after the incident that Sparks suspected, "Linden's group panicked after the shooting, took the German guards they had taken prisoner at the *Jourhaus,* and returned with them to the main gate."

On his way to the *Jourhaus,* Sparks saw prisoners stream from their barracks by the thousands and rush toward the wire that enclosed them. "Walking along the canal almost to the *Jourhaus,* I saw a large number of naked bodies stretched out along the ends of the barracks," he said. "I estimated there were about two hundred bodies there. I also spotted quite a few of my men at the *Jourhaus*. About this time, the camp erupted. The prisoners came out of the barracks shouting and screaming."

The arrival of the Americans caused pandemonium among the prisoners. Thousands of them dashed to the wire enclosure, emitting an unearthly howl—a howl of rage at what had befallen them, and a howl of joy at their redemption. Sparks said,

> I told Karl Mann, my interpreter, to yell at them and tell them that we couldn't let them out, but that food and medicine would be arriving soon. He yelled himself hoarse. Then I saw bodies flying through the air, with the prisoners tearing at them with their hands. I had Karl ask what was going on. The prisoners told him that they were killing the informers among them. They actually tore them to pieces with their bare hands. This went on for about five minutes until they wore themselves out. I had Karl tell them to send their leaders to the fence, where I told them to keep calm, that medicine and food would be coming soon. This seemed to settle them down.

Sparks recalled that he reached the *Jourhaus,* where he saw,

> a beautiful iron gate to the concentration camp itself . . . that had a sign on it that said in German, "Work makes you free," or something to that effect. Of course, they worked those prisoners to death, just on stupid tasks, like pushing a wagon around that was loaded with rocks—anything to humiliate them. I was standing there at the gate, talking to one of my officers about security

when, all of a sudden, I saw three jeeps coming up and they stopped at the end of the little bridge that spanned the canal [at the *Jourhaus*].[82]

In the jeeps were Brigadier Generals Linden and Banfill; Lieutenant Colonels Lucien E. Buldoc and Fellenz; Captain McLaughlin; Lieutenant Cowling; Sergeant Killiam; technical sergeants Veitch, Oddi, and Wells; and Private Chester Domanski along with several others, including Marguerite Higgins and the photographer Peter Furst.[83]

Karl Mann also remembered the 157th Regiment group being at the gate for ten or fifteen minutes before the Linden contingent reappeared.

I was probably talking with the trustee, while Colonel Sparks was probably doing something that I wasn't directly involved with—setting up communications or security or something. It was all very disorganized then; prisoners were at the gate and they were pressing against it. Earlier, when the GIs got to the fence, they began throwing candy bars and cigarettes over the fence to the prisoners until somebody said to stop it, because if you throw things to them, they're going to get hurt fighting over the items.[84]

William Donahue of the 42nd, however, recalled already being at the *Jourhaus* when Sparks's men arrived. "Pretty soon, the 45th came along from the north, along the moat. Some of them had been drinking. The general took a bottle from one of them and threw it in the moat. The prisoners were starting to rush the gate so the general sent me upstairs [in the *Jourhaus*], where some of the prisoners were climbing over their own bodies to get up to the windows and were trying to come in."[85]

Sparks said the jeeps stopped at the western end of the bridge that spanned the canal at the *Jourhaus* and he talked briefly with Linden, who did not get out of his jeep, about the situation. Sparks said Linden told him that the reporter (Higgins) wanted to enter the camp to interview the inmates. Sparks replied that his orders prohibited anyone but his men from entering the camp. Higgins then spoke up, demanding to be allowed inside the enclosure. She said, "Colonel, there are some famous people in there,"[86] and rattled off a list of names, including former Austrian Chancellor Kurt von Schuschnigg and his wife and daughter; Pastor Martin Niemöller, an anti-Nazi theologian; the former French Premier Léon Blum; Prince Frederick Leopold of Prussia; Prince Xavier of Luxembourg; Prince Louis de Bourbon; Hitler's former chief of staff Franz Halder; survivors of the Spanish Civil War—even a group of Hindus. (It was rumored that Stalin's son, Jacob, was among the group, but this was never confirmed. Most of the other prominent prisoners had been removed from the camp—along with 6,000–7,000 other inmates—by the SS on 26 April and force-marched seventy miles south to Tegernsee. Those who could not keep up were shot by their guards. The survivors were found and freed on 2 May by the 42nd Division.)[87]

Sparks reiterated his orders, adding, "Look at all those people pressing against the gate." Undeterred, Higgins ran to the gate, removed the bar that was holding it shut, and was nearly trampled by the mass of prisoners attempting to get out. Sparks said his men were forced to fire warning shots over the heads of the prisoners to regain order and reclose the gate. "When the firing started," Sparks said, "it scared this woman and she ran back to her jeep."[88]

John Lee was one of those at the *Jourhaus*. "While General Linden and Colonel Sparks were talking, Higgins went up to the gate and removed the restraining bar. This caused panic and the prisoners began rushing toward the gate. We were ordered to fire in the air and push the inmates back in behind the gates."[89]

While elements from the two divisions were gathered in front of the *Jourhaus,* trying to calm the excited inmates whose sole goal was to be released from their prison, another strange incident occurred. In his written report to General Linden, Lieutenant Cowling wrote,

> Just as the prisoners were pushed back inside the enclosure, an enlisted man of the 45th Division picked up a number of chains, shackles, etc., which had been used to chain the prisoners, and he rattled them at the crowd. General Linden ordered the man, who was standing directly in front of him, to drop the chains at once, as they were causing increased excitement among the prisoners and they were surging forward in an attempt to get through and grab the chains and again break out of the confines of the inclosure. The man, however, disobeyed the General's order and turned his back on him, raising the chains above his head and shaking them again. In an attempt to get the man's attention, General Linden tapped the man on the helmet with a stick he was carrying. The man turned and the General again directed him to drop his chains. This time the man dropped his chains and walked off, although he was very sullen, showing no military discipline or respect.

There is also evidence to suggest the soldier may have been drunk.[90]

At this point, a violent argument broke out between Sparks and Linden—an argument remembered clearly more than fifty years later by men from both divisions. Exactly what touched off the argument has never been conclusively determined. Sparks said it was because he refused to abdicate his responsibility of securing the camp and turn it over to an American general from a division that wasn't supposed to be there. It also may have concerned one or more I Company soldiers whom General Linden hit (or "tapped") on the head with his stick. (Sparks's recollection is that he ordered one of his men to escort Linden and his party from the area and that Linden struck the soldier on the helmet with his stick when he approached the jeep.) It may have been Marguerite Higgins trying to insert herself into the situation. Certainly Sparks's war weariness, brought on by nearly two years of almost continuous combat, played a significant role. Or the outburst could have been simply attributable to the incredible events of the day—the discovery of the "death train" and the corpses at the crematorium, Walsh's rampage, the killing by I Company men of the SS guards at the coal yard, and the line of German corpses at Tower B. Whatever the catalyst, Sparks contended that he briefly lost his composure and threatened the general with his .45 caliber pistol.[91]

John Lee related, "The general, who was not in charge there, was upset and told the colonel he would be court martialed. The general was so upset, he struck Sergeant Brumlow on the helmet."[92] Karl Mann also recalled much of the chaotic scene at the *Jourhaus*. "I remember this general who was short and . . . carried a riding crop or a stick. The general looked at the trustee who was with me and said, 'Hey, this fellow belongs on the inside,' so he was sent back inside the compound and we lost our unofficial guide. The general was trying to take over and Sparks was telling him it was his [Sparks's] responsibility. So they had this hassle and Sparks got pretty angry and red in the face." Mann confessed that he didn't see Linden hit the enlisted man; nor did he witness Sparks draw his pistol.

> I probably wasn't paying too much attention until they started having this big hassle and shouting at each other. That's the part I vividly remember. That drew everybody's attention. People were standing around, watching this like spectators. I don't know what they were shouting about; you don't think, fifty years later, that there's going to be much historical interest in what two officers are saying. Then the general threatened Sparks with a court-martial. But this was Sparks's assigned area and he wasn't going to let a small group of officers from some other division interfere with that.[93]

Sergeant Donald M. Lesch, a radio operator with Sparks's battalion, recalled seeing Sparks wave a pistol at an officer from the 42nd, but couldn't tell the man's rank.[94]

Acting Corporal Henry "Hank" Mills, of the 3rd Battalion's Intelligence and Reconnaissance Platoon, said, "I remember distinctly that Sparks put a gun to that guy's head and said, 'If you don't get the "F" out of here, I'm going to blow your brains out.'"[95]

Sparks confirmed that he advised the general and his party to leave. The general shook his fist at Sparks and told him that he was relieved of his command. "That's when Colonel Fellenz came running up." The two lieutenant colonels exchanged threats. According to Sparks, "Fellenz said, 'I'll see you after the war.'

"I said, 'You son of a bitch—what's the matter with right now?'"

Fuming, Fellenz returned to his jeep and the group departed.[96]

• • •

Linden's testimony to the I.G. contains virtually none of the above. He said,

> About this time [which, if his estimated arrival time of 1530 hours is accurate, would be approximately 1600 hours], Colonel Fellenz of the 222nd had come in with about ten or twelve men in [jeeps] and had found the electrician of the stockade and pulled the switch. This, of course, increased the problem of keeping the prisoners in the stockade in that they literally tore the fence and [*Jourhaus*] with their bare hands. . . . We were able to keep control over those that poured through the holes in the fence along the moated roadway, but the surge through the gate house building and its bridge opening directly across the moat became a problem. By taking personal command of the situation and ordering all of the soldiers we had available at the bridge . . . we formed a cordon around the gate house and after about half an hour to an hour, we were able to push back all of those outside and relieved the pressure on the gate house, and after two hours restored order in a large measure through the prison inmate underground itself. Sometime during this period, Colonel Sparks of the Forty-fifth Division came up and stated that he had about a battalion moving through the camp and had some soldiers along the fence who, all this time, had helped to stem the flow of prisoners out of the stockade. I gave command of the stockade to Colonel Fellenz of the 222nd Infantry and directed the two commanders to execute relief of any Forty-fifth Division soldiers around the moat as soon as practicable. During this period, there was some shooting from the east flank tower, and other small arms fire from both flanks.

When asked by Whitaker if Sparks had made any statement about his orders or what his troops were doing in connection with the camp, Linden replied, "No, except that he said he was cleaning up the camp and I asked him if he had the rest of the camp in hand and he stated he had. That was part of the basis of putting him in command of the area he already occupied. I told him that the Corps and Army orders were to freeze the inmates in place and, therefore, we must concentrate on restoring order in this camp."

Linden made no reference to the shooting of the guards at Tower B, nor to tapping any 45th Division soldier on the helmet, nor to any argument with Sparks.[97]

During the "Battle of the Officers" at the gate, Lieutenant William Walsh said he returned to the *Jourhaus* from his visit to the barracks inside the wire. The prisoners were still streaming out of the barracks and filling the *Appelplatz* (roll-call square) to the east of the *Jourhaus*. Seeing the crowd in front of the guardhouse, he and the other two members of his party inconspicuously squeezed through the gate (probably with the help of the American soldiers guarding the gate) and observed Sparks in a hot argument with "some general from another division." Not wanting to become involved in this or to be noticed, the lieutenant left the *Jourhaus* and headed northward along the canal, in the direction of Tower B.[98]

The historian Hugh Foster wrote, "I believe it is entirely possible that Walsh was the first person to reach the Jourhaus, perhaps during the same period that Linden's aide was clearing the guards out of the southwest tower. . . . That Walsh did not mention this to the I.G. might be because Walsh knew he was not supposed to enter the concentration camp, having received orders to post an 'air-tight' guard on the place."[99]

Walsh may have also been less than honest in his testimony to the I.G. to keep from getting into more trouble than he already was. When questioned by Whitaker regarding the shooting at Tower B, Walsh said,

> Looking for a way through the crematory, we found a wall and on the other side of the wall was this big pen [the prisoner compound]. The shouting went up from the camp, the inmates shouting and yelling. Then . . . our platoon started to clear one of the towers and got about eight guards out of it. The [American] guards were attempting to line them up on the road outside. I think what provocated [*sic*] the killing of those men was that one of them had a gun which he pulled when they were trying to line them up. Then, I sent for my other two platoons to come to the pen and set up a guard and clear the rest of the towers. About that time, some units of the Forty-second Division showed up at the far side of this pen [probably at Tower G, at the southwest corner of the enclosure near the *Jourhaus*]. I understand that they had been in the camp also, because a couple of times they fired at some of my men who were bringing back prisoners. My first platoon was coming up to help on the main gate. Then, there was a fire fight with the guards in the main tower [the term "main tower" is misleading; Walsh was no doubt speaking of Tower B]. Then, I again met the battalion commander [Sparks] and he told me to deploy my company 'round the pen itself. Later on, we were relieved by the Forty-second Division.

Whitaker later recalled Walsh for additional testimony regarding this incident and received a slightly more detailed version: "I noticed that some of the men were concentrating around this tower [Tower B]. . . . I went down to the left to cross over on a bridge and while I was doing this, they were emptying the tower of the guards that were in it. As I approached the tower, it looked to me like a scuffle as my men were lining up these prisoners. I think what happened is somebody struck a rifle in one of the guards' hands and during this they opened up on the prisoners." When asked if he had seen any soldiers from the 42nd Division there, Walsh replied, "I didn't recognize any at that time."* Walsh also testified that he did not see any Germans pushed into the water or shot in the water; nor did he witness anyone shooting into the dead bodies of the Germans. (Naturally, if Walsh had been inside the prisoner compound with Guerisse, as he later con-

---

*Whitaker determined that at least two members of the 42nd were present and one took part in the incident.

tended, he could not have seen these incidents. But of course, he did not tell Whitaker about his visit inside the compound.)[100]

Once Linden and his group departed, Sparks said he saw no one from the group again. "After they left, I placed security around the camp. Walsh and some of his men went into the camp kitchens to see if there was any food, but there wasn't much. I never went into the confinement area."[101]

The 45th's chief of staff, Kenneth Wickham, commented, "I heard of the various discussions of the assistant division commander of the 42nd being there and the argument with one of our lieutenant colonels. At that moment, it didn't seem very important. General Frederick wasn't very concerned one way or the other—he thought the 42nd general was kind of out of line. I don't know who was first [at KL Dachau] or how much difference it made."[102] (Evidently, however, word reached Frederick that Linden had struck one of the 45th's enlisted men and he phoned General Collins on the evening of 29 April to inform him that he intended to prefer court-martial charges against the brigadier. After obtaining versions of the incident from Linden and Cowling and learning that Brigadier General Banfill was an eyewitness and would corroborate the other two officers' stories—and perhaps realizing there was some dispute as to whether Linden "struck" or "tapped" the soldier with his walking stick—Frederick let the matter drop.)[103]

• • •

By now, Sparks and I Company were totally confused as to what the 42nd was doing at the camp and who was supposed to be in charge. Wanting a clarification as to exactly in whose zone of responsibility the camp lay, the 45th Division operations officer queried XV Corps headquarters. The response was: "With reference to your TWX stating that Fury [code name for the 42nd Division] was attempting to relieve your guards at the Dachau PW camp (Y765700), the guarding of this camp is your responsibility as it is in your zone."[104] This order was evidently changed later, and the 42nd was put in charge of the prisoner compound, with the 45th assigned to secure the SS complex and the area outside the prisoner compound.[105]

The New York Times picked up Howard Cowan's story of the liberation, making it front-page news on 1 May:

> DACHAU, Germany, April 30—Dachau, Germany's most dreaded extermination camp, has been captured and its surviving 32,000 tortured inmates have been freed by outraged American troops who killed or captured its brutal garrison in a furious battle. Dashing to the camp atop tanks, bulldozers, self-propelled guns—anything with wheels—the Forty-second and Forty-fifth Divisions hit the notorious prison northwest of Munich soon after the lunch hour yesterday. Dozens of German guards fell under the withering blasts of rifle and carbine fire as the soldiers, catching glimpses of the horrors within the camp,

> raged through its barracks for a quick clean-up. . . .* Prisoners with access to records said that 9,000 captives had died of hunger and disease or been shot in the past three months and 14,000 more had perished during the winter. Typhus was prevalent in the camp and the city's water supply was reported to have been contaminated by drainage from 6,000 graves near the prison.[106]

Chaplain Leland Loy recalled that the situation was still chaotic that afternoon.

> That afternoon, when I went back to take pictures, my assistant and my driver and the first sergeant were standing beside my jeep . . . and one of the German soldiers came running around a corner and we grabbed him as he came to our jeep, and a Forty-second Division soldier came around the corner right behind him. We were standing not over three feet apart and this Forty-second Division man whirled the guy around and said, "Here you are, you S.O.B.," and machine-gunned him. . . . I said, "Look, fella, you're crazy. This guy was a prisoner." [He replied,] "Gotta kill 'em, gotta kill 'em, gotta kill 'em." This guy was psycho.[107]

At 1635 hours, a very weary Felix Sparks radioed back to regiment that he had opened his command post in Dachau. It was the first time he had been in radio contact with higher headquarters for several hours. About an hour after the Linden party left, a soldier told Sparks a lieutenant colonel wanted to see him at the camp headquarters. "I went back to the headquarters," Sparks said,

> and this lieutenant colonel said he was from the Inspector General department of Seventh Army and had been sent there to investigate the incident between me and General Linden. About that moment, there was a huge crash. A soldier from one of our artillery battalions had taken his rifle butt and smashed the glass case with the antique weapons. I told him to get his ass out of there. The colonel from the I.G. said, "Can't you control your own men?" I said he wasn't one of mine, he was an artilleryman. Then I said, "Look, I don't have time for this now," and the I.G. colonel stalked out.

"Later," said Sparks, "I took General Frederick and Colonel O'Brien, the regimental commander, around the camp and told them about the massacre and the incident with Linden. General Frederick told me not to worry about it, that he'd take care of it."†[108]

---

*Another of Cowan's curiously inaccurate articles; there were no tanks, bulldozers, or self-propelled guns at KL Dachau on 29 April with either I Company, 157th, or Linden's advance party. Nor was there a "furious battle."

†Frederick evidently was so sickened by the conditions he found in Dachau that, when asked about the situation by assistant division commander Paul Adams, Frederick refused to discuss the matter (Paul Adams, oral history taken May 6, 1975, U.S. Army Military History Institute).

Many of the soldiers were thankful they had reached the camp in time to save countless lives but discovered it was virtually impossible to avoid being repelled by the awful conditions in the camp. Sidney C. Horn, a member of I Company, 157th, recalled the terrible overcrowding and the lack of proper sanitation: "The people wanted to hug you and love you for what you were doing, but the stench was so bad, you couldn't keep from running from them."[109]

Chaplain Loy was staggered by what he saw at Dachau. "It was horrible beyond imagining. I simply could not believe that human beings could treat each other in such a way. The inmates were unbelievably grateful for their liberation. Many of them broke down and cried and kissed our hands. We conducted religious services for them; it didn't matter what their religions were, or even if they spoke English or not. They were just so thankful to be alive, after all they had been through."[110]

As the gray, sunless day settled into a cold, dank night, a sense of relief spread over the inmates of KL Dachau. From the barracks, for the first time in twelve years, came sounds of laughter, sounds of singing, sounds of prayers of thanksgiving. There was little joy among their American liberators, however. Although they had undoubtedly helped save thousands of lives, many of the men of I Company, 157th, felt sick and depressed over the sights and events of the day, and the stench of death was still heavy in the air.

John Lee recalled,

> That night was when the realization really hit. We had to guard the bakery, our squad. I remember [a buddy] saying, "I'll never make it through the night," because he had been smelling the bodies all day long, the stench and everything. You were sick to your stomach to begin with. No one ate chow that night . . . everyone was sick. . . . I was sick constantly all night long. I don't think there was a guy who slept that night, and I don't think there was a guy who didn't cry openly that night.[111]

Many of the I Company men were also sickened by the realization of what some of their comrades had done that day. Hank Mills said, "We came over here to stop this bullshit and here we've got somebody doing the same thing. Once [the German guards] were unarmed, they were prisoners. You can't shoot 'em, you can't do that. That's an atrocity, I'm sure."[112]

John Lee added, "I really didn't feel good about what happened there, but also I have to admit there was a certain amount of revenge and, in a way, I felt that even though these [guards] may not have been the men who perpetrated this sort of thing, at least you paid back a little bit for these people, what happened to them. I realized you can't resolve it by doing that—it was wrong, what happened there, but you had to have been there to see what we saw."[113]

On the evening of 29 April, at 1903 hours, Sparks received a message that I and L Companies were to relieve C Company, which had moved into the concentration camp. Then, at 2010 hours, Major Carroll, the S-3, made the following entry in his journal: "Colonel Brown [Lieutenant Colonel Lawrence Brown, who had just taken command of the 157th from Colonel O'Brien] to Blue Three [Blue Three was the radio code sign for the 3rd Battalion operations officer]—You are to surround the camp with your whole battalion. Blue Three says Forty-second Division has a company there. Colonel Brown tells him they are to move out and, if they don't, have their company commanding officer or battalion commanding officer report to this CP."[114]

At 2045 hours, the 42nd's 222nd Regiment reported to division that A and F Companies are "at concentration camp," and other units were scattered in various other locations. At 2100 hours that evening, the regiment reported, "Concentration camp situation well in hand." The 222nd remained in the Dachau area until the next day, 30 April, when it pushed forward and opened a new CP at 1840 hours in Munich. Thus, the 42nd's association with Dachau ended.[115]

At 2300 hours on 29 April, the 45th Division messaged the XV Corps: "Concentration camp at Dachau captured by I Company 179th [*sic*] Inf with thousands of political prisoners. . . . Entire Third Battalion trying to contain hysterical liberated. Rumored horrors unexaggerated."[116] At 2350 hours that night, the G-5 detachment from Corps arrived to take control of the camp.[117] To further clarify the issue (or confuse it, depending on which side one stands), the XV Corps's G-3 report for 30 April concludes: "Results of Operations: . . . Forty-fifth Inf Div liberated political PW camp at Dachau." Farther on in the report, the G-3 added:

> Status of Camp on Morning of 30 April. At 0800 an inspection was made of the camp by Corps G-5 together with the Regimental Commander of the 157th Infantry. . . . The exterior of the camp was then under guard by elements of the Forty-fifth Division, while the interior was being guarded by elements of the 42d Division. By coordination between the various commanders, responsibility for the camp's security were allocated, and the elements of the two divisions rendered excellent coordination and each had a clearly defined security zone. At 0945, responsibility for the camp was taken over by the XV Corps and temporary command of the camp was assumed by Corps G-5. On 1 May . . . command of the camp was turned over to Colonel Barrett, Inspector General of XV Corps.[118]

The next morning, Lieutenant Colonel Ralph Krieger's 1st Battalion, 157th, took all of the division's attached armor and pushed ahead to attack Munich but came to an abrupt halt before getting very far. Krieger's men had come across, and liberated, a satellite camp a few kilometers away at

Corporal Larry Mutinsk of A Company, 157th Infantry Regiment, handing out cigarettes to prisoners at Allach, one of Dachau's satellite camps. (Courtesy of U.S. Army Military History Institute)

Allach, on the northwest outskirts of Munich. It turned out to be a slave labor camp with 9,454 inmates.[119]

"An artillery battalion relieved 3rd Battalion at Dachau and we followed 1st Battalion into Munich," Sparks said. "We took over an apartment building for our headquarters, then I got a message to go back and relieve the artillery battalion that had relieved us. Next morning, May first, it snowed a little. I took L Company back and relieved the artillery battalion, then went back to my headquarters in Munich. L Company remained at Dachau until May third, when the 179th came in."

On 1 May, however, Sparks was relieved of command of the 3rd Battalion, apparently, he thought, as a result of his threatening a general officer.*

> On May first, General Frederick came to see me in Munich. He said, "Things are getting hot. General Linden is raising a stink. I'm going to send you back to the States immediately. Our division is scheduled to invade Japan and I'm sending you back. You can take a leave and rejoin us when we come back to the States." Next morning, a command car showed up at my headquarters. I took my driver and interpreter and a rifleman. I didn't have any written orders; Frederick just said to go to Le Havre and I'd get my orders there.[120]

Sparks called his company commanders together, told them he was being sent back to the States, and bade them farewell. According to the 3rd Battalion journal, Sparks asked the company commanders "to pass message on to their men and to carry on for new C.O. as they have for him. He feels badly about leaving this unit." By 1345 hours, he was gone.[121]

• • •

Lieutenant Colonel Joseph Whitaker, Seventh Army's assistant inspector general, spent several weeks interviewing as many participants and witnesses to the events of 29 April as he could reach, then wrote up his findings. Once his report, stamped "Secret," was complete, it was sent to the office of the Seventh Army Judge Advocate General, who recommended that Lieutenant Walsh, Lieutenant Busheyhead, Technician third grade Wells, and Private Albert Pruitt (who had finished off the four Germans whom Walsh had herded into the railroad car) should be charged with murder and tried by court-martial. Furthermore, the JAG recommended

*According to the historian Hugh Foster, "The term 'relieved' is a touchy word, if not fully explained in relation to the times. Today, a commander who is 'relieved' is dishonored, for the term today means the officer did something wrong; it means being fired for cause. However, during World War II, the term did not hold that connotation, necessarily. It *could* mean being fired, but it could also refer to a normal change of a commander, that is, a change without prejudice. Sparks's view is that he was not 'fired,' but was taken out of command in order to be sent back to the States—to get him out of the way of Linden's charges" (Hugh Foster, letter to author, Mar. 16, 1997).

that Lieutenant Drain be court-martialed for failure to perform his duty for not attempting to stop the commission of a criminal act, and Lieutenant Howard Buechner, the 3rd Battalion, 157th's battalion surgeon, be charged with failure to perform his duty for failing to render aid to wounded enemy soldiers (even though, according to Sparks, Buechner did not arrive on the scene until at least two hours after the shooting).[122]

Wade Haislip, who had succeeded Alexander Patch as commander of Seventh Army, however, refused to proceed with the recommended courts-martial, citing the fact that the I.G. had failed to take into account the emotional state of the troops, who had been in nearly continuous combat for more than a month. Haislip only approved of charging Walsh and Pruitt with shooting the four SS soldiers in the box car and stalled long enough for his Seventh Army to be reorganized and ordered to push on into Austria; Patton's Third Army, relocating its headquarters from Regensburg to Bad Tölz, south of Munich, would take control of Bavaria. Because the 45th Division was reassigned to become part of Third Army, the matter was handed over to Third Army for disposition.[123] Patton, not uncharacteristically, also chose to take no disciplinary action. His position, no doubt, was that it was the *Germans* who were the enemy; the SS had run the concentration camps and if some of them got killed in the process of liberation, that was just too damn bad. Besides, Patton had never shown any inclination to sully the reputation of the American Army and especially that of the 45th Division. (The decision to court-martial the two 45th Division soldiers after the massacre of German and Italian POWs on Sicily was Bradley's not Patton's; Patton would have been happy simply to sweep the incidents under the rug. After Bradley had reported the matter to Patton, Patton hinted strongly that the reports should be altered to make it appear that the enemy dead had been snipers or had tried to escape. At Bad Tölz, he had no Bradley to act as his conscience.)[124] Furthermore, the surviving leaders of the Nazi regime were being rounded up and imprisoned in anticipation of war crimes trials that were to take place in the upcoming months at Nürnberg; to conduct a court-martial of the 45th Division men involved in the Dachau massacres would not only besmirch the honor of the American fighting man but could seriously weaken the Allies' case against the Nazis accused of atrocities. According to Felix Sparks, Patton, in his presence, destroyed Whitaker's report and no courts-martial were ever conducted. Only a single copy of the report survived, and it lay undetected in the bowels of the National Archives for half a century.[125]

The 45th Division chief of staff, Kenneth Wickham, recalled, "General Patton, who had taken over the Army area, kind of said, 'To hell with it [the I.G. investigation],' and that was it. We didn't go further into it and General Frederick wasn't concerned much one way or the other. He was just kind of annoyed by it."[126]

To Sparks, the I.G.'s investigation into the shooting of the guards at Dachau was a curious affair. For one thing, neither he nor Lieutenant Colonel Buldoç was ever questioned or called as witnesses. ("I was back in France, but the Army knew where I was. My only guess," Sparks surmised, "is that Buldoc refused to go along with a made-up story.") Sparks said, "In his sworn testimony to the I.G., Linden doesn't mention anything about our altercation. He says he placed me in charge of the outer portion of the camp and placed Colonel Fellenz in charge of the prisoner area. It's like we were buddy-buddy. I never saw him again."

Sparks continued, "Neither Linden nor anyone else in the 42nd Division ever mentioned Marguerite Higgins in their testimony. In the whole course of the investigation, there was not one mention of her. They were embarrassed by it, because I think they were in Dachau only because of her—they were escorting her around. But they made one mistake; the 42nd's Division Journal for that day showed she had reported in to headquarters that morning. They forgot to take that out."[127]

The civilians living in or near Dachau, who claimed they knew nothing of the horrors being committed in their backyard, were given a lesson in the brutality of their countrymen. The medic Peter Galary recalled that once the camp was in American hands, "We made the civilians who lived around there parade past the boxcars full of dead bodies, and they said, 'We never knew about it.' They cried, but what good is crying going to do?—it wouldn't bring any of those people back to life."[128]

Like Sparks, Walsh, too, was relieved of his command, but it may not have been a benign, administrative move. Sent back to a staff job at regimental headquarters, he realized that he and some of his men were probably in hot water over the incidents of 29 April. "It wasn't a real legitimate fight . . . if there is such a thing," he said.

> But some of the SS guys had died in defense of that camp, and some Goddamn day, when I go to hell with the rest of them, I'm going to ask how the hell they could do it and what they were doing up there, and if they knew? I don't think there was any SS guy that was shot or killed in the defense of Dachau that wondered why he was killed. . . . I have a funny feeling that every one of them that died in the defense of Dachau knew why he died, and maybe he felt very proud dying for the . . . Fatherland and the defense of the SS and the practices that went on in Dachau.[129]

And what of the inmates—all 31,432 of them? "Overjoyed" is too mild a term to adequately describe their feelings of redemption. And certainly, whether their redeemers wore a Thunderbird patch or a rainbow or anything else was of absolutely no concern to them. The Americans had come, they were alive and free, and that was all that mattered. Medical teams from XV Corps immediately went to work in an attempt to save as many of the critically ill former inmates as possible. Their best efforts often went unrewarded, as a further 2,466 died of illness between 29 April and 16 June. The emaciated but surviving prisoners were carefully nourished, inoculated, sprayed with DDT to kill body lice, and given fresh clothing. As the danger of the spread of typhus was high, the inmates were quarantined in the camp for a few more weeks. Their situation, however, had been immeasurably improved, and soon they were readied for repatriation to their former homelands.[130]

One of the inmates, a Pole named Walenty Lenarczyk, told Whitaker through an interpreter,

> After this shooting [at Tower B], prisoners swarmed over the wire and grabbed the American soldiers and lifted them to their shoulders amid many cries. I helped to lift the soldiers. . . . During this celebration, there must have been a hundred, maybe 200, of the camp prisoners surrounding these Americans, boosting them up. All that could were crowding in to kiss their hands and clothes. . . . At this time, four German SS guards ran. It is impossible to say where they came from but they ran across the front . . . and it was impossible for the Americans to shoot them because they were surrounded with camp prisoners. And, while this was going on, other prisoners caught the SS men and killed them. The SS men were always proud, and as the crowd of prisoners closed around them, they would go through. The first SS man elbowed one or two prisoners out of his way, but the courage of the prisoners mounted, they knocked them down, and nobody could see because of the great group whether they were stomped or what, but they were killed. All we could think about were Americans. For the past six years we had waited for the Americans, and at this moment the SS were nothing. We were all these years animals to them. . . . It was ordered by Himmler that the SS kill all prisoners before the Americans come, and so when they came fast, it was truly our second birthday.[131]

• • •

As with the advance on Rome nearly a year earlier, every unit wanted the honor of being the first into Munich. The 3rd, 42nd, and 45th Infantry Divisions were all racing toward the city, along with the 12th and 20th Armored Divisions. The Seventh Army history reports the race was a dead heat.[132]

On 29 April, moving down the *Autobahn* from the north on tanks and tank destroyers and other vehicles of the 106th Cavalry Group, the 179th, now under Lieutenant Colonel William P. Grace (who had succeeded Colonel Preston Murphy when the latter was wounded on 16 April) bypassed Dachau and attacked the city of Munich, which had been heavily damaged by aerial assaults but had not been completely reduced to rubble as had so many other German cities. The 3rd Division attacked from the south while the 42nd entered from the northwest. Only light resistance was encountered by the 179th on the northern outskirts and, as each block

Sergeant Arthur E. Peters, 45th Infantry Division, relaxing on a sofa with a copy of Mein Kampf *in Hitler's Munich apartment, May 1945. (Courtesy of Life magazine, David Scherman photographer/Life Magazine © Time Inc.)*

passed, the Thunderbirds expected to catch hell from hordes of fanatical Nazis defending the birthplace of National Socialism. But aside from some isolated pockets of resistance, the city's defenders gave up with barely a whimper, thanks in large measure to an anti-Nazi underground movement within the city. By 1 May, Munich had been secured, and the 45th moved in to garrison the city while the rest of Seventh Army drove south to link up with Truscott's Fifth Army at the Brenner Pass. The linkup occurred on the morning of 4 May.[133] The 179th set up its command post in what had once been Hitler's apartment, and the 157th established its CP in the famed *Hofbrauhaus* beer hall, where Hitler's oratory had once stirred the masses to a fever pitch.[134]

At Munich, one of the division's major tasks was to ride herd on a POW compound holding some 125,000 of the vanquished enemy. On 3 May, another 7,400 men from the 9th Hungarian Division joined the ranks of enemy POWs. The 45th was also assigned the tremendous responsibility of occupation: securing supply installations, maintaining public facilities, and controlling the civilian population, including a mass of restless refugees who wanted only to return to their homes.[135]

Up north, as the Soviets closed in on Berlin, Adolf Hitler killed himself in his bunker on 30 April. Resistance throughout Germany slowly came to an end as the Allies strangled the Nazi empire from east and west. Finally, it was done. Nearly six years of total war in Europe had ended, a war that had left a continent utterly destroyed, a war in which tens of millions had died. To signal the end of the fighting, a simple, unadorned message was issued by Eisenhower's headquarters: "The mission of this Allied force was fulfilled at 0241 local time, May 7, 1945." The crusade in Europe was over.[136]

To the weary men of the 45th, it all seemed like a dream come true. No more amphibious landings. No more unending artillery bombardments. No more pitched battles on snowy mountain peaks. No more crouching in water-filled foxholes waiting for the enemy's charge. No more crawling through minefields to burn enemy troops out of their fortifications. No more picking up the nightmarish remains of what had once been one's best friend.

Just peace.

Glorious peace.

Or was it? Half a world away, Japan remained fiercely defiant, unconquered. The Army needed experienced combat units for its planned invasion of the Japanese home islands, which was expected to cost a million American casualties. And the 45th was just what the Army was looking for.

Epilgoue: Things of Beauty

My guide and I came on that hidden road to make our way back to the bright world; and with no care for any rest, we climbed—he first, I following—until I saw, through a round opening, some of those things of beauty Heaven bears. It was from there that we emerged, to see—once more—the stars.

—Dante Alighieri, *The Inferno*, Canto XXXIV

ON 30 MAY 1945, UNDER A BRILLIANT BLUE SKY, the 45th Division took part in a Memorial Day ceremony in Munich's capacious *Königsplatz* where, eight years earlier, Hitler and Mussolini had watched the cream of the German Army march by on its way to touching off the most destructive war in history.

Here in the city that Eisenhower had called "the cradle of the beast," the assembled troops, standing in ranks before the red-white-and-blue–bedecked wooden platform set up in front of the neoclassical Propylaea on Briennerstrasse, stood a little taller, a little straighter, as the 45th's commanding officer stepped to the microphone to address the division he had inherited in December. The American flag behind him hung at half staff.

"Today," said Major General Robert T. Frederick,

> in the very heart of a conquered Germany, we pause to pay tribute to our comrades who gave the fullest measure of sacrifice for their country. They fell facing an enemy whose object was the destruction of those ideals which Americans hold dear. They fell in the glorious tradition of the American heritage that fights for the right to live in freedom.
>
> Those men were our friends. With them we shared our dangers, our successes, and our hopes. We cannot bring them back, but we can do our part to insure the endurance of those principles for which they died.

A portion of the 45th Division assembled for Memorial Day ceremony, May 1945. (Courtesy of 45th Infantry Division Archives)

Thinking of the Japanese foe that was down but not yet out, Frederick continued,

> Today we stand at the halfway point of the greatest of all wars. Some of us will carry on the fight in other active theaters; others will remain here in Europe; and still others will return to their homes in America. I hope that, wherever we go, we shall not forget our debt to our fallen comrades. I ask that you not merely pay tribute to their memory, but carry on their fight for peace—even after the last armistice is signed. Only by carrying on that fight, unceasingly and without wavering, can we fulfill our obligations to our brothers in arms who lie dead in foreign soil.[1]*

A chaplain then said a prayer and a bugler blew "Taps." It was over.

• • •

Near the end of May, Patton's Third Army moved into nearby Bad Tölz but wanted Munich for itself. The 45th Division found itself unceremoniously evicted. Brigadier General Paul D. Adams, the 45th's assistant division

---

*During the course of the war, which consumed some 50 million human lives, 4,080 men of the 45th Division were killed in action or died from their wounds. Another 16,913 were wounded—many more than once. Another 3,617 were reported as missing in action. Of the eighteen National Guard divisions that saw combat in World War II, none suffered higher casualty figures than the 45th. In fact, only three Regular Army divisions lost more men in Europe (John K. Mahon, *History of the Militia and the National Guard* [New York: Macmillan, 1983], p. 191).

commander, remembered, "I asked this Third Army Chief of Staff, 'Well, where do you want us to go?' And he said, 'We don't give a damn, just get the hell out of town, we want it.' So the Third came in and put their CP in Munich. And we had the last word, though; as we moved out of town the Engineers put a sign on every significant road leading into town. . . . It read, 'Third Army Area—By Courtesy of the Forty-fifth Division.'"[2]

To look at the 45th's total effort in the whole of the war, the men of the 45th had performed magnificently the job for which they had been trained. Few other divisions were ordered to do more than the Thunderbirds, and none performed with greater valor. In its 511 days of actual combat (the artillery battalions, which were often attached to support other divisions, had even more), the 45th covered thousands of miles from Sicily to Munich, liberated hundreds of villages, towns, and cities, and captured nearly 125,000 of the enemy. The number of German dead and wounded inflicted by the Thunderbirds is unknown but must surely stretch into the tens of thousands. By any measure, the 45th's contribution to the defeat of Germany was enormous.

The division received the praise of those corps and theater commanders under which it had served. On 16 July, General George S. Patton called a number of the 45th Division officers and enlisted men together for a brief ceremony, telling them that the 45th was one of only three divisions he knew of that conducted itself like a veteran division on its first day of combat. Then he wished them well and departed.

The war in Europe was over, but one more foe remained to be conquered. That summer, the 45th moved from Germany to Camp Saint Louis near Le Havre, France, to await further deployment. Although the troops hoped that their next and final stop would be the good old U.S.A., most also realized that they would probably soon be invading the Japanese home islands—an invasion that was expected to cost a million American casualties. Throughout the summer, the men of the 45th trained once more in the terrible skills of warfare, preparing their minds and bodies for another all-out conflict, one that was expected to be even bloodier than the one that they had just endured. Then, on 6 August 1945, an atomic bomb exploded above the Japanese city of Hiroshima. Three days later, another one wiped the city of Nagasaki off the map. The Japanese Empire, the last remaining member of the unholy Axis alliance, surrendered.

The 45th Infantry Division came sailing home in September 1945. It was a far different division from the one that had left Virginia on 4 June 1943. Very few of the original Thunderbirds were still with the outfit. Many had been maimed for life. Others lay buried in makeshift American military cemeteries throughout Sicily, Italy, France, and Germany or had completely vanished. Those who had survived were old beyond their years.[3]

As the troopships steamed into their East Coast ports (the 179th and 180th Regiments landed at New York; the 157th debarked at Boston),

Men of the 45th Division coming home by troop ship, August 1945. (Courtesy of 45th Infantry Division Archives)

bands played, confetti danced in the air like snowflakes, and pretty girls greeted the soldiers with hugs and kisses. Some of the girls were even the wives or girlfriends of the soldiers. Many held in their arms infants—the sons and daughters of Thunderbirds who had been born while their fathers were overseas. More than one child on the docks cried while being hugged and kissed by a man he or she had never seen before.

There was the usual hurry up and wait as the men were processed and received new orders or, if they had accumulated enough "points,"* were given their discharge papers and mustering-out pay of $300. The majority received a forty-five-day "rest-and-recuperation" furlough and were told to report to Camp Bowie, near Brownwood, Texas, at the end of their R&R.[4]

As they traveled to their destinations, many of the men were amazed by the sights and sounds of an America that they had all but forgotten, sights and sounds that contrasted so vividly with the wreckage and carnage of war that had become the norm throughout the continent of Europe. The American cities through which the Thunderbirds passed were intact and unbombed. Instead of roads choked with endless lines of pitiful refugees, the streets were filled with happy, prosperous, and well-dressed civilians. Instead of long stretches of olive-drab jeeps and trucks and tanks, civilian cars and buses and taxis crowded the boulevards. The planes that flew overhead carried passengers, not bombs. The air was fragrant with the scent of summer flowers, not redolent with the odor of cordite and decomposing bodies. Not a soul seemed worried about buried mines, snipers, or strafing, and no one scanned the block ahead with binoculars, looking for likely ambush sites. Stores were filled with the types of goods the GIs had only dreamt about for two years. Instead of cracking open another K ration box or peeling the top off a C ration can, they could actually walk into a restaurant and order a steak, smothered with mushrooms or onions. Grateful civilians slapped them on the back and pumped their hands and bought them drinks and thanked them for the job they had done, even though few of them could tell a 45th Division patch from a 101st Airborne "Screaming Eagle" emblem. But everyone knew what a Combat Infantryman's Badge

*The Army devised a complicated-but-fair demobilization system. On each individual's Adjusted Service Rating Card were such categories as Service Credit (one point for each month of service between 16 September 1940, and 12 May 1945), Overseas Credit (one point for each month served overseas between the above two dates), Combat Service (five points for the first and each additional award of the Distinguished Service Cross, Legion of Merit, Silver Star, Distinguished Flying Cross, Soldier's Medal, Bronze Star, Air Medal, Purple Heart, or bronze battle or campaign participation stars worn on theater ribbons), and Parenthood Credit (twelve points for each child, age eighteen or under, born before 12 May 1945, up to a limit of three children). To be released from the service, an enlisted man needed a total of eighty-five points. Some soldiers, however, could be kept on active duty if their C.O.s listed them as "essential" (*Yank* Magazine, June 1, 1945, pp. 20–21).

looked like, and they had all had heard of Sicily and Salerno and Anzio and Dachau. They knew the man in uniform was someone very special. They knew he was a soldier.

Then, one by one, each man found his way home, fell into the arms of his wife, his children, his mother or father, his sister or brother. Tears flowed freely—tears of complete, absolute, and unbounded joy.

It was good, at long last, to be home.

For those who remained in the Army, the furloughs ended all too quickly. The men had become, in just a short time, already too accustomed to civilian life and civilian cooking, sleeping in a real bed in a room instead of in a hole in the ground or in a rowdy barracks with dozens of others. But the Army had called and it was time to return to duty. They shouldered their duffle bags; bade their loved ones farewell once more; boarded buses, trains, or cars; and headed for Camp Bowie, Texas, near Brownwood, southeast of Camp Barkeley. It was clear that with massive demobilization of the nation's armed forces, the days of the 45th Infantry Division were numbered. The officers were determined to throw the biggest farewell bash Texas had ever seen. Unable to round up the requisite number of steaks locally, Brigadier General Paul Adams sent Army trucks all the way to Kansas City, where they picked up 2,200 thick, juicy T-bones.[5]

Now under the command of Brigadier General Henry J.D. Meyer, who had commanded the 45th's Division Artillery after the departure of General McLain, the division was inactivated on 7 December 1945—exactly four years to the day since Japanese aircraft attacked the American Pacific Fleet at Pearl Harbor and brought the United States into World War II. Ironically, the inactivation orders were signed by the very man whose Anzio beachhead they had once helped save—Major General John Porter Lucas.

In his farewell message to the division, Meyer wrote,

> As of 2400 hours, 7 December 1945, the 45th Infantry Division will cease to be an active unit of the United States Army. It somehow seems right and appropriate that we should victoriously complete our great task upon the anniversary of the declaration of war which started us on our crusade. In official language, the Division is being "inactivated." The word "inactivated" imparts a status of inertia; a word never used in conjunction with the 45th and therefore strange to you. Subsequent to its inactivation, and until further orders, the Division will become dormant for the first time since 16 September 1940. . . . There are some things about the Division which can never be inactivated. Many events have been engraved in the minds of men, and some of them have been recorded in the annals of our nation's history.

Meyer then detailed the division's many successes—the victorious march across Sicily, the saving of the Salerno beachhead, the suffering in the wintry mountains around Venafro, the steadfastness at Anzio, the landings in southern France and the drive through the Vosges and Alsace, the sacrifices at Reipertswiller, the splintering of the Siegfried Line, the battles for Aschaffenburg, Nürnberg, and Munich.

"Never let us forget," he continued,

> our comrades who gave their lives to protect and insure for our country those blessings of Life, Liberty, and the Pursuit of Happiness which they cannot now enjoy with us. Their crosses blaze the trail of the Division from Comiso Airport to Munich. Never let us forget our living comrades now hospitalized, whose courageous demeanor belies the fact that their wounded bodies are racked with pain. The Forty-fifth paid heavily for maintaining our American heritage. . . . There is also the remarkable spirit of cooperation and brotherhood which has characterized the personnel of the Division from the date of its induction until these, its last days in Federal Service.
>
> Yes, these are the things which we can never forget—the friendships, the joys, the sorrows, the suffering, and the glorious accomplishments of 511 days of combat. Whatever destiny may hold in store for our great country and however long that country's military history may continue, readers in the future will search long before finding a chapter more brilliant than that written by the quill dipped in the blood of the Thunderbirds. Being a Thunderbird has been a source of great pride to me. I shall remember my service with you, as Artillery Commander and as your Commanding General, as one of the outstanding honors and pleasures of my life. Farewell to all of you, and may God bless you.[6]

Brigadier General Henry J.D. Meyer (right), the 45th's last World War II commander. (Photo courtesy of 45th Infantry Division Archives)

Since the end of the war, the veterans of the 45th have often mused over and discussed among themselves how they—members of a National Guard division—were able to stop the best the Germans could send against them, time after time. The men have differing but similar answers.

Chester Powell, M Company, 180th, said, "We was raised up hard in the '30s. We was poor. What meat we got, we shot. The Army didn't have to teach us to shoot, especially the boys from Oklahoma. I'm not putting down any of the boys from the East Coast, 'cause some of them turned into real good soldiers. I believe by nature we was pretty rough customers; we had to depend on each other. At Anzio, there was heaven above us and hell below us and the sea behind us and the Germans in front of us. There wasn't but one way for us to move."[7]

Thinking of such outstanding leaders as Key, Middleton, Eagles, Frederick, Ankcorn, McLain, and Darby, William C. Pullum, K Company, 157th, said, "We stopped the Germans because of leadership. We were blessed with some exceptional leadership—from junior officers right up into the division. I think it showed."[8]

Glen K. Hanson, L Company, 157th, offered, "Teamwork. Everybody worked together. Everybody knew what he was supposed to do and everybody did it. If somebody saw a hole in the line, they didn't say what do we do? They plugged it."[9]

Philip Burke, HQ Company, 157th, replied, "I think our success was due to our training in the States, which was fantastic, and also to our commanders and junior officers. You couldn't hate anybody more for the way they drove us, but it really paid off later. Of course, all the experience we got in Sicily and going up the center of Italy and on the Volturno made us a tough, sharp, street-wise outfit."[10]

Henry Havlat put it succinctly: "The Germans found out who the 'master race' was when they met us."[11]

• • •

With the war over and the need for a large standing army vanished, most of the men of the 45th returned to civilian life and either returned to school or to careers cut short by the war or tried to start life anew, faced with daunting challenges.

Although he lost both legs at Anzio, Edward "Don" Amzibel became the chief maintenance clerk for Union Carbide in Ohio. He lives in Ashtabula, where he has been honored for his sacrifice on many occasions.

Clay Barnes, who commanded the 157th's Anti-Tank Company, attended Harvard Business School and entered the fledgling automotive rental field with Hertz and Avis. He lives today in Homestead, Florida.

Hubert Berry, who was evacuated with trench foot at Anzio, became a district sales manager for Moorman Manufacturing in Texas. Today he lives in Goldthwaite, Texas.

The twice-wounded artilleryman James Bird earned the Silver Star and returned to New Jersey, where he worked for thirty-seven years for the State Department of Public Safety and became deputy superintendent of the Department of Weights and Measures. He is a charter member of the United States Holocaust Museum, has been active in the Boy Scout program for nearly forty years, and lives in Medford, New Jersey.

Philip Burke, a lieutenant wounded during the escape from the caves at Anzio, went to medical school and became a surgeon. He lives in Worcester, Massachusetts.

Pete Conde, who lost a foot in France in October 1944, lives in Denver and volunteers his time with a seniors' services center.

Nicholas Defonte, who was attached to the British at Anzio to serve as an interpreter and POW interrogater, became a customs broker. He resides in Wantagh, New York.

Alex Dryden became a Catholic priest. He lives in Pennsauken, New Jersey.

Charlie Dunham, who came home on points just before his company—E Company, 157th—was wiped out at Anzio, worked for the Colorado Department of Revenue. He lives in Lamar, Colorado.

Platoon Sergeant Everett Easley of the 179th, who was wounded four times and received the Bronze Star, returned to California and the logging industry. He lives today in Fall River Mills, California.

The medic George Ecker also earned the Bronze Star. He returned to teach at the University of Connecticut. He lives in the college town of Storrs.

Daniel Ficco, who now resides in Petaluma, California, became self-employed, opening his own grocery store and bar after the war.

Ralph Fink joined the 45th as a replacement and ended up as a platoon sergeant. He was awarded three Bronze Stars and two Purple Hearts. He said,

> Many soldiers, including myself, in our quiet moments, feel a sense of guilt in having survived, when we lost so many good men along the way. This, along with the overpowering experience of seeing man's cruelty to man at Dachau, later led my wife and myself to seek employment in a helping occupation. I had been raised in a wonderful school as an orphan boy at Milton Hershey School. My wife Clarabel and I found our niche in life there as houseparents for thirty-one years. Over our long career, we cared for and nurtured nearly three hundred boys in the eleven-to-fifteen age bracket, each for a period of up to four years.[12]

He still lives in Hershey, Pennsylvania.

Bernard Fleming earned three Bronze Stars, three "V" for Valor devices, and two Purple Hearts. He worked as an electrician after the war. He lives in Hyannis, Massachusetts.

Robert Joseph "Doc Joe" Franklin, recipient of the Silver Star with Oak Leaf Cluster, who still remembers his Army serial number (39240192), returned to California, where he worked as a teacher and photographer. Due to the sounds of the big guns, his ability to hear high tones, such as the ringing of a phone, has been permanently impaired. He lives in Sylmar, California.

William Gordon, who once shot at tanks at Anzio, worked for the New Jersey Department of Agriculture. He resides in Vineland, New Jersey.

John Griffin, who had his jeep destroyed at Anzio, lives in Canfield, Ohio. After the war, he worked as a steelworker and in the data processing field.

Glen Hanson, who earned the Silver Star, Bronze Star, and Purple Heart, left the service in May 1945, became an office manager, then rejoined the Army in 1950, retiring in 1968. He has returned to his old hometown of Cortez, Colorado.

Henry Havlat, who was wounded at Bloody Ridge in Sicily, worked for the Department of Defense after he recovered from his wounds. He lives in Englewood, Colorado.

Captured near the caves at Anzio, Henry Kaufman spent the rest of the war in German POW camps, including Dachau. After the war, he owned a number of successful California corporations, became a charter member of the U.S. Holocaust Memorial Museum, and published a book on his experiences. He lives today in Los Angeles.

Charles Keffler earned two Bronze Stars and a Purple Heart. He returned to Canton, Ohio, to resume his career with the utility company. He lives there today.

Kenneth Kindig, the sniper who helped hold off the enemy at the Overpass, earned a Bronze Star and Purple Heart. Returning to Denver, Colorado, he entered the trucking and construction business. He died in 1997.

Robert LaDu, a platoon leader in the 179th, earned a Purple Heart and Bronze Star with Oak Leaf Cluster. He became a veterinarian after the war and now resides in Marshall, North Carolina.

Karl Mann, Felix Sparks's interpreter in the 3rd Battalion at Dachau, returned to school. He received his bachelor's degree at American University, earned a master's at Wisconsin and his Ph.D. in Industrial and Labor Relations at Cornell, and then spent over thirty years teaching at the college level, including twenty-seven years at Ryder College in New Jersey. He lives in Yardley, Pennsylvania.

Four-times wounded, Alvin "Bud" McMillan followed a number of career paths after the war, including athletic director and accounting. The recipient of both the Silver Star and Bronze Star (with Oak Leaf Cluster and "V" for valor), he calls Myrtle Beach, South Carolina, home.

Jack McMillion, who lost a leg at Anzio, returned to Colorado, where he ran for the state legislature. As a write-in candidate, he won by a 2 to 1 margin and served several terms. He later owned a car dealership in Akron, Colorado, and also was elected mayor of the town. He now lives in nearby Fort Morgan.

Jack Montgomery, the Cherokee who received the Medal of Honor, Silver Star, Purple Heart with Oak Leaf Cluster, and the Italian Military Cross of Valor, went to work for the Veterans Administration after the war. He resides in Muskogee, Oklahoma.

Sid Pollock, a twice-wounded Bronze Star winner from Philadelphia, became an auto mechanic after the war. He has retired and lives in Maitland, Florida.

Chester Powell spent much of his prewar life on a farm. After the war, he became a home builder and a minister. He currently lives in Fletcher, Oklahoma.

Bill Pullum, first sergeant of K Company, 157th, received a battlefield commission prior to the invasion of southern France in August 1944. After the war, he worked as an electrician and then rejoined the Army. He has retired to Sun City, Arizona.

Charles Reiman, a former platoon commander from Kansas City who managed to avoid capture at Anzio, became a teacher. He lives in Stevensville, Montana.

Bill Rolen today lives in Alexandria, Virginia. A former prisoner of war, he worked for thirty-four years for the Department of Defense and was the executive director of the National Ex-POW Association.

Ken Vogt, a platoon sergeant with E Company, 157th, enjoys his retirement in Knoxville, Kentucky.

Howard Walton became a school teacher and principal after the war. He lives in Salinas, California.

Ray Williams, a miner before the war and a machinist after it, now lives in Coarse Gold, California.

John Lee, who today lives in West Lake, Ohio, can never forget what he saw at Dachau but worries that others might.

> Many times I have been asked to describe the sights and smell of the Dachau camp. As I have told students and others, the horrifying scene that we came upon was the most traumatic shock I ever went through in my life. It gave you such a helpless feeling to think that so many of these people could only look forward to death in order to get relief. As the survivors and liberators get older and older and fewer and fewer, it is going to be harder to make the younger generations believe that it *did* happen and could happen again. Groups like the Institute for Historical Review work hard to convince the public that the Holocaust is a historical lie and an exaggeration of special-interest groups. My response to these people is, "I know what I saw at Dachau and it was no mirage, but the work of barbaric and uncivilized minds that have no place in this world."[13]

Vere "Tarzan" Williams, who was seriously wounded in France and missed the drive into Germany, came home in Army hospital pajamas. In his duffle bag was his uniform jacket with an assortment of ribbons over the pocket: the European Theater ribbon and five battle stars, four Purple Heart medals (the Army said two of his six wounds did not officially qualify for the award), and his most prized possession—the Silver Star for gallantry under fire. Only 360 other members of the regiment received the Silver Star, the nation's fourth-highest award for valor.

He recalled that while he was in a military hospital in England before being sent back to the States, a colonel walked into the ward. Williams said,

> There were two majors and two or three captains and all the nurses on the wards around us. The colonel said, "It gives me great pleasure to present a man such a great honor as this." He said, "Sergeant Vere L. Williams," and I stood up. He had a piece of paper and read that, for courage above and beyond the call of duty, I was awarded the Silver Star. He said that it was a great honor for him to give me that award, that they never got to give anyone a citation like that. He shook my hand and saluted me. The other officers shook my hand and congratulated me, and the nurses hugged me and kissed me. I was really somebody around there.

After three months, the cast was finally taken off Williams's arm and he was informed he soon would be going home. Williams celebrated by hitting six Bristol pubs in one night. But instead of the promised plane ride home, Williams was sent home aboard the Queen Elizabeth, which reached New York from Glasgow in just five and a half days. Then there was a cross-country train trip scheduled from New York to a hospital in Vancouver, Washington, but, in Chicago, Williams was rerouted to Denver and received his discharge on 14 June 1945. His twenty months of overseas duty finally had come to an end.

While he had been away, his mother and father sold the family farm at Snyder, Colorado, and moved to the railroad town of Minturn, not far from where the ski resort of Vail would spring up some twenty years later. His two younger brothers were also in the service; Claude was a Navy man and Paul was in the Army, serving in the Pacific.

Reflecting back on his truncated military career, Williams said, "I would have liked to gone into Germany, but I may have been killed getting there."[14]

For other Thunderbirds, the Army became their way of life. The Medal of Honor recipient Van Barfoot spent twenty years in the service and retired at the rank of lieutenant colonel. He lives today in Ford, Virginia, where he enjoys playing golf as frequently as possible. As with the other obstacles he has faced in life, he has successfully battled cancer.

The Medal of Honor recipient Ernest Childers lives in Coweta, Oklahoma. After being brought back to the United States for a war bond tour, he was reassigned to a combat unit and took part in the invasion of southern France. He was part of the occupation force in Japan after the war ended. He remained in the service, retiring in 1965 at the rank of lieutenant colonel. He then worked for many years with the Department of the Interior. A school in his hometown, Broken Arrow, was named in his honor and a nine-foot bronze statue depicting him, sculpted by the noted Chiricahua-Apache artist, Allan Houser, was dedicated in Broken Arrow fifty-one years after the exploits that earned him the Medal of Honor.

Lieutenant Colonel Ralph Krieger, C.O. of the 157th's 1st Battalion, received the Legion of Merit—one of only sixteen awarded to men of the 157th. After retiring from the service, he studied pharmacy at the University of Texas, became a pharmacist, and then returned to the Army, where he became a brigadier general and assistant commander of the 36th Division. He retired to Abilene, Texas, not far from the site of Camp Barkeley. He died in 1996.

After retiring from the service, Lieutenant Colonel Leland Loy, a chaplain with the 157th, returned to being a civilian Methodist minister and was very active in the 157th Infantry Regiment Association. After retiring, he divided his time between Brooklyn, New York, and San Antonio, Texas. Like Krieger, he passed away a few months after being interviewed for this book.

Jeremiah Moher, a platoon commander with E Company, 157th, who was taken prisoner on 16 February 1944, vividly recalled his experiences: "About the second day [after being captured], they interrogated me, but they didn't find out much. Then they took us back another two miles. We had to take cover from a bomber strike that went over. Then they got us up and marched us to a railroad center and put us in box cars. We went from there to northern Italy. We stayed in a hospital for five days and I got cleaned up." Moher and his group were then transferred to another train that crossed the Alps, went through Austria, and stopped at a prisoner of war camp in Poland. "There were about 900 other officers there," he said. In January 1945, with the Soviet Army closing in, the POWs were moved.

> They marched us from there to east of Berlin. I didn't want to go there, so another guy and I—he was from the 1st Ranger Battalion—we got away and hid out in a barn. The next day the Germans were gone. We stayed there for three days and the Russians came. We told them we'd like to go home, so they let us get away and we rode every kind of vehicle we could get—a train or a truck—down to Lublin. There we took shelter in a big school where we stayed for a week with about 2,000 others. They put us in boxcars and took us to Odessa. We got good treatment all the time, but the Russians kept us locked up behind barbed wire. There was a British ship in the harbor and we told the Russians we would like to go. Two American majors from the embassy came to see how we were doing and told us they'd help us get out of there and back to the States. A couple of days later, the majors reappeared and said, "Let's go." They put us on a train that took us to Port Said, Egypt. We stayed there for four days in a big tent city and then, in April of '45, we came home.[15]

He was awarded the Bronze Star and Purple Heart. The wounds he suffered caused him limited use of his left arm but did not prevent him from making lieutenant colonel. He lives in Alexandria, Virginia.

Anse "Eddie" Speairs, commanding officer of C Company, 157th, received the Legion of Merit, Silver Star, four Bronze Star medals, and four Purple Hearts. He served with the 45th Infantry Division again during the Korean Conflict and had a one-year tour of duty in Vietnam before retiring with the rank of colonel. He lives today in Melbourne, Florida.

Kenneth P. Stemmons, C.O. of B Company, 157th, who knew how to lay out a minefield at Salerno and was awarded the Silver Star, Bronze Star, and Purple Heart, also retired at the rank of lieutenant colonel and then went to work for the Department of the Army as a military transportation specialist. He lives today in Galena, Missouri.

Bill Whitman remained in the Army, fought in Korea (where, he says, he may have been the last non-POW American soldier to leave North Korea), and retired after twenty years of service. Some of his decorations include the Silver Star, Bronze Star, and three Purple Hearts. He published his memoirs and lives today in San Francisco.

Felix Sparks stayed in the Reserves, earned a law degree, and became a Justice of the Colorado State Supreme Court. In 1961, he was recalled to active duty during the Cuban Missile Crisis. In 1968, he was promoted to brigadier general and became commander of the Colorado National Guard. He founded the 157th Infantry Regiment Association and has been its longtime secretary. He remains the most eloquent and ardent spokesman for the division as a whole and the 157th in particular. He is held in high esteem by virtually all members of the 157th Regiment, and there is little doubt in their minds that he should have received greater recognition for his deeds than the two Silver Star medals the Army bestowed on him. One of the men who served under him, Bud McMillan, remained in awe of his courage and expressed the sentiments of many of Sparks's men: "Sparks should have received about three Medals of Honor. I don't know how he survived the war. He's about the luckiest guy who ever lived."[16]

To varying degrees, the surviving members of the 45th Division are still suffering from their wartime experiences. Those who lost limbs—such as Pete Conde and Jack McMillion and Don Amzibel—are the most obvious, whereas others' wounds are not visible until they open their shirt or pull up a pants leg. They remain fiercely proud of their battle scars, their "red badges of courage." Still others carry emotional scars as deep as any wound caused by a bullet or piece of shrapnel. Tarzan Williams, for example, still suffers from posttraumatic shock syndrome; any sharp, loud noise immediately sends his mind racing back to his nearly two years under fire.

When the final curtain at last fell on the tragedy known as World War II, the main actors left the stage for other roles. General Mark Clark went on to command the United Nations ground forces during the Korean Conflict, after President Harry Truman fired Douglas MacArthur. Following Korea, Clark served as president of The Citadel military college in South Carolina from 1953 to 1965. He died on 17 April 1984 at the age of eighty-seven, the last of America's great World War II commanders.[17]

Clark's nemesis, *Generalfeldmarschall* Albert Kesselring, who was rushed from Italy to the western front, was unable to restore Hitler's collapsing Reich. Following Germany's surrender, he was arrested, tried as a war criminal, and received the death sentence. But Churchill and Alexander both pleaded for clemency, and his sentence was eventually commuted to life imprisonment. Suffering from ill health, Kesselring was released in 1952 and died in 1960 at age seventy-four.[18]

After turning over his division to William Eagles, Troy Middleton went on to command the VIII Corps as it followed up the first wave of the Normandy Invasion. Middleton and the VIII Corps took part in Operation Cobra (the breakout from the beachhead), and then he saw his units hard hit when Hitler launched his desperate Christmas offensive known as the Battle of the Bulge. Unlike his steady, reliable, battle-hardened Thunderbirds, the untested 106th Infantry Division tried in vain to hold back the unexpected, overwhelming German assault through the snowy Ardennes; over half of the 106th was killed or captured. In spite of this debacle, he earned a third star before retiring in 1945, then returned to Louisiana State University and served as its president until 1962. He died on 9 October 1976, three days shy of his eighty-seventh birthday. He is buried in the Baton Rouge Military Cemetery.[19]

After recovering from his wounds, William Willis Eagles went on to serve as the commander of the Ryukus Command in Okinawa in 1948. Beginning the next year, he served in the Office of the Secretary of the Army at the Pentagon until his retirement in 1953. He died on 19 February 1988 in Bethesda, Maryland, just five weeks past his ninety-third birthday.[20]

Robert T. Frederick, the 45th's last World War II combat commander, was head of U.S. forces in Austria following the war, then commanded the 4th Infantry Division at Fort Ord, California. His last official post was as chief of the Joint U.S. Military Aid Group to Greece. He had made enemies and it is said that political intrigues cost him that post and forced him into an early retirement in 1952. He passed away in 1970 at the age of sixty-three.[21]

Ernie Pyle, the war correspondent and the 45th's friend, was killed by a Japanese bullet on the island of Ie Shima during the battle for Okinawa on 18 April 1945.[22]

John Porter Lucas, the scapegoat of Anzio, left Italy bitter, depressed, and worn out. After being relieved of his VI Corps command, he briefed Eisenhower's staff on the lessons learned at Anzio and then returned to the States to take charge of the Fourth Army, with its headquarters at Fort Sam Houston, Texas. By that time, however, there wasn't much of a Fourth Army left; most of the units had either already departed for overseas assignments or were on orders to do so. From 1946 to 1948, Lucas headed the U.S. Army military advisory group in China. His last assignment was as Fifth Army deputy commander in Chicago. He died in 1949, still believing he had won something of a victory at Anzio.[23]

And, in fact, he had, albeit not swiftly.

America has always preferred the immediate success, the rapier thrust as opposed to the prolonged bludgeoning. Patience is not necessarily an American virtue; we respect the tortoise but emulate the hare. We breed sprinters, not marathoners. Although the public and Lucas's superiors may have wanted or expected an all-out, hell-bent-for-leather dash from Anzio to Rome, hindsight has shown that such a move would most likely have met with disaster, given his understrength Corps, with the chance of reinforcement, owing to inadequate shipping, piecemeal at best. Because Clark sensed the risks involved, he did not press his subordinate to take chances. Establish a beachhead, Lucas was ordered, and establish a beachhead was precisely what he did—piling up tons of supplies and ammunition and adding more units to withstand the massive counterattacks he knew the Germans eventually would launch against his forces. Had he recklessly plunged ahead, the possibility that the Anzio invasion force would have been wiped out or at least seriously decimated was very real.

By 1944, Hitler was in desperate need of a victory; his forces had not had a major battlefield win since February 1943 when Rommel's Afrikakorps scored a temporary triumph in Tunisia as it overwhelmed an inexperienced American force at Faid and Kasserine Pass. A German victory at Anzio would have shaken the Americans and British, but it would not have won the war or even the battle for Italy. Such a victory would have been a brief public relations coup for the Axis, but it would not have held back the Red tide on the eastern front or forestalled the Allies from hitting the beaches at Normandy. The Allies would have most likely pulled as many men as possible from the Anzio beachhead and reinstalled them along the Gustav Line, where the war of attrition would have continued. The lessons learned by a defeat at Anzio would have been employed in Normandy, as were lessons learned in the setback at Dieppe in August 1942. The ultimate outcome of the war would not have changed.

So the question then becomes, if an Allied defeat at Anzio would have made no difference in the outcome of the war, did the eventual Allied triumph there contribute materially to victory? The answer would have to be a qualified yes, given the fact that other eventualities springing from a German success are pure speculation and conjecture. With or without a victory in Italy, the Allies would have still won the war. That ultimate victory may have taken longer, however, and cost more lives if Hitler had been able to redeploy his forces tied down on the Italian peninsula—twenty-seven divisions of them—elsewhere. These divisions may not have been able to do much to stop the vast Soviet armies, but they could have been strategically employed at Normandy to thwart the American and British landings.

The success of Operation Overlord, one must remember, was never a given, never a sure thing. For several days after D day, Ike carried a note in his pocket that was to be issued to the press in the event of failure.* The operation's ultimately favorable outcome was due in large measure to the fact that key German divisions could not be transferred from Italy to the northern coast of France. Although he railed against the plodding manner in which Lucas conducted the operation, Winston Churchill nevertheless was convinced of Anzio's value:

> We now know that early in January, the German High Command had intended to transfer five of their best divisions from Italy to Northwestern Europe. Kesselring protested that in such an event he could no longer carry out his orders to fight south of Rome and he would have to withdraw. Just as the argument was at its height, the Anzio landing took place. The High Command dropped the idea, and instead of the Italian Front contributing forces to Northwest Europe, the reverse took place. . . . It proves that the aggressive action of our armies in Italy, and specifically the Anzio stroke, made its full contribution towards the success of Overlord.[24]

A stronger German presence along the Normandy coast, coupled with a swifter German response to the initial phase of the invasion, could have turned the battle in Hitler's favor. In all likelihood, a failed invasion, possibly reattempted at a later date, would have allowed the Soviets the honor of single-handedly defeating Germany and "liberating" the rest of Europe. The people of Hungary, Czechoslovakia, Poland, and others knew all too well what being "liberated" by the Soviet Union meant. With a Soviet-dominated Europe, the entire history of the world since 1945 would have been radically different from what we know, in ways no one can say. So the Allied victory at Anzio, as costly and as delayed as it was, and purchased in large measure with the lives of the men of the 45th Infantry Division, must be seen as being very significant indeed!

Just as surely as the sun will rise tomorrow, humankind will continue to experience conflicts between nations. Whether these conflicts will be of a local, regional, or global nature, no one can say for certain. One thing *is* certain, however: The United States, as the world's remaining "superpower," will continue to be called on to take part in these conflicts. One

---

*The note read: "Our landings in the Cherbourg-Havre area have failed to gain a satisfactory foothold and I have withdrawn the troops. My decision to attack at this time and place was based upon the best information available. The troops, the air, and the Navy did all that bravery and devotion to duty could do. If any blame or fault attaches to the attempt, it is mine alone" (Eisenhower Museum, Abilene, Kans.).

can only hope that America's young soldiers—whether Regular Army or National Guard—who are called on to put their lives on the line in the defense of liberty have the same level of courage, perseverance, and devotion to duty possessed in such great measure by those who, more than fifty years ago, wore the patch of the Thunderbird.

Postscript

In the summer of 1996, fifty-two years after the smoke and din of the battle had faded away, I visited Anzio and many of the other places where the men of the 45th had fought and bled and died. As in so much of Europe where titanic struggles have taken place, the scars of World War II have been virtually wiped clean. The cities of Germany, France, and Italy, which had been flattened by the war, today show virtually no signs that the war ever passed their way, and the visitor often must make a special effort to find the places of historical significance. Remnants of the Siegfried Line fortifications still exist, the concrete dragon's teeth moss covered and stained by time; most of the bunkers and pillboxes were destroyed by Allied engineers shortly after the war. Much of the concentration camp at Dachau still remains, although severely sanitized, and it is one of Germany's major "tourist attractions," drawing hundreds of thousands of visitors each year. In Italy the town of Cassino and the abbey above it have both been totally rebuilt, although the castle below the abbey remains a pockmarked wreck. Tour buses filled with aging veterans of both sides wind their way up the mountain road daily to tour the reconstructed abbey and remember again their long-dead comrades. The crumbling ruins of San Pietro, close to Venafro, are still there, but a new village has grown up below them. Venafro itself is a bustling little town. Anzio has returned to its former existence as a prosperous seaside resort. Children play in the waves that lap the shore, and couples laugh and dine in trendy seafood restaurants, apparently oblivious to the fact that once Anzio was a household name known around the world as a place of death and destruction.

It is only the profusion of military cemeteries that silently speak of a different reality. On the outskirts of Venafro there lies a cemetery filled with the bodies of French colonials from Morocco and Algeria. On a hillside behind the Abbey of Monte Cassino sits a large Polish Army cemetery. At Anzio, two well-tended British cemeteries, containing the remains of 3,369 British and Commonwealth soldiers are located; a cemetery for 7,862 American dead is in Nettuno. The German cemetery at Pomezia contains the remains of 27,470 soldiers.

Yet, when one visits Anzio, one is aware that something is wrong. Time marches on, and valuable land must be returned to productive use; people cannot live forever amid the ruins of battle. But, at Anzio, the past has been too well obliterated, the ghosts too completely exorcised. Unlike the sites of other major battles, such as Gettysburg, Waterloo, Verdun, and Normandy, the Italians have allowed extensive development to take place on this hallowed ground.

The once-barren fields—over which armies wrestled and thousands of men died horrible, violent deaths—have been desecrated by stores, car dealerships, factories, warehouses, and gas stations. A huge factory just northwest of the Overpass now sprawls where so many gave their lives. The area of the caves where the remnants of the 157th's 2nd Battalion held out for a week is being bulldozed. Houses and commercial enterprises sit on the crest of Buon Riposo Ridge, which, like the other battlefields around Anzio and Nettuno, is unmarked by signs or monuments telling of the awesome struggle that took place there.

Aprilia, which once had fewer than thirty buildings, is now a booming residential and industrial area of nearly 100,000 inhabitants. The only evidence that Aprilia was once the focus of such bitter fighting is the shrapnel-punctured bronze statue of San Michele in the main square. One must look carefully to gain the slightest glimpse of the area's importance to military and world history. A small sign near the Overpass declares laconically in English, Italian, and German, "Campo di Carne—On this site, thousands of men fought and died." The sign is virtually hidden by an overgrown tangle of vines. It is as though Italy is trying to forget the war altogether.

Perhaps to further this agenda, a number of the towns and geographical features in the area have had their names changed in the intervening decades. The Mussolini Canal is now the Canale di Moscarello. Littoria has been changed to Latina, Conca is now Borgo Montello, and the ominously named town of Campo Morto (Field of Death) has been rechristened Campo Verde (Green Field), more befitting a freshly built American suburb than a battlefield.

The name of the main Rome-Anzio highway, for which so many fought and died, has been changed from the Via Anziate to the Via Nettunese, also known as Highway 207. The Dead End Road now goes by the name Strada del Giardini (Street of the Gardens), and the Lateral Road, once the final beachhead defensive line, is now a major highway clogged with large trucks traveling at typically Italian breakneck speeds. The Bowling Alley never received its railroad track and was converted into a four-lane, high-speed *autostrada* known as Highway 148, leading from Rome to Terracina. The unnamed road located to the east of the caves across the Via Anziate is now known as Via della Mecchanica, probably due to all the truck repair facilities situated along it.

Many of the magnificent umbrella pines of the Padiglione Woods still stand, but the forest itself has been considerably cut back as the land is cleared for other uses. The tomb of Menotti Garibaldi, once so bitterly contested for by the Germans and the 45th, has been rebuilt in a style that resembles the original. Unfortunately, due to poor signage at Carano and being completely hidden by a thick grove of bamboo, the tomb is extremely difficult to find.

It is only in the museums that the past is preserved. A small but excellent museum that details the battle is the Museo Dello Sbarco in Anzio. The museum also operates a bookshop and gift store. Another outstanding effort to document and preserve artifacts of the battle, the Museum of the Allied Landing, is located in Nettuno.

Many of the divisions and smaller units who fought here have erected small markers and monuments at various points, recording for all posterity their contributions to the battle. But, because their veterans' association does not endorse the placing of monuments or memorials outside the United States, the contributions and sacrifices of the men of the 45th Infantry Division at Anzio are conspicuously absent.

Notes

Chapter 1

1. Shelby L. Stanton, *World War II Order of Battle* (New York: Galahad Books, 1984), pp. 108, 126, 131.

2. Vere Williams, interview with author, Denver, CO, Aug. 30, 1994; and Doris Kearns Goodwin, *No Ordinary Time* (New York: Touchstone, 1995), p. 23.

3. George A. Fisher, *The Story of the 180th Infantry Regiment* (San Angelo, TX: Newsfoto Publishing Co., 1947), pp. 5–6.

4. Guy Nelson, *Thunderbird: A History of the 45th Infantry Division* (Oklahoma City, OK: 45th Infantry Division Association, 1970), pp. 11–13.

5. *National Guard of the State of New Mexico: Pictorial Review 1939* (Atlanta: Army-Navy Publishing Co., 1939), pp. 16–17.

6. D. Shaw Duncan, *National Guard of the State of Colorado: Pictorial Review 1939* (Atlanta: Army-Navy Publishing Co., 1939), pp. 14–16.

7. Alvin M. Josephy, Jr., *The Civil War in the American West* (New York: Knopf, 1991), pp. 78–92.

8. Duncan, pp. 15–16.

9. Josephy, p. 290.

10. Duncan, p. 16.

11. *National Guard of the State of Arizona: Historical Review 1938–1939* (Atlanta: Army-Navy Publishing Co., 1939), pp. xvii–xviii.

12. Duncan, p. 17.

13. *National Guard of the State of Arizona,* p. xviii.

14. Duncan, p. 19.

15. Charles F. Barrett, *National Guard of the State of Oklahoma: Historical Annual 1938* (Baton Rouge, LA: Army-Navy Publishing Co., 1938), p. 11.

16. Duncan, p. 137.

17. *National Guard of the State of New Mexico,* p. 17.

18. *National Guard of the State of Arizona,* p. xix; and Barrett, p. 11.

19. Duncan, p. 138.

20. *National Guard of the State of Arizona,* p. xx.

21. Duncan, p. 138.

22. *National Guard of the State of Arizona,* p. xx.

23. Duncan, p. 139.

24. Carlo D'Este, *Patton: A Genius for War.* (New York: HarperCollins, 1995), pp. 156–163, and John K. Mahon, *History of the Militia and the National Guard* (New York: Macmillan, 1983), pp. 151–152.

25. Peter G. Chronis, "Villa's Attack on Town Recalled." *Denver Post*. Mar. 10, 1996.

26. Duncan, p. 139.

27. Barrett, p. 13; and D'Este, *Patton*, p. 184.

28. Barrett, p. 13; and Duncan, pp. 139–140; and *National Guard of the State of Arizona,* pp. xxiii–xxiv; and *National Guard of the State of New Mexico,* p. 18.

29. *National Guard of the State of Arizona,* p. xxiv.

30. "Thunderbird Legends: William Schaffer Key," *45th Division News,* Jan. 1989.

31. Warren P. Munsell, Jr., *The Story of a Regiment: A History of the 179th Regimental Combat Team* (Place unknown: Privately published, 1946), p. 1; Felix Sparks, interview with author, Lakewood, CO, Oct. 12, 1996.

32. William L. O'Neill, *A Democracy at War: America's Fight at Home and Abroad in World War II* (New York: Free Press, 1993), p. 9.

33. G. Fisher, p. 5; and Nelson, p. 16.

34. Duncan, pp. 140–142.

35. A. H. Speairs, telephone interview with author, Oct. 15, 1996.

36. Munsell, p. 1; and Felix Sparks, interview with author, Lakewood, CO, Oct. 12, 1996.

37. Alison R. Bernstein, *American Indians and World War II* (Norman and London: University of Oklahoma Press, 1991), p. 55.

38. Ibid., p. 44.

39. Louis Scott, "Evolution of Unit Shoulder Patches: The Thunderbird Story," *45th Division News,* Jan. 1992.

40. G. Fisher, p. 1.

41. Jack Montgomery, telephone interview with author, May 5, 1996.

42. Nelson, p. 14.

43. G. Fisher, p. 9.

44. Nelson, pp. 15–17.

45. "Coleman Mayor Lauds 45th Troops"; and "Abilene Citizens Aid in Morale Program"; and "New Home of the 45th Division" (Photo caption), *Abilene Reporter-News,* dates unknown, but possibly April or May 1941.

46. G. Fisher, p. 11.

47. Ibid., pp. 10–11.

48. Ricky Robertson, "The Great Louisiana Maneuvers," *Army Motors,* Nos. 65, 66, 67 (1993–1994).

49. G. Fisher, pp. 11–12.

50. Ibid., p. 12.

51. Munsell, p. 2.

52. Leland Loy, telephone interview with author, Jan. 9, 1995.

53. Nelson, pp. 14–18; and Stanton, pp. 8–14; and O'Neill, p. 18; and Felix Sparks, interview with author, Lakewood, CO, Oct. 15, 1996.

54. Nelson, pp. 14–18; and Stanton, p. 228.

55. G. Fisher, pp. 13–14.

56. Ibid., pp. 13–14.

57. Frank J. Price, *Troy H. Middleton: A Biography* (Baton Rouge: Louisiana State University Press, 1974), p. 168.

58. G. Fisher, p. 15; and Don Robinson, *News of the 45th* (New York: Grosset & Dunlap, 1944), pp. 36–39.
59. G. Fisher, p. 15.
60. Vere Williams, interview with author, Denver, CO, Aug. 30, 1994.
61. G. Fisher, p. 16.
62. Price, passim, pp. 1–129; and "Thunderbird Legends: Troy Houston Middleton," *45th Division News*, Oct. 1990.
63. Emajean Buechner, *Sparks: The Combat Diary of a Battalion Commander* (Metarie, LA: Thunderbird Press, 1991), p. 61.
64. Vere Williams, interview with author, Denver, CO, Aug. 30, 1994.
65. Nelson, pp. 19–20.
66. Buechner, p. 61.
67. Quoted in Leo V. Bishop, George A. Fisher, and Frank J. Glasgow, *The Fighting Forty-Fifth: The Combat Report of an Infantry Division* (Baton Rouge, LA: Army-Navy Publishing Co., 1946), p. 38.
68. Quoted in G. Fisher, p. 55.
69. Price, p. 143; and Samuel E. Morison, *History of United States Naval Operations in World War II: Sicily-Salerno-Anzio,* vol. 9 (Boston: Little, Brown, 1954), p. 128.
70. Vere Williams, interview with author, Denver, CO, Aug. 30, 1994.
71. Price, pp. 143–145.
72. Buechner, p. 63.
73. Louis Scott, "If Only We Had Known . . . ," *45th Division News,* Oct. 1993.
74. Vere Williams, interview with author, Denver, CO, Aug. 30, 1994.
75. Omar N. Bradley, *A Soldier's Story* (Chicago: Rand McNally, 1951), p. 108.
76. Buechner, pp. 64–65.
77. Vere Williams, interview with author, Denver, CO, Aug. 30, 1994.
78. Bishop et al., p. 7.
79. Bradley, p. 118.
80. Bishop et al., p. 7.
81. D'Este, *Patton,* p. 509; and *Bitter Victory: The Battle for Sicily, 1943* (New York: Dutton, 1988), pp. 612–613.
82. D'Este, *Bitter Victory,* p. 317.

Chapter 2

1. D'Este, *Bitter Victory,* p. 153; and G. A. Shepperd, *The Italian Campaign: 1943–45* (New York: Praeger, 1968), p. 30.
2. D'Este, *Bitter Victory,* pp. 138–141.
3. Shepperd, pp. 43–44.
4. Shepperd, p. 43; and Bradley, p. 106; and D'Este, *Bitter Victory,* pp. 142–158, pp. 262–263.
5. Bishop et al., pp. 13–14; and Morison, p. 126.
6. Trevor Evans, telephone interview with author, Jan. 11, 1997.
7. Raymond McLain diary (*Diary of the Sicilian Campaign*), p. 1, 45th Infantry Division Archives, Oklahoma City, OK.

8. Morison, pp. 129–133.
9. Ibid., p. 130.
10. McLain diary, pp. 2–3.
11. Morison, p. 136
12. Ibid., p. 130
13. Ibid., p. 136
14. Glen Hanson, telephone interview with author, Apr. 28, 1996.
15. Morison, p. 137
16. Ibid., p. 131
17. Bishop et al., pp. 13–18
18. A. H. Speairs, telephone interview with author, Jan. 19, 1995.
19. Vere Williams, interview with author, Denver, CO, Aug. 30, 1994.
20. Pete Conde, interview with author, Denver, CO, Aug. 25, 1994.
21. Morison, p. 140.
22. Bishop et al., pp. 16–17.
23. Pete Conde, interview with author, Denver, CO, Aug. 25, 1994.
24. McLain diary, p. 6.
25. Buechner, p. 67.
26. Morison, p. 140.
27. McLain diary, pp. 6–7; and Price, p. 148.
28. Bill Whitman, *Scouts Out!* (Los Angeles: Authors Unlimited, 1990), pp. 6–7.
29. G. Fisher, p. 24; and Morison, p. 145.
30. G. Fisher, p. 31; and Whitman, p. 18.
31. G. Fisher, p. 23.
32. Whitman, pp. 20–21.
33. Price, p. 143.
34. Bishop et al., pp. 16–22.
35. McLain diary, pp. 10–11.
36. Paul A. Cundiff, *45th Division CP—A Personal Record from World War II* (privately published, place and date unknown), p. 104.
37. Bradley, p. 130.
38. Morison, p. 146.
39. D'Este, *Bitter Victory*, pp. 307–309.
40. Robert Wallace, *The Italian Campaign* (New York: Time-Life Books, 1981), p. 25.
41. McLain diary, p. 22.
42. Bradley, p. 135.
43. McLain diary, pp. 19–20.
44. Leland Loy, telephone interview with author, Jan. 9, 1995; and Jack Hallowell et al., *History of the 157th Infantry Regiment* (Rifle) (privately published, place and date unknown), pp. 23–24.
45. Trevor Evans, telephone interview with author, Jan. 11, 1997.
46. Hallowell et al., pp. 24–25.
47. *45th Division Quartermaster Operation Report*, Jan. 18, 1944, 45th Infantry Division Archives, Oklahoma City, OK.
48. Bradley, pp. 134–136.
49. Price, p. 150.

50. Bradley, pp. 134–136.
51. McLain diary, p. 31.
52. Hallowell et al., p. 25; and D'Este, *Bitter Victory,* pp. 327–328.
53. Hallowell et al., p. 25.
54. Price, pp. 150–151.
55. Whitman, p. 19.
56. D'Este, *Bitter Victory,* pp. 318–319, 612–613.
57. Bishop et al., p. 23.
58. Bradley, pp. 140–141.
59. McLain diary, pp. 33–35.
60. Bishop et al., pp. 24–26.
61. Charlie Dunham, telephone interview with author, Nov. 18, 1995.
62. Bradley, p. 139; and Price, p. 153.
63. Price, p. 157; and D'Este, *Bitter Victory,* p. 612–613.
64. Price, p. 160.
65. H. Esseme, *Patton: A Study in Command* (New York: Scribner, 1974), pp. 109–117; and D'Este, *Patton,* pp. 533–538.
66. Price, p. 154.
67. Bishop et al., pp. 27–28; and D'Este, *Bitter Victory,* p. 456.
68. Munsell, p. 18.
69. Hallowell et al., p. 27; and Munsell, pp. 17–18.
70. Price, p. 154.
71. G. Fisher, pp. 44–45.
72. Whitman, pp. 27–28.
73. Bishop et al., pp. 29–30; and G. Fisher, p. 48.
74. McLain diary, p. 41.
75. Bishop et al., p. 30; and Hallowell et al., p. 28.
76. G. Fisher, p. 49.
77. Hallowell et al., p. 28.
78. Glen Hanson, telephone interview with author, Apr. 28, 1996.
79. G. Fisher, p. 49.
80. Henry Havlat, telephone interview with author, Oct. 28, 1995.
81. Robert Franklin, telephone interview with author, Apr. 21, 1996.
82. Hallowell et al., p. 28.
83. Vere Williams, interview with author, Denver, CO, Aug. 30, 1994.
84. Robert Franklin, telephone interview with author, Apr. 21, 1996.
85. Hallowell et al., p. 29.
86. Bishop et al., p. 31.
87. Bishop et al., pp. 30–33; and Hallowell et al., pp. 27–30.
88. D'Este, *Bitter Victory,* p. 453.
89. Price, p. 156.
90. Esseme, pp. 108–109.
91. Bradley, pp. 158–159; and Lucien K. Truscott, *Command Missions* (New York: Dutton, 1954), pp. 67–72.
92. D'Este, *Bitter Victory,* pp. 482–483.
93. A. H. Speairs, telephone interview with author, Jan. 19, 1995.
94. Bishop et al., p. 38.

95. D'Este, *Bitter Victory*, p. 518.
96. Ibid., pp. 513–553; and Shepperd, p. 69.
97. Munsell, p. 19.
98. Ray Williams, telephone interview with author, Jan. 7, 1995.
99. A. H. Speairs, telephone interview with author, Jan. 19, 1995.
100. Quoted in Bishop et al., p. 31.
101. Shepperd, p. 86.
102. Matthew Cooper, *The German Army 1933–1945: Its Political and Military Failure* (New York: Stein & Day, 1978), p. 404.
103. Shepperd, pp. 88–91.
104. Martin Blumenson, *Salerno to Cassino*, vol. 3 in the "U.S. Army in World War II; The Mediterranean Theater of Operations" series (Washington, DC: Center of Military History, 1969), pp. 12–16.
105. Ibid., pp. 20–21.
106. D'Este, *Bitter Victory*, pp. 430–432; and W. G. F. Jackson, *The Battle for Italy* (New York: Harper & Row, 1967), pp. 68–73.
107. Martin Gilbert, *The Second World War* rev. ed. (New York: Henry Holt, 1989), p. 430.
108. Blumenson, *Salerno to Cassino*, p. 31.
109. Ibid., p. 39; and Richard Lamb, *War in Italy: A Brutal Story* (New York: St. Martin's, 1993), p. 23.
110. Bishop et al., p. 39.
111. Truscott, p. 229.
112. Quoted in G. Fisher, p. 55.

Chapter 3

1. Blumenson, *Salerno to Cassino*, pp. 43–57.
2. Bishop et al., p. 39; and D'Este, *Fatal Decision: Anzio and the Battle for Rome* (New York: HarperCollins, 1991), p. 30.
3. *The German Operation at Anzio; German Military Document Section; A Study of the German Operations at Anzio Beachhead from 22 Jan. 44 to 31 May 44*. War Department, Military Intelligence Division, Camp Ritchie, MD, 1946, 45th Infantry Division Archives, Oklahoma City, OK, p. 2.
4. Shepperd, pp. 94–95.
5. O'Neill, p. 184.
6. Ray Williams, telephone interview with author, Jan. 7, 1995.
7. *45th Division Quartermaster Operation Report*, Jan. 18, 1944, 45th Infantry Division Archives, Oklahoma City, OK.
8. Stanton, p. 9.
9. *45th Division Quartermaster Operation Report*, Jan. 18, 1944, 45th Infantry Division Archives, Oklahoma City, OK.
10. Shelford Bidwell, "Albert Kesselring," in *Hitler's Generals*, ed. Correlli Barnett (New York: Grove Weidenfeld, 1989), pp. 265–289; and Albert Kesselring, *The Memoirs of Field Marshal Albert Kesselring* (Novato, CA: Presidio Press, 1989), passim.

11. Martin Blumenson, *Mark Clark: The Last of the Great World War II Commanders* (New York: Congdon & Weed, 1984), passim, pp. 1–128.
12. Blumenson, *Salerno to Cassino,* p. 31.
13. Blumenson, *Mark Clark,* passim.
14. Blumenson, *Salerno to Cassino,* p. 53; and Morison, p. 260.
15. Blumenson, *Salerno to Cassino,* p. 74.
16. Ibid., pp. 29–34; and Eric Morris, *Circles of Hell: The War in Italy 1943–1945* (New York: Crown, 1993), pp. 28–29.
17. Bishop et al., pp. 40–41.
18. Blumenson, *Salerno to Cassino,* pp. 73–75; and Morison, pp. 260–261.
19. Bishop et al., p. 41.
20. Stephen E. Ambrose, *Eisenhower; Soldier, General of the Army, President-Elect, 1890–1952* (New York: Simon & Schuster Touchstone edition, 1985), p. 260.
21. Blumenson, *Salerno to Cassino,* pp. 16–22.
22. Ibid., pp. 54–56.
23. Ibid., p. 73.
24. Morison, pp. 247–248.
25. Morison, pp. 273–275; and Blumenson, *Salerno to Cassino,* p. 73.
26. Morison, pp. 261–265; and Blumenson, *Salerno to Cassino,* pp. 77–78.
27. Morison, p. 269; and Blumenson, *Salerno to Cassino,* pp. 80–85.
28. Wallace, pp. 58–59.
29. Des Hickey and Gus Smith, *Operation Avalanche: The Salerno Landings, 1943* (New York: McGraw-Hill, 1984), pp. 170–171.
30. Morison, p. 298.
31. Ibid., p. 280.
32. Bishop et al., pp. 40–42.
33. Trevor Evans, telephone interview with author, Jan. 11, 1997.
34. Blumenson, *Salerno to Cassino,* p. 106.
35. Buechner, p. 71.
36. Blumenson, *Salerno to Cassino,* pp. 85–104.
37. Hallowell et al., p. 31; and Munsell, p. 23.
38. Bishop et al., p. 42.
39. Bishop et al., pp. 42–43; and Hickey and Smith, pp. 163–164.
40. Munsell, pp. 14–25.
41. Bishop et al., p. 44; and Blumenson, *Salerno to Cassino,* p. 107.
42. Munsell, p. 24.
43. Bishop et al., p. 44.
44. Munsell, p. 26.
45. Mark Clark, *Calculated Risk* (New York: Harper & Bros., 1950), p. 197.
46. Munsell, pp. 26–27.
47. Bishop et al., p. 44.
48. Price, p. 165.
49. Pete Conde, interview with author, Denver, CO, Aug. 25, 1994.
50. Ray Williams, telephone interview with author, Jan. 7, 1995.
51. Hickey and Smith, pp. 193–195.
52. Munsell, pp. 23–27.

53. Daniel Witts, telephone interview with author, Mar. 31, 1996.
54. Munsell, pp. 25–26; and Blumenson, *Salerno to Cassino,* pp. 104–108.
55. A. H. Speairs, telephone interview with author, Jan. 19, 1995.
56. Bishop et al., pp. 44–45; and Blumenson, *Salerno to Cassino,* pp. 108–109.
57. Price, p. 166.
58. Blumenson, *Salerno to Cassino,* pp. 110–113.
59. Trevor Evans, telephone interview with author, Jan. 11, 1997.
60. Bishop et al., pp. 40–44.
61. *45th Division Artillery Operations Report,* Apr. 25, 1944, 45th Infantry Division Archives, Oklahoma City, OK.
62. Bishop et al., p. 45.
63. Ibid., pp. 46–48; and Blumenson, *Salerno to Cassino,* pp. 114–115.
64. Blumenson, *Salerno to Cassino,* pp. 116–117.
65. Clark, p. 197.
66. Blumenson, *Salerno to Cassino,* p. 115.
67. Eric Morris, *Salerno: A Military Fiasco* (New York: Stein & Day, 1983), p. 170; and Chester G. Starr, *From Salerno to the Alps: A History of the Fifth Army 1943–1945* (Washington, DC: Infantry Journal Press, 1948), p. 28.
68. Clark, p. 202.
69. Pete Conde, interview with author, Denver, CO, Aug. 25, 1994.
70. Blumenson, *Salerno to Cassino,* p. 119; and Morris, *Salerno,* p. 190.
71. Price, p. 166.
72. A. H. Speairs, telephone interview with author, Jan. 19, 1995.
73. Kenneth Stemmons, telephone interview with author, Mar. 21, 1995.
74. A. H. Speairs, telephone interview with author, Jan. 19, 1995.
75. Blumenson, *Salerno to Cassino,* pp. 117–121, 127.
76. Ibid., pp. 122–126.
77. Ibid., pp. 127, 134–136.
78. Ibid., pp. 131–132.
79. Price, p. 166.
80. Jack Montgomery, telephone interview with author, May 5, 1996.
81. Blumenson, *Salerno to Cassino,* p. 130.
82. Price, p. 166.
83. Clark, p. 206.
84. Blumenson, *Salerno to Cassino,* pp. 148–152.
85. Price, p. 166.
86. Whitman, p. 39.

Chapter 4

1. Hallowell et al., p. 41.
2. Bishop et al., p. 50.
3. Blumenson, *Salerno to Cassino,* pp. 154–187.
4. Glen Hanson, telephone interview with author, Apr. 28, 1996.
5. Hallowell et al., p. 42.
6. Wallace, p. 101.

7. Blumenson, *Salerno to Cassino,* pp. 149–152, 158; and Morris, *Salerno,* p. 188.
8. G. Fisher, pp. 64–70.
9. Ernest Childers, telephone interview with author, Mar. 21, 1997.
10. "Thunderbird Legends: James D. Slaton." *45th Division News,* Jan. 1992.
11. Nelson, p. 46.
12. Hallowell et al., p. 42.
13. Nelson, p. 46.
14. Mel Craven, telephone interview with author, Sept. 30, 1994.
15. Nelson, p. 46.
16. Hallowell et al., pp. 42–43.
17. G. Fisher, p. 79; and Whitman, p. 48.
18. Bishop et al., pp. 52–53.
19. Leland Loy, telephone interview with author, Jan. 9, 1995.
20. Ray Williams, telephone interview with author, Jan. 7, 1995.
21. G. Fisher, pp. 79–82.
22. Ibid., p. 82; and Whitman, p. 50.
23. G. Fisher, p. 79.
24. Jack Montgomery, telephone interview with author, May 5, 1996; and G. Fisher, pp. 82–84.
25. Blumenson, *Salerno to Cassino,* pp. 188–190.
26. Ibid., pp. 193–194.
27. Ibid., p. 195.
28. Ibid., p. 194.
29. Munsell, p. 32.
30. Nelson, p. 47; and Blumenson, *Salerno to Cassino,* p. 195.
31. Blumenson, *Salerno to Cassino,* p. 195; and Bishop et al., pp. 54–56.
32. Hallowell et al., p. 44.
33. Gilbert, p. 467.
34. Whitman, pp. 52–56.
35. Bishop et al., p. 55; and Hallowell et al., p. 45; and Munsell, p. 33.
36. Ray Williams, telephone interview with author, Jan. 7, 1995.
37. Munsell, p. 33; and Blumenson, *Salerno to Cassino,* p. 213.
38. Hallowell et al., pp. 44–45.
39. Blumenson, *Salerno to Cassino,* pp. 213–214.
40. Munsell, p. 33.
41. Hallowell et al., p. 45.
42. Nelson, pp. 47–48.
43. Munsell, p. 35.
44. Blumenson, *Salerno to Cassino,* p. 220.
45. Bishop et al., p. 57.
46. Munsell, p. 35.
47. Ray Williams, telephone interview with author, Jan. 7, 1995.
48. Bishop et al., p. 58.
49. G. Fisher, p. 94.
50. Munsell, pp. 36–37.
51. A. H. Speairs, telephone interview with author, Jan. 19, 1995.

52. Ray Williams, telephone interview with author, Jan. 7, 1995.
53. Daniel Witts, telephone interview with author, Mar. 31, 1996.
54. Munsell, pp. 39–40.
55. Blumenson, *Salerno to Cassino,* p. 224.
56. Ibid., p. 233.
57. Ibid., pp. 253–256.
58. Ibid., pp. 252–254.
59. Bishop et al., p. 63.
60. Vere Williams, interview with author, Denver, CO, Aug. 30, 1994.
61. Ray Williams, telephone interview with author, Jan. 7, 1995.
62. Hallowell et al., p. 49.
63. Minor Shirk, interview with author, Denver, CO, Aug. 30, 1994.
64. Daniel Witts, telephone interview with author, Mar. 31, 1996.
65. Jack McMillion, interview with author, Denver, CO, Aug. 30, 1994.
66. Charlie Dunham, telephone interview with author, Nov. 18, 1995.
67. George Nalley, interview with author, Denver, CO, Aug. 30, 1994.
68. Morty Carr, telephone interview with author, Mar. 21, 1995.
69. Robert Franklin, telephone interview with author, Apr. 21, 1996.
70. Price, pp. 168–170.
71. Munsell, p. 41; and Stanton, p. 164.
72. Martin Blumenson, *Anzio: The Gamble That Failed* (Philadelphia & New York: Lippincott, 1963), p. 145.
73. Munsell, p. x.
74. *The German Operation at Anzio,* pp. 2–7.
75. Blumenson, *Salerno to Cassino,* pp. 293–294.
76. Ibid., pp. 235–256; and D'Este, *Fatal Decision,* pp. 74–75.
77. D'Este, *Fatal Decision,* pp. 76–78.
78. Morison, pp. 323–326.
79. Blumenson, *Salerno to Cassino,* pp. 300–304.
80. Ibid., pp. 303–304, 353; and Wynford Vaughn-Thomas, *Anzio* (London: Longmans, Green, 1961), p. 20.
81. Blumenson, *Salerno to Cassino,* p. 313.
82. Ibid., pp. 300–303.
83. Morison, pp. 323–327.
84. Blumenson, *Salerno to Cassino,* pp. 260–289.
85. Morison, pp. 326–327.
86. Blumenson, *Salerno to Cassino,* p. 302.
87. Bishop et al., p. 69; and Lamb, p. 185.
88. Ralph Krieger, telephone interview with author, Mar. 20, 1995.
89. Felix Sparks, interview with author, Lakewood, CO, Oct. 15, 1996.
90. Robert LaDu, telephone interview with author, Apr. 3, 1995.
91. Glen Hanson, telephone interview with author, Apr. 28, 1996.
92. Morty Carr, telephone interview with author, Mar. 21, 1995.
93. Pete Conde, interview with author, Denver, CO, Aug. 25, 1994.
94. *179th Operations Report,* Jan. 1–31, 1944, 45th Infantry Division Archives, Oklahoma City, OK.
95. Bishop et al., p. 69.

96. *180th Operations Report,* Jan. 1–31, 1944, 45th Infantry Division Archives, Oklahoma City, OK.

97. Oliver R. Birkner, letter to editor, *45th Division News,* Feb.1995.

98. *157th Operations Summary,* Jan. 1–31, 1944, 45th Infantry Division Archives, Oklahoma City, OK.

99. *45th Division Operations Report,* Jan. 1–31, 1944, 45th Infantry Division Archives, Oklahoma City, OK.

100. G. Fisher, p. 119.

101. A. H. Speairs, telephone interview with author, Jan. 19, 1995.

102. Bishop et al., p. 70; and Munsell, p. 47.

103. Edward Amzibel, monograph (*The War Years of Edward "Don" Amzibel,* 1995), 45th Infantry Division Archives, Oklahoma City, OK; and telephone interview with author, Mar. 4, 1995.

104. *The German Operation at Anzio,* pp. 3–7.

105. Morison, p. 329.

106. Ibid., p. 332.

107. Blumenson, *Salerno to Cassino,* p. 355.

108. Morison, p. 329.

109. Truscott, p. 304.

110. Blumenson, *Salerno to Cassino,* p. 355.

111. Ronald Lewin, *Ultra Goes to War* (New York: McGraw-Hill, 1978), pp. 20–21.

112. D'Este, *Fatal Decision,* p. 109.

113. Blumenson, *Salerno to Cassino,* pp. 313–321.

114. Ibid., p. 320.

115. Ibid., p. 322.

116. Ibid., p. 332.

117. Dominick Graham and Shelford Bidwell, *Tug of War: The Battle For Italy: 1943–45* (New York: St. Martin's, 1986), pp. 148–149.

118. Blumenson, *Salerno to Cassino,* pp. 321–347.

119. Ibid., p. 347.

120. Vaughn-Thomas, pp. 30–31.

121. Ibid., pp. 28–30.

122. Blumenson, *Salerno to Cassino,* p. 355.

123. Vaughn-Thomas, p. 39.

124. Blumenson, *Salerno to Cassino,* pp. 356–357.

125. Ibid., p. 356.

126. Vaughn-Thomas, p. 44.

127. John P. Lucas diary, Jan. 20, 1944, U.S. Army Military History Institute Collection, Carlisle, PA.

Chapter 5

1. James C. Fahey, *The Ships and Aircraft of the United States Fleet* (New York: Gemsco, 1944), p. 60.

2. Blumenson, *Salerno to Cassino,* p. 356; and Christopher Hibbert, *Anzio: The Bid for Rome* (New York: Ballantine, 1970), p. 45.

3. John Bowditch III, ed., *Anzio Beachhead*, vol. 14 in the "American Forces in Action" series (Washington, DC: Department of the Army Historical Division, 1947), p. 14.

4. Lucas diary, Jan. 10, 1944; and Blumenson, *Salerno to Cassino,* pp. 356–357.

5. *The German Operation at Anzio,* p. 10; and Ennio Silvestri, *The Long Road to Rome* (Latina, Italy: Etic Grafica, 1994), p. 148.

6. Bowditch, p. 14.

7. Hibbert, p. 45.

8. Blumenson, *Salerno to Cassino,* p. 358.

9. William O. Darby and William H. Baumer, *We Led The Way: Darby's Rangers* (San Rafael, CA: Presidio Press, 1980), pp. 147–149; and Silvestri, p. 7.

10. Blumenson, *Salerno to Cassino,* pp. 358–360.

11. Bowditch, p. 18.

12. Fred Sheehan, *Anzio: Epic of Bravery* (Norman: University of Oklahoma Press, 1994 [originally published 1964]), p. 33.

13. Blumenson, *Salerno to Cassino,* pp. 360–365; and *The German Operation at Anzio,* pp. 10–12.

14. Silvestri, p. 314; and Morison, p. 335; and G. Fisher, p. 131; and Hallowell et al., p. 52; and Jasper Ridley, *Garibaldi* (New York: Viking, 1976), passim; and Elma Sant'Anna, *Menotti: Il Garibaldi "Brasiliero"* (Aprilia, Italy: Assessoria Grafica e Editorial, 1966), pp. 13–14.

15. Silvestri, pp. 159–160; and G. Fisher, pp. 131–133.

16. Ernie Pyle, *Brave Men* (New York: Henry Holt), pp. 159–162.

17. William Fraser, *Hic et Ubique* (London: Sampson, Low, Marston, 1893), p. 88.

18. J. H. Green, "Anzio," *After The Battle*, No. 52 (1986), p. 12; and Vaughn-Thomas, p. 64; and Diego Cancelli, *Aprilia 1944: Immagini Quotidiane di Una Guerra* (Aprilia, Italy: Poligraf, 1994), pp. 19–24.

19. Sheehan, p. 58.

20. Silvestri, p. 206; and Pyle, p. 163; and Vaughn-Thomas, p. 85; and D'Este, *Fatal Decision,* p. 149.

21. Bowditch, pp. 3–5.

22. Hibbert, p. 24.

23. Vaughn-Thomas, p. 59; and Morison, p. 344.

24. Blumenson, *Salerno to Cassino,* p. 392.

25. Winston Churchill, *The Second World War: Closing the Ring* (Boston: Houghton Mifflin, 1951), p. 488; and Vaughn-Thomas, pp. 111–112.

26. Morison, pp. 345–346.

27. Morty Carr, telephone interview with author, Mar. 21, 1995.

28. Nicholas Defonte, telephone interview with author, Mar. 21, 1995.

29. Munsell, pp. 48–49.

30. Ray Williams, telephone interview with author, Jan. 7, 1995.

31. Robert LaDu, telephone interview with author, Apr. 3, 1995.

32. Hibbert, pp. 65–66.

33. D'Este, *Fatal Decision,* p. 146.

34. Sheehan, pp. 67–68.

35. Blumenson, *Salerno to Cassino,* pp. 386–387.

36. Lucas diary, Jan. 25, 1944.

37. Hibbert, p. 65.
38. Blumenson, *Salerno to Cassino,* p. 388.
39. Clark, pp. 293–294.
40. Blumenson, *Salerno to Cassino,* p. 389.
41. Churchill, p. 488.
42. Hibbert, p. 68.
43. Munsell, p. 51.
44. Robert LaDu, telephone interview with author, Apr. 3, 1995.
45. Mel Craven, interview with author, Denver, CO, Aug. 30, 1994.
46. Vere Williams, interview with author, Denver, CO, Aug. 30, 1994.
47. Hallowell et al., pp. 52–53.
48. Alvin McMillan, telephone interview with author, Oct. 30, 1994.
49. Hallowell et al., pp. 52–53.
50. Mel Craven, interview with author, Denver, CO, Sept. 30, 1994.
51. Henry Kaufman, *Vertrauensmann: Man of Confidence* (New York: Rivercross, 1994), p. 19.
52. A. H. Speairs, telephone interview with author, Jan. 19, 1995.
53. Edward Amzibel, telephone interview with author, Mar. 4, 1995.
54. Hallowell et al., pp. 52–53.
55. Alvin McMillan, telephone interview with author, Oct. 30, 1994.
56. Hibbert, p. 72; and Bowditch, p. 26.
57. Vaughn-Thomas, p. 74; and George F. Howe, *The Battle History of the 1st Armored Division* (Washington DC: Combat Forces Press, 1954), pp. 282–283.
58. Vaughn-Thomas, p. 70.
59. Howe, p. 283.
60. Bowditch, pp. 28–30; and Darby and Baumer, pp. 159–172.
61. Bowditch, p. 30.
62. Ibid., pp. 32–35.
63. Churchill, p. 493.
64. Bowditch, p. 26; and Howe, p. 290.
65. Howe, pp. 287–289.
66. Lucas diary, Feb. 1, 1944.
67. Whitman, pp. 78–79.
68. G. Fisher, p. 133.
69. D'Este, *Fatal Decision,* pp. 76–77.
70. G. Fisher, p. 133
71. Vere Williams, interview with author, Denver, CO, Aug. 30, 1994.
72. John Griffin, telephone interview with author, May 10, 1996.
73. Chester Powell, telephone interview with author, Mar. 13, 1995.
74. Morty Carr, telephone interview with author, Mar. 21, 1995.
75. Pyle, p. 173.
76. Ralph Fink, telephone interview with author, May 1, 1995.
77. Alvin McMillan, telephone interview with author, Oct. 30, 1994.
78. Ray Williams, telephone interview with author, Jan. 7, 1995.
79. G. Fisher, pp. 133–134 .
80. Bill Mauldin, *Up Front* (New York: Norton, 1991), p. 35.
81. Vere Williams, interview with author, Denver, CO, Aug. 30, 1994.

82. G. Fisher, p. 134.
83. Mel Craven, interview with author, Denver, CO, Aug. 30, 1994.
84. George Ecker, telephone interview with author, Mar. 13, 1995.
85. Hallowell et al., p. 53.
86. Bowditch, p. 40.

Chapter 6

1. *The German Operation at Anzio,* pp. 25–28.
2. Ibid., p. 32.
3. Sheehan, p. 136.
4. D'Este, *Fatal Decision,* pp. 89, 146, 186–188.
5. Vaughn-Thomas, pp. 93–96.
6. Ibid., pp. 99–108.
7. *The German Operation at Anzio,* p. 32.
8. Vaughn-Thomas, pp. 99–108.
9. *The German Operation at Anzio,* p. 30.
10. Vaughn-Thomas, pp. 99–108.
11. Sheehan, pp. 98–99.
12. *The German Operation at Anzio,* p. 33.
13. Hallowell et al., p. 54.
14. *The German Operation at Anzio,* p. 35.
15. Hallowell et al., pp. 54–55.
16. Ibid., p. 54.
17. Glen Hanson, telephone interview with author, Apr. 28, 1996.
18. Bishop et al., pp. 71–72; and Hallowell et al., pp. 54–56.
19. Jack McMillion, interview with author, Denver, CO, Aug. 30, 1994.
20. Edward Amzibel, telephone interview with author, Mar. 4, 1995.
21. Hallowell et al., p. 56.
22. Alistair Horne, *The Price of Glory: Verdun 1916* (New York: Penguin unabridged edition, 1993), p. 254.
23. Hallowell et al., p. 56.
24. Blumenson, *Salerno to Cassino*, p. 396; and D'Este, *Fatal Decision,* p. 213.
25. Bowditch, pp. 56–57.
26. Ibid., p. 60.
27. Sheehan, p. 108.
28. Hibbert, p. 103.
29. Bowditch, p. 60.
30. Sheehan, p. 106.
31. Bowditch, p. 60.
32. Sheehan, pp. 108–109.
33. Churchill, pp. 488–489.
34. Hibbert, p. 103.
35. Munsell, pp. 53–54; and Sheehan, pp. 109–110.
36. G. Fisher, p. 139.
37. A. H. Speairs, telephone interview with author, Jan. 19, 1995.
38. Munsell, p. 53; and Sheehan, p. 110.
39. Chester Powell, telephone interview with author, Mar. 13, 1995.

40. Robert Rogers, letter to author, Feb. 20, 1995.
41. Munsell, p. 54.
42. George Ecker, telephone interview with author, Mar. 13, 1995.
43. Munsell, p. 53.
44. Ray Williams, telephone interview with author, Jan. 7, 1995.
45. Munsell, p. 54.
46. Ray Williams, telephone interview with author, Jan. 7, 1995.
47. Munsell, pp. 53–54; and Sheehan, p. 111.
48. Clay Barnes, telephone interview with author, Jan. 19, 1995.
49. Ralph Fink, telephone interview with author, May 1, 1995.
50. Vere Williams, interview with author, Denver, CO, Aug. 30, 1994.
51. Pyle, p. 48.
52. J. W. Rolen, telephone interview with author, Mar. 21, 1995.
53. Kenneth Stemmons, telephone interview with author, Mar. 21, 1995.
54. Robert Franklin, telephone interview with author, Apr. 21, 1996.
55. Bishop et al., p. 73.
56. D'Este, *Fatal Decision,* p. 206.
57. Hallowell et al., p. 57.
58. G. Fisher, p. 135.
59. Amzibel monograph.
60. Charlie Dunham, telephone interview with author, Nov. 18, 1995.
61. Fisher, p. 136.
62. Joseph Bosa diary, Paul's Valley, OK, Feb. 14, 1944.
63. Bishop et al., p. 73.
64. J. W. Rolen, telephone interview with author, Mar. 21, 1995.
65. Ralph Fink, telephone interview with author, May 1, 1995.
66. Minor Shirk, interview with author, Denver, CO, Aug. 30, 1994.
67. Munsell, p. 54.
68. Clay Barnes, telephone interview with author, Jan. 19, 1995.
69. Minor Shirk, interview with author, Denver, CO, Aug. 30, 1994.
70. Bosa diary, Feb. 15, 1944.
71. Sheehan, pp. 141–144.
72. Vere Williams, interview with author, Denver, CO, Aug. 30, 1994.
73. David Brinkley, *Washington Goes to War* (New York: Ballantine, 1988), p. 35.
74. Al Bedard, interview with author, Denver, CO, Aug. 30, 1994.
75. Whitman, pp. 88–89.
76. Clay Barnes, telephone interview with author, Jan. 19, 1995.
77. Sheehan, p. 117.
78. D'Este, *Fatal Decision,* pp. 224–226; and Kesselring, p. 194; and Lamb, p. 97.
79. Kesselring, p. 196.
80. Ibid., pp. 195–196.
81. Sheehan, p. 117; and Vaughn-Thomas, p. 161.

Chapter 7

1. Hallowell et al., p. 57.
2. Daniel Witts, telephone interview with author, Mar. 31, 1996.
3. Ralph Krieger, telephone interview with author, Mar. 20, 1995.

4. Bishop et al., p. 73; and D'Este, *Fatal Decision,* p. 226.
5. D'Este, *Fatal Decision,* p. 231.
6. Blumenson, *Salerno to Cassino,* p. 420.
7. Bishop et al., pp. 73–74.
8. Felix Sparks, interview with author, Lakewood, CO, Oct. 15, 1996.
9. Munsell, pp. 54–56.
10. Daniel Witts, telephone interview with author, Mar. 31, 1996.
11. William Gordon, telephone interview with author, Mar. 13, 1995.
12. Hibbert, pp. 110–111.
13. Felix Sparks, interview with author, Lakewood, CO, Oct. 15, 1996.
14. Pete Conde, interview with author, Denver, CO, Aug. 25, 1994.
15. Alvin McMillan, telephone interview with author, Oct. 30, 1994.
16. Robert LaDu, telephone interview with author, Apr. 3, 1995.
17. Charles Reiman, monograph, Feb. 7, 1987, 45th Infantry Division Archives, Oklahoma City, OK.
18. Everett Easley, telephone interview with author, Jan. 18, 1995.
19. Daniel Ficco, telephone interview with author, Apr. 19, 1995.
20. Kenneth Stemmons, telephone interview with author, Mar. 21, 1995.
21. Amzibel monograph.
22. D'Este, *Fatal Decision,* p. 313.
23. Whitman, p. 90.
24. Chester Powell, telephone interview with author, Mar. 13, 1995.
25. D'Este, *Fatal Decision,* p. 231; and Kesselring, p. 196.
26. Blumenson, *Salerno to Cassino,* p. 240; and D'Este, *Fatal Decision,* p. 231; and *The German Operation at Anzio,* p. 54.
27. Mel Craven, interview with author, Denver, CO, Aug. 30, 1994.
28. James Bird, telephone interview with author, May 1, 1995.
29. Felix Sparks, interview with author, Lakewood, CO, Oct. 15, 1996.
30. Hallowell et al., pp. 60–61.
31. Ibid., p. 61.
32. Vere Williams, interview with author, Denver, CO, Aug. 30, 1994.
33. Bishop et al., p. 75.
34. Munsell, p. 139.
35. William Gordon, telephone interview with author, Mar. 13, 1995.
36. George Ecker, telephone interview with author, Mar. 13, 1995.
37. Leland Loy, telephone interview with author, Jan. 9, 1995.
38. Daniel Ficco, telephone interview with author, Apr. 19, 1995.
39. *157th Operations Report,* Feb. 1944, 45th Infantry Division Archives, Oklahoma City, OK.
40. *179th Operations Report,* Feb. 1944, 45th Infantry Division Archives, Oklahoma City, OK.
41. Munsell, p. 55.
42. Ibid., pp. 55–56.
43. Robert LaDu, telephone interview with author, Apr. 3, 1995.
44. Munsell, p. 55; and Blumenson, *Salerno to Cassino,* p. 459.
45. Everett Easley, telephone interview with author, Jan. 18, 1995.
46. Munsell, pp. 55–56.

47. Hallowell et al., p. 64.
48. Alvin McMillan, telephone interview with author, Oct. 30, 1994.
49. Felix Sparks, interview with author, Lakewood, CO, Oct. 15, 1996.
50. Robert Franklin, telephone interview with author, April 21, 1996.
51. Whitman, pp. 91–92.
52. G. Fisher, p. 139.
53. Howe, p. 295; and D'Este, *Fatal Decision,* p. 235.
54. G. Fisher, pp. 139–140.
55. *157th Operations Report,* Feb. 1944, 45th Infantry Division Archives, Oklahoma City, OK.
56. *45th Division Artillery Operations Report,* Feb. 1944, 45th Infantry Division Archives, Oklahoma City, OK.
57. D'Este, *Fatal Decision,* p. 232.
58. Jeremiah Moher, telephone interview with author, May 2, 1995.
59. Whitman, pp. 92–93.
60. Bosa diary, Feb. 16, 1944.

Chapter 8

1. D'Este, *Fatal Decision,* pp. 230–231.
2. Ibid., p. 237.
3. *The German Operation at Anzio,* pp. 53–54; and Vaughn-Thomas, p. 155.
4. G. Fisher, p. 146.
5. Sheehan, p. 122.
6. Bosa diary, Feb. 17, 1944.
7. Vaughn-Thomas, p. 21.
8. Hallowell et al., p. 66.
9. Hibbert, pp. 111–112.
10. Kaufman, p. 20.
11. D'Este, *Fatal Decision,* p. 235; and Hibbert, p. 112; and Green, p. 25.
12. Hibbert, pp. 112–113; and Green, p. 28; and Howe, p. 296.
13. Edward A. Raymond, "The Caves of Anzio," *Field Artillery Journal,* Dec. 1944, p. 852.
14. Kaufman, p. 21.
15. Raymond, p. 852.
16. D'Este, *Fatal Decision,* p. 232.
17. Bowditch, pp. 75–77.
18. Felix Sparks, interview with author, Lakewood, CO, Oct. 15, 1996.
19. Bowditch, pp. 75–77.
20. Hallowell et al., p. 65.
21. Pete Conde, interview with author, Denver, CO, Aug. 25, 1994.
22. Bill Hemingway, "The Anguish of Anzio," *Denver Post,* Empire sec., Nov. 19, 1978.
23. Al Bedard, interview with author, Denver, CO, Aug. 30, 1994.
24. Bishop et al., p. 76; and Hallowell et al., pp. 66–67.
25. Kaufman, p. 21.

26. Al Bedard, interview with author, Denver, CO, Aug. 30, 1994.
27. Kaufman, p. 22.
28. Raymond, p. 852.
29. Hallowell et al., p. 66.
30. Philip Burke, telephone interview with author, Oct. 19, 1994.
31. Kaufman, pp. 21–22.
32. Hallowell et al., p. 65.
33. D'Este, *Fatal Decision,* pp. 236–240.
34. William Pullum, telephone interview with author, Jan. 14, 1995.
35. Hallowell et al., p. 65.
36. *The German Operation at Anzio,* p. 56.
37. Ibid., p. 59.
38. D'Este, *Fatal Decision,* p. 247; and Hibbert, p. 113.
39. Bowditch, p. 80.
40. *The German Operation at Anzio,* pp. 56–57.
41. Sheehan, p. 123; and Fisher, p. 143.
42. Hallowell et al., pp. 65–67; and D'Este, *Fatal Decision,* pp. 236–238; and Hibbert, pp. 112–113.
43. Jack McMillion, interview with author, Denver, CO, Aug. 30, 1994.
44. Glen Hanson, telephone interview with author, Apr. 28, 1996.
45. D'Este, *Fatal Decision,* p. 236.
46. Munsell, pp. 55–56.
47. Hibbert, pp. 114–115.
48. Hallowell et al., pp. 66–67; and D'Este, *Fatal Decision,* p. 243.
49. Bowditch, p. 81.
50. D'Este, *Fatal Decision,* pp. 240–242.
51. Hallowell et al., p. 67; and D'Este, *Fatal Decision,* p. 243.
52. Robert Franklin, telephone interview with author, Apr. 21, 1996.
53. Jack McMillion, interview with author, Denver, CO, Aug. 30, 1994.
54. Edward Amzibel, monograph and telephone interview with author, Mar. 4, 1995.
55. Hubert Berry, telephone interview with author, Dec. 7, 1995.
56. Bernard Fleming, telephone interview with author, Jan. 14, 1995.
57. Robert Franklin, telephone interview with author, Apr. 21, 1996.
58. Kenneth Kindig, telephone interview with author, Nov. 1, 1995.
59. Vere Williams, interview with author, Denver, CO, Aug. 30, 1994.
60. Bernard Fleming, telephone interview with author, Jan. 14, 1995.
61. George Nalley, interview with author, Denver, CO, Aug. 30, 1994.
62. Jack McMillion, interview with author, Denver, CO, Aug. 30, 1994.
63. Robert Franklin, telephone interview with author, Apr. 21, 1996.
64. Munsell, p. 56; and Sheehan, p. 121.
65. Blumenson, *Salerno to Cassino,* p. 423.
66. D'Este, *Fatal Decision,* p. 244.
67. Blumenson, *Salerno to Cassino,* p. 423; and Michael J. King, *William Orlando Darby: A Military Biography* (Hamden, CT: Archon Books, 1981), p. 160.
68. King, p. 160.
69. *45th Division Artillery Operations Report,* Feb. 1944, 45th Infantry Division Archives, Oklahoma City, OK.

70. King, p. 160.
71. Ibid., pp. 160–175.
72. Ralph Fink, telephone interview with author, May 1, 1995.
73. Charles Reiman, letter to author, June 10, 1995.
74. Alex Dryden, telephone interview with author, Feb. 23, 1997.
75. G. Fisher, p. 140.
76. Ibid., p. 147.
77. Ibid., pp. 143–144; and Sheehan, p. 133.
78. Bosa diary, Feb. 18, 1944.
79. George F. Dennis, monograph (*Activities of Pfc. Lloyd C. "Blackie" Greer*), 45th Infantry Division Archives, Oklahoma City, OK.
80. Morris, *Circles of Hell,* p. 288.

Chapter 9

1. Churchill, p. 491; and Hibbert, p. 102.
2. Vaughn-Thomas, pp. 187–189; and Shepperd, p. 222; and Siegfried Westphal, *The German Army in the West* (London: Cassel, 1951), pp. 160–161.
3. Sheehan, p. 137; and D'Este, *Fatal Decision,* pp. 244–249.
4. Howe, pp. 296–299.
5. Whitman, pp. 94–95.
6. Sheehan, p. 138.
7. Bosa diary, Feb. 19, 1944.
8. Munsell, p. 56.
9. Pete Conde, interview with author, Denver, CO, Aug. 25, 1994.
10. Charles Reiman, letter to author, June 10, 1995.
11. *45th Division Artillery Operations Report,* Feb. 1944, 45th Infantry Division Archives, Oklahoma City, OK.
12. G. Fisher, pp. 143–144; and *45th Division News,* Jan. 1991; and Bowditch, pp. 81–83.
13. Bosa diary, Feb. 19, 1944.
14. *The German Operation at Anzio,* pp. 8–9.
15. Bosa diary, Feb. 19, 1944.
16. G. Fisher, p. 150.
17. Whitman, p. 93.
18. Munsell, p. 59.
19. Robert LaDu, telephone interview with author, Apr. 3, 1995.
20. Pyle, p. 174.
21. Kenneth Stemmons, telephone interview with author, Mar. 21, 1995.
22. Bosa diary, Feb. 22, 1944.
23. Hemingway, *Denver Post,* Nov. 19, 1978.
24. Kaufman, pp. 22–29.
25. Robert LaDu, telephone interview with author, Apr. 3, 1995.
26. Felix Sparks, interview with author, Lakewood, CO, Oct. 15, 1996.
27. Hallowell et al., p. 69; and Bowditch, p. 94; and Raymond, p. 853; and Eric Linklater, *The Campaign in Italy* (London: His Majesty's Stationery Office, 1951), p. 206.

28. Felix Sparks, interview with author, Lakewood, CO, Oct. 15, 1996.
29. Hallowell et al., pp. 69–70.
30. Jack Montgomery, telephone interview with author, May 5, 1996.
31. Al Bedard, interview with author, Denver, CO, Aug. 30, 1994.
32. Hallowell et al., p. 70; and Raymond, p. 853.
33. Felix Sparks, interview with author, Lakewood, CO, Oct. 15, 1996.
34. Hemingway, *Denver Post,* Nov. 19, 1978.
35. Philip Burke, telephone interview with author, Oct. 19, 1994.
36. Pete Conde, interview with author, Denver, CO, Aug. 25, 1994.
37. Bowditch, p. 94; and *The German Operation at Anzio,* p. 67.
38. Felix Sparks, interview with author, Lakewood, CO, Oct. 15, 1996.
39. Bosa diary, Feb. 23, 1944.
40. Blumenson, *Salerno to Cassino,* pp. 423–424; and Shepperd, p. 217.
41. Hallowell et al., p. 71.
42. Donald G. Taggart, ed., *History of the Third Infantry in World War II* (Washington, DC: Infantry Journal Press, 1948), p. 107.
43. Hallowell et al., p. 51.
44. Munsell, p. 57.
45. Blumenson, *Anzio,* p. 137.
46. G. Fisher, p. 148.
47. Morris, *Circles of Hell,* p. 287.
48. Blumenson, *Anzio,* p. 139; and Hibbert, p. 120.

Chapter 10

1. Bowditch, pp. 96–100.
2. Bosa diary, Feb. 29, 1944.
3. Bowditch, pp. 100–104.
4. G. Fisher, pp. 156–157.
5. Bishop et al., p. 82.
6. Bishop et al., p. 82; and Munsell, p. 61.
7. Bosa diary, Mar. 5, 1944.
8. Ibid., Mar. 7, 1944.
9. Bishop et al., p. 83.
10. Museum display, Museo Vesuvio, Naples.
11. Bishop et al., p. 83.
12. Daniel Witts, telephone interview with author, Mar. 31, 1996.
13. Ralph Fink, telephone interview with author, May 1, 1995.
14. V. I. Minahan, letter to editor, *45th Division News,* Nov. 1944.
15. J. W. Rolen, telephone interview with author, Mar. 21, 1995.
16. Alvin McMillan, telephone interview with author, Oct. 30, 1994.
17. Vere Williams, interview with author, Denver, CO, Aug. 30, 1994.
18. Hibbert, pp. 137–138.
19. Nelson, p. 62; and Shepperd, p. 218; and D'Este, *Fatal Decision,* p. 413.
20. Bowditch, p. 104.
21. Bishop et al., p. 83.

22. Ibid., p. 84.
23. Morty Carr, telephone interview with author, Mar. 21, 1995.
24. Nelson, p. 64.
25. Vaughn-Thomas, pp. 196–197.
26. Mel Craven, interview with author, Denver, CO, Aug. 30, 1994.
27. Ralph Fink, telephone interview with author, May 1, 1995.
28. Felix Sparks, interview with author, Lakewood, CO, Oct. 15, 1996.
29. Bishop et al., p. 84.
30. Edward Amzibel, telephone interview with author, Mar. 4, 1995.
31. Robert Franklin, telephone interview with author, Apr. 21, 1996.
32. Pyle, p. 174.
33. D'Este, *Fatal Decision,* pp. 6, 226, 454–457; and Clark, p. 326.
34. Chester Powell, telephone interview with author, Mar. 13, 1995.
35. Ralph Fink, telephone interview with author, May. 1, 1995.
36. J. W. Rolen, telephone interview with author, Mar. 21, 1995.
37. Leland Loy, telephone interview with author, Jan. 9, 1995.
38. George Ecker, telephone interview with author, Mar. 13, 1995.
39. Minor Shirk, interview with author, Denver, CO, Aug. 30, 1994.
40. Kaufman, p. 20.
41. Vere Williams, interview with author, Denver, CO, Aug. 30, 1994.
42. Daniel Witts, telephone interview with author, Mar. 31, 1996.
43. Pyle, p. 176.
44. Ralph Fink, telephone interview with author, May. 1, 1995.
45. Morty Carr, telephone interview with author, Mar. 21, 1995.
46. Vere Williams, interview with author, Denver, CO, Aug. 30, 1994.
47. Silvestri, p. 195.
48. James Bird, telephone interview with author, May 1, 1995.
49. Morty Carr, telephone interview with author, Mar. 21, 1995.
50. Robert LaDu, telephone interview with author, Apr. 3, 1995.
51. Pete Conde, interview with author, Denver, CO, Aug. 25, 1994.
52. Bishop et al., p. 83.
53. Howe, p. 304.
54. Dennis monograph.
55. James Bird, telephone interview with author, May 1, 1995.
56. Charles Keffler, letter to Canton, OH, electrical utility company. Date unknown, but probably March 1944.
57. Bosa diary, Mar. 9–12, 1944.
58. *The Battle for Italy* (video documentary), Polygram Video International, 1996.
59. Blumenson, *Salerno to Cassino,* pp. 432–448.
60. G. Fisher, p. 160.
61. Vaughn-Thomas, pp. 194–195; and Hibbert, pp. 130, 134.
62. Munsell, p. 64 ; and G. Fisher, p. 159.
63. Pyle, p. 172.
64. Whitman, pp. 127–128.
65. *157th Operations Report,* Mar. 1–31, 1944, 45th Infantry Division Archives, Oklahoma City, OK.

66. A. H. Speairs, monograph (*An Anzio Experience*), 45th Infantry Division Archives, Oklahoma City, OK.
67. Bishop et al., p. 86.
68. Ibid.; and Bowditch, pp. 107–108.

Chapter 11

1. Bowditch, pp. 105–107; and Ernest Fisher, *Cassino to the Alps*, vol. 2, Part 4 in the "U.S. Army in World War II, The Mediterranean Theater of Operations" series (Washington DC: Center of Military History, 1984), p. 110; and Shepperd, pp. 248–253.
2. Fisher,, pp. 21–26.
3. Shepperd, pp. 252–253, p. 269.
4. Ibid., p. 255.
5. Ibid., pp. 255–256.
6. E. Fisher, pp. 106–107.
7. D'Este, *Fatal Decision*, pp. 294, 413; and Green, p. 34.
8. Munsell, pp. 64–65.
9. Jack McMillion, interview with author, Denver, CO, Aug. 30, 1994.
10. Vaughn-Thomas, p. 212.
11. Daniel Witts, telephone interview with author, Mar. 31, 1996.
12. Shepperd, pp. 258–259; and E. Fisher, pp. 42–62.
13. E. Fisher, pp. 79–80.
14. Shepperd, pp. 258–259; and E. Fisher, pp. 42–62.
15. E. Fisher, pp. 66–76.
16. Dan Kurzman, *The Race for Rome* (Garden City, NJ: Doubleday, 1975), pp. 226–237.
17. E. Fisher, p. 80.
18. Kurzman, pp. 244–251.
19. Silvestri, pp. 109–110.
20. Kurzman, p. 233.
21. Kurzman, pp. 226–253; and Shepperd, p. 269.
22. E. Fisher, pp. 86–97.
23. D'Este, *Fatal Decision*, pp. 355–359; and Hibbert, pp. 145–148; and Sheehan, pp. 196–198.
24. E. Fisher, p. 117.
25. Ibid., p. 115.
26. G. Fisher, pp. 172–173.
27. Leland Loy, telephone interview with author, Jan. 9, 1995.
28. Felix Sparks, interview with author, Lakewood, CO, Oct. 15, 1996.
29. Hallowell et al., pp. 84–85.
30. Robert Franklin, telephone interview with author, Apr. 21, 1996.
31. Hallowell et al., p. 87; and Nelson, p. 66; and Van Barfoot, telephone interview with author, Aug. 11, 1996.
32. Glen Hanson, telephone interview with author, Apr. 28, 1996.
33. Jack McMillion, interview with author, Denver, CO, Aug. 30, 1994.

34. Edward Amzibel, monograph and telephone interview with author, Mar. 4, 1995.
35. Howe, pp. 322–323.
36. Felix Sparks, interview with author, Lakewood, CO, Oct. 15, 1996.
37. Daniel Witts, telephone interview with author, Mar. 31, 1996.
38. G. Fisher, pp. 175–179.
39. J. W. Rolen, telephone interview with author, Mar. 21, 1995.
40. E. Fisher, pp. 118–141; and Kurzman, p. 288.
41. E. Fisher, p. 140.
42. G. Fisher, p. 179.
43. Bishop et al., p. 87.
44. E. Fisher, p. 137.
45. Felix Sparks, interview with author, Lakewood, CO, Oct. 15, 1996.
46. Sid Pollock, telephone interview with author, Mar. 14, 1995.
47. Robert Franklin, telephone interview with author, Apr. 21, 1996.
48. Kenneth Stemmons, telephone interview with author, Mar. 21, 1995.
49. A. H. Speairs, telephone interview with author, Jan. 19, 1995.
50. Ken Vogt, telephone interview with author, Feb. 11, 1995.
51. Morty Carr, telephone interview with author, Mar. 21, 1995.
52. Everett Easley, telephone interview with author, Jan. 18, 1995.
53. Daniel Witts, telephone interview with author, Mar. 31, 1996.
54. Felix Sparks, interview with author, Lakewood, CO, Oct. 15, 1996.
55. Vere Williams, interview with author, Denver, CO, Aug. 30, 1994.
56. Whitman, pp. 133–139.
57. E. Fisher, pp. 184–190; and Kurzman, pp. 288–322.
58. Kurzman, pp. 369–374.
59. E. Fisher, p. 542.
60. Ken Vogt, telephone interview with author, Feb. 11, 1995.
61. *Life*, May 28, 1944.
62. *45th Division Artillery Operations Report,* June 1944, 45th Infantry Division Archives, Oklahoma City, OK.
63. Hallowell et al., pp. 94–95.
64. Munsell, p. 86.
65. Charles Reiman, letter to author, Mar. 6, 1995.
66. G. Fisher, pp. 201–203.
67. Whitman, pp. 146–148.
68. Kurzman, pp. 369–380, pp. 417–418.
69. G. Fisher, pp. 199–208.
70. Minor Shirk, interview with author, Denver, CO, Aug. 30, 1994.
71. Felix Sparks, interview with author, Lakewood, CO, Oct. 15, 1996.
72. Hallowell et al., pp. 95–96.
73. G. Fisher, p. 213.
74. Hallowell et al., p. 97.
75. Everett Easley, telephone interview with author, Jan. 18, 1995.
76. Howard Walton, telephone interview with author, Jan. 22, 1995.
77. Ray Williams, telephone interview with author, Jan. 7, 1995.
78. Kenneth Stemmons, telephone interview with author, Mar. 21, 1995.

79. Bowditch, p. 116; and D'Este, *Fatal Decision,* p. 2.
80. Nelson, p. 67.
81. Sheehan, p. vii.
82. Hallowell et al., pp. 97–98; and Bishop et al., p. 92.

Chapter 12

1. Bishop et al., p. 92.
2. Vere Williams, interview with author, Denver, CO, Aug. 30, 1994.
3. Bishop et al., p. 92.
4. Mark Arnold-Forster, *The World at War* (New York: Stein & Day, 1973), p. 231.
5. Vere Williams, interview with author, Denver, CO, Aug. 30, 1994.
6. Bishop et al., pp. 97–107.
7. William B. Goddard, *The 7th United States Army Report of Operations: France and Germany, 1944–1945* (Heidelberg, Germany: Aloys Gräf, 1946), vol. 1, pp. 190–192.
8. Vere Williams, interview with author, Denver, CO, Aug. 30, 1994.
9. Goddard, vol. 1, p. 221.
10. Hallowell et al., p. 105.
11. Goddard, vol. 1, pp. 255–265.
12. Hallowell et al., p. 106.
13. Alan Wilt, *The French Riviera Campaign of August 1944* (Carbondale: Southern Illinois University Press, 1981), p. 155.
14. Hallowell et al., pp. 107–108; and Bishop et al., p. 8.
15. Goddard, vol. 1, pp. 269–272.
16. Bishop et al., p. 105.
17. Goddard, vol. 1, pp. 269–272.
18. Ibid., pp. 287–305.
19. Van Barfoot, telephone interview with author, Aug. 11, 1996.
20. Goddard, vol. 1, pp. 311–313.
21. Ibid., vol. 2, pp. 359–369.
22. Ibid., vol. 2, p. 380.
23. Vere Williams, interview with author, Denver, CO, Aug. 30, 1994.
24. Keith Bonn, *When the Odds Were Even: The Vosges Mountains Campaign, October 1944–January 1945* (Novato, CA: Presidio Press, 1994), pp. 110–115.
25. Bishop et al., pp. 120–121.
26. Bonn, pp. 119–123.
27. Bishop et al., pp. 120–125.
28. Bishop et al., p. 125; and Munsell, p. 98; and *45th Division News,* Jan. 1990; and Robert H. Adleman and George Walton, *The Devil's Brigade* (Philadelphia and New York: Chilton Books, 1966), pp. 19–33.
29. Bonn, p. 136.
30. Ibid., p. 119.
31. Goddard, vol. 2, pp. 464–467.
32. Bishop et al., pp. 127–128; and Hugh Foster, letter to author, Mar. 16, 1997.
33. Charles Whiting, *Siegfried: The Nazis' Last Stand* (New York: Stein & Day, 1982), p. xvii.

34. Bishop et al., p. 129.

35. Goddard, vol. 2, pp. 492–493; Hugh Foster, letter to author, Mar. 16, 1997.

36. Bonn, pp. 205–206; and James Lucas, *Hitler's Mountain Troops* (London: Arms & Armour Press, 1992), pp. 164–167; and Hugh Foster, letter to author, Sept. 11, 1997.

37. James Lucas, p. 165.

38. Bonn, p. 192.

39. Bishop et al., pp. 138–139.

40. Bonn, p. 208.

41. G. Fisher, pp. 297–300; Hugh Foster, letters to author, Mar. 16, 1997, and Sept. 11, 1997.

42. Hugh Foster, letters to author, Mar. 16, 1997, and Nov. 17, 1997.

43. Hugh Foster, letter to author, Sept. 11, 1997.

44. Bishop et al., p. 139.

45. Hallowell et al., p. 131.

46. Hugh Foster, letters to author, Sept. 11, 1997, and Nov. 17, 1997.

47. Hugh Foster, letter to author, Mar. 16, 1997.

48. Bernard Fleming, telephone interview with author, Jan. 14, 1995.

49. Buechner, pp. 110–119.

50. Hallowell et al., p. 133; and Bishop et al., p. 145.

51. Hallowell et al., pp. 135–136.

52. Bishop et al., pp. 145–146; and Hugh Foster, letter to author, Mar. 16, 1997.

53. G. Fisher, p. 297.

54. Bishop et al., pp. 149–151.

55. Hallowell et al., pp. 142–143.

56. G. Fisher, pp. 316–318.

57. Bishop et al., p. 11.

58. Hallowell et al., pp. 141–152.

59. Bishop et al., p. 161.

60. Ibid., p. 163.

61. Hallowell et al., pp. 152–162.

62. James Bird, letter to author, May 15, 1996.

63. Bishop et al., pp. 166–184; and Hallowell et al., pp. 157–162.

Chapter 13

1. *Historical Atlas of the Holocaust* (New York: Simon & Schuster Macmillan, 1996), p. 141.

2. Hugh Foster, letter to author, May 9, 1997.

3. Andrew Mollo, "Dachau," *After the Battle,* No. 27 (1994), pp. 1–21.

4. Michael Berenbaum, *Witness to the Holocaust* (New York: HarperCollins, 1997), p. 143.

5. Edwin Gorak, interviewed by James Strong, *The Liberation of KZ Dachau* (video documentary), Strong Communications, Coronado, CA, 1990.

6. XV Corps, G-5 Log, Box 4865, National Archives.

7. Ibid.

8. Ibid.

9. Felix Sparks, interview with author, Lakewood, CO, Dec. 19, 1996.
10. *45th Division G-2 Report #222,* Annex B, Box 10897, National Archives.
11. Kenneth Wickham, telephone interview with author, Feb. 9, 1997.
12. Paul Adams, oral history taken May 6, 1975, U.S. Army Military History Institute Collection, Carlisle, PA.
13. *157th S-3 Journal,* Apr. 28, 1945, Box 11072, National Archives.
14. Felix Sparks, interview with author, Lakewood, CO, Dec. 19, 1996.
15. *157th S-3 Journal,* Apr. 28, 1945, Box 11072, National Archives.
16. *157th S-3 Periodic Report #47,* Apr. 29, 1945, Box 10978, National Archives.
17. *157th S-3 Journal,* Apr. 28, 1945, Box 11072, National Archives; and *45th Division War Room Journal,* Apr. 29, 1945, p. 7, Serial 67, Box 10978, National Archives.
18. *157th S-3 Journal,* Apr. 28, 1945, Box 11072, National Archives.
19. Felix Sparks, interview with author, Lakewood, CO, Dec. 19, 1996.
20. William Walsh, interviewed by James Strong, *The Liberation of KZ Dachau,* 1990.
21. Mollo, p. 14; and Goddard, vol. 3, p. 832.
22. John Lee, letter to author, Nov. 12, 1997.
23. Peter Galary, telephone interview with author, Jan. 8, 1997.
24. Ralph Fink, quoted by Dick Evans, "Veteran Recalls Best and Worst of Times," *Lebanon* (PA) *Daily News,* May 3, 1995.
25. James Bird, telephone interview with author, May 1, 1995.
26. Sidney Olson, "Foreign News: Dachau," *Time*, May 7, 1945, p. 32.
27. Gilbert, p. 678.
28. Felix Sparks, interview with author, Lakewood, CO, Dec. 12, 1996.
29. Paul Adams, oral history taken May 6, 1975, U.S. Army Military History Institute.
30. William Walsh, interviewed by James Strong, *The Liberation of KZ Dachau,* 1990.
31. Felix Sparks, interview with author, Lakewood, CO, Dec. 19, 1996.
32. *157th S-3 Periodic Report #47,* Apr. 29, 1945, Box 10978, National Archives.
33. John Lee, letter to author, Nov. 12, 1997.
34. William Walsh, interviewed by James Strong, *The Liberation of KZ Dachau,* 1990.
35. Felix Sparks, interview with author, Lakewood, CO, Dec. 19, 1996; and *45th Division G-2 Report #222,* Apr. 30, 1945, Box 10897, National Archives.
36. Joseph M. Whitaker, "Investigation of Alleged Mistreatment of German Guards at Dachau," May-June 1945 (hereinafter referred to as "*I.G. Report*"); and Fred Randolph testimony, I.G. Report, Exhibit B, p. 106, National Archives.
37. Ibid., Harold Moyer testimony, p. 113.
38. Ibid., William Walsh testimony, p. 7; and Curtis Whiteway, letter to author, Jan. 6, 1997.
39. Felix Sparks, interview with author, Lakewood, CO, Dec. 19, 1996.
40. Hugh Foster, letter to author, Mar. 14, 1997.
41. Sidney Horn, telephone interview with author, Jan. 6, 1996.

42. William Walsh, interviewed by James Strong, *The Liberation of KZ Dachau,* 1990.
43. John Lee, letter to author, Nov. 12, 1997.
44. Felix Sparks, interview with author, Lakewood, CO, Dec. 19, 1996.
45. John Lee, letter to author, Nov. 12, 1997.
46. Felix Sparks, interview with author, Lakewood, CO, Dec. 19, 1996.
47. Peter Galary, telephone interview with author, Jan. 8, 1997.
48. Felix Sparks, interviewed by James Strong, *The Liberation of KZ Dachau,* 1990.
49. Felix Sparks, interview with author, Lakewood, CO, Oct. 15, 1996.
50. James Bird, telephone interview with author, May 1, 1995.
51. Henry Mills, telephone interview with author, Mar. 24, 1997.
52. Karl Mann, telephone interview with author, Dec. 28, 1996.
53. Felix Sparks, interview with author, Lakewood, CO, Dec. 19, 1996.
54. Stanton, p. 128–129; and Goddard, vol. 3, p. 664.
55. *222nd Unit Journal,* Apr. 29, 1945, Box 10692, National Archives.
56. Mollo, pp. 30–33.
57. Harry J. Collins, memoirs, U.S. Army Military History Institute Collection, Carlisle, PA.
58. Whitaker, *I.G. Report,* Henning Linden testimony, p. 52, National Archives.
59. John Veitch, telephone interview with author, Jan. 1, 1997.
60. Whitaker, *I.G. Report,* Henning Linden testimony, p. 52, National Archives; and *222nd Infantry Report of Operations,* Apr. 1945, Box 10692, National Archives; and Letter from Colonel (Ret.) John Linden to 45th Infantry Division Association Historian, Apr. 10, 1996.
61. John Veitch, telephone interview with author, Jan. 1, 1997.
62. Antoinette May, *Witness to War: A Biography of Marguerite Higgins* (New York & Toronto: Beaufort Books, 1983), passim.
63. *222nd Unit Journal,* p. 17, National Archives.
64. John Veitch, telephone interview with author, Jan. 1, 1997.
65. *222nd Regimental Narrative,* Apr. 1945, pp. 16–17, National Archives.
66. Whitaker, *I.G. Report,* Henning Linden testimony, p. 52, National Archives.
67. William Donahue, telephone interview with author, Jan. 25, 1997.
68. Whitaker, *I.G. Report,* Henning Linden testimony, p. 52, National Archives.
69. Hugh Foster, letters to author, Jan. 24, 1997, and Mar. 14, 1997.
70. William Walsh, interviewed by James Strong, *The Liberation of KZ Dachau,* 1990.
71. Howard Cowan, "Dachau Captured by Americans Who Kill Guards, Liberate 32,000." *New York Times,* May 1, 1945.
72. William Donahue, telephone interview with author, Jan. 25, 1997.
73. Whitaker, *I.G. Report,* Henning Linden testimony, p. 52, National Archives.
74. John Veitch, telephone interview with author, Jan. 1, 1997.
75. Guido Oddi, telephone interview with author, Jan. 27, 1997.
76. Whitaker, *I.G. Report,* Walter Fellenz testimony, pp. 55–58, National Archives.
77. Whitaker, *I.G. Report,* Henry Wells testimony, pp. 74–79, National Archives.

78. Whitaker, *I.G. Report,* Marion Okrutnik testimony, p. 50, National Archives.

79. Whitaker, *I.G. Report,* John Bauerlein testimony, p. 67, National Archives.

80. Whitaker, *I.G. Report,* Walter Fellenz testimony, p. 94, National Archives.

81. John Veitch, telephone interview with author, Jan. 1, 1997.

82. Felix Sparks, interview with author, Lakewood, CO, Dec. 19, 1996.

83. Whitaker, *I.G. Report,* passim, National Archives.

84. Karl Mann, telephone interview with author, Dec. 29, 1996.

85. William Donahue, telephone interview with author, Jan. 25, 1997.

86. Felix Sparks, interview with author, Lakewood, CO, Dec. 19, 1996.

87. Marcus J. Smith, *The Harrowing of Hell: Dachau* (Albuquerque: University of New Mexico Press, 1972), pp. 268–279; and Cowan, *New York Times,* May 1, 1945; and "Say Schuschnigg Lives," *New York Times,* May 3, 1945.

88. Felix Sparks, interview with author, Lakewood, CO, Dec. 19, 1996.

89. John Lee, letter to author, Nov. 12, 1997.

90. Lt. William Cowling Report to Brig. Gen. Linden, May 2, 1945, U.S. Army Military History Institute.

91. Felix Sparks, interview with author, Lakewood, CO, Dec. 19, 1996.

92. John Lee, letter to author, Nov. 12, 1997.

93. Karl Mann, telephone interview with author, Dec. 29, 1996.

94. Donald Lesch, telephone interview with author, Jan. 28, 1997.

95. Henry Mills, telephone interview with author, Mar. 24, 1997.

96. Felix Sparks, interview with author, Lakewood, CO, Dec. 19, 1996.

97. Whitaker, *I.G. Report,* Henning Linden testimony, pp. 52–54, National Archives.

98. Hugh Foster, letter to author, Jan. 24, 1997.

99. Ibid.

100. Whitaker, *I.G. Report,* William Walsh testimony, pp. 8, 100, National Archives.

101. Felix Sparks, interview with author, Lakewood, CO, Dec. 19, 1996.

102. Kenneth Wickham, telephone interview with author, Feb. 9, 1997.

103. Art Lee, letter to David Israel, Sept. 29, 1993.

104. *XV Corps G-3 Journal File, Operation Phone Pad,* 0405 hours, Apr. 30, 1945, Box 4827, National Archives.

105. *XV Corps G-3 Report #264,* National Archives.

106. Cowan, *New York Times,* 1 May 1945.

107. Leland Loy, interviewed by James Strong, *The Liberation of KZ Dachau,* 1990.

108. Felix Sparks, interview with author, Lakewood, CO, Dec. 19, 1996.

109. Sidney Horn, telephone interview with author, Jan. 6, 1995.

110. Leland Loy, telephone interview with author, Jan. 9, 1995.

111. John Lee, interviewed by James Strong, *The Liberation of KZ Dachau,* 1990.

112. Henry Mills, interviewed by James Strong, *The Liberation of KZ Dachau,* 1990.

113. John Lee, interviewed by James Strong, *The Liberation of KZ Dachau,* 1990.

114. Felix Sparks, interview with author, Lakewood, CO, Dec. 19, 1996; and *157th S-3 Journal,* Apr. 29, 1945, Box 11072, National Archives.

115. *222nd Regimental Journal,* Apr. 29–30, 1945, Box 10860, National Archives.

116. *XV Corps G-3 Journal,* Apr. 29, 1945, Box 4827, National Archives.

117. *157th S-3 Journal,* Apr. 30, 1945, Box 11072, National Archives.

118. *XV Corps G-3 Report #264,* National Archives.

119. *XV Corps G-5 Report,* May 5, 1945, Box 4865, National Archives.

120. Felix Sparks, interview with author, Lakewood, CO, Dec. 19, 1996.

121. *3rd Battalion, 157th Journal,* May 1, 1945, Box 11075, National Archives.

122. Informal Routing Slip from Judge Advocate to 7th Army Chief of Staff, June 9, 1945, National Archives; and Felix Sparks, interview with author, Lakewood, CO, Dec. 19, 1996.

123. Informal Routing Slip from Judge Advocate to 7th Army Chief of Staff, June 9, 1945, National Archives; and Felix Sparks, interview with author, Lakewood, CO, Dec. 19, 1996; and Memorandum from William H. Craig, Asst. Chief of Staff, 7th Army, to 7th Army Inspector General, June 18, 1945, Box 2673, National Archives.

124. D'Este, *Bitter Victory,* p. 318.

125. Felix Sparks, interview with author, Lakewood, CO, Dec. 19, 1996.

126. Kenneth Wickham, telephone interview with author, Feb. 9, 1997.

127. Felix Sparks, interview with author, Lakewood, CO, Dec. 19, 1996.

128. Peter Galary, telephone interview with author, Jan. 8, 1997.

129. William Walsh, interviewed by James Strong, *The Liberation of KZ Dachau,* 1990.

130. Hallowell et al., p. 167; and Mollo, p. 15.

131. Whitaker, *I.G. Report,* Walenty Lenarczyk testimony, p. 51, National Archives.

132. Goddard, vol. 3, p. 835.

133. Bishop et al., pp. 185–189; and Goddard, vol. 3, pp. 835–847.

134. Munsell, p. 128; and Hallowell et al., p. 171.

135. Bishop et al., p. 188.

136. Harry C. Butcher, *My Three Years with Eisenhower* (New York: Simon & Schuster, 1946), p. 834.

Epilogue

1. Bishop et al., pp. 187, 196.
2. Paul Adams, oral history taken May 6, 1975, U.S. Military History Institute.
3. Bishop et al., pp. 189–202; and Hallowell et al., pp. 176–178.
4. G. Fisher, p. 357.
5. Paul Adams, oral history taken May 6, 1975, U.S. Military History Institute.
6. Bishop et al., p. 200.
7. Chester Powell, telephone interview with author, Mar. 13, 1995.
8. William Pullum, telephone interview with author, Jan. 14, 1995.
9. Glen Hanson, telephone interview with author, Apr. 28, 1996.

10. Philip Burke, telephone interview with author, Oct. 19, 1994.
11. Henry Havlat, telephone interview with author, Oct. 28, 1995.
12. Ralph Fink, telephone interview with author, May 1, 1995.
13. John Lee, letter to author, Nov. 12, 1997.
14. Vere Williams, interview with author, Denver, CO, Aug. 30, 1944.
15. Jeremiah Moher, telephone interview with author, May 2, 1995.
16. Alvin McMillan, interview with author, Denver, CO, Aug. 31, 1994.
17. Blumenson, *Mark Clark,* pp. 260–289.
18. Samuel W. Mitcham, Jr., and Friedrich von Stauffenberg, The Battle of Sicily: *How the Allies Lost Their Chance for Total Victory* (New York: Orion, 1991), p. 308.
19. "Thunderbird Legends: Troy Houston Middleton," *45th Division News,* Oct. 1990.
20. *Register of Graduates and Former Cadets* (West Point, NY: United States Military Academy, 1995).
21. Adleman and Walton, p. 232.
22. David Nichols, ed., *Ernie's War: The Best of Ernie Pyle's World War II Dispatches* (New York: Random House, 1986), p. 33.
23. D'Este, *Fatal Decision,* p. 421.
24. Churchill, p. 494.

Bibliography

Published Sources/Books

Adleman, Robert H., and Walton, George. *The Devil's Brigade*. New York: Chilton Books. 1966.

Ambrose, Stephen F. *D-Day; June 6, 1944: The Climactic Battle of World War II*. New York: Simon & Schuster. 1994.

______. *Eisenhower: Soldier, General of the Army, President-Elect, 1890–1952*. New York: Simon & Schuster (Touchstone edition). 1985.

Arnold-Forster, Mark. *The World at War*. New York: Stein & Day. 1973.

Barrett, Charles F. *National Guard of the State of Oklahoma: Historical Annual 1938*. Baton Rouge, LA: Army & Navy Publishing Co. 1938.

Berenbaum, Michael. *Witness to the Holocaust*. New York: HarperCollins. 1997.

Bernstein, Alison R. *American Indians and World War II*. Norman & London: University of Oklahoma Press. 1991.

Bidwell, Shelford. "Albert Kesselring." in *Hitler's Generals*, ed. Correlli Barnett. New York: Grove Weidenfeld. 1989.

Bishop, Leo V., George A. Fisher, and Frank J. Glasgow. *The Fighting Forty-Fifth: The Combat Report of an Infantry Division*. Baton Rouge, LA: Army & Navy Publishing Co. 1946.

Blumenson, Martin. *Anzio: The Gamble That Failed*. Philadelphia & New York: Lippincott. 1963.

______. *Mark Clark: The Last of the Great World War II Commanders*. New York: Congdon & Weed. 1984.

______. *Salerno to Cassino,* vol. 3 in the "U.S. Army in World War II, The Mediterranean Theater of Operations" series. Washington, DC: Center of Military History. 1969.

Bonn, Keith E. *When The Odds Were Even: The Vosges Mountains Campaign, October 1944–January 1945*. Novato, CA: Presidio Press. 1994.

Bowditch, John, III, ed. *Anzio Beachhead*, vol. 14 in the "American Forces in Action" series.Washington, DC: Department of the Army Historical Division. 1947.

Bradley, Omar N. *A Soldier's Story*. Chicago: Rand McNally. 1951.

Bradley, Omar N., and Blair, Clay. *A General's Life*. New York: Simon & Schuster. 1983.

Brinkley, David. *Washington Goes to War*. New York: Ballantine Books. 1988.

Buechner, Emajean. *Sparks: The Combat Diary of a Battalion Commander*. Metarie, LA: Thunderbird Press. 1991.

Cancelli, Diego. *Aprilia 1944: Immagini Quotidiane di una Guerra*. Aprilia, Italy: Poligraf. 1994.

Churchill, Winston S. *The Second World War: Closing The Ring*. Boston: Houghton Mifflin. 1951.

Clark, Mark W. *Calculated Risk*. New York: Harper & Bros. 1950.

Cooper, Matthew. *The German Army 1933–1945: Its Political and Military Failure*. New York: Stein & Day. 1978.

Cundiff, Paul A. *45th Division CP—A Personal Record from World War II*. Privately published. Place and date unknown.

D'Este, Carlo. *Bitter Victory: The Battle for Sicily, 1943*. New York: Dutton. 1988.

_____. *Fatal Decision: Anzio and the Battle for Rome*. New York: HarperCollins. 1991.

_____. *Patton: A Genius for War*. New York: HarperCollins. 1995.

Darby, William O., and Baumer, William H. *We Led the Way*. San Rafael, CA: Presidio Press. 1980.

Duncan, D. Shaw. *National Guard of the State of Colorado: Pictorial Review 1939*. Atlanta, GA: Army-Navy Publishing Co. 1939.

Embry, John. *The 45th Infantry Division at Anzio* (Monograph No. 8). Oklahoma City, OK: 45th Infantry Division Museum. 1986.

Esseme, H. *Patton: A Study in Command*. New York: Scribner's. 1974.

Fahey, James C. *The Ships & Aircraft of the United States Fleet*. New York: Gemsco. 1944.

Fisher, Ernest F., Jr. *Cassino to the Alps*, vol. 2, Part 4 in the "U.S. Army in World War II" series. Washington, DC: Center of Military History. 1984.

Fisher, George A. *The Story of the 180th Infantry Regiment*. San Angelo, TX: Newsfoto Publishing Co. 1947.

Gilbert, Martin. *The Second World War* (rev ed.). New York: Henry Holt. 1989.

Goddard, William B., et al. *The 7th United States Army Report of Operations: France and Germany, 1944–1945*, vols. 1, 2, 3. Heidelberg, Germany: Aloys Gräf. 1946.

Graham, Dominick, and Bidwell, Shelford. *Tug of War: The Battle for Italy: 1943–45*. New York: St. Martin's. 1986.

Grigg, John. *1943: The Victory That Never Was*. New York: Hill & Wang. 1980.

Hallowell, Jack, et al. *History of the 157th Infantry Regiment (Rifle)*. Privately published. Place and date unknown.

Harrison, Walter M. *Log of the 45th*. Privately published. Place unknown. 1941.

Hibbert, Christopher. *Anzio: The Bid for Rome*. New York: Ballantine Books. 1970.

Hickey, Des, and Smith, Gus. *Operation Avalanche: The Salerno Landings, 1943*. New York: McGraw-Hill. 1984.

Historical Atlas of the Holocaust. United States Holocaust Memorial Museum. New York: Simon & Schuster Macmillan. 1996.

Howe, George F. *The Battle History of the 1st Armored Division*. Washington DC: Combat Forces Press. 1954.

Jackson, W.G.F. *The Battle for Italy*. New York: Harper & Row. 1967.

Josephy, Alvin M., Jr. *The Civil War in the American West*. New York: Knopf. 1991.

Kaufman, Henry. *Vertrauensmann: Man of Confidence*. New York: Rivercross Publishing. 1994.

Kemp, Anthony. *The Maginot Line: Myth & Reality*. New York: Stein & Day. 1982.

Kesselring, Albert. *The Memoirs of Field-Marshal Kesselring*. Novato, CA: Presidio Press. 1989.

King, Michael J. *William Orlando Darby: A Military Biography*. Hamden, CT: Archon Books. 1981.

Kurzman, Dan. *The Race For Rome*. Garden City, NY: Doubleday. 1975.

Lamb, Richard. *War in Italy: A Brutal Story*. New York: St. Martin's. 1993.

Lewin, Ronald. *Ultra Goes to War*. New York: McGraw-Hill. 1978.

Linklater, Eric. *The Campaign in Italy*. London: His Majesty's Stationery Office, 1951.

Lucas, James. *Hitler's Mountain Troops*. London: Arms & Armour Press. 1992.

Mahon, John K. *History of the Militia and the National Guard*. New York: Macmillan. 1983.

Mauldin, Bill. *Up Front*. New York: Norton. 1991.

May, Antoinette. *Witness to War: A Biography of Marguerite Higgins*. New York & Toronto: Beaufort Books. 1983.

Mitcham, Samuel W., Jr., and von Stauffenberg, Friedrich. *The Battle of Sicily: How the Allies Lost Their Chance for Total Victory*. New York: Orion Books. 1991.

Morison, Samuel E. *History of United States Naval Operations in World War II: Vol. 9. Sicily-Salerno-Anzio*. Boston: Little, Brown. 1954.

Morris, Eric. *Circles of Hell: The War In Italy 1943–1945*. New York: Crown. 1993.

______. *Salerno: A Military Fiasco*. New York: Stein & Day. 1983.

Munsell, Warren P., Jr. *The Story of a Regiment: A History of the 179th Regimental Combat Team*. Place unknown: Privately published. 1946.

National Guard of the State of Arizona: Historical Review 1938–1939. Baton Rouge, LA: Army & Navy Publishing Co. 1939.

National Guard of the State of New Mexico: Pictorial Review 1939. Atlanta, GA: Army-Navy Publishing Co. 1939.

Nelson, Guy. *Thunderbird: A History of the 45th Infantry Division*. Oklahoma City, OK: 45th Infantry Division Association. 1970.

Nichols, David, ed. *Ernie's War: The Best of Ernie Pyle's World War II Dispatches*. New York: Random House. 1986.

O'Neill, William L. *A Democracy at War: America's Fight at Home and Abroad in World War II*. New York: Free Press. 1993.

Operations in Sicily & Italy. West Point, NY: Department of Military Art and Engineering, United States Military Academy. 1947.

Otte, Alfred. *The HG Panzer Division*. West Chester, PA: Schiffer. 1989.

Pond, Hugh. *Salerno*. Boston & Toronto: Little, Brown. 1961.

Price, Frank J. *Troy H. Middleton: A Biography*. Baton Rouge: Louisiana State University Press. 1974.

Pyle, Ernie. *Brave Men*. New York: Henry Holt. 1944.

Ridley, Jasper. *Garibaldi*. New York: Viking. 1976.

Robinson, Don. *News of the 45th*. New York: Grosset & Dunlap. 1944.

Rowe, Vivian. *The Great Wall of France: The Life and Death of the Maginot Line.* New York: G. P. Putnam. 1959.

Salerno: American Operations from the Beachhead to the Volturno. Washington, DC: Military Intelligence Division, War Department. 1944.

Salpeter, Norbert, ed. *Ready in Peace and War: A Brief History of the 180th Infantry Regiment.* Munich: F. Bruckmann KG. 1945.

Sant'Ana, Elma. *Menotti: Il Garibaldi "Brasileiro."* Aprilia, Italy: Assessoria Grafica e Editorial. 1995.

Sheehan, Fred. *Anzio: Epic of Bravery.* Norman: University of Oklahoma Press. 1964. Reprint 1994.

Shepperd, G.A. *The Italian Campaign: 1943–45.* New York: Frederick A. Praeger. 1968.

Silvestri, Ennio. *The Long Road to Rome.* Latina, Italy: Etic Grafica. 1994.

Smith, Marcus J. *The Harrowing of Hell: Dachau.* Albuquerque: University of New Mexico Press. 1972.

Stanton, Shelby L. *World War II Order of Battle.* New York: Galahad Books. 1984.

Starr, Chester G., ed. *From Salerno to the Alps—A History of the Fifth Army, 1943–45.* Washington, DC: Infantry Journal Press. 1948.

Taggart, Donald G., ed. *History of the Third Infantry Division in World War II.* Washington, DC: Infantry Journal Press. 1947.

Thunderbird Review: 45th Infantry Division: World War II/Korean Conflict. Atlanta, GA: Albert Love Enterprises. Date unknown, but probably 1951.

Tregaskis, Richard. *Invasion Diary.* New York: Random House. 1944.

Trevelyan, Raleigh. *The Fortress: A Diary of Anzio and After.* London: Collins. 1956.

Truscott, Lucien K. *Command Missions.* New York: Dutton. 1954.

Vaughn-Thomas, Wynford. *Anzio.* London: Longmans, Green. 1961.

Verney, Peter. *Anzio 1944: An Unexpected Fury.* London: B. T. Batsford. 1978.

Wagner, Robert L. *The Texas Army: A History of the 36th Division in the Italian Campaign.* Privately published. Place unknown. 1972.

Wallace, Robert. *The Italian Campaign.* New York: Time-Life Books. 1981.

Westphal, Siegfried. *The German Army in the West,* London: Cassel. 1951.

Whiting, Charles. *Siegfried: The Nazis' Last Stand.* New York: Stein & Day. 1982.

Whitman, Bill. *Scouts Out!* Los Angeles: Authors Unlimited. 1990.

Wilt, Alan F. *The French Riviera Campaign of August 1944.* Carbondale: Southern Illinois University Press. 1981.

Published Sources/Articles

45th Division News. Various issues.

Adams, Caralee Johnson. "Search Begins for Unheralded Medal Winners." *Tulsa* (OK) *Tribune.* July 4, 1989.

Bishop, Wayne. "Childers Dedication Set Sept. 24." *Broken Arrow* (OK) *Ledger.* July 17, 1994.

Chronis, Peter G. "Villa's Attack on Town Recalled." *Denver Post.* Mar. 10, 1996.

Cole, William. "Silver Star Recipient Earned the Right to Speak His Mind." *Burlington* (NJ) *County Times*, July 3, 1992.

Cowan, Howard. "Dachau Captured by Americans Who Kill Guards, Liberate 32,000." *New York Times.* May 1, 1945.

Deatherage, Jackie. "Broken Arrow School Named for Medal of Honor Winner." *Tulsa (OK) World*. Nov. 11, 1985.
Evans, Dick. "Veteran Recalls Best and Worst of Times." *Daily News* (Lebanon, PA). May 3, 1995.
"The First Attack: Italy." *Life*. May 29, 1944.
Green, J. H. "Anzio." *After the Battle*. No. 52. 1986.
Greiner, John. "Ceremony to Honor 45th Division." *The Daily Oklahoman*. Apr. 10, 1989.
______. "Thank God It's Over: Memories Vivid for Medal Winner." *The Daily Oklahoman*. Apr. 9, 1990.
Hemingway, Bill. "The Anguish of Anzio." *Empire* section. *Denver Post*. Nov. 19, 1978.
Johnson, Jeffery W. "Childers Immortalized in Bronze Sculpture." *Broken Arrow (OK) Ledger*. Dec. 10, 1991.
Levy, Paul M.G. "Nous Libérions. . . . Dachau!" *L'union des Services de Renseignment et d'action*. Apr. 1946.
Miller, Matt. "Dachau Still Haunts Memory; Area Veteran Can't Forget Horrors He Saw 50 Years Ago." *The Patriot* (Harrisburg, PA). Apr. 29, 1995.
Mollo, Andrew. "Dachau." *After the Battle*. No. 27. 1980.
Myers, Jim. "45th Wins Special Status." *Tulsa (OK) World*. Aug. 31, 1994.
Olson, Sidney. "Foreign News: Dachau." *Time*. May 7, 1945.
"Plan to Honor Childers Advances." *Tulsa (OK) World*. Oct. 21, 1992.
Raymond, Edward A. "The Caves of Anzio." *Field Artillery Journal*. Dec. 1944.
Robertson, Ricky. "The Great Louisiana Maneuvers." *Army Motors*, Nos. 65, 66, 67. 1993–1994.
"Say Schuschnigg Lives." *New York Times*. May 3, 1945.
"Statue Will Honor Childers." *Tulsa (OK) World*. Jan. 27, 1993.
"Thunderbirds Get New Charge." *Broken Arrow (OK) Ledger*. Sept. 6, 1994.
Valenti, Sabrina. "War Hero's Wife Was Surprised by Attention." *Broken Arrow (OK) Ledger*. Nov. 11, 1993.
Watertown (NY) *Daily Times*. May 12, 1958.
Whitlock, Flint. "Allied Agony at Anzio." *World War II*. Jan. 1994.

Videos/Films

Aitken, Andy, director. *The Battle of Italy*. *Battlefield* series. Polygram Video International. 1996.
Strong, James K., director and producer. *The Liberation of KZ Dachau*. Coronado, CA: Strong Communications. 1990.

Unpublished Sources/Monographs/Letters

Adams, Paul D. Oral history taken May 6, 1975. U.S. Army Military History Institute Collection. Carlisle, PA.
Amzibel, Edward J. Monograph: "The War Years of Edward 'Don' Amzibel." 1995. 45th Infantry Division Archives. Oklahoma City, OK.
Bird, James. Letters to author.
Bosa, Joseph. Wartime diary. Pauls Valley, OK.

Collins, Harry J. Memoirs. U.S. Army Military History Institute Collection. Carlisle, PA.

Cowling, William. "Report of the Surrender of Dachau Concentration Camp." May 2, 1945. U.S. Army Military History Institute Collection. Carlisle, PA.

Dennis, George F. Monograph, "Activities of Pfc. Lloyd C. 'Blackie' Greer." 45th Infantry Division Archives. Oklahoma City, OK.

XV Corps Reports and Journals. National Archives. Washington, DC.

45th Division Operations Reports and Journals. 45th Infantry Division Archives, Oklahoma City, OK; and National Archives, Washington, DC.

42nd Division Operations Reports and Journals. National Archives, Washington, DC.

Foster, Hugh. Letters to author.

Gay, Hobart R. Wartime diary: April-July 8, 1945. U.S. Army Military History Institute Collection. Carlisle, PA.

The German Operation at Anzio; German Military Document Section; A Study of the German Operations at Anzio Beachhead from 22 Jan. 44 to 31 May 44. War Department,Military Intelligence Division, Camp Ritchie, MD. 1946. 45th Infantry Division Archives. Oklahoma City, OK.

Israel, David. Letters to author.

Lucas, Maj. Gen. John P. Diary. U.S. Army Military History Institute Collection. Carlisle, PA.

McLain, Brig. Gen. Raymond S. "Diary of the Sicilian Campaign." 45th Infantry Division Archives. Oklahoma City, OK.

Reiman, Charles R. Monograph, Feb. 7, 1987. 45th Infantry Division Archives. Oklahoma City, OK.

Speairs, A. H. Monograph (undated). "An Anzio Experience." 45th Infantry Division Archives. Oklahoma City, OK.

Whitaker, Lt. Col. Joseph. M., Assistant Inspector General, 7th Army. "Investigation of Alleged Mistreatment of German Guards at Dachau." May-June 1945. National Archives. Washington, DC.

Whiteway, Curtis. Letters to author.

Index

Commands and forces are organized by order of battle; regiments are listed under division to which they belong.